Alan Simpson's
Windows® Me Bible

Alan Simpson's Windows® Me Bible

Alan Simpson with Brian Underdahl

IDG BOOKS WORLDWIDE

IDG Books Worldwide, Inc.
An International Data Group Company

Foster City, CA ✦ Chicago, IL ✦ Indianapolis, IN ✦ New York, NY

Alan Simpson's Windows® Me Bible

Published by

IDG Books Worldwide, Inc.

An International Data Group Company
919 E. Hillsdale Blvd., Suite 400
Foster City, CA 94404
www.idgbooks.com (IDG Books Worldwide
Web site)

ISBN: 0-7645-3489-0

Printed in the United States of America

10 9 8 7 6 5 4 3

1B/QT/QY/QQ/FC

Distributed in the United States by IDG Books Worldwide, Inc.

Distributed by CDG Books Canada Inc. for Canada; by Transworld Publishers Limited in the United Kingdom; by IDG Norge Books for Norway; by IDG Sweden Books for Sweden; by IDG Books Australia Publishing Corporation Pty. Ltd. for Australia and New Zealand; by TransQuest Publishers Pte Ltd. for Singapore, Malaysia, Thailand, Indonesia, and Hong Kong; by Gotop Information Inc. for Taiwan; by ICG Muse, Inc. for Japan; by Intersoft for South Africa; by Eyrolles for France; by International Thomson Publishing for Germany, Austria, and Switzerland; by Distribuidora Cuspide for Argentina; by LR International for Brazil; by Galileo Libros for Chile; by Ediciones ZETA S.C.R. Ltda. for Peru; by WS Computer Publishing Corporation, Inc., for the Philippines; by Contemporanea de Ediciones for Venezuela; by Express Computer Distributors for the Caribbean and West Indies; by Micronesia Media Distributor, Inc. for Micronesia; by Chips Computadoras S.A. de C.V. for Mexico; by Editorial Norma de Panama S.A. for Panama; by American Bookshops for Finland.

For general information on IDG Books Worldwide's books in the U.S., please call our Consumer Customer Service department at 800-762-2974. For reseller information, including discounts and premium sales, please call our Reseller Customer Service department at 800-434-3422.

For information on where to purchase IDG Books Worldwide's books outside the U.S., please contact our International Sales department at 317-596-5530 or fax 317-572-4002.

For consumer information on foreign language translations, please contact our Customer Service department at 800-434-3422, fax 317-572-4002, or e-mail rights@idgbooks.com.

For information on licensing foreign or domestic rights, please phone +1-650-653-7098.

For sales inquiries and special prices for bulk quantities, please contact our Order Services department at 800-434-3422 or write to the address above.

For information on using IDG Books Worldwide's books in the classroom or for ordering examination copies, please contact our Educational Sales department at 800-434-2086 or fax 317-572-4005.

For press review copies, author interviews, or other publicity information, please contact our Public Relations department at 650-653-7000 or fax 650-653-7500.

For authorization to photocopy items for corporate, personal, or educational use, please contact Copyright Clearance Center, 222 Rosewood Drive, Danvers, MA 01923, or fax 978-750-4470.

Library of Congress Cataloging-in-Publication Data

Simpson, Alan, 1953-
    [Windows Me bible]
    Alan Simpson's Windows Me bible/ Alan Simpson with Brian Underdahl.
        p. cm.
    ISBN 0-7645-3489-0 (alk. paper)
    1. Microsoft Windows (Computer file)
2. Operating systems (Computers) I. Title:
Windows Me bible. II. Underdahl, Brian. III. Title
QA76.76.O63 S5594   2000
005.4'469--dc21   00-044987
                                                   CIP

ABOUT IDG BOOKS WORLDWIDE

Welcome to the world of IDG Books Worldwide.

IDG Books Worldwide, Inc., is a subsidiary of International Data Group, the world's largest publisher of computer-related information and the leading global provider of information services on information technology. IDG was founded more than 30 years ago by Patrick J. McGovern and now employs more than 9,000 people worldwide. IDG publishes more than 290 computer publications in over 75 countries. More than 90 million people read one or more IDG publications each month.

Launched in 1990, IDG Books Worldwide is today the #1 publisher of best-selling computer books in the United States. We are proud to have received eight awards from the Computer Press Association in recognition of editorial excellence and three from Computer Currents' First Annual Readers' Choice Awards. Our best-selling ...For Dummies® series has more than 50 million copies in print with translations in 31 languages. IDG Books Worldwide, through a joint venture with IDG's Hi-Tech Beijing, became the first U.S. publisher to publish a computer book in the People's Republic of China. In record time, IDG Books Worldwide has become the first choice for millions of readers around the world who want to learn how to better manage their businesses.

Our mission is simple: Every one of our books is designed to bring extra value and skill-building instructions to the reader. Our books are written by experts who understand and care about our readers. The knowledge base of our editorial staff comes from years of experience in publishing, education, and journalism — experience we use to produce books to carry us into the new millennium. In short, we care about books, so we attract the best people. We devote special attention to details such as audience, interior design, use of icons, and illustrations. And because we use an efficient process of authoring, editing, and desktop publishing our books electronically, we can spend more time ensuring superior content and less time on the technicalities of making books.

You can count on our commitment to deliver high-quality books at competitive prices on topics you want to read about. At IDG Books Worldwide, we continue in the IDG tradition of delivering quality for more than 30 years. You'll find no better book on a subject than one from IDG Books Worldwide.

John Kilcullen
Chairman and CEO
IDG Books Worldwide, Inc.

Eighth Annual
Computer Press
Awards ≥ 1992

Ninth Annual
Computer Press
Awards ≥ 1993

Tenth Annual
Computer Press
Awards ≥ 1994

Eleventh Annual
Computer Press
Awards ≥ 1995

Credits

Acquisitions Editor
David Mayhew

Project Editors
Kurt Stephan
Colleen Dowling

Technical Editor
Rick Darnell

Copy Editor
Nancy Rapoport

Proof Editor
Patsy Owens

Project Coordinator
Marcos Vergara

Cover Image
Joann Vuong

Graphics and Production Specialists
Robert Bihlmayer
Jude Levinson
Michael Lewis
Victor Pérez-Varela
Ramses Ramirez

Quality Control Technician
Dina F Quan

Illustrators
Brian Drumm
Gabriele McCann

Proofreading and Indexing
York Production Services

About the Author

Alan Simpson is a freelance computer/Internet nerd and veteran author of digilit (digital literature). Although he's a bit of a computer guru, Alan is best known for his light, conversational writing style, which appeals to most people who are put off by the dense, unintelligible text that fills so many manuals and large computer books. Prior to writing books full time, Alan taught introductory and advanced computer programming courses at San Diego State University and UCSD Extension. He also worked as a freelance programmer and computer consultant. He maintains the www.coolnerds.com Web site (when time permits), and can be reached at alan@coolnerds.com.

To Susan, Ashley, and Alec, as always

Preface

Welcome to the Windows Me Bible.

Who Should Read This Book

Windows Me is an operating system for home and small business computers. Microsoft has gone to great lengths to put all aspects of computing into the reach of regular folks who have no formal training in computer science. This book is geared to exactly the same kind of people — people who want to put their computers to work right now.

Unlike many Windows books, which go on and on about underlying theoretical issues, driver models, architecture, and so forth, this book is a hands-on guide. Each feature is explained, not in theoretical terms, but in terms of what it can do for you. Step-by-step instructions for using the feature usually come next. This way, when you find some feature that may be helpful to you, you can start putting that feature to work immediately.

Features of This Book

Like most books, this one has the standard table of contents up front and an index at the back to help you find information on an as-needed basis. Within chapters, lots of pictures and step-by-step instructions are provided to help you get more out of your PC, right away. Here's what's in each part:

Part I: Know This or Suffer

This part covers all the basics of opening and closing things, finding stuff, navigating your computer, getting instant help, creating shortcuts, and more.

Part II: Becoming an Internet Guru

The first chapter in this part tells you everything you need to get online from your own PC. Then you learn to use all the most popular features of the Internet including the World Wide Web, channels, e-mail, newsgroups, conferencing, and chat.

Part III: Have It Your Way

In this part, you learn how to customize your work environment to suit your needs. Some important basic skills covered here include creating folders, moving, copying, and deleting files, and personalizing Windows Me to your tastes.

Part IV: Work and Play

Here, you discover general techniques for working with text, numbers, and graphic images (pictures). You learn how to copy items from one document to another using cut-and-paste, as well as scraps. You also learn about printing and fonts — those fancy typefaces you see in professionally published books and magazines. Fun stuff includes multimedia (sound and video), Web TV, DVD, and the new Windows Movie Maker.

Part V: Growth, Maintenance, and General Tweaking

This part helps you perform routine maintenance tasks to keep your PC running at maximum speed. You also learn how to install new programs and eliminate old ones. Part III also covers Multiple Display Support, which enables you to extend your Windows desktop across two or more monitors. Finally, if you share a computer with other people, this part will help you set up your own personal workspace on the PC that other users cannot tamper with or alter.

Part VI: Build Your Own Network

Here, you find out how to set up a local area network (LAN) using the new Home Networking wizard and modern hardware that lets you connect computers through existing telephone wiring and power outlets.

Part VII: Advanced Stuff

This part covers some of the more advanced topics that may not be relevant to everyone. Also, I go deeper into some of the more technical stuff that normally stays hidden behind the scenes — things like the Registry, file associations, and so forth.

The book also has some margin icons:

 This icon signifies your basic tip: a trick, technique, or other tidbit worth calling special attention to so you don't miss it.

 This icon points out a technique you need to think about before you act. Tread carefully, because if you make a mistake, it'll be difficult — or impossible — to undo.

 This icon refers to a source of additional information on a topic (just in case I didn't already tell you enough to bore you to tears).

 This icon identifies a piece of information that's especially noteworthy for some reason other than one of the above.

Acknowledgments

Even though only the author's name appears on the cover, every book is actually a team effort. Many people were involved in the creation of this book. My sincere thanks to all the people whose skills and talents helped to make this book become a reality.

First of all, many, many thanks to everyone at IDG Books Worldwide who made this book happen. You were all very supportive, very professional, and very patient. In particular, I'd like to thank Kurt Stephan and Colleen Dowling, project editors; David Mayhew, acquisitions editor; Nancy Rapoport, senior copy editor; Rick Darnell, technical editor; Marcos Vergara, production coordinator; and Danette Nurse, graphics technician,

I greatly appreciated the work of Forrest Houlette who helped with the writing of this book.

Many thanks to everyone at Microsoft for helping me get an early start on this great product and for all the support and answers provided along the way.

To Matt Wagner and everyone at Waterside: Thanks for getting this opportunity to me and for making the deal happen.

And, of course, to my family: Thank you, thank you, thank you for your patience and understanding. I really had to concentrate on this one and I appreciate all your support.

Contents at a Glance

Contents

Part V: Growth, Maintenance, and General Tweaking 635

Part VI: Building Your Own Network   733

Know This
or Suffer

◆   ◆   ◆   ◆

◆   ◆   ◆   ◆

What Is Windows Millennium Edition?

As you probably know, a computer is a general-purpose device that enables you to play (or run) programs. If you've visited any kind of computer superstore lately, you know hundreds of programs are available for the PC: educational programs for kids from ages 1 to 100; tons of programs to help with business, including word processing programs, spreadsheets, and databases; every sort of game imaginable; and programs contributing to a whole new era of digital photography and video.

Thanks to the advent of the Internet and online services such as America Online and the Microsoft Network, the PC has also become a valuable tool for communications. There's e-mail, the World Wide Web, chat, teleconferencing, and more. The ongoing integration of TV, radio, telephone, the Internet, and the PC promises to change the very nature of the ways in which we communicate with one another and entertain ourselves.

Just as you can pick and choose CDs for your stereo and movies for your VCR, you can also pick and choose programs for your PC. You can use as many different programs and as many different online services as you like. One program is mandatory on all PCs, though. This program is called the *operating system* (pronounced with the emphasis on the op). The operating system (OS) is sort of the home base program from which all other programs are launched. The operating system essentially defines the interface between the computer and you, the user. Or, more simply stated, the operating system defines how you work your PC.

What Is Windows Me?

Windows Me (short for Millennium Edition) is an operating system. You may have heard of some of the other operating systems out there, such as the old DOS and the Mac OS used on Macintosh computers. There are also Linux and UNIX, used mainly in large businesses. And there are other flavors of Windows, known as Windows NT, recently renamed to Windows 2000. Like Linux and UNIX, Windows 2000 is geared toward medium- to large-size businesses. Windows Me, on the other hand, is geared to home users and small businesses. Whereas Windows 2000 and NT are oriented toward processing a large volume of business transactions and maintaining security, Windows Me is geared more toward multimedia, gaming, entertainment, and human creativity. While the Windows 2000 product line is geared toward taking advantage of the latest business tools, like doing e-commerce via the Internet, Windows Me is oriented toward taking advantage of new consumer technologies like interactive TV, DVD, digital photography, the Internet, and so forth.

If you're familiar with Windows, it might help to understand that Windows 2000 is essentially version 5 of the Windows NT product line. Windows Me is the next generation of a series of operating systems from the Windows 3.0, Windows 95 and Windows 98 product lines. If you're an experienced Windows 98 user, and want to know specifically what's new in Windows Me, Appendix B provides a more detailed summary of the new features in Windows Me.

By the way, I don't want to imply that Windows Me isn't good for doing work. To the contrary, Windows Me supports all the most popular "work-oriented" programs out there, including (of course) the entire Microsoft Office suite of applications. Hence, Windows Me is well-suited to the home office and even small businesses that require some networking of computers. Perhaps what's most important to small businesses is that Windows Me is easy enough to install, use, and maintain that you don't need a degree in computer science, nor a full-time system administrator, nor IT (Information Technology) staff just to baby-sit the computers.

Hardware and Software Basics

For those of you who are new to computers, this section discusses some basic terminology. Computer *hardware* is the stuff you can see and touch; if you throw it off the roof of a building, it will probably break. Your basic PC consists of the hardware components shown in Figure 1-1. Each component plays some role in helping you use the computer:

✦ **Monitor:** The big TV-like thing. Probably has its own on/off switch as well as brightness, contrast, and other buttons for fine-tuning the display onscreen.

✦ **Screen:** The part of the monitor where all the action takes place — similar to the screen on a TV set.

✦ **System unit:** The main body of the computer. Houses the main on/off switch plus access to the floppy disk and CD-ROM drives.

✦ **Mouse:** Your main tool for navigating (getting around) and for making the computer do what you want. I'll talk about mice in more detail in a moment.

✦ **Keyboard:** Laid out like a standard typewriter, the keyboard is used for typing and, in some cases, can also be used as an alternative to the mouse.

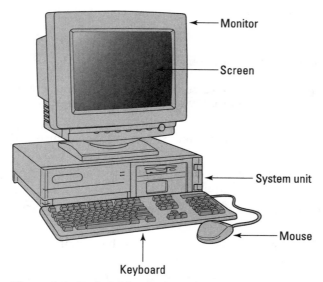

Figure 1-1: Basic PC hardware

Computer software is the stuff that makes the PC worth owning. Like the music for a stereo, software is stuff recorded on a CD-ROM, a floppy disk, perhaps inside a digital camera, or maybe even stored on some computer somewhere. The software won't do you any good without a PC on which to run it. And, as I've mentioned, a PC won't do you any good until you have some software (programs) to run on it. Of course, neither the hardware or software will do you any good if you don't know how to work it. So let's take a look at the most basic of basic skills required to use your hardware and software.

Mouse Basics

Right away, the one piece of hardware you must get comfortable with is the mouse. If you've never used a mouse before, here's where you'll learn how. The basic idea is you place your right hand comfortably on the mouse, with your index finger resting (but not pressing on) the left mouse button, as shown in Figure 1-2. When the computer is on, you'll see a little arrow, called the mouse pointer, on the screen. As you roll the mouse around on a mouse pad or your desktop, the mouse pointer will move in the same direction you move the mouse.

Figure 1-2: Rest your hand comfortably on the mouse, with your index finger near the button on the left.

Here's some basic mouse terminology you should know:

✦ **Mouse button (or primary mouse button):** Usually the mouse button on the left — the one that rests comfortably under your index finger when you rest your right hand on the mouse.

✦ **Right mouse button (or secondary mouse button):** The mouse button on the right.

✦ **Point:** To move the mouse so the mouse pointer is touching some object onscreen.

✦ **Click:** To point to an item, and then press and release the primary mouse button.

✦ **Double-click:** To point to an item and then click the primary mouse button twice in rapid succession — click click!

✦ **Right-click:** To point to an item and then press and release the secondary mouse button.

✦ **Drag:** To hold down the primary mouse button while moving the mouse.

✦ **Right-drag:** To hold down the secondary mouse button while moving the mouse.

Windows Me is geared toward two-button mouse operation. If your mouse has a little wheel in the middle, you can use that for scrolling, as discussed in Chapter 2. If your mouse has three buttons on it, you can ignore the button in the middle. I'll show you how you can get some hands-on experience in using your mouse in a moment.

You can configure a mouse for left-hand use. Doing so makes the button on the right the primary mouse button and the button on the left the secondary mouse button (so your index finger is still over the primary mouse button). If you're a lefty, see Chapter 16 for information on customizing your mouse.

How to Start Windows Me

If Windows Me is already installed on your PC, starting Windows Me is a simple task. Follow these steps:

Caution If Windows Me has not been installed on your PC already, please refer to Appendix A for information on system requirements and instructions on installing Windows Me.

1. If your computer has a floppy disk drive (Figure 1-3), check to make sure no disk is in that drive. If you think a disk is in that drive, push the little button on the front of the drive to pop out the disk.

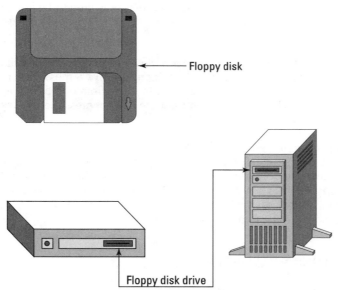

← Floppy disk

Floppy disk drive

Figure 1-3: Remove any floppy disks from the floppy disk drive before turning on your computer.

2. Turn on all peripherals attached to your PC, such as your monitor and printer, and any other connected device that has its own on/off switch.

3. Turn on the main power on the system unit.

4. Wait a minute or so for your computer to *boot up* (start itself and load Windows Me for you).

You'll probably hear some whirring and buzzing as the computer boots up. You might see some little messages (highly technical ones) go by on the screen. For the most part, you needn't worry about those. That's only the computer getting all the various components working and in sync with one another.

Depending on how your computer is currently configured, one of the first prompts you'll need to respond to is the request for a user name and password. The request appears in a *dialog box* that will look like one of the examples shown in Figure 1-4. If your computer is *not* connected to other computers in a network, you may see the dialog box asking for the Windows password. The Windows user name and password are actually optional. If you're the only person who uses this PC, you can actually leave the user name and password boxes empty by clicking the Cancel button in the dialog box, or by pressing the Escape (Esc) key on your keyboard. If you do so the very first time you start Windows Me, it won't ask for a password in the future. If several people will be using this computer, and each person wants to be able to create his or her own unique settings, then each person who logs in should create their own user name and password.

Tip
As you'll learn in the next chapter, the term *dialog box* is used to describe any little box on the screen that asks for information, displays a message, or presents some set of options for you to choose from. To move from one option to another in a dialog box, just click the option you want to fill in or press the Tab key on your keyboard.

If your computer is connected to other computers in a network, you'll be asked to enter a network user name and password. If you want to have access to other computers in the network, you should enter a valid user name and password. If you work in a company that has a network administrator, you should ask that person for your user name and password. Then type those into the blanks in the dialog box. Then click the OK button in the dialog box.

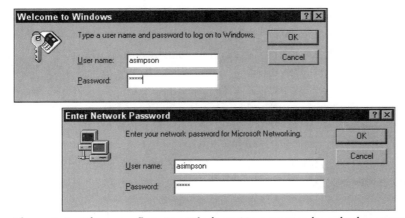

Figure 1-4: When you first start Windows Me, you may be asked to enter a user name and password in a dialog box that looks something like one of these.

Why no floppy disk?

Floppy disks and CD-ROMs are used to transport software, like CDs and cassette tapes are used to transport music, from the factory to your PC. Software that you use all the time, such as Windows Me, is stored on the *hard disk* inside your computer. You never see this hard disk directly because it cannot be removed from the computer.

When you first turn on a computer, it may check to see if a floppy disk is in drive A (the floppy drive). If there is a disk in that drive, the PC attempts to boot up (load the operating system) from that floppy. If the floppy doesn't contain an operating system, then the PC won't start. Instead, some message like "Non-System disk or disk error. Replace and press any key when "ready" appears onscreen.

If that happens, remove the floppy disk from the floppy disk drive. On most computers, you need to push the little button on the front of the drive and the disk will pop out (if a disk is in the floppy drive). Then press any key on the keyboard (like the spacebar, the Enter key, or some letter) to resume startup. Your PC will then automatically go to your hard drive (drive C, as it's called) and load the operating system from that drive.

 Caution

If you do enter a user name and password, you should write both down on a piece of paper, immediately, to make sure you don't forget what they are. Forgetting your user name or password can make using Windows Me very difficult!

Whenever you type in a password, each letter is represented by an asterisk (*). Thus, anything you type will look like a bunch of asterisks. This is normal, so keep typing. The purpose of the asterisks is to prevent someone from peeking over your shoulder to learn your password (technically known as "shoulder surfing").

Finally, I should point out that no matter what you do, you're not making any big commitment. You can always change your password, and even change if, and how, Windows requests a user name and password. Chapter 29 explains how to make those changes.

Help and Support

When Windows Me is fully loaded and ready for action, you might see a window titled Help and Support, shown in Figure 1-5, when you first start up your PC. You have several choices there.

✦ If you want to get some immediate hands-on training in using your mouse and keyboard, click the Tours & Tutorials option in the bar beneath the Search box. The click the first option under Windows Tour (or any other blue underlined text) and follow the onscreen instructions.

✦ If your computer or your copy of Windows Me is brand new and unregistered, you can register your software. If you have access to the Internet, you can use the Registration Wizard to register. Otherwise, you should (eventually) fill out and mail in the registration card that came with Windows Me.

Tip   Don't worry—you can use Windows Me right here and now without registering it. Eventually, however, you should register your copy of Windows Me so Microsoft can find you when they need to announce an update or a fix to the product.

✦ When you want to eliminate the Help and Support window, click the Close (X) button in the upper-right corner of the Welcome to Windows ME window. You'll be given a choice as to whether this window appears automatically each time you start your PC. Click either the Yes or No button.

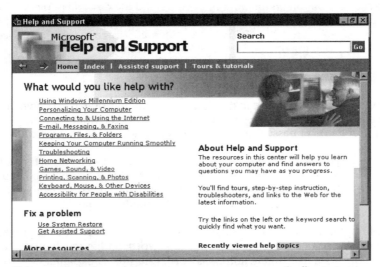

Figure 1-5: Help and Support may appear automatically at startup.

If the Help and Support program doesn't start automatically but you want to try it, click the Start button near the lower-left corner of the screen, then click on Help in the menu that appears.

What's with the ⇨?

Throughout this book, I'll use the symbol ⇨ to separate options you choose in a series. For example, "Click the Start button and choose Programs ⇨ Accessories ⇨ Notepad" is a short-cut way of saying "Click the Start button, and then choose the Programs option, and then choose the Accessories option, and then click the Notepad option."

The Windows Me desktop

For your daily use of your PC, most activity will take place through the Windows Me desktop, shown in Figure 1-6. In this figure, I labeled the various doodads on the desktop you'll use to interact with your computer. Becoming familiar with those names is a good idea, as you'll come across them constantly in your work with Windows Me.

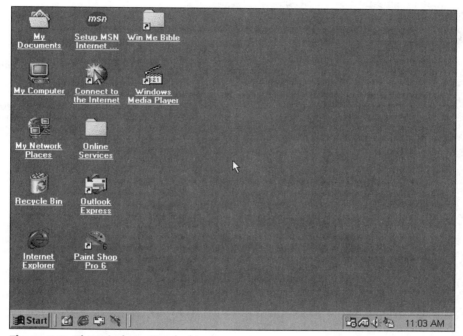

Figure 1-6: The Windows Me desktop

Note

Your Windows Me screen won't look exactly like the one shown in Figure 1-6 because everyone's computer is a little different. But you should see some icons, the taskbar, and so forth.

Once Windows Me is started, it remains available throughout the entire session (that is, until you turn off the computer). So even when you run some other program, Windows Me remains in the background, ready for action. When you finish using a program and close it, you're returned back to Windows Me.

In other words, you might think of Windows Me as a sort of home base. No matter where your mouse and keyboard take you, you can always return to the Windows Me desktop. You'll learn more about starting and exiting programs in Chapter 2. For now, let's look closely at the various doodads pointed out in Figure 1-6.

The desktop and icons

The desktop is the large blank area that acts like your real (wooden or metal) desktop; it's always there. The desktop enables you to choose the programs you want to run. Each little picture on the desktop is an *icon*. Each icon represents some program or some service you can access. To open an icon, you either click or double-click it, depending on how your copy of Windows Me is currently configured. The section titled "To Single-Click or Double-Click?" later in this chapter shows you how to choose one method or the other.

The mouse pointer

The mouse pointer is a little indicator that moves when you move the mouse. Sometimes it appears as a hollow arrow. Other times, it has a different shape, depending on where it's currently resting. When the computer is busy doing something, the mouse pointer turns to a little hourglass symbol. That means "Wait — the computer is doing something." Wait until the mouse pointer changes back to a little arrow (or some other symbol) before you try clicking anything else onscreen.

The Start button, taskbar, Quick Launch toolbar, and indicators

The taskbar normally appears along the bottom edge of the screen. The taskbar can easily be dragged to any edge of the screen, though, so look along all four edges of the screen if you don't see it along the bottom.

If you don't see the taskbar at all, it's probably hidden (out of the way for the moment). Typically, to bring the taskbar into view, you must move the mouse pointer down to the very bottom of the screen.

The Start button on the taskbar is one starting point for launching programs. Clicking that button reveals a menu of options, which I'll discuss as we go along. For now, it's sufficient to know the taskbar is there, it has a name, and it holds the Start button, Quick Launch toolbar, and indicators.

You'll learn lots of techniques for using the taskbar and customizing it to your liking in Chapters 2, 3, 4, and 17. For now, it's sufficient to know where the taskbar and Start button are located.

To Single-Click or Double-Click?

You can choose from two different methods for opening icons on your desktop. The first method, sometime referred to as the "Classic" method, requires that you double-click an icon to open it (or right-click the icon and choose Open from the menu that appears). The alternative approach is to use what's sometimes called "Web view" because of its similarity to using the World Wide Web. With Web view, you don't need to double-click an icon to open it. Just click the icon once. Choosing one approach or the other is simply a matter of personal taste. Though I suspect most people would rather click than double-click. You can tell which style is currently in use by looking at your desktop icons:

✦ If the text beneath the icon is underlined as in the upper left example of Figure 1-7, or if that text suddenly becomes underlined when you touch the icon with your mouse pointer, then you're probably using Web-style navigation, where you can open an icon by slicking it once. Also, with Web-style navigation, whenever the mouse pointer is resting on an icon, the pointer turns into a pointing hand symbol to indicate that the item is clickable.

✦ If the text beneath the icon is not underlined, and the mouse pointer doesn't change to a little hand when it touches the icon, you're probably using the Classic navigation style. To open an icon, you must double-click it. But try clicking once first, just to make sure. If the item doesn't open, you need to double-click.

Figure 1-7: Underlines beneath icon text and pointing hand mouse pointer indicate single-click Web view. Non-underlined text with arrow pointer indicates Classic double-click view.

To choose between the Web and Classic styles of icons:

1. Click the Start button in the lower left corner of the screen.

2. Choose Settings ⇨ Control Panel from the menu that appears.

3. Open the icon titled Folder Options to get to the dialog box titled Folder Options shown in Figure 1-8. To *open* an icon click it or double-click it, depending on which view you've selected.

Tip

If you don't see an icon titled Folder Options, you're probably viewing the brief, simplified version of the Control Panel. Click the ". . . view all Control Panel" option within the Control Panel to view all Control Panel icons.

4. Near the bottom of the dialog box, choose either the "Single-click to open an item" or "Double-click to open an item" option depending on whether you'd prefer to use single-click or double-click.

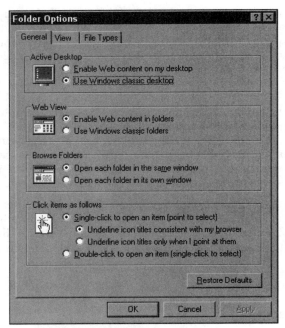

Figure 1-8: The Folder Options dialog box

5. If you do opt for single-click you can decide if you want icon titles to be under-lined all the time, or just when you point to them. This selection just defines how the icons *look* on the screen and won't change how you go about clicking the item.

6. Click the OK button down near the bottom of the dialog box.

Once you've completed all the steps, the dialog box closes (disappears from the screen) and you're returned to the Windows desktop. From now on, whichever set-tings you chose while in the Folder Options dialog box will remain in effect. Should you change your mind in the future, just repeat the steps and choose whatever option(s) you want. Do bear in mind, however, that when I use the term "open the icon," you'll either need to click the icon, or double-click it, depending on which option(s) you chose in the Folder Options dialog box.

How to Get Help with Anything

The Discover Windows Me program provides a good hands-on tour of Windows Me and is a good way to get your cyberfeet wet. But a guided tour can do only so much. Sometimes you need an answer to a question. And many questions not covered in the tour are bound to arise in your daily use of Windows.

Obviously, this book is one good resource for getting your questions answered. But a complete online help system is also at your beck and call. The online help isn't an entertaining tutorial. Instead, it's an electronic reference guide containing mostly text. The online Help system is a great way to find specific information fast, when you need it, even when you don't have a book or manual around.

Instant help through ToolTips

Before I get into the intricacies of the complete online Help system, let me point out some simple techniques you can use to get help and information immediately. The simplest help is the ToolTip, which is a small explanatory message that appears when you rest — but don't click — the mouse pointer on some item for a few seconds. For example, if you rest the mouse pointer on your My Computer icon for a few seconds, a ToolTip like the one shown in Figure 1-9 appears.

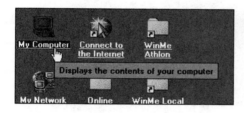

Figure 1-9: ToolTip for the My Computer icon

If you point to (rest the mouse pointer on) the Start button or any of the little icons in the taskbar, you'll see most of those have ToolTips, too. Not all items on your desktop will have ToolTips, but there's a simple technique you can use to see if an item has one. Just rest the mouse pointer on the item for a few seconds to see if a ToolTip appears!

Right-clicking and shortcut menus

Another good technique for getting some quick hints about what an item is or what it can do is to right-click the item to view its shortcut menu. For example, if you move the mouse pointer to the desktop (so it isn't touching an icon, the taskbar, or anything else) and then press and release the secondary mouse button (typically the mouse button on the right), you'll see a shortcut menu for the desktop, as in Figure 1-10.

While the shortcut menu doesn't give you any specific information, it does present a list of options — things you can do to, or with, the object. For instance, if you choose Properties from the shortcut menu for the desktop, you'll be taken to the Display Properties dialog box shown in Figure 1-11. There, you can customize the appearance of the desktop by choosing a tab (near the top of the dialog box) and then making selec-tions from the options that appear below the tab.

The Settings tab in the Display Properties dialog box, shown in Figure 1-11, is especially useful in setting up the size of items on your screen, and the quality of the color, as discussed in Chapter 15. For now, just be aware that right-clicking is yet another way to get information about an item on the screen.

When you finish with the dialog box, click its OK button to save your changes or its Cancel button to bail out without making any changes. After that, you can right-click other items. For instance, try right-clicking the taskbar or Start button to explore what kinds of options they have to offer.

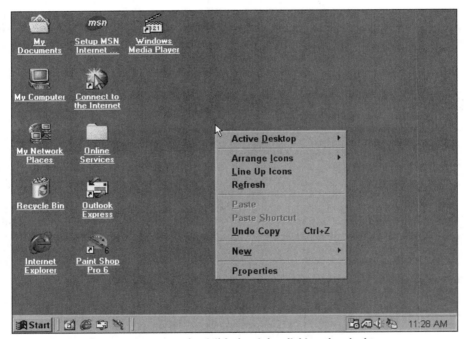

Figure 1-10: Shortcut menu made visible by right-clicking the desktop

Context-sensitive help

The term *context-sensitive help* refers to help that's available and directly relevant to what you're currently trying to do. You have four ways to get to the context-sensitive help (when it's available):

✦ If you see a tiny button with a question mark on it, usually near the upper-right corner of a dialog box (see Figure 1-12), click that button. Then click the item with which you need help.

✦ Right-click the item you're curious about and choose What's This? (if available) from the shortcut menu that pops up.

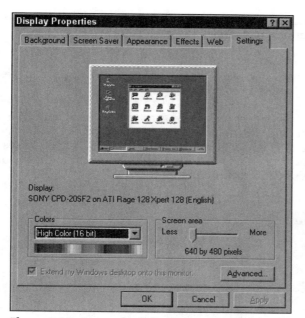

Figure 1-11: A sample dialog box accessed through a shortcut menu

Figure 1-12: When you need help in a dialog box, look for the little Help buttons on the left, or right-click the item to see if it displays a "What's this?" prompt.

✦ If you see a button labeled Help, click it.

✦ Press the Help key (the key labeled F1 near the upper-left corner of your keyboard).

The first option—clicking the question mark (?) button—displays a brief description of whatever you clicked after clicking the question mark (?) button. For example, try these steps:

1. At the far-right edge of the taskbar (most likely near the bottom-right corner of the screen) you should see the time of day (for example, 11:00 AM). Right-click on the time shown and choose Adjust Date/Time to open the Date/Time Properties dialog box.

2. Click the question mark (?) button near the upper-right corner of the dialog box. The mouse pointer now has a small question mark attached to it.

3. Click any item (such as the calendar) for brief help.

4. After reading the brief help message (Figure 1-13), click on or near that message box, or press the Esc key, to remove the message.

The message disappears and the mouse pointer returns to its normal appearance and functionality. If you want help with another item, you must first click the question mark (?) button and then the item with which you want help. In many cases, pressing the F1 key or clicking the Help button will take you straight to the full-on Windows Help system. I discuss how to work that next.

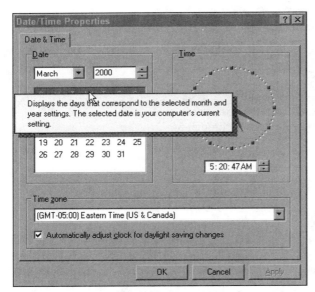

Figure 1-13: Sample brief help message that appears after clicking the question mark (?) button and then the item

The Windows Help system

In addition to the little ToolTips and other help messages, Windows Me offers a complete online help reference. To get to it:

1. Click the Windows Me Start button down near the lower-left corner of the screen.

2. Click the Help option that appears in the menu. You'll be taken to the Help and Support "home page" within the Windows Help system, as shown in Figure 1-14.

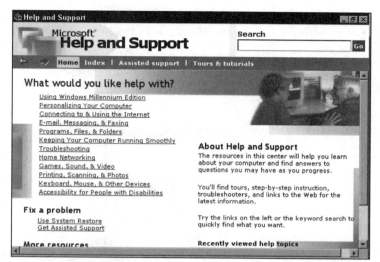

Figure 1-14: The Help and Support home page of Windows' built-in Help

The figure shows the Help page opened to full-screen size. If yours opens as a smaller window and you want to expand that to full-screen size, do either of the following:

✦ Click the Maximize button near the upper-right corner of the Help window. (It's the one with the large square; a ToolTip will show "Maximize" when you're pointing to the correct button.)

✦ Optionally, you can double-click on the title bar across the top of the window.

As will be discussed in Chapter 2, you can use either method above to switch between full-screen and a smaller window size at any time, in any window that appears on the screen.

 If you're at the Windows desktop, you can also press the Help key (F1) to get to Windows Help. Remember, however, that the F1 key is context-sensitive. So if you press F1 while some other dialog box or program is on the screen, you're likely to get help with that particular item or program.

Browsing the Help system

As you can see on the screen, the Help system is pretty self-explanatory. Essentially, any underlined text is a link that you can click to learn more about the topic. As you click on topics to read about, you'll notice that a frame with the options to Print and Change View appears, as in Figure 1-15. For simplicity, we can refer to that frame as a second column here. In general, the left column acts as a table of contents. The actual Help text appears in the right column. Note, too, the Change View icon near the top of the window on the right. Clicking that icon will hide, or display, the Table of Contents column on the left. Very handy if you want to shrink down the Help window without losing sight of the help text.

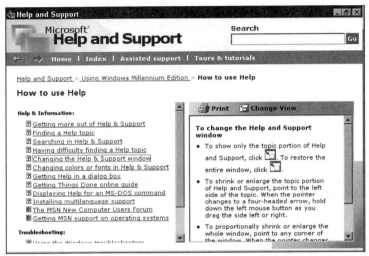

Figure 1-15: Much of the time, the Help system displays two columns of information, topics to choose from on the left, and a Help page on the right.

The icons across the top of Help window offer easy navigation through the Help system. The function of each is described below. Although the first three icons aren't labeled, pointing to them will reveal their names in a ToolTip.

✦ **Back:** After you change to a new page, the Back button is available to take you back to the previous page you were on.

✦ **Forward:** After you click the Back button, the Forward button becomes available. Clicking that button will go back to whatever page you were on before you clicked the Back button.

✦ **Print Current Page:** Prints a copy of the currently displayed Help page.

✦ **Home:** Takes you back to the opening Help page shown back in Figure 1-14.

✦ **Index:** Takes you to an index of Help topics, which you can use like the index at the back of a book. See "Searching the Help System" below for more information.

✦ **Assisted Support:** If your PC is connected to the Internet, takes you to the new Assisted Support feature of Windows Me. See Chapters 5 and 6 for information on connecting to the Internet, and Chapter 8 for more information on Assisted Support.

✦ **Tours & Tutorials:** Provides user-friendly graphical tutorials and tours to further simplify learning Windows Me.

✦ **Exit:** Closes the Help system window.

Searching the Help system

Browsing the Help system is useful when you're just looking to learn about general features and concepts. But for specific information on a topic, you're probably better offer looking up a specific word or phrase. There are a few ways to do so. On the Help home page (or any other page that provides such a prompt), click in the Search Help and Support box, type the word or phrase you're looking for, and then click the Go button. The left column will fill with topics having to do with the word or phrase you search for. Just click any listed topic to see its Help screen in the column to the right.

If you're in the Help system but don't see a "Search " box, you can click the Index option near the top of the Help window instead. The left column will change to an alphabetized listing of keywords. You can scroll down the list of topics using the scroll bar to the right of the index, or by putting the mouse pointer anywhere in the list and spinning your mouse wheel (if your mouse has a wheel). As an alternative to scrolling through the index, you can just click anywhere in the box labeled "Type in the keyword to find." Then, type any word or phrase. As you type, the highlighter bar in the index will attempt to jump to the topic that best matches your typed word or phrase.

Note

If you don't know how to work scroll bars or your mouse wheel yet, sit tight. You'll learn all about that stuff in Chapter 2.

What's with the Internet Connection Wizard?

Some of the choices within the Help system will attempt to access the Internet to provide you with the most current information. If you're computer isn't connected to the Internet, you'll end up at a dialog box titled "Internet Connection Wizard" instead of at the appropriate Internet page. As discussed in Chapter 5, you'll need some kind of modem and an account with an Internet Service Provider (ISP) to get beyond the Internet Connection Wizard to the Help page you were actually supposed to see. Part II of this book, "Becoming an Internet Guru" will tell you everything you need to know. For now, if you simply want to close the Internet Connection Wizard without setting up an account, click the Cancel button near the lower-right corner of the Internet Connection Wizard dialog box.

Once you find an index entry that looks like it might help, you can just double-click the topic to display the appropriate Help page in the column on the right. Or, just click the Help topic once and then click the Display button down near the lower-right corner of the index. The column on the right will display the Help page you requested.

Closing Help

When you've finished using the Help system, you can close it by clicking on the word "Exit" near the upper-right corner of the Help window. Optionally, you can use the same techniques you use to close any other open Window, as discussed in Chapter 2. For example, you can click the Close (X) button in the upper-right corner of the window to close it.

Backing Out of Jams

Sometimes, especially as a beginner, you might open some item and then not know what to do with it. In this case, you'll probably want to back out of that selection until you get to more familiar territory. When you find yourself in unfamiliar territory, try any of these techniques or buttons (see Figure 1-16) to back out gracefully:

✦ Press the Escape key (labeled Esc) on the keyboard. This key is so named because it enables you to escape from unfamiliar territory.

✦ Or, look for a button labeled Cancel and click it.

Figure 1-16: The Escape key, and any of these buttons, will help you back out of unfamiliar territory.

✦ Or, if you see a button labeled Back, click that until you find yourself in more familiar territory.

✦ Or, close the item by clicking the Close (X) button near the upper-right corner of the item.

✦ If all else fails, press Alt+F4 (on the keyboard, hold down the key labeled Alt, press and release the key labeled F4, and then release the Alt key). Doing so will close whatever window is currently open.

If you can remember these five techniques, you should be able to back your way out of any jam, no matter how lost you feel. If you really, really, really get stuck and none of the previous techniques works, you may have to go to the special Close Program dialog box and terminate the current program or reboot the system. This is the least desirable approach because it doesn't give you a chance to save any work. But if the whole computer is hung (won't do anything), this may be your only hope. To get to the Close Program dialog box, press Ctrl+Alt+Del (hold down the Ctrl key, hold down the Alt key, hold down the Delete (Del) key for a moment, and then release all three keys). Chances are you'll be taken to a dialog box that lists all running programs. The hung program (if any) will have the words "not responding" after its name. Click the name of that faulty program and then click the End Task button. If problems persist, you can press Ctrl+Alt+Del again to reboot the system. Or, click the Shut Down button at the bottom of the Close Programs dialog box to shut down your system and start all over again.

Caution   Remember, the techniques discussed here are only for bailing out of unfamiliar territory. If you actually want to save some settings you made in a dialog box, click the OK button to save and activate those settings.

Shutting Down Your PC

One of the most common mistakes newbies make when using a PC is simply to turn off the PC when they're done. This is not good because it doesn't give you, or your computer, a chance to save any changes you made or any work you accomplished. The proper way to shut down your PC at the end of the day is to follow these steps:

1. Click the Start button and then choose Shut Down. You'll come to the dialog box shown in Figure 1-17.

Figure 1-17: Shut down Windows before turning off your computer.

2. If Shut Down doesn't appear in the text box, click the down arrow at the right edge of the text box and choose Shut Down.

3. Click the OK button or press the Enter key.

4. If you've left behind any unsaved documents, you'll be given an option to save them before the computer shuts down. You should choose Yes to save anything you forgot to save earlier.

Note   You'll learn about creating documents and saving your work in Chapter 3. For now, remember you should always shut down Windows Me properly before turning off your PC.

The only safe time to turn off your computer is when you see the message "It's now safe to turn off your computer." If your computer was made within the last couple of years, it may shut down automatically shortly before, or after, that message appears. In that case, you don't need to turn the computer off yourself. If the "It's now safe . . ." message stays on the screen, then you can turn off the main power switch on the PC. You can then turn off any peripheral devices, such as monitor, printer, and exter-nal modem, after you've shut down the PC. Of course, if your printer doubles as a fax machine, you'll probably want to leave it on so it can accept faxes while the computer is off.

To restart your computer and get back to Windows Me at any time in the future, repeat the steps listed under "How to Start Windows Me" earlier in this chapter.

Summary

In this chapter, you learned the most important of Windows Me basic skills. My goal in this chapter has been to help those of you who are new to this program become comfortable with using the mouse and get a sense for the way things work. I'll get into more basic skills in the next chapter. But before you go on, let's review the most important items you've learned in this chapter:

✦ Windows Me is the "consumer" version of Microsoft's Windows product line, designed mainly for home, office, and small business use.

✦ To start Windows Me, simply start your computer (first make sure no floppy disk is in drive A).

✦ To *click* or *click on* something means to move the mouse pointer so it's touching the item you want. Then press and release the primary mouse button.

✦ On a right-handed mouse, the primary button is the one on the left — the one that rests comfortably under your index finger when you're resting your hand properly on the mouse.

✦ To get instant help with a topic, press the F1 key. Or, in a dialog box, click the button labeled Help. Or, click the question mark (?) button and then the item with which you need help.

✦ To get to the full online help for Windows Me, click the Start button and then choose Help from the Start menu that appears.

✦ You should always exit Windows Me before you shut down your PC. Simply click the Start button, choose Shut Down, and click the OK button.

✦   ✦   ✦

Getting Around
Like a Pro

This chapter expands upon what you learned in Chapter 1. In this chapter, you'll improve your basic Windows Me navigational skills. As in Chapter 1, this chapter points out basic skills you need to know to use your PC and Windows Me effectively. This chapter goes into more detail, however. You'll learn techniques for managing windows and dialog boxes, and also how to explore your computer.

Understanding Icons

Imagine a desk with all the usual accoutrements: telephone, calculator, calendar, pens and pencils, and documents you're using. Now imagine you have the power to touch any one of those objects and shrink it to the size of a pea, just to get it out of the way temporarily. That power would certainly help unclutter your desktop. When you need to use one of those pea-sized objects, you could tap it with your finger, and bingo — the object would open in its natural size.

Of course, no real-world desktop works this way. The Windows Me desktop, however, works exactly that way. You can make things appear and disappear just by touching them with your mouse.

A pea-sized object on your computer screen is called an *icon*. Initially, you'll see several icons on your Windows Me desktop, including one named My Computer and another named Recycle Bin. As you start opening icons into windows, you'll see those windows often contain still other icons (see Figure 2-1).

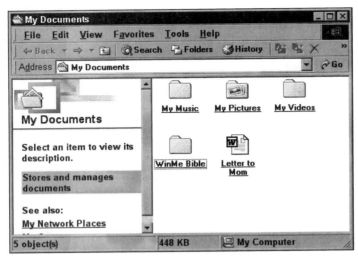

Figure 2-1: Some examples of icons in Windows Me

The appearance of an icon gives you some clue about what kind of stuff is inside the icon and what is likely to appear when you open the icon. The following list summarizes the main types of icons you'll come across:

✦ **Desktop icon:** Some icons on the desktop, including those for My Computer and Recycle Bin, are permanent and cannot be deleted. These provide easy access to commonly used Windows Me tools. Some, such as My Computer and My Documents, open into a window containing more icons. Others, such as Internet Explorer, open into a program.

✦ **Folder icon:** Represents a folder. Opening a folder icon displays the contents of that folder which, in most cases, will be a collection of more icons. In Figure 2-1, My Pictures, and WinMe Bible are all examples of folder icons.

✦ **Program icon:** Represents a program. When you open a program icon, you start the program it represents. For example, opening the Internet Explorer icon launches the Microsoft Internet Explorer program.

✦ **Document icon:** Represents a document; typically this is something you can change and print. The icon usually has a little dog-ear fold in the upper-right corner to resemble a paper document, like the Letter to Mom icon in Figure 2-1. Opening a document icon typically launches whatever program is required to view, change, and print that document, as well as launching the document itself.

✦ **Shortcut icon:** The little arrow in the lower-left corner of an icon identifies that icon as a shortcut to some program, document, folder, or Web site. As you learn in Chapter 4, you can easily create shortcut icons to your own favorite things.

You also come across icons that don't fall into any of these categories. Some icons represent disk drives, printers, help files, settings, and so on. But you can manipulate virtually all icons by using the set of basic skills in the following list:

✦ To open an icon, double-click it if you're using the Classic double-click navigation style, or click it once if you're using the single-click Web-style of navigation discussed in Chapter 1. The icon's contents appear in a window (discussed in the following section).

✦ To move an icon, drag it to any new location on the screen.

Tip

Remember, to drag something means to rest the mouse pointer on the item you want to move, and then to hold down the mouse button as you move the mouse pointer to the new location. To drop the item at the new location, simply release the mouse button.

✦ To see all the options available for an icon, right-click the icon to open its shortcut menu.

✦ To organize all the icons on the desktop or in a window, right-click an empty part of the desktop or window. Point to Arrange Icons on the shortcut menu that appears, and then click whichever option you prefer (By Name, By Type, and so forth).

✦ To have Windows Me automatically arrange icons for you (even if you resize the window), right-click an empty part of the desktop or the window and choose Arrange Icons ➪ Auto Arrange. To turn off the automatic arrangement, repeat this step. When Auto Arrange has a check mark next to it, that means that that feature is currently turned on.

When you put icons on the desktop in alphabetical order by name, the permanent icons remain in their original order starting at the upper-left corner of the screen. But any custom shortcut items you add will be alphabetized after the permanent icons.

When you open an icon, a window appears. Learning how to work those windows is an important part of using your PC. As you learn in the next section, you have quite a bit of control over the size and shape of every window that appears on your screen.

Managing Windows

In the olden days of computers, when you ran a program, that program took over the entire screen. To use a different program, you had to exit the one you were in and then start the other program. That program, in turn, hogged the entire screen. With Windows, you can run as many programs as you want [well, as many programs as you can fit into your PC's random access memory (RAM)]. Rather than hogging the entire screen, each program occupies only a window onscreen. In Figure 2-2, for example, two programs are running and visible on the screen.

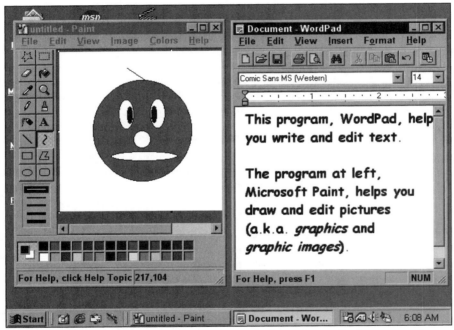

Figure 2-2: Two programs, Microsoft Paint and Microsoft WordPad, open on the desktop, each in its own window

Window dressing

Every window you open will have its own unique contents. But if you look closely, you may notice the frames surrounding those windows are similar. The reason for this similarity is simple: All the tools you use to manage the window are in this frame. Because of this arrangement, no matter how perplexed you may be by the contents of a window, you can always use the tools on the window's border to manipulate the window. Figure 2-3 shows the tools that frame most windows.

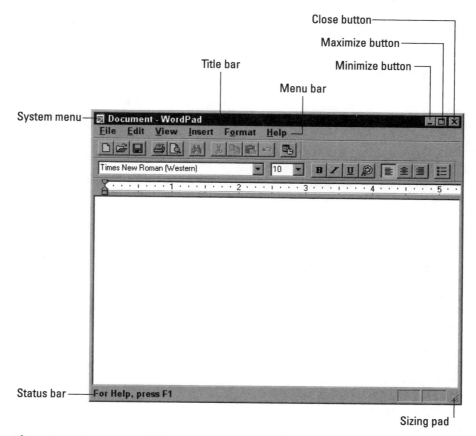

Figure 2-3: Features available on most windows that open on your screen

Most windows have all of the tools shown in Figure 2-3. The following sections describe how you work with each tool. (If you want to open the WordPad window on your own screen, click the Start button and choose Programs ➪ Accessories ➪ WordPad.)

Title bar

The title bar shows the System Menu icon, the title of the window or name of the program being run in the window, and the buttons for resizing and closing the window. The title bar alone offers some handy features:

✦ To expand a window to full-screen size or to shrink it back to its original size, double-click its title bar.

✦ To move a window to some new location on the screen, drag the window by its title bar.

Remember, to *drag* something means to put the mouse pointer on it and then to hold down the mouse button while moving the mouse. You can only move a window if it's smaller than the entire screen.

Minimize button

When you click the Minimize button, the window disappears and shrinks to a button in the taskbar. Doing so gets the window out of the way for the moment so you can see the desktop behind that window. To reopen a minimized window, click its button in the taskbar.

As an alternative to using the Minimize button in the window frame, you can click the window's button down in the taskbar to show/hide that window. You can minimize all the windows onscreen by choosing Minimize All Windows from the taskbar's shortcut menu. To open the shortcut menu, you need to right-click some neutral part of the taskbar. To redisplay the minimized windows, right-click the taskbar again and choose Undo Minimize All.

Windows Me always leaves a little extra space between the last (rightmost) button in the taskbar and the indicators. That little gray patch is the neutral area for you to right-click.

Maximize button

Clicking the Maximize button expands the window to full-screen size (a quick way to hide other windows that may be distracting you). When the window is full-screen size, the Maximize button turns into the Restore button, and you cannot move the window on the desktop. To return the window to its previous size, click the Restore button. That button will show two little windows on its face and will always be between the Minimize and Close buttons in the window. When you point to the button, its ToolTip reads "Restore."

Instead of using the Maximize and Restore buttons, you can double-click the title bar to switch between a maximized and restored view of the window.

Combination keystrokes (*key+key*)

Combination keystrokes, for which you hold down one key while tapping another, are common in Windows, although most are optional alternatives to using the mouse to do something. The combination keystrokes always consist of one of the "special keys" labeled Alt (Alternate), Ctrl (Control), or Shift (uppercase). You hold down that key, tap (press and release) the second key, and then release the first key.

For example, Ctrl+A means hold down the Ctrl key, press and release the letter A, and then release the Ctrl key. Shift+F1 means hold down the Shift key, press and release the function key labeled F1, and then release the Shift key. Alt+Enter means hold down the Alt key, press and release the Enter key, and then release the Alt key.

Close button

Clicking the Close button closes the window, taking it off the screen and out of the taskbar as well. If you've been working on a document and haven't saved your work, you'll be given a chance to do so before the window closes. You learn more about creating and saving documents in Chapter 3, "Opening Programs and Documents."

Border and sizing pad

The frame, or border, that surrounds a window is an important tool. You size the window by dragging its border. Many windows have a large sizing pad in the lower-right corner; this pad is especially easy to drag. (No sizing pad will appear if the status bar is turned off.) Of course, you can size any window by dragging any corner. The sizing pad only gives you a little larger area on which to position the mouse.

To size and arrange all the open windows instantly — so you can see their title bars — right-click any neutral part of the taskbar. Next, choose Cascade Windows from the shortcut menu that appears.

Toolbars

Some windows also have a toolbar just below the menu bar. The toolbar provides one-click access to the most frequently used menu commands. Most toolbars provide ToolTips, a brief description that appears on the screen after you rest the mouse pointer on the button for a few seconds.

In many programs you can display toolbars with or without labels under or next to the button icons. Just right-click the toolbar, or any button on the toolbar and choose Customize from the shortcut menu that appears. In the Customize Toolbar dialog box that appears choose one of the following options from the Text Options drop-down list:

Tip

To open a drop-down list, click its small down-arrow button. To choose an option from the menu that appears, just click the option you want.

✦ **Show text labels:** Displays a label on each button to briefly describe what the button does. Good for beginners but makes the toolbar tall thereby taking up more space on the screen.

✦ **Selective text on right:** Shows labels to the right of some (but not all) button icons in the toolbar. Sort of an intermediate step between "Show text labels" and "No text labels" for intermediate users. Keeps the toolbar narrow, but may require scrolling to the left and right to view all buttons.

✦ **No text labels:** Removes all text labels showing only the button icons. Good for experienced users who know the meaning of each icon because it makes the toolbar as small as possible. Pointing to a button will still display its ToolTip as well.

If the window you're viewing at the moment isn't wide enough to display all the buttons in the toolbar, you'll see the symbol >> at the right edge of the toolbar, or the symbol << at the left edge of the toolbar. Click on that << or >> to scroll in that direction to view more buttons.

Sometimes, several toolbars are available in a program's window, but may be "turned off" (invisible). In programs that offer multiple toolbars you can usually see what's available, and choose to show or hide toolbars, by choosing View ➪ Toolbars from the window's menu bar. Currently visible toolbars will have a check mark next to their name in the menu that appears. To show, or hide, a toolbar, click the name of the tool. You can hide or display as few or as many toolbars as you wish. You can also arrange toolbars by dragging the little vertical bar that appears at the left edge of a toolbar. Drag the vertical bar left or right to widen/narrow the toolbar. Drag the vertical bar up or down to combine two toolbars into one or to separate toolbars onto separate rows.

Status bar

The status bar along the bottom of a window shows you the status of various things inside the window. You'll see some examples as you go along in this book. For now, be aware that in many windows you can hide or display the status bar by choosing View ➪ Status Bar. The Sizing Pad at the lower-right corner of a window is visible only when the Status Bar is visible. To show or hide the status bar, choose View ➪ Status Bar from the window's title bar.

Menus

Many windows that you open will have a menu bar across the top. To view one of those menus, click whatever menu you want to open. If your hands happen to be on the keyboard rather than the mouse, you can hold down the Alt key and type the underlined letter in the menu command. For example, pressing Alt+F would open the File menu (if the current window has a menu bar with a File option in it).

Once the menu opens, you'll see more options. On an open menu, you can select any option by clicking it, or by pressing the underlined letter in the command on your keyboard. It's not necessary to hold down the Alt key first once the menu is open. You can also use the arrow keys to move around through menu options. Press Enter when the option you want is highlighted.

Some menus will show symbols like right-pointing arrows, down-pointing arrows, and shortcut keys, as in the example shown in Figure 2-4. A right-pointing arrow indicates that there are more options on a submenu. Clicking (or just pointing to) that option will open the submenu. Down-pointing arrows indicate that not all options are currently visible. Pointing to, or clicking on the down-pointing arrow(s) expands the menu to show the full range of options. The shortcut key shows you what key you can press as an alternative to using the menu. For example, the File menu shown in the figure has a Save option on it. The Ctrl+S combination keystroke tells you that as an alternative to going through the menus, you can just press Ctrl+S on the keyboard to save your work.

The icon to the left of some options shows you the toolbar alternative to going through the menu. For example, rather that choosing File ⇨ Save or pressing Ctrl+S, you could also just click the little disk icon in the program's toolbar.

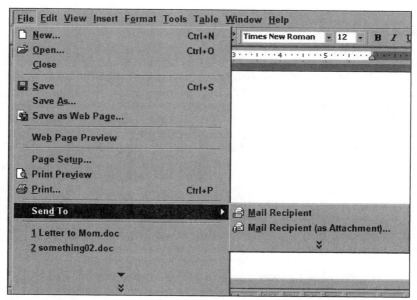

Figure 2-4: Sample open menu

Should you ever open a menu by accident and want to close it without making a selection, you can do either of the following:

✦ Press the Escape (Esc) key.

✦ Or, click some neutral area just outside the menu.

Incidentally, all these basic menu bar concepts apply to the Start menu and the small menu that appears when you right-click an icon. You can also open the Start menu by pressing the Windows key (if you have one) on your keyboard. That's the key with the little flying window on it. If you don't have a Windows key on your keyboard, pressing Ctrl+Esc or Alt+S will also open the Start menu.

Occasionally, you'll come across a menu option that acts as a *toggle*. Which is to say the option represents some feature that can be turned on, or turned off. The Auto Arrange option described earlier in this chapter is an example of a toggle in that it's a feature that can be either turned on, or turned off. If a toggle option is currently turned on, a check mark will appear next to it in the menu. If the option is currently turned off, no check mark appears. When you click a toggle option in a menu, you switch it to the opposite state. If you open a menu and see a toggle option that's already in the state you want it to be, you can just press the Escape (Esc) key or click outside the menu to close it without changing the current setting.

System menu

The System menu enables you to move, size, and close the window by using the keyboard rather than the mouse. You might find this handy if you do a lot of typing and prefer not to take your hands off the keyboard to manage a window. To open the System menu, press Alt+Spacebar (hold down the Alt key, press and release the spacebar, and then release the Alt key) or click the System menu icon in the upper-left corner of the window. Once the System menu is open, you can choose options in the usual manner. Click the option you want. Or, on the keyboard, type the underlined letter of the option you want; for example, type the letter *n* to choose the Minimize option.

If several windows are open on the screen, pressing Alt+Spacebar opens the System menu for the current window only (the one with the darkened title bar). To make some other window the current window, click anywhere in that window. Or, hold down the Alt key and press the Tab key until the program you want to use is framed in the dialog box that appears, and then release the Alt key.

If you choose the Move or Resize option, you can then move or resize the window using the arrow keys. When you finish moving or resizing the window, press the Enter key. As with earlier versions of Windows, you can close any open window by double-clicking its System menu icon.

Closing versus minimizing a window

Think of minimizing a window as taking some document on a real desktop and sliding it into a desk drawer. The document is not cluttering your desk anymore, but it is within easy reach. Just click the document's taskbar button, and you're back in action. Closing a window, on the other hand, is more like putting a real folder back in the file cabinet. You still can get back to the document when you want it. But you'll need to restart the program from scratch, at which point it opens up with no document. Then you need to open the document you want to work with using options on the program's File menu, as discussed in Chapter 3.

From a technical standpoint, closing a window has two advantages: It frees the memory (RAM) the program was using, and it gives you an opportunity to save your work. Minimizing a window does neither of those; it just shrinks the window to a taskbar button to get it out of the way for the moment.

Top ten tips for managing windows

If all the gizmos on the window's border have your mind reeling, perhaps it would be easier to consider what you actually want to do with the windows open on your desktop. The following are the main things you need to know:

✦ To open a window, double-click its icon (if you're using Classic style) or click its icon (if you're using Web style).

✦ To hide an open window temporarily (to unclutter your desktop a bit), click the window's Minimize button or click that window's taskbar button.

✦ To view an open window that is covered by other windows or is minimized, click that window's taskbar button.

✦ To move a window, drag it by its title bar to some new location onscreen.

✦ To size a window, drag its lower-right corner or any border.

✦ To enlarge a window to full-screen size so it completely covers any other windows, double-click its title bar or click its Maximize button.

✦ To restore a maximized window to its previous size, double-click its title bar or click its Restore button.

✦ To arrange all open windows in a stack with their title bars showing, right-click any neutral area of the taskbar and choose Cascade Windows from the shortcut menu.

✦ To close a window, click the Close (X) button in the upper-right corner of the window.

To reopen a closed window, you must repeat whatever steps you took to open it the first time. Closing a window also removes its button from the taskbar.

Using the Taskbar

The taskbar at the bottom of the screen contains a button for each open window on the desktop. At first, it may seem stupid to show buttons only for open windows. If a window is already open, why do you also need to see a button for it? The answer: Having a window open is no guarantee you can see that window. Windows can (and often do) overlap or completely cover one another. The beauty of the taskbar is you can bring any open window from hiding simply by clicking its taskbar button.

You can do many cool things with the taskbar, as summarized in the following list:

✦ To bring an open window to the forefront, click its taskbar button.

✦ To minimize an open window so it shrinks to a button on the taskbar, click its taskbar button.

✦ To see the options for a particular window, right-click its taskbar button.

✦ To arrange all the open windows on the desktop, right-click a neutral spot on the taskbar and then choose Cascade Windows, Tile Windows Horizontally, or Tile Windows Vertically. Experiment with these options whenever you have two or more open windows on the desktop, to see for yourself how each option arranges the windows. (Tile Windows Vertically is my personal favorite.)

✦ To minimize (or restore) all windows, right-click a neutral spot on the taskbar and then choose Minimize All Windows or Undo Minimize All.

✦ To move the taskbar to some other edge of the screen, position the mouse pointer in a neutral area of the taskbar. Then hold down the mouse button, drag the taskbar to some new location, and release the mouse button.

✦ To size the taskbar (to make it thinner or thicker), drag its inner edge (the edge nearest the center of the screen) up or down.

Figure 2-5 shows an example of the Windows desktop with several program windows open, and arranged in a "cascading" format where the windows are arranged like a stack of paper, but with the each window's title bar visible. To cascade the open windows like that, right-click the taskbar and choose Cascade Windows. Although it isn't always obvious at first, each button in the taskbar corresponds to one open window on the desktop.

The more open windows you have, the more buttons there are in the taskbar. At some point, the buttons may be too small to see much information about the window the button represents. If you rest the mouse pointer on a taskbar button, however, a ToolTip appears showing the complete title of the window the button represents. For example, in Figure 2-5, the mouse pointer is resting on a button with only "Wi..." visible. The ToolTip informs us the button actually represents the window titled Windows Media Player.

You can personalize the taskbar in a variety of ways to suit your own work style and environment. I discuss those options in Chapter 17, "Organizing Your Virtual Office." For now, the basic skills you've learned should hold you. At this juncture, I'd like to turn your attention to some basic concepts about how things are organized in your computer.

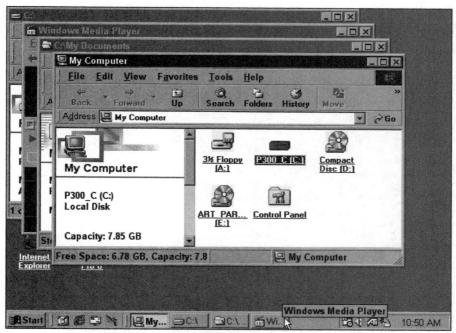

Figure 2-5: Several open windows displayed in a cascading format

Dialog Boxes and Common Controls

A dialog box is sort of like a window. But rather than representing an entire program, a dialog box generally contains some simple settings from which you can choose. The term *dialog box* comes from the fact that you carry on a kind of "dialog" with the box by making selections from the options it presents. Controls within a dialog box are similar to the controls on any other kind of machine, be it a car, dishwasher, or stereo. Controls let you control how a program behaves and looks.

You've already seen a few examples of dialog boxes. For instance, the Display Properties dialog box enables you to control your display (screen). To get to the Display Properties dialog box now and look at some examples of controls, follow these steps:

1. Right-click some neutral area of the desktop.

2. In the shortcut menu that appears, choose Properties.

The Display Properties dialog box opens, looking something like Figure 2-6.

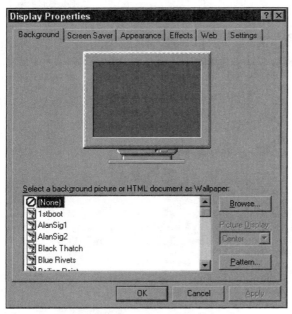

Figure 2-6: The Display Properties dialog box

Within the dialog box, you see examples of some common controls. In the following sections, I'd like to explain briefly how to work all the different kinds of controls you may come across in your daily use of Windows. The sample Display Properties dialog box doesn't offer all the controls I discuss here. But trust me, you will eventually come across all the controls described in the next few sections.

Tabs

Some dialog boxes contain more controls than can actually fit into the box. In this case, options are split into two or more tabs. For example, the Display Properties dialog box shown in Figure 2-6 contains tabs labeled Background, Screen Saver,

Appearance, Effects, Web, and Settings. To view the options offered by a tab, click the tab you want. Alternatively, you can hold down the Ctrl key while pressing the Tab key to move from one tab to the next. Pressing Ctrl+Shift+Tab moves through the tabs in the opposite order, from right to left.

Buttons

You've already seen plenty of examples of buttons (and you'll see plenty more!). Buttons are simple. You click them with your mouse. If a button has an underlined letter in its label, you can optionally hold down the Alt key and tap on the key that represents the underlined letter. For example, as an alternative to clicking a button labeled Pattern, you could press Alt+P.

You might notice one button in a group has a slightly darker border than the others, like the OK button shown in Figure 2-7. That darker button is called the *default button* and, as an alternative to clicking directly on that button, you can press the Enter key. Many dialog boxes will also have a Cancel button, which enables you to escape gracefully from the dialog box without saving any changes. As an alternative to clicking the Cancel button, you can press the Esc key.

Figure 2-7: Examples of buttons

If your hands happen to be on the keyboard rather than the mouse, and you want to choose a button, you can press the Tab key to move forwards from one control to the next, or Shift+Tab to move backward through the controls until the button you want to press is highlighted with a dotted line. Then press Enter to push that highlighted button.

The buttons play an important role in dialog boxes. Keeping them straight is important. To summarize:

✦ The Apply button (if available and enabled) applies your selection right now, without closing the dialog box.

✦ The OK button applies your selection(s) and then closes the dialog box.

✦ The Cancel button closes the dialog box without applying or saving any options you selected (except any you already applied).

✦ Similarly, closing the dialog box by using the Close (X) button or pressing Alt+F4 without having first clicked the Apply button closes the dialog box without saving any of your selections.

Don't forget the handy Help (?) button displayed near the top of many dialog boxes. You can click this button and then click any option within the dialog box to learn more about that option.

Dimmed (disabled) controls

Sometimes you'll come across controls that appear to be dimmed or grayed out, like the Apply button back in Figure 2-6. No, these are not mistakes. When a control is dimmed (aka *disabled*), it means that the control isn't relevant or meaningful at the moment. So there would be no point in selecting it. For example, the Apply button in Figure 2-7 is dimmed because I haven't made any selections from the dialog box yet, and hence there's nothing to apply to the actual screen. As soon as the situation changes and the control becomes meaningful, it will automatically be *enabled* (un-dimmed).

Option buttons and check boxes

Option buttons (also called radio buttons) are a set of two or more mutually exclusive options. The name radio button comes from the buttons on old-fashioned car radios, where pushing a button to select a station automatically unpushed whatever button was previously pressed. The left side of Figure 2-8 shows a hypothetical group of radio buttons. Choosing a radio button automatically deselects whichever button was selected before making the change. Thus, you can only select one radio button.

Even though many people call them radio buttons, the official name of those doohickeys in Windows is *option buttons*. Apple Computer originally created radio buttons as part of the Macintosh operating system. When Microsoft put radio buttons into Windows, Apple balked because it had come up with the concept and term. So rather than take this option out of Windows, Microsoft renamed them option buttons. Hence, the two different names for exactly the same type of options.

Clicking a radio button using your mouse is simple. In many cases, you can even click the text to the right of the radio button to select that button. Choosing radio buttons with the keyboard is a little trickier. Within the dialog box, you need to press the Tab or Shift+Tab keys until one of the radio button options is selected (has a little gray border around it or its label). Then you can use the arrow keys to move that gray border to the option you want. To move out of the radio button group, press the Tab or Shift+Tab keys.

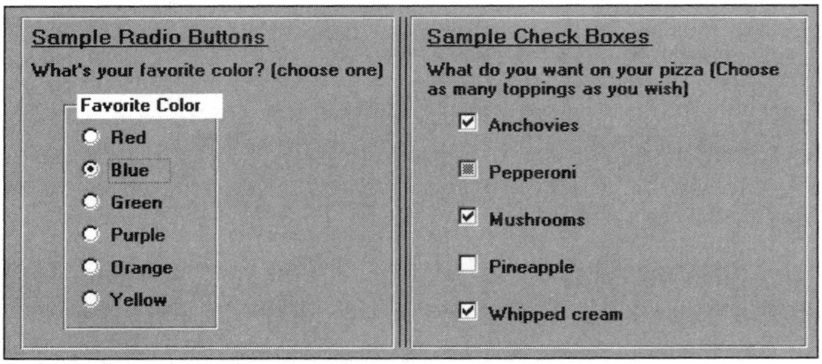

Figure 2-8: Hypothetical examples of radio buttons and check boxes

Check boxes, like the examples shown in the right side of Figure 2-8, enable you to turn some option on or off. When a check box is selected (contains an X or a check mark), then the option is turned on. When the check box is empty (clear) the option is turned off. If the check box is gray in the middle, that usually means that some, but not all, of a subset of options is selected. (But don't worry about that right now.) To select, or clear, a check box, click it. Often, you can click the text to the right of a check box to turn it on and off.

While the mouse is the simplest way to turn a check box on or off, you can also do so with the keyboard. Press Tab or Shift+Tab until the option you want has a gray border around it. Then press the spacebar to select and deselect the check box.

Sliders and scroll bars

Sliders and scroll bars enable you to adjust settings or to scroll to text currently out of view. Some examples of sliders and scroll bars are shown in Figure 2-9. Working sliders and scroll bars with the mouse is easy. To move the slider:

✦ Drag the little slider box to some new place along the slider bar.

✦ Or, click somewhere along the slider bar to move the slider box to (or in the direction of) the place you clicked.

✦ If buttons are on either end of the slider, you can click those to move the slider box a small amount in either direction.

✦ If your mouse has a wheel, spinning the wheel will scroll up and down through the options. If it doesn't work the first time you try it, try clicking on, or to the left of, the scroll bar. Then spin the wheel again.

You can sometimes work slider bars using the keyboard. Often, pressing an arrow key or the Page Up (PgUp) and Page Down (PgDn) keys enables you to scroll through underlying text. In situations where no underlying text exists, as in the sample Screen area slider, you can move the focus (little gray frame) to the control by pressing the Tab or Shift+Tab keys. Once the slider control is framed, you can use the left and right arrow keys to move the slider left and right.

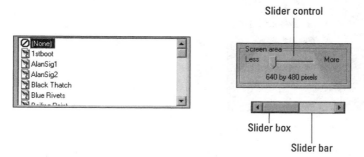

Figure 2-9: Some examples of sliders and scroll bars

Drop-down lists

A drop-down list (also called a combo box) is a small control containing some text and a little down-pointing arrow. Clicking that down-pointing arrow opens a list of choices, as in the right-hand side of Figure 2-10. To make a selection from the list, click whatever option you want.

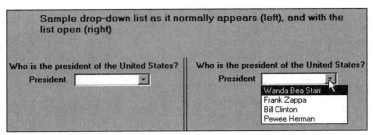

Figure 2-10: A drop-down list box closed (at left) and open (on the right)

Like other controls, it is possible to work a drop-down list via the keyboard. The trick is to press Tab or Shift+Tab until the blinking cursor is inside the control you want. To display the drop-down list, press Alt+Down Arrow (hold down the Alt key, press the down arrow key on the keyboard, and then release both keys). Once the list is open, you can select an option by moving the highlighter up and down using the up and down arrow keys. When the option you want is highlighted, press Alt+Enter.

Lists

A list or list box is a list of alternative options. To choose an option from a list, click it. If the list has a scroll bar next to it, as in the examples shown in Figure 2-11, you can use this scroll bar to scroll up and down the list to view options that are scrolled out of view.

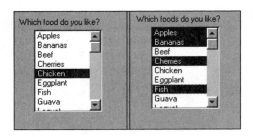

Figure 2-11: Sample list box control

Combination clicks (key+click)

In many situations you can hold down one of the "special keys" while clicking the mouse button to change the effect of the click. For example, Shift+click means "Hold down the Shift key, click the item, and then release the Shift key." Ctrl+click means "Hold down the Ctrl key, click the item, and then release the Ctrl key.

Some lists enable you to choose multiple items, as in the right-hand side of the figure. To select multiple items from a list, use these techniques:

✦ To select one item, click it.

✦ To select an additional item without unselecting the first one, Ctrl+click the option you want (hold down the control (Ctrl) key while clicking the item you want).

✦ You can also deselect a single selected item using Ctrl+click.

✦ To select a range of options, use Shift+click. That is, click (or Ctrl+click) the first option you want, and then Shift+click the last item in a group you want.

✦ You can hold down both the Ctrl and Shift keys while clicking to select a range of options without deselecting any currently selected items.

You can also make selections from a list box using the keyboard. Press Tab or Shift+Tab until the focus (the gray frame) is inside the list box. Then use the up and down arrow keys to move the highlighter to the option you want and press Enter."

To jump to the bottom of a list, press Ctrl+Down Arrow. To jump back up to the top of the list, press Ctrl+Up Arrow. You can also select a range of objects using the keyboard. Move the highlighter to the first option you want, and then hold down the Shift key while pressing the down or up arrow key to extend the selection up or down.

Text boxes

Text boxes enable you to type in text or numbers. A text box can be small, only large enough to handle a name, word, or short phrase. But you might also come across some larger text boxes capable of handling multiple lines of text. Some text boxes, particularly those displaying numbers or dates, also have spin buttons next to them. Figure 2-12 shows some examples.

Figure 2-12: These are examples of text boxes. The last one has a spin button attached.

To type text into a text box, you must first move the blinking cursor into the text box. You can do so by either clicking the text box or pressing Tab or Shift+Tab until the blinking cursor is in the text box you want. Then start typing.

Changing text

Several general rules apply to typing and editing (changing) text in text boxes, as well as most forms of text in general. To make simple changes or corrections, you can position the blinking cursor where you want to make a change, either by clicking the spot or by using the arrow keys. Then:

✦ To delete the character to the right of the cursor, press the Delete (Del) key.

✦ To delete the character to the left of the cursor, press the Backspace key.

✦ To insert new text, start typing.

✦ To choose between insert and overwrite mode, press the Insert (Ins) key.

Let me explain the difference between insert mode and overwrite mode. Let's say a text box already contains this text:

```
Wanda Starr
```

Next, you place the cursor just to the left of the S in Starr. If you then type Bea and a space, in insert mode, the new text is inserted, like this:

```
Wanda Bea Starr
```

If you typed Bea followed by a blank space in overwrite mode, the new text would replace existing text, like this:

```
Wanda Bea r
```

In the previous example, the new letters Bea and the blank space that follows have replaced the letters Star.

Selecting text

To change or delete a chunk of text, you can also select that text first. To select text, do one of the following:

✦ Drag the mouse pointer through the text you want to select.

✦ Position the blinking cursor to the start or end of the text you want to select, and then hold down the Shift key while you press the arrow keys to extend the selection.

✦ In some cases, you can select all the text in a text box by clicking the label next to the text box.

✦ Select a single word by double-clicking that word.

The selected text will be highlighted, typically as white letters against a blue background. Once you select a chunk of text, you can:

✦ Press Delete (Del) to delete the selected text.

✦ Or, start typing new text.

When you type new text, whatever you type replaces what was previously selected. Here's an example: At the top of Figure 2-13 is a text box that already contains some text — `http://www.microsoft.com` — (that's a Web site address, or a URL, but the technique I'm discussing here works with any text).

The middle example in the figure shows how the text looks after I selected only the *microsoft* portion. The final example shows how the text looks after I type *coolnerds*. The new text has completely replaced the selected text.

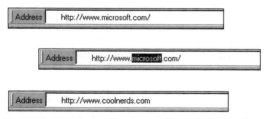

Figure 2-13: Example of selecting and replacing text

Using spin buttons

If a text box displays a number, a date, or a time, the text box may have a pair of little spin buttons attached to it, like the bottom example shown back in Figure 2-12. You can type and change text inside the text box using any of the techniques previously described. You can also increase or decrease the number(s) in the box by clicking the spin buttons. If the box contains several distinct numbers, like the time of day shown near the bottom of Figure 2-12, you can click any single number in the text box, and then use the spin buttons to increase or decrease only the number near the blinking cursor.

How Files Are Organized

Everything I've discussed so far is vitally important to using Windows Me because you must be able to manipulate the various objects on your screen to get anything done. Managing windows and icons onscreen is as important as managing papers and other objects on your real desktop. Where you get the stuff that appears on the desktop differs between your real desktop and your virtual Windows Me desktop. In a real-world desktop, most of the documents you work with probably are stored in a file cabinet. On a computer, all the objects you can bring to the desktop are stored on a computer disk.

In a real-world file cabinet, you go through the following steps to fetch whatever you want:

1. Go to the appropriate file cabinet.
2. Open the appropriate drawer.
3. Pull out the appropriate file.

On a computer, you do this instead:

1. Go to the appropriate disk drive.
2. Open the appropriate folder(s).
3. Open the appropriate file icon.

You're probably somewhat familiar with these terms from earlier computer experience. To play it safe, however, the following sections define those terms.

Drives

Anything in the computer is stored on a disk. The disk spins so the computer can read and write stuff to the disk. The device that actually spins the disk around is called a disk drive (or drive for short). A disk drive generally has a one-letter name. Your floppy disk drive, for example, is named A; you may have a second floppy disk drive named B. In general, you use the floppy disk drives to copy files to and from the hard disk inside your computer, to make backups, or to copy stuff from one PC to another.

Most of the stuff in the computer is stored on your hard disk drive, which usually is named C. Unlike floppy disks, the hard disk usually isn't visible to you because it's sealed up tight inside the PC. Typically, a hard disk can hold as much information as thousands of floppy disks.

You may have some other drives attached to your computer. If you have a CD-ROM drive, it may be named D.

Why your screen doesn't look like mine

If you followed along with this section by opening My Computer and other icons on your own PC, your screen probably won't match mine exactly. That's because every PC starts out as sort of a big, empty electronic file cabinet. You fill this file cabinet by adding whatever folders and files are appropriate to your own work.

One way to create files is to create and save documents, as discussed in Chapter 3. You also can create folders and files by using menu commands, as discussed in Chapter 18, Also, when you install a new program, the installation procedure automatically creates folders and files for storing that particular program, as discussed in Chapter 25.

To see what drives are available on your computer, open the My Computer icon on the desktop. When the My Computer window opens, you see an icon for each drive (and perhaps a few folders that represent other hardware and special features on your computer). In Figure 2-14, for example, you can see that My Computer has a 3½-inch floppy drive named A, a hard disk named C, and two CD-ROM drives named D and E.

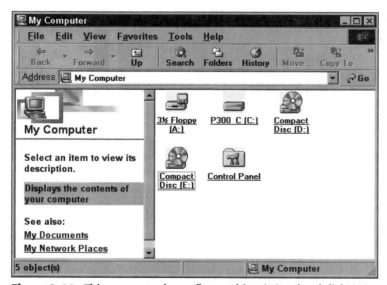

Figure 2-14: This computer has a floppy drive (A:), a hard disk (C:), and two CD-ROM drives (D: and E:).

Note

In case you're wondering why I have two CD-ROM drives, one is a regular CD-ROM drive that just reads CDs. The other is a CD-RW drive for creating CDs.

Folders

A hard disk or CD-ROM can contain hundreds, even thousands, of files. If you put all those files on the disk without organizing them, finding things later could be difficult. The process would be similar to taking all the files from your file cabinet and dumping them into a large box.

Many folders are created automatically when you install new programs. If I were to open the icon for drive C, a new window would open, showing the names of the folders (and files, if any) on that drive, as shown in Figure 2-15. You'll learn how you create, manage, and delete folders in Chapter 17, "Organizing Your Virtual Office." For now, it's sufficient to know a folder can contain many files and also other folders.

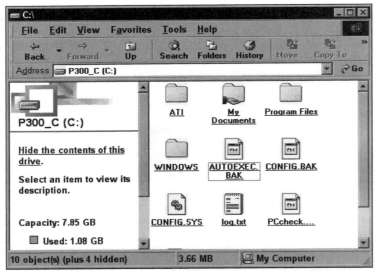

Figure 2-15: Opening a drive icon displays the names of folders and/or files on the disk in that drive.

Tip   If you're an experienced DOS, Windows 3.*x*, or Unix/Linux user, you may be familiar with the term *directory*. A Windows Me folder is actually a directory.

Files

A file is most like the contents of a manila file folder in a file cabinet. Each item in the computer is in its own file. For example, if you use a word processing program to type a letter and then save that letter, the letter will be stored in its own file. As you'll learn in Chapter 3, whenever you create a file of your own, you can give it whatever filename you want. For example, filenames such as *Letter To Mom* and *Summer 2000 Quarterly Sales* are perfectly valid. They're very descriptive and you can guess what's in the file just by looking at its name. The only thing you *don't* want to do when naming a file is use punctuation marks like periods, asterisks (*), slashes (/), backslashes (\), question marks (?) and such, as these have special meaning. You'll learn the roles played by various punctuation marks as you progress through this chapter and the next. For now, it's sufficient to know that every file has a name. And no two files within a single folder can have the same name.

As mentioned earlier, a file's icon gives you some clue about the type of information in the file. Program files have icons that represent those programs. Opening a program generally starts this program. Opening a document file generally opens this document, as well as a program that can help you view, change, and print this document. You'll see many examples as you proceed through the chapters ahead.

Filename extensions

Many filenames have *extensions*. The extension usually contains three or four characters preceded by a period at the end of the filename. For example, the filename "index.htm" has the .htm extension. The filename "index.html" has the extension .html. The extension gives Windows (and you) some clue as to what's contained within the file. For example, a file with the .htm or .html extension is usually a Web page. When you click (or double-click) on such a file's icon, Windows "knows" that it needs to open a Web browser — such as Microsoft Internet Explorer or Netscape Navigator — to display the contents of that file on the screen. Another way of stating that is that Windows *associates* all files with the .htm or .html exten-sion to your Web browser program. As you'll learn a little later in this chapter, you can decide whether you want the extensions to be visible, or invisible, in My Computer and other programs that let you browse through your files. The default (normal) setting is to hide the filename extensions.

If you try to open a document file that's not associated with any particular program on your computer, Windows will pop up a list of programs for you to choose from. As a beginner, it's not always easy to know which program to use to open a specific file. Chapter 34 discusses these issues in depth. For now, it's sufficient to know that files have names and, often, a small extension at the end of the filename that tells Windows something about the contents of that file.

Paths

A drive can hold a lot of files. To help keep things organized, you can divide a drive into folders, where each folder can hold its own set of related files. For example, you might put all the letters you type into a folder named My Letters. You could put all your spreadsheets (or whatever) into some other folder. The exact location of a file on the disk is often referred to as a *path*. The path is a string of names, separated by one colon (for the drive) and backslashes for the folders, leading from the most general location (the drive) to the most specific (the actual folder and filename). The general syntax looks like this: *drive*:*folder(s)**filename*.

For example, c:\windows\whatever.com refers to a file named "whatever.com" in the folder named "windows" on disk drive C. In other words, to get to the file named "whatever.com" the computer has to follow a path that starts with drive C, and then goes to the folder named "windows." There it will find the specific file named "whatever.com."

Here's another example — c:\backups\documents\letter.doc refers to a file named "letter.doc." To get to this file, the computer has to follow a path that starts with drive C, and then goes to the folder named "backups." Within this folder, the next step in the path is to open the folder named "documents," which leads to the file named "letter.doc."

Note the role played by the backslashes. If I were to type a path like this — d:backupsdocumentsletter.doc — the computer would think I was referring to a file named "backupsdocumentsletter.doc" in the root directory or in drive D. The backslashes separate the various names that make up the path, so the computer can see the series of locations: d:, the drive; \backups, the folder; \documents, the folder inside the backups folder; and, finally, \letter.doc, the last item, which is always the name of the specific file. You must use backslashes (\). Forward slashes (/) will not work. If you are a Unix, Linux, or Internet user, this can be especially confusing because their paths use forward slashes, to separate names in the path, as in /home/asimpson or as in the URL http://www.cool-nerds.com/winME.

Exploring Your Files

Finding stuff in the computer is pretty challenging for most beginners. To help simplify things, Windows Me offers three different programs to help you explore what's on your computer. These programs are

- ✦ **My Computer:** Lets you browse around and see what's available, using a simple one-window-at-a-time method.
- ✦ **Windows Explorer:** Lets you explore your computer using a two-pane window.
- ✦ **Search command on the Start menu:** Lets you search for a file based on its name, contents, creation date, or some other known bit of information.

You'll learn about each of those programs in the sections that follow.

Browsing with My Computer

The icon labeled My Computer, usually displayed at or near the upper-left corner of the Windows desktop, is perhaps the easiest tool for browsing the contents of your PC. To open My Computer, click (if you're using the newer Web view) or double-click (if you're using the Classic view) the My Computer icon. Initially you'll see icons for disk drives that are on your PC, as well as some folders, as in the example in Figure 2-16. Once the My Computer window is open on your desktop, you can use these simple techniques to do some basic exploring:

✦ To see what's on the disk in a particular drive, open that drive's icon.

✦ To see what's in a folder, open that folder.

✦ To see what's in a file, open that file's icon.

✦ To close anything you opened, click the Close (X) button in the upper-right corner of the window you want to close.

Figure 2-16: The My Computer icon opened into a window on the desktop

Drilling down (and back up)

My Computer enables you to navigate and explore your computer by going from the general to the specific. Or, looking at it another way, My Computer enables you to drill down to more specific areas of the disk. For example, you may open My Computer and open the C: drive to look on drive C. Then you may open a folder to drill down and see what's in that folder. Within that folder, you may open yet another folder to drill down and see what's in there.

You also can work your way back up through the drill-down procedure or even jump to an entirely different drive, folder, or whatever using buttons in the Standard and Address toolbars as follows:

✦ To move up to the parent folder (the folder above the current folder, if any), click the Up button, or press the Backspace key.

✦ To move back to wherever you just left, click the Back button.

✦ After moving back, you can click the Forward button to return from where you just backed up.

✦ To jump to another place altogether, click the down-arrow button near the word "Address" on the Address toolbar. A drop-down list will open and you can click a destination in the list that appears.

Remember, both the Standard and Address toolbars are optional. You can choose View ➪ Toolbars to hide or display the Standard and Address toolbars.

Changing your view in My Computer

When you first open a window in My Computer, the contents usually appear in Large Icons view. You can decide for yourself how you want to view the contents. Your choices are

✦ **Large Icons:** Each icon and title is fairly large, hence, easy on the eyes.

✦ **Small Icons:** Each icon is small so you can see more icons at a time within the window.

✦ **List:** Similar to Small Icons view, but names are alphabetized down columns.

✦ **Details:** Shows filename, size (if appropriate), type, and the date and time the file was last modified.

✦ **Thumbnails:** If the folder contains any files that are graphical images, a small "thumbnail" of the image appears instead of an icon.

Figure 2-17 shows examples of each type of view. Of course, there is no right or wrong view. You can choose whichever view is currently most convenient. For example, if relatively few icons appear within the window, the Large Icons view may be easiest on your eyes. If the window contains many icons, you can use the Small Icons or List view to see more icons within the window. Both views show only a tiny icon for each file. The Small Icons view alphabetizes names across columns, like the Large Icon view. The List view alphabetizes names down columns, like the telephone directory. The Details view is handy when you want to see more information about each folder or file. The Thumbnail view works best when viewing folders that contain a lot of graphic images, such as the My Documents\My Pictures folder found on many Windows computers.

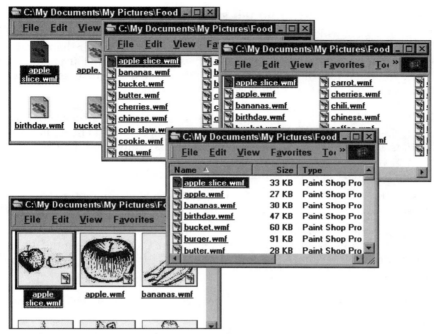

Figure 2-17: Five ways of viewing a window's contents in My Computer

It's simple to choose a view — so simple, in fact, you can try out all five views to see which works best currently. Techniques for changing your view include:

✦ Click View in the window's menu bar and then choose either Large Icons, Small Icons, List, or Details from the drop-down menu that appears.

✦ Or, if the Standard toolbar is open and the Views button is visible, you can click the Views button repeatedly to switch from one view to the next. Or, you can choose a view by clicking the little down-pointing triangle, just to the right of the Views button.

Feel free to experiment with the various views on your own PC. You certainly can't do any harm!

Tip

Choose View ➪ Toolbars ➪ Standard Buttons from My Computer's menu bar to hide/display the Standard toolbar. The Views button is at the extreme right end of this toolbar.

Special features of the Thumbnail view

The thumbnail view, which is new in Windows Me, is especially good for viewing the contents of folders that contain a lot of graphic images. Rather than showing an icon for each folder, you'll see a small *thumbnail* of the graphic image inside the file. When you point to a thumbnail (or click it, if you're using the Classic view), the image appears in the lower-left corner of the window.

The small toolbar across the top of the image in the lower-left corner allows you to work with the small image. Pointing to any button will display its name in a toolbar. The buttons are pretty self explanatory, but here's basically what they do:

✦ **Zoom In:** Click the Zoom In button, and then click the picture to magnify it.

✦ **Zoom Out:** Click the Zoom Out button, and then click the picture to un-magnify it.

✦ **Image Preview:** Click this button to see the picture full-size in the Image Preview window. To close the preview, click the Close button in the upper-right corner of the Image Preview window.

✦ **Print:** Prints a copy of the picture.

✦ **Rotate:** Lets you rotate the picture (not available for all image types, however).

The "View Pictures As Slideshow" option, in the top half of the left pane, lets you view all the pictures in the folder full-screen in a slide-show manner. Each picture will appear on the screen for a few seconds. To hurry along to the next picture, just click anywhere on the picture you're currently viewing. A toolbar will also appear momentarily. From that toolbar, you can choose to start the slide show, stop it, go to the previous picture, go to the next picture, or close the slide show and return to the My Computer window.

Tip   If you don't see the left pane in your Thumbnail view, first make sure the window is sized wide enough for the left column to appear. If the left column still doesn't appear, choose View ➪ Customize this Folder from My Computer's menu bar. In the wizard that appears, choose Next ➪ Choose Or Edit An HTML Template For This Folder ➪ Next ➪ Image Preview ➪ Next ➪ Finish.

You'll also notice an option that reads "Get pictures from a scanner or camera." That option works only after you've set up Windows to use your camera or scanner. That topic is discussed in Chapter 21.

Arranging My Computer contents

In addition to deciding the size of the icons in a My Computer window, you can choose the order in which you view those items. The normal order is to list all the folders (if any) within the current folder in alphabetical order, followed by all the files (if any) within the current window, also in alphabetical order. To change the order, follow these steps:

1. Choose View ⇨ Arrange Icons.

2. Click one of the following options:

   - By Name: Presents folders and files in alphabetical order by name (the usual method).

   - By Type: Organizes the folders by type, either by filename extension or the program associated with the filename extension.

   - By Size: Organizes everything by size (smallest to largest).

   - By Date: Organizes files by date last modified, with most recently modified files listed first. (This option is handy when you're looking for a file you created recently, whose name you can't quite remember.)

Details view (the one that shows all the file details) offers a shortcut for rearranging the icons within the window. Click the column heading to sort everything by that column; click the heading a second time to reverse the sort order in that column. If you click the Modified column heading, for example, the icons are instantly arranged by ascending date (newest to oldest). Clicking Modified a second time reverses the sort order (oldest to newest).

Here's another little trick that pertains only to Details view: You can widen or narrow the columns. Point to the vertical line that separates two column heads until the mouse pointer turns into a two-headed arrow and crosshair, and then drag the column line to the left or right. Or, if you want the column to fit snugly around the widest text in that column, double-click the vertical separator line between the column heads.

Web content in folders

You also have the option of choosing between a single-column My Computer window, which displays only icons, as well as a double-column window that displays additional information about the folder and contents of files. The information that appears in the left column is called "Web content." However, it's not information that's coming from the Internet's World Wide Web. Rather, it's text – often with blue underlined *hypertext* that you can click to get more information. Furthermore, the left column is capable of displaying a thumbnail view of the contents of any file that contains information that could be published on the Web. That includes text documents that have the `.htm` or `.html` filename extension, as well as graphic images stored in the `.gif` and `.jpeg` formats that are widely used on the Web. Figure 2-18 shows an example of a folder with Web content turned on (lower right), and also turned off (upper left).

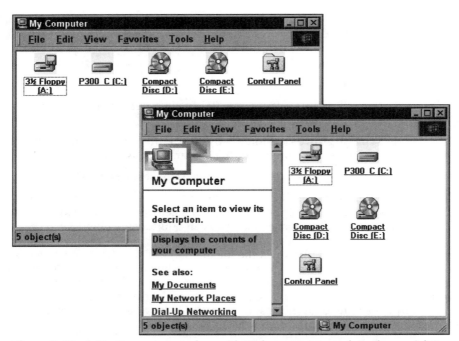

Figure 2-18: A My Computer window with Web content turned on (lower right) and off (upper left)

Even with Web content turned on, you won't see that left column information if the window is too narrow to display it. The window has to be wide enough to accommodate the entire left column, plus some portion of the right column. So if you're expecting to see Web content, but don't, try widening the window.

Operating system and hidden files

Normally, Windows hides *system files* that it needs for its own use, such as dynamic link libraries (.DLL), system files (.SYS), and device drivers (.VXD, .386, and .DRV). That's because there's no need for the average user to ever mess with these. And, in fact, deleting system files — whether intentionally or accidentally – can cause your computer to stop working altogether.

Hidden files are files that a user, like yourself, has opted to hide from other users who might be using the same computer. You can hide individual files as well as entire folders. Simply right-click the file or folder's icon and choose Properties. To hide the file or folder, choose the Hidden option so that it contains a check mark. To unhide a hidden file or folder, clear that check box. Then click the OK button.

Of course, if you could *never* see operating system or hidden files, there would be no way to ever get to them. So, as you'll learn in the next section, you can choose to show, or hide, system and hidden files at any time.

Viewing and hiding file info

Windows is very flexible, and you can choose to show or hide paths, Web content, filename extensions, and so forth. You can set up some general rules that apply to all windows that show files by making some selections from the Folder Options dialog box. Here's how:

1. Click the Start button and choose Settings ⇨ Control Panel.

2. Open the Folder Settings icon to display the options shown in Figure 2-19.

Tip Remember, if you don't see an icon in Control Panel, it may just be temporarily hidden. Click "View all Control Panel options" in the Control Panel window to see all of its icons.

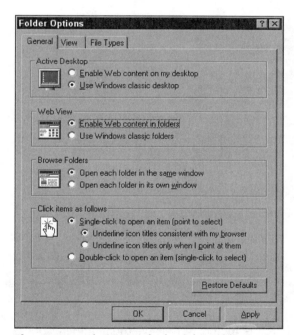

Figure 2-19: The General tab of the Folder Options dialog box

3. If you want to view Web content in your folders, choose the "Enable Web content in folders" option under Web View. To hide Web content, choose "Use Windows classic folders."

4. Click the View tab near the top of the dialog box to get to the options shown in Figure 2-20. Select whichever options you like by clicking the check box to the left of the option. A check mark in the box means the option is turned on. No check mark indicates that the option is turned off.

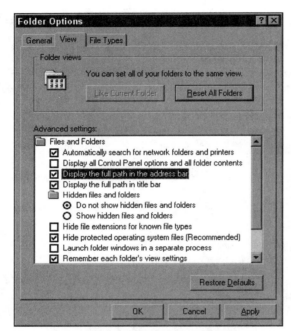

Figure 2-20: The View tab of the Folder Options dialog box

- **Display the full path in title bar:** If selected, the title bar of the window shows the complete path to the folder you're currently viewing. If not selected, only the name of the current folder appears in the title bar.

- **Hidden files and folders:** Here you can choose whether to bring hidden files and folders out of hiding, or to leave them hidden. (Does not apply to operating system files.)

- **Hide file extensions for known file types:** If selected, filename extensions are invisible if Windows knows which program is associated with that type of document. If not selected, filename extensions are visible for all files.

- **Hide protected operating system files:** If selected, the critical operating system files are safely hidden from view. If not selected, those files will be visible when browsing around your computer.

- **Remember each folder's view settings:** If selected, you can customize views on a folder-by-folder basis. If not selected, each folder's view returns to the default settings defined here when you first open the folder.

5. Click the OK button after making your selections to close the Folder Options dialog box.

6. You can also close the Control Panel window by clicking its Close (X) button.

The choices you made will be apparent as you start browsing through your files with My Computer. I should point out that you can make the same choices from any folder that's currently open. Just choose View ➪ Customize this folder, and a wizard will appear to help you make your selections. Be aware, however, that the options you select for the current folder will disappear as soon as you close the folder, unless you've selected "Remember each folder's view settings" from the Folder Options dialog box described earlier.

Tip   Options on the View tab of the Folder Options dialog box also apply to Windows Explorer, described next. However, in Windows Explorer the left column is reserved for showing folder names, so your Web content selections won't apply to Windows Explorer.

What the heck are known or registered files?

In Windows Me, certain types of files are automatically identified or known as belonging to certain programs. This is called being *registered*. Files with the .doc extension, for example, are registered to WordPad, or to Microsoft Word if that program is installed. This means if you open an icon for a file with the .doc extension, Windows Me automatically opens Microsoft Word and then displays the document you opened.

This approach has two advantages. First, you needn't go through the usual method of opening a program and then choosing File ➪ Open within that program to open a specific document. Instead, you simply open the document by clicking its icon in My Computer. Second, a naive user needn't know which program was used to create a particular document. Suppose Kyle Klewless, who knows nothing about computers, wants to see what's in a file named "Please review me Kyle." He needn't know what program is required to open that document; he simply has to open the document.

Because Windows Me generally handles all the registration business behind the scenes automatically, you rarely need to display filename extensions. Showing Kyle Klewless the filename "Please review me Kyle.doc" does him no good; the name "Please review me Kyle" is sufficient. This is the reason extensions on registered filenames are hidden by default in Windows Me.

Of course, the automatic associations for registrations may not always be exactly as you want them. You can change them. In Chapter 4, "Shortcuts and Other Cool Tricks," I show you many shortcuts for opening documents, including techniques for associating different types of files with different programs.

Refreshing the My Computer icons

If your computer is connected to a local area network (LAN) or you are creating, moving, copying, or deleting a lot of files, an open My Computer window may get out of sync with what's really inside a folder. To make sure a My Computer window is showing you accurate information, you can refresh its view by choosing View ➪ Refresh from My Computer's menu bar or by pressing the F5 key.

Minimizing window pileups

Piling up My Computer windows eats up system resources. If memory is tight, you probably should avoid these pileups. Also, the pileups can waste a lot of space on your screen and can be confusing. If you don't want My Computer sub-windows stacking up as you drill down through folders, follow these steps:

1. Choose View ➪ Folder Options, and then click the General tab.

2. Choose Custom, and then click the Settings button.

3. Under Browse Folders as Follows, choose the first option — Open Each Window in the Same Folder.

4. Choose OK twice.

Should you change your mind, repeat the steps but choose the opposite option. Or, choose the Classic Style or Web Style option.

Even if you minimize window pileups in My Computer, you still have to drill down through folders one window at a time. Although this procedure is fine for many people, more experienced users may prefer to use Windows Explorer to browse their PCs.

Browsing with Windows Explorer

Like My Computer, Windows Explorer is a tool for browsing around on your hard disk (or on any disk, for that matter) to see what's available. Windows Explorer doesn't use the one-window-at-a-time technique. Instead, it presents your drives, folders, and files in a single window with two panes, and you navigate within that window. To open Windows Explorer, do any of the following:

✦ Click the Start button, point to Programs, and then click Windows Explorer.

✦ Or, right-click the My Computer icon and then choose Explore.

✦ Or, right-click a disk drive or folder icon in any My Computer window and then choose Explore.

Regardless of which method you use to start Windows Explorer, you open the Exploring window, which will look something like Figure 2-21. The icons displayed will depend on what you are currently viewing.

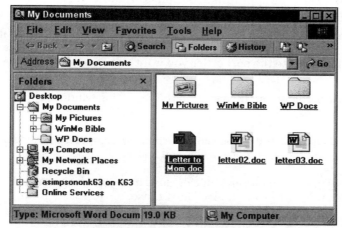

Figure 2-21: Windows Explorer's Exploring window

To use Windows Explorer to go exploring, follow these steps:

1. As with My Computer, you can choose View ⇨ Toolbar from Explorer's menu bar to decide which toolbars you want to use.

2. If you want to go to a different drive, click the drop-down list button in the Address toolbar, and then click the drive you want to explore. (This step is optional.)

3. In the leftmost pane, click the drive or folder whose contents you want to view. This step selects the drive or folder.

4. If additional folders are within the selected folder in the leftmost pane, you see a plus (+) sign next to the folder name; click that plus sign to view the names of folders within the folder. (You can click the minus sign to hide the folders within the folder again.)

5. Repeat Steps 3 and 4 until you've drilled down to and selected the folder you want to view.

6. To see what's in the selected folder, look in the rightmost pane (to the right of the folder list).

7. When you finish exploring, click the Close button in the upper-right corner of the Exploring window.

Many of the tricks discussed in the section, "Browsing with My Computer" also work in Windows Explorer, including the following:

✦ To view large icons, small icons, a list, or details in the rightmost pane of the Exploring window, click the appropriate button in Windows Explorer's toolbar, or choose View and then click the appearance you want.

✦ To sort the icons, choose View ➪ Arrange Icons from the menu bar, or right-click inside the right page and choose Arrange Icons from the shortcut menu that appears. Then choose the sort order you want (for example, By Name or By Date).

✦ To update the list of folder and filenames in the Exploring window, choose View ➪ Refresh or press F5.

Cross-Reference As you'll learn in Chapters 3 and 4, you can use either My Computer or Windows Explorer to open, copy, move, and delete files and folders.

When you finish with Windows Explorer, you can close it as you would any other window: Click its Close (X) button, or choose File ➪ Close.

Searching for lost files

It's not unusual, especially among beginners, to lose files on their hard disk. You may create a document, or download a file from the Internet, and save it to your hard disk, and then sometime later forget what you named the file, and what folder you put it into. When it comes to finding files you've lost track of, the Windows Search tool will probably serve you better than either My Computer or Windows Explorer.

Before I explain how to find a lost file, let me tell you how to *avoid* losing files in the first place. Whenever you save a file — be it something you created or something you downloaded — you'll always be given a chance to decide where you want to save it, and what you want to name it. Most of the time, the Save As dialog box shown in Figure 2-22 will appear to allow you to make those decisions.

The first thing you want to do is take a close look at the selection next to "Save in" at the top of the dialog box, as that tells you where you're about to save the file. In the figure, the Save As dialog box is suggesting the folder named My Documents. That's usually a good choice because if you always keep your documents in that folder, you'll always know where to find them. However, you're free to choose any drive and folder you wish. Just open the drop-down list and make your selection.

Tip If you want the downloaded or saved file's icon to appear right on your Windows desktop, choose Desktop from the "Save in" drop-down list.

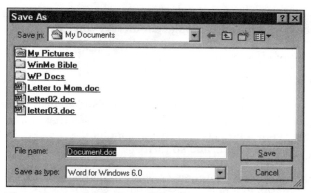

Figure 2-22: The Save As dialog box

If you prefer to save the file on some other drive or in some other folder, you can choose any available drive from the drop-down list. Then choose a folder from those that appear beneath the "Save in" drop-down list.

Next, you'll want to give the file a name that you can easily remember. Use the File name text box to give the file a name. In the figure, the Save As dialog box is suggesting using the name Document.doc. That's not a very good name, however, because it's too general. You should try to think of a better, more descriptive name to give the file. But don't change the filename extension. Windows uses that to determine which program is best suited to opening the file later.

Finally, after you've selected your folder and typed in a filename, click the Save button. The file will be saved and, I hope, you'll be able to remember where you saved it, and what you named it, in the future.

Of course, even with that forethought, it's still possible to misplace a file. And when that does happen, the Search tool will be your best ally. To open the Search tool, follow these simple steps:

1. Click the Windows Start button.

2. Choose Search ➪ For Files or Folders.

A dialog box will appear. There, you'll want to give Windows as much information about the file as you can to help you locate it. Your options are described in the sections that follow.

Search for files or folders named

If you know any part of the name of the file you're looking for, type that into the text box under "Search for files or folders named." For example, if you think the name "smith" appears somewhere in the filename, you can just type the word "smith." You can use the wildcard characters * and ? as placeholders if you like:

✦ *: Matches any number of characters

✦ ?: Matches any single character

For example, a search for `*.doc` would find all files that have the extension .doc regardless of the filename. A search for `letter*` would find all files that start with "letter" followed by any other characters and extensions, including `Letter To Mom.doc`, `letterbe.exe`, `letter99.txt`, and so forth.

Since the question mark character only matches a single character, it limits the search to files with an exact match in length. For example, a search for `??.exe` would list all files that have exactly two letters in the file name, followed by the extension .exe.

Do remember that the wildcard characters are entirely optional. Omitting them will actually give you the broadest search. For example, the search for `smith` would match `NoteToSmith.doc`, `NoteFromSmith.doc`, `Smithsonian.gif`, `Albert Smith MD.txt`, and any other file that has the letters "smith" somewhere in the filename.

If you don't remember anything about the name of the file you're trying to find, you can leave the "Search for files or folders named" text box blank, and base your search on other known information, as discussed below.

Containing text

Sometimes you might be looking for a document you created, such as a letter you wrote to someone, but you can't remember anything about the filename. You may, however, remember something about the contents of the file. For example, if the file contains a letter to someone named Sally Salerno, then there's a good chance her name appears somewhere within the document (for example, "Dear Ms. Salerno"). In that case, you could use the "Containing text" option to search the contents of files, as opposed to their names. Entering `Salerno` into the Containing Text textbox would find all files that have the name Salerno somewhere inside the file.

Be forewarned, however, that it takes Windows a lot longer to read through the contents of all the files than it does to read just their filenames. So you may have to wait a while for the results of a "Containing text" type of search.

If you don't know anything about the contents of the file (which is usually true if you're looking for a program rather than a document you created), you can leave the Containing Text text box blank.

Look In

The Look In option lets you specify where you want to perform the search. In most cases, you'll probably want to search your local hard drive since that's the place you're most likely to be saving files. But you can choose other drives, and even specific folders to search, using options from the Look In drop-down list.

Once you've completed one of the first two options and chosen where to look for the file(s), Windows will probably have enough information to conduct the search. Just click the Search Now button, and the search will begin. If, on the other hand, you didn't know enough about the filename or its containing text, you can choose from other search options to pinpoint your file. You can also use the search options to narrow down your search to including only "recently created" files, or files that are Microsoft Word documents, and so forth.

Search options

The Search options enable you to describe still more about the file you're looking for. If the Search options aren't visible in the left column, just click the >> to expand those options. Then you can use the search options described below to tell Windows more about the file you're looking for.

Date

The Date option is ideal for locating files that you created or saved recently, but cannot remember where or under what name. Click in the Date check box, and then choose an option that describes something about the file you're looking for. For example, if you're looking for a file that you saved yesterday, you could choose "File created" under Date, and then choose "In the last 2 days." That's a huge help when you have no other information to go on.

Type

If you happen to remember the type of file you're looking for, you can select the Type option, and then choose the type of file to search for from the drop-down list that appears.

Size

While you're not likely to remember the exact size of a file, you might remember if it as unusually large or small. For example, if it took all night to download some file off the Internet, it's probably several megabytes in size (one megabyte equals 1,000K). So you could narrow your search by specifying files that are *at least* 1,000K in size.

Combining the above options will really help you narrow your search. For example, if you search for "Files created in the last 2 days" that are "at least 4,000K in size," you'll end up with a list of all the large files on your system that were created (or downloaded) within the last 48 hours. And that might be all the information you need.

Tip In the case of a downloaded file, you could also go back to the Web site from which you downloaded the file and just look for the name of the file you downloaded. Then search for that filename.

Advanced options

The Advanced options enable you to broaden or narrow the search further still, as summarized below:

✦ **Search subfolders:** For the widest possible search, you'll want to select "Search subfolders" to ensure that all folders on the disk (or all subfolders within the currently selected folder) are searched. If you wanted to just search a single folder, such as My Documents, you'd choose My Documents from the Look In options and then clear the Search Subfolders check box.

✦ **Case sensitive:** In the unlikely event that you happen to remember the exact upper and lowercase letters of the file you're searching for, you can choose the "Case sensitive" option.

Regardless of which options you choose, remember that you'll need to click the Search Now button in the left column to actually perform the search. If that button scrolls out of view, just use the scrollbar (or your mouse wheel) to scroll it back into view so you can click it. As Windows searches for files that match your criteria, it lists their names over in the right column of the window. That right column works much like the main window in My Computer and Windows Explorer in that you can choose different views from the View menu, click column headings (in Details view) to put the files into alphabetical order by name, or in chronological order by date modified, and so forth.

If you're new to computers, all of this might seem a bit overwhelming. For the moment, the most important points to remember about the Search utility in Windows is that there's no need to panic when you misplace a file. There's a good chance Search can locate it. But perhaps more importantly, an ounce of prevention is worth a ton of cure. You won't misplace as many files if you pay attention to where you're putting them and what you're naming them via the Save As dialog that appears whenever you save a file.

Summary

The concepts and basic skills you've learned in this chapter are important, and most of them you'll use in your day-to-day interaction with your computer. Of course, they won't become second nature to you until you've had some hands-on practice. Still, it's important to know what can be done, and how to do it. Here's a quick recap of the topics discussed in this chapter:

✦ An icon is a small picture that opens into a full window.

✦ To open an icon, click it if you're using Web-style navigation or double-click it if you're using Classic-style navigation.

✦ To close an open window, reducing it once again to an icon, click the Close (X) button in the upper-right corner of that window.

✦ Information in your computer is stored in files.

✦ Files are organized into folders and subfolders.

✦ The thing that stores the folders, subfolders, and files is called a disk drive, or a drive for short.

✦ Each drive has a short, one-letter name. For example, your main hard disk is probably drive C.

✦ Dialog boxes present controls that enable you to choose among various options a particular program or device offers.

✦ The My Computer icon offers an easy one-window-at-a-time method of exploring your computer.

✦ Windows Explorer offers a two-pane method of exploration, in which a hierarchical tree of folders appears in the left pane and the names of subfolders and files within the selected folder appear in the right pane.

✦ The Search utility will search an entire disk, or even several disks, for a file based on information you provide about the file you're trying to find.

✦   ✦   ✦

Opening Programs and Documents

Most daily use of your PC involves using programs. If you use your computer for work, you might use some of those programs to create your own documents. Opening programs and, perhaps, documents, are two tasks you're likely to do dozens of times a day. Windows Me offers many ways to do these tasks. There is no right or wrong way to do them, of course. Choosing a method is simply a matter of deciding what's most convenient at the moment. Before I get into the details, however, let's discuss the term *program*.

Understanding Programs

The term *program* generally refers to something you buy to run on your computer. When you walk into the software section of a computer store, each shrink-wrapped box on the shelves contains some program you can buy, install, and use on your computer. Programs also are called *applications* (*apps*, for short). Small programs, such as the accessories that come with Windows, sometimes are called *applets*.

These days, people often download programs off the Internet and install them on their computers as well. But regardless of how you get a program, or whether the program is used for work or play, all programs are computer software. Specifically, they're files that contain instructions that tell the computer how to do whatever the program makes the computer do.

Chances are, many programs are already installed on your PC and you can experiment with them right now. But you may also have some new program in hand you want to try. If you want to use a new program, you must install that program first. Chapter 25 discusses installing new programs in detail. For now, let's assume you want to start some program already installed on your PC.

Opening programs

By *opening* a program, I mean bringing the program to the screen so you can use it. People use all kinds of words in place of "open" when they discuss the act of running a program. For example, the terms *launch* a program, *run* a program, *start* a program, *execute* a program, and *fire up* a program all mean the same as *open* a program.

The typical scenario for opening a program in Windows Me is simply to locate that program's startup icon in the Start menu and then click that icon. Here are the exact steps:

1. If the program requires a CD-ROM in the CD-ROM drive, put the appropriate CD into the CD-ROM drive. (If you're unsure, leave the CD-ROM drive empty.) Wait a few seconds to see if the program starts automatically. If a program does open, you can skip the remaining steps.

2. Click the Start button. If you see an icon for the program you want to start, click this icon instead and skip the remaining steps.

3. Point to (or click) Programs.

4. If you see the program's icon, click it. Or, point to the group on the Program menu that contains the program's startup icon and then click the program's icon.

For example, in Figure 3-1, I clicked the Start button, pointed to Programs, and then pointed to Accessories. I am about to open a program named Calculator.

After you launch a program, you can use it normally. Depending on the program you open, you may or may not get some help in using that program right on the screen. When many programs open, they assume you can figure out what to do or that you have already read the associated documentation; hence, you know what to do. For instance, the Calculator program that comes with Windows Me opens in a window with the usual title bar, menus, and such, as well as some buttons like the ones you find on your average pocket calculator, as shown in Figure 3-2.

You work the Calculator program like you work a regular calculator. For instance, if you click 1 and then click the plus sign (+) and then click 5 and then click the equals sign (=) you get the answer 6, because one plus five equals six.

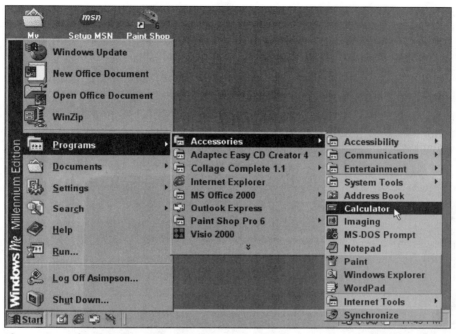

Figure 3-1: About to open a program named Calculator

Figure 3-2: The Calculator program open on the desktop

Getting help in programs

Most programs come with their own online help, similar to Windows' online help. The help a program offers, however, is geared toward that particular program rather than toward Windows Me. To get to a program's online help, while you're in that program, try either of these methods:

✦ Choose Help ➪ Help Topics (or some similar option from the Help menu).

✦ Or, press the Help key (F1).

The Help window that appears will be about the program you're currently using. For example, Figure 3-3 shows the help that appears when you request help while using the Calculator program. In this example, I've already opened the Performing Calculations book and I'm viewing the help for Perform a Simple Calculation.

Figure 3-3: The Calculator program's online help

When both the program and its online help are open, you can bring either window to the forefront by clicking its button in the taskbar. To close the help window, click the Close (X) button in the upper-right corner of that window. Or, right-click the Help button in the taskbar and choose Close from the shortcut menu that appears.

Opening from the taskbar

Once a program is open, it stays open until you specifically close it. If a program gets buried by other windows onscreen or if you minimize the program's window to get it out of the way momentarily, you can get back to that program without restarting it. Just look for the open program's button in the taskbar and then click that button to bring the program to the forefront on your screen.

**My instructions say something about
Program Manager**

When you're running or installing a program designed for Windows 3.x, your instructions may tell you to go to Program Manager or to choose Run from Program Manager's File menu. This can be confusing for Windows 95 and Windows Me users because neither of these versions of Windows have a Program Manager window.

The Windows Me equivalent to Program Manager is the Start menu. Any icon that's supposed to appear in Windows 3.x Program Manager will probably appear instead, after you click the Start button and point to Programs, in the Start menu.

If your instructions say to choose Run from the Program Manager's File menu, do this in Windows Me: Click the Start button and choose the Run option. Then type whatever you are supposed to type into the small Run dialog box that appears onscreen.

Tip   In Chapter 4, you'll learn cool tricks for creating your own shortcuts to favorite programs.

Closing a program

When you finish using a program, you should close it. I've already discussed different ways to go about closing things, but here's a quick review. Use any of the following methods to close an open program:

✦ Click the Close (X) button in the upper-right corner of the program's window.

✦ Or, choose File ➪ Exit or File ➪ Close from the program's menu bar.

✦ Or, right-click the program's button in the taskbar and choose Close.

✦ Or, press Alt+F4.

The program's window will close and you'll be back to the Windows Me desktop.

Working with Documents

Unlike a program, which is something you generally purchase, a document is usually something you create on your own. A document can be a letter, a report, a picture, a collection of names and addresses — whatever. To open a document means to bring the document to the screen so you can see, and perhaps work with, that document.

Creating a document

If you've never created, saved, or opened a document before and you want to try it, you can use the following steps, right now, to create a simple document using the WordPad program that comes with Windows Me. Here we go:

1. Starting from the Windows Me desktop, click the Start button and choose Programs ➪ Accessories ➪ WordPad. The WordPad program opens on your screen as in Figure 3-4.

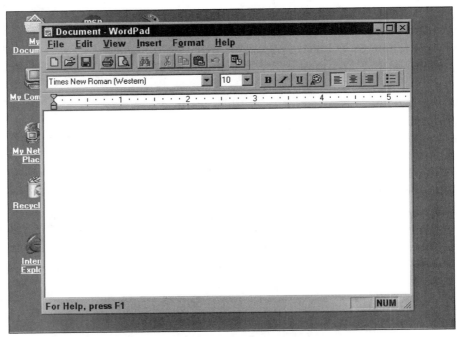

Figure 3-4: The WordPad program open on the screen

2. Type some text in the large white document window. For example, you might type a simple sentence, like "My dog has fleas," as in Figure 3-5.

So now you have a tiny document you created with WordPad. Your document has not been saved yet, however, and it has no filename. Let's discuss general techniques for saving any kind of document, using this little WordPad document as an example.

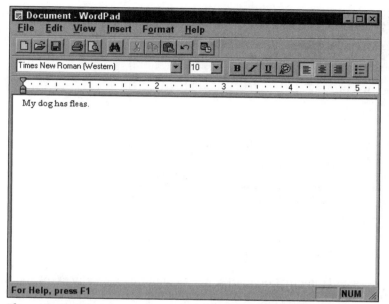

Figure 3-5: A tiny document containing the sentence "My dog has fleas" in WordPad

Saving a document

When you start creating documents, remember this: *Any work you do is not saved unless you specifically save it*. This is important because many beginners spend considerable time creating a document. Then, unwittingly, they close the program or turn off the computer unaware that, in doing so, they just lost all the work they finished.

Saving a document is easy. The only trick is remembering to do it once in a while. Anyway, here's how you save a document:

1. Choose File ➪ Save from the program's menu bar (that would be WordPad's menu bar, in this example). The Save As dialog box introduced in Chapter 2 appears, as in Figure 3-6.

2. Remember, you must pay attention to *where* you're saving the document. For simplicity, you can use the suggested My Documents folder (this folder is already selected next to Save in: in the dialog box). If you want to save to a different folder, you can click the drop-down list button next to the "Save In" prompt and choose a different drive and/or folder. You can also use the Up One Level button next to the "Save in" text box to navigate to a higher-level folder.

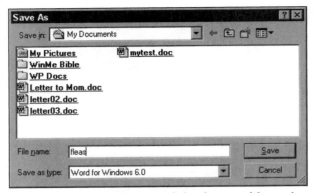

Figure 3-6: A typical Save As dialog box used for saving a document

3. In the File Name text box, type in a filename. Choose a name that will be easy to find or recognize later. The name can be up to 255 characters and can contain blank spaces and punctuation marks, but it cannot include any of the following characters: * ? / \: < > |. A short, meaningful name is best. For this example, you can type **fleas** as the filename.

4. Click the Save button.

The Save As dialog box disappears and you're returned to your program and document. You might notice the title bar of the program now shows the name of the document on which you're working.

When you save a document, you save all work you've done up until the moment you save. If you change or add to the document, you must specifically save the document again to save those changes or additions. To save a document that already has a filename, choose File ⇨ Save from the program's menu bar once again. Or, you can click the little Save button in the toolbar (if any), or press Ctrl+S. You won't be prompted to enter a filename again because you already gave the document a filename the first time you saved it.

If you want to save the current version of a document under a new name, so you don't alter the original copy, choose File ⇨ Save As from the program's menu bar. You'll be prompted to choose a folder and enter a filename once again.

Closing a document

You can close a document in many ways. If you want to close a document and the program you used to create the document, close the program using any method described under "Closing a program" earlier in this chapter. For example, you can click the Close (X) button in the upper-right corner of WordPad's window now to close the fleas document and the WordPad program.

Some programs (although WordPad isn't one of them) enable you to close a document without closing the program. Such programs will support one or more of the following approaches to close only the document:

✦ Choose File ➪ Close from the program's menu bar.

✦ Or, click the Close (X) button near the upper-right corner of the document.

Some programs will have a Close button for the program and another Close button near the upper-right corner of the document. Make sure you click the innermost Close button when you want to close only the document, but not the program.

Opening a document

You can open documents many ways in Windows Me. The simplest way is to use the Documents menu. This menu keeps track of recently used documents. So if you recently created or worked on the program, you can follow these steps to open the document again, right from the Windows Me desktop:

1. Click the Start button and point to Documents. The Documents menu opens, as in the example shown in Figure 3-7.

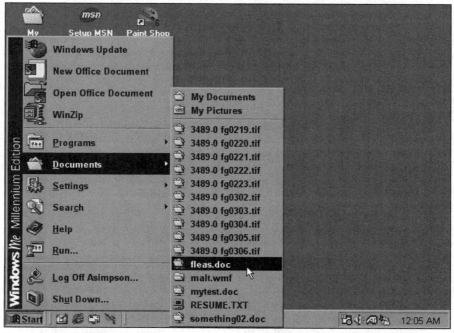

Figure 3-7: The Documents menu is accessible from the Start menu.

2. If you see the name of the document you want to open, click that name and skip the steps that follow.

3. Choose My Documents from the top of the Documents menu. A My Computer-style window opens, showing the names of all the files in the My Documents folder, as in Figure 3-8.

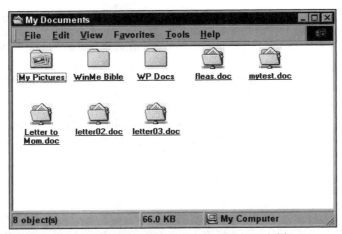

Figure 3-8: The contents of the My Documents folder on one of my computers

4. Click (or double-click, if you're using Classic-style navigation) the name of the document you want to open.

The document opens, most likely in the same program you used to create the document. Note, however, that the document might open in some other program. For example, if you have Microsoft Word installed on your computer, the fleas.doc file might open in Microsoft Word rather than WordPad because files with the .doc extension are registered to open in Microsoft Word. But don't worry about this. In Chapter 4, I'll show you how to customize the Send To menu so you can open a document with any one of several different programs.

Browsing to a document's icon

The Documents menu keeps track of recently used documents. If you try to open a document but you don't find it on the Documents menu, you can use My Computer, Windows Explorer, or Find to locate and open the document. For example, if you know the document is in the My Documents folder of drive C, you could start either My Computer or Windows Explorer. Then open the icon for the C: drive, open the My Documents folder, and then click (if underlined) or double-click the icon for the document you want to open.

If you don't remember where you placed a document, use the Search tool described in Chapter 2 to search the entire C: drive (or whatever drive you used) for the name of the document you want to open.

Using the program's File menu

Yet another way to open a document is to use the File menu inside the program you want to use to edit the document. Although the exact steps may vary a little from program to program, this procedure does work in most programs:

1. If you haven't already done so, start the program you want to use to edit the document you want to open.

2. From this program's menu bar, choose File.

3. Often, the File menu will display a list of recently saved documents, as in the example shown in Figure 3-9. If you see the document you want to open, click it and skip the rest of the steps.

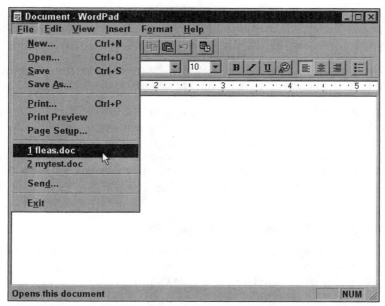

Figure 3-9: The File menu on some programs keeps track of recently edited programs.

4. Choose Open to get to the Open dialog box shown in Figure 3-10.

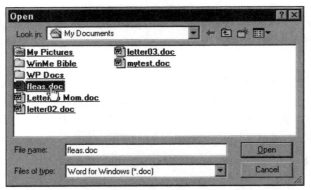

Figure 3-10: Dialog box that appears after choosing
File ⇨ Open from a program's menu bar

5. If you see the name of the document you want to open, click that filename, and then click the Open button.

6. If necessary, use the Look In drop-down list and/or the Up One Level button to navigate to the document's folder. Then open the document by clicking the filename and then the Open button.

In the Open dialog box, you can double-click the name of the file you want to open as an alternative to clicking once on the file and then clicking the Open button.

Your best bet for finding documents actually starts when you save the document. If you make a habit of storing all your documents in a single folder, like the My Documents folder on drive C, then you'll always know to search only this folder when you're looking for a document. Also, giving each document a meaningful, easy-to-remember filename will make locating the file much easier in the future. If all else fails, you can use the Search program described in Chapter 2 to find a document.

Opening unregistered documents

Occasionally, you might try to open a document that has never been registered to any particular program on your system. When this happens, you're automatically taken to the Open With dialog box shown in Figure 3-11.

In this dialog box, you can scroll through the list of programs installed on your PC until you find the program you want to use to open the document. Click (once) the name of this program. If you want to open all documents of the current type in the selected program, then make sure to choose the Always Use This Program To Open This File option by placing a check mark in the check box (click the check box, if necessary).

Figure 3-11: The Open With dialog box used to open unregistered document types

If you wish, you can also type a brief, plain-English description of the type of document you're about to open as a personal reminder for the future. Choose OK, and the document will open in the requested program (if possible).

Caution   If you open a document in the wrong program, you're likely to see only a bunch of weird looking characters on the screen. *Do not save that file!* Close the program and, when asked if you want to save any changes, choose No. Choosing Yes could ruin the file so that no program can open it!

Do not register documents to programs arbitrarily. Most programs can only work with certain kinds of documents. For example, word processing programs can open documents containing text. Graphics programs can open documents containing pictures. Before you permanently register a document type to a program, make sure the program can, indeed, open the type of document you're trying to open. If you run into any major problems, you can refer to Chapter 34 for more in-depth information on registering documents with programs.

Creating New Documents

In the olden days (DOS and Windows 3.*x*), the typical method of creating a new document was to start the appropriate program, and then either start typing or choose File ➪ New to start a new document. You still can use this method in Windows Me. But you also can use an alternative technique that enables you to create and name the document, give it a desktop icon, and launch the appropriate program, all in one fell swoop. Follow these steps:

Tip   If you have Microsoft Office 2000 you can click the Start button and choose New Office Document to start a new document from scratch.

1. If you want to put the new document in a particular folder, open that folder using My Computer or Windows Explorer. Or, if you want to put the icon for the new document right on your Windows Me desktop, stay at the desktop.

2. Right-click an empty part of the open window or desktop, and then choose New from the shortcut menu that appears. A menu of document types you can create this way appears, as shown in Figure 3-12.

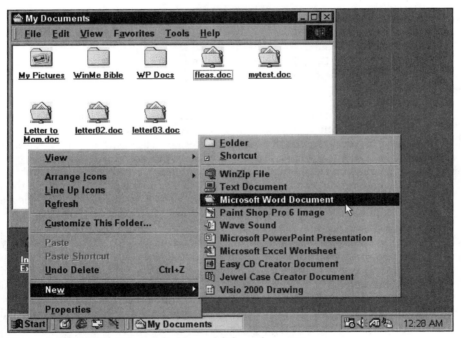

Figure 3-12: Right-click the desktop and then choose New.

3. If you see an option for the type of document you want to create, click that option. (If you don't see such an option, you can use the Start button method to start the program and create the document.)

4. An icon for the document appears on the desktop, along with a suggested name (for example, New Microsoft Word Document).

5. If you want to change the name of this new document, type the new name — for example, `letter.doc` if you are viewing filename extensions for known file types or `letter` if you are not — and press Enter.

6. To launch the program needed to edit the new document, open the new document icon by clicking it (if you're using Web-style navigation) or by double-clicking it (if you're using Classic-style navigation).

The program appears with a new, blank editing window and the document is already named and saved under the filename you specified in Step 4 or 5. Now you can start using the program normally to create the document. When you finish working on the document, save it normally.

 Tip Remember, when you want to tidy up your icons, right-click the neutral area outside an icon and then choose Arrange Icons ⇨ By Name from the shortcut menu that appears.

If, at some later time, you decide to change the name or location of this new document, you can do so using all the standard techniques discussed in Chapter 5. That chapter will also discuss, in more detail, options for creating, changing, and deleting associations between programs and document filename extensions.

Starting and Using DOS Programs

Some of you may still want to use your favorite DOS programs on your Windows Me PC. Any DOS program should be able to run perfectly on Windows Me. But you might not have a convenient icon to click the Start menu to get that program going. If this is the case, you can use My Computer, Windows Explorer, or Find to locate the icon for the DOS program you want to start, and then open that icon to launch the DOS program.

Or, you can use this DOS command-line approach to open the DOS program:

1. Click the Start button and choose Programs ⇨ Accessories ⇨ MS-DOS Prompt.

2. At the C:\> (or C:\WINDOWS>) prompt, type the appropriate DOS command and press Enter to start that program.

If you're trying to start WordPerfect 5.1 for DOS, for example, type `cd\wp51` to get to the appropriate directory (folder), and then press Enter. Then, to start the program, type `wp` and press Enter.

Using a DOS program

When you have your DOS program running, use it exactly as you use it in DOS. You should remember a few things, however. The toolbar that appears across the top of the DOS window (see Figure 3-13) belongs to Windows Me, not to DOS. If you don't see this toolbar, it may be turned off. To display this toolbar, click the System Menu icon in the upper-left corner of the DOS window — or press Alt+Spacebar — and then choose toolbar (if available). Buttons on the toolbar enable you to mark and copy text inside the DOS window. You then can paste this text into any DOS or Windows Me window.

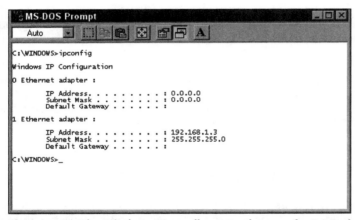

```
MS-DOS Prompt                                        _ □ ×
Auto     ▼  [ ]  ▣ ▣  ▣   ▣ ▣  A

C:\WINDOWS>ipconfig

Windows IP Configuration

0 Ethernet adapter :

        IP Address. . . . . . . . : 0.0.0.0
        Subnet Mask . . . . . . . : 0.0.0.0
        Default Gateway . . . . . :

1 Ethernet adapter :

        IP Address. . . . . . . . : 192.168.1.3
        Subnet Mask . . . . . . . : 255.255.255.0
        Default Gateway . . . . . :

C:\WINDOWS>_
```

Figure 3-13: The Windows Me toolbar near the top of a DOS window

To switch between full-screen windowless DOS and windowed DOS, press Alt+Enter. Or, when you're in the windowed view, click the Full Screen button on the toolbar to expand the DOS window to full screen (press Alt+Enter to return to the windowed view).

Note   Some graphics-intensive DOS applications can run only in full-screen mode. If the program you want to run falls into this category, you'll see a message indicating the DOS program will be suspended when you leave full-screen mode.

When you're in a DOS screen, you can do the following:

✦ Press Alt+Esc to return to Windows Me.

✦ Press Ctrl+Esc to return to Windows Me with the Start menu open.

✦ Press Alt+Tab to switch to another running program.

✦ Do any other normal Windows operation outside the window, such as click the Start button, click an open program's button in the taskbar, and so forth.

Each of these techniques leaves a button for the DOS window in the taskbar. To return to your DOS program, click that taskbar button.

The Font toolbar button in the DOS window enables you to change the font the DOS window uses. Changing fonts in the DOS window, however, is nothing like changing document fonts in Windows. In the DOS window, a font change affects the entire screen, rather than only the selected text, and it does not affect anything you print from that window. A DOS-window font change simply sizes the screen text so it is comfortable for your eyes.

Closing a DOS window

You can use the standard title bar, the borders, and the Maximize, Minimize, and Restore buttons to size and shape the DOS window. You won't have as much freedom in sizing the window as you do with regular windows, however, and you may be unable to click the Close button on the window's border to close a DOS window. Instead, you may need to exit the DOS program by using whatever exit procedure is appropriate for that program (choosing File ➪ Exit works in many programs).

Don't forget to save any unsaved work before you exit. Also, remember DOS can read and write only 8.3-character filenames. Which means that the filename itself can contain no more than eight letters. That name can then be followed by a period (dot) and an extension up to three characters in length. You cannot enter a longer filename in DOS. When displaying a long filename created in Windows, a DOS program shows only the first six characters of the filename with any spaces removed, followed by a tilde (the character ~) and a number. For instance, a Windows Me document named Morph me baby.txt, for example, would appear as MORPHM~1.TXT to a DOS program.

Typing DIR and pressing Enter at the DOS prompt shows the short filenames (with tildes), the file sizes, modification dates and times, and the long Windows filenames.

If you end up at the C:\> or C:\WINDOWS> prompt inside the DOS window after exiting your DOS program and saving your work, type exit and press Enter to close the DOS window and return to Windows Me.

Summary

Running programs is what computers are all about. Many of us run programs that enable us to create our own documents, such as memos, letters, spreadsheets, databases, and so forth. This chapter has covered all the basic skills you need to open (start) and close programs and documents. To recap the most important points:

✦ Generally, a program is something you purchase to use on your PC. A document is something you create on your PC, using some program.

✦ The easiest way to start a program is to click the Start button, point to Programs, and then locate and click the icon for the program you want to start.

✦ If you're starting a program to resume work on a document you saved earlier, click the Start button, click Documents, and then click the name of the document you want to open.

✦ If the Start menus don't offer an icon for the program you want to start, you can browse to the program using My Computer, Windows Explorer, or Find. Then click the icon for the program you want to start.

✦   ✦   ✦

Shortcuts and Other Cool Tricks

In this chapter, you learn about one of Windows Me's best features — *shortcuts*. Shortcuts give quick access to all your favorite programs, documents, folders, and more. The shortcuts are easy to create on the fly and just as easy to get rid of when you don't need them anymore. So you can make lots of shortcuts for whatever project you're doing. When that project is done, you can easily eliminate the shortcuts and start building a new set of convenient shortcuts for the next project.

What Is a Shortcut?

A shortcut is an icon that provides easy access to any program, document, folder, or nearly any other resource. A shortcut icon generally looks like the original icon, but it has a small arrow in the lower-left corner, as in Figure 4-1.

Figure 4-1: Sample shortcut icon

The original (nonshortcut) icon for a program, document, or folder represents the actual file. So, if you delete the original icon, you delete the entire underlying file. As a rule, *this is not good*, unless you really know what you're doing. A shortcut, on the other hand, is a small link to the original icon. You can create, move, copy, and delete shortcuts at will, without worrying about accidentally deleting the actual underlying file.

Best of all, you can put shortcuts anywhere—even right on the Windows Me desktop. This way, you can get to a favorite resource right from the desktop without having to navigate though My Computer, Windows Explorer, or the Start menu.

In addition to all the information on shortcuts you'll learn in this chapter, there's plenty of help available. Click the Windows Me Start button, choose Help, click the Index option, type shortcut, and then click any subtopic that looks interesting.

On a more technical level, a shortcut is a tiny file that provides a link to some larger file. This file has the extension .lnk and usually has an icon matching the file's original icon, with the little shortcut arrow displayed.

Creating Desktop Shortcuts

You can put shortcuts to folders, programs, documents—and even to other computers—right on your desktop. The job is a pretty simple one. Here are the steps:

1. Using My Computer, Windows Explorer, or Search, locate the icon for the folder or document to which you want to create a shortcut. For example, in Figure 4-2 (see the next section), I've opened the My Documents folder, which contains a folder I created and named Windows Me Bible.

2. Right-click the icon to which you want to create a desktop shortcut and choose Send To ➪ Desktop (as shortcut).

That's all there is to it. The icon will be named something like "Shortcut to" followed by the original name of the folder or file. If you want to rename the icon, just right-click it, and use the basic editing techniques described in Chapter 2 to change the name to whatever you want. Optionally, to get your icons in order, right-click the desktop and choose Arrange Icons ➪ By Name.

From now on, you can click (if you're using Web-style navigation) or double-click (if you're using Classic style) the icon right on the desktop to get to the document or folder. There's no need to navigate through folders with My Computer, Windows Explorer, or Search.

Shortcuts to Start Menu Programs

If you get tired of going through the Start menu to launch a favorite program, you can easily put a shortcut to that program right on your desktop. Use the exact same technique used to create a shortcut to a file or folder:

1. Click the Start button, and work your way to the option that allows you to start the program to which you want to create a shortcut. But don't click that option.

2. Right-click the menu option instead and choose Send To ➪ Desktop (create shortcut).

Again, a new shortcut icon appears on the desktop, which you can click (or double-click) from now on whenever you want to start that particular program. As with any icon, you can also right-click the shortcut icon and choose Rename to give the shortcut icon a new name, if you like.

While the desktop is a handy place for storing shortcuts, there is one small inconvenience to contend with. Any open windows on your desktop could easily cover those icons. But here are a couple of tricks you can use to temporarily get those open windows out of the way and get full view of your desktop:

✦ Click the Show Desktop icon in the Quick Launch toolbar (see Figure 4-2).

✦ Or, if you don't see the Quick Launch toolbar, right-click the taskbar and choose Minimize All Windows.

Figure 4-2: Use the Show Desktop button in the Quick Launch toolbar to quickly display the entire desktop.

Whichever technique you use will make all open windows suddenly "disappear" from the desktop. But don't panic. Each open window is just minimized and is still represented by a button in the taskbar. To bring a window out of hiding, just click its taskbar button. Or, to bring all the windows out of hiding in one fell swoop, click the Show Desktop button in the Quick Launch toolbar again. Or right-click the taskbar and choose Undo Minimize All.

Using the Quick Launch Toolbar

The Quick Launch toolbar is yet another handy place to store icons to programs, folders, and documents that you access frequently. First, a few facts about that toolbar:

✦ To display or hide the Quick Launch toolbar, right-click an empty part of the taskbar and choose Toolbars ➪ Quick Launch.

✦ To find out what a Quick Launch button does, point to it. A descriptive ToolTip, as in the example shown back in Figure 4-2, pops up near the mouse pointer.

✦ To expand or shrink the Quick Launch toolbar so you can see more or fewer buttons, double-click the double vertical bar at the left edge of the toolbar. Or, drag the vertical bar to the right of the Quick Launch toolbar to the left or right to make more/less room for that toolbar.

✦ To display or hide text descriptions of the toolbar's buttons, right-click an empty part of the Quick Launch toolbar, or its vertical bar, and choose Show Text.

Where is that darn taskbar?

The taskbar normally rests across the bottom of the Windows Me desktop, but it's movable. So if you share a computer with others, you might have to go looking for the taskbar.

If you don't see the taskbar at all, but you do see a thin gray line along the bottom edge — or any other edge — of the screen, you can move the mouse pointer to that thin gray line. The taskbar will stay in view as long as the mouse pointer is touching it. Then it will hide itself after you take the mouse pointer away. If you prefer the taskbar not to hide itself when you aren't using it, click the Start button, point to Settings, and then choose Taskbar & Start Menu. In the dialog box that appears, click the Taskbar Options tab, clear the Auto Hide check box, and then click the OK button.

If none of the above bring the taskbar into view, perhaps it's currently too narrow to see. Move the mouse pointer to the thin gray bar at the bottom of the screen (or perhaps some other edge of the screen) until the mouse pointer turns into a two-headed arrow. Then drag that edge up toward the center of the screen a little to widen the taskbar.

If you want to make sure the taskbar never gets covered by other stuff on the screen, click the Start button, point to Settings, and choose Taskbar & Start Menu. On the General tab, select (check) the Always On Top option. Click the OK button, as usual, to save the change and close the dialog box.

✦ To display or hide the Quick Launch toolbar title, right-click an empty part of the Quick Launch toolbar, or its vertical bar, and choose Show Title.

✦ To rearrange buttons in the toolbar, drag any button to some new location within the toolbar, and then release the mouse button.

✦ To stack the toolbar and taskbar, drag the top edge of the toolbar up toward the center of the screen until its width doubles. To unstack, drag the top of the toolbar a little, down toward the bottom of the screen.

✦ To separate the Quick Launch toolbar from the taskbar, point to the toolbar's vertical bar, until the mouse pointer turns into a two-headed arrow. Then drag the mouse pointer up toward the center of the screen and release the mouse button.

✦ To rejoin the Quick Launch toolbar to the taskbar, drag the Quick Launch toolbar into the taskbar.

Adding buttons to the Quick Launch toolbar

Now that you know what the Quick Launch toolbar is and the kinds of things you can do with it, let's discuss how you can customize it to contain buttons to your favorite programs, documents, and folders. The procedure couldn't be much simpler than it is. Here are the steps:

1. Be sure the Quick Launch toolbar is visible. If it isn't, right-click an empty part of the taskbar and choose Toolbars ➪ Quick Launch.

2. Point to any icon to which you want to create a shortcut. The icon can be any icon on the desktop, in the Start menu, or in any folder you open with My Computer, Windows Explorer, or Search. The icon can even be an existing shortcut icon.

3. Hold down the right mouse button and right-drag the icon into the Quick Launch toolbar. A little black vertical line appears showing you where the button will be placed. You can right-drag the icon to wherever you want the button to be placed within the toolbar.

4. Release the right mouse button and choose Create Shortcut(s) Here.

That's all there is to it. The icon appears as a button on the toolbar. Pointing to this button displays a ToolTip matching the name of the program, document, or folder. Clicking this button opens the program, document, or folder the button represents.

Removing a button from the toolbar

Removing a button from the Quick Launch toolbar is even easier than putting it there. If you want to remove the button completely, right-click it and choose Delete from the menu that appears. Choose Yes when you're asked for permission to send the button to the Recycle Bin.

In case you haven't noticed, the secondary (right) mouse button is a darn good one for finding out what kinds of things you can do with an object. Whenever you want to do something with an object, but don't know how, right-clicking the object is a good way to start looking for clues. Right-clicking works in most Windows programs, as well as in Windows Me itself.

If you want to move the button onto the desktop, rather than delete it altogether, you can drag the button from the Quick Launch toolbar onto the desktop. Now let's look at other ways to create shortcuts to favorite programs.

Customizing Your Send To Menu

As you learned in Chapter 3, you can usually click (or double-click) any document icon to open that document in whatever program is associated with that type of document. For example, opening an icon named My Letter.doc would cause that document, My Letter, to open in the Microsoft Word program (if you have it), or the smaller WordPad program that comes with Windows Me.

In some cases, however, you may want the flexibility to send a particular type of document to any one of several programs. Suppose you create your own Web pages for publishing on the Internet's World Wide Web. Web page documents generally have the filename extension .htm. When you open a document whose filename extension is .htm, Windows Me automatically displays that page in a Web browser program, such as Microsoft Internet Explorer or Netscape Navigator.

This technique may be a bit advanced if you're unaccustomed to creating and editing your own documents. If you can 't think of any good reason to customize your Send To menu right now, don't worry. Just remember, the Send To menu is yet another way to create convenient shortcuts to favorite programs.

Now let's suppose, as the creator of Web pages, you'd sometimes like to open .htm files in the Web browser, to view them as the public will see them. But, at other times, you'd like to open a .htm file using some kind of editing program such as Notepad. A simple way to achieve this goal is to customize your Send To menu to include whatever programs to which you want to send programs.

To see the Send To menu, right-click any document file's icon and then point to Send To. A list of programs or devices to which you can send the file appears, as in Figure 4-3. You could click any option in that Send To menu to send the current document file to that device or program.

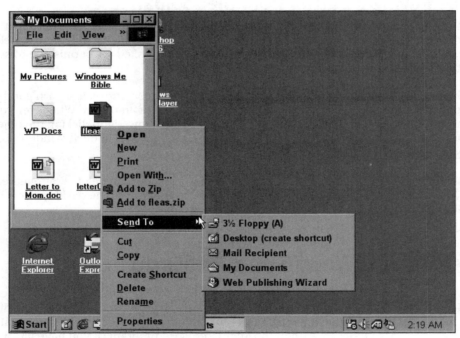

Figure 4-3: The Windows Me Send To menu

You can customize the Send To menu so it contains shortcuts to all your own favorite programs. This way, whenever you want to open a document in a particular program, you can right-click the document's icon, choose Send To, and then choose the name of the program with which you want to open the document.

To begin, you need to open the C:\Windows\SendTo folder on your computer. This folder is usually hidden to prevent beginners from making mistakes with it. But I'll explain how to avoid the type of mistake they're worried about. To bring hidden files and folders out of hiding:

1. Click the Start button and choose Settings ⇨ Control Panel.

2. Open the Folder Options icon.

3. Click the View tab.

4. Choose the Show Hidden Files and Folders option.

5. Click the OK button at the bottom of the dialog box.

6. Click the Close (X) button in the upper-right corner of the Control Panel window.

Now you can open the usually hidden SendTo folder by following these steps:

1. Double-click your My Computer icon.

2. Click drive C. If no icons appear, click on View The Entire Contents Of This Drive at the left side of the window.

3. Open the folder named Windows. If you see a message warning you not to rename or delete any files in the folder, choose Show Files. You won't be renaming or deleting any files here.

4. Open the folder named SendTo.

Once this folder is open, you may want to size it (by dragging the sizing pad in the lower-right corner or any border). Then move the folder (by dragging its title bar) so it's visible but not hogging too much room on the screen, as in Figure 4-4. Note that each icon in the SendTo folder represents one of the options in the actual Send To menu shown back in Figure 4-3.

To add shortcuts to the Send To menu, you can right-drag shortcut icons from the Start menu, desktop, Quick Launch toolbar, or any place else, into the SendTo folder. Then release the mouse button and choose Copy Here. Optionally, you can right-drag any non-shortcut icon into the SendTo folder, drop it there, and then choose Create Shortcut(s) Here. But what's important is that you add *only* shortcut icons to the SendTo folder. You don't want to move or copy a regular icon into that folder because doing so would move the underlying file into that folder, which could cause the program to stop working altogether! This is probably the main reason that the SendTo folder is usually hidden — to prevent beginners from making such a mistake. This bears repeating, so here goes.

Figure 4-4: The C:\Windows\SendTo folder is open in My Computer.

Caution   When adding programs to your SendTo folder, make sure you only create *shortcuts* in that folder. You never want to move or copy a program's actual file into the C:\Windows\SendTo folder.

Let's take a look at an example. Suppose you want to add shortcuts to Microsoft Internet Explorer and WordPad to your Send To menu. Since there's an icon for Internet Explorer right on your desktop, you can just right-drag that icon from the desktop into the SendTo folder. Drop it there (release the right mouse button) and then choose Create Shortcut(s) Here from the menu that appears. A new icon titled Shortcut to Microsoft Internet Explorer appears and has the characteristic shortcut arrow in its lower-left corner.

There is no icon for Notepad on the desktop. So to create a shortcut to that program you'll need to right-drag its option off of the Start menus. Here's how:

1. Click the Start button to open the Start menu.

2. Navigate your way to the program you want to add to the SendTo folder. In this example, you want to choose Programs ➪ Accessories and then point to (but don't click) Notepad. (You may need to click the down-pointing arrows at the bottom of the menu to see the Notepad option.)

3. Right-drag the icon (for Notepad in this example) from the menu into the SendTo folder and drop it there.

4. Choose Create Shortcut(s) Here from the menu that appears.

If things have gotten a little messy in your SendTo folder, just choose View ➪ Arrange Icons ➪ by Name from its menu bar. If you want to rename an icon (for example, the one titled "Shortcut to Internet Explorer") just right-click that icon, choose Rename, and type the new name. Choose View ➪ Arrange Icons ➪ by Name again to resort the names into alphabetical order. Figure 4-5 shows how my SendTo folder looks after adding shortcuts to Internet Explorer and Notepad and arranging the icons by name.

Figure 4-5: Shortcut icons to Internet Explorer and Notepad added to the C:\Windows\SendTo folder

When you finish, you can close the C:\Windows\SendTo folder by clicking its Close (X) button. To verify that the items have been added to your Send To menu, right-click any icon and choose Send To. For example, in Figure 4-6 you can see where Internet Explorer and Notepad have been added to the Send To menu. Since you're just looking for verification here, you can press the Escape key or click outside the Send To menu without making a selection to close that menu.

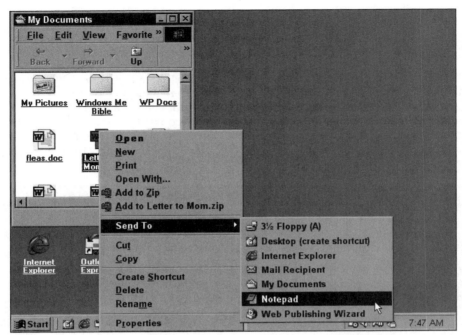

Figure 4-6: Internet Explorer and Notepad added to the Send To menu

You're not limited to adding programs to your Send To menu. You can add virtually anything that's capable of accepting a file, including disk drives and folders. In fact, your Send To menu probably already contains shortcuts to your floppy disk drive and My Documents folder. The main thing to remember is that you only want to add shortcuts to these other items to the C:\Windows\SendTo folder. Don't move or copy icons into that folder.

You might want to take a moment now to put your hidden files and folders back into hiding, just to keep them safe. Just open the Folder Options dialog box in the Control Panel again, as you did near the beginning of this section. Then choose "Do Not Show Hidden Files And Folders" from the View tab and click OK.

Auto-Starting Favorite Programs

You can have Windows Me automatically start any program after you turn on your PC, and Windows has started. This way, the program will be onscreen waiting for you shortly after you start your PC. To have a program start up automatically, you need to add a shortcut icon for that program to the C:\Windows\Start Menu\Programs\ StartUp folder. A quick and easy way to open this folder is to right-click the Start button and choose Open. Then open the folder named Programs, and then open the folder named StartUp. You may want to size and position this window off to the right edge of the screen, as in Figure 4-7, so you can see it after you open the Start menu.

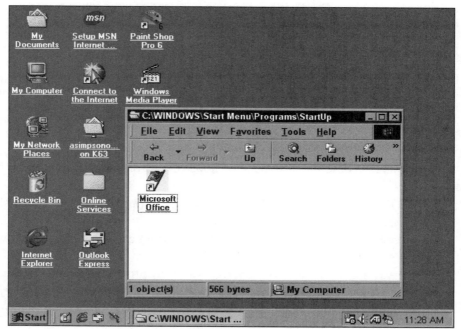

Figure 4-7: The C:\Windows\Start Menu\Programs\Startup folder

If your PC is already auto-starting programs, you'll see icons for those programs in that StartUp folder. To add a new program to the folder, you can click the Start button, choose Programs, and then work your way to the startup option for any program you want to auto-start. Don't click that icon, though. Instead, right-drag it from the menu into the StartUp folder, drop it there, and choose Create Shortcut(s) Here. Each time you start your computer in the future, that program will be loaded automatically. If you change your mind in the future and don't want to auto-start the program any more, just delete its shortcut icon from the C:\Windows\Startup folder.

Summary

This chapter ends Part I of the book. I focused on both basic skills necessary to use Windows Me and some optional, though useful, techniques for creating shortcuts to make getting to whatever you need on your PC easier. Remember, practice makes perfect. It takes time to become fluent in the many tricks and techniques Windows Me offers to get around and use your system. And don't forget, whenever you need help, you can always look things up in the online help.

From this point, you probably know enough about Windows to skip to virtually any chapter in this book that interests you. I've opted to discuss connecting to the Internet in Part II, only because I suspect that so many of you will want to get connected right away. Before we get to that, however, here's a quick recap of the most important topics covered in this chapter:

✦ A shortcut offers quick access to any folder, document, or program.

✦ To create a desktop shortcut to a favorite program, folder, or document, right-drag its icon onto the desktop and choose Create Shortcut(s) Here from the menu that pops up.

✦ The Quick Launch toolbar offers quick access to the Internet and to any short-cuts you add to it.

✦ To display or hide the Quick Launch toolbar, right-click an empty place on the taskbar and choose Toolbars ⇨ Quick Launch.

✦ To create a Quick Launch button, right-drag any program, folder, or document icon into the Quick Launch toolbar and then choose Create Shortcut(s) here.

✦ If you want to send a document from the desktop right into a favorite program, place a shortcut icon to that program in your SendTo folder (C:\Windows\SendTo).

✦ If you want a program to start automatically right after Windows itself starts up, add a shortcut to that program to the C:\Windows\Start Menu\Programs\StartUp folder on your PC.

✦   ✦   ✦

Becoming an
Internet Guru

Choosing and Installing a Modem

The Internet, and online services like America Online, MSN, CompuServe and so forth are radically different from the programs you run on your computer in one huge way. They don't exist on your computer at all. To use the Internet or online services, you typically need some kind of modem, which is a gadget that connects your computer to telephone lines, cable lines, or some other medium. Some large services, such as America Online, offer their own connection service. When you sign up for an account, they'll suggest what kind of modem to purchase, how to set it up, and so forth.

The Internet, which isn't owned by any one company, generally requires that you sign up with an Internet service provider (ISP). (However, you can access the Internet through most of the large online services.) You can find ISPs in your area through your local newspapers or Yellow Pages. If you're specifically looking for Internet access, the first thing you'll need to decide is what type of connection you want, as discussed in the sections that follow.

Choosing a Connection Type

As I mentioned, there are lots of ways to get your computer online and connected to the Internet. The major differences between your options, from a consumer point of view, are the speed and the cost. Basically, the faster the connection the more it costs. A faster connection means less time waiting. But whether or not the saved time is worth the added expense of a fast connection is something everyone has to decide for themselves. In the sections that follow, I'll briefly summarize the options that may (or may not) be available in your area.

My computer already has a modem

If your computer came with a modem built into it, then there's really no need to install anything. Just connect the "Line" jack on the back of the computer to the phone jack on the wall. Then, if you'll be using the same phone line for voice conversations, connect the Phone jack on the back of the computer to the telephone. You can use standard telephone cables and connectors for both connections. You can then skip right down to the section titled "Defining Your Dialing Rules" later in this chapter.

Cable modem

Many cable TV companies have gotten into the Internet service business, using their existing cable infrastructure to deliver high-speed Internet access to homes and small businesses. The exact cost of this service is entirely up to your cable provider. The only way to find out what's available is to check with all the cable service providers in your area, and find out if they offer Internet access and what they charge. Typically, there's an initial setup fee, plus a monthly fee.

Cable connections require cable modems. You don't want to go shopping around for a cable modem prior to setting up your account. In fact, most cable services will provide the modem as part of their service, and will even come to your location to install it. If you do go with a cable service, chances are the rest of this chapter won't even be relevant to you, simply because your modem will be selected and installed for you, as part of the service.

If you have a satellite TV service, you might also be able to get an Internet connection through your satellite provider. You'll need to call them for pricing and availability. As with cable connections, your service provider will most likely choose and install an appropriate modem for you.

Digital Subscriber Line

Digital Subscriber Line, also known as DSL, ADSL and xDSL, is the newest option for high-speed Internet access from the home and small business. DSL uses standard telephone lines but is not at all limited to the 56 Kbps speeds offered by standard modems. To the contrary, DSL can attain theoretical speeds of up to 8 Mbps (or 8,000 Kbps). However, even 1.5 Mbps is more than sufficient for even the most demanding user!

Note   The speed or *bandwidth* of a connection is measured in bits per second — abbreviated bps. A thousand bits per second is expressed as kilobits per second (Kbps). A million bits per second is expressed as megabits per second (Mbps). A larger bps number means a higher bandwidth, which translates to faster speed and shorter wait times. The term *broadband* is a generic term that refers to all high-bandwidth, high-speed access media.

Aside from sheer bandwidth, DSL offers a couple of other advantages over other high-speed connection types. For one, DSL uses POTS (Plain Old Telephone System) lines, which eliminates the cost of running new, special lines to your location. Secondly, with DSL you can purchase only as much bandwidth as you want or can afford. For example, you can purchase 144 Kbps, 256 Kbps, 768 Kbps, and so forth, usually up to at least 1.5 Mbps (which equals 1,500 Kbps). The monthly cost of your service is based on the bandwidth you choose.

DSL does *not* use the standard dial-up modems that most of this chapter focuses on. So don't go out and buy a modem until you've signed up with a DSL provider. That provider will then either provide you with an appropriate modem, or recommend modems that are compatible with your service. If you do need to install the modem yourself, you'll need to follow the instructions that come with the modem as opposed to the instructions for dial-up modems presented in this chapter.

Currently, DSL is available mainly in large metropolitan areas and nearby outlying areas. Contact your local phone company for pricing and availability. If you already have Internet access, you can learn more about DSL services from www.flashcom. com, www.freedsl.com, and http://whatis.com/dsl.htm.

ISDN

Integrated Services Digital Network (ISDN) is another service that works through telephone lines. However, unlike DSL, ISDN requires that you have special lines installed (by the phone company). Also unlike DSL, you don't get a wide selection of speeds to choose from. The standard ISDN installation consists of two 64K lines giving you an overall access rate of about 128K. So ISDN's days as a popular Internet access option may be numbered as DSL becomes faster, cheaper, and more widely available.

Still, if neither cable nor DSL are available in your area, and you're looking for something that's faster than the standard dial-up account, ISDN may be an option. Check your local Yellow Pages for Internet service providers that offer ISDN connections, and also your local phone company for pricing and availability.

Like cable and DSL, ISDN does not use standard dial-up modems. Instead, ISDN requires an *ISDN Terminal Adapter* (though it's often called an *ISDN modem* just to avoid confusion.) Before choosing a terminal adapter you'll want to set up accounts with your phone company and Internet service provider, and then have them help you choose the best terminal adapters for your service.

T1, T2, frame relay, and such

Historically, large businesses have used T1, T2, T3, and 56K leased lines for internet-working and connecting to the Internet. While these services are certainly fast, they can also be frightfully expensive and woefully complex to maintain and install. Unless you happen to be part of a large corporation with an entire information technology (IT) department at your disposal, you'll probably want to ignore these options altogether.

Dial-up accounts

Least glamorous of the lot is the standard dial-up connection to the Internet. This type of connection uses standard phone lines, and has a top speed of about 56 Kbps. Though far from being speedy, it's probably the most widely-used connection type among consumers because it's been around for a long time, it's available virtually everywhere that there are telephones, and it's generally the least expensive connection you can get.

To get a dial-up connection to the Internet, you need only check your local newspaper or Yellow Pages for Internet Service Providers in your area. Pricing and availability will vary. But you can probably expect to spend at least $20.00 per month. To keep the service inexpensive, ISPs who offer dial-up accounts will rarely choose or install modems for you. You're on your own for that, and you'll be lucky if you can get any support at all. Thus, the rest of the chapter really focuses on the type of modem you'll be installing and using with a standard dial-up connection to the Internet (or some other online service). We'll start with a discussion of choosing a dial-up modem.

Choosing a Dial-Up Modem

Before you buy a modem, consider which features you need. Some modems are strictly data modems; some modems have auto-answer capabilities; still other modems offer fax and voicemail capabilities. Here, in a nutshell, are the reasons why you might want these features:

✦ **Data modem:** You use this basic modem to connect to the Internet, online services, bulletin board systems (BBSs), and other PCs. Few modems today are data only.

✦ **Call waiting:** If you'll be using a single phone line for both voice and modem calls, and you have call waiting on your phone service, this feature will prevent call waiting from disrupting your modem communications and also allow you to talk on the phone without losing your modem connection.

✦ **Auto-answer modem:** If you plan to use dial-up networking (see Chapter 24), you need a modem with auto-answer capability. You'll also need this capability if you want to accept incoming calls from other PCs.

✦ **Data/fax modem:** A data/fax modem adds the capability to send and receive faxes directly from your PC, without printing them.

✦ **Data/fax/voice modem:** A voice modem can handle voice phone calls as well as standard data/fax modem capabilities. Calls are made using voice-call software and your computer's speakers and microphone. You can also purchase modems with speakerphones built into them.

✦ **Cellular modem:** A cellular modem fits into the PCMCIA slot of a laptop computer and connects to a cellular phone. This modem enables you to make fax/data transmissions on the road (that is, from your car or in a plane).

Internal, external, and PC Card modems

You can buy modems in three main configurations: internal, external, and PC Card. No real difference exists among the types in terms of performance. The following list summarizes the types of modem configurations:

✦ **External modem.** *Upside:* Easy hookup; you don't have to disassemble the computer. *Downside:* You must have a spare serial (COM) port and the modem takes up a little space on your desktop.

✦ **Internal modem.** *Upside:* The modem stays inside your PC and doesn't take up any space. *Downside:* You need to disassemble the computer to install the modem.

✦ **PC Card.** A PC Card (PCMCIA) modem fits into the PCMCIA slot. Most modern laptops have at least one PCMCIA slot. When you buy a PCMCIA modem, make sure it's compatible with your PCMCIA slot type. Desktop PCs usually do not have PCMCIA slots.

Performance considerations

Modem speed determines how long it takes to send and receive files. Today, dial-up modems enable data transfer at a maximum of about 56 Kbps over standard phone lines. There's really no need to buy anything slower than that. In fact, if you go to your local computer or electronics store and take a look at the modems available, chances are they will all be 56 Kbps modems.

You might also find a few different modem *protocols* including 56Kflex, X2, and V.90. You should check with your service provider to see which protocols they support before selecting a modem. But I can tell you right now that about 99.9 percent will be supporting V.90. So you're pretty safe with that protocol.

There's a good chance the modem will come with all the instructions you need. And if you're able to follow them, by all means do so. Sometimes, however, the instructions make everything a little more complicated than it needs to be. So if you don't have any instructions, or need a little support in understanding the instructions you have, feel free to read the general instructions provided in the next section.

Installing the Modem

Once you've purchased a modem, the first step at home or in the office will be to install the modem hardware. Follow the modem manufacturer's instructions to do this. With an internal modem, this will require shutting down and unplugging the computer (*very* important!), opening the computer case, installing the modem card into an available expansion slot, and closing the case back up.

External and PC Card modems exist outside the computer case and hence don't require any real installation, per se. However, you will need a *modem cable* to connect the external modem to a serial port on the back of you computer. Your dealer can help you select the appropriate cable. With a PC Card modem, you merely need to slide the modem into the PCMCIA slot on your laptop computer.

The next step is to connect the modem to a phone jack on the wall. You can use a standard phone line cable, available at any electronics or computer store, to make that connection. Your modem might have two phone-sized plugs on it. Connect the one labeled "Line" or "Jack" to the telephone jack on the wall. The one labeled "Phone" should never be connected to a phone jack on the wall. Instead, if you need to use the same phone line for phone conversations, you can connect your telephone to the "Phone" jack on the modem, and use the same phone line for both voice and modem communications. Though not necessarily at the same time! The only alternative there is to have the phone company add a second phone line with a different number, which you can use solely for the modem.

If you're installing an external modem, you'll also need to plug it in for power. The modem should come with the appropriate cable. The external modem is also likely to have an on/off switch, which must be switched to "On" before you start up your computer.

Installing modem drivers

The next step to installing a modem will usually be the installation of the modem drivers and other software. Again, your best bet is to follow the instructions that came with the modem. While I can't possibly write instructions for every make and model of modem ever made, I can give you a sense of what the most likely scenario will be at this phase. This is especially true if you're installing a Windows plug-and-play modem, which is highly likely given that most Windows modems manufactured since 1995 are plug-and-play modems. Follow these steps if you have no other instructions to rely on:

1. Gather your original Windows Me CD-ROM, but don't put it into the CD-ROM drive yet. Keep any disks that came with the modem handy as well. If your computer came with Windows Me pre-installed, you may not need to bother with the Windows Me CD.

2. Turn on the computer normally. If asked to enter your user name and password, do so normally.

3. If Windows is able to detect your modem during startup, you'll see a dialog box titled New Hardware Found. What happens next depends on the hardware:

   • If there's already a driver for the modem available on the hard disk, Windows installs the driver, and you're not asked for any more information.

- If Windows recognizes the modem and has a driver for it on its CD-ROM, you'll be prompted to put the Windows Me CD into your CD-ROM drive. Just follow the instructions on the screen until you get to the Windows desktop.

- If Windows can't find a driver for your modem, you'll need to install the driver from the CD or disk that came with the modem. Prompts on the screen will help you along, but you'll want to follow the instructions that came with the modem as well, to provide the information requested on the screen.

4. You'll eventually get to the normal Windows desktop.

You should then check, and follow, the instructions that came with your modem for information on installing other software for that modem. If Windows was unable to find a driver for your modem, you may need to run a setup.exe or similar program from the disks that came with your modem to get that driver installed. Sorry I can't give you any more information than that. But there are just too many different makes and models of modems out there to cover all the bases.

Defining Your Dialing Rules

Before you try using the modem, you'll want to verify that it has been installed, know where it's dialing from, and is set to run at the highest possible speed. Follow these steps at the Windows desktop:

1. Click the Start button and choose Settings ➪ Control Panel. If you see an underlined option reading View All Of Control Panel Options, click it.

2. Double-click the Modems icon. If this is the first time you've opened the icon since installing the modem, you should be taken to the Location Information dialog box shown in Figure 5-1. Otherwise, you're taken straight to the Modems Properties dialog box described after these steps.

 Note If Windows starts looking for a modem after you open the Modems icon, that means Windows isn't aware of your modem yet. You may have missed something while physically installing your modem. Shut down the computer, carefully check *all* connections, and restart the computer.

3. Choose your country from the drop-down list, and type your area code into the appropriate text box.

4. If you need to dial a 1 or 9 or some other number to get to an outside line from your current location (as is often the case is businesses and hotels), type that number into the second text box.

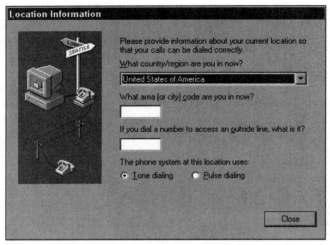

Figure 5-1: The Location Information dialog box

5. Leave the last setting at Tone Dialing unless you're in an area that still uses the old-fashioned pulse dialing of rotary phones.

6. Click the Close button.

At this point you'll be taken to the Modem Properties dialog box described next.

Assuming everything has gone smoothly up to this point, you should now be at the Modems Properties dialog box shown in Figure 5-2. Your modem should appear in the list of installed modems, as in the figure where I've installed the Sportster V.90 56K Faxmodem. Your dialog box might look slightly different, depending on your modem's features, but don't worry about that. To set the modem's properties, make sure the modem is selected in the list and then click the Properties button in the dialog box.

On the General tab of the Properties dialog box that appears (also shown in Figure 5-2), you can adjust the modem's speaker volume to your liking. This, essentially, determines the loudness of the weird noises you hear when first logging onto a remote system with your modem. Under Maximum Speed, *make sure you choose the highest possible number, typically 115200.* If you don't, the modem may not be able to run at its highest possible speed. This bears repeating!

Caution   If the Maximum Speed setting is not set to 115200 or higher, your modem may not be able to run at its highest possible speed!

On the Connection tab, shown in Figure 5-3, the settings shown in the figure should work fine for most modems. The last option, "Disconnect call if idle . . .," is optional. But it protects you from inadvertently leaving the modem on (and hence, the phone off the hook) for hours on end should you forget to disconnect at the end of a modem session. The settings shown in the figure will automatically disconnect the call and hang up the phone if the modem has just been sitting there with no activity for 15 minutes.

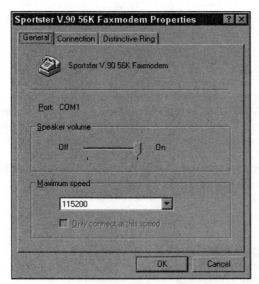

Figure 5-2: The modem's Properties dialog box

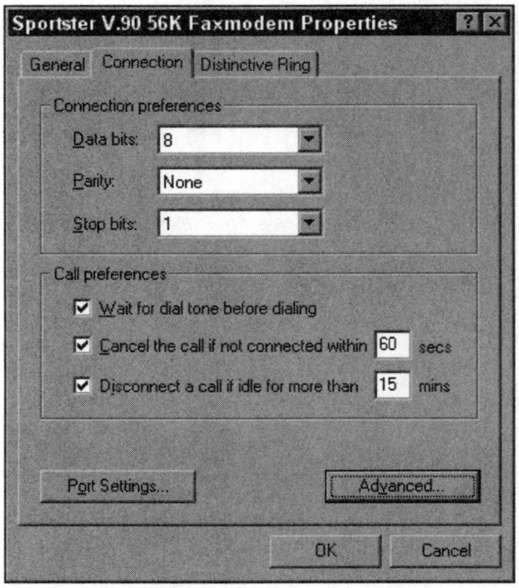

Figure 5-3: The Connection tab of a modem's Properties dialog box

The remaining options in the modem's Properties dialog box aren't relevant to a wide range of modems. If your modem and/or telephone service supports "Distinctive Ring" or other advanced features, the manual that came with the modem or service will explain how to use them. However, they're entirely optional and you needn't mess with them now if you don't want to. For now, you can just click the OK button at the bottom of the modem's Properties dialog box to close it. You needn't close the general Modems Properties dialog box just yet.

Setting dialing properties

The Location Information dialog box shown earlier in this chapter asked some basic information about the phone from which you'll be dialing. With all the new rules regarding area codes these days, those settings might not be sufficient. You should check your dialing properties now to make sure you comply with the area code rules in your locale. To do so, click the Dialing Properties button in the Modems Properties dialog box. (If you've already closed that dialog box, you can open the Control Panel, and then double-click the Telephony icon in the Control Panel). Either way, you'll end up in the Dialing Properties dialog box shown in Figure 5-4.

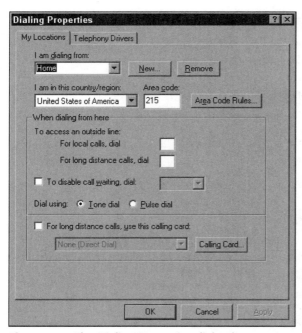

Figure 5-4: The Dialing Properties dialog box

The first thing you'll want to do is change the "I am dialing from" option from New Location to something more descriptive. While it's not absolutely necessary to do so, it can be helpful. Particularly if you're working with a laptop computer that you'll be taking traveling. The remaining settings will reflect the basic selections you made from the Location Information dialog box earlier. You can change those if you now realize you made a mistake.

More importantly, however, you'll want to click the Area Code Rules button and check to make sure your settings are correct. When you first open the Area Code Rules dialog box, its options will all be unselected and blank, as in Figure 5-5. Those settings work in areas within the U.S. that use the following rules:

✦ Local calls (within the same area called) are dialed as 7-digit numbers.

✦ Calls outside the current area code are dialed with a 1, followed by the 3-digit area code plus the 7-digit phone number.

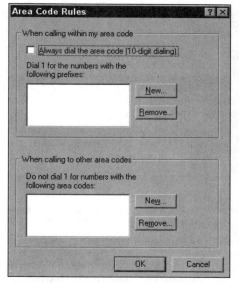

Figure 5-5: Settings in an empty Area Code Rules dialog box apply to some, but not, all area codes in the U.S.

Some areas require that you always dial the area code. For example, in the 215 area code in the eastern United States, you must dial the area code and the phone number, even when dialing within your own area code. You don't, however, dial a 1 first in that case. When you're dialing outside the 215 area code, then you must dial a 1, followed by the 10-digit area code plus phone number. Figure 5-6 shows how to set up the Area Code Rules dialog box for the 215 area code. Note that the "Always dial the area code (10-digit dialing)" option is selected. To prevent the modem from dialing a 1 before dialing a 10-digit number within the 215 area code, I used the New button to add the area code 215 to the list of numbers for which a 1 should *not* be dialed when dialing a 10-digit number. So in other words, the modem will always dial the area code, as is required in the 215 location. But it won't dial a 1 before dialing numbers within the 215 area code, as is required in that location.

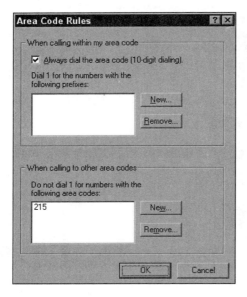

Figure 5-6: Area code rules changed to always use 10-digit dialing. However, numbers within the 215 area code will not be preceded by dialing a 1.

When you've finished making your selections, you can close the Area Code Rules and Dialing Properties dialog boxes by clicking their OK buttons. If the Control Panel is open as well, you can click its Close (X) button to get it out of the way. Now would be an ideal time to test the modem because there are things that can go wrong later down the road when connecting to an ISP or other online service. Ensuring that the modem is working correctly now will eliminate the need to check the modem should you have any problems later when connecting to specific services. A simple tool for testing your modem is the Windows Speed Dialer.

Testing Your Modem with Phone Dialer

Windows Me comes with a handy little Phone Dialer. Like the speed dialer on some phones, this device enables you to keep a list of frequently called numbers and to dial those numbers with the click of a button. Phone Dialer is especially handy if your modem shares the same phone number as your voice phone, because you can use Phone Dialer to dial out. But even if you don't plan on using the Windows Phone Dialer in your day-to-day use of your PC, it's a good tool for testing your modem connection for the first time.

If Phone Dialer isn't in your Communications menu, you can install it now. See Chapter 25 for information. When you get to the Windows Setup tab, click the Communications component, and then click the Details button to find Phone Dialer.

To use the Phone Dialer to test your modem and dialing properties, follow these steps:

1. Click the Start button.
2. Choose Programs ➪ Accessories ➪ Communications ➪ Phone Dialer.

Now you're ready to test your modem. To see if your dialing properties are set up to dial local numbers correctly, type a 7-digit phone number into the Phone Dialer drop-down list. Or, click the appropriate numbers on the dialing keypad just as you would on a pushbutton phone. This can be any number — even the number you're dialing from. All you care about here is that the modem be able to get a dial tone, dial accurately, and get a ring, busy signal, or recorded message as an answer. For example in Figure 5-7 I'm about to dial the seven-digit number 846-1212, which is the local Time in my area. After you've typed a test number, click the Dial button and listen for any activity.

Figure 5-7: About to dial a local 7-digit number

You should see a dialog box titled "Dialing" followed by a dialog box titled "Call Status." If your modem volume is loud enough, you should also hear a dial tone, the number being dialed, and some sort of response from the other end. If you called an actual person, and this line also has a voice phone on it, you can pick up the phone and click "Talk" to speak or leave a message. When you're ready to hang up, just click the Hang Up button in the Call Status dialog box. If your modem made any reasonable connection at all, it's properly installed and your dialing properties are set correctly. If an error message appears saying there is no dial tone, or no modem, or some other problem that prevents Phone Dialer from dialing out, see the Troubleshooting section later in this chapter for help resolving common problems.

You might also want to try dialing a long-distance number, just to make sure your long-distance dialing properties are set correctly. Type any 10-digit number into the "Number to dial" box, or punch in the phone number on the dialing keypad. Click the Dial button, and listen to ensure that the number is dialed correctly. Unless you specified otherwise in your dialing properties, the Phone Dialer should automatically dial a 1 before dialing any number outside your own area code. Again, if you have any problems, refer to the Troubleshooting section near the end of this chapter for help.

More on the Phone Dialer

If you have a regular voice phone connected to your modem line, Phone Dialer is good for more than just testing your modem. You can use it to dial the phone hands free, and wait for someone (or something) to answer, without taking your hands away from the computer. As with any program, you can create a desktop shortcut and/or Quick Launch button that will allow you to pop the dialer up on your screen with a single click. You can store frequently-called numbers and dial them with a single mouse click. Since it sends the same tones that the buttons on your phone does, you can even use it to work your way through those voice systems that make you choose from a series of options before you actually reach a human being. You don't have to pick up the phone until it's time to actually start talking.

To store a phone number in phone dialer, just click any blank speed-dial button, fill in the blanks, and click the Save button. Or to change a Speed Dial button, choose Edit ⇨ Speed Dial from Phone Dialer's menu bar. The "Number to dial" drop-down list also keeps track of recently dialed numbers so you can redial a number simply by choosing it from that drop-down list. Phone Dialer will even maintain a log of all your incoming and outgoing calls is you like: Choose Tools ⇨ Show Log to see the log and choose your options. For more information on using Phone Dialer, choose Help ⇨ Help Topics from its menu bar.

Removing a Modem

If you plan to remove an external or internal modem, such as when you plan to upgrade to some other modem, you should remove the current modem's driver before you physically remove the modem from the computer. The simple way to do so is to click the Windows Start button and choose Settings ⇨ Control Panel. In the Control Panel, open the Modems icon. In the Modems Properties dialog box that appears, click the modem you plan to remove, and then click the Remove button. Finally, click the OK button.

If Windows asks if you want to restart your computer, choose No. Then, shut down the computer normally (Start ⇨ Shut Down ⇨ Shut Down ⇨ OK). Once the computer is shut down, then you can remove the existing modem. You can install the new modem at that time as well.

Troubleshooting a Modem

If you have any problems with your modem, use the Troubleshooter to track down and correct the problem. Follow these steps:

1. Click the Start button and choose Help.
2. Choose Troubleshooting from the left column.
3. Choose "Hardware & System Device Problems."
4. Choose "Hardware, Memory, & Others."
5. Choose Modem Troubleshooter and then start answering questions in the right column (Figure 5-8), clicking the Next button after answering each question.

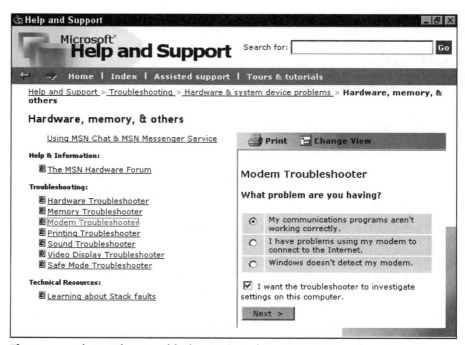

Figure 5-8: The Modem Troubleshooter in Help & Support

Some other things you might want to check if you're having trouble with your modem are listed below:

✦ If you are using an external modem, make sure the modem is plugged in and turned on.

✦ Make sure the "Line" plug on the modem is connected to the phone jack on the wall.

✦ Make sure the phone is not off the hook. The modem can't dial without a dial tone.

✦ Check your voicemail. Strange as this might seem, the little beeps used by some voicemail systems to indicate calls in your message box can confuse some modems.

✦ If you have call waiting, and your modem doesn't support that feature, incoming calls might mess up your modem connection. You can have the modem disable call waiting to prevent interruptions via the Telephony icon in the Control Panel.

✦ If you're not dialing from your usual location, use the Telephony options in the Control Panel to set up a new location suited to your current situation. Remember, in hotel rooms and such you often need to dial an 8 or a 9 to get an outside line before you dial the actual phone number. Options in Telephony enable you to specify the number needed to reach an outside line.

Summary

Here are the main points to remember when choosing and installing a modem:

✦ Remember, cable, DSL, and other services don't use "traditional" dial-up modems. Before you choose a modem, select your ISP or other online service provider, and make sure you get a modem that's compatible with their service.

✦ If your PC came with a modem already installed, you need only connect its "Line" plug to the phone jack on the wall using a standard telephone line cable.

✦ Use the "Phone" jack on the modem only to connect the modem to an actual voice phone. Doing so is necessary only if you plan to use the same phone number for voice calls.

✦ Test your modem with the Phone Dialer program first, just to make sure it's working before you start setting up a connection to the Internet or other online service.

✦ If you have problems with your modem, the Modem Troubleshooter in Help & Support can help you track down and fix the problem.

✦   ✦   ✦

Connecting to the Internet

You've undoubtedly heard of the Internet — the huge network that connects millions of computers from around the world. I'm sure many of you are already connected to the Internet. This chapter is for those of you who have no access to the Internet yet. Here, you'll learn all the different options for getting online and the step-by-step procedures needed to create a dial-up connection to the Internet from your own PC.

When to Ignore This Chapter

Before you dig into the many options and complexities of connecting your computer to the Internet, you should be aware that the vast majority of Internet service providers offer programs that you can run to set up your connection in an instant. This is especially true of new cable and DSL connections. But even the more common dial-up connections discussed in this chapter have largely been automated by most ISPs.

Tip If you already have Internet access, you can learn more about DSL, cable, and other *broadband* connections at www.windowsmedia.com/broadband. If you don't have Internet access, you can find information in Windows Help by searching for the word "broadband."

Therefore, once you've chosen your ISP and received account information and instructions from them, you should definitely follow *all* of their instructions before you even look at this chapter. Chances are, by the time you've finished following their instructions, your connection will work just fine and everything that follows in this chapter will be largely irrelevant. You'll only need to use this chapter if your ISP doesn't provide any sort of installation or setup instructions at all.

Will you use Internet Connection Sharing?

Windows Me comes with a feature called Internet Connection Sharing, in which several computers that are connected together in a network can share a single modem and Internet account. To use that feature, you first need to set up your network as discussed in Part VI of this book. Then, you'll set up your Internet connection on one computer in the network — typically the computer to which the modem is physically connected. To set up Internet connections on the remaining computers in the network, you'll use the Internet Sharing Client Disk, as discussed in Chapter 32. So in other words, even if you do need to use this chapter to set up your Internet account, you'll only need to do so on one computer in the network. All other computers in the network will require a completely different setup procedure.

Are you already connected?

Some of you may already have access to the Internet and not know it. For example, if you have an account with one of the large commercial online services such as CompuServe, America Online, Prodigy, or the Microsoft Network (MSN), you already have access to the Internet through that service. To get to the Internet, hunt for the word "Internet" within that service for more information. Then you can skip the rest of this chapter because you already have access to the Internet.

If you work for a large organization, you may be able to access the Internet through your computer at work. If you're in doubt, ask your network administrator, or whoever is in charge of granting network access to workers, for assistance.

What You Need to Connect to the Internet

If you don't have any access to the Internet or an online service, you need to do some things before you can get connected to the Internet. Specifically, you must install and set up a modem, as discussed in Chapter 5. Then, you need to set up an account with an ISP.

Unfortunately, I can't help you much with the second item. Thousands of ISPs exist in the world and choosing one that's good for you is something you must do on your own.

One of the most important factors (for most people anyway) is to make sure the connection is a local call so you don't get charged by the phone company for connect time. Check your local telephone directory for a list of dialing prefixes you can dial free.

Tip Most of the national ISPs listed in the Internet Connection Wizard, described later in this chapter, have local dialing numbers in all the major cities and outlying suburbs.

Then, try to locate an ISP that can set up an account for you with one of the free dialing prefixes. Here are some resources you can check to find an appropriate ISP:

✦ Start the Internet Connection Wizard (Start ➪ Programs ➪ Internet Explorer ➪ Connection Wizard); choose the first option, "I want to choose an Internet Service Provider and set up a new account" when given setup options; click the Next button; and follow instructions onscreen.

✦ Check your local Yellow Pages (under Internet) or newspaper for local Internet services.

✦ Call your local phone company and ask if they offer a service.

✦ Call 1-888-ISP-FIND for an automated referral service.

✦ If you have access to the Internet through work or a friend, visit ISP FIND at http://www.ispfinder.com.

✦ Go to your local computer store or bookstore and ask for *Boardwatch* magazine's Internet service provider's book.

You'll probably be presented with a ton of options when you contact an ISP. For starters, you can get a basic account that offers e-mail and access to the World Wide Web and newsgroups. As you gain experience with the Internet, you may find you want to upgrade your account to include more options, such as your own Web site. But upgrading an account after the fact is usually pretty easy so there's no harm in starting off with the basic services.

When you set up an account with a local ISP, it may (or may not) provide you with a lot of information about your account. If you are provided with such information, make sure you file it away where you'll always be able to find it. Also, keep it handy as you work through this chapter. You can fill in the blanks in Table 6-1 right here in the book if you like. If your ISP doesn't provide you with all the information presented in Table 6-1, then they will probably provide you with a setup program or procedure that automatically enters the appropriate information into all the right places in Windows.

Table 6-1
What You Need to Know to Set Up a Dial-Up Connection

Information	Fill in Your Info
Your IP address:	
Your subnet mask:	
Your gateway IP address:	
Your computer's user host name:	
Your ISP's domain name:	

Continued

Table 6-1 *(continued)*	
Information	*Fill in Your Info*
Your ISP's primary DNS server IP address:	
Your ISP's secondary DNS server IP address (if any):	
Your ISP's domain suffix:	
Your ISP's telephone number:	
Your login name:	
Your password:	

Caution   For obvious security reasons, you may not want to write your password in Table 6-1, especially if other people might be peeking at your answers. But you could put in a hint – a word or phrase that will remind you of the password.

As mentioned, if your ISP offers some kind of easy program for setting up your account, go ahead and use that program. But if you have no such program to work with, the Internet Connection Wizard should make for a nice alternative.

Using the Internet Connection Wizard

Aside from following your ISP's installation instructions, the easiest way to set up a dial-up connectoid (connection icon) to the Internet is to run the Internet Connection Wizard. The wizard will pose questions for you to answer and give you blanks to fill in. Use the information from Table 6-1 to fill in the blanks as questions are posed to you. Here's how to get started:

1. Click the Start button and choose Programs ➪ Accessories ➪ Communications ➪ Internet Connection Wizard.

Tip   You can also get to Dial-Up Networking by opening your my Computer icon. If the Dial-Up Networking icon doesn't appear right away, click Dial-Up Networking in the left column, or open the Control Panel and scroll down to the Dial-Up Networking icon.

2. From the first wizard screen, shown in Figure 6-1, choose whichever option best describes what you want to do. For clarification, here's what they mean:

   • **I want to sign up for a new Internet account:** Select this option only if you've never contacted an ISP or set up an account, and you want to purchase an account right now.

- **I want to transfer my existing Internet account to this computer:** If you've set up an account with an ISP, have a username and password (and perhaps some other information from Table 6-1), choose this option.

- **I want to set up my Internet connection manually:** To use this third option, you must have an account and information from Table 6-1. Or your computer must be connected to a network, and one of the computers on the network already has Internet access.

Cross-Reference The third option will also apply to any client computers on a local area network after one computer has already been set up with a shared account. Refer to Chapter 32 for more information.

3. After making your choice, click the Next button.

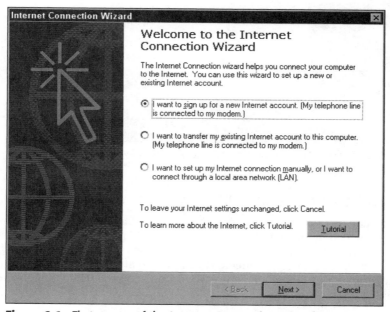

Figure 6-1: First screen of the Internet Connection Wizard

Theoretically, the rest should go smoothly and easily. I can't take you step-by-step through the wizard because exactly how you progress through the wizard depends on how you answer questions. It's important, however, to pay attention to the following warning.

Caution Usernames and passwords are usually case-sensitive. Any time the Internet Connection Wizard asks you to type a username or password, make sure you type it using the *exact* upper/lowercase letters provided by your ISP.

When you finish working your way through the wizard pages, you should see a screen like the one in Figure 6-2. Click the Finish button. If any more instructions appear onscreen, be sure to follow them carefully.

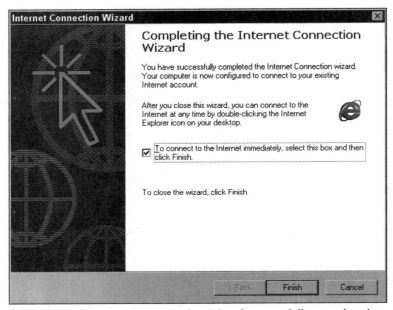

Figure 6-2: The Internet Connection Wizard successfully completed

Making the connection

Now you can test your Internet connection. If you have an external modem, make sure it's plugged in, turned on, and ready to go. Then click the Start button and choose Programs ➪ Accessories ➪ Communications ➪ Dial-Up Networking. You should see an icon for the connectoid you just created. For example, the CTS Internet connectoid, shown in Figure 6-3, is one I created using the Internet Connection Wizard.

Tip   If you want to create an easy shortcut to your Dial-Up Networking connectoid, right-drag its icon out of the Dial-Up Networking folder onto the desktop or Quick Launch toolbar (see Chapter 4). When you release the right mouse button, choose Create Shortcut(s) Here.

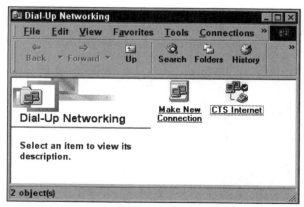

Figure 6-3: I created the CTS Internet connectoid using the Internet Connection Wizard.

Open the connectoid's icon by clicking (if you're using Web-style navigation) or double-clicking. The Connect To dialog box (see Figure 6-4) appears. If you filled out all the questions correctly in the Internet Connection Wizard, all the information you need to log on will already be filled in. Click the Connect button.

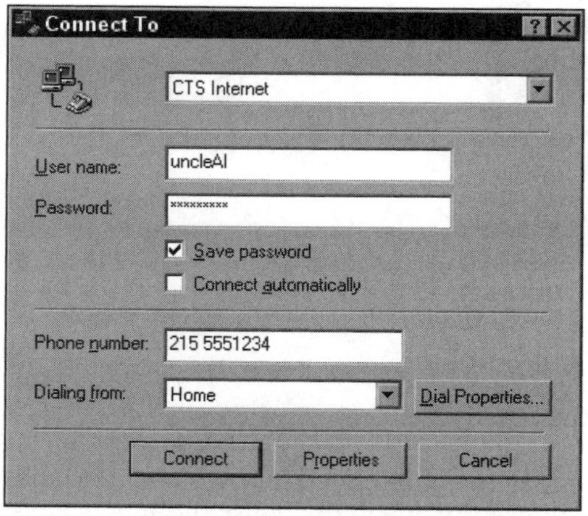

Figure 6-4: The Connect To dialog box

You should see a small dialog box that keeps you informed of what's going on (dialing, connecting, and so forth). Wait until you see the dialog box shown in Figure 6-5 (or something similar). You can close this dialog box after it appears by clicking its Close (X) button.

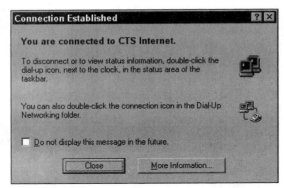

Figure 6-5: Success! This computer is connected to the Internet.

When you're connected, a small network icon (two monitors) appears in the taskbar. Pointing to this icon shows some information about the connection. Double-clicking this little icon shows more information, as shown in Figure 6-6.

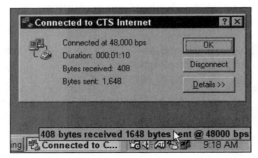

Figure 6-6: A two-monitor icon in the taskbar indicates you are connected.

Once you're connected, you'll stay connected until you specifically break the connection. If you now open some Internet program, such as Microsoft Internet Explorer, you should be taken to some home page, as in the example shown in Figure 6-7. The page you see won't look at all like the one in the figure though, because the default home page in your Web browser isn't likely to be www.coolnerds.com. You'll learn how to visit Web pages, and how to choose a default home page in Chapter 7. For now, just the fact that you can see any home page is sufficient.

Figure 6-7: Example of a successful Internet connection using the Internet Explorer program

Disconnecting from the Internet

Remember, (especially if you're paying phone charges) as long as that little two-monitor icon is visible in the taskbar, you are connected to your ISP. When you're done cruising the Internet, you should always disconnect, using whichever of the following methods you prefer:

✦ Right-click the little two-monitor icon and choose Disconnect.

✦ Double-click the little two-monitor icon in the taskbar and then click the Disconnect button in the dialog box that appears.

✦ Open My Computer ➪ Dial-Up Networking, right-click the connectoid's icon, and choose Disconnect.

Once you're disconnected, programs that access the Internet will stop working. You'll need to reconnect, by repeating the procedure under "Making the Connection" earlier in this chapter before you can access the Internet.

Tip   Actually, most of your Internet programs can be configured to connect to the Internet automatically so you may never need to open the Dial-Up Networking connectoid again! I'll talk about automatic connections as we progress through these chapters.

If you're able to connect to the Internet at this point, there's really no reason to continue reading in this chapter. What follows is only relevant to those of you who may need to jump through some additional flaming hoops to get your Internet connection working.

Creating a Connectoid Manually

If the Internet Connection Wizard doesn't do the trick to connect you to the Internet, you can manually go through all the pieces required to make a connection to look for, and correct, any problems. Remember, however, if you are already able to connect to the Internet, reading the rest of this chapter is unnecessary. The wizard will have already set up all the items necessary to make your connection.

Installing Dial-Up Networking

The program that makes your connection to the Internet is called Dial-Up Networking. To ensure this component is installed, click the Start button and choose Programs ➪ Accessories ➪ Communications. If the resulting submenu is compressed, click the double arrows at the bottom to see all its options. If you do see an option for Dial-Up Networking, as in Figure 6-8, then Dial-Up Networking is already installed. Skip to the section "Installing TCP/IP networking" later in this chapter.

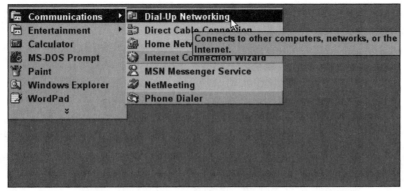

Figure 6-8: Dial-Up Networking is already installed on this computer.

If you don't see a Dial-Up Networking icon in My Computer, you need to install this component now. Here's how:

1. Close all open programs and save any work in progress.

2. Gather your original Windows Me CD-ROM or floppy disks (unless your computer doesn't require those).

3. Click the Start button and choose Settings ⇨ Control Panel.

4. Open the Add/Remove Programs icon.

5. Click the Windows Setup tab.

6. Click Communications and then click the Details button.

7. Select (check) Dial-Up Networking, as in Figure 6-9.

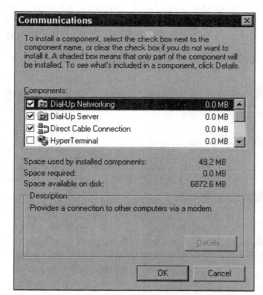

Figure 6-9: Ready to add the missing Dial-Up Networking component

8. Click the OK button to close the Details box.

9. Click the OK button to close Add/Remove Programs and then follow any instructions that appear onscreen.

When the installation is complete, you can close the Control Panel, if you wish. Be sure to restart your computer if any instructions appear telling you to do so.

Installing TCP/IP networking

The Internet is based on a communication protocol named TCP/IP, which stands for Transmission Control Protocol/Internet Protocol. Windows Me has built-in TCP/IP, but it may not be installed on your PC. To find out, and to install it, if necessary, follow these steps:

1. Close all open programs and, if relevant, save any work in progress.

2. Gather your original Windows Me CD-ROM or floppies (unless your computer doesn't require those to install components).

3. Click the Start button and choose Settings ➪ Control Panel.

4. Open the Network icon.

5. Click the Configuration tab and scroll down through the list of installed components. If you see the TCP/IP ➪ Dial-Up Adapter protocol listed already, as in Figure 6-10, you don't need to install this now. Click OK, close the Control Panel, and skip down to the section "Creating a new connectoid" later in this chapter.

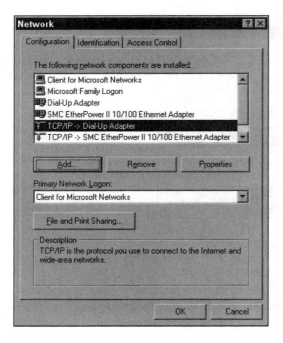

Figure 6-10: In this example, TCP/IP protocol is already installed.

6. If you don't see TCP/IP listed as a protocol, click the Add button below the list of installed network components. The Select Network Component Type dialog box appears. Click Protocol to highlight this one option.

7. Click the Add button, and then click Protocol. In the next dialog box that appears, click Protocol, and then click the Add button. Then choose Microsoft in the left column and TCP/IP in the right column, as in Figure 6-11.

8. Click the OK button and follow the instructions that appear onscreen.

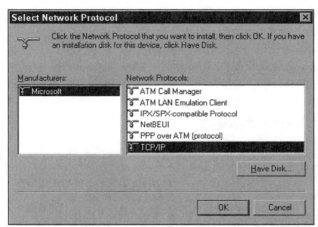

Figure 6-11: About to install Microsoft TCP/IP networking protocol

Click the OK button as necessary to work your way back to the Windows Me desktop and restart the computer if requested to do so. When you get back to the Windows Me desktop, you're ready to proceed with the next main step, configuring TCP/IP for a dial-up connection to the Internet. You may notice a new icon, named Network Neighborhood, on your desktop. That's good — it shows your computer is now ready for networking.

Creating a new connectoid

Now that Dial-Up Networking and TCP/IP are installed, you can set up a connectoid to dial into the Internet. A *connectoid* is a small file containing the information necessary to make a connection between your PC and your ISP. When completed, the connectoid will appear as an icon in your Dial-Up Networking folder. Follow these steps to create a connectoid:

1. Click the Start button and choose Programs ➪ Accessories ➪ Communications ➪ Dial-Up Networking.

2. If the Welcome to Dial Up Networking Wizard does not appear, open the Make New Connection icon to start the Make New Connection Wizard, shown in Figure 6-12.

3. Type a name (anything you like) for this connection. For example, I named mine "My Internet Connectoid" in the figure shown.

4. If the "Select a device" option does not display the name of the modem you want to use, choose the correct modem from the drop-down list.

5. Click the Next button to move onto the next wizard dialog box.

6. In the next wizard dialog box, type in the area code (even if it's your own area code) and phone number the ISP told you to use for making your Internet connection, as in the example shown in Figure 6-13.

7. The next wizard dialog box will inform you that you successfully created a dial-up networking connection. Click the Finish button.

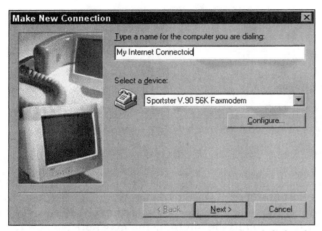

Figure 6-12: The Make New Connection Wizard dialog box

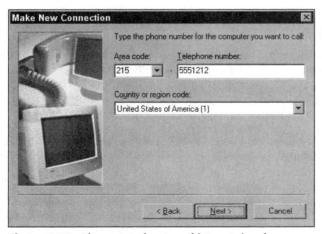

Figure 6-13: Phone number typed into a wizard page

Is your modem okay?

Throughout these troubleshooting steps, I assume your modem is connected correctly, turned on (if it's an external modem), and ready to go. If you haven't used this particular modem in a while, you may want to run a quick test on it using the Phone Dialer applet, as discussed in Chapter 5.

Also, you may want to check your modem and COM port settings in Device Manager. Click the Start button and choose Settings ➪ Control Panel, and then open the System icon. Click the Device Manager tab. If you see any little *problem* icons on either your modem or the COM port to which the modem is connected, you must solve this problem (or those problems) first. To do so, click the Start button and choose Help. Open the Troubleshooting link and work your way through the hardware and modem troubleshooters.

The Dial-Up Networking dialog box will now include an icon for the connectoid you just created. To test the connectoid, open it as discussed under "Making the connection" earlier in this chapter. If you have any problems, skip to the following section, "Troubleshooting a Connectoid."

Troubleshooting a Connectoid

If you're reading this section, then you already created a Dial-Up Networking connectoid using either the Internet Connection Wizard or the more manual method previously described. But this connectoid doesn't seem to be working. In the following sections, I look at the many options involved in getting a connectoid to work. Before we do that, it's important you understand your best ally in solving any connection problems is your ISP (not me and not Microsoft). Your ISP knows its system best, and it knows exactly what's needed on your end to make a successful connection. While the following sections can help you solve problems, you may need information from your ISP to fill in all the blanks. To begin exploring (and, I hope, fixing) your connectoid, follow these steps:

1. Click the Start button and choose Programs ➪ Accessories ➪ Communications ➪ Dial-Up Networking.

2. Open the connectoid that's giving you trouble by clicking it (or double-clicking if you're using Classic Windows navigation style). The Connect To dialog box appears, as in the example shown in Figure 6-14.

Caution

Remember, passwords for login names are case-sensitive on many computers. When typing these on your machine, make sure to type uppercase and lowercase letters exactly as specified by your ISP!

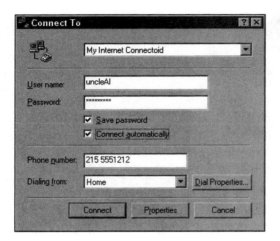

Figure 6-14: This is the first dialog box to appear when you open a connectoid.

3. Now check, and correct, as necessary, the following:

- Make sure the User name option exactly matches your login name as provided by your ISP and as you wrote in Table 6-1.

- Because you can't see your password, carefully retype it, being careful of uppercase and lowercase letters, as per the information you wrote next to "Your password" in Table 6-1.

- Make sure the phone number shown is exactly the number you're supposed to dial, as written next to "Your ISP's telephone number" in Table 6-1. You can omit the hyphen between the prefix and suffix, if you like, as in the example shown in the figure.

- Click the Dial Properties button to get to the dialog box shown in Figure 6-15.

- Make sure the "I am dialing from" option represents the number from which you're really dialing. Or, create a new profile by clicking the New button.

- Carefully check to see if anything looks amiss. For example, is the area code from which you're currently dialing correct? Are the Area Code Rules (accessible from the button by the same name) correct for this dialing location? Do you need to dial some special number to dial out, such as 8 or 9? If so, fill in the appropriate blanks. Does this phone line have call waiting? For more information on other options, click the question mark (?) button near the upper-right corner of the dialog box and then click the option with which you need help.

4. Click the OK button to return to the Connect To dialog box.

5. Click the Connect button to try again.

It may take a while to get connected. If you do get connected, proceed now to Chapter 7. Otherwise, continue with the next section to do more troubleshooting.

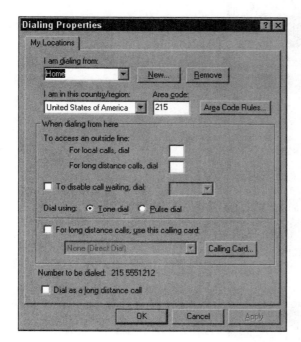

Figure 6-15: Dialing properties for an Internet connectoid

More troubleshooting

If you completed the preceding troubleshooting steps and you still can't get connected, we need to dig a little deeper. Follow these steps:

1. Click the Start button and choose Programs ➪ Accessories ➪ Communications ➪ Dial-Up Networking.

2. Right-click the connectoid giving you trouble and choose Properties.

3. On the General tab (see Figure 6-16) make sure the area code, phone number, country code, and "Connect using" accurately reflect the dialing information provided by your ISP. And make sure your modem is presented under "Connect using." If you found any mistakes, correct them now.

4. Next, click the Networking tab. Choose the settings shown in Figure 6-17, unless your ISP specifically told you to do otherwise.

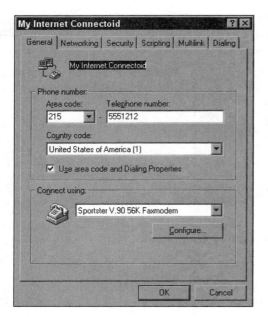

Figure 6-16: The General tab of a connectoid's properties dialog box

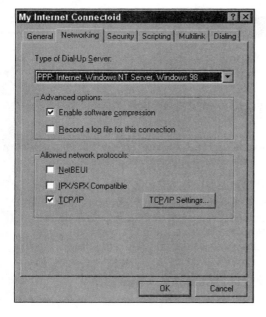

Figure 6-17: Typical server type settings for an Internet connection

5. Next, click the TCP/IP Settings button to get to the TCP/IP Settings dialog box, shown in Figure 6-18. Now you have a few decisions to make:

- If your ISP did not give you a specific IP address and/or DNS servers (way back in Table 6-1), leave the settings, as shown in Figure 6-18.

- If you have a specific IP address and DNS name server in Table 6-1, select "Specify an IP address" and type in the IP address assigned by your ISP. Likewise, choose "Specify name server addresses" and fill in the blanks with the appropriate information for your account, as in the example shown in Figure 6-19.

6. Click OK to return to the previous dialog box.

7. Click the OK button to close the next dialog box.

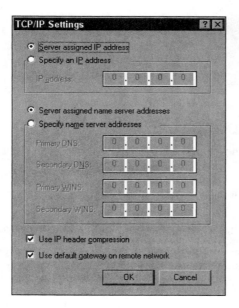

Figure 6-18: TCP/IP settings for an ISP that assigns IP addresses dynamically when you log on

If you see any additional instructions onscreen, follow them. If you made any changes in the preceding steps, now is a good time to test your connectoid again. Open it to try to get connected to the Internet as described previously under "Making the connection." If the problem appears solved, you can skip the rest of the chapter and move on to Chapter 7. If problems persist, read on.

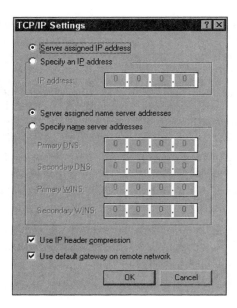

Figure 6-19: Sample TCP/IP settings for an ISP that doesn't assign addresses dynamically

Still more troubleshooting

If you're still having troubles connecting to the Internet, follow these steps to check your modem settings:

1. Once again click Start and choose Programs ➪ Accessories ➪ Communications ➪ Dial-Up Networking.

2. Right-click the connectoid that's giving you grief and choose Properties.

3. On the General tab, click the Configure button. You're taken to the modem properties dialog box similar to the one shown in Figure 6-20.

4. Now check and, if necessary, correct all the following:

   - On the General tab, make sure the correct Port is selected (COM1 if your modem is connected to COM Port 1 or COM2 if your modem is connected to COM Port 2).

   - If you want, you can adjust the volume of the modem. Also, set the Maximum Speed to 115200 (as shown in Figure 6-20) or to whatever value is highest on your PC.

   - Click the Connection tab and make your settings look something like the ones in Figure 6-21.

   - Click the Advanced button and then set up your options, as in Figure 6-22. If your ISP told you to add any extra settings to your modem, fill in the appropriate information under "Extra settings" near the bottom of the dialog box.

• Click the OK button and then click the Options tab. Again, I suggest matching your settings to the ones shown in Figure 6-23, unless your ISP provided different instructions.

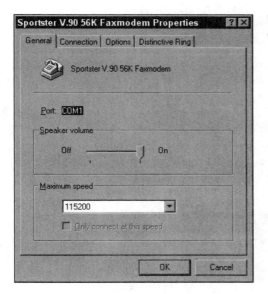

Figure 6-20: The modem properties dialog box

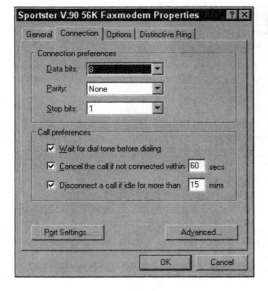

Figure 6-21: The Connection tab in the modem properties dialog box

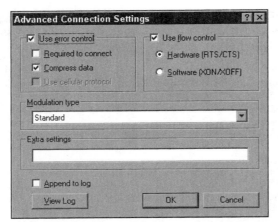

Figure 6-22: Advanced configuration settings for an Internet connectoid

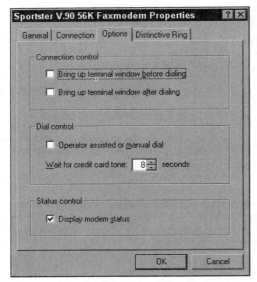

Figure 6-23: Options tab of the modem properties dialog box

5. Click the OK button to close the modem properties dialog box and then click the OK button to close the connectoid's properties dialog box.

If you made any changes at all, try connecting again as described under "Making the connection" earlier in this chapter. If you are able to connect — great! — go on to Chapter 7 and ignore the rest of this chapter.

If problems persist beyond this point, you may need to ask your ISP for more information. You may want to have your ISP fax all the information necessary to complete Table 6-1 and any other additional information required. Then try creating another connectoid or changing an existing connectoid to the correct settings your ISP provided.

Automating Your Connection

If you want your computer to dial in to the Internet as soon as you open Microsoft Internet Explorer, follow these steps:

1. Open Internet Explorer using its icon on the desktop or Quick Launch toolbar. Or, click the Start button and choose Programs ➪ Internet Explorer. If your Connect To dialog box appears, you can skip it for now by clicking its Work Offline button.

2. Choose Tools ➪ Internet Options from Internet Explorer's menu bar.

3. Click the Connections tab.

4. If you have more than one connection defined, click the one that you'll use as the default, and then click the Set Default button (if it's available).

5. Choose "Always dial my default connection," as in Figure 6-24.

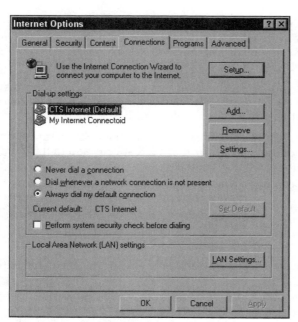

Figure 6-24: Internet Explorer automatically connects using a Dial-Up Networking connectoid named CTS Internet.

Click the OK buttons to close the dialog boxes and to return to the desktop. From this point, you should be able to browse the Web at any time, just by opening your Microsoft Internet Explorer program.

The ISDN Connection

Integrated Services Digital Network (ISDN) is an alternative to using a standard (analog) modem to connect to telephone lines. The top-end speed for a standard modem is about 56K. An ISDN connection can communicate at 128K — more than twice as fast.

Unfortunately, ISDN isn't as readily available as the regular phone lines modems use. Some cities don't even have ISDN yet. And ISDN isn't easy to set up and it doesn't come cheap.

Finally, with the advent of *x*DSL, which provides much faster connections than ISDN, using regular phone lines, choosing ISDN to connect to the Internet looks less and less attractive. I suppose one could say ISDN's days are numbered. Nevertheless, if you already have an ISDN phone line, or ISDN is the best option for your location for whatever reason, Windows Me will support an ISDN connection.

The total procedure to get set up for ISDN is pretty complicated. But in general it will go like this:

1. Find out whether your ISP supports ISDN. If the answer is No, stop right here or get an account with an ISP that does. If the answer is Yes, make sure you can get a true 128K connection and ask how much it will cost. A monthly ISDN connection is likely to cost you more than a standard telephone connection.

2. Find out whether your telephone company supports ISDN. If the answer is No, stop right here. If the answer is Yes, make sure you can get a 128K connection and ask how much the installation and monthly service will cost.

3. Find out what hardware your ISP has tested with its ISDN connection. Choosing hardware that can perform at 128K speeds and that is compatible with your ISP's equipment is essential.

4. Order ISDN service from your local telephone company.

5. Purchase the hardware — an ISDN modem or ISDN terminal adapter — needed to connect your PC to an ISDN line.

6. Set up your ISDN account with your ISP.

7. Install the ISDN adapter hardware and software, as per the manufacturer's instructions.

Unfortunately, I can't help you much with all these items because so many different brands of ISDN adapters and so many ISPs exist. But I can offer a few alternatives that may save you some headaches:

✦ Search for local ISPs that offer a complete ISDN package, where they come to your home or office and set up everything for you.

✦ If you already have some kind of Internet connection, read about current events and products in the ISDN arena at `http://www.microsoft.com/windows/getisdn`.

ISDN information you'll need

An ISDN phone line is different from a regular phone line in that you need some specific information to make it work. If you decide to get an ISDN account with your local telephone company, make sure it gives you the information listed in Table 6-2, which will be necessary to make your connection. You should get two phone numbers and two Service Profile IDs (SPIDs). The SPIDS are typically the same as the phone numbers with a 00 or 01 on the end. Fill in the blank cells in the third column of Table 6-2 with information provided by your telephone company.

Table 6-2 **Information Needed from Your Phone Company to Make ISDN Work**		
Info from Phone Company	*Example*	*Fill in Your Info*
Switch Protocol	ATT: AT&T ESS 5, or NI1 (National ISDN), or NTI (Northern Telecomm DMS 100)	
Phone number #1	5550687	
SPID #1	760555068700	
Phone number #2	5550761	
SPID #2	760555076100	

Installing the ISDN modem

If you purchase an external ISDN modem, you'll want to install it as you would any other external modem. Be sure to follow the modem manufacturer's installation instructions closely, as you'll be using their configuration software to set up your connection.

If you purchased an internal ISDN modem, go ahead and install that one as per the manufacturer's instructions. When the installation is complete and you've restarted your computer, you may get some added help from the ISDN Configuration Wizard, as described next.

Using the ISDN Configuration Wizard

Some internal ISDN modems (those that act like a network card, rather than a modem emulator) will automatically launch the Windows Me ISDN Configuration Wizard after you install the modem and restart your computer. When the wizard first appears, you see an introductory wizard dialog box with ISDN Configuration in the title bar. As with any wizard, you need just fill in the blanks and click the Next button on each page that appears.

When you complete the wizard, you may see a brief reminder to set up a Dial-Up Networking connectoid to the Internet. Run the Make New Connection Wizard inside Dial-Up Networking, as discussed earlier in this chapter, to set up your connection. Be sure to choose your ISDN device when prompted by the wizard to pick your connection device.

Note   Once the ISDN Configuration Wizard has been called into play by Windows, you can access it from the Start menu. This will be handy if you need to change some settings you made the first time going through the wizard.

Caution   Don't be alarmed if your internal ISDN modem doesn't appear under Modems in Device Manager or the Control Panel. You'll probably find it listed in Network Adapters in Device Manager.

If you can't get connected to your ISP after installing your ISDN modem (or terminal adapter), your best bet is to contact your ISP for support. Your ISP knows best what's needed to make a successful ISDN connection to its network.

Virtual Private Networking and PPTP

Virtual Private Networking (VPN) is a means of accessing networks and, in some cases, even the Internet, through a secure tunneling protocol. VPN works with Point-to-Point Tunneling Protocol (PPTP), which some (but not all) ISPs offer as

an alternative to regular PPP. Virtual Private Networking is often used in large cor-
porate environments where companies interact with one another via *extranets* —
private networks that use the Internet for their wiring, and are similar to the
Internet in look and feel. To this extent, they tend to be more commonly used in
"Enterprise" operating systems such as UNIX/Linux or Windows NT/Windows 2000.
Nonetheless, if you need a VPN connection to a network, you can get one through
Windows Me.

To use VPN you first need a *terminal adapter* (a device similar to a modem) that
supports VPN. You'll also need to set up a PPTP account with an ISP or your company's network administrator. Assuming you overcome those hurdles, you can
install the Windows Me Virtual Private Networking. You can install this component
like any other Windows component, by following these steps:

1. Click the Start button and choose Settings ➪ Control Panel.

2. Open the Add/Remove Programs icon.

3. Click the Windows Setup tab and wait for Windows to detect your components.

4. Click the Communications category and then click the Details button.

5. Scroll down to Virtual Private Networking (see Figure 6-25). If this component
   isn't checked, select (check) it now. (If Virtual Private Networking is checked
   already, then this component is already installed and needn't be reinstalled.)

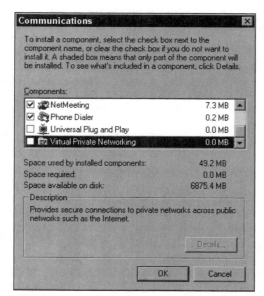

Figure 6-25: Virtual Private Networking in
Windows Setup

6. Click the OK button to close the Communications dialog box and then click the next OK button to close the Add/Remove Programs dialog box.

When you finish, you won't see anything new on the desktop or Start menus. To verify that VPN is installed, you can follow these steps to take a look at the Device Manager window:

1. Click the Windows Me Start button and choose Settings ⇨ Control Panel.

2. Open the System icon and then click the Device Manager tab.

3. Expand the Network Adapters category by clicking the plus (+) sign next to that category name. You should see a Virtual Private Networking adapter and Dial-Up adapter with VPN support.

4. Click the Cancel button to return to Windows Me.

Once you have the information you need from your ISP to connect to your PPTP account, you can set up a Dial-Up Networking connectoid in the usual manner, as described earlier in this chapter. But when you open the Select a Device option in the Make New Connection Wizard, choose Microsoft VPN Adapter. Then click the Next button and fill in the remaining information required for connecting to your ISP.

For information on using VPN to connect across a LAN, across the Internet, or to your corporate network, contact your ISP or corporate network administrator. You can also find some relevant information in Help: Click the Start button, choose Help, click the Index tab, and type **virt** to get to that section of the index. Then click Virtual Private Networking and click the Display button.

Summary

In this chapter, I reviewed all the steps required to connect your PC to the Internet. To recap the main points:

✦ You can use any standard modem to connect to the Internet.

✦ If you have an account with one of the large online services such as AOL, CompuServe, MSN, or Prodigy, you already have Internet access. Go to that service and look for information on using the Internet.

✦ Another way to access the Internet is through a local Internet service provider (ISP), which you can find in your Yellow Pages (under Internet), local newspaper ads, or by calling 1-888-ISP-FIND.

✦ To access the Internet through a local ISP, you'll probably need to run the Internet Connection Wizard (Start ⇨ Programs ⇨ Accessories ⇨ Communications ⇨ Internet Connection Wizard).

✦ If you have any problems making a connection with your ISP, see the trouble-shooting sections in this chapter.

✦ Also, if you have problems, try running the Windows Me Troubleshooters to test and, possibly, fix your modem and Dial-Up Networking settings.

✦ ISDN offers a faster means of accessing the Internet. For information on getting an ISDN account, first contact your ISP.

✦ Windows Me supports PPTP Virtual Private Networking (VPN). You can install VPN from the Communications category of Windows Setup, in Add/Remove Programs.

✦ ✦ ✦

Browsing the World Wide Web

T he Internet offers many services, including the wildly popular Word Wide Web (aka the Web). The Web provides an easy point-and-click interface to a vast amount of information, free software, technical support, and just plain fun. Even if you haven't actually been on the Internet yet, you've undoubtedly seen Web site addresses — those www. whatever.com things — in ads, letterhead, or elsewhere. In this chapter, you'll learn how to get to those addresses and much more about using the Web.

Getting on the Web

Getting on to the World Wide Web is easy. The exact way you go about it, though, depends on your Internet connection and your Internet service provider (ISP). For example, if you work for a company that provides a permanent connection to the Internet, you may have to log on to your company's network and then start your Web browser. If you're going through one of the big online services such as America Online, CompuServe, or Prodigy, you'll probably need to start the browsing software those services come with and then click a "Connect to the Internet" button. If you have a dial-up connection of the sort discussed in Chapter 6, you may need to open the connectoid to your ISP first.

But, as a general rule, you probably can get right on to the World Wide Web by opening Microsoft Internet Explorer. You can do this in three different ways. Use whichever method is most convenient:

- ✦ Open the Internet Explorer icon on your desktop.
- ✦ Click the Launch Internet Explorer Browser icon in the Quick Launch toolbar.
- ✦ Choose Start ➪ Programs ➪ Internet Explorer.

If an Internet Connection Wizard dialog box appears, read it carefully and follow its instructions to set up your Internet connection. (You'll only need to do this step the first time you start your browser.)

Most browsers, including Internet Explorer, automatically prompt you to connect to the Internet if you're not connected already. This means you can start your browser without bothering to connect first. If you are prompted to connect, simply click the Connect button that appears.

Your Web browser will start and connect to its default home page. For example, the default home page for Internet Explorer is Microsoft's Web site at http://www.msn.com. While there's no telling how this page will look when you get there, because Web pages change often, you'll probably see something resembling Figure 7-1.

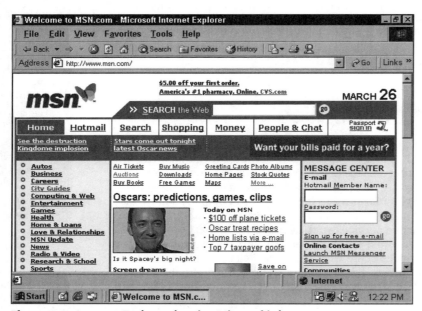

Figure 7-1: Internet Explorer showing Microsoft's home page

Visiting a Web Site

Every Web site has its own unique address, or Uniform Resource Locator (URL). Most start with http://www (for Hypertext Transfer Protocol, World Wide Web). Most also end with a three-letter extension, such as .com. For example, my personal Web site's URL is http://www.coolnerds.com. (In most Web browsers, including Internet Explorer, you don't have to type the http:// at the beginning of the URL.)

To visit a Web site, point your Web browser to that site by typing the site's URL into the Address text box of your Web browser. Here are the exact steps:

1. Click the URL currently in the Address bar (`http://www.msn.com` in this example). The current URL will be selected (highlighted).

Tip If you don't see the Address Bar toolbar, choose View ➪ Toolbars ➪ Address Bar from Internet Explorer's menu bar. If no text box appears next to the Address Bar toolbar, double-click the vertical bar to the left of the word Address and the text box will appear.

2. Replace the address currently shown with the address to which you want to go. You can type over the highlighted address or use standard text-editing techniques to change the current URL to the URL you want.

3. Press Enter.

4. Wait for the page to appear.

While you're waiting, the icon near the upper-right corner will spin to let you know the browser is working. The status bar at the bottom of the screen will present messages to inform you of the browser's progress. When the "Done" message appears in the left side of the status bar, the entire page has been down-loaded to your PC. Figure 7-2 shows the page for my Web site after I entered the URL `http://www.coolnerds.com` into the Address box.

Tip If you don't see a status bar at the bottom of the Web browser window, choose View ➪ Status Bar from Internet Explorer's menu bar. (When the status bar is visible, the View ➪ Status Bar option has a check mark next to it.)

Internet Explorer keeps track of sites you visit and tries to fill in the blanks of any partial Web site addresses you type. This feature is called AutoComplete. Suppose, for example, you visited Coolnerds in the past and now you want to revisit this site. You could click whatever URL is currently shown in the Address box to select that entire address and then start typing **www.coolnerds**. Chances are, by the time you've typed cool, Internet Explorer will finish typing the rest of the URL, at which point you can press Enter to go there. If Internet Explorer tries to complete the address for you, but gets the wrong address, don't worry. Keep typing the address you want. If you end up with some extra stuff to the right of the address you typed, press Delete (Del) as needed to delete it.

Tip To enable or disable AutoComplete, choose Tools ➪ Internet Options from Internet Explorer's menu bar. Click the Advanced tab. Under the Browsing category in the list that appears, you can click the check box next to Use Inline AutoComplete to turn this feature on (checked) or off (no check mark).

Figure 7-2: Now viewing the page at `http://www.coolnerds.com`

Using hyperlinks

One of the best features of the Web is its use of hyperlinks — hot spots on the
screen — which, when clicked, take you to images, videos, audio clips, or other
Web pages. Most hyperlinks appear as underlined text, but any text, or even part
of a picture, can be a hyperlink. When the mouse pointer is touching a hyperlink,
it changes to the little pointing hand. A ToolTip showing a description of the hyperlink or the address to which the hyperlink will take you also may appear near the
mouse pointer. The status bar typically will show the hyperlink's address. To follow
the link to its destination, click the left mouse button and wait for the new page to
appear on your screen.

Note   While you cruise the Web, Internet Explorer may occasionally display Security Alert
dialog boxes. These alert you to the possible security risks of carrying out an
action, although usually they're just a lot of crying "Wolf!" and you can ignore
them. Nonetheless, you should read the box carefully and then choose Yes to continue or No to cancel the operation. You can customize the security options, as
explained in "Personalizing Your Browser," later in this chapter. For more information about Internet security, look up *Security* in the Internet Explorer Help index.

Creating a Favorites list

As you follow links and explore the Web, you're sure to find sites you'll want to revisit in the future. You can make the return trip easier by adding the site to your Favorites while you're there. Here's how:

1. While viewing the page you want to add, choose Favorites ⇨ Add To Favorites from Internet Explorer's menu bar. You'll see the Add Favorite dialog box, shown in Figure 7-3.

2. Type in a name for this favorite item or accept the suggested name.

3. Click the OK button.

As a shortcut, you can go to the page you want to add to Favorites and then press Ctrl+D. Internet Explorer adds the page to your Favorites list without displaying the Add Favorite dialog box.

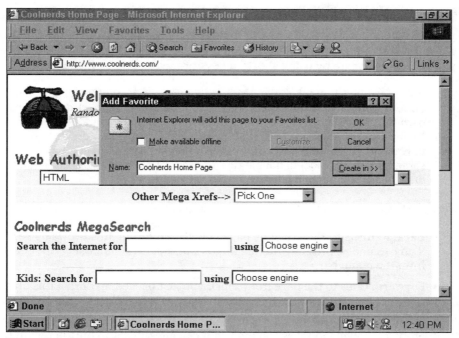

Figure 7-3: The Add Favorite dialog box

Revisiting a favorite page

When you want to revisit this site in the future, you needn't type its address. Instead, follow these steps:

1. Click the Favorites menu in Internet Explorer's menu bar.

2. If your favorite page is stored in a subcategory (or folder) on the Favorites menu, point to or click that folder.

3. Click the name of the site you want to revisit.

You'll be whisked back to the favorite page you chose.

Tip Later in this chapter, you'll learn how to organize your Favorites list into subcategories — such as Cooking, Stock Investments, or Pets — so you can find your favorite places more easily.

Using other navigation tools

The Standard Buttons toolbar across the top of Internet Explorer's window provides some additional, simple navigation buttons (refer to Figures 7-1 and 7-2). You also can navigate by using shortcut keys or menu options, if you prefer.

Note If the Standard Buttons toolbar isn't visible, choose View ⇨ Toolbars ⇨ Standard Buttons from Internet Explorer's menu bar. If you don't see text descriptions on each button (as shown in Figures 7-1 and 7-2) and you want to, choose View ⇨ Toolbars ⇨ Customize, and select Show text labels in the Text options list box to turn them on. Click Close to close the Customize Toolbar dialog box. Finally, if some buttons are hidden, double-click the vertical bar next to the Back button or drag the vertical bar to the left.

Here are the navigation buttons, shortcuts, and menu options you can use:

✦ **Back:** Returns to the previous page you visited during this browsing session, if any. (Same as pressing Alt+left arrow, Backspace, or choosing Go ⇨ Back from the menu bar.)

✦ **Forward:** Goes to the page from which you just backed up during this browsing session (if any). (Same as pressing Alt+right arrow, or choosing Go ⇨ Forward from the menu bar.)

✦ **Stop:** If a download takes too long, you can click the Stop button to end the download. This frees the browser so you can visit elsewhere. (Same as pressing Esc or choosing View ⇨ Stop from the menu bar.)

✦ **Refresh:** Ensures you are viewing the absolute latest version of the current page. (Same as pressing F5 or choosing View ⇨ Refresh from the menu bar.)

✦ **Home:** Returns you to your default home page — http://www.msn.com — in our example. (Same as choosing Go ➪ Home Page from the menu bar.)

✦ **Search:** Displays a Search Explorer bar in the left-hand frame of the screen. (Same as choosing View ➪ Explorer Bar ➪ Search.) This frame enables you to search the Internet for all kinds of good stuff, as explained later in this chapter. (If you choose Go ➪ Search the Web from the menu bar, you'll be taken to the Web page for a search engine rather than the Search Explorer bar.)

✦ **Favorites:** Displays the Favorites Explorer bar in the left-hand frame of the screen. (Same as choosing View ➪ Explorer Bar ➪ Favorites from the menu bar.) Like the Favorites menu, this frame enables you to jump quickly to your favorite Web sites. I'll explain more about working with the Favorites Explorer bar later in this chapter.

✦ **History:** Displays the History Explorer bar in the left-hand frame of the screen. (Same as choosing View ➪ Explorer Bar ➪ History from the menu bar.) You can use the History frame to revisit places you've been before, even if they aren't your favorites. I'll give you a History lesson later in this chapter.

The Search, Favorites, and History buttons are toggles. If you choose them by accident, don't worry. You can quickly return the screen to its previous appearance by clicking whatever toolbar button you clicked to display the frame or full screen in the first place. See "Clever Explorer bar tricks" later in this chapter for other tips on using the Explorer bars.

✦ **Mail:** Takes you to Internet e-mail, as discussed in Chapter 9.

✦ **Print:** Prints the Web page you're viewing. (Same as choosing File ➪ Print from the menu bar, or pressing Ctrl+P.)

✦ **Messenger:** Opens the MSN Messenger service. (Same as choosing Tools ➪ MSN Messenger Service from the menu bar.) This enables you to send and receive *instant messages* with your buddies when you both are online.

Tip

To jump to a specific Web page you visited recently, click the little down-arrow button next to the Back button, Forward button, or Address text box. Then click the name of the page you want to revisit in the drop-down list that appears. You also can use the History list to revisit pages, as explained in "Going Places You've Gone Before (History 101)," later in this chapter.

Every Web site you visit is bound to have hyperlinks to take you to other sites in which you're interested. So the few skills you've learned so far will enable you to explore the Web forever! At some point, however, you may get tired of being led around the Web and you may start asking "How do I find information on such and such?" The *such-and-such* part can be any topic that interests you. And I do mean any topic because the Web is loaded with millions of pages of information. The next section explains how to find just about everything, from apples to zoonoses, on the Internet.

Searching the Web

Internet Explorer offers you several ways to search for information on the Internet. Perhaps the handiest is the built-in Search Explorer bar. To use it, click the Search button on the Standard Buttons toolbar, or choose View ➪ Explorer Bar ➪ Search from the menu bar. The viewing area splits into two frames, as in the example shown in Figure 7-4. Whatever page you were viewing scoots over to the frame on the right. The new frame on the left acts as your Search browser.

Figure 7-4: Click the Search button to open the Search Explorer bar in the left side of the screen.

Now, to search for your topic on the Internet, follow these steps:

1. If you wish, choose a search engine by clicking the Customize button at the top of the Search Explorer bar. The Search Explorer bar options below the Choose Provider list will change to reflect the search engine you picked.

2. Choose whichever options best describe how you want to perform the search (i.e. All Words or Any Words).

3. Begin your search as follows, depending on what you want to do:

   • If you want to search for a specific topic, click in the text box below the name of the search engine, type the topic you're looking for (for example, **zoonoses**), and then click the Search button.

   • If the search engine offers a list of categories, and you want to search in a category, click the hyperlink for the category.

4. The Search Explorer bar frame will list hyperlinks that satisfy your search. (Be sure to scroll up and down through the entire frame to see what's available and look for any "Next Page" or "Previous Page" hyperlinks that take you to additional matches for your search.) Now, click the hyperlink of the item you want to explore.

Soon the Web page you're searching for will appear in the right-hand frame. Now you can explore the Web page in the right-hand frame, just as you'd explore any Web page. (If you want to see the page without the left-hand frame, click the Search button in the toolbar. When you want to return to the Search Explorer bar, click this Search button once more.) You'll be amazed at how quickly you can home in on the information you seek.

If you don't find what you're looking for, you can repeat any of Steps 1 through 4. For example, start with Step 1 and try another search engine, or start with Step 4 and click a different hyperlink in the Search Explorer bar. Very convenient!

Caution   Remember, just because you read something on the Web doesn't make it so! When doing online research, always try to get corroboration from several sources and use your own common sense before you believe any "facts" you find.

Searching from a Web page

You can search the Internet from the Web site for a specific search engine if you want. For example, you can go straight to the Yahoo! Web site by entering `http://www.yahoo.com` into the Address box. Or, visit the Lycos search engine at `http://www.lycos.com`. Other popular search engines can be found at `http://www.excite.com` (**Excite**) and `http://www.infoseek.com` (**Infoseek**).

Once you get to the search engine's Web site, simply complete Steps 2 through 4, as you would when using the Search Explorer bar.

What's a search engine, anyway?

A *search engine* is a front-end program that helps you find resources on the Internet, including Web pages, newsgroups, and more. When you start a search, the engine looks through a predefined database—not the Internet itself—so the search isn't really live. (Because the search isn't live, the results may include entries for out-of-date sites or for sites that no longer exist or have moved. Similarly, some great sites may not be listed because the database hasn't been updated recently enough.)

The Internet offers dozens of search engines in addition to those shown in the Customize Search Settings dialog box. Those listed are among the best and most popular, though. You can access most of these extra search engines by choosing the "Use the Search Assistant for smart searching" option in the Customize Search Settings dialog box.

Different search engines use different methods for populating their databases with links to Internet locations. For example, some engines index frequently appearing keywords on Web pages. Others rely on submissions by people who want their own Web sites listed. And still others are updated by specially trained humans who consider certain sites to be of special interest. (Most engines use a combination of these methods to fill their databases.) For these reasons, checking several search engines is a good idea when you're doing serious online research.

Most search engines enable you to enter complex search criteria, such as zoonoses *and* rabbits. Unfortunately, the methods for doing these fancier searches depend on the engine you choose. Luckily, most search engines offer Help buttons or hyperlinks you can click for more details and examples, but you may need to visit the search engine's Web site to get this help.

Searching from the Address bar

In a hurry? Then why not do an *autosearch* right from the Address Bar? It's as easy as following these steps:

1. Click the Address text box.

2. Type **go** or **find** followed by a space.

3. Type the topic you seek.

4. Press Enter.

For example, type **go llamas** or **find llamas** or **? llamas** and press Enter. This will fire up the Internet Explorer MSN search engine and begin searching the Web for the topic you entered.

Going Places You've Gone Before (History 101)

Maybe history wasn't your best subject in school, but it can be a lifesaver when you're cruising the Internet. Let's say you've been quite the Internet butterfly, flitting from site to site as you visit the Internet's most interesting spots. Now further suppose you want to return to a page you visited yesterday or the day before, but you forgot to add this page to your Favorites list. Are you stuck? Of course not! Returning to this page is no sweat if you use the History list, which Internet Explorer updates for you automatically.

Note　The History list is a special folder within the Windows folder on drive C (C:\ Windows\History). The History Explorer bar, discussed next, makes it easy for you to work with the History list.

Opening the History Explorer bar

The first step in working with the History list is to open the History Explorer bar. To do this, click the History button on the Standard Buttons toolbar or choose View ➪ Explorer Bar ➪ History from Internet Explorer's menu bar. The screen will split into two frames, with the left-hand frame showing the History Explorer bar and the right-hand frame showing whatever Web page you're currently viewing. Figure 7-5 shows an example containing two days of history information.

Finding what you found

Every so often, your searches will retrieve a page that doesn't seem to belong there. Say, for example, you're looking for Mikhail Baryshnikov and up pops a page about football. You can't for the life of you figure out what Baryshnikov and football have in common. When you visit the page, you still have no idea. This is where the faithful Find feature comes in handy. Choose Edit ➪ Find from Internet Explorer's menu bar (or press Ctrl+F), type the specific word you're looking for (in this case, *Baryshnikov*), and click the Find Next button. The Find feature will try to locate the word you're looking for on the current Web page. In the case of the ballet-football mystery, I had done a Find for Barysh (just part of the word will often do), and discovered the sports writer said the quarterback "leapt with the grace of Baryshnikov." Mystery solved! There's nothing a search engine can do about synonyms, homonyms, and creative metaphors, but at least now we know what our pal Mikhail was doing in the end zone.

Figure 7-5: Viewing your place in history with the History Explorer bar

Once the History Explorer bar is open, jumping to a previously visited page is easy:

1. Click the hyperlink for the day you want to revisit. For example, in Figure 7-5, I clicked the hyperlink for Today. (If several weeks of history exist, click the hyperlink for the week you want and then click the hyperlink for the desired day.)

2. Click the hyperlink for the site you want to revisit (sites are marked with a folder icon). A list of pages you visited at this site will appear below the folder in the History Explorer bar.

3. Click the page you want to revisit. The page is marked with a globe and paper icon.

That's all there is to it! The page you chose to revisit will appear in the right-hand frame, ready for you to explore (if you really like this page, adding it to your Favorites list is a good idea, as explained earlier).

You can repeat the preceding three steps to revisit any of the pages for any date in the History Explorer bar. When you finish using the History Explorer bar, you can hide it again by clicking the History button on the toolbar.

Rewriting history

Internet Explorer updates the History list each time you visit another page on the Internet. This happens automatically whether or not the History Explorer bar is visible. You can customize the History list in several ways, including the following:

✦ To delete an item from the History list, right-click it in the History Explorer bar and choose Delete from the pop-up menu.

✦ To empty the History list, choose Tools ➪ Internet Options from the Internet Explorer menu bar, choose the General tab, click the Clear History button, and then click Yes.

✦ To view or change the number of days pages are kept in the History list, choose Tools ➪ Internet Options from the Internet Explorer menu bar, choose the General tab, and then look at or change the "Days to keep pages in History" option.

Getting the Most from Your Favorites List

You've already seen how the Search and History Explorer bars and the Favorites menu can help you navigate the Internet more quickly. There's also a Favorites Explorer bar to speed your visits to favorite spots on the Net. To display it, click the Favorites button on the Standard Buttons toolbar or choose View ➪ Explorer Bar ➪ Favorites from the menu bar. As usual when you choose an Explorer bar, your screen will split into two frames, with the Favorites Explorer bar on the left and the current Web page on the right, as shown in Figure 7-6.

Choosing a favorite page from the Favorites Explorer bar is a lot like revisiting a page in the Favorites menu:

1. If your favorite page is stored in a subcategory (or folder), click that folder in the Favorites Explorer bar. Folders are listed alphabetically, which makes them easy to find.

2. Click the name of the site you want to revisit.

As usual, the page you chose will appear in the right-hand frame. When you're ready to hide the Favorites Explorer bar, click the Favorites button on the toolbar.

Figure 7-6: The Favorites Explorer bar makes quick work of jumping to your favorite Web pages.

Adding folders to your Favorites list

You can organize your Favorites list into subcategories (or folders), just as you group your computer files into folders. For example, suppose you discovered a bunch of great cooking sites and you want to add them to a Cooking category in your Favorites list. Grouping the cooking links this way is much more convenient than scattering them all over your Favorites list.

Several ways exist to create new folders in your Favorites list. Perhaps the easiest is to set up the folder when you add a Web page to your Favorites list. Here's how:

1. Go to the page you want to add and then choose Favorites ➪ Add To Favorites from Internet Explorer's menu bar. You'll see the Add Favorite dialog box, shown earlier in Figure 7-3.

2. Type a name for this favorite item or accept the suggested name.

3. Click the Create In button. The Add Favorite dialog box will expand, as shown in Figure 7-7.

4. If you want the new folder to appear below one of the existing folders in the Favorites list, click that folder name.

5. Click the New Folder button, type a name for your new folder, and then click OK. Your new folder will appear in the Create In list and it will be selected automatically. (When a folder is selected, its icon appears open.)

6. Be sure the folder in which you want to store your favorite page is selected. If it isn't, click it.

7. Click the OK button to add your favorite page to the selected folder.

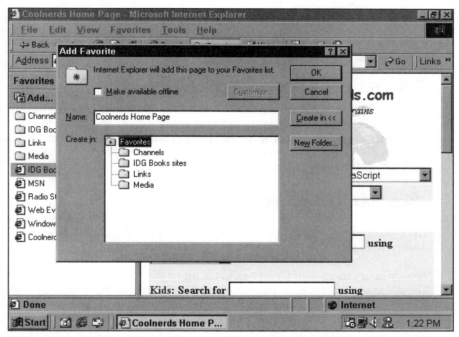

Figure 7-7: Click the Create In button to choose (or create) folders for organizing your favorite pages.

Adding favorite items to existing folders

If the Favorites folder in which you want to store a favorite item already exists, your job is even easier. Just complete Steps 1, 2, 3, 6, and 7 from the previous section (skip Steps 4 and 5).

If drag-and-drop is more your style, you'll love this trick for adding new items to the Favorites list:

1. Open the Favorites Explorer bar.

2. Go to the page you want to add to Favorites or to any page that offers a hyperlink to the page you want to add.

3. If you're currently viewing the page you want to add, position the mouse pointer on the tiny icon just to the left of the URL in the Address box. If you're viewing a page that offers a hyperlink to the page you want to add, position the mouse on the hyperlink.

4. Drag the icon or hyperlink to the appropriate folder in the Favorites Explorer bar. When the black horizontal marker appears at the place where you want the new favorite item, release the mouse button.

Reorganizing your Favorites list

You may want to reorganize your Favorites list or clean it up occasionally. For example, you might want to move some favorite pages from one folder to another, delete old favorites you no longer want, or change a folder name so it's more descriptive. You can do all this from the Organize Favorites dialog box or by using drag-and-drop and other file management techniques.

Using the Organize Favorites dialog box

To use the Organize Favorites dialog box, choose Favorites ➪ Organize Favorites from the Internet Explorer menu bar. You'll see the Organize Favorites dialog box, shown in Figure 7-8.

How you organize your Favorites list is up to you. If you're already comfortable with the file management techniques covered in Chapter 5, you'll quickly realize using the Organize Favorites dialog box is much like using My Computer, although it's a tad more friendly. Try these tricks for starters:

✦ To open a folder, click the folder. The folder you opened will appear in the list along the right of the Organize Favorites dialog box.

✦ To create a new folder inside whatever folder is shown in the folder list, click the Create Folder button, type a new folder name, and press Enter.

✦ To delete a folder or a favorite item, select it (by clicking it) and then click the Delete button or press your Delete key. Click Yes when asked about moving the item to the Recycle Bin.

✦ To move a folder or a favorite item, select it and then click the Move to Folder button. When prompted to browse, click the folder in which the selected item belongs and then choose OK.

✦ To rename a folder or a favorite item, select it and then click the Rename button. Type a new name and then press Enter.

When you finish using the Organize Favorites dialog box, click its Close (X) button.

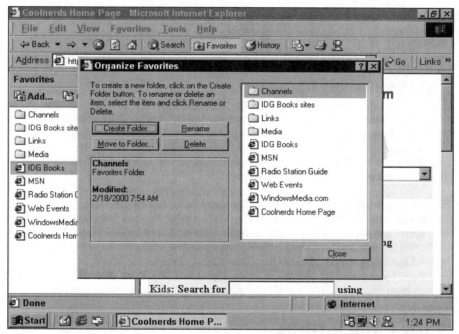

Figure 7-8: You can use the Organize Favorites dialog box to set up your Favorites list any way you like.

Using file management techniques

The Favorites folder is just another folder on your computer, which means you can use all the standard file management tricks to reorganize items when the Organize Favorites dialog box or Favorites Explorer bar is open. For example, you can right-click items and choose options from the pop-up menu and you can use drag-and-drop to move and copy items. You also can use My Computer or Windows Explorer to organize the Favorites list if you want. The Favorites folder is located inside your Windows folder on drive C (C:\Windows\Favorites).

Clever Bar Tricks

I've already mentioned several ways to use the various bars in Internet Explorer. In this section, I'll summarize the basics, in case you feel like looking them up in one place. The browser has three types of bars: toolbars, the status bar, and Explorer bars. To display or hide one of these bars, simply choose the appropriate option from the View menu, as described here:

✦ To display or hide one of the toolbars, choose View ➪ Toolbars and then either Standard Buttons, Address Bar, Links, or Radio.

✦ To display or hide text labels on the Standard Buttons toolbar, choose View ➪ Toolbars ➪ Customize and select Show text labels from the Text Options drop-down list. Then click the Close button.

✦ To display or hide the status bar, choose View ➪ Status Bar.

✦ To display or hide an Explorer bar, choose View ➪ Explorer Bar and then either Search, Favorites, History, or Folders. (You also can click the Search, Favorites, or History buttons on the Standard Buttons toolbar.)

Remember, if a toolbar's option is checked on the View menu, that bar will be visible. If it isn't checked, you won't see that bar.

Note   The Links bar offers buttons that can take you to handy places on the Internet and it contains the same entries as the Links folder in your Favorites list. The initial items are set up as a gift to you from Microsoft, but you can update them if you want. To add an item, drag a Web page hyperlink or the icon next to the URL in the Address box to the place in the Links bar or Links folder where you want the new item to appear. To delete an item, right-click the item and choose Delete. To change the URL of the item, right-click the item and choose Properties.

Clever toolbar tricks

You can reposition the toolbars if you want. (It's easy to do this accidentally and then have a fit as you search in vain for the toolbar you moved.) To reposition a toolbar, move your mouse to the left side of the toolbar (between the vertical bar and the first button on the bar). Then, drag the bar up, down, left, or right (as you drag, the mouse pointer changes to a four-headed arrow). When the bar pops into place, release the mouse button.

You also can resize the toolbars, making them narrower (to show fewer buttons) or wider (to show more buttons). To resize a toolbar, drag the vertical line next to the toolbar name to the left or to the right. The mouse pointer changes to a two-headed arrow when it's safe to drag. If you want to shrink or expand the toolbar quickly, double-click the vertical line instead.

Tip   To display or hide a toolbar quickly, right-click a blank spot in any visible toolbar and then click the name of the toolbar you want in the pop-up menu.

Most of the figures in this chapter show the Internet Explorer title bar, menu bar, and each of the toolbars in separate rows along the top of the window. Figure 7-9 shows Internet Explorer's window after moving and resizing Standard Buttons, Address, and Links toolbars.

Clever Explorer bar tricks

When you click the Search, Favorites, History, or Channels buttons on the Standard Bars toolbar (or you choose the equivalent options on the View ➪ Explorer Bar menu), the screen splits into two frames (see Figures 7-4, 7-5, and 7-6). The left frame shows the Explorer bar and the right frame shows the current Web page. Now, here are some ways to put any Explorer bar through its paces:

Figure 7-9: Here are the menu bar and the Standard Buttons, Address Bar, and Links toolbars after moving and resizing some of them.

✦ To hide the Explorer bar, click the same button on the Standard Buttons toolbar you clicked to display it originally. Or, right-click the gray title bar at the top of the Explorer bar and choose Close. Or, click the Close (X) button on the Explorer bar's gray title bar.

✦ To refresh the Search Explorer bar with any recent updates, right-click its gray title bar and choose Refresh.

✦ To display the Search Explorer bar in a separate window, right-click its gray title bar and choose Open In Window. A new window will open and it will contain the Search Explorer bar information only.

✦ To narrow or widen an Explorer bar, move your mouse pointer to the border on the right side of the bar until the pointer changes to a two-headed arrow. Then drag the border to the left or to the right.

Clever full-screen tricks

When you choose View ➪ Full Screen, or press the F11 key, the current Web page is displayed without the added clutter of the status bar, menu bar, Address Bar, or Links toolbar (see Figure 7-10). You can quickly toggle between the normal display shown in earlier figures and the full-screen display by pressing F11.

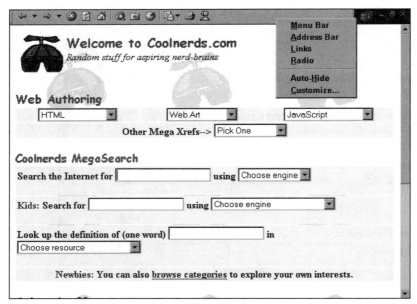

Figure 7-10: This is Internet Explorer in full-screen view. In this example, I right-clicked the Standard Buttons toolbar.

You can customize full-screen view in several ways:

✦ To display or hide the menu bar, Address Bar toolbar, or Links toolbar, right-click the Standard Buttons toolbar and choose Menu Bar, Address Bar, or Links (as appropriate).

✦ If the Menu Bar, Address Bar, or Links toolbar are visible, you can resize or move them as described earlier. Note, however, that you can move them to the left or right only.

✦ To toggle the *auto hide* feature for the Standard Buttons toolbar, right-click the toolbar and choose Auto Hide. When auto hide is on, the Standard Buttons toolbar is invisible until you point your mouse to the top of the screen, where the toolbar magically reappears. When auto hide is off, the Standard Buttons toolbar is always visible in full-screen view.

Browsing Without Your Browser

Practically everything in Windows Me is capable of connecting you to the Internet, whether you've fired up Internet Explorer or another browser first. For example, when you open My Computer, Windows Explorer, or the Address toolbar on the taskbar, you can type an Internet address or a search command (such as `find llamas`) into the Address text box (see Figure 7-11) and press Enter, just as you do in Internet Explorer. Instantly the window will have all the basic features of Internet Explorer and you can surf the Net as usual.

Figure 7-11: You can browse the Internet from My Computer, Windows Explorer, and the Address toolbar on the Windows taskbar.

Tip   To display or hide the Address toolbar on the taskbar, right-click the taskbar and then choose Toolbars ➪ Address.

You also can choose options on the View or Favorites menus in My Computer or Windows Explorer to use the toolbars, Explorer bars, and Favorites lists you learned about in this chapter. And, anytime you click a hyperlink *anywhere* — on your desktop, in a document, or on a button—the Internet features will kick in exactly as you'd expect. This Internet-awareness in Windows Me is a huge bonus because you never have to plan your Internet travels ahead of time. Just do what's convenient and Windows Me will handle the rest.

Adding Internet Links to the Desktop

Windows Me offers tons of ways to integrate the Internet with your desktop. I'll dive deeper into those features in Chapter 8. To whet your appetite for what's to come, I want to explain a few quick ways to create links to the Internet right on your Windows desktop. To begin, go to the Web page you want to add to your desktop or go to a Web page *containing* a hyperlink you want to add. Now, do any of the following steps to add a hyperlink to your desktop:

✦ To add a link to the current page, choose File ⇨ Send ⇨ Shortcut to Desktop from the Internet Explorer menus.

✦ To drag-and-drop a link to the current page, be sure you can see the desktop (click the Restore button in your browser if you need to). Then, drag the little icon shown next to the URL in the Address box to your desktop and release the mouse button (see Figure 7-12).

✦ To drag-and-drop a link that's somewhere on the current Web page, point to the link so the mouse pointer changes to a pointing hand. Then drag the link to your desktop and release the mouse button (see Figure 7-13).

A shortcut to the Internet hyperlink will appear on your desktop. Now, you can open it as you'd open any shortcut on your desktop (for example, by double-clicking or clicking it) and the Web page you linked to will open in your browser.

Of course, what goes on the desktop can easily be swept off it. If you no longer want the desktop shortcut, simply drag it to the Recycle Bin.

Tip You can drag-and-drop Internet shortcuts to the Start button, to the Favorites or Channels Explorer bars, or to any toolbar on the taskbar.

Downloading from the Web

Downloading means to copy a file from the Internet to your own PC. Tons of things exist on the Web for you to download—mostly in the form of free programs, updates to existing programs, and shareware (try-before-you-buy) programs. Downloading from the Web is remarkably easy, almost effortless. Typically, you'll find a link to the program or file you want to download, as in the example shown in Figure 7-14. The links shown are available at `http://www.coolnerds.com/books/msaccess/accfree.htm` (another great place for downloadable software is Microsoft's site at `http://www.microsoft.com/msdownloads/search.asp?`).

Figure 7-12: Start dragging at mouse pointer to create a desktop hyperlink to the current page.

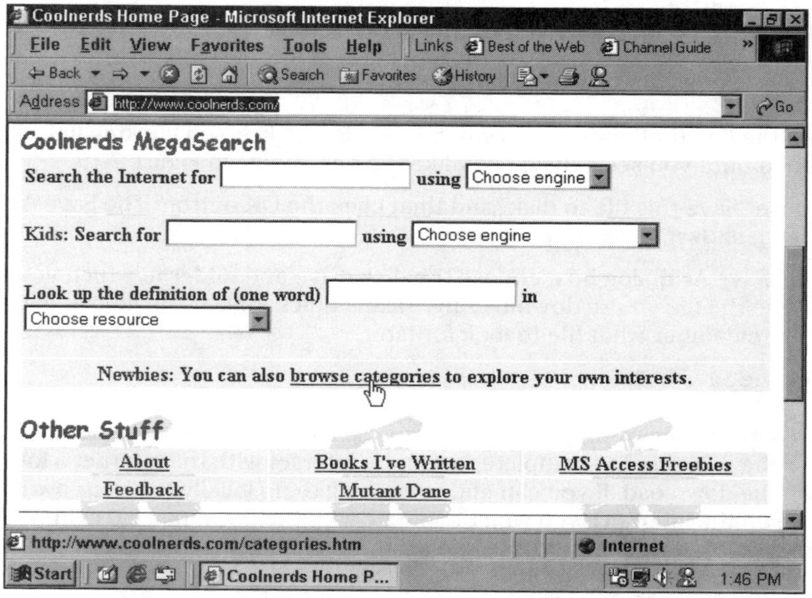

Figure 7-13: Start dragging at mouse pointer to create a desktop hyperlink to a hyperlink contained on the current page.

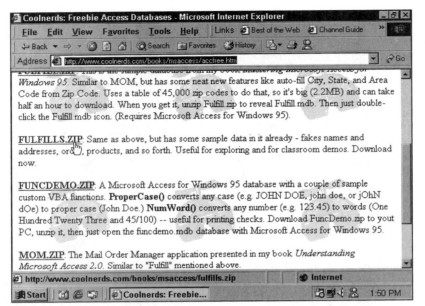

Figure 7-14: Links like these — for downloading files — are available on many Web sites.

Downloading when a link exists

To perform the download when a link exists:

1. Click the link that offers to download the file and keep on clicking links as needed until you see a dialog box like the one shown in Figure 7-15.

2. Choose "Save this file to disk" and then click the OK button. The Save As dialog box, shown in Figure 7-16, appears.

3. In the Save As dialog box, choose the disk drive and folder in which you want to store the file you're downloading. Take a quick look at the filename, too, so you'll remember what file to look for later.

4. Click the Save button.

The download will begin and you'll see a progress meter. You can do other work while waiting for the download to complete, but if you interact with the Internet a lot, you'll slow down the download. If you can find something to do locally (on your own PC, rather than on the Internet), you won't compete with the download. Of course, if the file you're downloading is a large one, going out to lunch isn't a bad idea!

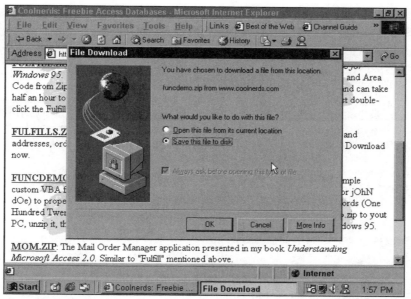

Figure 7-15: This dialog box asks what you want to do with a Web file.

Figure 7-16: Tell Internet Explorer where to put the file you're downloading.

Inoculating your computer against viruses

Occasionally, high-tech vandals sneak nasty little programs, called *viruses*, into files. If you download a file containing a virus, you probably won't know it until the virus starts doing damage (or playing little tricks, if it's not an overly hostile virus).

You can purchase software that prevents viruses from being downloaded to your PC and also scans for and eliminates existing viruses. Such products are available at most computer stores. If you'd like to shop around first from the comfort of your PC, you can visit the Web sites of these anti-virus software publishers: McAfee Network Security and Management at `http://www.mcafee.com`, or Symantec at `http://www.symantec.com/avcenter`. For a more broad overview of viruses, go to a search engine such as `http://www.lycos.com` and search for virus or anti-virus software.

A note on Zip files

Some of the files available for download on the Web are compressed (or *zipped*), so they'll download more quickly. These files typically have the extension .zip on their filenames. Before you can use such a file, you must decompress (or *unzip*) it. To do this, you need to add the Compressed Folders tool. You will find this tool as one of the optional components in the System Tools category on the Windows Setup tab of the Add/Remove Programs dialog box. See Chapter 25 for more information on adding Windows Me components.

Downloading when no link exists

In some cases, you might see a picture in a Web page, or some other item that offers no real download option. Chances are, you can download a copy of that item right to your own PC by following these steps:

1. Right-click the link or the item you want to download to your own PC.

2. From the pop-up menu that appears, choose Save Target As or Save Picture As (or whichever option implies you can save the item you just right-clicked).

3. When the Save dialog box appears, choose the disk drive and folder in which you want to store the file and remember to take a quick look at the filename.

4. Click the Save button to begin the download.

As with any download, you'll see a dialog box keeping you informed of the download's progress. When the download is complete, that dialog box disappears from the screen.

Caution

Of course, you should *never* steal any Web page, pictures, sounds, or videos without permission. *Always* treat everything on the Web as copyrighted material, unless you're given explicit swiping rights in writing.

Saving a Web page

You can save an entire Web page, which is handy if you want to design a page similar to an existing page on the Web. To save the page, choose File ⇨ Save As from the Internet Explorer menus. From the Save As Type drop-down list choose one of the following options:

✦ **Web Page, complete (*.htm,*.html):** Saves the Web page and any graphics that go along with it. But graphics and text are stored in separate files.

✦ **Web archive, single file (*.mht):** Saves the Web page and its graphic images in a single file with the .mht extension.

✦ **Web Page, HTML only (*.htm,*.html):** Saves only the text and HTML (formatting) codes, but no graphics.

✦ **Text File (*.txt):** Saves only the text with no graphics or HTML formatting.

Then enter a name for the page, and click the Save button.

Personalizing Your Browser

Part III of this book explains many ways to personalize your Windows Me system. As you might expect, your browser and Internet settings are fully customizable, too, and you may want to look at your options if things aren't working exactly as you'd like. You can get started in either of two ways:

✦ Choose Start ⇨ Settings ⇨ Control Panel from the Windows taskbar and then open the Internet Options icon in the Control Panel.

✦ Choose Tools ⇨ Internet Options from the Internet Explorer menu bar.

You'll see the Internet Options dialog box, shown in Figure 7-17. Like most dialog boxes that enable you to customize stuff in Windows Me, this one offers several tabs at the top, which you can click to choose various categories of settings. The basic drill goes like this:

1. Choose the tab containing the settings you want to change. (Figure 7-17 shows the General tab.)

2. Change the settings as needed. (If you need help with a particular setting, click the question mark (?) button at the upper-right corner of the dialog box and then click the setting about which you want to know more.)

3. Repeat Steps 1 and 2 as needed.

4. When you finish making changes, click OK as needed to save your changes and close the dialog box. Or, click Cancel to discard the changes and close the dialog box. Or, click Apply to save your changes and stay in the dialog box.

The following offers a quick run-down of each tab:

✦ **General:** Enables you to choose your home page, to delete or change settings for temporary Internet files the browser stores in a special cache so you can view them more quickly, and to adjust your History folder settings. You also can choose colors, fonts, languages, and other formatting (accessibility) options.

✦ **Security:** Enables you to set the security level for various zones of Web content you visit on the Internet.

✦ **Content:** Enables you to control the Internet content that can be viewed on your computer; to use security certificates to identify sites, publishers, and yourself; and to adjust personal information and the Microsoft Wallet used for Internet shopping.

✦ **Connections:** Enables you to change your Internet connection settings using an automated wizard or manual options to specify a corporate proxy server, or to use automatic configuration settings stored on a network server.

✦ **Programs:** Enables you to specify the default programs to use for mail, news, and Internet phone calls, as well as your calendar and contact list. You also can have Internet Explorer check to see whether it is the default browser.

✦ **Advanced:** Enables you to customize advanced options for accessibility, browsing, multimedia, security, Java VM, printing, searching, toolbars, and HTTP 1.1.

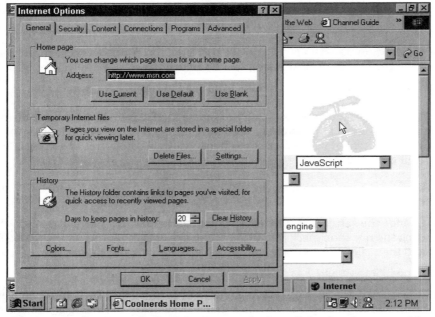

Figure 7-17: The General tab of the Internet Options dialog box for customizing your Internet settings

Getting Support Online

One of the great things about the Internet is Web sites and other online documents can be updated daily or even more frequently. Microsoft's Web site, particularly its support documents and online Knowledge Base, uses this to great advantage. If Microsoft finds a bug in its software or updates a software component, it (and you) no longer must wait for the next release to get a fix or an upgrade. The most recent versions of the Help files are a major part of the Knowledge Base, as are problems reported by users (and how to fix them). Microsoft's support area starts at the Support home page, shown in Figure 7-18. You can quickly reach this page by choosing Help ➪ Online Support from the Internet Explorer menu bar.

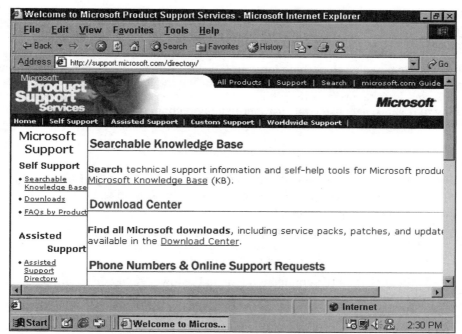

Figure 7-18: You'll find an array of choices for technical support at Microsoft's Support page.

The Support site consists of several key areas you can familiarize yourself with by browsing around, clicking hyperlinks, choosing items from drop-down lists, typing text into search boxes, and clicking buttons as needed.

Tip   Automatic Updating, covered in Chapter 8, is the quickest and easiest way to keep your system up to date and free of bugs.

Choosing your own home page

You're not stuck with using Internet Explorer's default home page. In fact, you can specify any starting page you want, use the page you're currently viewing, or start with a blank one. To do this, choose Tools ➪ Internet Options from Internet Explorer's menu bar. Click the General tab. Next, fill in the Address text box in the Home Page area with the address of your favorite starting Web page or click the Use Current button to select the current page you're browsing as your home page. Click the Use Default button to revert to Microsoft's site as the home page. Or, click the Use Blank button to save a few seconds when you fire up Internet Explorer because it won't go looking for your home page. Finally, choose OK to save your changes.

Disconnecting from the Web

Even if you pay next to nothing for your Internet connection, disconnecting from your dial-up line when you're not actively surfing the Internet is a good idea. This way, you don't tie up your own line or the one owned by your ISP. Disconnecting is easy to do and, because your browser usually reconnects whenever it needs to, you have nothing to lose by disconnecting.

Here are some ways to disconnect your dial-up connection:

✦ Choose Disconnect Now if a Disconnect dialog box asks if you want to close the connection to your ISP. This dialog box usually pops up when you close Internet Explorer and other programs that connect to the Internet automatically.

✦ Double-click the little connection icon in the lower-right corner of the taskbar and click the Disconnect button in the dialog box that appears. (The connection icon shows two computers tied together.)

✦ Right-click the little connection icon in the lower-right corner of the taskbar and choose Disconnect from the pop-up menu.

Summary

This chapter has been something of a whirlwind tour of the World Wide Web and the Internet Explorer browser that comes with Windows Me. The techniques presented here represent the most important everyday skills you need to use the Web successfully. To recap:

✦ To browse the World Wide Web, connect to the Internet and then start your Web browser program.

✦ Every site on the World Wide Web has a unique address, or URL, often in the format http://www.whatever.com.

✦ To go to a specific Web site, type its address (URL) into the Address text box near the top of the Web browser window and then press Enter.

✦ You can browse the Web by clicking *hyperlinks* — hot spots that appear on the various pages you visit.

✦ To keep track of your favorite Web pages, add them to your Favorites list. That is, visit the Web page and then choose Favorites ➪ Add To Favorites from the menu bar.

✦ To revisit a favorite page at any time, open the Favorites menu and click the name of your favorite page.

✦ To search for specific information on the Web, use a search engine. Click the Search button on the Standard Buttons toolbar to begin your search.

✦ To download a file means to copy it from the Internet to your own PC.

✦ To download a file from the Web, click the download link and choose "Save this file to disk" in the dialog box. Or, right-click the link or item you want to download and choose the Save As option from the pop-up menu.

✦   ✦   ✦

Maximum Web

Windows Me, and the Microsoft Internet Explorer Version 5.5 that comes with it, provide some features that are designed to make your use of the Internet, and the time you spend browsing the Web, more productive and entertaining. In this chapter, you'll learn about those features including Assisted Support, Automatic Updates, Offline Browsing, and Active Desktop. You'll also take a look behind the scenes to see how the Web *really* works so you can learn how to turn waiting time into productive time.

Using Assisted Support

Assisted Support is a new feature of Windows Me that's designed to round out the basic built-in support with added support from the Internet. You can browse forums and message boards to see if the question in your mind has already been answered. You can even post a question using the new Ask Maxwell feature.

To use Assisted Support, you need to have your Internet connection up and running. That's why I didn't mention this type of help back in Chapter 2 when Help was first introduced. But once you have a working Internet connection, using Assisted Support is simple. To get started:

1. Click the Start button and choose Help.

2. In the Help and Support window that appears, click Assisted Support.

3. Choose an option from the left column of the Help and Support window (see Figure 8-1).

4. If you're not already connected to the Internet and you select an option that requires online access, you'll see the Connect To dialog box. Click the Connect button and wait a moment for the connection to be made.

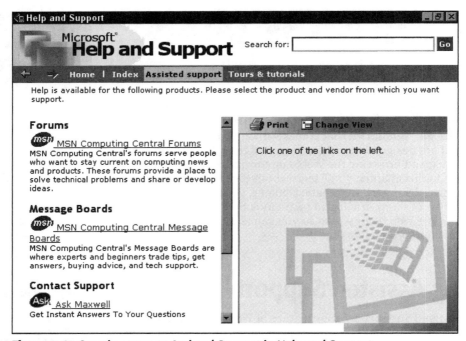

Figure 8-1: Opening page to Assisted Support in Help and Support

From here on out, you'll be online and the rest should be self-explanatory. (At least I hope it is, since I can't really predict how anything online is going to look on the specific day that you visit.) Be aware, though, that much of the online content will appear in your Internet Explorer Web browser, not within the Help and Support window. But clicking the Help and Support button in the taskbar will take you back to that window instantly.

Automatic Updates

Automatic Updates enable you to keep your computer up-to-date with changes, enhancements, and bug fixes in Windows Me, without your making an effort to find them. When activated, Automatic Updates will either automatically download new files as they become available, or at least notify you of those updates so you can decide for yourself whether or not to update. A third option, of course, is to completely deactivate Automatic Updates and do them all yourself using Windows Setup, as discussed later in this section. To activate or deactivate Automatic Updates:

1. Click the Start button and choose Settings ➪ Control Panel.

2. Open the Automatic Updates icon. You'll come to the options shown in Figure 8-2.

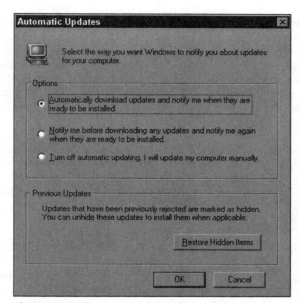

Figure 8-2: The Automatic Updates dialog box

3. Your first three options are pretty self-explanatory. Just choose one and then click the OK button.

If you choose either of the first two options, at some point you may see a message on your screen like the one shown in Figure 8-3. As instructed, you'll want to click on the indicator. The Updates Wizard will open on your screen, at which point you'll need to accept the License Agreement that appears. That's all there is to that step. From here on, it's just a matter of waiting to see if and when any updates become available. But of course you don't want to wait idly because there's no telling how long it will be before something becomes available. Just go about your business normally with the confidence of knowing that if Microsoft comes up with anything important, you will be notified.

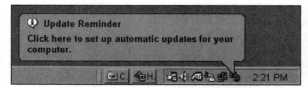

Figure 8-3: Reminder to set up Automatic Updates

When updates do become available, you'll see a window titled Ready To Install (if the updates have already been downloaded to your computer), or a window titled Available Updates (if you opted to perform the downloads manually). If you're too busy to perform the download or install the updates, you can choose Remind Me Later from the options presented. You can then specify when you want to be reminded, and Windows won't bother you again until that time has elapsed. When you are ready to install, double-click the icon that appears in the taskbar each time an update has been downloaded and is ready to be installed. Then click the Details button and choose which updates you do/don't want to install from the options presented. Only those updates that are selected with a check box will be installed, and you'll see a message that tells you when the installation is complete. Follow any instructions that appear on the screen.

Should you decide to not to install updates, by clearing their check marks in the Details dialog box, Windows will hide those options to keep them out of your way during future sessions. If at any time you want to review those updates you opted not to install, click the Start button and choose Settings ⇨ Control Panel and then once again open the Automatic Updates icon. Click the Restore Hidden Items button under Previous Updates in the dialog box that appears.

As an alternative to using Automatic Updates, you can use Windows Update to check for, download, and install updates from time to time. Click the Start button and choose Windows Update from the menu. You'll be taken to the Window Update Web site at `http://windowsupdate.microsoft.com`. There you'll find a list of available updates, as well as information on choosing and installing those updates.

The Floating Address Bar

It's not actually necessary to pop open your Web browser every time you want to view online Web content. Instead, you can use the Address on the taskbar, or in a free-floating manner, to give yourself rapid access to commonly-visited Web sites. To open the Address bar, right-click the taskbar, point to Toolbars, and choose Address. The Address bar will be added to the taskbar. But, you can drag it anywhere on the screen by the little vertical bar at its left side. When the Address toolbar is separated from the taskbar, as in Figure 8-4, you can ensure it never gets obscured by another window. Just right-click the Address toolbar and choose Always On Top.

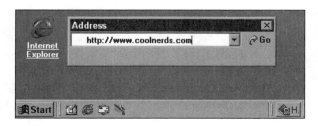

Figure 8-4: The free-floating Address bar provides quick access to local and Internet resources.

Once the Address toolbar is visible, you can use it to navigate anywhere on your computer or on the Internet. For example, to jump to the coolnerds Web site quickly, you can type its URL into the text box and press Enter or click the Go button to the right. Microsoft Internet Explorer opens and takes you straight to the site. To browse something locally, such as the contents of your C: drive, type in the address **C:** and press Enter or click Go. Whenever you need to make a quick return trip to some site or resource, open the drop-down list. If you see the address of the resource you want, just click it.

How the Web Really Works

The remaining topics discussed in this chapter may make more sense to you if I give you some background into how the World Wide Web *really* works. When you're browsing the Web, you may get the impression it's like TV. For instance, when you go to a URL such as `http://www.microsoft.com`, you see what's on the Web site — sort of like your Web browser is a telescope peering at pages far away, although, technically, that's not exactly how it works.

Actually, when you browse to a URL your screen doesn't just show the contents of that distant computer. Instead, your Web browser just tells that distant computer to send files from its hard disk to your computer's hard disk. After the files are down-loaded to your PC, your Web browser shows them to you. So what the browser is actually showing you on your screen is files that are on your *own* PC, not files that are on the remote (distant) computer!

If you have standard modem/dial-up access to the Internet, you may have noticed the first time you visit a page it takes quite a while for the page to show on your screen. That delay is the amount of time it takes to copy files from the remote com-puter's hard disk to your own hard disk. But subsequent visits using the Back but-ton, History list, or whatever, are much faster. That's because whenever you point your Web browser to a URL, the first thing Internet Explorer does is check to see if the materials of this URL have already been downloaded to your PC. If they have, then your Web browser reads the material from your local hard disks, which is much, much faster than downloading from the Web site.

This approach is good because it makes your Web browsing go much faster and it helps keep traffic on the Internet to a minimum. But it also means that when you view a Web page, you may be viewing it as it looked a while ago and not as it really looks right now. For example, suppose I point my Web browser to `http://www.coolnerds.com`. Then I cruise around some other sites for 15 minutes or so, and then I return to the coolnerds Web site. The page I'm viewing at that moment is the one I downloaded 15 minutes ago. If the author of the coolnerds page made any changes in the past 15 minutes, I wouldn't see those changes.

Fortunately, this is not a big issue because most Web sites only update their contents weekly or monthly. Furthermore, you can always force your Web browser to download the latest version of a page by clicking the Refresh button in your Web browser's toolbar. Finally, with *Offline Browsing* discussed a little later in this chapter, you can control exactly when all the time-consuming downloads take place.

Files downloaded from Web sites are stored on your hard drive in your Internet *cache* (pronounced like *cash*). You're probably unaware of it because it's hidden behind the scenes. But you can control both the size of the cache and how often pages are updated. Here's how:

1. Start Microsoft Internet Explorer.

2. Choose Tools ➪ Internet Options and click the General tab of the dialog box that opens. You'll see a section titled Temporary Internet Files, as in Figure 8-5.

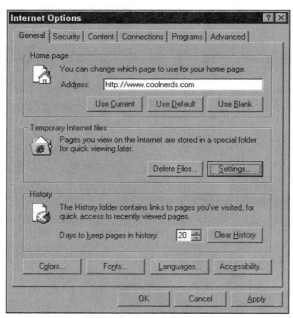

Figure 8-5: The Internet Options dialog box

3. Click the Settings button in the Temporary Internet Files pane to get to the dialog box shown in Figure 8-6.

Figure 8-6: Settings for temporary Internet files

The Settings dialog box provides several options for controlling how these tempo-rary Internet files are handled. You can choose how often the temporary files are updated:

✦ **Every visit to the page:** Ensures every visit to a Web site is fresh but forces you to wait for a fresh download each time you visit the page, even if you visited only a minute ago.

✦ **Every time you start Internet Explorer:** When you close Internet Explorer, it *forgets* about all the pages in the Internet cache. So next time you fire it up and start browsing the Web, it always downloads fresh material from each Web site.

✦ **Never:** Always takes material from the Internet cache (if possible). The only way to ensure you're getting fresh material is to click the Refresh button when you get to a page.

You can use the slider bar to decide how much disk space you want to sacrifice to the Internet cache. The larger the cache, the more pages can be stored and the faster your browsing goes. A small cache saves disk space but doesn't allow for many temporary Internet files to be stored locally. This, in turn, may slow down your browsing because only enough room exists to store information from, say, the last two or three sites you visited.

The default folder used for the Internet cache is C:\Windows\Temporary Internet Files. You can change this using the Move Folder button. You can view its contents using the View Files button. If you want to clean out your Internet cache, you can click the OK button to close the Settings dialog box. Then click the Delete Files button in the Internet Options dialog box. But all these options represent sort of a brute force approach to try to balance disk usage, download time, and how often material in your Internet cache is updated. Offline Browsing, described a little later in this chapter, provides a more elegant solution.

Downloaded program files

The View Objects button in the Settings dialog box lists "helper" and "player" programs that you've downloaded from the Internet. These are programs that generally add functionality to a Web page. For example, Macromedia (www.macromedia.com) offers Shockwave and Flash players, capable of displaying complex animation and multimedia. These programs tend to be large, so you wouldn't want to have to download them each and every time you visit a Web site that uses the features of these players. To prevent the players from being cleared out every time you empty your Internet cache, they're stored in a separate folder, typically C:\Windows\ Downloaded Program Files.

If, for whatever reason, you do want to delete a downloaded program file, going through the Settings dialog box might not be the best approach. Instead, go to Add/Remove Programs in the Control Panel and see if you can find the program listed on the Install/Uninstall tab. If you find it there, click its name and then click the Add/Remove button. That way, you'll get rid of the program file as well as any settings within Windows that "expect" to find that file in your Downloaded Program Files folder.

Saving Time with Offline Browsing

As mentioned, Offline Browsing offers a way to control when time-consuming downloads take place so that you can make the time you spend on the Web more productive. Essentially, Offline Browsing lets you update your favorite Web content during off-hours (such as when you're asleep) so that when you do come back to review your favorite Web pages, they will have already been downloaded to your computer, and so will appear instantly as you go through their links. In fact, since you don't even need to be online to view the pages, you could review them on a laptop on your way to work or whatever (assuming you're not driving a car).

You can set up specific schedules for when different pages are downloaded. For example, you might want to download certain favorites once a day starting at, say, 2:00 a.m. You can also *synchronize* your pages at any time with just a couple of mouse clicks. However, you still need to wait for the downloads in that case. Still, you could perhaps start a synchronization just before going to lunch, so all the pages are downloaded and ready for viewing by the time you get back.

Pages that can be downloaded during off hours or with a synchronization procedure are called *offline favorites* in Internet Explorer 5.5 jargon. Creating an offline favorite is simple and works with any Web site. While you're viewing, in Internet Explorer, a page or site that you'd like to add to your offline favorites, just follow these steps to get started:

1. Choose Favorites ➪ Add to Favorites from Internet Explorer's menu bar. You'll come to the dialog box shown in Figure 8-7.

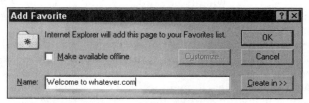

Figure 8-7: The Add Favorite dialog box

2. Choose Make Available Offline. Then click the Customize button.

3. The Offline Favorite Wizard appears. If you want to avoid seeing this introductory wizard page in the future, click the check box.

4. Click the Next button to proceed.

At this point you're taken to the first "real" page of the Offline Favorite Wizard, shown in Figure 8-8. If the page you're viewing is the *only* page from this site you want to download and view offline, choose "No" so that only the current page will be downloaded. If you want to be able to view additional pages from this same site, choose "Yes." Then indicate how many pages deep, in terms of hyperlinks, you want the download to follow.

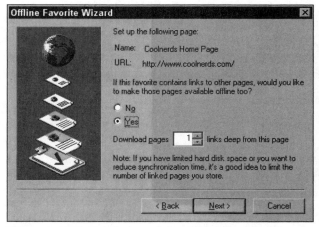

Figure 8-8: First real page of the Offline Favorite Wizard

For example, let's say you're adding a page that contains thumbnails of graphic images that you can click for a larger view. The photos change daily. By extending the download to pages that are one link deep from the page you're viewing, you're telling Internet Explorer to also download the larger graphic images that can be accessed by clicking the thumbnails. Thus, you're ensuring that both the page you're viewing with its thumbnails, and the larger graphic images that those thumbnails are linked to, will be downloaded automatically. Later, when you're browsing offline, clicking a thumbnail image will display the larger image instantly because Internet Explorer can just read it out of the Internet cache.

You do need to keep in mind, however, that graphic images and other multimedia files are large, and therefore do consume a lot of disk space. You'll want to be generous when defining the size of your Internet cache to make sure there's enough disk space to accommodate the large files. Remember, you can adjust the size of your Internet cache at any time using the Settings dialog box described earlier in this chapter.

After you've made your selections from the first wizard page, click the Next button to get to the next page, which might look something like Figure 8-9. If you want to Internet Explorer to download the page(s) during off-hours, then you need to select a schedule (if you've already defined schedules), or select "I would like to create a new schedule" if you've never defined a schedule in the past. Click the Next button to get to the options shown in Figure 8-10. There, you need to define when you want the pages to be downloaded. In the example shown, I've opted to download pages daily at 2:00 in the morning. Selecting the check box ensures that Windows will make the appropriate modem connection at 2:00 a.m. so that it can perform the download. I've named my schedule "Favorites Updates," although you can name yours anything you like.

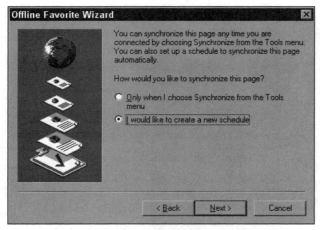

Figure 8-9: Second page of the Offline Favorite Wizard

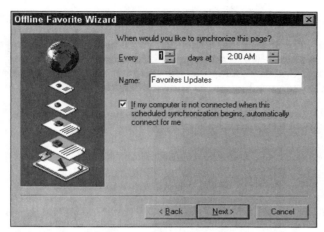

Figure 8-10: Third page of the Offline Favorite Wizard

 Caution   Updating favorites during off hours can only happen if you leave your computer on during those off hours. If you turn off your computer, or even just turn off your external modem, the download can't happen!

Clicking Next will take you to the fourth page of the wizard, shown in Figure 8-11. You need only select "Yes" if the site you'll be downloading from requires that you enter a user name and password. Don't add the user name and password for your Internet account or ISP here. If the page you'll be downloading isn't restricted and doesn't require a user name and password, select "No." Click the Finish button, and you're done.

Figure 8-11: Fourth page of the Offline Favorite Wizard

If you're online at the moment, Internet Explorer will download the pages now. But you can cancel that if you'd prefer to have the pages downloaded according to your schedule. Once you've created at least one schedule, you'll be given the option to choose that schedule in the future when adding new offline favorites. For example, after creating my "Favorites Updates" schedule, the third wizard page will allow me to add new favorites to that same schedule, as shown in Figure 8-12.

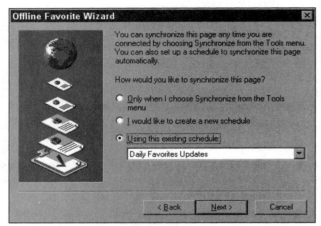

Figure 8-12: Update schedules appear as an option in the Offline Favorite Wizard.

 Tip   If you've already added a page to your Favorites and now want to convert it to an offline favorite, choose Favorites ➪ Organize Favorites from Internet Explorer's menu bar. Then right-click on the name of the page you want to convert to an offline favorite, and choose Make Available Offline. Then just step through the Offline Favorite Wizard normally.

Updating pages manually

If you ever want to update all of your offline favorites on the spur of the moment, get online and choose Tools ➪ Synchronize from Internet Explorer's menu bar. You'll need to wait for the downloads, of course. But when the download is complete, the pages in your Internet cache will indeed be in sync with the latest pages on those favorite Web sites.

Managing download schedules

You can change your download schedules, add new schedules, and have Internet Explorer send you an e-mail whenever a site has been updated — at any time. Just open Internet Explorer and choose Favorites ➪ Organize favorites. Right-click the offline favorite that you want to change (or any offline favorite, if you want to alter a schedule), and choose Properties from the menu that appears. Options on the Web Document, Schedule, and Download tabs will allow you to change scheduling characteristics of that one page.

To change or add a schedule, click the Schedule tab in that Properties dialog box to get to the options shown in Figure 8-13. To create a new schedule, click the Add button. To delete a schedule, click whichever one you want to delete, and then click the Remove button. To change a schedule, click its name in the list and then click the Edit button.

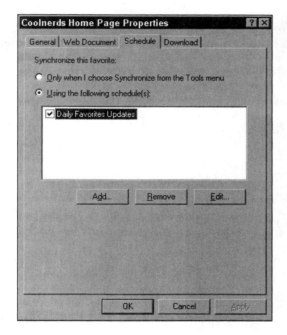

Figure 8-13: Options for adding, deleting, and changing Web page download schedules

Browsing offline

Whenever you want to view the updated pages on your PC, you should browse through your favorites offline, so that Internet Explorer doesn't attempt to go out and download the pages *again* during the current session. To browse offline, just start Internet Explorer in the usual manner. If you have a dial-up connection, and the option to connect pops up on the screen, choose Work Offline to avoid connecting.

If you're connected to the Internet automatically when Internet Explorer starts, you'll need to disconnect in order to browse offline. Just choose File ➪ Work Offline from Internet Explorer's menu bar. If you have a dial-up account and the little modem indicator in the taskbar remains active, you can right-click that indicator and choose Disconnect to go completely offline.

Using the Active Desktop

Active Desktop is a feature of Windows that lets you place "live" objects on your screen that can constantly receive data from the Internet. For example, you could put a stock ticker on your Windows desktop, which in turn would show you the current price of any stocks you're following. The Active Desktop items work especially well with "always on" connections such as DSL, many cable connections, and dedicated lines, because they can update themselves at regular intervals. But even if you don't have an "always on" connection, the desktop object will stay up-to-date as long as you're connected to the Internet through your dial-up account.

To use the Active Desktop feature, you first need to make sure it's turned on. To do so, right-click any neutral portion of your desktop and choose Properties. Or click the Start button and choose Settings ⇨ Control Panel and then open the Display icon. Either way, you'll come to the Display Properties dialog box. There, click the Web tab to view the options shown in Figure 8-14.

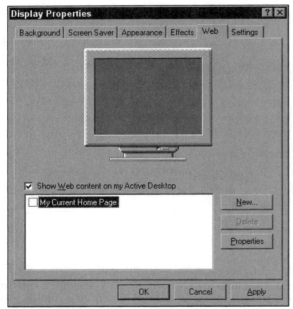

Figure 8-14: The Web tab of the Display Properties dialog box

To ensure that any Active Desktop items you add to your desktop will be visible, you'll need to select the "Show Web content on my Active Desktop" option. Once you've done that, the rest is simply a matter of finding items you like, and downloading them to your computer. The easiest way to do so is as follows:

1. Click the New button.
2. Click the Visit Gallery button in the wizard screen that appears.
3. If necessary, choose Connect to get online.

The rest is easy. Just look through the categories of desktop items and choose any you like. Then follow the instructions that appear on the screen to complete the download and add the item to your desktop. Once the item is visible on your desktop, you should be able to point to it to display a window border around it, as in the example in Figure 8-15. You can then move the item around by dragging the title bar at the top of the border and size the item by dragging any border or corner.

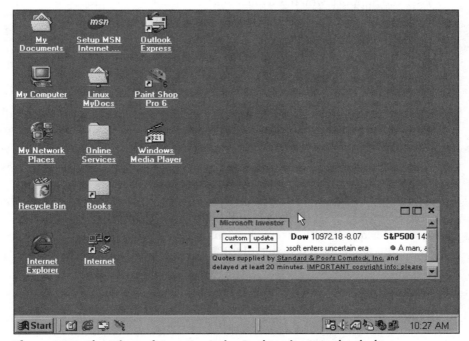

Figure 8-15: The Microsoft Investor Active Desktop item on the desktop

Tip   If your Active Desktop items are currently covered by other windows on the screen, clicking the Show Desktop button in the QuickLaunch toolbar will quickly hide those windows so you can see your desktop. Click that same button a second time to bring the hidden windows back into view.

To customize the item, look for a "custom" or "customize" option, or some kind of menu button. Or, you may need to right-click the item and choose Properties. That all depends on the specific item you're working with. But in general they're easy to install and use, and I doubt you'll have any trouble. If you do need help with a specific desktop item, your best resource will be the Web page visited to get that item in the first place.

Summary

In this chapter, you've learned a little about how the Internet works behind the scenes and some good tricks for getting the best out of your Internet time with Windows Me and Internet Explorer 5.5. To recap:

✦ Assisted Support, which is available as an option within the more general Help & Support, provides online access to forums and other sources of additional help and information.

✦ Automatic Updates will keep you posted when new programs for Windows Me become available. Use the Automatic Updates icon in the Control Panel to enable or disable these updates. Use Windows Setup to perform manual updates.

✦ The Address toolbar, available from the taskbar's Properties menu, provides quick access to any resource, online or local, to your PC, and can be made to float independently on your desktop.

✦ Any Web content you view is actually on your computer by the time you see it, stored inside a folder known as the Internet cache.

✦ Offline Browsing lets you pre-download Web pages at off-hours so that when you're ready to view them, you don't have to wait for the downloads.

✦ Active Desktop items present "live" information from the Internet while your computer is connected to the Internet.

✦   ✦   ✦

Internet E-mail

Perhaps the busiest feature of the Internet is electronic mail, e-mail for short. And no wonder. Unlike regular snail mail, which takes days to reach its destination, e-mail usually takes only a few seconds, no matter how far the message has to travel.

In the e-mail world, every person has a unique address. You've probably seen dozens of Internet e-mail addresses, which all tend to look something like `someone@someplace.com`. For example, my e-mail address is `alan@coolnerds.com`.

In this chapter, you learn to send and receive Internet e-mail messages. The program you use to do all this is called Microsoft Outlook Express. This program is built into Windows Me and the Internet Explorer program, discussed in Chapter 7. Do remember, though, I'm only using Internet Explorer and Outlook Express as examples. The basic concepts presented in this chapter will work with nearly any e-mail program (or e-mail client, as it's called). You need to explore the menus and help system of whatever e-mail client you choose to determine where to plug in the information required for your e-mail addresses and servers.

What You Need for Internet E-mail

Using Internet e-mail is pretty easy, but there are a few things you will need first. To send and receive Internet e-mail, you need the following:

- ✦ Some kind of connection to the Internet, as discussed in Chapter 6

- ✦ An e-mail client (a program for managing Internet e-mail)

- ✦ An e-mail address and other information about your mail server, which you get from your Internet service provider (ISP)

For the last item, you especially need the information presented in Table 9-1. The second column in this table is blank, so you can fill in your own information. The only place to get this information is from your ISP — the company or organization providing you with access to the Internet.

Table 9-1 Information You Need from Your ISP to Send and Receive E-mail	
Information to Get	*Write It in This Column*
Outgoing (SMTP) mail server address	
Incoming mail server type (POP3 or IMAP)	
Incoming mail server address	
Your e-mail address	
Your e-mail account name	
Your e-mail password	

Once you gather the information you need from your ISP, setting up nearly any e-mail client should be a breeze.

Starting Outlook Express

The program for sending and receiving e-mail is called Outlook Express. You can start this program in any of several ways. Use whichever method is most convenient:

✦ Open the Outlook Express icon on your desktop.

✦ Click the Launch Outlook Express button on the Quick Launch toolbar (if it's visible on your taskbar).

✦ Click the Start button and choose Programs ⇨ Outlook Express.

✦ If you're in Internet Explorer, click the Mail button on the Standard Buttons toolbar and then click the Read Mail option.

✦ If you're in Internet Explorer, choose Tools ⇨ Mail and News ⇨ Read Mail from the Internet Explorer menu bar.

When Outlook Express starts, you'll probably be viewing its Inbox, which looks something like Figure 9-1. From this one window you can compose, send, and read Internet e-mail messages, as I'll discuss throughout this chapter.

Menu bar · Message list · Tool bar

Outlook bar · Folder list · Folder bar

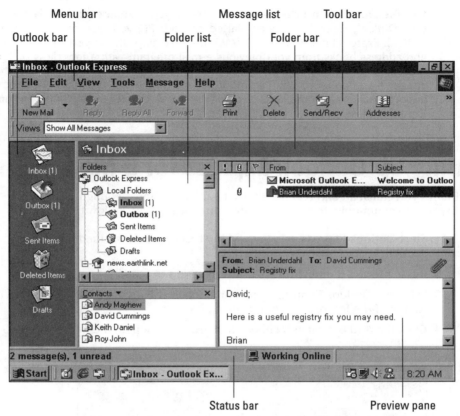

Status bar · Preview pane

Figure 9-1: Compose, send, and read messages using Outlook Express's Inbox.

Note   Figure 9-1 shows the folder list and all the bars Outlook Express can display. You can customize the Outlook Express window in many ways by choosing options on the View menu (try View ➪ Layout if you're curious). You'll learn more about customizing the program later in this chapter under "Personalizing Outlook Express."

If you don't see the Inbox, click the Inbox icon in the Outlook bar or folder list. Or, if you're viewing the main Outlook Express pane, click the Read Mail link.

If this is the first time Outlook Express has ever been started on your PC, you may be taken straight to the Internet Connection Wizard, which will help you configure the program using your own information from Table 9-1. If you don't get the Internet Connection Wizard or if you need to make changes to your configuration after going through the wizard, you can use the technique described in the next section.

Tip

If you've previously installed e-mail software on your computer and this is the first time Outlook Express has been started on your PC, you may be taken to the Outlook Express Import Wizard. This wizard enables you to import the messages and address books from your previous e-mail program with a few clicks of your mouse. To start importing, click the Next button and then follow the prompts that appear. If you prefer to skip the import for the time being, click Cancel (you can import the items anytime, as explained later in this chapter under "Importing and Exporting Messages").

Setting Up Outlook Express for E-Mail

Before you can send and receive Internet e-mail, you must configure Outlook Express to communicate with your Internet e-mail server. Follow these steps:

1. Start Outlook Express using any of the techniques described in the previous section.

2. If the Internet Connection Wizard starts, skip to Step 5.

3. From the Outlook Express menu bar, choose Tools ➪ Accounts. You'll see the All tab of the Internet Accounts dialog box.

4. Click the Add button and choose Mail from the pop-up menu (see Figure 9-2).

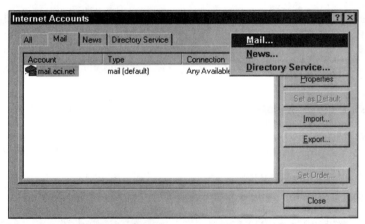

Figure 9-2: The Mail tab of the Internet Accounts dialog box after clicking the Add button

5. When the Internet Connection Wizard kicks in, fill in the blanks and options in each dialog box and then click the Next button to move on to the next dialog box. When you reach the last dialog box, click the Finish button.

The Internet Connection Wizard will ask you to supply a descriptive name for the account, the name that should appear in the From field of your outgoing messages, your e-mail address, and other information you wrote in Table 9-1. You also must specify the type of connection you'll use for this account (phone line or local area network).

Tip   If you have multiple e-mail accounts with one service provider or you have e-mail accounts with several service providers, you can use the Internet Connection Wizard to configure each e-mail account.

Changing an E-Mail Account Setting

Viewing or changing the settings for any e-mail account is easy after you use the Internet Connection Wizard to set it up:

1. Go to the Internet Accounts dialog box if you're not there already (choose Tools ⇨ Accounts from the Outlook Express menu bar).

2. Click the Mail tab if you want to focus on your e-mail accounts without the added clutter of news and directory service accounts. Or, click the All tab if you want to see all your accounts at once (see Figure 9-3).

Tip   News and directory services enable you to participate in newsgroups and to find people in cyberspace. I discuss directory services later in this chapter and newsgroups in Chapter 10.

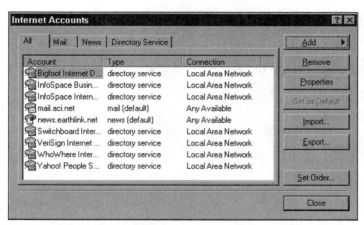

Figure 9-3: The All tab of the Internet Accounts dialog box shows all your accounts at once.

3. Click the account name you want to view or change and then do one of the following:

- To make the highlighted account your default e-mail account, choose Set As Default (available only if you have more than one e-mail account).

- To delete the highlighted account, click Remove and then click Yes to confirm.

- To change the settings for the selected account, click the Properties button (or double-click the account name). Then fill in or change the fields on the General, Servers, Connection, Security, and Advanced tabs of the mail account Properties dialog box, as needed. For example, to have Outlook Express connect using your network connection, click the Connection tab and select your connection from the "Always connect to this account using" drop-down list (see Figure 9-4). When you finish changing the account properties, click OK.

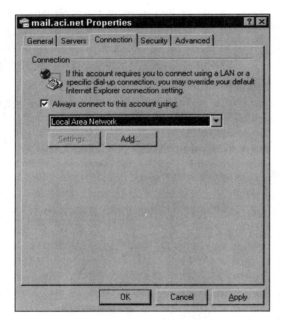

Figure 9-4: The mail account Properties dialog box for an e-mail account named mail.aci.net

4. Choose Close to return to Outlook Express.

Tip   Anytime you need help with one of the options in an Outlook Express dialog box, click the question mark (?) button at the upper-right corner of the dialog box and then click the field or option that's puzzling you. A pop-up description appears near the mouse pointer. Press the Esc key to hide the description again. Try it, you'll like it!

Composing a Message

Once you start Outlook Express, typing an e-mail message is easy. Try any of these three ways to begin:

✦ Click the New Mail button on the Outlook Express toolbar.

✦ Choose Message ⇨ New Message from the Outlook Express menu bar.

✦ Press Ctrl+N when a mail folder is open.

Regardless of how you start, the New Message window for composing your e-mail message will appear onscreen, looking something like Figure 9-5. To compose your message, first fill in the address portion of the window as explained in the following steps.

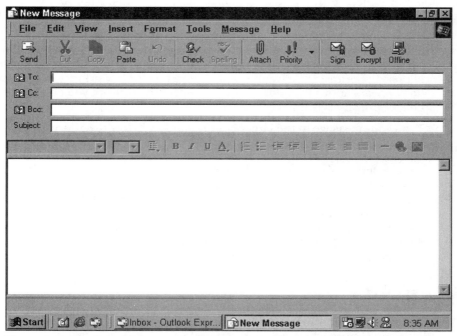

Figure 9-5: The New Message window for composing a new e-mail message

1. In the To: box, type the complete mailing address of each recipient. For example, typing **alan@coolnerds.com** addresses the message to me. To send the message to multiple recipients, type in each e-mail address separated by a semicolon (;).

Instead of typing in an e-mail address, you can choose one from your Address Book by clicking the little Rolodex card icon. You'll find more about this topic under "Using the Address Book" later in this chapter. (By the way, sending messages to yourself when you're trying new features in your e-mail program is a good idea.)

2. In the Cc: box, type the e-mail address of anyone to whom you want to send a carbon copy of this message. Again, you can type multiple recipients as long as you place a semicolon between each address.

3. In the Bcc: box, type the e-mail addresses of anyone who is to receive blind carbon copies. Separate multiple addresses by a semicolon.

A carbon copy of an e-mail address shows the recipient who also received a copy of the message. A blind carbon copy does not display the names of its recipients, so the other recipients don't know who else received this message.

4. In the Subject: box, type a brief subject description. This part of the message appears in the recipient's Inbox and is visible prior to opening the message.

5. If you want to set the priority or importance of the message, choose Message ➪ Set Priority from the New Message toolbar and then choose High, Normal, or Low. Or, click the Priority icon just above the address area and choose the priority you want. If you choose high or low priority, a message line appears above the address area to reflect the priority you chose. The default priority is Normal.

6. Type your message in the larger editing window below the address portion. Information on basic editing techniques appears later in the chapter.

If you want to take a break while composing your message, choose File ➪ Save from the New Message window menu bar and then click OK if you see a dialog box informing you that the message has been saved in your Draft folder. Then close the New Message window (File ➪ Close). When you're ready to finish composing the message, click the Draft folder in the Outlook bar or the folder list and then double-click the message in the message list. Finish editing your message and send it as the following explains.

Sending the message

When you finish composing your message, you have some alternatives for sending it and you can choose whichever one you prefer:

✦ To send the message immediately, click the Send button near the upper-left corner of the New Message window toolbar (see Figure 9-6) or press Alt+S. If you have multiple service providers, the message will be sent using your default service provider.

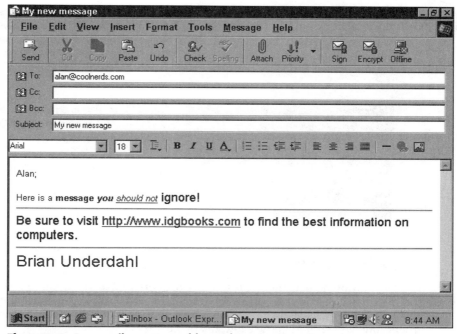

Figure 9-6: An e-mail message addressed to alan@coolnerds.com

✦ To send the message immediately, using a specific service provider, choose File ➪ Send Message Using and then click the name of the service provider you want. (This option is available only if you have set up more than one e-mail account in the Internet Accounts dialog box.)

✦ To send the message later, choose File ➪ Send Later. Or, if you have more than one e-mail account, choose File ➪ Send Later Using and then click the name of the service provider you want.

Sent messages will go out right away only if the Send Messages Immediately option on the Send tab of the Options dialog box is selected (see the section titled "Send options" later in this chapter). If this option is *not* selected, clicking the Send button places the message in your Outbox. To send a message from the Outbox, you need to choose Tools ➪ Send and Receive from Outlook Express's menu bar.

What happens next depends on how Outlook Express is set up on your computer and how you chose to send the message:

✦ If Outlook Express is set up to check the spelling of your messages automatically, the spelling checker will kick in and help you to fix any spelling errors it finds in the message (you also can check your spelling manually before sending the message). I'll explain more about checking your spelling later in this chapter under "Spell checking your message."

✦ If your outgoing message is placed in the Outbox, you may see a message like the one shown in Figure 9-7. This is a healthy reminder that the message is taking a side trip to your Outbox (and not being sent over the Internet). You can send it later, as discussed under "More About Sending and Receiving Messages."

Figure 9-7: This is a reminder that your new message is going to your Outbox so you can send it later.

Basic editing techniques

If you know how to use Microsoft Word, WordPerfect, WordPad, or some other Windows word processing program, you already know the basic skills you need to type and edit a message in Outlook Express. In case you're unfamiliar with word processing, you should know a few key facts.

First, the text will automatically wrap to the next line when the insertion point (or cursor) reaches the right edge of the editing window. So when you type a paragraph, press Enter only to end the paragraph or to end a short line. When you press Enter, the insertion point will move to the next line.

Tip

Outlook Express can create messages in either HTML format (the default "looks like a Web page" format) or plain text format. See "Formatting your messages" later in this chapter for more information.

As you type, you can use the buttons in the Formatting toolbar (shown just above the message) to format your text, insert a horizontal line, or add a picture to your e-mail. More on these topics under "Formatting your messages" a little later in this chapter.

If you need to change the text in your message, use either of the following techniques:

✦ Position the insertion point where you want to make the change (for example, click your mouse or press the arrow keys on your keyboard). Then type new text, or press Backspace or Delete to delete text, or press Enter to break the paragraph or line in two.

✦ Select a chunk of text (for example, drag the mouse pointer through it). Then, delete the chunk by pressing Backspace or Delete, or format it by choosing buttons on the Formatting toolbar. (If you select the wrong chunk of text, click the mouse outside the selection or press an arrow key to deselect it.)

Tip   To select all the text in the message, choose Edit ➪ Select All from the New Message window menu bar or press Ctrl+A.

You can use standard Windows Clipboard techniques or drag-and-drop to copy or move text and objects in the message. To begin, select the chunk of text or click an object you want to move or copy. Then do any of the following:

✦ To copy the selection using the Windows Clipboard, choose Edit ➪ Copy (or press Ctrl+C, or click the Copy button on the toolbar). Position the insertion point where the copied item should appear and choose Edit ➪ Paste (or press Ctrl+V, or click the Paste button on the toolbar).

✦ To move the selection using the Windows Clipboard, choose Edit ➪ Cut (or press Ctrl+X, or click the Cut button on the toolbar). Position the insertion point where the moved item should appear and choose Edit ➪ Paste (or press Ctrl+V, or click the Paste button on the toolbar).

✦ To copy the selection with drag-and-drop, hold down the Ctrl key while dragging your selection to a new place in the message.

✦ To move the selection with drag-and-drop, drag your selection to a new place in the message without pressing any keys.

Attaching a file

You can attach one or more files to an e-mail message. The attachment can be virtually any kind of file on your PC — a word processing document, a graphic image, a program, whatever. If the attached file is large, and both you and the recipient have a compression/decompression program, such as WinZip (available at http://www.winzip.com), you'd be wise to compress (zip) the file(s) before attaching them. Doing so will shrink the files so they transfer more quickly and with less chance of damage during the transfer.

Tip   Don't forget that you can use the Windows Me Compressed Folders option to create and open ZIP files.

Anyway, to attach one or more files to your e-mail message, click the Attach File toolbar button (the little paperclip) or choose Insert ➪ File Attachment from the New Message window menu bar. When the Insert Attachment dialog box appears, browse to the file you want to attach and then click the filename and click the Attach button (or double-click the filename). You can attach as many files as you wish. Each attached file will be represented by an icon at the bottom of the address area, as in the example shown in Figure 9-8.

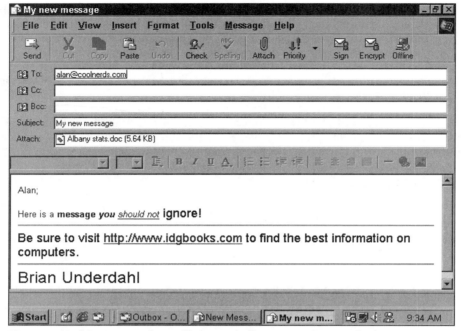

Figure 9-8: This message has a file named Albany stats.doc attached.

Tip

If you change your mind about an attachment, you can click its icon and press the Delete key to eliminate it. Or, right-click the icon and choose Remove from the shortcut menu that appears.

Formatting your messages

By default, Outlook Express sends messages in rich text (HTML) format rather than as plain text. With rich text format, your messages can resemble full-fledged Web pages complete with headings, images, fancy fonts, hyperlinks, cool background colors, and more. Your decorative options are almost unlimited. Figure 9-9 illustrates some of the possibilities by showing the welcome message that appears in your Inbox after you install Microsoft Outlook Express.

If you'd rather create your message as plain text, without any HTML formatting, choose Format ➪ Plain Text from the New Message window menu bar. You can change the default message format if you want, as explained later in the section "Customizing the default mail options" later in this chapter.

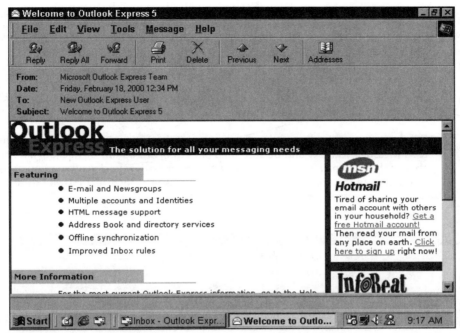

Figure 9-9: The Microsoft Outlook Express welcome message

Caution

Not everyone is lucky enough to own an e-mail program that understands rich text HTML. If the recipient's e-mail program can't deal with HTML formatting, your message usually appears as plain text with an HTML attachment (or sometimes as plain text with HTML statements in it). To view the formatted HTML message, the recipient can save the HTML attachment or text as an HTML file (with a .htm extension) and then open the saved file in any Web browser. For best results, use plain text format when sending messages to recipients whose e-mail programs do not handle rich text HTML messages.

Using the Formatting toolbar

When you begin editing a rich text message, the Formatting toolbar appears between the message header section (To:, Cc:, Bcc:, and Subject:) and the message editing area, as shown in Figure 9-10. You can use buttons on the toolbar to help you decorate your message in many ways. The basic steps for using the Formatting toolbar are simple:

1. Position the insertion point where you want to make a change or select a chunk of existing text to format.

2. Click a button on the toolbar. (To determine the purpose of any Formatting toolbar button, point to it with your mouse. After a moment, a descriptive ToolTip will appear near the mouse pointer.)

3. If a drop-down menu appears below the button, click the option you want. If a dialog box opens, fill in the dialog box and choose OK.

4. If necessary, type new text. (Be careful! If you selected text in Step 1, your typing will replace the existing text.)

Tip

If you don't see the Formatting toolbar, open the View ⇨ Toolbars menu in the New Message window and be sure the Formatting Bar option is checked. If it isn't, choose the option. If it is checked, press the Alt or Esc key to close the menu. If you still don't see the Formatting toolbar, choose Format ⇨ Rich Text (HTML) from the New Message window menu bar.

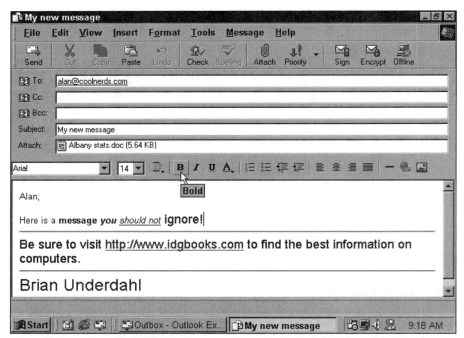

Figure 9-10: The Formatting toolbar across the middle of the window makes it easy to format a message.

By the way, most of the options on the Formatting toolbar are available on the Insert and Format menus in the New Message window. You also can choose formatting options from the shortcut menu that appears when you right-click within selected text or at a particular spot in the message.

Changing the font, style, color, and size

You can use any of the first seven buttons on the Formatting toolbar to change the appearance of text in the message. Here's how:

1. Position the insertion point where you want to type new text, or select a chunk of existing text.

2. Click the Font or Font Size drop-down arrow, or click the Style Tag, Bold, Italic, Underline, or Font Color button. If you chose Font, Font Size, Style Tag, or Font Color, click the option you want from the drop-down menu that appears. Repeat this step as needed.

3. Type new text (assuming you didn't select text in Step 1).

Figure 9-11 shows a sample message after I went crazy with the first seven buttons on the Formatting toolbar. This figure resembles a ransom note, but it isn't.

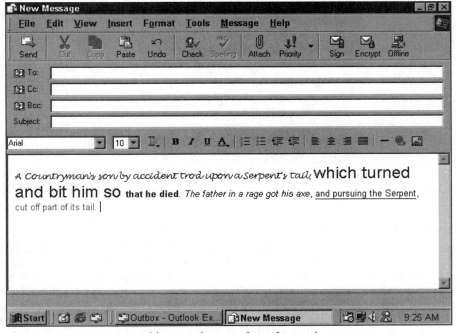

Figure 9-11: A message with several types of text formatting

Tip   If you want to apply a formatting style to text you've already typed, select the text by dragging the mouse pointer through it or by holding down the Shift key while pressing the arrow keys. When the text you want to format is highlighted, choose your format.

The Bold, Italic, and Underline buttons are toggles. Click them once to turn on the effect; click them again to turn off the effect. You also can press shortcut keys to turn the effects on and off. Use Ctrl+B for bold, Ctrl+I for italic, and Ctrl+U for underline.

Instead of using shortcut keys or buttons on the Formatting toolbar, you can choose Format ➪ Font from the New Message window menu bar and then choose the font name, style, size, underlining, and color from one convenient Font dialog box (see Figure 9-12). After making your selections, click OK to save your changes.

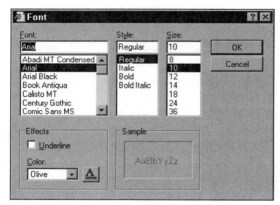

Figure 9-12: Choose font options using the Font dialog box.

Aligning text

Your text usually is left-aligned, but you can center, right-align, or justify text if you want (see Figure 9-13). To alter the text alignment, click in the paragraph or short line you want to change, or click where you're about to type a new paragraph or line. If you want to adjust several paragraphs or short lines at once, select them. Now click the Align Left, Align Center, Align Right, or Justify button on the Formatting toolbar, or choose Format ➪ Paragraph from the New Message window menu bar, and then choose Left, Center, Right, or Justify.

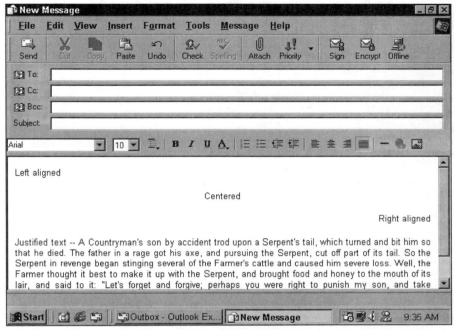

Figure 9-13: Some examples of left, center, and right text alignment

Indenting and outdenting text

You can indent a paragraph by moving it in one tab stop (about five spaces) toward the right or you can outdent a paragraph by moving it out one tab stop toward the left, as shown in Figure 9-14. This is an excellent way to make certain paragraphs — such as quotations — stand out. The steps should be familiar by now:

1. Click the paragraph or short line you want to indent or outdent, or click where you're about to type a new paragraph or line. If you want to adjust several paragraphs or short lines at once, select them.

2. Click the Increase Indentation or Decrease Indentation button on the Formatting toolbar or choose Format ➪ Increase Indent or Format ➪ Decrease Indent from the New Message window menu bar.

That's all there is to it! As you'll see next, indenting and outdenting is also useful when you're typing lists.

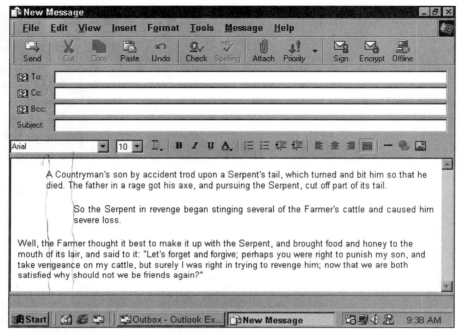

Figure 9-14: Indented and outdented text

Typing lists

I'm a great fan of bulleted and numbered lists because they make it easier to understand a series of choices or a logical sequence of steps. You can create lists like the ones shown in Figure 9-15 with a few keystrokes and mouse clicks. When you create a numbered list, new items are numbered automatically in their proper sequence. If you delete an item in the list, the numbering adjusts accordingly, as you would expect.

Typing a new list

Here's how to type a new list:

1. Click where you want the new list to start.

2. Do one of the following:

   - To create a numbered list, click the Formatting Numbers button on the Formatting toolbar or choose Format ➪ Style ➪ Numbered List from the New Message window menu bar. A number appears at the insertion point and the Formatting Numbers button will appear pushed in.

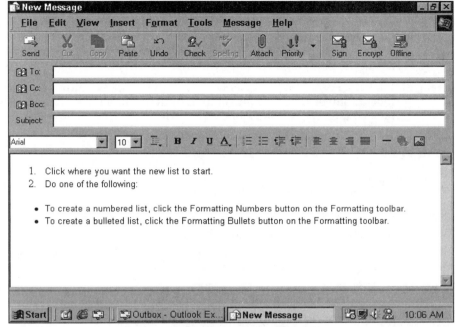

Figure 9-15: A numbered list with an indented bulleted list

- To create a bulleted list, click the Formatting Bullets button on the Formatting toolbar or choose Format ➪ Style ➪ Bulleted List from the New Message window menu bar. A bullet appears at the insertion point and the Formatting Bullets button will appear pushed in.

3. If you want to indent or outdent the current item, click the Increase Indentation or Decrease Indentation button on the Formatting toolbar (or choose the equivalent options on the New Message window's Format menu).

4. Type the next list item and press Enter. A new number or bullet will appear.

5. Repeat Steps 2 through 4 as needed.

When you finish typing the list, follow the steps given in the section "Removing numbers and bullets." (Basically, you repeat the previous Step 2 to turn off the list.)

Tip   The Formatting Bullets and Formatting Numbers buttons and the equivalent menu options are toggles. Choosing the button or option once turns on the numbered or bulleted list. Choosing it again turns off the list.

Creating a list from existing text

If your message already includes some paragraphs or short lines that would work better as a list, converting them is easy:

1. Select the paragraphs or lines you want to format into a list.

2. Click the Formatting Numbers or Formatting Bullets buttons and the Increase Indentation or Decrease Indentation buttons on the Formatting toolbar as needed (see Steps 2 and 3 of the procedure for typing a new list).

Creating a list within a list

You can even create a list within a list, like the bulleted list within the numbered list shown in Figure 9-15. As usual, you can make the change while you're typing a new list or by selecting text first. Follow these steps:

1. Position the insertion point where you want the indented list item to appear or select the existing paragraphs or lines you want to indent.

2. Click the Increase Indentation button on the Formatting toolbar or choose the equivalent menu options until you get the indentation level you want.

3. If you want to change the type of list, click the Formatting Numbers or Formatting Bullets button, or choose the equivalent menu options. A number or bullet appropriate to the indentation level appears.

4. If you did not select text in Step 1, type your list items, pressing Enter after each one.

Of course, you can return list items to their previous levels by outdenting. Simply repeat the previous four steps except, in Step 2, click the Decrease Indentation button on the Formatting toolbar as needed.

Removing numbers and bullets

You can remove the numbers or bullets from list items at any time. Simply select the items or position the insertion point anywhere in the item from which you want to remove the number or bullet. Then click the Formatting Numbers button (if it's a numbered item) or the Formatting Bullets button (if it's a bulleted item) on the Formatting toolbar until the number or bullet disappears. If necessary, increase or decrease the indentation level.

Tip

You can remove numbers and bullets *and* return the text to its leftmost position by repeatedly clicking the Decrease Indentation button.

Inserting a picture

A great-looking picture of your pet, spouse, kid, or newest possession can spice up an e-mail message. You can insert many types of pictures, including scanned images and clip art, by following these steps:

1. Click in the message editing area where you want the image to appear.

2. Click the Insert Picture button on the Formatting toolbar, or choose Insert ➪ Picture from the New Message window menu bar. You'll see the Picture dialog box shown in Figure 9-16.

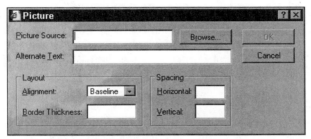

Figure 9-16: Add graphics to your e-mail messages using the Picture dialog box.

3. In the Picture Source box, type the complete filename of the picture. Or, click the Browse button and then locate and double-click the picture's filename in the dialog box that appears (see Figure 9-17).

Figure 9-17: Select the picture you want from the list.

4. If you want to specify alternate text or various layout and spacing options, fill in the appropriate Alternate Text, Layout, and Spacing fields.

5. Choose OK.

Your picture appears at the insertion point. Recipients who don't have rich text e-mail clients will see the image as a regular attachment, not as an inline image. Recipients whose e-mail clients have no graphics capability will see only the alternate text.

Alternate text will appear in place of the image if the recipient's e-mail client has pictures turned off or cannot display them. Alternate text also appears while the image is loading.

Outlook Express can import images in GIF, JPEG (JPG), bitmap (BMP), Windows metafile (WMF), XBM, and ART formats. The default import formats are GIF and JPEG. You can choose a different format from the Files Of Type drop-down list shown at the bottom of Figure 9-17.

Inserting a hyperlink

By now, you've probably had experience browsing the World Wide Web and you know you can click hyperlinks on a Web page to jump to another place on the Internet or to perform some action, such as sending e-mail or downloading a file. Well, guess what? You can insert your own hyperlinks into any e-mail message (see Figure 9-18).

Outlook Express automatically creates hyperlinks from valid e-mail addresses and URLs as soon as you type them into a message and press the spacebar or Enter key. For example, after I type my e-mail address (alan@coolnerds.com) or the URL of my home page (http://www.coolnerds.com) and press the spacebar or the Enter key, Outlook Express automatically converts the text to an underlined blue hyperlink. The message recipient simply clicks the hyperlink to send me an e-mail message or to jump to my home page on the Web.

You also can create hyperlinks manually, using any text you want. For example, you may want your message to include a sentence, such as:

```
Click here to send me an e-mail message or click here to
download a heavenly recipe.
```

In this example, the first appearance of the word "here" is a hyperlink that sends me an e-mail message; the second appearance of the word "here" is a hyperlink that sends my favorite recipe for cinnamon rolls to your computer (just kidding, I don't cook).

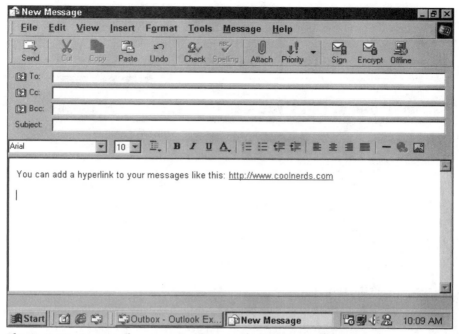

Figure 9-18: An e-mail message with an underlined hyperlink:
`http://www.coolnerds.com`

To create a hyperlink manually from any existing text, follow these steps:

1. Select the text you want to use as a hyperlink.
2. Click the Insert Hyperlink button on the Formatting toolbar. You'll see the Hyperlink dialog box, shown in Figure 9-19.
3. Click the drop-down arrow in the Type box and select one of the types listed in Table 9-2. The type you select is filled in as the prefix in the URL box.
4. Click after the prefix in the URL box and type the rest of the URL.
5. Click OK.

The selected text becomes a hyperlink in your message.

Figure 9-19: The Hyperlink dialog box

To change a hyperlink you created manually, repeat the preceding Steps 1 through 5. To change a manual hyperlink to plain text, select the hyperlink text, delete it, and then retype it.

Table 9-2
Types of URLs You Can Use to Create Hyperlinks

Type	Description	Sample Entry in the URL Box
file:	Opens the file specified in the URL box	`file://c:/windows/desktop/wrinkled_paper.bmp`
ftp:	Downloads the file specified in the URL box	`ftp://ftp.winzip.com/winzip/winzip95.exe`
gopher:	Goes to the Gopher site specified in the URL box	`gopher://gopher.well.com`
http:	Goes to the Web page specified in the URL box	`http://www.branchmall.com`
https:	Goes to the secure Web page specified in the URL box	`https://www.branchmall.com`
mailto:	Sends a new message to the e-mail address specified in the URL box	`mailto:alan@coolnerds.com`
news:	Goes to the newsgroup specified in the URL box	`news:news.newusers.questions`
telnet:	Establishes a Telnet link to the computer specified in the URL box	`telnet:compuserve.com`
wais	**Establishes a link to a Wide Area Information Server (wais)**	`wais:info.cern.ch`

Changing the background color or picture

Normally your e-mail message will have whatever background color is the default for the recipient's e-mail program or browser. You can, however, specify the background color or even use a picture as the background, as I did in Figure 9-20.

Specifying a colored background

To specify a colored background, choose Format ➪ Background ➪ Color from the New Message window menu bar and then choose a color from the menu that appears. You should try to pick a color that won't obliterate the message text (or reformat the text if necessary). For example, your recipient will have a hard time reading a message typed with black text on a purple background. The text might look rather cool, however, if you reformat it in boldface, a larger size, and the color white. (See the section "Changing the font, style, color, and size" earlier in this chapter.)

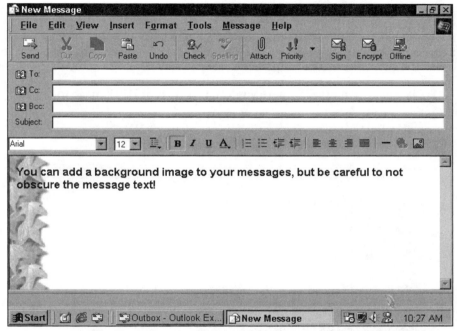

Figure 9-20: This message uses a picture of ivy, which comes with Outlook Express, as a background and big bold text for added readability.

Specifying a picture background

To use a favorite picture or texture as a background, follow these steps:

1. Choose Format ➪ Background ➪ Picture from the New Message window menu bar. The Background Picture dialog box appears.

2. In the File box, type the path of a file on your own computer or click the drop-down arrow next to File and choose one of the picture files that comes with Outlook Express. Or, you can click the Browse button and then locate and double-click the picture file you want to use.

3. Choose OK.

The picture or texture you chose will be repeated as needed to fill up the background, as in Figure 9-20. Again, be careful to choose a picture that won't obscure the text in your message and type the message in an easy-to-read format.

Tip   The pictures that come with Outlook Express are in the folder C:\Program Files\Common Files\Microsoft Shared\Stationery. You can copy your favorite GIF, JPEG (.JPG), or bitmap (.BMP) pictures to this folder. Then, they'll appear in the File drop-down list of the Background Picture dialog box and you can select them more quickly.

Inserting a text file or an HTML file

Let's suppose you already put together a plain text file containing your message (perhaps using Notepad) or you have an HTML Web page prepared. Now you want to e-mail the text or Web page to someone else. No sweat. Here's what you should do:

1. Click in your message where you want the text or HTML page to appear.

2. Choose Insert ➪ Text From File from the New Message window menu bar. The Insert Text File dialog box appears (see Figure 9-21).

Figure 9-21: Use the Insert Text File dialog box to include a text or HTML file in your message.

3. Choose the type of file you want to insert from the Files of type drop-down list near the bottom of the dialog box. You can choose either Text Files (*.txt) to insert a plain text file or HTML Files (*.htm,*.html) to insert an HTML file.

4. Locate and double-click the file containing your text.

The plain text or HTML page appears in your message.

What is HTML?

HTML stands for *Hypertext Markup Language,* a language Web browsers and many e-mail programs interpret to display Web pages. You can create HTML pages from scratch, using Windows Notepad or other simple word processors, or you can use fancier word processors and specialized Web page design programs to create What You See Is What You Get (WYSIWYG) Web pages. Microsoft Word and Corel WordPerfect are two word processors that can create Web pages. Microsoft FrontPage, FrontPage Express, FrontPad, and Publisher, along with Netscape Compose, are examples of Web page design programs.

Fixing "Broken" HTML Pictures and Links

If the HTML file you inserted is at all fancy, it may have broken picture icons like the "view from my office" icon shown in Figure 9-22 and sometimes the hyperlinks won't work when the recipient clicks them.

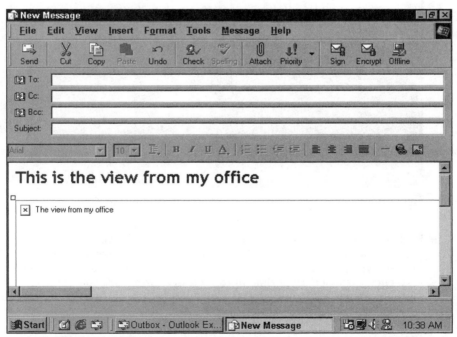

Figure 9-22: This HTML page includes a broken picture icon. I've selected the icon in this example.

Try the following methods to solve these problems:

✦ Broken picture icons are indicated by an *x* and an empty frame where the picture should appear. To fix a broken picture icon, click the icon and then click the Insert Picture button on the Formatting toolbar (or right-click the icon and choose Properties). Now complete the Picture Source box as explained earlier under "Inserting a picture." Figure 9-23 shows the page from Figure 9-22 after I fixed the broken picture icon.

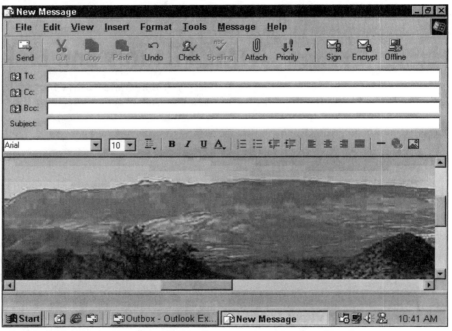

Figure 9-23: The HTML page after I fixed the broken image icon

✦ Broken hyperlinks aren't obvious just by looking at them; however, they'll point to files or URLs unavailable to the recipient of your message. To fix a broken hyperlink (or to check a hyperlink for accuracy), select the hyperlink text, click the Insert Hyperlink button on the Formatting toolbar, and complete the Hyperlink dialog box, as explained earlier, in the section "Inserting a hyperlink."

Note   Outlook Express will not let you save or send your messages until you fix all broken picture icons.

Sending a Web page from the Internet

You can send a Web page directly from the Internet, if you like. To begin, open Microsoft Internet Explorer and visit the Web page you want to send. Then choose File ➪ Send ➪ Page By Email from the menu bar. Outlook Express will open and place the entire Web page — including all its pictures and hyperlinks — in a New Message window. When the page is finished loading into the New Message window, you can fill in the recipient's address, a subject, and any additional message text you want. Then send the message.

Spell checking your message

No one wants to seem careless or ignorant, especially when using e-mail to communicate with other people. One way to avoid bad impressions is to send messages free of embarrassing spelling errors. Outlook Express offers a built-in spelling checker that makes checking your spelling a breeze.

Note   To be honest, Outlook Express doesn't have its *own* spelling checker. Instead, it uses the spelling checker provided with the Microsoft Office 95 or Office 97 programs (including Microsoft Word, Microsoft Excel, or Microsoft PowerPoint). If you do not have one of these programs installed, the spelling features are not available.

If the spelling checker doesn't start automatically when you click the Send button (or you want to spell check the message while you're composing it), choose Tools ➪ Spelling from the New Message window menu bar, or press F7. The spelling checker will start. If it doesn't find any errors, a dialog box informs you the spelling check is complete (click OK to clear it). If the spelling checker does find an error, you'll see a Spelling dialog box like the one in Figure 9-24. The unrecognized word appears in the Not In Dictionary box just below the title bar.

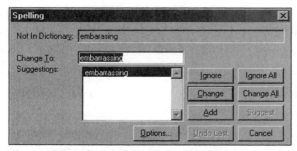

Figure 9-24: The Spelling dialog box detects misspelled (or unrecognized) words.

Tip
If the Spelling dialog box is covering part of the message, simply drag the dialog box by its title bar to move it out of the way.

Be aware, the spelling checker isn't all-knowing. Sometimes it fumes about a perfectly acceptable word. As I'll explain in a moment, you can add unrecognized (but properly spelled) words to the spelling checker's custom dictionary and you can change the spelling options so the spelling checker doesn't complain so much.

The buttons in the Spelling dialog box are as follows:

✦ **Ignore:** Click Ignore to ignore this error and move on to the next one.

✦ **Ignore All:** Click Ignore All to ignore this error throughout the entire message.

✦ **Change:** Click the word you want to use as a replacement in the Suggestions list (if it's not highlighted already) or edit the word in the Change To box. Then click the Change button to change the misspelled word to the word shown in the Change To box.

✦ **Change All:** Click the word you want to use as a replacement in the Suggestions list (if it isn't already highlighted) or edit the word in the Change To box. Then click Change All to change the same misspelled word throughout the entire message to the word shown in the Change To box.

✦ **Add:** Click this button to add the unrecognized word to the spelling checker's custom dictionary.

✦ **Suggest:** Type a word into the Change To box and then click Suggest to look up the word and display other possible spellings in the Suggestions list.

✦ **Options:** Click Options to open the Spelling Options dialog box (shown in Figure 9-25), which enables you to customize the current spelling options. You can check or clear the check boxes, choose a language from the Language drop-down list, and even edit the custom dictionary, which contains words you've added via the Add button, plus any words you type in manually.

✦ **Undo Last:** Click Undo Last to undo your most recent change (if any) and skip back to the previous misspelled word.

✦ **Cancel (or Close):** Click Cancel or Close to stop the spelling check immediately.

A message appears when the spelling check is complete. Click OK to clear the message.

Tip
Your choices in the Spelling Options dialog box affect the current spelling check session and all future spelling check sessions. You'll learn another way to change the spelling checker options in "Customizing the default mail options," later in this chapter.

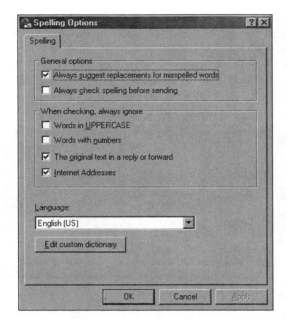

Figure 9-25: Use the Spelling Options dialog box to customize the spelling checker.

More About Sending and Receiving Messages

As mentioned earlier in this chapter, you can send your messages immediately — by clicking the Send button on the New Message window toolbar, for example. If you prefer to stack up your messages in your Outbox until you're ready to send the whole bunch, you can use the File ➪ Send Later options instead. Assuming you have some messages stacked in your Outbox, follow these simple steps to send them:

1. Open Outlook Express using whichever method you prefer (see "Starting Outlook Express").

2. If you want to see a list of messages waiting to be sent, click the Outbox icon in the Outlook bar or the folder list. A list of messages waiting to be sent appears in the message list, as in the example shown in Figure 9-26.

3. Do one of the following:

   • To send all the current messages and also to receive any messages waiting for you, click the Send/Recv button on the toolbar or press Ctrl+M. If you have more than one account, Outlook Express will send and receive e-mail for all your accounts automatically.

- To send all the current messages and also receive any messages that are waiting for you, you also can choose Tools ➪ Send and Receive ➪ Send and Receive All. If you have multiple accounts, you'll see a list with options for choosing which account to use.

- To send the pending messages without retrieving new ones, choose Tools ➪ Send and Receive ➪ Send All from the menu bar.

Figure 9-26: Messages waiting to be sent appear in Outlook Express's Outbox.

A dialog box will keep you posted on the progress and your computer will dial your service provider (if you use a modem to connect). When all the messages have been sent, the Outbox will be empty. Copies of the sent messages will be stored in the Sent Items box.

Tip   You can change any message waiting in your Outbox. Simply open the Outbox, double-click the message you want to change in the message list, and change the message as needed. Then click the Send button on the toolbar (or press Alt+S) or choose File ➪ Send Later from the New Message window menu bar.

If you close Outlook Express while unsent messages are still in your Outbox, you'll see a box telling you the following:

```
You have unsent messages in your Outbox. Do you want to send
them now?
```

This is a friendly reminder in case you composed a message and forgot to send it. You can choose Yes to send the messages immediately or choose No to leave them in the Outbox to send them later.

Reading Your Messages

Retrieving and viewing new Internet e-mail messages is easy. Just follow these steps:

1. Open Outlook Express using any of the techniques described in the section "Starting Outlook Express" earlier in this chapter.

2. Click the Send/Recv button (or press Ctrl+M).

You'll see some progress dialog boxes as Outlook Express sends any messages in your Outbox and then copies new messages from your e-mail server on the Internet to your PC.

To view the new messages, open the Inbox (a number appears next to the Inbox to indicate the number of unread messages it contains). New messages you haven't read yet are listed in boldface in the message list and are preceded by a closed envelope icon, as in the example shown in Figure 9-27. Messages containing attached files are preceded by a paperclip icon and those with a high or low priority are preceded by an exclamation point (!) or a down arrow, respectively.

 Caution Don't panic if the boldface attribute suddenly disappears from the message line. This means you viewed the message for about five seconds (an interval you can adjust, as explained later in "Customizing the default mail options").

To read a specific message, click it. The preview pane at the bottom shows the contents of the e-mail message. If you prefer to open the message in a separate window, double-click it.

 Tip If you already have messages stored in one of the more popular e-mail programs, you can import them into Outlook Express. Importing old messages can be especially handy when you're switching from some other e-mail program to Outlook Express. See the section "Importing and Exporting Messages" for details.

When you finish reading the message, you can do any of the following:

✦ **Reply:** To send a reply to the author of the e-mail, click the Reply toolbar button or press Ctrl+R. Type your reply and click the Send toolbar button.

✦ **Reply All:** To reply to everyone who received the message (including those who received carbon copies), click the Reply All toolbar button or press Ctrl+Shift+R. Type your reply and click the Send button.

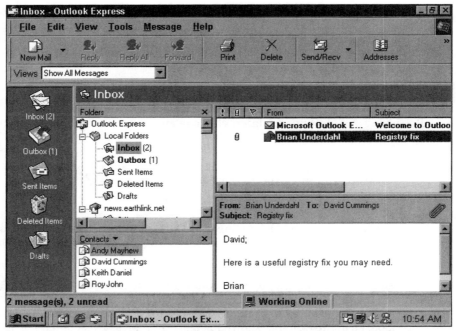

Figure 9-27: The Outlook Express Inbox with two unread messages, listed in boldface

✦ **Forward:** To forward the message to someone else, click the Forward (or Forward Message) toolbar button, or press Ctrl+F. Type the new recipient's name, type a message describing the forwarded information (optional), and then click the Send button.

✦ **Forward As Attachment:** To forward the message to someone else as an attachment to a message you've written, choose Message ⇨ Forward As Attachment from the menu bar. Type the new recipient's name, type a message describing the forwarded information (optional), and then click the Send toolbar button.

✦ **Delete:** To delete the message, click the Delete button or press Ctrl+D. Outlook Express moves the message to the Deleted Items folder.

✦ **Print:** To print the message, choose File ⇨ Print from the menu bar, or press Ctrl+P, or click the Print toolbar button if it's available.

✦ **Mark As Unread:** To mark the message line with boldface as a reminder to reread it later, choose Edit ⇨ Mark As Unread from the menu bar.

✦ **Mark As Read:** To remove the boldface and mark a message as read, choose Edit ⇨ Mark As Read, or press Ctrl+Q.

✦ **Mark All As Read:** To mark all the messages as read, choose Edit ➪ Mark All As Read.

✦ **View the Next Message:** To view the next message in the folder, click the Next button on the toolbar (if it's available) or press Ctrl+> (Ctrl plus the greater than symbol), or choose View ➪ Next ➪ Next Message from the menu bar. To read the next unread message, press Ctrl+U.

✦ **View the Previous Message:** To view the previous message in the folder, click the Previous button on the toolbar (if it's available), or press Ctrl+< (Ctrl plus the less than symbol), or choose View ➪ Previous Message from the menu bar.

✦ **View the Message Properties:** To view details about the message, choose File ➪ Properties from the menu bar. Then click the General tab (to see general information) or the Details tab (to see the Internet headers for this message). To view the message headers and HTML source text, select the Details tab and then click the Message Source button. When you finish viewing the properties, click the Close (X) and OK buttons as needed.

Instead of using the toolbar buttons to reply to or forward the message, you can choose options from the Message menu. And if you're viewing the message in the message list (rather than in a separate window), you can right-click the message and decide its fate by choosing an option from the shortcut menu that appears. You'll find more about replying to messages, forwarding them, and deleting them in the later sections "Replying to a Message," "Forwarding a Message," and "Deleting Messages."

Working with several messages at once

Working with several messages at once is often handy. For example, you might want to delete several messages, mark them as read (or unread), move them to another folder, open them in separate windows, and more. The first step is to click the folder containing the messages with which you want to work. Next, select (highlight) the messages, using any of the following techniques:

✦ To select one message, click it in the message list.

✦ To select all the messages, choose Edit ➪ Select All, or press Ctrl+A.

✦ To select several adjacent messages, click the first message you want to select and then hold down the Shift key while clicking the last message you want to select (this technique is called Shift+click).

✦ To select several nonadjacent messages, click the first message you want to select and then hold down the Ctrl key while clicking each additional message you want to select (this technique is called Ctrl+click). If you select a message by accident, Ctrl+click it.

A few words about junk mail (spam)

If people are sending you unwanted junk mail (also known as *spam*), never respond to the spammer directly. Instead, try to find out more about where the spam message came from by viewing its header information. To do this, open your Inbox, highlight the message, choose File ⇨ Properties, select the Details tab, and look for an e-mail address next to the "From:" lines. You might see something like this:

```
From: "A. Spammer" <aspammer@spammerISP.com>
```

Unfortunately, the message header can be rather cryptic and it may be false if the spammer is masquerading as someone else. Nonetheless, this header information can help your Internet service provider (ISP) and the spammer's ISP to filter out the spam or to cancel the spammer's account.

Many ISPs have a specific policy about junk mail. You should check with your own ISP for details about how you can fight spam. Some ISPs ask you to notify their "abuse" or "postmaster" e-mail account when you receive spam. In this case, forward the spam message to your own ISP (for example, to `abuse@myISP.com` or `postmaster@myISP.com`) and to the spammer's ISP (for example, to `abuse@spammerISP.com` or `postmaster@spammerISP.com`). At the top of the forwarded message, type something like this:

```
I received the attached spam e-mail, and I would appreciate
anything you can do to discourage this spammer from sending such
messages in the future. Many thanks!
```

When you finish typing this introductory text, send your message, and then delete the original spam from your Inbox.

Later in this chapter, you learn how to filter out unwanted messages from specific e-mail addresses. This tool can be handy for weeding out messages from repeat spammers. For more tips and information on dealing with junk e-mail, check out the antispamming Web site at `http://www.dgl.com/docs/antispam.html`.

Now you can work with all the selected messages at once. Here are some things you can do with them:

✦ Right-click any of the selected messages and choose an option from the shortcut menu that appears. Right-clicking is perhaps the easiest way to work with multiple messages.

✦ Choose File ⇨ Open or nearly any option from the Edit menu.

✦ Click the Forward Message or Delete button on the toolbar.

✦ Drag any of the selected messages to another folder in the folder list (all the selected messages are moved to the new folder).

✦ Hold down the Ctrl key while dragging any of the selected messages to another folder in the folder list (all the selected messages are copied to the new folder).

Note   You can create your own folders to organize your e-mail messages, and you can have the Inbox Assistant automatically move or copy incoming messages to specific folders.

Finding and sorting messages

Eventually, you may end up with a huge number of messages in your Inbox and other folders within Outlook Express. Finding a particular message in that pile of mail could be like looking for the proverbial needle in the haystack. But thanks to the Find Message feature, it's easy to search for messages. Follow these steps to find the message(s) you want:

1. Starting from the main Outlook Express window, click the folder you want to search.

2. Choose Edit ⇨ Find ⇨ Message from the menu bar or press Ctrl+Shift+F. You'll see the Find Message dialog box.

3. To narrow the search, fill in as much information as you need about the messages you want to find. (It doesn't matter whether you type uppercase or lowercase letters.)

4. If you want to search a different message folder, click the Browse button. You also can choose whether to include subfolders of the selected folder by checking or unchecking the Include Subfolders box.

5. Click the Find Now button to begin the search.

Tip   In Step 3, you can specify partial words or names in the From, To, Subject, and Message fields. If you enter information into more than one field, Outlook treats each field as an *and*. For example, Outlook Express interpreted the find in Figure 9-28 as "Find any message that both contains the word *Brian* in the From line and has an attachment."

After you click Find Now, the Find Message dialog box expands to include an area for showing messages that match your search. If matches exist, they'll appear in the list, as shown in Figure 9-28. If no matches exist, the list will be empty and you'll see "0 message(s)" in the status bar at the bottom of the dialog box.

The Find Message dialog box offers many cool ways to work with messages. For example, you can conduct another search by repeating Steps 3 through 5 of the previous find procedure. You also can do just about anything that works in the main Outlook Express window, including the following:

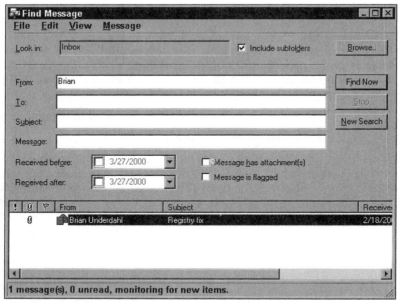

Figure 9-28: The Find Message dialog box after searching for messages that contain the word registry and an attachment

✦ Double-click a message to open it.

✦ Select one or more messages and then choose options from the File, Edit, View, or Compose menus in the Find Message dialog box.

✦ Select one or more messages, right-click your selection, and then choose an option from the shortcut menu.

✦ Select one or more messages and then delete them by pressing the Delete key. (For more information about deleting messages, see "Deleting Messages," later in this chapter.)

When you finish using the Find Message dialog box, you can close it by choosing File ➪ Close from the Find Message menu bar, by pressing Alt+F4, or by clicking the Close (X) button in the upper-right corner of the dialog box.

Sorting the message list

Another quick way to find a message is to sort the message list. You can sort the list by any column in either ascending (A to Z) or descending (Z to A) order. To begin, click the icon for the folder you want to sort. Then, use any of the following methods to sort the message list:

✦ Click the column button at the top of the message list. For example, click the Subject column button to sort the messages by subject. If you click the column button again, the sort order is reversed. A small up-pointing triangle on the button indicates an ascending sort; a down-pointing triangle indicates a descending sort.

✦ Right-click the column button at the top of the message list and choose either Sort Ascending or Sort Descending.

✦ Choose View ➪ Sort By from the menu bar and then choose the column by which you want to sort. If you want to toggle the current sort order between ascending and descending order, choose View ➪ Sort By ➪ Sort Ascending. If the Sort Ascending option is checked, the list is sorted in ascending order. If it isn't checked, you get a descending sort.

You can add and remove columns in the message list, as explained later in "Customizing the Outlook Express window."

Finding text within a message

In addition to searching for a specific message, you can search for text within the message you're currently viewing in the message list or in a separate window. To do this, choose Edit ➪ Find Text in this message from the menu bar. Type the text you're looking for in the Find box and choose any options you want. You can decide whether to match the whole word only, whether to match the uppercase and lowercase letters you typed, and the search direction (up or down). Click the Find Next button to start the search. Find will highlight the next match it finds. You can continue clicking Find Next and highlighting matches until you find the match you want. When you finish searching, click Cancel.

Viewing and saving attachments

If a message includes an attachment, a paper-clip icon appears next to the message in the message list and also at the upper-right corner of the message in the preview pane. The icon for the actual file appears below the address header anytime you view it in a separate window. Figure 9-29 illustrates the same message opened in both the preview pane (left side of figure) and in a separate window (right side of figure).

Viewing or saving the attachment is easy:

✦ If you highlighted the message in the preview pane, click the paperclip icon at the upper-right corner of the message and then click the filename of the attachment you want to open.

✦ If you opened the message in a separate window, double-click the attachment icon. Or, for even more processing options including Open, Print, and Save As, right-click the attachment icon and choose an option from the shortcut menu.

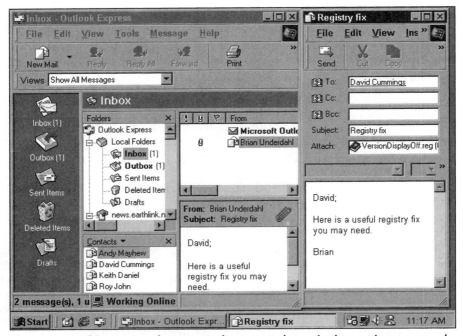

Figure 9-29: This message has an attachment, as shown in the preview pane and in a separate window.

What happens next depends on the type of information the attachment contains. If the attachment is an e-mail message, it will open in a separate window. If it's a compressed file (such as a .zip file), it may open in your file compression program (such as WinZip or PKUNZIP). If it's a program or data file (such as a spreadsheet or word processing document), you'll usually see the Open Attachment Warning dialog box, shown in Figure 9-30. Now take either of the following actions:

✦ To open the attachment, click Open it, choose OK, and then respond to any dialog boxes that appear.

✦ To save the attachment to disk, choose "Save it to disk" and choose OK. When the Save Attachment As dialog box appears, specify a filename in the File Name box (optional), choose a disk drive and folder location in the Save In: area near the top of the dialog box, and then click the Save button or press Enter.

Caution Be careful about opening a file if you haven't checked it for viruses. It's okay to save a file to disk and then check it for viruses, but once you open the file (by choosing "Open it" in the Open Attachment Warning dialog box or by double-clicking it in My Computer or Windows Explorer), you can expose your computer to any viruses the file contains. See Chapter 7 for more information about viruses in general and about the popular virus checkers from McAfee and Symantec.

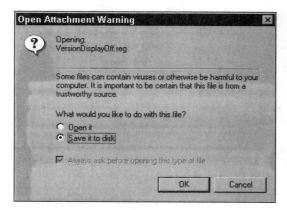

Figure 9-30: This dialog box enables you to open the attached file or to save it to disk.

Replying to a Message

You can reply to any message you highlighted in the message list or that you're viewing in a separate window. First, do one of the following:

✦ To send a reply to the author of the e-mail, click the Reply toolbar button or press Ctrl+R (or choose Message ➪ Reply To Sender).

✦ To reply to everyone who received the message (including the people who received carbon copies), click the Reply All toolbar button or press Ctrl+Shift+R (or choose Message ➪ Reply To All).

A Reply window will open, as shown in Figure 9-31. Notice the To: box in the address area is already filled in with the recipient's e-mail name and the Subject line displays Re: (for reply) followed by the original subject name. The insertion point is positioned above the original message, which appears in the lower portion of the editing area. (If the message originally contained an attachment, the attachment is not included.)

Type your reply using any of the editing and formatting techniques discussed in the section "Composing a Message." Although you shouldn't need to, you also can change any items in the address and subject areas. When you finish typing your reply, send the message as usual (for example, click the Send button in the Reply window or press Alt+S).

Tip   You can choose whether to include the original message in the reply, as explained in the section "Customizing the default mail options." For the best reminder about what you're replying to, include the original message. You can always delete any extraneous text from the original message using standard editing techniques.

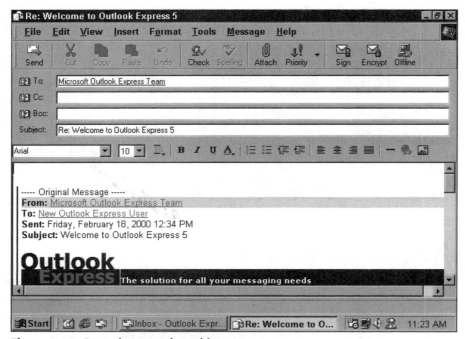

Figure 9-31: Preparing to reply to this message

Forwarding a Message

You can forward any message to someone other than the original author or carbon copy recipients. Forwarding a message is similar to sending a reply, although these differences exist: Attachments are included in the forwarded message; the To: box in the address area is not filled in automatically; and the Subject: line is filled in with Fw: (for forward) followed by the original subject or it is blank.

To forward a message, follow these steps:

1. Highlight the message you want to forward in the message list or open it in a separate window.

2. Do one of the following:

   - To forward the message exactly as it originally appeared in your Inbox, click the Forward toolbar button or press Ctrl+F (or choose Message ➪ Forward). A Forward (Fw) window opens and shows the original message and its attachments, if any.

- To forward the message as an attachment, choose Message ⇨ Forward As Attachment. A New Message window opens with the original message appearing as an attachment icon.

3. Type the recipient's e-mail address in the To: box or use your Address Book to fill in the address (see "Using the Address Book" later in this chapter). If you want to forward the message to more than one recipient, type a semicolon between each recipient's e-mail address.

4. If you forwarded the message as an attachment, type a subject in the Subject: box.

5. Click the message editing area and type an introduction to the message you're forwarding. This introduction is optional, but it's helpful to tell recipients why you're forwarding the message.

6. Send the message as usual (for example, click the Send toolbar button or press Alt+S).

Deleting Messages

Deleting an unwanted message from any folder is easy. First, open the folder containing the message and open the message or select it in the message list. Then, click the Delete button on the toolbar or press Ctrl+D. If you selected messages in the message list, you can delete them in two other ways: Either press the Delete (Del) key on your keyboard or drag the selection to the Deleted Items folder.

Note   You can empty your Deleted Items folder automatically as soon as you exit Outlook Express, as explained in the section "Customizing the default mail options" later in this chapter

When you delete a message from any folder except the Deleted Items folder, you actually move it to the Deleted Items folder. So if you ever need to undelete a message, you can just move it to another folder. To do so, open the Deleted Items folder and select the message(s) you want to undelete in the message list. Then right-click the selected message(s), choose Move To from the shortcut menu, and double-click Inbox or whatever folder to which you want to move the message(s). Or, you can select messages in the Deleted Items folder and drag them to another folder in the folder list or the Outlook bar.

Caution   When you delete a message from the Deleted Items folder, the message is removed from your hard disk and it cannot be undeleted.

Backing Up Your Messages

It's a good idea to back up your Outlook Express message folders to a floppy disk, Zip disk, or network drive. Backups can protect you against the loss of all your saved messages in the event of a hard disk crash and they provide some extra insurance just before or after you do a major cleanup in your message folders.

Each Outlook Express message folder is actually a file on your hard disk with a .dbx extension.

The general steps for backing up your messages are as follows:

1. Open the folder that contains your Outlook Express messages using Find, Windows Explorer, or My Computer. See the following section, "Finding your Outlook Express messages," for some tips on locating this folder.

2. Copy the message files to a backup folder on your computer, to a floppy disk or Zip disk, or to a network drive. Note, some message files may be too large to fit on a floppy disk.

Finding your Outlook Express messages

You can use the Windows Find command to find and open the folder containing your Outlook Express message files. Follow these steps:

1. Click the Start button on the Windows taskbar and choose Search ➪ Files Or Folders.

2. In the Named box of the Find dialog box, type ***.dbx;**.

3. Click the drop-down arrow next to the Look In box and select your hard drive (C:).

4. Click the Search Now button.

5. When the search is complete, highlight one of the files shown in the Search Results dialog box (for example, highlight Drafts.mbx) and then choose File ➪ Open Containing Folder from the menu bar.

The folder containing your Outlook Express messages opens on the Windows desktop. Note that if you share your PC with other users you will want to be careful to open the folder that shows your user name.

Compacting a folder

Outlook Express compacts your message folders automatically to eliminate wasted space. You also can compact a folder manually at any time. First, open the folder you want to compact. Then choose File ➪ Folder ➪ Compact and wait a moment while the compactor cleans up the wasted space. (If you prefer to compact all the folders at once, choose File ➪ Folder ➪ Compact All Folders instead.)

Tip Compacting is not the same as compressing. Outlook Express can directly use any folders it has compacted; you needn't decompress them in any way.

Importing and Exporting Messages

If you recently switched from Eudora Pro, Eudora Light, Microsoft Exchange, Microsoft Internet Mail For Windows 3.1, Microsoft Outlook, Microsoft Windows Messaging, Netscape Communicator, or Netscape Mail, you may have a bunch of messages you want to import for use in Outlook Express. Conversely, you may want to export your Outlook Express messages for use in Microsoft Outlook or Microsoft Exchange, predecessors of Outlook Express. As the following sections explain, importing and exporting messages between Outlook Express and other e-mail programs is easy.

Note The first time you start Outlook Express on your PC, you may be taken to the Outlook Express Import Wizard, which asks if you want to import messages from previously installed e-mail software.

Importing messages

To import messages from another e-mail program into Outlook Express, use the following steps:

1. Open Outlook Express and choose File ➪ Import ➪ Messages from the menu bar. An Outlook Express Import dialog box appears.

2. From the "Select an e-mail client to import from" list, choose the type of file to import. Your choices are Eudora Pro or Light (through V3.0), Microsoft Exchange, Microsoft Internet Mail (32-bit Version), Microsoft Internet Mail For Windows 3.1, Microsoft Outlook, Microsoft Outlook Express 4, Microsoft Outlook Express 5, Microsoft Windows Messaging, Netscape Communicator, and Netscape Mail (V2 or V3).

3. Click Next.

4. Respond to any prompts that appear. The prompts will depend on your choice in Step 2.

When importing is complete, the messages will appear in the appropriate Outlook Express folders (of course, all the original messages are still intact in your old e-mail program). To view the imported messages, simply click the Outlook Express folder in which you're interested.

Tip   If necessary, Outlook Express will create new folders to hold messages from the original e-mail program. For example, if the old e-mail program contained messages in a folder named "Good Stuff," a Good Stuff folder will appear in the Outlook Express folder list and Outlook bar, and it will contain messages from the Good Stuff folder in your old program.

Exporting messages

Use the following steps to export your Outlook Express messages to either Microsoft Outlook or Microsoft Exchange:

1. Open Outlook Express and choose File ➪ Export ➪ Messages from the menu bar.

2. When you see the message "This will Export messages from Outlook Express to Microsoft Outlook or Microsoft Exchange," click OK.

3. When the Choose Profile dialog box appears, choose a Microsoft Outlook or Microsoft Exchange profile from the Profile Name drop-down list and then click OK. (If you have no idea what profiles are, click the Help button in the Choose Profile dialog box.)

4. When prompted to select the folders to export, choose All Folders or choose Selected Folders, and then click, Shift+click, or Ctrl+click the folders you want to export.

5. Choose OK to export the messages.

Using the Address Book

Outlook Express has a handy address book you can use to record, maintain, and find people's addresses, phone numbers, and, of course, e-mail addresses. You also can use the Address Book to fill in the e-mail addresses of your recipients automatically when you compose a new message or when you reply to or forward a message.

To get to the Address Book, use any of the following approaches:

✦ From the Windows Me desktop, click the Start button and choose Programs ➪ Accessories ➪ Address Book.

✦ From any Outlook Express window, choose Tools ➪ Address Book from the menu bar or press Ctrl+Shift+B.

The Address Book window opens, perhaps empty if you've never used it before, as in Figure 9-32. Now you can add new contacts and new groups, change the properties of or delete any existing entry, search or print the Address Book, send mail to anyone in the Address Book, and more. When you finish using the Address Book window, click its Close (X) button in the upper-right corner or choose File ➪ Exit from its menu bar.

Tip

As a shortcut while using Outlook Express, you can open the Address Book by clicking either the Addresses toolbar button or the Select Recipients toolbar button, whichever is available. If you click the Addresses button, you'll see the Address Book dialog box shown in Figure 9-32. If you click Select Recipients, you'll see the Select Recipients dialog box, shown later in Figure 9-38.

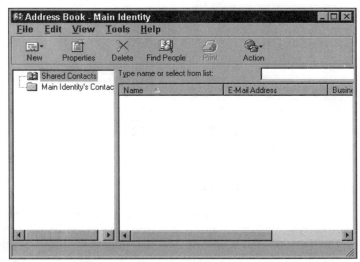

Figure 9-32: The Address Book prior to entering any names and addresses

Adding names and addresses

Adding people's names and addresses to the Address Book is simple. First, open the Address Book. Then, click the New button on the toolbar or choose File ➪ New Contact from the menu bar, or press Ctrl+N. The Properties dialog box, like the one shown in Figure 9-33, appears.

Tip

Anytime you're viewing an e-mail message in a separate window, you can quickly copy any underlined address in the From:, To:, Cc:, or Bcc: area to your Address Book. Simply right-click the address and choose Add To Address Book from the shortcut menu. You'll be taken to the Name tab of a Properties dialog box and you can complete the contact information as explained in this section. (You cannot enter duplicate addresses.)

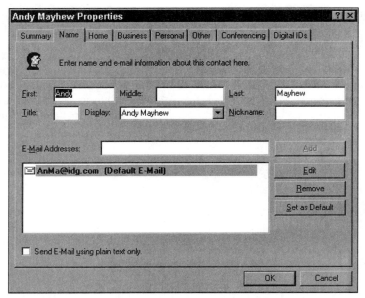

Figure 9-33: Sample entry for the Name tab of the Address Book

You can type in any person's name and (if applicable) e-mail address.

Note When you enter the First, Middle, and Last name fields, Outlook Express automatically fills in the Display name field from your entries (you can edit the Display name field, of course). The Name column of your Address Book shows the Display name.

If the person has several e-mail addresses, you can type one at a time, clicking the Add button to record each one. The first address you enter is automatically assigned as the default e-mail address. You can change that, however, by clicking the e-mail address you'll send to most often and then clicking the Set as Default button. If you want to remove an e-mail address from the list, click it and then click the Remove button. To change an e-mail address, click it, click the Edit button, change the address, and press Enter.

Tip If the contact has an e-mail program that cannot read HTML-formatted mail, select the Send E-Mail Using Plain Text Only box.

The Home, Business, Personal, Other, Conferencing, and Digital IDs tabs enable you to record additional information about this person. For example, in Figure 9-34, I've typed some sample information into the Home tab.

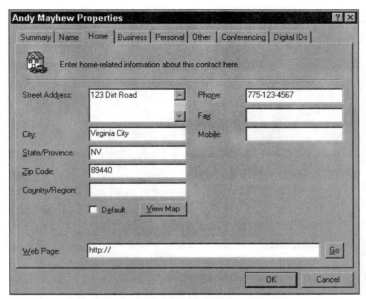

Figure 9-34: More sample information for one person in the Address Book

As explained in the section "Customizing the default mail options," which appears later in this chapter, you can have your Address Book updated automatically with the address of every e-mail message to which you respond. And if you already have an address book in Eudora Light, LDIF-LDAP Data Interchange Format, Microsoft Exchange, Microsoft Internet Mail for Windows 3.1, Netscape, Netscape Communicator, or a comma-separated text file, you can import it into your Address Book and save yourself a bunch of time as explained later in "Importing and exporting address books."

Creating groups and mailing lists

Suppose you have a group of friends who like to receive jokes by e-mail, or you're organizing a family reunion, or maybe you're a project leader. When sending e-mail to all these folks, you certainly won't want to specify each person's e-mail address individually. Instead, you'll want to enter the name of a group — such as Joke list, or Reunion list, or Project team — and have Outlook Express automatically know to send your message to each address on the list. Creating a group of e-mail addresses is easy. As always, begin by opening the Address Book. Then follow these steps:

1. Choose File ➪ New Group from the menu bar or press Ctrl+G. A Properties dialog box appears. (Figure 9-35 shows a completed example.)

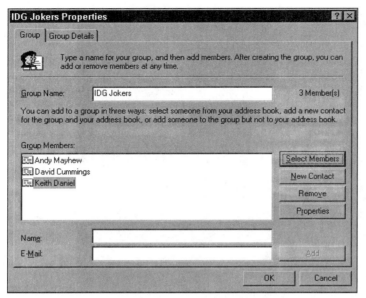

Figure 9-35: A completed group in the group Properties dialog box

2. In the Group Name box, type the name for your group (for example, Project Team).

3. Do any of the following, as needed:

- To select addresses already in your Address Book, click the Select Members button and then double-click the names of the people or groups you want to add to your group. When you finish, click OK.

- To create a new Address Book entry on the fly and add it to the group, click the New Contact button, fill in the Properties dialog box (shown back in Figure 9-33), and click OK.

- To remove an entry from the group, click it and then click the Remove button. This does not remove the entry from your Address Book, just from the group itself.

- To update the details about any group member, click the member's entry and then click the Properties button (or double-click the member's entry). Edit the entry as needed and click OK.

4. If you want to add some notes about the group, click in the Notes box and type away.

5. When you finish creating the group, click OK in the Properties dialog box.

The group name will appear in the Address Book in boldface text, with a little group icon beside it. If you point to the group name with your mouse, a list of the group members will appear near the mouse pointer.

Tip   You can point to any entry in the Address Book and Outlook Express will display the name and e-mail address in a pop-up box. Very cool! (If you don't see the pop-up box right away, try clicking an empty area in the list of names and e-mail addresses and then pointing to an entry.)

Once you've set up some groups, you can click any group in the list to see only the members of that group or click Address Book to view the entire Address Book.

Tip   You can quickly send a message to group members while you're viewing the Groups List in the Address Book. To send a message to everyone in the group, click the name of the group and then choose Tools ➪ Action ➪ Send Mail. Or, to send to selected people in the group, click the name of the group, use the Shift+click or Ctrl+click technique to select the members in the right side of the window, and then choose Tools ➪ Action ➪ Send Mail. A New Message window will open with the group members listed automatically in the To: box of the message. This feature is cooler than an Eskimo's igloo!

Changing and deleting Address Book entries

Of course, you'll probably need to change the entries in your Address Book occasionally. It's easy. First, open the Address Book window and click the entry you want to change. Then, click the Properties button on the Address Book toolbar, or choose File ➪ Properties from the menu bar, or press Alt+Enter. As a shortcut, you can double-click the entry you want to change. Now change the entry using the same techniques you used to create it in the first place. When you finish, click OK to return to the Address Book window.

To delete an entry, highlight it in the Address Book. Or, if you want to delete multiple entries, select them by using the same Shift+click or Ctrl+click techniques discussed earlier in the section "Working with several messages at once." Then, click the Delete button on the Address Book toolbar, or choose File ➪ Delete from the menu bar, or press the Delete key. When prompted for confirmation, click Yes. Poof! The entries are gone.

Searching the Address Book

As your Address Book grows, you may have trouble finding a particular entry simply by scrolling up and down. But it's no problem at all because you can search for entries in several ways. The easiest method is to click the Type Name Or Select From List box and then type the first part of the name you're trying to find. As you type, Outlook Express highlights the closest matching entry. The more information you type, the narrower the search. In Figure 9-36, for example, I typed **ke** and Outlook Express immediately highlighted the name Keith.

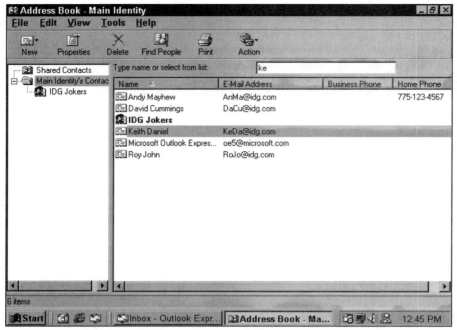

Figure 9-36: I'm searching for a person whose name begins with *ke*.

You also can find entries quickly by sorting your Address Book. The techniques are similar to those already discussed in the section "Sorting the message list." To sort by a particular column, click the column heading (click it again to reverse the sort order). You also can choose options from the View ⇨ Sort By menu.

Doing fancy Find People searches

You can do an even fancier Find People search of your Address Book or various online directory services. To begin, click the Find button on the Address Book toolbar, or choose Edit ⇨ Find from the menu bar, or press Ctrl+F. When the Find People dialog box appears, choose the name of the address book or directory you want to search in the Look in drop-down list, fill in the blanks with the text you want to look for on the People tab, and then click Find Now. (If you chose an online directory service, you may be prompted to connect to the Internet.) Figure 9-37 shows the results of searching for Alan Simpson in the WhoWhere online directory.

Note You'll learn more about online directory services in the section "Using online directory services" later in this chapter.

You can work with any address shown at the bottom of the Find People dialog box. First, click the entry to highlight it. Then, do one of the following:

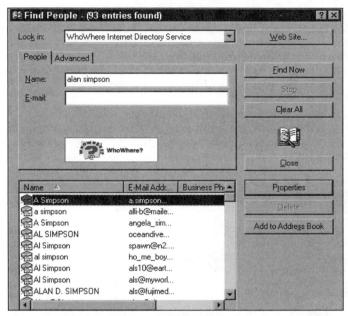

Figure 9-37: The Find People dialog box after choosing the WhoWhere directory, typing **alan simpson** in the Name box, and then clicking Find Now

✦ To view or change the entry, click the Properties button or double-click the entry.

✦ To delete the entry, click the Delete button or press Delete and then choose Yes to confirm the deletion (available only if you're searching the Address Book).

✦ To add the entry to your Address Book, click the Add to Address Book button (available only if you're searching an online directory service).

If you want to do a new search, click the Clear All button; then, choose an address book or directory to search, fill in the boxes on the People tab, and click Find Now. If you want to visit the Web site for the currently selected online directory service, click the Web Site button. When you finish using the Find People dialog box, click Close and you'll return to the Address Book.

Choosing recipients from your Address Book

Several ways exist to choose recipients from your Address Book when you're composing a new message, replying to a message, or forwarding a message.

If you're starting from the Address Book, select the addresses you want to include in the To: box of a new message. You can use the click, Shift+click, and Ctrl+click selection methods discussed earlier. Now click the Action button on the toolbar and choose Send Mail or choose Tools ➪ Action ➪ Send Mail. A New Message window opens and the To: box includes the addresses you selected.

If you're starting from the New Message window, the Reply window, or the Forward window, click the little Rolodex card next to the To:, Cc:, or Bcc: box. You'll see a Select Recipients dialog box, like the one shown in Figure 9-38. From here you can take any of the following actions as needed:

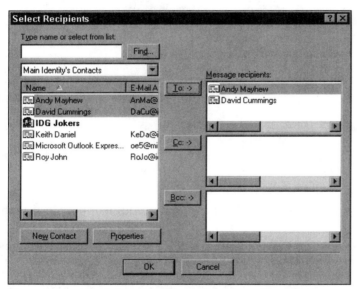

Figure 9-38: The Select Recipients dialog box after selecting two recipients and clicking the To: button

✦ To select the name(s) you want from the Name list, use the click, Shift+click, and Ctrl+click methods described earlier in the section "Working with several messages at once." Then, click the To:, Cc:, or Bcc: button depending on whether you want to add the names to the To:, Cc:, or Bcc: address boxes in your message.

✦ To highlight a name quickly in the Name list, click the "Type name or select from list" box and type the first part of the name (see "Searching the Address Book"). Now select the name you want (if it isn't highlighted already) and then click the To:, Cc:, or Bcc: button as appropriate.

✦ To do a Find People search, click the Find button and search as explained earlier in "Doing fancy Find People searches." After clicking Find Now, select the names you want and then click the To:, Cc:, or Bcc: button as appropriate.

When you finish using the Select Recipients dialog box, click OK. The e-mail recipient names you selected will appear in the address boxes of your message. (If you added a name by accident, simply click the name in the address box to select it and then press the Delete key.)

Now that you're an ace with your Address Book, why not try this great shortcut for specifying e-mail recipients? It works anytime you're using the New Message window, the Reply window, or the Forward window:

1. Click the To:, Cc:, or Bcc: box of the message as usual.

2. Type any part of a name or e-mail address that you know is in your Address Book. For example, type **alan** or **simpson** or **coolnerds** if you've entered my name and e-mail address in your Address Book. If you want to enter more than one recipient, type a semicolon, and then type the next name or e-mail address.

3. Repeat Steps 1 and 2 as needed.

4. If the correct recipient names aren't filled in automatically when you finish entering names, click the Check Names button on the toolbar or press Ctrl+K, or choose Tools ➪ Check Names from the menu bar.

Outlook Express will do its best to match and fill in the names you chose. If it needs your help to decide which address to include, you'll see a Check Names dialog box, as shown in Figure 9-39. Click the address you want to use and then click OK (or click Show More Names, highlight the name you want, and then click OK).

Tip If "Automatically complete e-mail addresses when composing" is checked on the Send tab of the Options dialog box—as it is by default—Outlook Express will fill in any match it finds in your Address Book as you type in the To:, Cc:, or Bcc: box of the message and you can skip Step 4. If more than one entry matches your typing, Outlook Express matches only the first entry it finds. For example, if your Address Book includes two Alans—Alan A. Abalone and Alan C. Simpson—Outlook Express matches Alan A. Abalone if you type **alan.** To match the entry for Alan C. Simpson in this example, enter **simp** or part of the e-mail address, such as **cool.** See the section "Personalizing Outlook Express" later in this chapter for information on customizing the Send options.

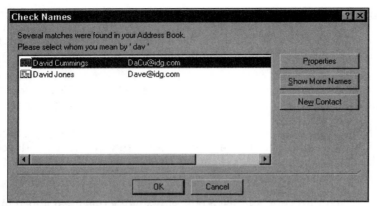

Figure 9-39: If Outlook Express can't match a name you entered, it displays the Check Names dialog box.

Printing your Address Book

Who was it that said you can't take it with you? If they were talking about the Address Book, they were wrong. You can easily print a paper copy of your Address Book to take on a trip or to drop into your little black book by following these steps:

1. Open the Address Book (click the Addresses button on the main Outlook Express toolbar).

2. If you only want to print certain addresses, select them with the usual click, Shift+click, Ctrl+click, or Find methods.

3. Click the Print button on the Address Book toolbar or choose File ➪ Print from the menu bar, or press Ctrl+P.

4. In the Print dialog box (see Figure 9-40), choose a printer, a print range, a print style, and the number of copies to print.

5. Click OK to start printing.

Using online directory services

The Internet is swarming with online directory services that enable you to look up e-mail addresses. Outlook Express can automatically access several of the most popular online directory services — Yahoo! People Search, Bigfoot, InfoSpace, InfoSpace Business, SwitchBoard, VeriSign, and WhoWhere — but you can add others, if necessary. Once a directory service is added to the list, you can search that directory from Outlook Express, as explained earlier in the section "Doing fancy Find People searches."

To view or change the directory lists Outlook Express can search, choose Tools ➪ Accounts from the Address Book or main Outlook Express menu bar, and then click the Directory Service tab in the Internet Accounts dialog box (if it isn't selected already).

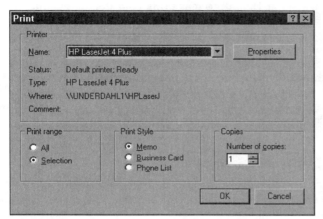

Figure 9-40: Use the Print dialog box to print a copy of your Address Book.

If you want to add a new directory service to the list, click the Add button (or click Add and then choose Directory Service). You'll be taken to the Internet Connection Wizard, which will prompt you for information including the Light Directory Access Protocol (LDAP) server, whether the server requires you to log on, whether you want to check e-mail addresses using this directory service, and the name of the Internet directory service. Fill in each box and click Next or Finish to continue (you may need to contact the directory service if you're uncertain how to fill in the dialog boxes). When you finish adding the service, you'll see it in the list, as shown in Figure 9-41.

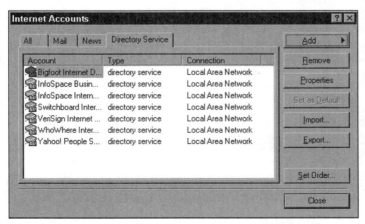

Figure 9-41: This is the Directory Service tab, which lists the online directory services.

Updating the directory service list is easy. First, click the name of the directory service you want to change. Then, click Remove to remove the service from the list, click Properties to view or change the settings you assigned in the Internet Connection Wizard, or click Set as Default to make this your default account. If you want to change the order used to check names when you send e-mail, click Set Order, move the directory services up or down in the list that appears, and choose OK. When you finish using the Internet Accounts dialog box, click Close.

Tip   Although you can have Outlook Express check names against the online directory service when you're sending e-mail, everything will go faster if you search the online directory occasionally and add selected addresses to your local Address Book (as explained in the section "Doing fancy Find People searches").

Backing up your Address Book

Just as you'll want to back up your message folders, you'll also want to back up your Address Book. The Address Book is stored in a file named username.wab in the folder C:\Windows\Application Data\Microsoft\Address Book, where *username* is your e-mail name or network user name.

Even a large address book like mine will fit conveniently on a floppy disk, so compressing the Address Book files before backing them up isn't important. Simply use My Computer, Windows Explorer, or Find to open the C:\ Windows\Application Data\Microsoft \Address Book folder. Then select the Address Book file and copy it to your backup disk.

Importing and exporting address books

If you used another e-mail program before switching to Outlook Express, you probably already have a bunch of addresses stored in an address book. Back in the bad old days, switching to a new e-mail program was a major pain; you had to re-enter all your contact information from scratch. There was no way to import existing addresses into the new address book. Fortunately, those bad old days are over, at least where Outlook Express is concerned. You can import address books from several different e-mail programs into the Address Book. Likewise, you can export your Address Book to a file many other e-mail programs can import and use in their address books.

Importing an address book

To import an address book from another e-mail program into your Address Book, follow these steps:

1. Choose File ➪ Import ➪ Other_Address Book from the Address Book or the main Outlook Express menu bar.

2. When the Address Book Import Tool dialog box appears, click the import format you want. Your choices are shown in Figure 9-42.

3. Click Import.

4. Respond to any dialog boxes that appear next. The prompts will depend upon your choice for the import format in Step 2.

5. When you see the message "Address book import has completed successfully," click OK and then click Close to exit the Address Book Import Tool dialog box.

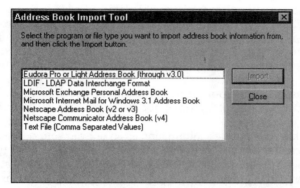

Figure 9-42: The Address Book Import Tool dialog box

Tip

When you import address books (or vCards), Outlook Express will check to see whether an address you're importing already exists in your Address Book. If it does, you'll be asked whether you want to replace the old entry with the new one. Choose Yes to replace the old entry or No to keep it.

The next time you open your Address Book, it will include any addresses you had before, plus all the addresses you imported.

Exporting your Address Book

Exporting your Address Book to a format another e-mail program can use is equally easy:

1. Choose File ➪ Export ➪ Address Book from the Address Book or the main Outlook Express menu bar.

2. When the Address Book Export Tool dialog box appears, click the export format you want. Your choices are Microsoft Exchange Personal Address Book and Text File (Comma Separated Values). Most e-mail programs can import comma-separated value text files if they can import any files at all. Click Export.

3. Respond to any additional dialog boxes that appear. The prompts will depend on your choice for the export format in Step 2.

4. When you see the message "Address book export has completed successfully," click OK and then click Close to exit the Address Book Export Tool dialog box.

Importing and exporting vCards

vCards — or business cards in Outlook Express parlance — are a standardized electronic business card that can be exchanged between e-mail, address book, communications, personal planner, and other types of programs. vCards can even be exchanged between different types of devices and platforms, including desktop computers, laptops, personal digital assistants (PDAs), and telephony equipment. Thus, vCard files (which have a .vcf file extension) offer a flexible, universal format — something like Esperanto for the computerized address book world.

Outlook Express can import and export vCard files with ease. (Unfortunately, you can import or export just one vCard at a time, not an entire address book. Oh, well.)

 Importing a vCard file adds the file's information as an entry in your Address Book. Exporting a vCard creates a vCard file from an entry in your Address Book (you can send that vCard file to other digital devices and operating systems that accept them). You also can add vCards as signatures to outgoing messages, as explained in the section "Setting up an automatic signature," later in this chapter.

Importing from vCards

Follow these steps to import an address from a vCard file into your Address Book:

1. Open the Address Book and choose File ➪ Import ➪ Business Card (vCard) from the menu bar.

2. When prompted for a filename, locate and double-click the vCard file you want to import.

The selected address appears in a Properties dialog box like the one you use to create new e-mail addresses. Enter any additional information you want on the Personal, Home, Business, Other, NetMeeting, or Digital IDs tab, and then click OK. Voila! The new address appears in your Address Book.

Exporting to vCards

To export an address from your Address Book to a vCard file, follow these steps:

1. Open the Address Book.

2. Select the address you want to export. You can select only one address and groups aren't allowed.

3. Choose File ⇨ Export ⇨ Business Card (vCard) from the menu bar.

4. When prompted for a filename, type a filename for the address (for example, **alan**) and choose a drive and folder location, if you wish. You can omit the .vcf extension because Outlook Express will add it automatically.

5. Click Save.

The selected address is saved in vCard format to the location you specified in Step 4.

Personalizing Outlook Express

You can personalize both the appearance and behavior of Outlook Express to your liking. First I'll describe ways to customize the Outlook Express window. Then I'll explore ways to change the program's behavior, to create folders, and to filter incoming messages using the Inbox Assistant.

Customizing the Outlook Express window

Throughout this chapter, I've shown you examples of the Outlook Express window in which the Outlook bar, folder list, folder bar, tip of the day, toolbar, status bar, preview pane, and preview header are visible. The toolbar buttons include explanatory text, the message text appears in a medium-sized font, and the preview pane appears below the messages. You'll probably find the default setup easiest to use, but you certainly can change things, if you like.

Tip By default, all the doodads mentioned appear in the Outlook Express window, except the Outlook Bar.

Choosing what appears in the window

You can use options on the View menu of the main Outlook Express window to choose which features appear onscreen. The options are controlled by the Window Layout Properties dialog box, shown in Figure 9-43. To open this dialog box, choose View ⇨ Layout from the main Outlook Express menu bar.

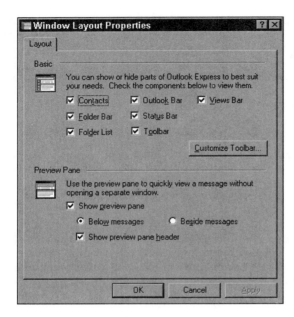

Figure 9-43: These are the options for the Window Layout Properties dialog box. Choose View ⇨ Layout to get here.

Arranging the preview pane

The preview pane enables you to preview your message by clicking it in the message list. You can hide the preview pane altogether or display it below messages or beside them. To begin, choose View ⇨ Layout from the main Outlook Express menu bar. Then, in the Window Layout Properties dialog box, do any of the following:

✦ To display the preview pane, check Show Preview Pane; to hide the preview pane, uncheck Show Preview Pane. When the preview pane is hidden, you must double-click a message in the message list to read it.

✦ To split the window so the preview pane appears next to the messages (see Figure 9-44), check Show Preview Pane and choose Beside Messages.

✦ To split the window so the preview pane appears below the messages (as shown throughout this chapter, except in Figure 9-44), check Show Preview Pane and choose Below Messages.

✦ To display or hide the preview pane header (the gray band above the message in the preview pane), check Show Preview Pane and check or uncheck Show Preview Pane Header.

✦ When you finish making changes, choose OK.

Resizing the lists, panes, and columns

You can resize the lists, preview pane, or columns for easier viewing of the information they contain. Here's how:

1. Move the mouse pointer to the dividing line for the pane or the column you want to resize. The mouse pointer changes to a two-headed arrow (see Figure 9-44).

2. Drag the mouse in the direction of the arrows.

3. When the pane or the column is the size you want, release the mouse button.

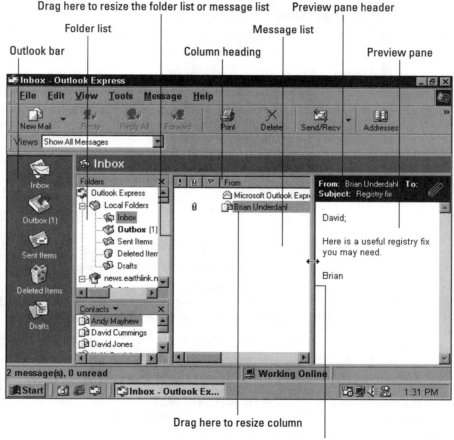

Figure 9-44: The Outlook Express screen with the preview pane displayed next to the messages and the mouse pointer poised to resize the preview pane

That's it! If you don't like the results, simply repeat these three steps.

Configuring columns in the message list

In addition to resizing the columns, you can add or remove columns in the message list or reposition them by following these steps:

1. Choose View ⇨ Columns from the main Outlook Express menu bar. You'll see the Columns dialog box, shown in Figure 9-45.

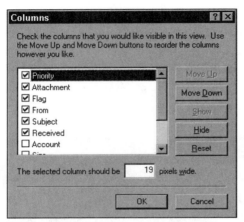

Figure 9-45: Use the Columns dialog box to configure columns.

2. Do any of the following:

   • To add a column to the message list, select the column you want to add.

   • To remove a column from the message list, deselect it.

   • To reposition a column in the message list, click its name and then click Move Up or Move Down as needed (this moves the column heading to the left or right, respectively, in the actual message list).

   • To return to the default columns for the message list, click the Reset button.

3. Click OK.

The new list of columns will appear in the Outlook Express message list. If necessary, you can resize the columns as explained in the previous section.

Tip　If you only want to reposition an existing column, you can skip the Columns dialog box altogether and use the drag-and-drop technique. That is, drag the column button left or right along the top of the message list until the column is where you want it, and then release the mouse button.

Customizing the toolbar

The main Outlook Express toolbar is customizable. You can add or remove its buttons, change its position, and choose whether to display its text labels. To begin, go to the main Outlook Express window and choose View ➪ Layout and click the Customize Toolbar button. Or, right-click the toolbar and choose Customize from the submenu that appears.

You'll see the Customize Toolbar dialog box shown in Figure 9-46. The techniques for customizing the toolbar buttons are similar to those for customizing the columns in the message list. You can double-click a button under Available Buttons to add it to the toolbar or double-click a button under Toolbar Buttons to remove it. To reposition a button, click it under Toolbar Buttons and then click the Move Up or Move Down button as needed. Anytime you want to return to the default toolbar, click Reset. You can experiment with the alignment options and turn the text labels on and off by clicking the option you want. When you finish making changes, click Close.

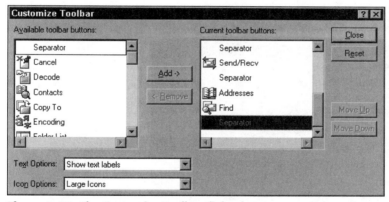

Figure 9-46: The Customize Toolbar dialog box

Tip   As a shortcut, you can drag the items from the Available Buttons list in the Customize Toolbar dialog box to the Toolbar Buttons list and vice versa. You also can drag items in the Toolbar Buttons list up or down to reposition them.

Customizing the default mail options

Tons of options exist for customizing the way Outlook Express behaves and most of them are available from the Options dialog box. To open this dialog box, choose Tools ➪ Options from the main Outlook Express menu. Next, click the tab you want to use, change the settings as needed, and then click OK to save your changes. In the following sections, we look at the General, Send, Read, and Connection tabs in the Options dialog box.

Tip

You can learn more about any option in the Options dialog box. Simply select the tab you want to use, click the question mark (?) button at the upper-right corner of the dialog box, and then click the option puzzling you. A description appears near the mouse pointer. To clear the description, press Esc.

General options

The General tab of the Options dialog box offers features that don't fall neatly into any other category (hence, the name General). As Figure 9-47 shows, all the options are toggles: When you check them, the feature is turned on; when you uncheck them, the feature is turned off. For example, you can choose whether to play a sound when new messages arrive, whether to check for new messages automatically and how often to check, whether to empty deleted messages from the Deleted Items folder when you exit Outlook Express, and whether to put e-mail addresses of people you reply to in your Address Book automatically. The settings shown in Figure 9-47 are the ones I find most convenient.

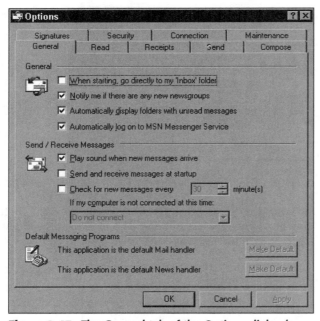

Figure 9-47: The General tab of the Options dialog box

Note

The tabs in the Options dialog box contain some options that apply to e-mail and others that apply to newsgroups (the topic of Chapter 10).

Send options

Figure 9-48 shows the Send tab of the Options dialog box. As you can see, the Mail Sending Format area on this tab controls the format of messages you send. Check or clear the boxes as needed.

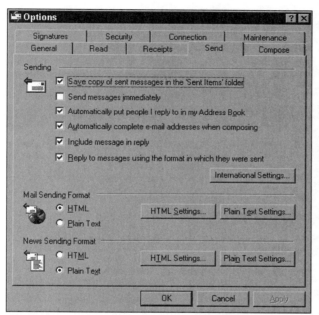

Figure 9-48: Use the Send tab of the Options dialog box to specify your sending options.

The default format for sending mail is HTML, but you can select either HTML or Plain Text in the Mail Sending Format area and then click the appropriate Settings button to change the settings as needed.

Tip　If you want to change the format of a message on which you're currently working, choose Format ➪ Rich Text (HTML) or Format ➪ Plain Text from the menu bar on the New Message, Reply, or Forward windows.

Read options

The options on the Read tab of the Options dialog box (see Figure 9-49) control what happens when Outlook Express delivers new messages from your service provider. You can choose whether to mark previewed messages as read and how long to wait before marking them. You also can choose the font used to display your messages.

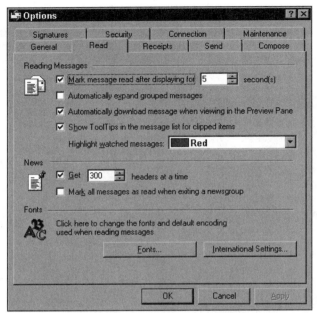

Figure 9-49: Use the Read tab of the Options dialog box to specify incoming message options.

Connections options

The Connection tab of the Options dialog box, shown in Figure 9-50, makes life easier for people with modem connections to the Internet. From here, you can specify which connection to use. You also can choose whether you want Outlook Express to warn you to cancel a connection that isn't working (if you have more than one dial-up networking connection) and whether to hang up automatically when sending, receiving, or downloading messages.

Setting up an automatic signature

Outlook Express can automatically insert a signature at the bottom of your messages, which will save you time and trouble. To use the automatic signature options, choose Tools ➪ Options from the Outlook Express menu bar and select the Signatures tab, shown in Figure 9-51. Now, click the New button to enable the Edit signature box, shown in Figure 9-52. Choose the options you want, as described in the list that follows. When you finish, choose OK.

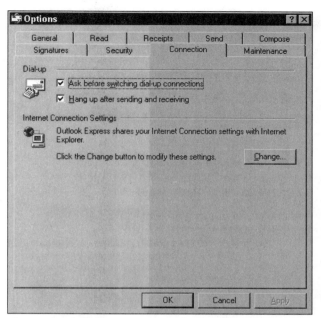

Figure 9-50: The Connections tab of the Options dialog box enables you to control your modem options.

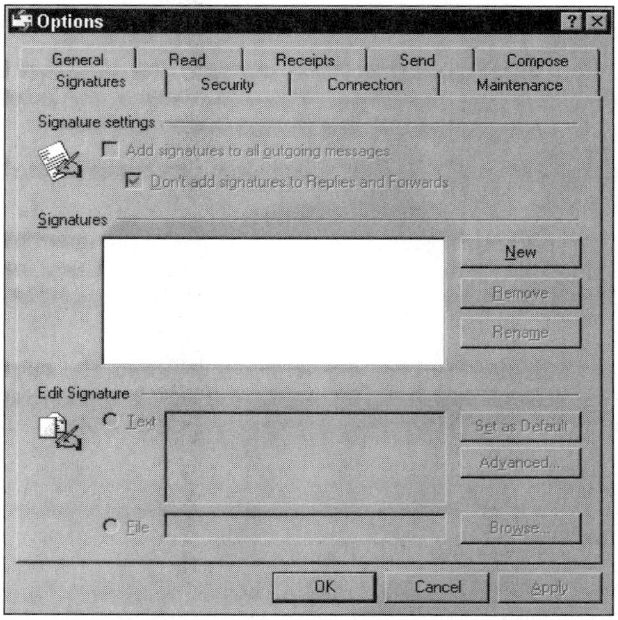

Figure 9-51: The Signatures tab of the Options dialog box

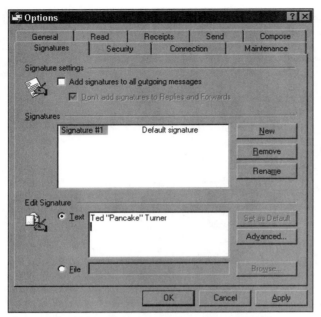

Figure 9-52: The Signature tab box, after I filled in a Text signature

You can choose any of these Signature options:

✦ **Add signatures to all outgoing messages:** When checked, the signature text appears at the bottom of outgoing messages. When unchecked, the automatic signature does not appear and you must sign the messages yourself.

✦ **Text:** When selected, the automatic signature uses text you typed in the box next to the Text option.

✦ **File:** When selected, the automatic signature uses text in the file specified next to the File option. (You can use the Browse button to help locate and insert the filename.) The signature file can be a text file (.txt) or an HTML file (.htm or .html).

✦ **Don't add signatures to Replies and Forwards:** When checked, the signature text is not added to replies and forwards. When unchecked, it is added to replies and forwards.

Of course, you insert signatures and business cards automatically, as described here. You also can insert them manually anytime you like:

✦ If you set up a signature text or file, you can manually insert your signature in a message. Starting from the New Message, Reply, or Forward window, position the insertion point where the signature should appear in the editing area of your message. Then choose Insert ⇨ Signature from the menu bar.

✦ If you set up a personal business card (vCard), you can insert it manually by choosing Insert ⇨ My Business Card from the message window menu. The vCard icon will appear below the stamp icon in the message window. (To remove the vCard, choose Insert ⇨ My Business Card again. The vCard icon will disappear.)

Tip

If you attach a vCard to your message or you receive a message with an attached vCard, the vCard appears in your message as a Rolodex card icon with a big *V* on it. You can then click or right-click the vCard icon and choose Open or Delete from the shortcut menu that appears.

Choosing custom stationery

People using snail mail (the slow stuff delivered by the post office) often pride themselves on the fancy stationery they use. With Outlook Express, your electronic mail messages can use stationery just as fancy. Or, if you'd rather not use fancy stationery, you can compose your messages in any font installed on your computer.

Caution

The stationery and font options work best for messages composed in rich text (HTML) format, rather than plain text format.

To use the automatic stationery options, choose Tools ⇨ Options and select the Compose tab in the Options dialog box. Now, choose any of the options that follow, and when you finish using the Options dialog box, click OK:

✦ **Compose Font:** Click the Font Settings button in the Compose Font area to select the font used for outgoing messages. When the Font dialog box appears, choose the Font, Font Style, Size, Effects, and Color options you want and choose OK.

✦ **Stationery:** Choose either Mail or News.

✦ **Select:** After choosing Mail or News, click the Select button to specify the stationery file you want to use for outgoing messages. You'll see the Select Stationery dialog box, shown in Figure 9-53. Now do any of the following, and then click OK to return to the Stationery dialog box:

• To select an existing stationery design, click its name in the Stationery list. A thumbnail view of the stationery appears in the Preview box.

- To select a design stored in a rich text (HTML) file on your computer, click the Look in list box and then locate and double-click the filename you want. HTML files have a .htm or .html extension.

- To edit a stationery design, click the design you want to edit in the Stationery list and then click the Edit button. When you finish editing, choose File ➪ Exit.

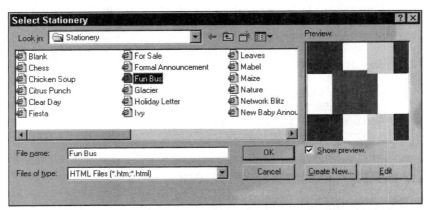

Figure 9-53: The Select Stationery dialog box appears when you click the Select button in the Options dialog box.

Tip

Before composing a new message, you can manually select a stationery file. Starting from the Outlook Express window, choose Message ➪ New Message Using and choose one of the stationery options listed. Or, choose Select Stationery and then locate and double-click the stationery file (.htm or .html) you want to use.

Leaving mail on the server

You already know how to customize your e-mail account settings by changing the settings in the mail account Properties dialog box, which opens when you choose Tools ➪ Accounts and double-click the name of the account you want to change. The Advanced tab in this dialog box offers a "Leave a copy of messages on server" option (see Figure 9-54). Most e-mail client programs have a similar option. As a general rule, if you use only one e-mail program, you'll want to leave this option deselected (unchecked) to keep mail from building up on your mail server.

If you use more than one program to check your e-mail, however, you should allow only one of those programs to remove the mail from the server. Otherwise, you may end up with some e-mail messages in one e-mail client program and some messages in another, which makes keeping track of messages difficult. If you choose to leave a copy of messages on the server, you also can choose when to delete the messages as Figure 9-54 shows.

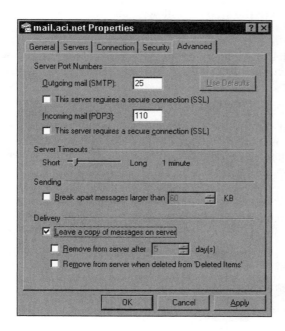

Figure 9-54: The Advanced tab of the mail account Properties dialog box enables you to choose whether to leave mail on your server and when to remove it.

Creating your own folders

Outlook Express automatically comes with the following folders for storing your e-mail messages:

- ✦ **Inbox:** Stores your incoming messages
- ✦ **Outbox:** Stores messages waiting to be sent
- ✦ **Sent Items:** Stores messages you already sent
- ✦ **Deleted Items:** Stores your deleted messages until you delete them manually or Outlook Express deletes them for you
- ✦ **Drafts:** Stores draft messages you've saved with the File ➪ Save command while composing them

Chances are, however, that you'll want to create some folders of your own to store copies of messages regarding specific projects or people. Folders offer a great way to organize your messages so you can find them easily.

Tip

When working with folders, be sure to display the folder list. If the folder list is not visible, choose View ➪ Layout, check Folder List, and choose OK.

Creating folders is a breeze. Here are the steps to follow:

1. Starting from the main Outlook Express window, choose File ➪ Folder ➪ New from the menu. Or right-click any folder except the "news" folder and choose New Folder from the shortcut menu. You'll see a Create Folder dialog box, as shown in Figure 9-55.

2. In the Folder Name box, type a name for the new folder.

3. Click the folder that should contain the new folder (that is, click the parent folder). If the parent folder is hidden within a higher-level folder, click the plus (+) sign next to the higher-level folders until you see the parent folder you want and then click the parent folder.

4. Choose OK.

In Figure 9-55, I created a folder named News Project inside the Inbox folder. I typed the new folder name into the Folder Name box; then I clicked the Inbox folder and chose OK.

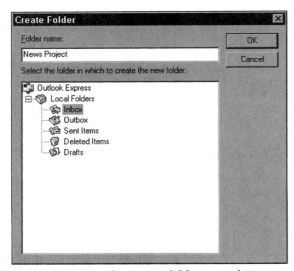

Figure 9-55: Creating a new folder named News Project below the Inbox folder

Using folders and subfolders

Any folders you create will appear in the folder list at the left side of the main Outlook Express window (top-level folders also will appear in the Outlook bar). Here's how to expand, collapse, and open a folder in the folder list:

✦ To expand a folder so its folders or subfolders are visible in the folders list, double-click the folder icon (for example, News Project, in Figure 9-56) or click the plus (+) sign next to the icon.

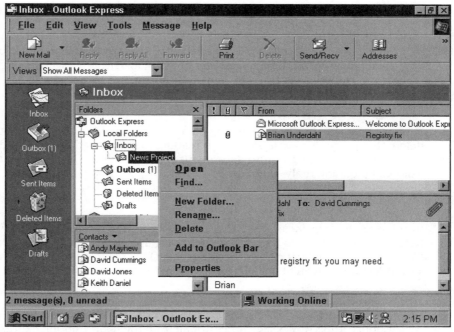

Figure 9-56: The News Project folder, which I right-clicked to display the shortcut menu

✦ To collapse a folder so its folders or subfolders are hidden, double-click the folder icon or click the minus (–) sign next to the icon.

✦ To open a folder so you can see its contents in the message list, click the folder icon (or right-click it and choose Open).

You can rename, delete, move, and copy any folder you create. Use the following techniques:

✦ To rename a folder, open the folder. Then right-click it and choose Rename, or choose File ➪ Folder ➪ Rename from the menu bar. Type a new folder name and choose OK.

✦ To delete a folder and the messages it contains, open the folder. Then, press the Delete (Del) key on your keyboard or right-click the folder and choose Delete. You also can choose File ➪ Folder ➪ Delete from the menu bar. When prompted for confirmation, choose Yes. (This action cannot be undone.)

✦ To move a folder and its contents to another folder, click the folder you want to move and drag it to the desired parent folder in the folder list.

 See "Working with several messages at once" earlier in this chapter for information about moving and copying messages between folders.

Using message rules

Suppose someone has been sending you annoying e-mail messages and you want to delete that person's messages without reading them. Or, perhaps you want to move or copy certain messages automatically to specific folders. Or, maybe you want to send an automatic reply, such as

```
Gone fishin' and I won't be back until the twelfth of never.
```

to some or all of the messages you receive. All this and more is possible with a little help from message rules that enable you to set up rules and actions to take when Outlook Express delivers your incoming mail. Once you get the hang of using message rules (and it won't take long), you'll appreciate the amount of time it saves.

To add a new rule, follow these steps:

1. Choose Tools ➪ Message Rules ➪ Mail from the main Outlook Express menu bar.

2. Select conditions for your rule.

3. Select actions to take on messages that meet the specified conditions.

4. In the lower portion of the dialog box, click an underlined item to edit it.

5. Click OK. You'll be returned to the Message Rules dialog box and your new rule will appear in the Description box, as shown in Figure 9-57.

You can repeat Steps 2–5 to set up as many rules as you need and you can adjust the rules, as I will explain in a moment. When you're happy with the list as it is, click OK. The next time you receive new messages, Outlook Express will process any messages that match the rules you set up.

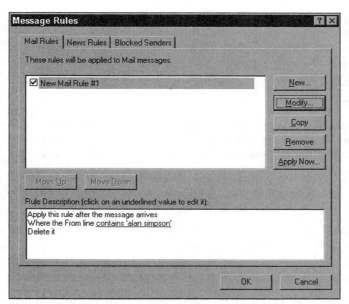

Figure 9-57: The Description box of the Message Rules after setting up some rules

Here are some points to remember about the Inbox Assistant:

✦ Outlook Express processes only the rules checked in the rules list. It ignores rules that appear in the rules list, but aren't checked.

✦ If an incoming message matches more than one rule, Outlook Express will process it according to the first rule it matches and ignore the others. (Of course, if you've set up multiple actions in a single rule, Outlook Express will take all the actions you requested.)

You can adjust the rules in the Message Rules dialog box at any time:

✦ To turn off a rule temporarily, deselect (clear) the check box next to the rule. To turn the rule back on again, check the box once more. Turning off a rule and turning it back on is easier than removing the rule and re-creating it later.

✦ To remove a rule permanently, click it in the rules list and then click the Remove button. Watch out! No prompt exists for confirmation. The rule is history the moment you click Remove.

✦ To change a rule, click it in the rules list and then click the Modify button (or double-click the rule's description). The Edit Mail Rule box will open and you can change any criteria or actions you want.

✦ To move a rule up or down in the Description list (and thus change the order in which the Inbox Assistant processes the rules), click the rule you want to move and then click the Move Up or Move Down button as needed.

Summary

Well, folks, that's about it for using Outlook Express. As you've seen, it's a powerful program that can simplify your electronic correspondence in dozens of ways. In the next chapter, we explore some more Internet goodies. But first, let's review the salient points covered in this chapter:

✦ Outlook Express comes with Windows Me and Internet Explorer and is installed automatically with those programs.

✦ To start Outlook Express from the Windows Me desktop, click the Start button and choose Programs ➪ Outlook Express.

✦ To start Outlook Express from within Microsoft Internet Explorer, choose Tools ➪ Mail and News ➪ Read Mail.

✦ To configure Outlook Express to your own e-mail account(s), start Outlook Express and choose Tools ➪ Accounts. Click the Add button and choose Mail to add a new account.

✦ To compose a new mail message, click the New Message button in its toolbar, or press Ctrl+N, or choose Message ➪ New Message from the menu bar. You'll be taken to a New Message window where you can compose your message.

✦ To send a composed message, click the Send button in the New Message window, or choose File ➪ Send Message from its menu bar. If you do not want to send the message immediately, choose File ➪ Send Later instead (the message will be placed in the Outbox).

✦ To send all messages from the Outbox to their recipients, choose Tools ➪ Send and Receive ➪ Send and Receive All from Outlook Express's menu bar, or click the Send/Recv button on the toolbar.

✦ To check for new incoming mail, click the Send/Recv button on the Outlook Express toolbar. Be sure to select the Inbox folder in the folder list or Outlook bar.

✦ To read a message, click it. The message content appears in the preview pane of Outlook Express's window. If you prefer to open the message in a new window, double-click the message.

✦ You can reply to the message you're currently reading in two ways. If you want to reply to the author only, click the Reply button on the toolbar. Or, to reply to everyone who received this message, choose Reply to All on the toolbar.

✦ To delete the message you just read, click the Delete button on the toolbar.

✦ To create and use an address book, click the Windows Me Start button and choose Programs ➪ Accessories ➪ Address Book. Or, if you're already in Outlook Express, click the Address Book button on the toolbar, or press Ctrl+Shift+B.

✦ To personalize the appearance of the Outlook Express window, choose options from the View menu.

✦ To personalize the way Outlook Express operates, choose Tools ➪ Options or Tools ➪ Accounts.

✦   ✦   ✦

Participating in Usenet Newsgroups

Usenet, like the World Wide Web, is another popular feature available on the Internet. Usenet is divided into many electronic bulletin boards, or newsgroups, where people gather to discuss a particular topic. The term newsgroup, however, is a little strange, because a newsgroup is not about news. Instead, it's sort of a forum where people with similar interests can share ideas, exchange information, ask questions, and post answers. Each newsgroup consists of messages written by members using software that's similar to an e-mail program.

To take advantage of newsgroups, you need an Internet account with access to Usenet newsgroups and a newsreader program, such as Microsoft Outlook Express, which comes with Windows Me and the Internet Explorer Suite.

Note In this chapter, I refer to the newsgroup reading part of Outlook Express as Outlook Express News and the e-mail part as Outlook Express Mail. Please read Chapter 9, which explains how to send and receive electronic mail with Outlook Express Mail. After you know the basics of using e-mail, you'll know how to use newsgroups practically by osmosis.

Newsgroup Factoids and Buzzwords

Newsgroups and e-mail are similar in many ways. For example, both are used to send messages electronically between networked computers. The techniques for composing, reading, and replying to e-mail and newsgroup messages are almost identical. Despite these similarities, you should know some important differences and a few newsgroup facts and buzzwords.

First, an important difference between e-mail messages and newsgroup messages: Unlike e-mail messages that go to specific electronic mailboxes, newsgroup messages go to specific newsgroups and stay there so that visitors can read past correspondence between members to find information and get a feel for discussions in progress. Anyone in the newsgroup can read its messages.

And now some buzzwords:

✦ Each message in a newsgroup is officially called an *article,* although I'll stick with the term *message* in this book. A series of messages on the same subject is called a *thread.* For example, if I post a message with the subject Llama Wanted, I've started a new thread. If anyone replies to my original message, or if anyone replies to that reply, all those messages will be part of the same thread. If I later post a new message with the subject Angora Rabbit Wanted, I've started a new thread.

✦ Many newsgroups are *moderated* by people who screen messages for suitability to the newsgroup; however, most newsgroups are *unmoderated* and messages pass through to the newsgroup unscreened.

✦ *Lurking* is hanging around a newsgroup to see what's being said without actually contributing anything. When you're new to a newsgroup, lurking for a while is a good idea — to get a feel for what's going on — before you start making contributions.

✦ *Flaming* is sending nasty messages to people in the group. If you don't lurk to find out what's going on in a group and, instead, start making irrelevant contributions, you're likely to get flamed. Also, anything that smacks of advertising in a newsgroup will surely result in flame mail directed at you!

✦ *Spamming* is sending blatant advertisements or sneaky ads disguised as newsgroup messages to a newsgroup. Highly unacceptable!

✦ *Netiquette* is observing proper newsgroup etiquette by not sending irrelevant comments and not spamming the group. A good *netizen* (network citizen) follows proper netiquette.

And some factoids:

✦ Newsgroups come and newsgroups go, and some aren't accessible on every newsgroup server. So don't be concerned if a newsgroup you read about in this book has disappeared by the time you sign on or if it is simply is unavailable.

✦ Some newsgroups contain offensive material. Please do not let your kids wander newsgroups (or any other part of the Internet) unsupervised!

Newsgroup categories

Each newsgroup discusses topics in a specific category. For example, the alt.humor. puns newsgroup covers punishing humor of this ilk:

```
Q: Why were the baby ants confused?
A: Because all their uncles were ants.
```

By contrast, the `rec.food.chocolate` newsgroup discusses the dark, gooey, fat-inducing sweet that has destroyed many a New Year's resolution to shed excess weight.

Caution

Before you post messages to a newsgroup for the first time, spend a while lurking in the newsgroup and absorb the local culture. If you post messages inappropriate for the category or the culture, newsgroup members may send you insulting messages in return (flaming). (Never send flame mail to anyone; it's rude!)

Newsgroup categories reflect a hierarchy, starting with the least specific category and ending with the most specific one, as you read from left to right. A period (.) separates each subcategory from the next. Using alt.humor.puns as an example, the newsgroup name goes from the broad category *alt* (for alternative topics), to the more specific subcategory of *humor,* to the still more specific humor subcategory of *puns.* Table 10-1 presents some examples of top-level categories. Later in this chapter, you'll learn how to display the complete list of newsgroups on your server and how to join any available newsgroup.

Table 10-1 Some Newsgroup Main Categories, Descriptions, and Names		
Main Category	*Description*	*Sample Newsgroup Names*
Alt	Alternative topics and lifestyles. Some material in this category may be offensive.	alt.humor.puns; alt.pets.rabbits; alt.test

Continued

Table 10-1 *(continued)*		
Main Category	**Description**	**Sample Newsgroup Names**
Bionet	Biology	bionet.microbiology; bionet.mycology
Bit	Bitnet, redistribution for BitNet Listserv mailing lists	bit.listserv.autism; bit.listserv.movie.memorabilia
Biz	Business	biz.comp.hardware; biz.comp.software
Comp	Computers	comp.human-factors; comp.jobs
Humanities	Arts and humanities	humanities.classics; humanities.music.composers.wagner
Misc	Miscellaneous	misc.books.technical; misc.computers.forsale; misc.test
News	Usenet news network and software	news.announce.newusers; news.answers; news.newusers.questions
Rec	Arts, hobbies, recreation	rec.food.drink.coffee; rec.food.chocolate
Sci	Science	sci.agriculture.beekeeping; sci.bio.food-science
Soc	Social topics and socializing	soc.culture.punjab; soc.geneology.surnames
Talk	Debates, opinions, and general yakkety-yak	talk.environment; talk.politics medicine

A little advice for the newcomer

If you're a newcomer to newsgroups (that is, a newsgroup *newbie*), you should be aware that the Usenet world, like the real world, is something of a jungle, which is home to both benign and malevolent critters. To avoid being bitten by the bad guys and to make your newsgroup safaris as much fun as possible, consider these tips:

✦ Learn to use the newsreader software (Outlook Express News) with help from this chapter.

✦ Read the *FAQs* (frequently asked questions) in the newsgroups you visit and lurk in a newsgroup for a while before posting any messages.

✦ Learn more about how newsgroups work in news.announce.newusers and news.newusers.questions. If you're still unsure about how to use newsgroups, post a question in news.newusers.questions.

✦ Post some test messages in alt.test or misc.test.

Here's some advice on netiquette, which, if heeded, will make you a better netizen as you post messages to newsgroups:

✦ Post your message only to the most appropriate newsgroup.

✦ Do not ask questions answered in the newsgroup's FAQ message.

✦ Make the Subject line of your message concise, but descriptive, like a headline in a newspaper or magazine.

✦ Keep the message text brief, but don't omit important details or background information that other newsgroup members may not know.

✦ When responding to newsgroup messages, consider responding directly to the author by e-mail if your answer requires some privacy or if it won't interest the entire group.

✦ Never send flames, advertisements, offensive material, chain letters, jokes (unless you're writing for a humor newsgroup), or anything illegal to a newsgroup.

✦ If someone is sending you flames or other unwanted messages via the newsgroup or e-mail, ignore them or complain to the author's system administrator.

Spams and scams

Unsolicited e-mail messages (spam) that advertise goods or services or are downright scams are a big problem on the Internet. Sooner or later, you're likely to get spammed if you post messages to a bulletin board on an online service or the Internet, post to a Usenet newsgroup, visit chat rooms (as discussed in Chapter 12), or are listed in an online service's member directory.

Although you probably can't avoid spam entirely, you can minimize it. First, never respond to the e-mail address of the spammer or to any e-mail address the spammer claims you can use to get yourself off the spam list. Instead, send an e-mail complaint along with a copy of the original spam message to the spam-stopper e-mail address at the spammer's Internet service provider (ISP). Typically, this e-mail address is `postmaster@spammersDomain` (or `abuse@spammersDomain`), where you replace `spammersDomain` with the domain of the person sending the spam.

The spammer's domain name is often buried in the header of the message you receive. Look on the From:, X-Sender:, or Sender: line, one of the Received: lines, or other headers that carry machine identification including Message-ID: or Comments. Suppose you receive a message from slime@spammers-are-us. com and you're pretty certain spammers-are-us.com is the real domain name of the spammer's Internet service provider. In this case, you'd send your complaint and attached spam message to postmaster@spammers-are-us.com.

Note If you want to view the detailed header of an e-mail message, highlight or open the message, choose File ➪ Properties, and click the Details tab in the dialog box that appears. See Chapter 9 for more about viewing message properties.

Responding to the demand for less spam in the world, America Online, Netcom, EarthLink, InterRamp, and other ISPs have set up special e-mail addresses for handling complaints about spam originating from their machines. Examples of these special e-mail addresses include abuse@aol.com, abuse@netcom.com, and abuse@interramp.com.

To learn more about reading message headers and avoiding spam, point your browser to this finger-twisting URL:

```
http://www.yahoo.com/Computers_and_Internet/Communications_and_
Networking/Electronic_Mail/Junk_Email/
```

or this one:

```
http://www.dgl.com/docs/antispam.html
```

You also can search for *spam* or *antispam* in your favorite search engine, including Yahoo! at http://www.yahoo.com, Microsoft's all-in-one search page at http://home.microsoft.com/access/allinone.asp, and the search engines available from the Internet Explorer Search bar (see Chapter 7).

Starting Outlook Express News

All righty! You're ready to explore newsgroups. Getting started is a breeze, especially if you've already set up your e-mail client as explained in Chapter 9. For the examples in this chapter, I assume that you've done this already and that you're using Microsoft Outlook Express as your e-mail client and newsreader. Of course, you can use any e-mail client and newsreader you want, but the setup will be a little different.

Starting for the first time

Before starting the Outlook Express newsreader for the first time, you need the same information you needed to set up your Outlook Express e-mail client (see Chapter 9). You also need the name of your Internet news (NNTP) server. You can get all this information from your ISP.

Tip For the acronymically interested, NNTP stands for Network News Transfer Protocol, the method your ISP's news server uses to communicate with your newsreader. If you don't know the name of your ISP's news server, try Microsoft's news—msnews.microsoft.com—which offers newsgroups that provide help with Microsoft products.

Now you're ready to start Outlook Express News and set it up. Follow these steps:

1. Connect to the Internet as explained in Chapter 6. Or, if you've set up your computer to dial into the Internet automatically, skip this step and let your computer dial up whenever it feels the need.

2. Use any of the following methods to start Outlook Express News:

   • Starting from Outlook Express (see Chapter 9) choose Tools ➪ Newsgroups from the menu bar (if you have already set up a news account).

   • Starting from Internet Explorer (see Chapter 7), choose Tools ➪ Mail_and News ➪ Read News from the menu bar.

   • Starting from Outlook Express, click Outlook Express at the top of the folder list or Outlook bar (in the left side of the window) and then click Read News.

   • Starting from Internet Explorer, click the Mail button on the Internet Explorer toolbar and then choose Read News.

Tip From Internet Explorer, you also can click the Address box, type **news:** followed by the name of the newsgroup you want to visit, and then press Enter. For example, enter **news:rec.crafts.textiles.needlework** into the Address box to start Outlook Express News and select the rec.crafts.textiles.needlework newsgroup automatically.

3. If the Internet Connection Wizard kicks in, simply read the instructions in each dialog box and answer the questions presented, just as you did when setting up your e-mail account. Click the Next or Finish button to move to the next dialog box. When you finish the last step, the Connection Wizard will download the list of newsgroups available on the server. This may take a while, but you only have to do it once.

4. If you see the message shown in Figure 10-1, click Yes and then continue with Step 5. If you don't see the message, you'll be taken to the main Outlook Express News window (shown later in Figure 10-2) and you can start browsing the newsgroups immediately.

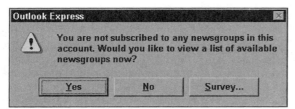

Figure 10-1: This message appears if you haven't yet subscribed to any newsgroups.

5. The Newsgroup Subscriptions dialog box will open (see Figure 10-2). If more than one news server appears in the News Servers list in the left side of the dialog box, click the name of the server you want to use.

6. In the Display newsgroups which contain box, type the name (or any part of the name) of the newsgroup that you want to join, as shown in Figure 10-2. The list under Newsgroup will match your typing. To start over again with the full list of newsgroups, simply delete the text in the box (for example, by pressing the Backspace key repeatedly).

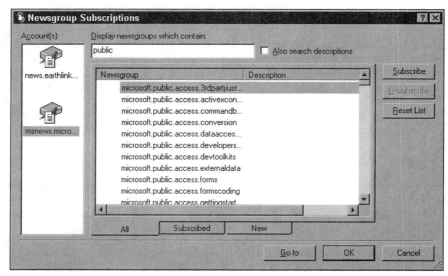

Figure 10-2: The Newsgroup Subscriptions dialog box with the msnews News Server selected and the word *public* typed in

7. Scroll through the Newgroup list until you find the newsgroup you want to join, and then click its name. Now, do one of the following:

- To subscribe to the selected newsgroup, so you can get to it more quickly in the future, click Subscribe. Then click Go To to open the newsgroup.

- To open the selected newsgroup without subscribing to it first, click Go To.

You'll see the main Outlook Express News window, shown in Figure 10-3. Notice it's almost identical to the Outlook Express Mail window. Its toolbar and menus, however, are for use with newsgroups rather than e-mail. Now you're ready to browse the newsgroups, as explained later under "Browsing Newsgroup Messages."

Tip

Anytime you click any of the e-mail folders in the folder list or Outlook bar (for example, Inbox, Outbox, or Sent Items), the toolbar and menus automatically switch to those for Outlook Express Mail and you can use Outlook Express Mail, as explained in Chapter 9. To return to the Outlook Express News toolbars and menus from Outlook Express Mail, simply click the name of your news server (or any newsgroup) in the folder list or Outlook bar, or choose Tools ➪ Newsgroups from the menu bar.

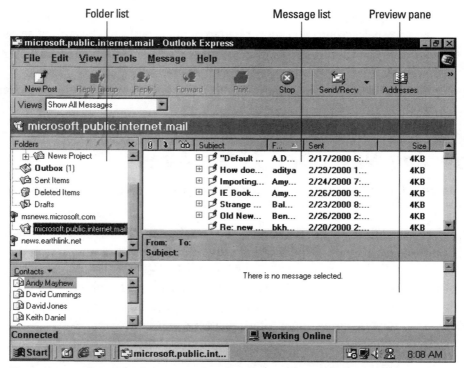

Folder list   Message list   Preview pane

Figure 10-3: The Outlook Express News window with the msnews News Server selected and a newsgroup and its messages visible

Starting later

Once you set up Outlook Express News, you can start it the same way you started it the first time. That is, connect to the Internet (if you haven't set up your computer to dial automatically) and use any of the methods given in Step 2 of the "Starting for the first time" procedure to fire up the program.

Here are two more quick ways to start Outlook Express News automatically. Starting from Outlook Express Mail (see Chapter 9), click the name of a news server or newsgroup in the Outlook bar or folder list. Or, starting from a browser, such as Internet Explorer, click a hyperlink to a newsgroup or newsgroup message in a Web page (see Chapter 7).

If you subscribed to any newsgroups, you'll be taken directly to the Outlook Express News window, shown in Figure 10-3. If you haven't subscribed, simply follow Steps 4 to 7 of the first-time procedure to choose and/or subscribe to a newsgroup. Like the Outlook Express Mail window described in Chapter 9, the Outlook Express News window usually is divided into several parts:

✦ **Outlook bar** (at the left): Displays your top-level e-mail folders and your newsgroup server(s). (The Outlook bar is hidden in the figures in this chapter to make the remaining elements easier to see.)

✦ **Folder list** (at the left): Displays your e-mail folders, your newsgroup server(s), and any newsgroups you subscribed to or opened during the current session.

✦ **Message list** (at the right): Displays the headers (summary information) of messages in the currently selected newsgroup.

✦ **Preview pane** (below the message list): Displays the contents of the currently selected message.

Browsing Newsgroup Messages

Browsing the newsgroup messages is easy. To begin, you must choose the newsgroup that you want to read, as explained here:

1. Connect to the Internet and start Outlook Express News, as explained earlier.

2. If you have set up more than one newsgroup server, click the name of the server that you want to use in the folder list or Outlook bar.

3. Do one of the following, depending on your setup and your whim:

   • If you haven't subscribed to any newsgroups yet, repeat Steps 4 to 7 of the procedure under "Starting for the first time."

- If you subscribed to the newsgroup you want to view, click its name in the folder list under the server you selected or double-click its name in the message list. If the subscribed newsgroups are hidden in the folder list, click the plus (+) sign icon next to the server name to expand the list and then click the name of the newsgroup. (The plus (+) sign changes to a minus (–) sign, which you can click to hide or collapse the list of newsgroups again.)

- If you want to view a newsgroup that isn't on your subscription list, return to the Newsgroups dialog box by clicking the Newsgroups button on the Outlook Express News toolbar or by choosing Tools ➪ Newsgroups from the menu bar. Now repeat Steps 5 to 7 of the procedure under "Starting for the first time."

After you select the newsgroup that you want to read, reading a message is basically the same as reading an e-mail message. Click the message that you want to view in the message list and the message will appear in the preview pane at the bottom of the screen (see Figure 10-3).

If you prefer to view the message in its own window, double-click it in the message list. Figure 10-4 is an example of a newsgroup message opened in a separate window. When you finish viewing the message, click the Close (X) button in the upper-right corner of the open message window, or choose File ➪ Close, or press Alt+F4 to return to the main Outlook Express News window.

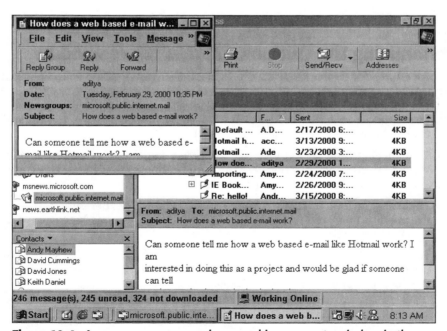

Figure 10-4: A newsgroup message is opened in a separate window in the upper-left portion of this figure.

Note In the message list, unread messages are boldface and preceded by yellow paper icons. After you read a message, the boldface is turned off and the yellow icon turns into a white full-sheet paper icon (see Figure 10-3).

Replying to newsgroup messages — the short of it

Anytime you're viewing a message, you can reply to it in any of these ways:

✦ Post a reply to this message that anyone in the newsgroup can read. To begin, click the Reply Group button on the toolbar, or choose Message ➪ Reply To Group, or press Ctrl+G.

✦ Post a reply, via e-mail, to the author of the message. Only the author will see your reply. To get started, click the Reply button on the toolbar, or choose Message ➪ Reply To Sender, or press Ctrl+R.

✦ Forward the message to someone else, via e-mail. Only the recipient will see your forwarded message. To begin, click the Forward button on the toolbar, or choose Message ➪ Forward (or Message ➪ Forward As Attachment), or press Ctrl+F.

After choosing a reply option, you reply to the message as you would any standard e-mail message. When you're ready to send your reply, click the Post Message or Send Message button on the toolbar (or choose File ➪ Send Message or press Alt+S). See "Replying to newsgroup messages — the long of it" later in this chapter for more details.

Customizing the Outlook Express News window

The procedures for customizing the Outlook Express News window are identical to those discussed in Chapter 25. Here are some reminders:

✦ To display or hide the toolbar or the status bar, choose View ➪ Layout and choose Toolbar or Status Bar, respectively.

✦ To display or hide the Outlook bar, folder list, folder bar, or views bar, choose View ➪ Layout. Select or deselect the appropriate options in the Basic area and then click OK to save your changes.

✦ To display or hide the preview pane or the message header information above the preview pane and to position the preview pane, choose View ➪ Layout. Set options in the Preview Pane area and then click OK.

✦ To position the toolbar, show or hide text on toolbar buttons, or customize the buttons, choose View ➪ Layout. Click the Customize Toolbar button, set the Toolbar options, and then click OK.

✦ To reposition the columns in the message list, drag the buttons at the top of the message list to the left or right. Or, choose View ➪ Columns from the menu bar and complete the Columns dialog box.

✦ To sort the messages by a particular column in the message list, click a column heading button at the top of the message list or right-click a button and choose Sort Ascending or Sort Descending from the shortcut menu. Or, choose View ➪ Sort By from the menu bar and choose an option from the submenu that appears.

Tip After sorting the messages by the Subject or From column, you can type the first letter of the Subject or From item you're looking for and quickly highlight the next message matching that letter.

Limiting the current view and finding messages

If you're viewing a newsgroup that contains many messages, you may become daunted by the sheer number of messages that you must wade through to find those that you really want to read. One way to find messages more quickly is to sort them, as explained earlier.

You also can limit the current message view by choosing options on the View ➪ Current View submenu. Here are your submenu choices:

✦ **Show All Messages:** Displays all messages in the newsgroup.

✦ **Hide Read Messages:** Displays only the messages you haven't read yet.

✦ **Show Downloaded Messages:** Displays only the messages you've downloaded from the server so far.

✦ **Hide Read or Ignored Messages:** Displays only the messages you haven't read or marked to ignore.

✦ **Show Replies To My Messages:** Displays replies to messages you have posted.

✦ **Group Messages by Conversation:** Displays message *threads* — messages and replies that belong together. See "Viewing, expanding, and collapsing threads" for details on message threads.

You also can use the Find command to find a message. This command works basically the same as it does for e-mail:

1. Go to the newsgroup you want to search.

2. Choose Edit ➪ Find ➪ Message or press Ctrl+Shift+F. You'll see the Find Message dialog box shown in Figure 10-5.

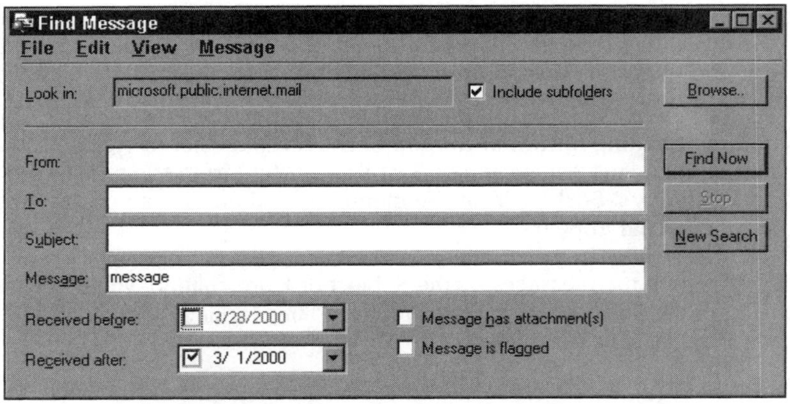

Figure 10-5: The Find Message dialog box in Microsoft Outlook Express News.

3. Specify the From:, Subject:, or date criteria for which you want to search. In the From: and Subject: boxes, you can type all or part of the text for which you're searching. In Figure 10-5, I'm searching for messages containing *message* in the Subject line and posted after March 1, 2000.

4. Click Find.

Find will highlight the first matching message (if it finds one). If you want to look for the next match, choose Edit ➪ Find Next or press F3. You can repeat this step until Outlook Express News reports no more messages were found and asks whether you want to start over from the top of the click. Click Yes to search again or click No to stop searching.

Viewing, expanding, and collapsing threads

Although the term *threads* may make you think I'm giving a sewing lesson or discussing the latest fashions, I'm not. A thread is simply an original message and any posted replies, as shown in Figure 10-6.

The threads are sorted and grouped according to the original title (or subject). The top level of each thread shows the original message. Below that, you see responses to the original message and any responses to the responses. As a simple example, suppose I post a message with this subject:

```
Wanted—Purple People Eater
```

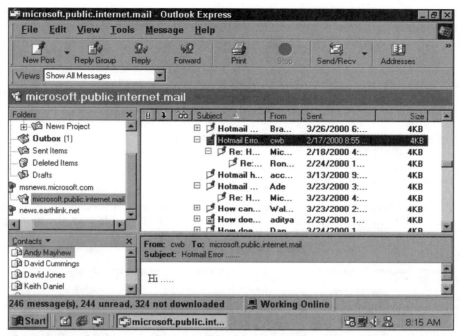

Figure 10-6: This message list is organized in a hierarchy of threads.

Finding messages in *any* newsgroup

You can search all of Usenet for newsgroup messages on nearly any topic. Two search engines—Deja News (http://www.deja.com/usenet) and AltaVista (http://altavista.digital.com)—specialize in helping you find newsgroup messages. Deja News is one of the best and a great place to start.

To begin your search, open your Internet browser (for example, Internet Explorer) and go to the Web site for the newsgroup search engine that you want to use. If the search engine provides an option for searching a particular archive or directory, choose the "Usenet" or "Newsgroup" option. Type the topic or phrase that you want to find in the appropriate search text box, and then click the Search, Find, or Submit button. When the search results appear, follow the hyperlinks until you reach the newsgroup or newsgroup message you seek. If you click the hyperlink for a newsgroup, you'll be taken to Outlook Express News automatically, and the newsgroup you selected will appear in the list of newsgroups on your newsgroup server. See Chapter 7 for more about searching the Internet.

My message will be at the top of a new thread. All replies to this message will have the subject:

```
Re: Wanted—Purple People Eater
```

and they'll appear below my original message in the thread.

If someone replies to my message and changes the subject to:

```
Wanted—Purple People Eater. Let's end this thread now! PPEs
don't exist.
```

that message automatically starts a new thread.

Although it's easiest to work with newsgroups if you group messages into threads, you can flatten out the hierarchy, as shown in Figure 10-7. This way, the message list looks more like the one for Outlook Express Mail.

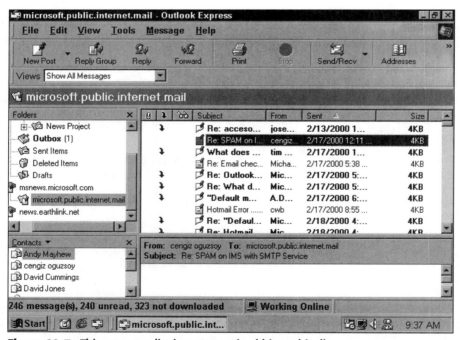

Figure 10-7: This message list is not organized hierarchically.

It's easy to turn the threading display on or off. Just choose View ⇨ _Current View ⇨ _Group Messages By Conversation. When the Group Messages By Conversation option is checked, the messages appear in a hierarchy, as in Figure 10-6. When it isn't checked, the messages appear in a long flat list, as in Figure 10-7.

When threading is turned on, you can expand or collapse any thread:

✦ To expand a thread, click the plus (+) sign next to the message icon in the message list. The plus (+) sign changes to a minus (–) sign and the subordinate messages appear in the message list.

✦ To collapse a thread, click the minus (–) sign next to the message's icon in the message list. The minus (–) sign changes to a plus (+) sign and the subordinate messages are hidden in the message list.

Keeping track of what you've read

Remember, unread messages appear in the message list in boldface text and are preceded by yellow icons; read messages are not bold and have a white icon. You can manually whitewash a message (that is, mark the message as read) or remove the whitewash (marking the message as unread). You can even mark an entire newsgroup, thread, or selected messages as read or unread. Here's how:

✦ To mark one message as read, click (select) the message and choose Edit ⇨ Mark As Read from the menu bar or press Ctrl+Q.

✦ To mark several messages as read, select those messages using the click, Ctrl+click, and Shift+click techniques explained in Chapter 9. Then, choose Edit ⇨ Mark As Read or press Ctrl+Q.

✦ To mark an entire thread as read, select any message in the thread and choose Edit ⇨ _Mark Conversation As Read or press Ctrl+T.

✦ To mark all messages in the newsgroup as read, choose Edit ⇨ Mark All As Read or press Ctrl+Shift+A.

✦ To mark messages in the newsgroup as unread, select the message or messages. Then choose Edit ⇨ Mark As Unread. This option is handy if you accidentally marked a message as read or you want to remember to read a message again later.

Instead of using the menu options, you can select one or more messages, right-click the selection, and choose Mark As Read, or Mark Thread As Read, or Mark As Unread from the shortcut menu.

Tip   Messages usually are marked as read after you preview them for five seconds. To change this, choose Tools ⇨ Options, click the Read tab, change the setting for the Message Is Read After Being Previewed For n Second(s) option, and click OK.

Replying to newsgroup messages — the long of it

You can reply to a newsgroup message that you're viewing in several ways, as the following sections explain. As you'll see, replying to a newsgroup message is similar to replying to an e-mail message.

Replying to the group

Normally you'll want to send your reply to the original newsgroup, so that everyone who visits the group — including the person to whom you're replying — can benefit from your gems of wisdom.

To reply to the group, first make sure that you're viewing the message to which you want to reply, either in the message list or in a separate window. That is, make it the current message. Now, follow these steps:

1. Click the Reply Group button on the toolbar, or choose Message ➪ Reply To Group from the menu bar, or press Ctrl+G, or right-click the message and choose Reply To Group from the shortcut menu. A new newsgroup Reply window will appear and the insertion point will be poised above the original message text, ready for you to type your answer (see Figure 10-8).

2. Type the reply as you'd type any standard e-mail reply (see Chapter 9). You also can use the techniques discussed later under "Posting New Newsgroup Messages" to update the Newsgroups:, Cc:, or Subject: information at the top of the reply and to attach a file, add a signature, or format your message.

3. When you're ready to send the message, click the Send button on the toolbar, or choose File ➪ Send Message, or press Alt+S.

Eventually your reply will make its way to all servers that carry your newsgroup and you'll see it under the thread for the original message.

Caution   Remember that if you change the text in the Subject: box, your reply will start a new thread and the person who posted the original message won't be able to find your answer.

Replying to the author

Perhaps you'd like to keep your reply a secret from the other members of the newsgroup or maybe the author of a message has specifically asked you to reply via e-mail. In this case, you'll want to reply by e-mail. The steps are similar to those for replying to the newsgroup. As usual, make sure you're viewing the message to which you want to reply. Then, follow these steps:

1. Click the Reply button on the toolbar, or choose Message ➪ Reply To Sender from the menu bar, or press Ctrl+R, or right-click the message and choose Reply To Sender from the shortcut menu. A new e-mail Reply window will appear (see Figure 10-9).

Type your reply here

Send message

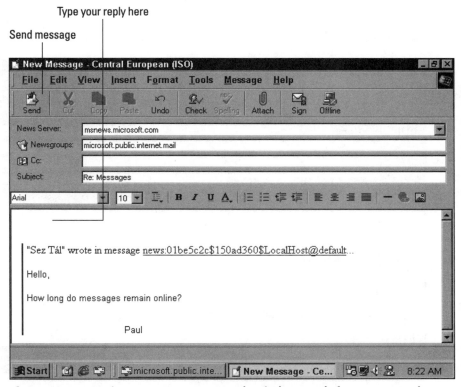

Figure 10-8: Here is a new newsgroup Reply window, ready for you to type in your reply.

2. Type the reply as you'd type any standard e-mail reply (see Chapter 9). You also can use the techniques discussed in Chapter 25 to update the To:, Cc:, Bcc:, or Subject: information at the top of the reply and to attach a file, add a signature, or format your message.

3. When you're ready to send the message, click the Send button on the toolbar, or choose File ➪ Send Message, or press Alt+S.

Your reply will go to the electronic mailboxes of the recipients listed in your message.

Tip If you prefer to plop the reply into your e-mail Outbox and send it later, choose File ➪ Send Later in Step 3. When you're ready to send the messages in your Outbox, choose Tools ➪ Send from the menu bar.

Type your reply here

Send message

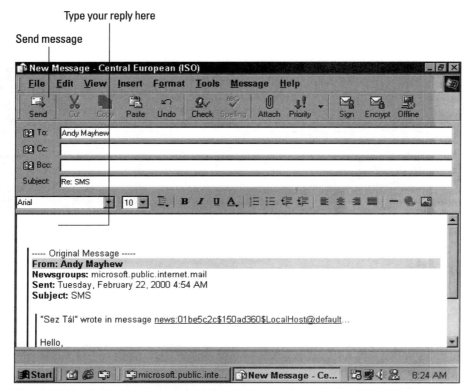

Figure 10-9: This is a new e-mail Reply window, ready for you to type in your reply.

Forwarding the message

Perhaps you have a buddy who's an expert in the topic a newsgroup member is asking about, but you doubt your buddy is a member of the newsgroup. In this case, you might want to forward the message to your friend's electronic mailbox and ask your friend to reply directly to the original author. To do this, select the message to which you want your buddy to reply, and then:

1. Do one of the following, depending on how you want the message to look:

- To forward the message as it appears in the newsgroup window, click the Forward button on the toolbar, or choose Message ➪ Forward from the menu bar, or press Ctrl+F, or right-click the message and choose Forward from the shortcut menu. A new e-mail Forward window appears. It looks just like the Reply window except the To: box is empty and the Subject: box says Fw: instead of Re:. A new e-mail forward window appears, as shown in Figure 10-10.

- To forward the message as an attachment, choose Message ➪ Forward As Attachment from the menu bar, or right-click the message and choose Forward As Attachment from the shortcut menu.

2. In the To: box, specify the e-mail address of the recipient using any of the techniques discussed in Chapter 9. You also can fill in the Cc: and Bcc: boxes if you want.

3. In the Subject: box, specify a subject for the message you're forwarding (if no subject appears automatically).

4. Click the message-editing area and type text that introduces your forwarded message. As usual, you can attach a file, add a signature, or format your message as needed.

5. Click the Send button on the toolbar, or choose File ➪ Send Message, or press Alt+S.

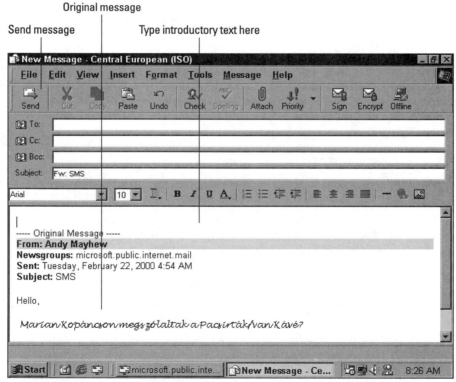

Figure 10-10: A new e-mail Forward window is ready for you to specify recipients, a subject, and a reply.

As usual, your message goes to the electronic mailboxes of the recipients.

Tip If you'd rather stack the reply in your e-mail Outbox and send it later, choose File ⇨ Send Later in Step 5. When you're ready to send the messages in your Outbox, choose Tools ⇨ Send from the menu bar.

Posting new newsgroup messages

Sometimes you'll be the one with a question or an opinion and you'll want to post it to the newsgroup of your choosing. This is easy to do, but please remember the two points of netiquette I mentioned earlier:

✦ Lurk in a newsgroup to absorb its culture before posting for the first time.

✦ Post only to the most relevant newsgroups. Do not post to multiple newsgroups unless it's absolutely necessary and do not post ads unless the newsgroup is specifically designated for advertising.

OK, now I'll get off my soapbox and list the steps for posting a new message to a newsgroup:

1. Go to the newsgroup where you want the message to appear.

2. Click the New Post button on the toolbar, or choose Message ⇨ _New Message from the menu bar, or press Ctrl+N. You'll see a New Message window, as shown in Figure 10-11.

3. Although this probably won't be necessary, you can choose a different newsgroup or specify additional newsgroups in the Newsgroups: box, as I'll explain soon under "Posting to multiple newsgroups."

4. If you want to send a copy of your message to an e-mail address, specify it in the Cc: box using any of the techniques discussed in Chapter 9.

5. In the Subject: line, specify the subject for your message. This subject will appear in the Subject column of the message list. Make it descriptive so that other newsgroup members will want to read it.

6. Click in the message editing area and type your message (again, be sure to follow the network etiquette advice given earlier in this chapter).

7. If you want, you can attach a file, add a signature, or format your message as explained under "Spiffing Up Your Newsgroup Messages" in a moment.

8. When you're ready to post the message, click the Send button on the toolbar, or choose File ⇨ Send Message from the menu bar, or press Alt+S.

After a while, your message will be propagated to all the servers that carry your newsgroup and it'll start a new thread in the message list.

Type your message here   Insert file

Send message   Type your subject here   Insert signature

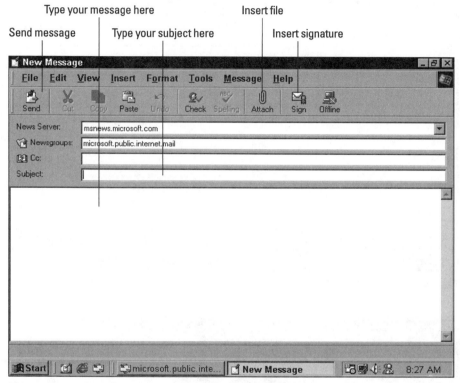

Figure 10-11: Use the New Message window to compose a new newsgroup message.

Posting to multiple newsgroups

You can post your new newsgroup message or your reply to more than one newsgroup, if necessary. There are two ways. First, you can type each newsgroup name, separated by a comma, in the Newsgroups: box, as shown in Figure 10-12.

If finger-twisting newsgroup names aren't exactly your cup of typing tea, you can pick the newsgroups that you want to receive your message. To begin, click the newspaper icon next to the Newsgroups: box or choose Tools ➪ Select Newsgroups from the menu bar. You'll see the Pick Newsgroups On dialog box shown in Figure 10-13.

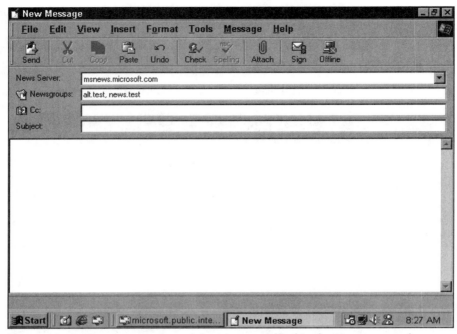

Figure 10-12: Two newsgroup recipients are specified in the Newsgroups: box

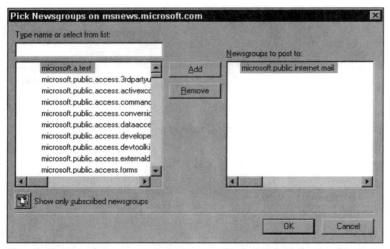

Figure 10-13: Choose your newsgroups in the Pick Newsgroups On dialog box.

Do any of the following to select the newsgroups to which you want to post:

✦ To show all the newsgroups for this server in the list below "Type name or select from list," click the button next to "Show only subscribed newsgroups" (in the lower-left corner of the dialog box). To limit the newsgroups to those you've subscribed to, click the button again.

✦ To display a subset of the newsgroups, type all or part of the name of the newsgroups you want to match into the "Type name or select from list" box. For example, if I typed **test** into the box, the list below "Type name or select from list" in Figure 10-13 would include only the alt.test and news.test newsgroups.

✦ To add a newsgroup to the "Newsgroups to post to" list, click that newsgroup name in the left side of the dialog box and then click Add (or double-click the name).

✦ To remove a newsgroup from the "Newsgroups to post to list," click that newsgroup name in the right side of the dialog box and then click Remove (or double-click the name).

When you've placed all the newsgroups that you want to post to in the right side of the dialog box, click OK. The selected newsgroups will appear in the Newsgroups: box of your message (see Figure 10-12).

Remember that it's considered bad netiquette to post messages to multiple newsgroups. Do this only if it's absolutely necessary.

Spiffing Up Your Newsgroup Messages

Normally your newsgroup messages are sent as plain text, without a predefined signature, and without any attached files. You can change all this if you want.

Formatting your messages

E-mail messages can come in two flavors: plain text and fancier rich text (HTML) that enables special formatting, such as boldface, italics, and so forth. In e-mail, the rich-text format is the default setting. Newsgroup messages also can come in the same two flavors. Plain text is the default, however, because most newsgroup readers do not support the rich-text HTML format that Outlook Express does.

Rich-text messages can display a lot of annoying HTML code in newsgroup readers that don't support rich text. I recommend that you stick with plain text for your newsgroup postings.

To change the format of a new newsgroup message or to that of one to which you're replying, choose Format ➪ Rich Text (HTML) or Format ➪ Plain Text. Choosing Format ➪ Plain Text displays the dialog box shown in Figure 10-14. Click OK to switch to the plain-text format that everyone can read or choose Cancel to stick with the HTML format (remember, however, that not everyone will be able to read your message).

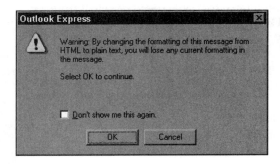

Figure 10-14: This dialog box reminds you that switching to plain-text format may cause a loss of formatting when the newsgroup message is sent.

If you do opt to use the rich-text format, you'll see the Formatting toolbar shown in Figure 10-15, and you can use any of its buttons to dress up your message. Chapter 9 explains how to use the Formatting toolbar and equivalent options on the menu bar.

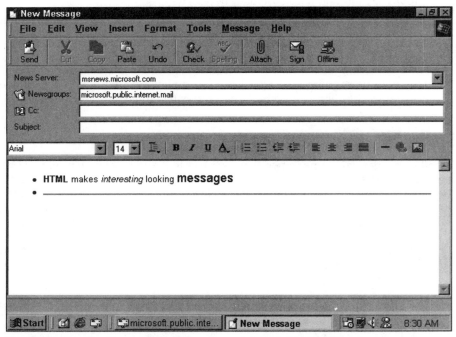

Figure 10-15: The Formatting toolbar for a rich-text (HTML) format message

Tip   To change the default format used for all newsgroup messages, choose Tools ⇨ Options from the Outlook Express menu bar, click the Send tab, choose the appropriate HTML and Plain Text options in the News Sending Format area, and click OK.

Inserting predefined signature text

If you set up some predefined signature text for newsgroup messages, you can add it to your message with one click of a button. First, position the insertion point where the signature text should appear. Then, choose Insert ⇨ Signature from the menu bar.

If you haven't set up a predefined newsgroup signature yet, the Insert ⇨ Signature option won't be available. See the later section "Automatically assigning signatures to newsgroup messages" for instructions on setting up a newsgroup message signature.

Tip   If you set up a personal business card (vCard) for newsgroups, you can add it to your message by choosing Insert ⇨ My Business Card from the message window menu. A vCard icon will appear near the upper-right corner of the message. (To remove the vCard information and its icon, choose Insert ⇨ My Business Card again. Or, click or right-click the vCard icon, and then choose Delete.) See Chapter 9 for more about vCards.

Attaching a file

You can attach files to a newsgroup message just as you attach them to e-mail messages (see Chapter 9). Here's a quick review of what to do:

✦ To insert plain text from a file, position the insertion point where the text should appear and choose Insert ⇨ Text From File. When the Insert Text File dialog box appears, locate and double-click the filename you want to insert. The text appears at the insertion point, just as though you had typed it in yourself.

✦ To attach a text file or a nontext file (which will appear as an icon in the message), click the Attach button on the toolbar (see Figure 10-11) or choose Insert ⇨ File Attachment from the menu bar. When the Insert Attachment dialog box appears, locate and double-click the filename you want to insert. An icon appears at the bottom of the address header, as shown in Figure 10-16. The reader usually can double-click the icon to display, open, run, or save the attached file.

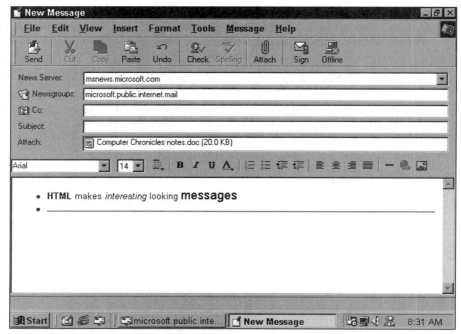

Figure 10-16: This is a newsgroup message that contains an attached file.

Automatically assigning signatures to newsgroup messages

Chapter 9 explains how to set up automatic signature text so Outlook Express will sign your e-mail messages automatically (or so you can insert the signature text manually whenever you want). These options work the same way in Outlook Express News. Here's how to begin:

1. Choose Tools ➪ Options and click the Signatures tab in the Options dialog box.

2. Specify one of these Signature options:

   - ___Text: **Display the text you type into the box next to the Text option.**

   - ___File: **Display the contents of the file listed next to the File option (you can click the Browse button to locate and fill in the filename).**

3. Specify whether to add the signature automatically or manually by selecting or deselecting Add This Signature To All Outgoing Messages and Don't Add Signature To Replies And Forwards. If you deselect the Add Signature . . . option, you can insert the signature manually, as explained earlier.

4. Click OK.

Filtering Out Unwanted Newsgroup Messages

Suppose you're tired of viewing old messages or you don't want to read any messages containing the word *spam* or *adult* in the Subject: line. No problem! You can filter out unwanted newsgroup messages using the Group Filters feature. Your filters can weed out messages by sender, subject, length in lines, or length of time they've hung around in the newsgroup. Like the message rules in Outlook Express Mail, news rules are a tool for defining rules for screening out messages in one or more newsgroups.

To add a new rule, follow these steps:

1. Choose Tools ➪ Message Rules ➪ News from the Outlook Express News menu bar. You'll be taken to a New News Rule dialog box that resembles Figure 10-17.

2. Select conditions for the rule.

3. Choose the actions you want to apply to the messages that meet the specified conditions.

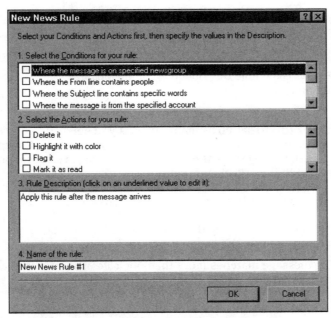

Figure 10-17: I'm setting up the criteria for weeding out unwanted newsgroup messages.

4. Click each of the underlined items in the rule description area and fill in the necessary information.

5. Click OK. You'll return to the Message Rules dialog box and your new rule will appear in the Rule Description list, as in Figure 10-18.

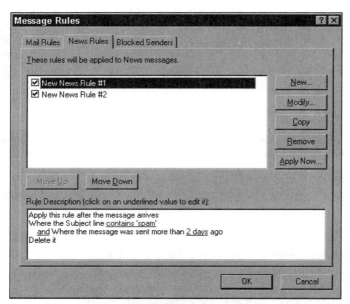

Figure 10-18: This is the Rule Description list of the Message Rules after setting up some rules.

You can repeat Steps 2 to 5 to set up as many rules as you need and you can adjust the rules, as I'll explain momentarily. When you're happy with the list, click OK. The next time you access the newsgroup, the Newsgroup message rules will process any messages that match the criteria you set up.

Here are some points to remember about the Message Rules:

✦ The Message Rules process only the rules selected in the list of rules. They ignore rules that appear in the list, but aren't selected.

✦ If an incoming message matches more than one rule, it's processed according to the first rule it matches and the others are ignored.

You can adjust the rules in the Message Rules dialog box at any time:

✦ To turn off a rule temporarily, deselect (clear) the check box next to the rule. To turn the rule back on again, select the box once more. It's easier to turn off a rule and turn it back on than it is to remove the rule and re-create it later.

✦ To remove a rule permanently, click it in the list and then click the Remove button. Be careful! No prompt exists for confirmation. The rule evaporates the moment you click Remove.

✦ To change a rule, click it in the list and then click the Modify button (or double-click the rule's description). The Edit News Rule dialog box will open and you can change any criteria you want.

✦ To move a rule up or down in the Description list (thus changing the order in which the rules are processed), click the rule you want to move and then click the Move Up or Move Down button as needed.

Subscribing and Unsubscribing

After a while, you'll discover some favorite newsgroups you'll want to return to again and again. That is, you'll want to subscribe to those newsgroups. Any newsgroup to which you've subscribed will appear below the appropriate newsgroup server name in the folder list. You can click the newsgroup in the folder list or message list to pay it a visit.

Note   If you don't see the subscribed newsgroups below the server in the folder list, click the plus (+) sign next to the server name. If you want to display the subscribed newsgroups in the message list instead, click the server name in the folder list.

It's easy to subscribe to (or drop a subscription from) any newsgroup your server offers. Follow these steps:

1. Starting from Outlook Express News, click the Newsgroups button on the toolbar or choose Tools ➪ Newsgroups. You'll see the Newsgroup Subscriptions dialog box, shown in Figure 10-19.

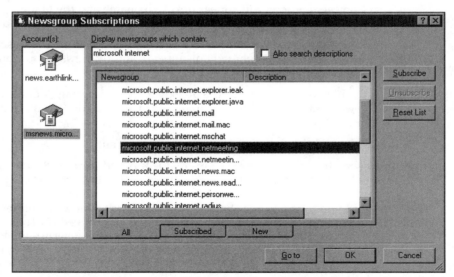

Figure 10-19: The Newsgroups dialog box with newsgroups that contain the words "microsoft" and "internet" selected

2. In the News Servers list at the left side of the window, click the server that you want to use (optional if only one server name appears).

3. If you want to download the latest list of newsgroups your server offers, click the Reset List button. Most news servers will automatically notify you of new newsgroups, so this step may not be necessary.

4. Choose whether to show all newsgroups, only the newsgroups to which you've subscribed, or new newsgroups on the server by clicking the All, Subscribed, or New tabs, respectively. Most often, you'll want to stick with the All tab so that you can see all the available newsgroups.

5. In the Newsgroup list, locate the newsgroup to which you want to subscribe or unsubscribe (newsgroups are listed in alphabetical order). You can use any of these techniques:

- Use the vertical scroll bar to scroll up and down in the Newsgroup list.

- Click in the Display newsgroups which contain box and type all or part of the newsgroup name, as shown in Figure 10-19. (To match more than one word or character sequence in the newsgroup name, type a space between each word or partial word, as in Figure 10-19, where I typed microsoft internet.) The Newsgroup list will display only the matching newsgroup names.

- Click the Display newsgroups which contain box and delete or edit the text it contains to redisplay the entire list or to correct a typing error.

6. Click the name of the newsgroup to which you want to subscribe or unsubscribe. Then do one of the following:

- To subscribe to the selected newsgroup, click the Subscribe button. A newspaper icon will appear next to its name and the newsgroup will appear in the folder list of the Outlook Express News window.

- To unsubscribe from the selected newsgroup, click the Unsubscribe button. The newspaper icon disappears and the newsgroup won't appear in the folder list.

- To subscribe or unsubscribe quickly to the newsgroup, double-click the newsgroup's name. The newspaper icon appears if it wasn't there before or disappears if it was previously there.

7. Repeat Steps 2 through 6 as many times as you want.

8. If you want to close the Newsgroups dialog box and jump to the currently selected newsgroup, click the Go To button; otherwise, click OK.

That's it! When you return to the Outlook Express News window, the folder list will show the newsgroups to which you've subscribed. If you clicked Go To in Step 8, but you didn't subscribe to the newsgroup you went to, that newsgroup also will appear in the folder list, but only during the current Outlook Express News session. It'll disappear from the folder list the next time you start Outlook Express News.

You can bypass the Newsgroups dialog box if the newsgroup to which you want to subscribe or unsubscribe already appears in your folder list. Simply right-click the newsgroup name in the folder list and choose Subscribe (if you haven't subscribed to it yet) or Unsubscribe (if you have).

Connecting to Multiple News Servers

You're not limited to viewing the newsgroups on your own ISP's news server. No indeed! Many publicly accessible and private news servers exist all over the Internet. To connect to them, you just have to find out the server name and plug it into your list of Outlook Express News accounts (as explained shortly).

Of course, the decision about whether to subscribe to a particular news server will depend on several factors, such as the groups the server offers and how much censorship the server imposes. Typically, your ISP will supply all the newsgroups you need. But you may want to set up additional newsgroup server accounts in the following situations:

✦ You need access to a private newsgroup server, which is available only to paid-up subscribers and usually requires a special account name and password.

✦ You need access to a private newsgroup server, which is free but accessible only to a select group of people, such as software beta testers. Again, access often requires a special account name and password.

✦ You have several ISPs and each offers special newsgroups that the others do not.

✦ You use a laptop computer and different Internet accounts, depending on whether you're at work or at home. For example, from work you access the Internet through a corporate server that doesn't offer its own newsgroups. From home, you access the Internet from a service provider that offers a full complement of newsgroups. In this scenario, you'll probably want to use two newsgroup servers: one generic server for your news reading activities at work, and another provided by your ISP for news reading at home.

One handy server for getting help and information on Microsoft products is msnews.microsoft.com and I recommend that you add it to your news server account list.

Once you find an interesting newsgroup server, you can plug it into Outlook Express News in either of two ways:

✦ By clicking the hyperlinks to those servers if you encounter them on a Web page. You'll be taken to Outlook Express News and asked if you want to download the list of newsgroups for the server. This method adds the server to the folder list of the Outlook Express News window during the current session only.

✦ By plugging the server names into the Internet Accounts dialog box in Outlook Express, as the following explains. This method adds the server to the folder list of the Outlook Express News window permanently (until you delete it).

To add a newsgroup server to your Internet Accounts, follow these steps:

1. Starting from Outlook Express News or Outlook Express Mail, choose Tools ➪ Accounts from the menu bar. The Internet Accounts dialog box appears.

2. To limit the account list to news servers only and reduce the clutter in the dialog box, click the News tab.

3. Click the Add button and choose News.

4. The Internet Connection Wizard will kick in just as it did when you first set up Outlook Express and you can follow the prompts to add the news server. As usual, fill in the dialog boxes that appear and click Next and Finish to continue.

5. When the wizard finishes, you'll be returned to the Internet Accounts dialog box, shown in Figure 10-20.

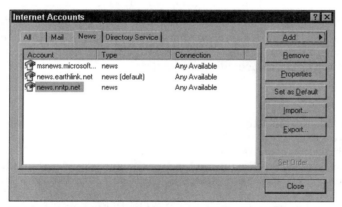

Figure 10-20: The Internet Accounts dialog box with three news servers added

The first server you set up will be the default server, but you can change this. Starting from the News tab in the Internet Accounts dialog box, click the name of the account you want to use as the default account and then click Set As Default. When you finish using the Internet Accounts dialog box, click Close. See Chapter 9 for more details about using the Internet Accounts dialog box and the Internet Connection Wizard.

Tip

The basic steps for setting up News accounts in the Internet Accounts dialog box are the same as for setting up Mail accounts, except that you choose the News tab to display only the News accounts and you choose News from the Add button, rather than Mail, to set up additional news servers.

Speeding Up Outlook Express News

Outlook Express News usually copies message headers and body text from the newsgroup to your local hard disk automatically. It also deletes read messages when you exit the program and only keeps unread messages for a limited time. You can customize this default behavior to make the program work more efficiently for your hardware setup.

If you're working with newsgroups over a slow connection, such as a 28.8Kbps modem, you may want to avoid downloading much information from a newsgroup onto your computer's hard disk until you're sure that you want to read it. Outlook Express News offers a useful way to serve up your newsgroup information in smaller bites — download fewer message headers at once. By default, Outlook Express News downloads 300 message headers.

To adjust the setting for downloading message headers, choose Tools ➪ Options from the Outlook Express News menu bar and then click the Read tab (see Figure 10-21). Now change the following option as needed:

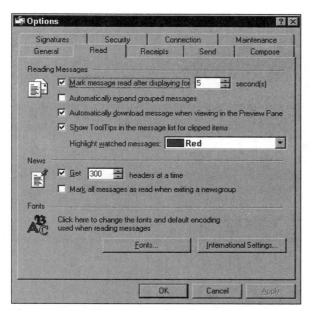

Figure 10-21: Change your download settings using the Read tab of the Options dialog box.

Select the **Get *n* Headers At A Time** option and then specify the number of headers you want to download at once — between 50 and 1000. If you deselect this option, Outlook Express News will download all the headers when you select a newsgroup, which can be time-consuming.

Click OK to save your settings. They'll take effect the next time you visit the newsgroup.

If you limited the number of headers to be downloaded at once, you can still display the next group of message headers. First, get online and connect to the newsgroup (if you haven't already). Then choose Tools ➪ Get Next *n* Headers (where *n* is the number you entered in the Options dialog box).

Downloading Messages for Later Viewing

If you're like most netizens, you pay a nominal flat rate fee for your Internet usage, regardless of how many hours you're actually connected to the Internet. But even if you do have unlimited flat-rate Internet access, it's best to disconnect from the Internet when you aren't using it and to read and compose newsgroup (and e-mail) messages offline whenever possible.

Outlook Express News offers many ways to read newsgroups offline and to copy (or download) messages to local files on your own computer, so you don't tie up valuable Internet resources (phone lines, LAN connections, and the like) while you read the daily news.

Marking messages for retrieval

Suppose you're not connected to the Internet, and when you click a message header in the message list, the following message displays in the preview pane:

```
This message is not cached. Please connect to your server to
download the message.
```

This message tells you that you're not connected and no local copy of the message exists on your hard disk for you to review. You have two choices:

✦ Go online now and view the message.

✦ Mark all the messages you want to view while you're offline. Then connect and download all the marked messages at once.

Follow these steps to mark the messages you want to download (you needn't be online):

1. Select the newsgroup you want to work with (if you haven't already).

2. Select the headers of the messages you want to download. You can use the standard click, Ctrl+click, or Shift+click technique to highlight the messages in the message list. To select all the messages at once, click any message in the message list and choose Edit ➪ Select All, or press Ctrl+A. (Chapter 9 explains more about selecting multiple items in the message list.)

3. Choose one of the following options from the Tools ➪ Mark For Offline submenu:

- ___Download Message Later: **Marks the selected messages for retrieval.**
- ___Download Conversation Later: **Marks the selected thread for retrieval.**
- ___Download All Messages Later: **Marks all messages in the newsgroup for retrieval.**

The messages you selected are marked with a little down arrow icon, as shown in Figure 10-22. You can repeat these steps for as many newsgroups as you want.

Tip

As a shortcut, you can mark one message for retrieval by right-clicking it and choosing Download Message Later from the shortcut menu or by clicking it and pressing Ctrl+M.

Unmarking messages for retrieval

If you change your mind about marking a message header for retrieval, it's easy enough to unmark it. First, select the messages you want to unmark using the usual click, Ctrl+click, Shift+click, or Ctrl+A methods given in the previous Step 2. Then choose Tools ➪ Mark For Offline ➪ Do Not Download Message.

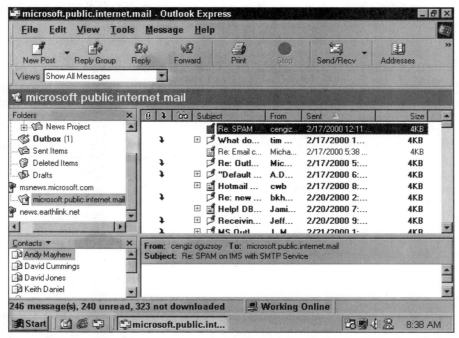

Figure 10-22: Several messages are marked for retrieval as indicated by the down arrow icons.

Downloading marked messages

Downloading marked messages is a breeze. Do either of the following:

✦ To download marked messages in *all* newsgroups, choose Tools ➪ Synchronize All. (This step also sends and receives all your e-mail messages.)

✦ To download marked messages in the currently selected newsgroup only, choose Tools ➪ Synchronize Newsgroup. You'll see the Synchronize Newsgroup dialog box, shown in Figure 10-23. Now, select Get messages marked for download, deselect Get the following items, and then click OK.

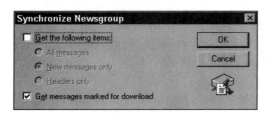

Figure 10-23: Use the Synchronize Newsgroup dialog box to download marked messages and/or specific items.

Outlook Express News will connect to the Internet and download the messages to your hard disk. Now you can view the messages by clicking (or double-clicking) their headers in the message list.

Getting new messages and headers

If you usually work offline, it is a good idea is to connect to the Internet occasionally and refresh the list of headers and/or messages in the newsgroups. You can refresh messages either for a specific newsgroup server or for a specific newsgroup.

Refreshing the list of new messages for a newsgroup server takes only a moment. First, select the newsgroup server that you want to refresh by clicking its name in the Outlook bar or the folder list. Then, choose Tools ➪ Synchronize All from the Outlook Express News menu bar.

If you prefer to refresh the list for a specific newsgroup, follow these steps instead:

1. Select the newsgroup that you want to work with, as explained earlier in this chapter.

2. Choose Tools ➪ Synchronize Newsgroup to open the Synchronize Newsgroup dialog box shown in Figure 10-23.

3. If you want to get marked messages in this newsgroup, select Get messages marked for download. If you don't want to get marked messages, deselect this option.

4. Select Get the following items and then do any of the following:

- To download new headers for the newsgroup, choose Headers only.

- To download new headers and messages for the newsgroup, choose New messages only.

- To download all headers and messages for the newsgroup, choose All messages.

5. Click OK.

Outlook Express News will connect to the Internet and download the headers and/or messages that you requested.

Tip While downloading takes place, an Outlook Express dialog box appears. It includes a progress bar, an option for specifying whether to hang up when finished, and three buttons: Hide, Stop, and Details. You can click the buttons as needed to hide the dialog box, to stop the download in its tracks, and to display or hide details of each download task and any errors that occurred. When downloading is complete, the dialog box will disappear.

Cleaning Up Your Local Files

Outlook Express News does a lot of cleanup on its own, so it doesn't leave a flotsam of unnecessary messages and headers floating around on your hard disk. You can control how often the program does garbage collection and you can manually clean up unnecessary files in a few ways.

To customize how often Outlook Express News does its automatic cleanup, follow these steps:

1. Choose Tools ➪ Options and click the Maintenance tab in the Options dialog box (see Figure 10-24).

2. Choose options in the Cleaning Up Messages area of the dialog box:

- **Delete news messages n days after being downloaded:** Select this option to delete downloaded messages automatically after they are n days old (where n is a number in days). Deselect this option if you never want to delete downloaded messages.

- **Delete read message bodies in newsgroups:** Select this option to toss out read messages when you exit Outlook Express. Deselect this option to keep read messages when you exit.

- **Compact messages when there is n percent wasted space:** Specify the amount of space that can be wasted before Outlook Express compacts the files automatically.

3. Click OK.

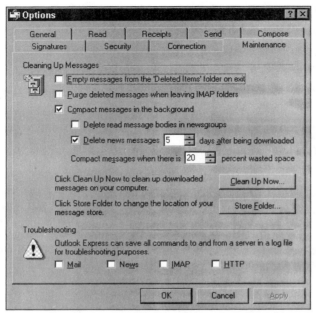

Figure 10-24: The Maintenance tab of the Options dialog box with the default options set

You also can manually clean up messages by following these steps:

1. Click the Clean Up Now button on the Maintenance tab of the Options dialog box (shown in Figure 10-24). The Local File Clean Up dialog box shown in Figure 10-25 will appear.

2. Click the Browse button to choose which messages to clean up. The account you select will appear in the Local file(s) for: list. You can choose Outlook Express or you can select a specific news server or newsgroup.

3. Click any of the following buttons as needed:

   • **Compact:** Reclaims disk space left over when you eliminated old unwanted messages and headers.

   • **Remove Messages:** Removes only the message bodies downloaded from the location you selected in Step 2, without removing any message headers.

   • **Delete:** Removes all message headers and bodies from the location you selected in Step 2. When asked for permission to delete the file of message headers and bodies, click Yes.

- **Reset:** Marks all articles as unread so you can re-download messages. When asked for permission to reset the information, click Yes.

4. Repeat Steps 2 and 3 for as many news servers and newsgroups as you want.

5. Click Close and OK (if necessary) to return to the main Outlook Express News window.

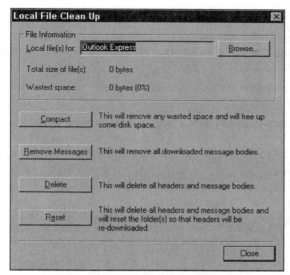

Figure 10-25: Clean up messages using the Local File Clean Up dialog box.

Other Ways to Customize Outlook Express News

You've already learned several ways to customize the behavior and appearance of Outlook Express News. Of course, many more ways exist and they'll be mighty familiar if you read Chapter 9.

If you'd like to experiment a little, choose Tools ➪ Options and explore the General, Send, and Read tabs in the Options dialog box. Also select the options on the View menu. You'll find the available options are easy to understand and to use.

Summary

In this chapter, you learned about Usenet newsgroups, yet another popular feature of the Internet. To summarize the main points:

✦ A newsgroup is a collection of messages sent to and from people who share an interest.

✦ You can use Outlook Express News to participate in Usenet newsgroups.

✦ To subscribe to a newsgroup in Outlook Express News, click the Newsgroups button on the toolbar. Then click any newsgroup that you want to join and click the Subscribe button.

✦ To read an article (message) within a newsgroup, click the message subject line in the message list.

✦ To view replies to a message, click the plus (+) sign to the left of the message subject line.

✦ To reply to a newsgroup message, click the Reply Group button (to reply to the entire group) or Reply Sender button (to reply to only the message author). Type your reply and click the Send button.

✦ To unsubscribe from a newsgroup, click the Newsgroups button in Outlook Express News, click the newsgroup you wish to leave, and then click the Unsubscribe button.

✦　　✦　　✦

NetMeeting: Your Free Long Distance Video Phone

The days of the long-distance telephone call seem to be coming to a close, as more and more people use the Internet to communicate in realtime, for free, over long distances. By *realtime,* I mean an actual ongoing two-way conversation, as opposed to e-mail where the message gets sent and you get a reply whenever you get a reply. Windows Me (though perhaps I should say Microsoft in general) offers two tools for such realtime communication. MSN Messenger enables any two or more people to communicate online in a "chat" fashion, where they type messages back and forth to one another. When you add NetMeeeting to the mix, you're no longer limited to typing. Instead, you can communicate by voice and video. You can even collaborate on projects, transfer files to one another, operate a remote computer as though it were on your desk, and more.

Using MSN Messenger

MSN Messenger, aka *MSN Instant Messaging,* is the service that's at the very root of online realtime conversations. No, you don't need to be a member of MSN to use this feature. In fact, it really doesn't matter who you use as your Internet Service Provider — you can still use MSN Instant Messaging. You do, however, need to set up an account with MSN.

Because that process takes place online and is subject to change, I can't give you exact step-by-step instructions for setting up an account. However, I can get you to the point where you'll be able to follow the simple onscreen instructions to get your account going.

Set up a Hotmail account

The first thing to do is set up a Hotmail account. Hotmail is Microsoft's free e-mail service. You don't actually have to use Hotmail or the Hotmail address you'll be creating by signing up (though you can use it if you want to). The main purpose of setting up a Hotmail account is to get you into the directory of MSN Instant Messenger users, and to get you a passport as well. Here's how to set up your Hotmail account:

Note   If you already have a Hotmail account, you don't need to perform any of the steps below!

1. If you have a dial-up account, you should first connect to your Internet Service Provider and log in normally so that you're online.

2. Open up Internet Explorer (or the Web browser of your choice) and go to http://www.msn.com.

3. Choose Hotmail from the options presented, then follow the instructions and options on the Web page that appears to set up a Hotmail account.

When you set up your account, be sure to write down your e-mail name (for example, wanda@hotmail.com) as well as your password. Again, you don't need to use the new e-mail address as your regular address, but you will need the name and password to use the Messenger and other services.

Setting up MSN Messenger

The next step is to set up the MSN Messenger Service. Again, much of this takes place online, so I can only give you enough instructions to get started.

1. If your Web browser is open, close it. But don't close your Internet connection.

2. If you're not connected to the Internet at the moment, log on to your ISP normally.

3. Click the Start button and choose Programs ➪ Accessories ➪ Communications ➪ MSN Messenger Service (or click the MSN Messenger icon if it appears in the System Tray).

4. You're taken to the first page of a setup wizard. Read it and then click the Next button.

From here on out, just follow instructions as they appear on the screen. Remember that you have, by now, set up a Hotmail account, so you don't need to sign up for a passport if/when you're given the option to do so. Instead, give whatever name and password you chose for your Hotmail account, and choose hotmail.com under "Provided by" as in the example shown in Figure 11-1.

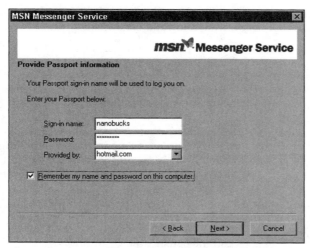

Figure 11-1: Specify your Hotmail account name and password as your Passport information.

You might also be given the option to download the latest version of MSN Messenger Service. If so, you should choose Yes and proceed with the download. When all is finished, the MSN Messenger Service window will be open on your screen. You can close that for the time being so that you can learn how to start and use the messenger service from scratch.

Creating your Contacts list

The next step is to create a contacts list, or "buddy list" as some services call it, of people with whom you want to interact online via the messenger service. After your account is set up, you might find that MSN Messenger has moved to your Programs menu. So startup will proceed as follows:

1. If you have a dial-up account, go ahead and connect to your ISP normally.

2. Click the Start button and choose Programs.

3. If you see MSN Messenger on the Programs menu, go ahead and select it. Otherwise, choose Accessories ➪ Programs ➪ Communications ➪ MSN Messenger Service.

Initially, MSN Messenger Service may start up telling you that you're not logged on. No problem; just click the link that enables you to log on, sign in with your Hotmail username and password, and click OK. If you've never set up a buddy list, you'll also see a message to that effect. To start building your buddy list:

1. Click the Add button in the MSN Messenger Service window.

2. Choose how you want to identify the contact. If all you know is the person's e-mail address, choose that first option and then click Next.

3. Type the complete e-mail address of the person you want to contact and then click Next.

At this point, the wizard will provide more options and feedback. Just follow the instructions on the screen and choose your options accordingly.

Once you've set up at least one buddy list person, starting MSN Messenger will show you which of those buddies is currently online, and which is not. For example, in Figure 11-2 one of my buddies, named Alec, is currently online so I could contact him directly. My other buddy, MediaMon2000@hotmail.com isn't currently online.

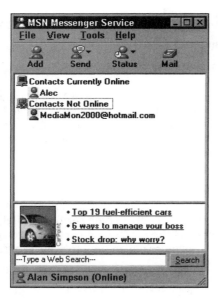

Figure 11-2: One buddy, Alec, is currently online; the other isn't.

Contacting a buddy

To contact a buddy who's currently online, double-click the buddy's name in the list. Or click the Send button and choose the buddy's name from the menu that appears. In the Instant Message dialog box that appears, type a message in the lower textbox, as in Figure 11-3, and then click the Send button.

Figure 11-3: Preparing to send a message to my buddy Alec using Instant Message

The buddy will hear a sound indicating an incoming call, and a button will flash in the taskbar. He or she just needs to click that button, and the online "typing" conversation can begin. Each party just types a message in the lower text box and clicks on Send to send the message.

To get other buddies to join in the conversation, just click the Invite button, and fill in the blanks as instructed. To end the session, just close the Instant Message dialog box. Or, should you get a weirdo on the line that you want to get rid of, just click the Block button to make him or her go away. However, that person won't be able to reach you in the future, so don't block people you intend to communicate with later.

You can also close the Instant Messenger dialog box. However, the MSN Messenger Service indicator will remain in the Indicators section of the toolbar, to let you know you're still logged on, and therefore other people can contact you.

Tip As a shortcut, you can just double-click the MSN Messenger Service icon in the Indicators section of the taskbar.

Receiving an Instant Message call

While you're online and logged into the messenger service, other people can contact you. You'll hear a little tone when someone calls you, and then see an Instant Messenger button blinking in the taskbar. To start the conversation, just click the blinking button.

Your "Do Not Disturb" option

If you don't want to receive Instant Messages, log off of the service. Just right-click the MSN Messenger Service icon in the Indicators section of the Taskbar and choose Log Off. Buddies will see your name listed under Contacts Not Online in the MSN Messenger Service and won't be able to bother you until you log back on. If your computer is still connected to the Internet, you can log on simply by right-clicking the MSN Messenger Service indicator in the taskbar and choosing Log On. If you go offline or shut down your computer, you'll need to connect to the Internet again, click the Start button, and choose Programs ➪ MSN Messenger Service to log back on.

More on MSN Messenger

As I write this chapter, MSN Messenger is still a fairly new service. By the time you read this, the service might have many more features. To supplement what you've learned here, and to keep abreast of changes, use these resources:

✦ For information about your current version of MSN Messenger, choose Help ➪ Help Topics from its menu bar.

✦ For more general information about the service, use your Web browser to visit http://messenger.msn.com.

Videophoning with NetMeeting

NetMeeting, which also comes with Windows Me, adds several dimensions to realtime communications over the Internet. Perhaps the most popular being voice and video. Once again, the phone companies are out of the picture when you're communicating with NetMeeting. So, not only do you get worldwide voice communications without long distance charges, but you also get a twenty-first century videophone for free.

NetMeeting requirements

Some of the hardware requirements to take full advantage of everything that NetMeeting offers go a bit beyond the basic requirements of running Windows Me. Here's what Microsoft suggests for basic voice communications:

✦ 90 MHz Pentium processor or better

✦ 16MB of RAM

✦ Microsoft Internet Explorer version 4.01 or later (Windows Me ships with Version 5).

✦ 28,800 bps or faster modem (faster is better)

✦ For voice communications, a sound card with microphone and speakers, or equivalent headset

For more advanced features of NetMeeting, including video and collaboration, the following hardware is recommended:

✦ A Pentium 133 MHz processor or better with at least 16MB of RAM

✦ 56,000 bps or faster modem, ISDN, or LAN connection

✦ Sound card with microphone and speakers or a headset (required for both audio and video communications)

✦ Video capture card, camera, or *Web cam* for videophone communications

Tip

There are dozens of inexpensive Web cams on the market that work great with NetMeeting. To see a list of compatible products online, choose Help ⇨ Get A Camera from NetMeeting's menu bar.

You'll also need to set up an account with one or more *directory servers*. A directory server is sort of like a telephone directory of addresses of people with whom you can communicate through NetMeeting. To get started, you might want to just set up a Hotmail account, the MSN Messenger service, and a buddy list, as discussed earlier in this chapter. If you've already done that, it's not necessary to do it again. The account you created there works with NetMeeting as well.

Starting NetMeeting

Starting NetMeeting is simple. Connect to the Internet in the usual manner for your PC. Then from the Windows Me desktop, click the Start button and choose Programs ⇨ Accessories ⇨ Communications ⇨ Microsoft NetMeeting.

The first time you start NetMeeting, you'll be taken to a wizard that helps you choose a directory server, identify yourself, and configure your audio gear. Like most wizards, it's pretty self-explanatory. The first page, shown in Figure 11-4, asks that you enter some basic information about yourself. This information is used to identify you in online meetings.

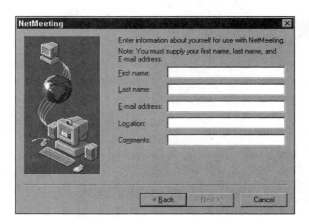

Figure 11-4: Enter information about yourself on this wizard page.

The second screen, shown in Figure 11-5, asks whether you want to be taken to a directory server as soon as NetMeeting starts. If you have, indeed set up a Hotmail and MSN Messenger account, go ahead and choose Microsoft Internet Directory as your default directory service, as in the figure. There's no cost for doing so. If you want to maintain your privacy you can choose the "Do not list my name in the directory" option.

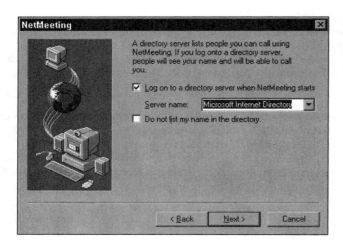

Figure 11-5: Choose your default directory server from this wizard screen.

In the third wizard screen, which is shown in Figure 11-6, choose your connection type. The fourth and fifth wizard screens will help you adjust the volume of your speakers and microphone, which you'll want to make sure are working and are sufficiently loud if you plan on having voice conversations with NetMeeting. When you've completed all the Wizard pages and clicked Finish, NetMeeting fires up, looking something like an ultramodern cell phone with a TV screen on it (Figure 11-7).

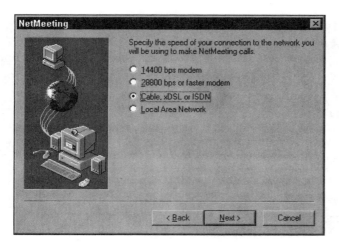

Figure 11-6: Choose your connection type from the third Wizard screen.

Figure 11-7: NetMeeting is ready for action.

Calling through Microsoft Internet Directory

Depending on how you responded to the Wizard prompts the first time you ran NetMeeting, you may or may not be connected to a server as soon as NetMeeting starts. Regardless, you can connect at any time the NetMeeting is running by following these steps:

1. If you have a dial-up connection to the Internet, go ahead and log in.

2. Choose Call ⇨ Directory. As with Instant Messenger, you'll see a list of "buddies" who are currently online, and off. (If you're not logged in automatically, choose Call ⇨ Log On to Microsoft Internet Directory first.)

3. Click the name of the person you want to call.

The recipient will see a message indicating that you are inviting them to use NetMeeting as in Figure 11-8. The recipient just needs to click on Accept, and the NetMeeting window will open on their screen. The message "In a call" appears in NetMeeting's status bar, to let you know that you can start communicating.

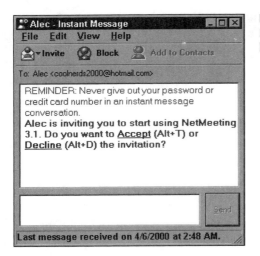

Figure 11-8: The recipient of a NetMeeting call sees a message like this one.

While you're in a call, use the three buttons below the video screen to fine-tune your audio and video settings. Pointing to a button, as always, displays the name of the button. Your choices are:

✦ **Start/Stop Video:** If you have video capability, use this button to start or stop your video display.

✦ **Picture In Picture:** To show or hide your video output on your own screen, click this middle button. To view your own video in a separate window, choose View ➪ My Video (New Window) from NetMeeting's menu bar.

✦ **Participant List/Adjust Audio Volume:** Switches between sliders for adjusting your microphone and speaker volume, as shown in the Figure 11-9, and a list of people currently participating in the call.

From here on out, the rest is easy. If both participants have sound capabilities, voice communications will start automatically and you can just start talking. If there's a problem, make sure the check boxes above the microphone and speaker sliders are selected, and their volumes are set comfortably. (If you see the participant list rather than the sliders, just click the Adjust Audio Volume button to view the sliders.) Use the leftmost of the first three buttons to start and stop video communications. The middle button enables you to see how your own image looks to the other person.

At this point, you're free to chat, use the whiteboard, transfer files, and so forth, and allow others to join in the conversation as well. The tools available to you, and the basic skills that you need to use those tools, are presented in the sections that follow. But before we get to that, you'll probably want to know how to end a NetMeeting call.

Figure 11-9: In a videophone call with Alec

Ending a NetMeeting call

When you're ready to hang up, just click the Hang Up button. If you're viewing the Participant List, you'll see it empty. The Not in a call indicator appears at the lower-left corner of NetMeeting's window when you're no longer in a call. And that, in a nutshell, is how you use the basic voice and video capabilities of NetMeeting. There are plenty of other tools and options to play around with though, as you'll learn in the sections that follow.

Holding an Online Meeting

Voice and video are certainly important parts of NetMeeting. And we'll look at some of the requirements and options for those two forms of communication in the sections that follow. But here you'll also learn about other communications tools that you can use while in a call in NetMeeting.

NetMeeting audio

To use voice (audio) features of NetMeeting, your computer must have a headset, and/or sound card with speakers and a microphone. If your computer lacks these, or if they're not properly connected, all of the audio features of NetMeeting are disabled.

Sound cards come in two basic "flavors," half-duplex and full-duplex. With half-duplex, the signal travels only one direction at a time. Therefore, only one person at a time can talk. Some of the early speakerphones used half-duplex. If you have experience with those, you'll know that the big downside to half-duplex is sound clipping. Each time one party starts talking, the first syllable or two tends to get cut off. Which can really drive you crazy.

If your sound card is half-duplex, there's no way around the problem, except to replace your existing sound card with one that supports full-duplex. If your sound card has full-duplex (or if you're not sure whether it does or not), and you're getting sound clipping, make sure the Enable full duplex audio so I can speak while receiving audio option in NetMeeting is turned on. To do so, choose Tools ➪ Options from NetMeeting's menu bar. Then click the Audio tab to get to the options shown in Figure 11-10. Make sure the Enable full-duplex audio so I can speak while receiving audio option is selected. If that option is disabled (dimmed), that means your sound card doesn't support full-duplex, and that there's no way to turn full-duplex on.

Note   The Audio tab in NetMeeting's Options dialog box is available only if your computer has audio capability.

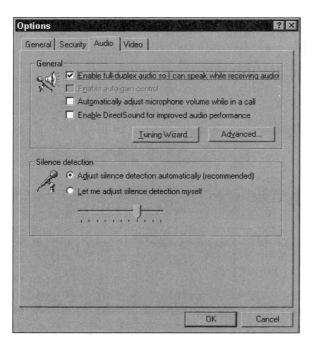

Figure 11-10: The Audio tab of NetMeeting's Options dialog box

Options on the Audio tab are summarized below. If an option is disabled in the dialog box, your sound card doesn't support that feature, and therefore it's not an option for you.

✦ **Enable full-duplex audio so I can speak while receiving audio:** This turns on your sound card's full-duplex capabilities. The only reason to disable this feature is to see whether half-duplex produces better sound quality.

✦ **Enable auto-gain control:** Some sound cards offer an auto-gain feature that automatically adjusts the microphone volume as you speak. If your sound card offers this feature, selecting this option will make sure that NetMeeting uses that feature.

✦ **Automatically adjust microphone volume while in a call:** If your sound card does not support auto-gain, selecting this option will provide the equivalent of an auto-gain feature.

✦ **Enable DirectSound for improved audio performance:** If your sound system supports DirectSound, choosing this option improves performance by shortening the time between when audio is sent and received.

✦ **Tuning Wizard:** Runs the audio tuning wizard that appeared the first time you ran NetMeeting. The wizard can't be used while you're in a call.

✦ **Advanced:** Lets you choose a compression/decompression (codec) method for compressing sound. Choose this option only if you have some compelling reason to manually select a codec other than the default.

✦ **Silence detection:** Selecting automatic silence detection enables NetMeeting to filter our background noise automatically. If you prefer to adjust that yourself, choose the Let me adjust silence detection myself option and then use the slider to increase or decrease silence detection.

While you're in a call, you can easily adjust audio settings without going to the Options dialog box. If you're currently viewing the Participant List, click the Adjust Audio Volume button to view audio sliders. To turn off your microphone, clear the check box next to the microphone icon. To turn off your speakers, clear the check box next to the speaker icon. To adjust the volume of each, first make sure the item's check box is selected and then move the slider left or right to decrease or increase the volume.

NetMeeting video

Anybody who uses NetMeeting can *receive* video from another party. But you can *send* video only if you have a Web cam or other video device installed on your computer. Options for fine-tuning your video are on the Video tab of the Options dialog box shown in Figure 11-11. In NetMeeting, choose Tools ➪ Options from the menu bar, and then click on the Video tab to get to those options. Note that if you don't have a video camera installed, most options will be disabled (dimmed).

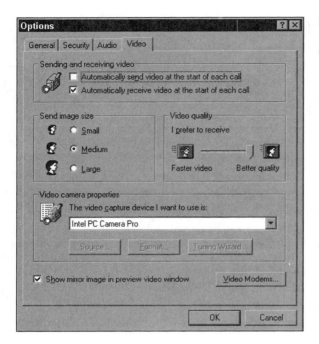

Figure 11-11: The Video tab in NetMeeting's Options dialog box

Your options are:

✦ **Automatically send video at the start of each call:** If selected, your video image is sent automatically as soon as the call starts. Otherwise, your video isn't sent until you click the Start Video button in NetMeeting, or choose Tools ➪ Video ➪ Send from the menu bar.

✦ **Automatically receive video at the start of each call:** If selected, a caller's video (if any) is displayed automatically. If not selected, a caller's video is hidden until you choose Tools ➪ Video ➪ Receive from NetMeeting's toolbar.

✦ **Send image size:** Determines the size of the video image you're sending. Larger images require more bandwidth (connection speed) to transmit smoothly.

✦ **Video quality:** Bandwidth-hungry video can be smooth, or can have high picture quality, but not always both. The Video quality slider lets you sacrifice picture quality for smoother motion if your bandwidth prevents you from having both qualities.

✦ **Video camera properties:** If you have multiple video devices attached to your computer, this option lets you choose which device to use with NetMeeting. The Format and Tuning Wizard buttons work differently with different types of cameras.

✦ **Show mirror image in preview video window:** If selected, your image is reversed like a mirror, which we're accustomed to by experience with everyday mirrors. However, deselecting this option can actually speed video transmissions because NetMeeting doesn't have to "calculate" a mirror image from the actual image.

✦ **Video modems:** If you have a video modem attached to your system, and NetMeeting isn't using it, the Video Modems button will start a wizard to help you configure and use that device.

While you're in a call, there's a lot more that you can do than just communicate with voice and video, as the sections below explain.

Typing messages with NetMeeting Chat

Chatting is a quick and easy method of communicating with others in a meeting. To chat, click the Chat button near the bottom of NetMeeting's window. Or choose Tools ➪ Chat from NetMeeting's menu bar. The Chat window opens, as in Figure 11-12, and its title bar indicates how many other people in your Current Call are using the same Chat window. Other peoples' messages will appear in the largest window automatically.

Figure 11-12: Using Chat in NetMeeting

To send a message, type whatever you want to say in the Message area. If you want to "whisper" (send a chat message to only one member of the meeting), choose that person's name from the Send To: drop-down list before you send the message. When you're ready to transmit the message, press Enter or click the large button to the right of the message area.

You also can control how chats are displayed on your screen using the Options menu in the Chat window. Choose View ⇨ Options from Chat's menu bar, and make your selections from the dialog box that appears. To save a chat session, choose File ⇨ Save from Chat's menu bar. Choose a folder and filename for the chat and then click the Save button. The chat is saved as a text (.txt) file that you can open later using Notepad, WordPad, or any word processing program. You'll also be given an opportunity to save the current chat session when you exit the Chat program (by closing the Chat window or choosing File ⇨ Exit from the Chat window's menu bar).

Using the Whiteboard

NetMeeting's Whiteboard is similar to Chat, but it lets you communicate with pictures rather than text. All the members of the current call can draw simultaneously. And everyone sees whatever is placed in Whiteboard. Think of Whiteboard as the regular chalkboard or white board often used in classrooms and meeting rooms. But, in this case, one person or several people can draw and write on the board at the same time. To start Whiteboard while in a NetMeeting call, just click the Whiteboard button near the bottom of NetMeeting's window. Or choose Tools ⇨ Whiteboard from its menu bar.

Whiteboard pops up on your screen, as well as on the screen of everyone else in the current call. With Whiteboard onscreen, you can draw using various tools, including Pen, Line, Unfilled Rectangle, Filled Rectangle, Unfilled Ellipse, and Filled Ellipse. To use a drawing tool, click the appropriate button on the toolbar and drag the tool across the large drawing area. If the drawing tools aren't visible, choose View ⇨ Tool Bar from Whiteboard's menus. You also can choose tools by right-clicking in the drawing area and making a selection from the shortcut menu that appears. Figure 11-13 shows the Whiteboard with some sample content.

Figure 11-13: The Whiteboard with some text, a drawing, and a pasted photo in it

Typing text in Whiteboard

You can type text using the Text toolbar button. After you click that button, you can choose a font and text color and font from options at the bottom of the Whiteboard window, or from the Tools menu in Whiteboard. Then click anywhere on the Whiteboard and type your text.

Pasting pictures into Whiteboard

Any pictures you paste into the Whiteboard are visible to everyone in the call who is viewing the Whiteboard. Use any of these techniques to paste an image into the Whiteboard:

✦ If the image is on the screen in a program, select and copy whatever you want to send, using whatever works in that particular program. Then click in the Whiteboard and choose Edit ➪ Paste.

✦ Optionally, you can click the Select Area button in Whiteboard, click OK if you see a message, drag a rectangle around anything on the screen that you want to paste, and then release the mouse button.

✦ Or, if you want to copy a specific window or dialog box into the Whiteboard, click the Select Window button. If a message appears, click its OK button. Then click on the window that you want to copy into the Whiteboard.

After you've pasted an image (or anything else, for that matter) into the whiteboard, you can easily move it. Click on the Selector button in the toolbar, click on the object you want to move, then drag that object to some new position.

Erasing from Whiteboard

You can erase material from Whiteboard in a few ways:

✦ To erase the entire Whiteboard at once, choose Edit ➪ Clear Page from the Whiteboard menu bar or press Ctrl+Delete. Then choose Yes when asked for confirmation.

✦ To erase a drawn object or block of text, click the Eraser tool. Then click the object or chunk of text you want to erase. (To undo the deletion, choose Edit ➪ Undelete from the menus or press Ctrl+Z.)

✦ To delete individual letters rather than a whole block of text, choose Tools ➪ Text (or click the Text toolbar button), select the letters that you want to erase, and then press the Delete (Del) key.

Other Whiteboard features

The Zoom button in Whiteboard enables you to double the size of the image in Whiteboard. The Lock Contents button locks the Whiteboard's contents so that other meeting members can't change it. The Remote Pointer button displays a pointing hand that you can drag with your mouse to call attention to parts of the screen.

You can store multiple pages in Whiteboard. To add a new page, click the Insert New Page button down near the lower-right corner of the Whiteboard window. Or, choose Edit ⇨ Insert Page Before or Edit ⇨ Insert Page After from the menus. A new, blank Whiteboard page appears on which you can draw, type, or paste pictures. To scroll through pages, use the First Page, Previous Page, Next Page, and Last Page buttons near the lower-right corner of the Whiteboard window. Or, type a page number into the Page text box (again, near the lower-right corner) and press Enter.

You can learn more about Whiteboard by choosing Help ⇨ Help Topics from its menu bar. If you plan on using the Whiteboard often in your work (or play), you'd do well to spend some time reading the Help pages, so that you'll know how to use everything that Whiteboard offers.

Sharing applications

One of the most amazing features of NetMeeting is its capability to share applications. In fact, you can share applications even if everyone in the meeting does not have the same software you are sharing! Sharing is easy to do. The only bummer is sharing can be a little slow. Nonetheless, if you want to try it:

1. Close any programs you do not want to share with others.

2. Start any program on your PC or open any document you want to share.

3. Click NetMeeting's Share button, or choose Tools ⇨ Sharing. Then click the name of the application that you want to share and click the Share button.

4. Optionally, you can click the Allow Control button if you want others to be able to control the program. Or click the Prevent Control button to prevent others from being able to control the program.

A window appears on everyone else's screen that contains your shared programs and documents, as in the example shown in Figure 11-14 where Alec Fraser is sharing Microsoft Outlook with me. Whether or not others can *do* anything with that application depends on whether or not you've opted to enable control or prevent control. If you did enable control, selecting the Automatically accept requests for control option will enable other viewers to take control of the program immediately. If you don't select that option, other viewers will have to choose Control ⇨ Request Control from their menu bars to request control. You'll see a message indicating that someone has requested control, at which point you can either accept or reject the request.

If you're the person who started sharing the application, you can stop sharing it just as easily by highlighting its name in the list of programs and choosing Unshare. Be careful what you share, especially when dealing with people you don't know well. For example, if you open My Computer and share that, you essentially give the other person complete control over your computer! If you have any worries, keep your hand near the Esc key. If the other person starts doing something you don't like, a quick tap on the Esc key removes control from them.

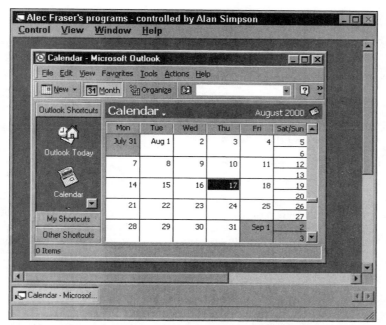

Figure 11-14: Microsoft Outlook's calendar function is shared using NetMeeting.

> **Tip**   Many programs in Microsoft Office 2000 have a Collaborate option on their tools menu, which you can use to schedule and start online meetings right on the spot.

If several people are working on a shared document, do remember that any and all changes made to the document are saved only if you save the changes (using File ➪ Save in that application). Furthermore, the changes are saved only on your computer. If you want others in the meeting to have copies of the completed document, you must send them copies as discussed in the next section. (Or as e-mail attachments — whichever you prefer.)

Transferring Files

To send files to someone in a NetMeeting call, click Transfer Files button near the lower right corner of NetMeeting's window. Or choose Tools ➪ File Transfer. Use the Add Files button to browse around your system and select the files you want to send. You can select as many files as you wish to transfer. For example, Figure 11-15 shows that I've opted to send three files.

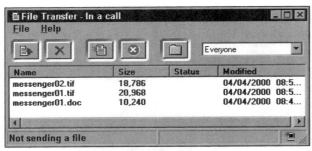

Figure 11-15: NetMeeting's File Transfer dialog box

You can use the drop-down list to choose to whom you want to send the file(s) — everyone or a specific member. When you're ready to send, click the Send All button. The recipient(s) of the file(s) will see a dialog box like that shown in Figure 11-16 for each file you send. As the dialog box shows, the recipient has the option to Accept, Open, or Delete the file (as do you when someone transfers a file to you.)

Figure 11-16: Receiving a file transferred by NetMeeting

By default, all files transferred by NetMeeting are stored in the \Program Files\ NetMeeting\Received Files folder on the computer that received the file. You can open that folder using My Computer or Windows Explorer when the transfer is complete. Then move, copy, or rename the files at your leisure. If you have any trouble finding a transferred file, but you know its name, you can always use the Search option on the Start menu to search the entire disk for the file.

Controlling One PC from Another

Remote Desktop Sharing (RDS) is a NetMeeting-related capability that enables you to thoroughly control one computer from another computer using that computer's mouse, keyboard, and monitor. This is great for certain types of technical support. For example, if you have a problem with your computer, you can turn control of the computer over to an expert who can examine things from his or her current location. The expert may even be able to fix the problem on your screen as you watch.

If you have an "always on" connection to the Internet (such as cable or DSL), and your computer has its own IP address on the Internet, you can also access that computer *remotely* (that is, from any other computer on the Internet). For example, you could use RDS to share your computer's entire desktop, and leave your computer on. Then, while you're out on the road, you could connect to the Internet, and actually control that home or office computer from wherever you happen to be located at the moment.

Setting up RDS on the computer to be shared

To share control of a PC, you first need to be at that PC and do some configuring. If you plan on accessing this computer from afar while it's unattended, you'll also need to create a password. Make the password a good one because you don't want just anyone guessing your password and gaining full access to your system via the Internet! As always, you must write the password down somewhere so you won't ever lose it. And don't forget that passwords are case-sensitive. After you've figured out a password, there's a wizard you can run to turn on RDS so that you can access the computer's resources remotely via the Internet.

1. Open NetMeeting. You do not need to be online or connected to a directory server.

2. Choose Tools ➪ Remote Desktop Sharing from NetMeeting's menu bar.

3. Read the first wizard screen and then click Next.

4. In the Enter Password wizard screen (see Figure 11-17), type your password. Then click OK.

Figure 11-17: Enter a password to use to access Remote Desktop Sharing.

5. The next wizard screen recommends that you enable a password-protected screensaver when RDS is interrupted. Choosing Yes prevents anyone who is near the computer from accessing it while you're controlling it from afar. Make your choice and then click Next.

6. If you chose Yes in step 5, you'll be taken to the Screen Saver tab of the Display Properties dialog box. Choose a screensaver from the drop-down list. Choose Password Protected, click the Change button, and create a password. Click OK to close the Display Properties dialog box and then click Next on the wizard page.

7. Read the last wizard screen and then click Finish.

That sets up your password-protection. Now there's one more step, discussed next, that you need to perform to make sure that the program will be accessible while you're away.

Finding your IP address

If you plan to access the computer yourself from afar, and there will be nobody at the computer to give you access, make sure you know the computer's IP address. To get that number, start NetMeeting and choose Help ➪ About Windows NetMeeting. Down near the bottom of the dialog box that appears you'll see the IP address, which will follow the standard dotted decimal notation *xxx.xxx.xxx.xxx* where *xxx* is any number in the range of 0 to 255. Write that information down along with your password and take it with you.

It's important to understand that if you *don't* have an "always on" connection to the Internet, the IP address you see will probably be accessible from the current LAN only, not from the Internet at large. Thus, you won't be able to access the computer through the Internet. However, you can access the computer from other computers in the same local area network, just by placing a secure call to the computer's IP address through NetMeeting, as described a little later in this chapter.

Making the computer accessible

Finally, you'll need to follow the steps below to make sure that RDS is enabled:

1. If NetMeeting isn't already open, open it.

2. Choose Tools ➪ Remote Desktop Sharing from NetMeeting's menu bar.

3. In the Remote Desktop Sharing Settings dialog box, select the Enable Remote Desktop Sharing on this computer option, as in Figure 11-18. Then click OK.

Figure 11-18: The Remote Desktop Sharing Settings dialog box

With Remote Desktop Sharing enabled, you should see a new icon in the Indicators section of the taskbar. When you point to that icon its ToolTip reads NetMeeting Remote Desktop Sharing. Right-click that icon as in Figure 11-19 and, if possible, select the Activate Remote Desktop Sharing option. If that option is dimmed and disabled, that just means that Remote Desktop Sharing is already active, which is good, because that's what you need if you want the computer to be accessible remotely.

Figure 11-19: Remote Desktop Sharing is enabled on this computer.

You can do several more things that will help RDS work better. For starters, consider changing the display resolution to 640×480. That will enable your entire desktop to fit inside a window on the calling computer, provided that computer is using some higher resolution. Also, if your computer has multiple monitors, you should disable all but the main monitor, as it's unlikely that the calling computer will be able to access the additional monitors. You can change the resolution and deactivate extra monitors via the Display Properties dialog box that appears when you right-click the desktop and choose Properties.

If you plan to leave the computer unattended while it's being used remotely, be sure that the computer is on and ready to accept the call when the time comes. If you're using power management options to power down your computer after a period of inactivity, disable those options before you leave the computer. Use the Power Options icon in Control Panel (Start ➪ Settings ➪ Control Panel) to set your System Standby option to Never. (It's OK to let the monitor and hard disk power down after a while.)

Some modern computers have a Wake on LAN capability built into them. This enables the computer to go into a suspended state while not in use, and then instantly "wake up" as soon as a request for resources comes through the network. If your computer has that capability, you'll probably need to set it up in the system BIOS. Typically the only way to get to the BIOS setup is to watch for a message that reads Press <*some key*> to Enter Setup right after you start the computer. You'll only have a few seconds to press the specified key. I can't give you much more advice than that though, because different computers have different BIOS chips and setup programs. You can check the written documentation that came with your system (or the system's motherboard) for more information on its BIOS capabilities and setup program.

The main thing to remember, though, is that if you want to access the computer from afar, and nobody will be sitting there to accept your NetMeeting call, then the computer has to be turned on and running when the call comes in.

Giving control to a caller

Once you've enabled RDS, you can give control of your computer to a tech support person or anyone else who contacts you through NetMeeting. Here, we're assuming that you are sitting at the computer when the NetMeeting call comes in. Just accept the call normally and then click the Sharing button near the bottom of the Net-Meeting window, or choose Tools ➪ Sharing from its menu bar. The Sharing dialog box will open, and the Desktop option at the top of the list should be enabled. Click on Desktop and then click on the Share button to share your desktop. Then click the Allow Control button and give control to the other party as in Figure 11-20.

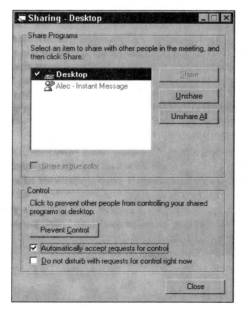

Figure 11-20: Control of this computer's desktop passed to a caller in NetMeeting

To close NetMeeting and give the other person complete control of your desktop, choose Call ⇨ Exit and Activate Remote Desktop Sharing from NetMeeting's menu bar.

The person at the other end of the NetMeeting call will see your desktop in a window. From that window choosing Control ⇨ Request Control will give them the power to operate your entire system from within that window. However, you still have the highest level of control. You'll be able to see everything the other user is doing. If you see something you don't like, just press the Esc key to instantly deny them that control.

Accessing an unattended desktop

If the computer has an always-on connection to the Internet, you (or anyone else) who's connected to the Internet, and knows the appropriate password, can access the computer's desktop and take control of the computer. Here's how:

1. On whatever computer you're using at the moment, connect to the Internet and start Microsoft NetMeeting.
2. Click the Place Call button.
3. In the To box, type the IP address of the remote computer.
4. Select Require Security For This Call so that it's check box is filled (this is important!).
5. Click the Call button in the dialog box.
6. When the remote computer answers you'll see a dialog box requesting a password. Type the password you created for accessing the remote computer and then click OK. Then wait a few seconds.

Eventually you should see a Meeting Properties dialog box that lists the types of things you can and cannot do. A large window that displays the desktop of the remote computer will follow. Any work you perform *inside* that window actually occurs on the remote computer. (In fact, if someone happened to walk by that computer, they'd see everything you're doing, as if a ghost were sitting there doing the work!).

Transferring files during RDS

As you're working a computer from afar, you might think that you can copy files from that remote computer to the current computer just using standard drag-and-drop techniques. However, that's not how it works. Instead, what you need to do is run NetMeeting on the remote computer and click the Transfer Files button in that computer's copy of NetMeeting. Go through the standard method described earlier in this chapter to select and send the files that you want to copy. After you click the Send button, the files will, of course, be sent to the computer you're currently sitting at. You can accept or reject them, just like you could had someone else sent them to you. If you're not given an option to place them in a specific folder on the local computer, they'll probably end up in the C:\Program Files\NetMeeting\Received Files folder, which is the default for storing transferred files.

Ending remote desktop access

When you've finished using the remote computer, disconnect it from its own end. That is, within the window displaying the remote desktop, click the Start button and choose Log Off. . . . Answer Yes to the Log Off dialog box that appears. If you left behind any unfinished work, you'll be prompted to save your changes. Select Yes to save your work. Finally, on the computer that you're still sitting at, click the Hang Up button in NetMeeting.

More on NetMeeting

NetMeeting has so many capabilities that it would take a small book to cover all the possibilities. Because I have only one chapter to work with, I've limited my coverage to just the most important and widely used features of the product. For the rest of this chapter, I'd like to point out some of those capabilities and point you in the right direction for getting more out of NetMeeting.

Using directory services

You are not limited to using the Microsoft Internet Directory as your directory server. NetMeeting is compatible with a wide range of directory servers. The best source for finding compatible servers us probably the NetMeeting Zone. As I write this chapter, the specific page of directory servers is at www.netmeet.net/bestservers.asp, but that could change. If you have any problems use your Web browser (that is, Internet Explorer) to visit NetMeeting Zone's homepage at www.netmeet.net.

There are a couple of ways to log on to a server other than Microsoft's. If you want to control whether or not your name will appear in that server, and whether or not you're logged on to a specific server when NetMeeting starts, you best bet is to add the directory server's URL to NetMeeting via the Options dialog box. Here are the exact steps:

1. From NetMeeting's menu bar choose Tools ➪ Options.

2. Under Directory Settings, replace the contents of the Directory drop-down list with the URL of the directory server that you're interested in. For example, you could drag the mouse pointer through the Microsoft Internet Directory option to select it. Then type in some new directory URL such as ils.visitalk.com.

Directory server URLs typically follow the format ils.*domainname.com* where ils is an acronym for Internet Locator Service (a service that finds people currently online). For example, the URL of the Microsoft Internet Directory is actually ils.microsoft.com. Of course, the URL of a directory server can be anything — the initial ils acronym is common, but by no means required!

3. If you don't want to be listed in that directory server's list of people online, select the Do not list my name in the directory option.

4. If you want to log on to a directory server automatically whenever NetMeeting starts, select the second option. Then choose the name of the directory that you want to log on to automatically from the Directory drop-down list.

5. Click OK.

You can also enter a new directory URL in the Select a directory drop-down list of the Find Someone dialog box, which opens after you choose Call ⇨ Directory from NetMeeting's menu bar.

Now whenever you're in NetMeeting and want to visit some server other than the one you're currently logged into, just choose Call ⇨ Directory from NetMeeting's menu bar. Open the Select a directory drop-down list as in Figure 11-21, and choose the directory that you wish to log on to. To place a call to anyone in the list, just click their name, and then click the Call button.

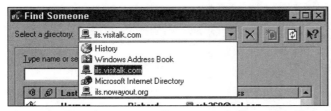

Figure 11-21: Choose your directory server from the drop-down list.

If you share this computer with other people, be aware that the drop-down list will display a "history" of the directory servers you've been visiting. If you prefer to keep that information private, you'll need to remember to delete the server name from the list before you exit. While the name is visible in the Select a directory drop-down list, just click the Delete (X) button to the right of that list.

Hosting a meeting

A NetMeeting meeting is really no different from any other type of call. However, you do need to make sure that everyone who is supposed to attend the meeting knows the time and place. The "place" should be a directory server, such as Microsoft Internet Directory, which everyone who is to attend the meeting will log on to before the meeting start time. If necessary, you may have to tell meeting participants how to set up Hotmail accounts to get onto the server, as discussed earlier in this chapter.

As the host of the meeting, you get to choose the meeting time, the meeting name, password, security settings, and the list of people who can be invited to the meeting. You can also define which tools (for example, Chat, Whiteboard) can be used during the meeting. When it comes time to actually go online and conduct the meeting, here are the steps to follow:

1. Start up NetMeeting and log on to the directory server you've chosen to act as the server.

2. Choose Call ⇨ Host Meeting from NetMeeting's menu bar.

3. In the dialog box that appears in Figure 11-22, enter the name of the meeting.

Figure 11-22: The Host a Meeting dialog box

4. Optionally, you can set these other meeting properties:

   • To require a password to enter the meeting, enter a Meeting Password.

   • To require security (discussed in detail in the section that follows), select the Require security . . . option.

   • To make yourself grand wazoo of who can join the meeting, select the Only you can accept incoming calls and Only you can place outgoing calls options.

   • Under Meeting Tools, choose the tools that meeting participants will be allowed to use.

5. Click OK.

As the host of the meeting you can now log into the appropriate server and start placing calls to meeting members. Probably the easiest way to do this would be by choosing Call ⇨ Directory to view people (or buddies) on the server. Then just click the name of the person whom you want to call. As with any other NetMeeting call, the recipient will hear a ring and be given the option to accept or reject the call.

As the host of the meeting, you can easily kick out anybody you want. Just right-click their name in the Participant's List and choose Remove From Meeting.

Tip   If you have Microsoft Office 2000, you can also conduct a meeting from most program's menu bars. Open the document you want to share, choose Tools ⇨ Online Collaboration. Then choose Meet Now. If Microsoft Outlook is installed, you can choose Schedule Meeting to schedule the meeting for a later time.

When you're ready to end the meeting, just click your Hang Up button. For more information on setting up and conducting meetings, meeting security, and so forth, choose Help ⇨ Help Topics from NetMeeting's menu bar. Then look up the word Host in the Index tab.

Note   Secure calls are data only, which means that you can't use voice and video during the meeting. You can learn more about different types of security available to you by looking up secure in NetMeeting's help index.

Gateways and gatekeepers

If you work for a large organization that uses gateways and/or gatekeepers to provide access to telephone and videoconferencing, you can log on to that server via NetMeeting. First, you'll need to get the address, password, and any other relevant information about the server from your company's network administrator or system administrator. That person can best tell you how to use the server. Some of those servers will even let you dial directly to normal telephones via NetMeeting. Should you ever need to dial directly, you can use choose View ⇨ DialPad from NetMeeting's menu bar to get to the dialing pad shown in Figure 11-23.

Figure 11-23: The DialPad works with gateways and gatekeepers that allow touch-tone dialing.

Still more

As I said earlier, a single chapter in a book can't really do justice to all that NetMeeting has to offer. But given that this is a book about Windows, rather than NetMeeting per se, a chapter is all I have to work with. But there is a lot more information available online that will help you expand the basic skills and concepts that you learned here. Of course, NetMeeting's own Help menu offers plenty of information — just choose Help ➪ Help Topics from NetMeeting's menu bar. On the Web you can learn about the many different directory servers that support NetMeeting, keep up with new events as the technology evolves, and learn about some of the more esoteric features of NetMeeting from any of these Web sites:

✦ Microsoft's NetMeeting Page at `www.micosoft.com/windows/netmeeting`

✦ MSN Messenger page at `http://messenger.msn.com`

✦ The NetMeeting Zone at `www.netmeeting-zone.com`

✦ VisiTalk's voice and video service at `www.visitalk.com`

✦ CamCrowd at `www.camcrowd.com`

✦ CU-SeeMee World at `www.cuseemeworld.com`

✦ Conflab.com at `www.conflab.com`

✦ NetMeetMe at `www.netmeetme.com`

✦ Helpmeeting at `www.helpmeeting.com`

✦ ILS Center at `www.ilscenter.com`

✦ MSN NetMeeting Community at `http://communities.msn.com/TheNetMeetingZone`

A search for the keywords "free long distance," "videoconference," "security certificate," or "NetMeeting" using any Web search engine is bound to turn up a lot more resources.

Summary

Windows Me comes with all the tools that you need to communicate online using MSN Messenger, the Microsoft Internet Directory, and virtually any other communications service on the Web. Here's a quick recap of the main topics covered in this chapter:

✦ To get started with MSN Messenger and NetMeeting, create a Hotmail account at `www.msn.com` or `http://messenger.msn.com`.

✦ To start MSN Messenger click the Windows Me start button and choose Programs ➪ MSN Messenger Service.

✦ Microsoft NetMeeting provides all the tools you need for videophoning across the Internet.

✦ NetMeeting also has additional options for hosting meetings, transferring files, collaborating on projects, and more.

✦ To start NetMeeting (on most computers), click the NetMeeting icon in the taskbar, or click the Start button and choose Programs ➪ Accessories ➪ Communications ➪ NetMeeting.

✦ To log on to a directory server with NetMeeting (if you're not logged on automatically), choose Call ➪ Log On To *Servername* from NetMeeting's toolbar.

✦ To see who's available at the server you're logged on to, choose Call ➪ Directory from NetMeeting's menu bar. To call someone in the Find Someone dialog box that appears, click (or double-click) his or her name.

✦ Remote Desktop Service (RDS) is an extension to NetMeeting that enables a separate computer to take control of your entire system over a network (including the Internet).

✦　　✦　　✦

Fun Online with Microsoft Chat

MSN Chat is a way to get answers to questions, get into heated debates on topics that interest you, flirt, and meet new people (in the virtual sense). Unlike NetMeeting's chat tool, with which you communicate with people who are specifically in your meeting, MSN Chat provides *chat rooms* in which people with common interests meet to chat. If you're used to the old Comic Chat from Windows 95 and 98, you'll notice a big change in MSN Chat. For one, there are no comic characters. And for another, you chat all through your Web browser rather than a separate "chatting" program. But it's all pretty easy, so this will be a short, easy chapter.

Chatting Basics

To get started with MSN Chat, you need to connect to the Internet in the usual manner. Then fire up Internet Explorer (or any other Web browser of your choosing), and visit the MSN Chat home page at `http://chat.msn.com`. Right off the bat you'll see some chat categories listed. Click any category that looks interesting, and you'll be taken to that chat room. You may need to download the current Chat component. If so, you'll see a message on the screen telling you so, and also how to do the download. You might also be asked to enter a nickname. You can type any nickname you like.

When you've finished downloading and answering any prompts, you'll be taken to your selected chat room. You'll see a message telling you when you're connected to the server. Then you'll see some introductory text as in Figure 12-1. Then you'll probably be able to see people within the room chatting (typing messages to each other).

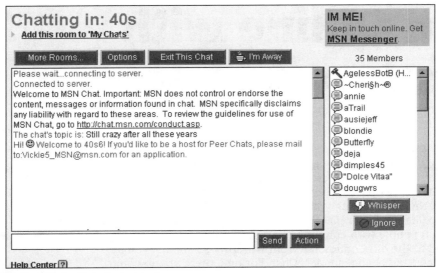

Figure 12-1: Entering a chat room

The large white pane on the left is where the conversations take place. The list of members to the right of that tell you how many people are in the chat room. For starters, you might just want to watch a while to see if any interesting topics come up. If you don't see any action, click the Exit This Chat button to return to the MSN Chat home page, where you can pick another category (room) to visit.

Joining a Conversation

Joining the conversation is easy. Just type whatever you want to say in the text box below the scrolling conversation, and then click the Send button. Or just press the Enter key. Your message appears on the screen preceded by your name, for all to see. Simple!

Whispering

You can also "whisper" to any one member so that only that person sees your message. To whisper, type your message normally. Then, in the members list, click the name of the person you want to whisper to. Optionally, you can whisper to several people by holding down the Ctrl key as you click on member names. Then click the Whisper button below the list of member names. Only the selected member(s) will see your message.

If someone whispers to you, a button will blink in your Windows taskbar. Click that button to see the message in the Whisper box. You can continue to hold a private conversation with that person by typing your messages in the Whisper box. To return to the room at large, just close the Whisper box.

Emoting and acting

To add a little emotion to your messages, you can add *emoticons*. Figure 12-2 shows the icons available to you. To "type" an icon, just type the characters shown to the right of that icon. For example, suppose you type the message below:

```
:-) Hello everyone
```

(That's a colon, hyphen, and closing parenthesis). When you press the Send button or hit Enter, the three characters are automatically converted to the happy face icon. As an alternative to typing all three of those characters, you can type just the colon and the parenthesis.

👍	(Y) (y)		♥	(L) (l)	
👎	(N) (n)		💔	(U) (u)	
😊	:-) :)		💋	(K) (k)	
😃	:-D :D :-d :d :-> ::		📷	(P) (p)	
😲	:-O :O :-o :o		🎁	(G) (g)	
😛	:-P :-p :P :p		🌹	(F) (f)	
😉	;-) ;)		🍸	(D) (d)	
😦	:-(:(:-< :<		🍺	(B) (b)	
😖	:-S :S :-s :s		💏	:-[:[	
😐	:-| :|		👤	(M) (m)	
🕺	(X) (x)		✉	(E) (e)	
🕺	(Z) (z)				

Figure 12-2: Emoticons you can use in MSN Chat

You can also show "action," where your text appears in purple italicized text. Type your text, but don't include your name. For example, you might type "is thinking" or "is laughing hysterically." Then click the Action button rather than the Send button.

Tip Chatters use some acronyms and abbreviations of their own. LOL means Laughing Out Loud. BRB means Be Right Back. NP means No Problem. K means OK. ROTFL means Rolling On The Floor Laughing, and CYA means See Ya.

Ignoring pests

If anyone in the chat room gets on your nerves, and you want to ignore that person, just click on his or her name in the members list. Then click the Ignore button below the list. Optionally, you can just right-click the member's name in the list and choose Ignore. The symbol to the left of the member's name turns to an international "no" sign.

In some cases, when a member is sending a huge number of messages to you, Chat's auto-ignore feature will click in and start ignoring the person for you. Either way, once you've opted to ignore a member, their messages won't disturb you until you repeat the process to un-ignore them. That is, right-click that member's name and choose Ignore again.

Taking a break

You might notice a little coffee cup icon to the left of some members' names in the members list. The coffee cup icon indicates that the person is away from his or her keyboard and won't be able to respond to any text you send. If you want to take a break from your keyboard, just click the I'm Away button. Your name will then get the coffee cup icon in the members list.

Styling your chat

The Chat Options dialog box, shown in Figure 12-3, enables you to customize some features of Chat to your liking. To get to that dialog box, just click the Options button above the conversation window. Change your nickname, the font and color used in your messages, or any of the other options to your liking. Then just click the OK button, as usual.

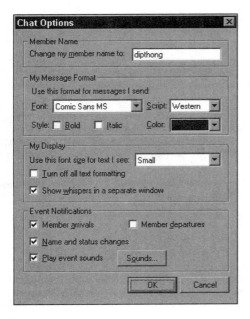

Figure 12-3: The Chat Options dialog box in MSN Chat

Creating Your Own Chat Room

To create your own chat room, navigate to the MSN Chat home page (http://chat.msn.com) and click the Create a Chat option. You'll be taken to the options shown in Figure 12-4. As instructed, fill in the blanks, and then click the Go button. Note that when selecting a category, if you choose Unlisted, your chat room won't be listed under any of the categories in the MSN's lists. Only people who know the exact name of your room will be able to join. This is a great way to use MSN Chat as you might use NetMeeting—to conduct a private meeting without outsiders joining in.

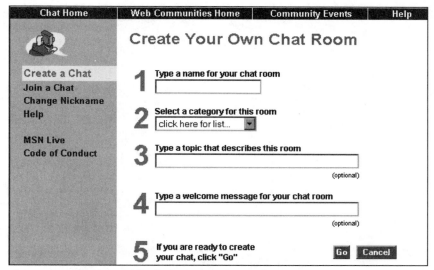

Figure 12-4: Web page for creating your own chat room

To invite people to your private chat room, tell them the exact name of your room, and have them browse to http://chat.msn.com. There they'll need to click the Join a Chat option in the left column of the page that opens. In the next page, have them type the exact name of your chat room, and then click the Go button.

Summary

As promised, this was a quick and easy chapter. Using MSN Chat is largely a matter of using your Web browser to visit http://chat.msn.com and just choosing options on the screen. This chapter covered the following points:

✦ To join a chat, just click any of the chat categories listed at http://chat.msn.com.

✦ Once you're in a chat, type a message and click the Send button to display your message to other members of the chat.

✦ To send a private message (whisper) to a member, type your message, click the name of the member you want to whisper to, and then click the Whisper button.

✦ To add emoticons to your typed messages, type the appropriate characters as listed back in Figure 12-2. For example, typing (F) or (f) will display a flower icon.

✦ To create your own chat room, click **Create a Chat** at `http://chat.msn.com`.

✦   ✦   ✦

Internet Games and Other Online Services

Windows Me is the operating system of choice for any sort of gaming. And you're not limited to playing alone, thanks to the Gaming Zone at MSN. In this chapter, you'll learn everything you'll need to know about Internet gaming. Of course, gaming is supposed to be fun and easy. And as you'll learn in this short, simple chapter, it is!

Playing Games

The games that come with Windows Me are all available from the Games option on the Program menu. So to play a game, the steps are simple:

1. Click the Start button.
2. Choose Programs ➾ Games to see the options shown in Figure 13-1.
3. Click on the name of the game you want to play.

If the Games option isn't available on your Programs menu, or if you're missing any of the games shown in the figure, you can install them using the Windows Setup tab of Add/Remove programs. See Chapter 25 for details.

For single-player games, use the Help option on the menu bar to learn how to play. Multi-player games come in two flavors — those you play with other people on your local area network, and those you play on the Internet. First I'll show you how to play on a local network, using Classic Hearts as the example. When you start that game, you're taken to the dialog box shown in Figure 13-2. Enter your name (any name will do). Then one person must opt to be the dealer. Then click OK. The message "Waiting for other players to join. Press F2 to begin with other players" appears in the status bar. If you press F2 with no other players, Hearts creates three imaginary players for you.

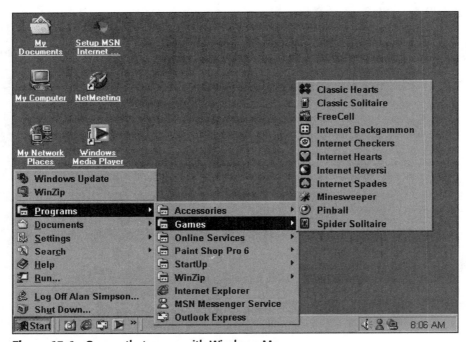

Figure 13-1: Games that come with Windows Me

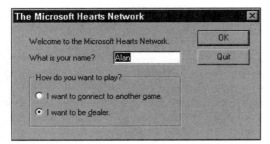

Figure 13-2: Starting a game of network Hearts

Note   The Hearts Network game assumes you're using two or more computers that are connected in a local area network (LAN). Part VI in this book explains how to set up such a network.

If you want other people on your local area network to join in, they'll first need to know you computer's name on the network. If you don't know the name of the computer you're sitting at as dealer, just right-click the My Network Places icon on your desktop, choose Properties, and then click the Identification tab. The name of your computer appears next to Computer Name. Click the Cancel button to close the dialog box without changing your network settings.

To play, other players need to start Classic Hearts (Start ➪ Programs ➪ Games ➪ Classic Hearts), enter a player name, and choose "I want to connect to another game." A dialog box appears asking for the name of the computer that the dealer is playing on. Type in the appropriate name and click OK. Names of everyone who is logged in will appear on all players' screens. When it's time the play, the dealer just needs to press the F2 key to get the game rolling. Instructions on the screen will tell all players when it's their turn, and how to play.

Installing and Using Game Controllers

If you've every played a video game, you know that the mouse and keyboard are not necessarily the best controls for all types of games. Video and arcade style games are often better played with Nintendo or PlayStation type controllers. A joystick is a must for any kind of game that involves flying. Driving and racing games might benefit from a steering wheel and foot pedals. All of these different types of game controllers are available for your computer, at any large computer store. You can also purchase and shop online. See the Gaming Zone's hardware page at www.zone.com/store_hw.asp for starters.

Once you've purchased a game controller, you need to install it per the manufacturer's instructions. Many game controls will plug into the gameport on the back of your sound card. You can also get controllers that plug into USB ports. Follow any instructions provided by the manufacturer for installing software for the device. Finally, to calibrate the installed device, follow these steps:

1. Click the Start button and choose Settings ➪ Control Panel.

2. Open the Gaming Options icon.

3. On the Controllers tab of the Gaming Options dialog box, click the name of the controller you want to calibrate. Then click Settings.

   If no controller is listed, click Add, choose your controller, and click OK to add the controller.

4. Choose Calibrate and follow the instructions on your screen.

If you ever need to change the port driver assigned to a controller, use the Controller IDs tab in the Gaming Options dialog box. To change a controller's ID click its name in the list and then choose Change. To change the port driver assignment, or polling of interrupts, choose the appropriate options from the Port Driver Assignment pane near the bottom of the Controller IDs pane.

Gaming on the Internet

Windows Me comes with five Internet games: Backgammon, Checkers, Hearts, Reversi, and Spades. Choosing one of the Internet games will display a dialog box. Clicking the Play button in that dialog box will connect you to MSN's Gaming Zone. If you have a dial-up connection and aren't connected, you'll be prompted to connect to your ISP first. Just follow the instructions that appear on the screen. Once you're connected, another dialog box that looks for players online appears. When enough players have been found, the game begins. (Or, if there aren't enough players, computer druids will be used as players!). Figure 13-3 shows an example with four players ready to begin a game of Internet Hearts.

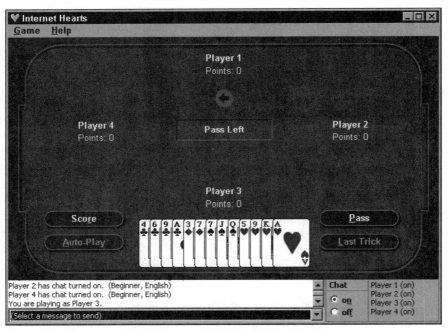

Figure 13-3: Internet Hearts game on MSN's Gaming Zone

As with any game, you can look to the Help menu, and other options on the menu bar, for help in getting going.

Chatting while gaming

Many Internet games give you the option to chat while playing. However, you're usually restricted to just a few phrases. For example, at the bottom of the Internet Hearts game board, you'll see the message "Select a message to send" in a drop-down list. To use chatting, first make sure the Chat option is turned on. Then select a message from the drop-down list. If any players speak some language other than the one you're using, those players will automatically see the message translated to their own language.

Some games will also support Voice Chat, with which you can communicate with other players by using a microphone and speakers or a headset. You'll need to enable voice chat on such games through the Control Panel. Here's how:

1. Click the Start button and choose Settings ⇨ Control Panel.

2. Open the Gaming Options dialog box.

3. Click the Voice Chat tab.

Note You may see the Sound Hardware Test Wizard the first time you enable Voice Chat. Just read and follow the instructions presented by that wizard to configure you sound hardware.

You'll see a list of games on your system that use DirectPlay but don't have their own integrated voice chat capabilities. If you don't see any games listed, that just means that you don't have any DirectPlay games without integrated voice. To enable voice chatting in any game list, just click the voice chat check box.

Even with all your voice hardware in place and all the appropriate options selected in the Gaming Options dialog box, you can still only communicate by voice under certain conditions. Specifically:

✦ You must be using a Web site or matchmaking service that supports voice chatting.

✦ The person hosting the game must enable voice chatting in his or her copy of the game and/or in his or her Gaming Options dialog box.

✦ If you're given connection options when you first enter a game, choose "Internet TCP.IP Connection for DirectPlay" (if available) to ensure that your voice communications will work.

✦ Any player can disable voice chat on his or her own computer. You cannot chat with a player who has disabled voice chat.

You also need to be aware that voice chatting during game play can greatly reduce the speed and performance of the game. This is especially true if you're using a dial-up connection rather than a faster broadband connection such as cable or DSL.

More Fun at the MSN Gaming Zone

The Internet games on the Windows Me Games menu are only a small selection of what's really available to play online. At the MSN Gaming Zone you'll find card games, adventures, sports, racing, and simulation games as well. In most cases, you can sign up for a game for free. Some games require subscriptions. However, you can usually use them for free on a trial basis. Note that you must be 13 or more years of age to play at the MSN Gaming Zone. To get to the Gaming Zone, open Internet Explorer, or any other Web browser, and go to www.zone.com.

If you're new to the Gaming Zone, you may want to sign up. It won't cost you anything to do so, and you'll have access to the widest selection of games, as well as the chance to play in tournaments. Just click on the Free Signup option on the www.zone.com home page and follow the instructions on the screen. Be sure to write down your Zone name and password so you don't forget next time to try to log on. You'll then be given the opportunity to download some core files for MSN gaming—go ahead and do so. Finally, you'll be given the opportunity to take a quick tour of the Gaming Zone. You'll want to choose that option as well.

When you get through all the rigmarole, you'll come to a list of free games, premium games, and more as shown in Figure 13-4. Additional games are available from the Game Index, which appears at the left side of the home page. Retail CD games are listed near the bottom of the page. To play a free game, just click its name and follow the instructions that appear on the screen. In most games you'll find a Getting Started option that you can click to learn more about that particular game. Some games will require you to download additional software. In those cases, you'll be given the option to download the necessary files right from the game's opening screen. Retail games, listed near the bottom of the MSN Gaming Zone's home page, require that you purchase and install the CD-ROM version of the game.

Once you choose a game, you'll be taken to a list of rooms in which that game is being played. In the left column of the list, you'll see the number of players in that room. To enter a room, just click its name. If you chose one of the free board or card games, you'll likely be taken to a gaming table. To join the game, click any empty chair in the table.

Tip To watch a game without playing, click any occupied chair around the gaming table.

Playing retail games

To play a retail game at the Zone, you'll first need to make sure you've purchased and installed the game you want to play. You'll probably need to leave the game CD in your CD-ROM drive as well. Then go to the Retail Games section of the Gaming Zone. There you can either host the game, or join an ongoing game.

If you're planning to host a game, be sure to exit the game before you go online. Go online and click the Quick Host option on the game's toolbar. You'll automatically be taken to the first free table where you can host the game. Optionally, if you see a Host option on the screen, you can click that and use chat features to recruit other players into your game.

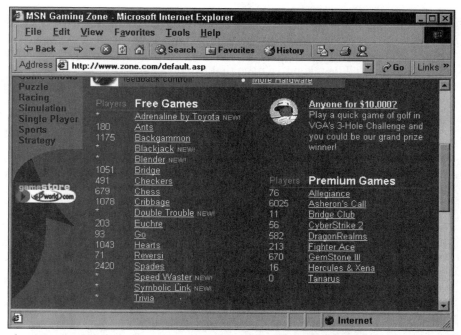

Figure 13-4: Some games to choose from at the MSN Gaming Zone

As the host of a retail game played at www.zone.com, you'll be able to set game parameters, including the name of the game, a description of the types of players (such as beginners, experts, and so on), and the number of players you'd like to have join. As host you can also opt to ignore quick joiners, which are people who click the Quick Join option to quickly join an ongoing game. The host can also opt to hold a private game. Just click the Private Game option, enter a password, and then click the OK button to close the dialog box.

Tip

> The Computer Games Forum at MSN Computing Central (www.computing central.com/topics/computergames) is another good place for gamers to visit.

Playing premium games

Premium games are heavily-enhanced, multi-player games that are unique to the Gaming Zone and heavily enhanced to support Internet play with many people. Most require you to pay a subscription fee to join. But most also have tournaments to play and prizes to win—the subscription fees go to all of that. Some of the premium games are also CD-ROM based, which means you'll need to purchase and install a Zone-enabled CD. Other games can be downloaded off the site for free.

To sign up for a premium game, just go to `www.zone.com` and click any game category at the left side of the page to see a wider selection of games. For example, Figure 13-5 shows the selection of Adventure games available on the day I visited. For more information on any game, just click its Info option. If the game is marked as "Premium" you'll be taken to a page that explains subscription fees and provides everything you need to sign up and become a member.

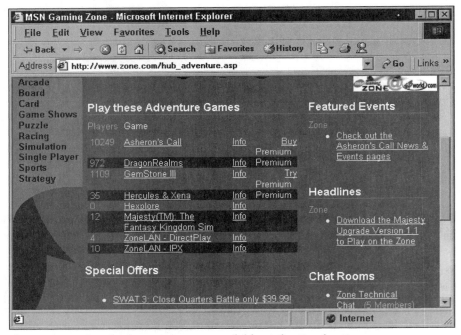

Figure 13-5: List of Adventure games available at the Gaming Zone

Summary

Gaming is fun and easy, and you can generally find out everything you need to know right from the game's Help menu or online opening page. There are game controllers for just about every kind of game you can think of. And thanks to the Internet, you can always find someone to play with. In summary:

✦ To see or play games that came with Windows Me, click the Start button and choose Programs ➪ Games.

✦ The Internet Games on the Games menu will automatically search the Internet for others playing that same game.

✦ For games that don't play well with mouse and keyboard, you can probably find a more suitable controller at any computer store — brick-and-mortar or online.

✦ To calibrate a game controller, open the Gaming Options icon in the Control Panel.

✦ For more information on the larger world of online gaming, visit MSN's Gaming Zone at www.zone.com.

✦ ✦ ✦

Have It
Your Way

General Housekeeping: Copying, Deleting, and So On

As you gain experience in using your computer, creating documents, and so forth, you may find you occasionally need to manage your files. The term "manage" includes copying, moving, deleting, and renaming folders and files. This chapter explains all the basic techniques you use to manage files and folders on your PC. As you see, many of these techniques build on basic skills you already learned in Part I, such as right-clicking and dragging. So you already know how to do much of what's described in this chapter!

Moving, Copying, and Deleting

Before we discuss general techniques for copying, moving, and deleting files and folders, let's discuss those three terms. To *copy* something means to make an exact duplicate of something, as you can with a photocopy machine. For example, if you copy a file named MyLetter.doc from your My Documents folder to a floppy disk in drive A, you end up with two identical copies of MyLetter.doc — the original copy still in the My Documents folder and a new copy on the floppy disk in drive A. (You could mail this extra copy to someone or keep it as a backup.)

To *move* a file means what the name implies — to change the file's location. For example, if you move the file named MyLetter.doc from the My Documents folder to a floppy disk in drive A, you still have only one copy of the MyLetter.doc file — the copy now on the floppy disk.

To *rename* a file simply means to change the name that appears under the icon. The file is not moved, copied, or deleted.

To *delete* a file or folder means to trash it permanently, so you end up with no copies of that file. Obviously, you need to use extreme caution when you delete things because you don't want to delete anything important. You'll occasionally want to delete files you no longer need to make more room for new stuff on your hard disk.

Renaming a file or folder

To rename a file or folder:

1. Right-click the icon of the file or folder you want to rename.

2. Choose Rename from the shortcut menu and then edit the current name or type a new one.

 Caution   If you change the extension at the end of a document filename, the document will no longer be associated with the same program as before. If you're in doubt, don't change the extension part of the name.

3. Click anywhere just outside the icon to save your change.

If you need a reminder of basic text-editing techniques you can use while renaming a file, see Chapter 2.

If you change your mind immediately after renaming a file, you can choose Edit ➪ Undo Rename from the menu bar of whichever program you're currently using (My Computer, Windows Explorer, or Search). Or, you can right-click the renamed icon and choose Undo Rename, or press Ctrl+Z, to get back to the original name.

Deleting a file or folder

Deleting a file is easy; just be careful about what you delete. Some important points to remember when you consider deleting something include:

✦ If you see the message "Are you sure you want to delete [filename]?," the file will be deleted immediately, not sent to the Recycle Bin. Think before you choose Yes.

✦ Remember that when you delete an icon, you delete everything the icon represents. The only exception is the shortcut icon, which you can delete without affecting the underlying disk files.

✦ Remember that if you delete a folder, you also delete all the files inside that folder! Use extreme caution here!

✦ Only items you delete from your local hard disk (typically, drive C) are sent to the Recycle Bin. Files on floppy disks, network drives, and other removable media are deleted permanently on the spot and they can't be undeleted.

Caution

Caution is the key to safe deleting. Always assume a worst-case scenario ("I won't be able to undelete this later") so you don't get cocky and careless. Also, never move things to the Recycle Bin just to get them out of the way temporarily. You may forget and permanently delete them later.

To remove an installed *program* (rather than a document file) from your PC, you should use the Add/Remove Programs icon inside the Windows Me Control Panel. Chapter 25 discusses this procedure in more detail.

If you are certain you want to delete a file or folder, follow these steps:

1. Use My Computer, Windows Explorer, or Search to locate the icon for the file you want to delete.

2. Right-click this icon and choose Delete (or press the Delete key, labeled Del on some keyboards).

3. When asked if you're sure you want to send the items to the Recycle Bin, choose Yes.

If you deleted from your local hard disk, the file or folder is moved into a special folder known as the Recycle Bin, which I'll discuss a little later in this chapter. You can still undelete the file if you deleted by mistake, as described in the section "Using the Recycle Bin" later in this chapter. In that sense, you can think of the Recycle Bin as being sort of a deletion "safety net."

If you delete one or more files and you realize your mistake immediately, you can easily undo the deletion by right-clicking some neutral area near where the deleted files were and choosing Undo Delete. If it's too late for this, you can still pull the files back out of the Recycle Bin, as discussed a little later in this chapter.

Moving and copying using drag-and-drop

Several ways exist to move and copy files. One is to use the drag-and-drop method. Here are the steps to follow if you want to use this method:

1. Use My Computer, Windows Explorer, or Search to locate the file you want to move or copy.

2. Browse to the destination drive or folder you want to copy the file to, again using My Computer, Windows Explorer, or Search.

3. Size and position the windows onscreen, so you can see both the name of the file you want to copy and the destination. For example, in Figure 14-1, you can see the folder for my My Documents folder. You can also see a folder for My Pictures.

4. Right-drag the file you want to move or copy from its current place into the destination folder. For example, to move or copy `Albany stats` from My Documents to My Pictures, you would right-drag that file's icon to any place within the My Pictures folder.

5. Release the right mouse button. Then choose either Move Here (if you want to move the file to the new location) or Copy Here (if you want to put a copy of the file in the new location).

Figure 14-1: Folders for my My Documents folder and My Pictures folder open on the desktop

That's it! If you copied the file, both windows now contain an icon for this file. If you moved the file, only the destination folder displays an icon for this file.

Using Cut and Paste to move and copy

As an alternative to using the drag-and-drop method, you can use the Cut and Paste or Copy and Paste method to move/copy a file from one location to another. Here are the exact steps:

1. Use My Computer, Windows Explorer, or Search to locate the file you want to move or copy.

2. Right-click the file's icon. In the menu that appears (Figure 14-2), choose Copy if you want to copy the file or choose Cut if you want to move the file.

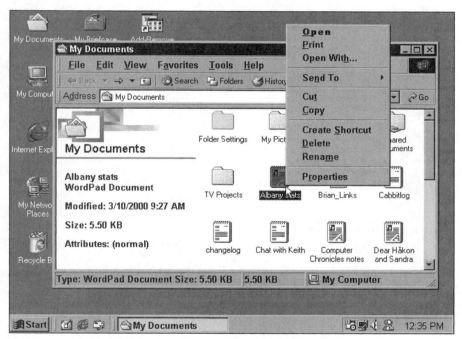

Figure 14-2: Right-click menu offers options to copy or cut.

Caution

Once you copy or cut a filename, *do not* cut or copy any others until *after* you paste the one currently being moved or copied. If you want to move or copy several files, select them all first as discussed under the following section, "Managing Multiple Files."

3. Open the destination folder or drive (the one to which you want to move/copy the folder). As usual, you can use My Computer, Windows Explorer, or Search to open this folder or drive.

4. Right-click some neutral area between icons inside the destination folder or drive to view the pop-up menu shown in Figure 14-3. Then select Paste from this menu.

The file's icon appears near where you right-clicked. As usual, you can choose View ➪ Arrange Icons ➪ By Name to put the icon into proper alphabetical order among all the icons in this folder.

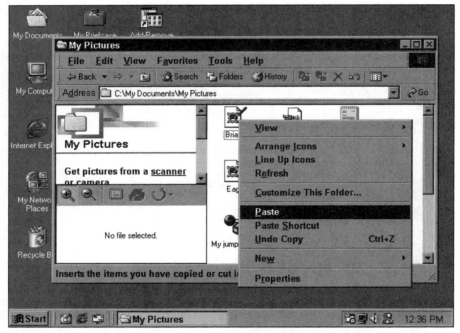

Figure 14-3: About to paste a cut or copied file into My Pictures

Managing Multiple Files

The general techniques previously described assume you only want to move, copy, or delete one file. If you want to move, copy, or delete a whole bunch of files—all in one fell swoop—you first need to select all the files. How you select the files depends a lot on whether you use Web-style or Classic-style navigation. But before we get into all this, let's take it from the top.

First, pick your view

You can decide how you want to view your icons. Your options (discussed in Chapter 2) are Large Icons, Small Icons, List, Details, and Thumbnails. You can choose a view from the Standard Buttons toolbar or from the View menu, or by right-clicking an open window and selecting View.

Tip   If you do not see the Standard Buttons toolbar, choose View ➪ Toolbar ➪ Standard Buttons from the menu. If the window isn't wide enough to show all the buttons you want to use, maximize the window. Or, point to the double-vertical bar at the left edge of the toolbar and drag it to another spot, or double-click it.

Then group things, if useful

If you plan to manage a group of files that have something in common, you can save some work by bunching those items in a list. To arrange the icons, choose View ➪ Arrange Icons. Then, choose an option based on the following possibilities:

✦ **By Name:** If the items you want to select have similar names (for example, they all start with the word "Chapter"), choose By Name to put the objects in alphabetical order by name.

✦ **By Type:** If the items you want to select are of a similar type (they all have the extension .BAK), choose By Type. Files with the same extension will be grouped in the list.

✦ **By Size:** If the items you want to select are the same size or you want to work with large items or small ones, choose By Size.

✦ **By Date:** If the items you want to select were created or modified on or near a particular date, choose By Date. Files with similar dates will be grouped in the list.

Remember, if you use Details view (choose View ➪ Details), you can see the name, size, type, and date modified for every file and you can sort by any one of those columns by clicking the column heading. (Click the column heading again to reverse the sort.)

Tip   You can also use Search to group files by some fractions of their names. For example, you could search `luau` in Search to isolate all files quickly with the word `luau` in the title.

Then select the items to move, copy, or delete

When you see the items you want to move, copy, or delete, you need to select the specific items. You can tell when an item is selected because it's colored differently than the unselected items. The methods for selecting differ, depending on whether you are using Classic-style clicking (in which you click to select and double-click to open) or Web-style clicking (in which you point to select and click to open).

Of course, you're not stuck using one style or the other. You can easily switch between Web and Classic styles by choosing Tools ➪ Folder Options from the current window's title bar. Then, on the General tab, choose either single-click (Web style) or double-click (Classic style).

Selecting in Classic style

If you are using Classic-style clicking, you can select items using a combination of keyboard keys and the mouse. As you may recall, to Ctrl+click something means to hold down the Ctrl key while clicking. To Shift+click means to hold down the Shift key while clicking. And to Ctrl+Shift+click means to hold down the Ctrl and Shift keys while clicking. You may find it easiest to use the List or Details view when working in this manner. Anyway, here's how it all works:

✦ To select one item, click it. Any previously selected items are unselected instantly.

✦ To add another item to a selection, Ctrl+click it.

✦ To extend the selection to another item, Shift+click where you want to extend the selection.

✦ To create another extended selection without disturbing existing selections, Ctrl+click the first item in the range and then Ctrl+Shift+click the last item in the range.

✦ To deselect a selected item without disturbing the current selections, Ctrl+click the item you want to deselect.

Figure 14-4 shows an example in which I have selected several filenames in Classic style. I started by clicking the topmost filename. The figure shows the keys I held down while clicking the mouse button to select other files in the list.

Selecting in Web style

If you are using Web-style clicking, you select items by pointing to them rather than clicking them. This approach can be tricky, especially if you're not all that adept at using a mouse yet. But it works, if you can get the hang of it:

✦ To select one item, point to it. Any previously selected items are unselected instantly.

✦ To add another item to a selection, Ctrl+point to it. To avoid mistakes, hold down the Ctrl key the whole time you move the mouse.

✦ To extend the selection to another item, Shift+point where you want to extend the selection. You can hold down the Shift key while you move the mouse pointer through the filenames you want to select.

Shift + click

Click Ctrl + click

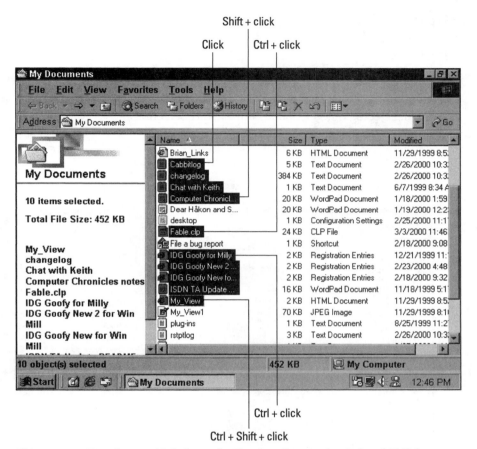

Ctrl + click

Ctrl + Shift + click

Figure 14-4: To select multiple items in Classic style, use the Ctrl and Shift keys while clicking.

✦ To create another extended selection without disturbing existing selections, Ctrl+point to the first item in the range and then Ctrl+Shift+point to the last item in the range.

✦ To deselect a selected item without disturbing the current selections, Ctrl+point to the item you want to deselect.

Figure 14-5 shows an example in which I selected several filenames in Web style. I started by pointing to the topmost filename. The figure shows the keys I held down while pointing the mouse to select other files in the list.

Selecting in either style

Some selection methods work the same way in both Classic-style clicking and Web-style clicking:

✦ To select all the items in the window, choose Edit ➪ Select All or press Ctrl+A.

✦ To invert the current selection (deselect all the selected items and select all the deselected ones), choose Edit ➪ Invert Selection.

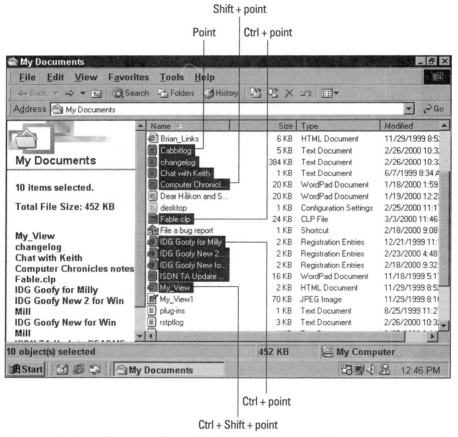

Figure 14-5: To select multiple items in Web style, use the Ctrl and Shift keys while pointing.

 Tip   The status bar at the bottom of the window shows how many files are selected currently and how much space, in kilobytes (KB), is required to store the selected files. If the status bar isn't visible, choose View ➪ Status Bar to turn it on.

Selecting by dragging

Yet another way to select multiple items is to drag a frame (also called a lasso) around them. This is especially handy when you're using the Large Icons view. Move the mouse pointer to just outside the first item you want to select. Then hold down the mouse button and drag a frame around all the items you want to select. The items will be selected as you drag and they will remain selected after you release the mouse button. Figure 14-6 shows how I selected a bunch of files by dragging a frame around them.

If you want to select additional items, hold down the Ctrl key while dragging frames around other items. To unselect a single item within the selection, Ctrl+click it. To unselect all the items, click an empty area within the window, outside any file or folder icons.

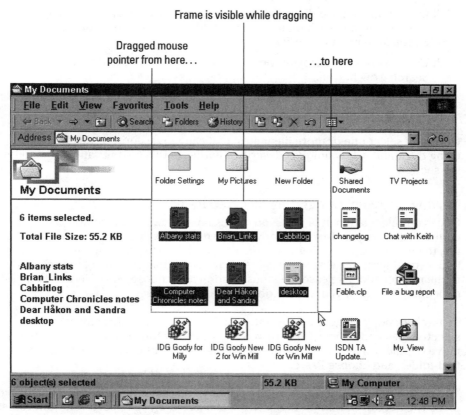

Figure 14-6: I selected all these filenames by dragging a frame around them.

Selecting across folders and drives

Both My Computer and Explorer work on a sort of a narrowing-down principle — you start by picking a drive, and then, perhaps, a folder on the drive, and you end up seeing files and other folders within that particular folder. Most of the time, this procedure is fine. But, occasionally, you may want to do something to all the files on a particular drive, regardless of which folder contains them.

Suppose disk space is getting tight and you want to eliminate old backup (.bak) files floating around on your hard drive. You don't care which folder each file is in; you want to make the deletions on an entire-hard-disk basis. The solution is simple: Use Search, rather than My Computer or Explorer, to isolate all the files. Follow these steps:

1. Click the Start button, point to Search, and click For Files Or Folders. (Or, right-click the Start button and choose Search.)

2. In the Look In drop-down list, select the drive you want to search (C, in my example) and make sure Include Subfolders is selected if you want to search all the folders on the drive.

3. Use the options to isolate the files you want to delete and then click the Search Now button.

4. In the right half of the Search Results window, select the files you want to copy, move, or delete. (Use extreme caution when selecting files to delete.)

Once you select one or more filenames, you can move, copy, or delete them using the standard techniques described earlier in this chapter and in the following section.

Moving, copying, or deleting selected items

Once you select a bunch of files, you can use the same basic techniques described earlier in this chapter to move, copy, or delete all the selected files at once. For example, to move or copy the files using the drag-and-drop method, open the destination folder (or at least make its icon visible). Then right-drag any one of the selected files to the new location. Release the mouse button and choose Move Here or Copy Here, depending on which you want to do.

To move or copy using the copy and paste method, right-click any one of the selected files and choose Copy (if you want to copy the files) or Cut (if you want to move the files). Then open the destination folder, right-click some neutral part of that folder, and choose Paste.

To delete all the selected files, right-click any one of them and choose Delete. Or, press the Delete (Del) key. Choose Yes when asked if you're sure you want to delete all the selected files.

You can't rename a group of selected files. If you do right-click one of the selected items and choose Rename, you can change the name of only the icon you right-clicked.

Making a copy in the same folder

Sometimes it's helpful to have two copies of the same file in a single directory. For example, let's say you have a file named January Newsletter.doc. When February rolls around, you want to use January's newsletter as the starting point for your new newsletter. Rather than altering January's newsletter directly, you can keep that one and use a copy as the starting point for the new newsletter.

You can use the simple copy and paste approach to make a copy of a file within the same folder. If you want to copy multiple files, select them all first. Then right-click the file you want to copy and choose Copy. Then right-click some neutral area within the same folder and choose Paste.

Initially, the new copy will have the same name as the original file, but it will be preceded by the words Copy of, as in the example shown in Figure 14-7. But you can easily right-click the new copy and choose Rename to give the copy some new name, such as February Newsletter.doc. Then you can put the icons into alphabetical order by right-clicking some neutral area between icons and choosing Arrange Icons ⇨ By Name.

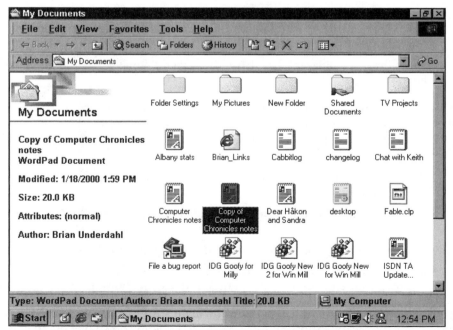

Figure 14-7: Copied file has same name as original file, preceded by the words "Copy of."

Undoing a move or copy

If you complete a move or copy operation and then change your mind, you can undo the action as long as you don't do any more moving or copying (you can only undo one move/copy operation — the one you performed most recently).

To undo a move or copy, go to the folder you copied or moved items to, right-click some neutral area between icons, and then choose Undo Move or Undo Copy from the pop-up menu. Or, you can choose Edit ⇨ Undo Copy or Edit ⇨ Undo Move from the menu bar (if any). Or, press the universal Undo key combination, Ctrl+Z. If you're asked to confirm the undo, choose Yes.

Drag-and-Drop Tips

When using drag-and-drop, your best bet is probably to use the secondary (right) mouse button to right-drag. Then, when you release the button you can decide if you want to move or copy the dragged items, or to create a shortcut. If you decide to ignore that suggestion and use the primary mouse button instead, you should know some things. First, two defaults:

✦ If you drag to a different folder on the same disk, the selected items are moved to that location.

✦ If you drag to a different disk drive, the selected items are copied to that location.

If you drag the files with the left mouse button and you aren't sure what Windows Me intends to do with those items, look at the mouse pointer (without releasing the mouse button). The icon near the mouse pointer tells you what Windows intends to do, as follows:

✦ If you see a plus sign (+), Windows intends to copy the files (add them to the disk or folder).

✦ If you see a small arrow, Windows intends to create shortcut icons at the destination.

✦ If you see neither symbol, Windows intends to move the files to that location.

✦ If you see an international prohibited symbol, Windows intends to do nothing because you're attempting an operation that's not allowed.

If Windows Me intends to do something you hadn't intended, you can force it to copy, move, or create a shortcut by pressing and holding down one of the following keys before you release the mouse button:

✦ **Ctrl:** Copies the selected item(s)

✦ **Shift:** Moves the selected item(s)

✦ **Shift+Ctrl:** Creates a shortcut to the selected files or folder

If you change your mind about a drag-and-drop procedure midstream, tap the Esc key before you release the mouse button. Windows Me will take no action on the dragged files.

Using the Recycle Bin

As mentioned earlier, the Recycle Bin acts as a temporary storage folder for files you deleted. When you delete a file from your hard disk, it disappears from the current folder. But a copy of it stays in the Recycle Bin, in case you change your mind later.

You can tell if trash is in the Recycle Bin by looking at its icon on the desktop. If the Recycle Bin is empty, the trash can will be empty, as in the right side of Figure 14-8. If the Recycle Bin contains any trash, then the trash can icon will also contain trash, as in the left side of Figure 14-8.

Recycle Bin (full)   Recycle Bin (empty)

Figure 14-8: Empty (right) and Full (left) Recycle Bin icons

Recovering files from the Recycle Bin

If you move folders and/or files to the Recycle Bin and then change your mind and want to bring them back, you can restore them. Follow these steps:

1. Open the Recycle Bin icon on the desktop to view its contents (see Figure 14-9). The Recycle Bin looks like any other folder except, of course, for the words Recycle Bin in the title bar. You can choose options on the View menu to control the appearance of items in the folder.

2. To save a file from deletion, right-click it and choose Restore. You can also select multiple files, right-click, and choose Restore to save them all from deletion. The restored files are placed back in their original folders.

Tip

If you want to restore all the files in the Recycle Bin, click the Restore All button.

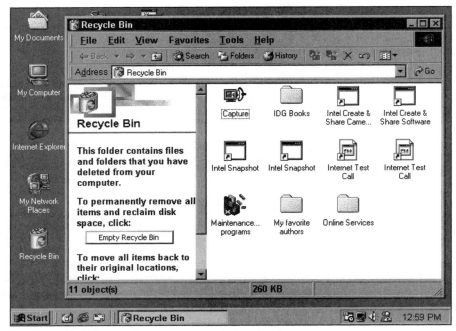

Figure 14-9: The Recycle Bin open on the desktop

Permanently deleting files

Deleted files and folders in the Recycle Bin still occupy as much disk space as they did before you deleted them. In fact, the files are still on your hard disk—they're just hidden from all browsing tools except the Recycle Bin. To recover the disk space occupied by those recycled files, you must delete those files permanently. This procedure is called emptying the Recycle Bin.

Caution   Remember, after you empty the Recycle Bin, you cannot restore the files!

To empty the Recycle Bin, follow these steps:

1. Open the Recycle Bin icon on the desktop.

2. Make certain only the files you want to delete permanently are listed. (This is your last chance to change your mind and restore any files in the Recycle Bin before sending them permanently to software heaven.)

3. Choose File ➪ Empty Recycle Bin, or click the Empty Recycle button.

4. Choose Yes when asked for confirmation.

The Recycle Bin is emptied and the space once occupied by those files is now free for other files.

 Caution Microsoft should have named the Empty Recycle Bin command something like Burn Recycle Bin, Nuke Recycle Bin, or something like that because it really does blast the files out of existence!

Personalizing your Recycle Bin

You can customize the way the Recycle Bin works on your PC. To see your options, first close the Recycle Bin if it's open, right-click the Recycle Bin icon, and choose Properties. You'll come to the Recycle Bin Properties dialog box, shown in Figure 14-10.

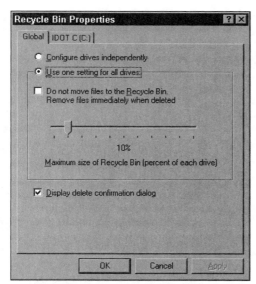

Figure 14-10: The Recycle Bin Properties dialog box

On the General tab, you can choose the "Use one setting for all drives" option if you have only one local hard disk or if you have multiple hard disks, but you want each drive to use the same settings. Then you can do the following:

✦ To disable the Recycle Bin so all files are permanently deleted immediately, check the "Do not move files to the Recycle Bin. Remove files immediately when deleted" check box. (You'll be taking away your own safety net if you choose this option!)

✦ You can set a maximum size for the Recycle Bin as a percentage of the total drive space.

✦ You can hide the usual "Are you sure...?" dialog box by clearing the check box next to "Display delete confirmation dialog" option.

If you have multiple hard disk drives and you want to configure each independently, choose the "Configure drives independently" option at the top of the General tab. Then use the other tabs to set preferences for each drive independently.

Choose OK after making your selections.

When you right-click the Recycle Bin, you'll probably notice an Empty Recycle Bin option. This option enables you to empty the Recycle Bin without opening it first. Unless you are absolutely certain you don't need any of the files in the Recycle Bin, this is dangerous to use!

Freeing Read-Only Files

Occasionally, you may come across a file flagged as Read-Only (sometimes abbreviated R/O), meaning you can view the file, but you can't make any changes to it. In a few cases, the file may be intentionally made Read-Only so you can't tamper with it. Files copied from CD-ROMs and downloaded from the Internet may be flagged as Read-Only for no good reason, though. To clear the Read-Only status, thereby converting it back to a normal Read-Write (R/W) file, follow these steps:

1. Close the file (if it's open) so you can get to its icon.

2. Use My Computer, Windows Explorer, or Search to get to the file's icon. Or, if you want to clear the Read-Only status from multiple files, select those files.

3. Right-click the file you want to convert to Read-Write (or right-click any one of the selected files) and choose Properties.

4. In the dialog box that appears, click the General tab (see Figure 14-11).

5. Clear the check mark from the Read-Only check box and then click the OK button.

The file (or selected files) will behave as normal Read-Write files from this point. To make a file Read-Only, repeat the steps but check — rather than clear — that Read-Only check box.

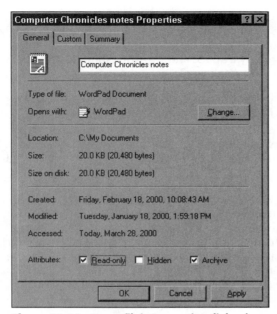

Figure 14-11: Use a file's Properties dialog box to change its Read-Only status.

Changing the Name of Your C: Drive

If you want to rename your C: drive for some reason, open My Computer and then right-click the icon for drive C. Choose Properties and type the new name in the box titled Label. (This name can be no more than 11 characters long.) Click OK when you finish.

You can use the same technique to name or rename a floppy disk in a floppy drive, but you can't rename Read-Only disks (including CD-ROMs).

Using DOS Commands to Manage Files

If you're familiar with DOS commands, you may be relieved to know you still can use the CD, COPY, ERASE, DEL, MOVE, DELTREE, XCOPY, and REN commands to navigate and to move, copy, and delete files and folders. (If you're unfamiliar with DOS commands, don't worry. You don't need to use them.)

To use the DOS commands, first click the Start button, point to Programs, Accessories, and choose MS-DOS Prompt. You see the MS-DOS prompt (typically C:\WINDOWS>), where you can enter DOS commands. For brief help with a command, enter the command followed by a space and /? — for example, **deltree /?**. (Remember, always press Enter after typing any DOS command.)

When you type folder (directory) and filenames at the MS-DOS prompt, use the shortened name — typically, the first six letters, followed by a tilde (~) and a number. Also, omit spaces in the file or folder name. To open a folder named Major Events on the current drive, for example, type cd \majore~1, and then press Enter. Alternatively, enclose the entire names in quotes, as in cd "\major events", and then press Enter.

When you use the DOS DIR command, the leftmost column shows the shortened name and the extension of each folder and file; the rightmost column displays the long name and the extension. You can use this display to discover the short DOS name for any long Windows Me name. Suppose you want to determine the short DOS name for a folder or file named Mathilda Misanthrope. You could enter the command dir mat*.* to search the current folder or dir c:\mat*.* /s to search all of drive C for names beginning with the letters *mat*. For a reminder of all the options you can use with DIR, enter dir /?.

To close the DOS window, enter the exit command at the MS-DOS prompt.

A number of books are available if you want to learn more about DOS. Check out *DOS For Dummies*, by Dan Gookin, published by IDG Books Worldwide, for an introduction to DOS.

Summary

Here's a quick recap of the most important points covered in this chapter:

✦ To rename an object, right-click the object and choose Rename from the shortcut menu.

✦ To select an object to move, copy, or delete, click the object (Classic style) or point to it with your mouse (Web style).

✦ To select several objects, you can drag a frame around them. Or, use Ctrl+click, Shift+click, and Shift+Ctrl+click with Classic-style clicking or Ctrl+point, Shift+point, and Shift+Ctrl+point with Web-style clicking.

✦ To move or copy selected objects, hold down the right mouse button and drag to the destination. Then release the mouse button and choose Copy Here or Move Here from the shortcut menu that appears.

✦ As an alternative to using drag-and-drop, you can right-click any selected file and choose Copy if you want to copy or Cut if you want to move. Then, open the destination folder, right-click some neutral area within that folder, and choose Paste.

✦ To delete selected objects, press the Delete key. Or, right-click a selected object and choose Delete from the shortcut menu.

✦ Remember, objects you delete from your local hard disk(s) (only) are sent to the Recycle Bin. They continue to use disk space until you empty the bin.

✦ To undelete deleted items, open the Recycle Bin, select the items you want to restore, and then choose File ➪ Restore from Recycle Bin's menu bar.

✦ To delete objects permanently in the Recycle Bin and recover their disk space, choose File ➪ Empty Recycle Bin from the Recycle Bin's menu bar.

✦ To convert a Read-Only file to Read-Write, right-click the file's icon and choose Properties. Then clear the Read-Only check box on the General tab of the dialog box that appears. Choose OK.

✦   ✦   ✦

Personalizing the Screen

This chapter looks at ways you can personalize your screen to suit your tastes and needs. Elements such as screen colors, the size of text and objects onscreen, the appearance of dates, times, and numbers, and the arrangement of the menu bar and toolbars in My Computer and Windows Explorer-type windows are all discussed. Fun stuff! This chapter doesn't explain techniques for organizing your desktop. Those topics are included in Chapter 17, which covers arranging files in folders, personalizing the Start menu, and customizing the taskbar.

Customizing the Screen

Personalizing the display properties — that is, your screen, wallpapers, and so on — is easy in Windows Me. But first, always, always, always adjust the brightness, contrast, and sizing controls (if any) on your monitor to get the best possible picture before you mess with the display properties. Then, if you do change the display properties in Windows Me, adjust those controls again when you finish to get the best possible picture from your new settings.

Follow these steps to change the display properties:

1. Right-click the desktop and choose Properties. Or, click the Start button and choose Settings ➪ Control Panel, and then open the Display icon. Either way, you see the Display Properties dialog box, shown in Figure 15-1.

2. Click any tab near the top of the dialog box and then choose any options within that tab. The sample monitor in the middle of the dialog box gives you a preview of the way your current selection will look onscreen.

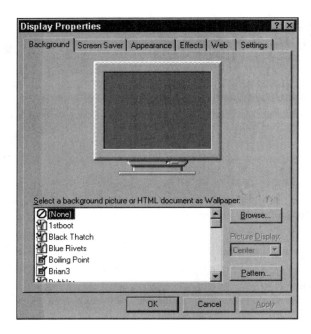

Figure 15-1: Use the Display Properties dialog box to personalize your screen.

3. To apply your selection to the screen without leaving the dialog box, click the Apply button.

4. When you finish, choose OK to save all your selections or click Cancel to save only the settings you already applied (if any).

The following sections describe in detail the various options in the Display Properties dialog box. You also can get instant help in the Display Properties dialog box by clicking the question mark (?) button and then clicking the option with which you need help. Or, click the option you need help with and then press the Help key (F1).

Choosing color palette and resolution

The Settings tab in the Display Properties dialog box (see Figure 15-2) may include the most important display property options. Use the options in this tab to set up the general appearance of your screen, as discussed in the following sections.

Changing the display type

You first want to be sure Windows Me is taking advantage of whatever features your graphics adapter and monitor have to offer. To do this, click the Advanced Properties button on the Settings tab. Windows Me displays the Advanced Display Properties dialog box, shown in Figure 15-3. The title of that dialog box will match the make and model of your video card, and options on some of the tabs will be unique to your computer's video card. If you need help with those settings, your best bet would be to refer to the manual that came with your video card or PC.

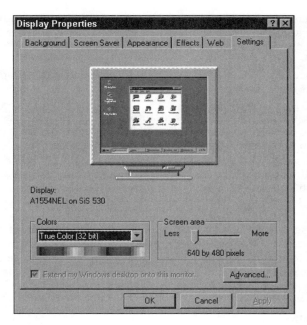

Figure 15-2: Use the Settings tab of the Display Properties dialog box to choose a color depth and screen resolution.

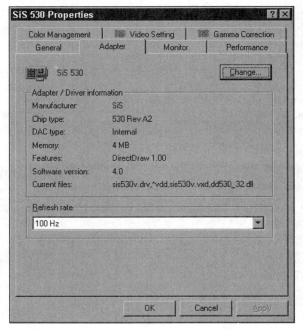

Figure 15-3: Use the Advanced Display Properties dialog box to specify your monitor and other settings.

Chances are Windows Me has detected your adapter card and monitor type automatically. If this is so, those settings already appear near the top of the Adapter and Monitor tabs of the dialog box and you can click Cancel.

Note   If you do purchase a new graphics adapter, use the Add New Hardware Wizard (described in Chapter 26) to install it.

If you recently installed a new graphics adapter or monitor, the current settings may be incorrect. To choose the correct settings, first gather up your original Windows Me CD-ROM. If your adapter or monitor came with disks, keep those disks handy, too. Next, click the tab for the device you want to change (Adapter or Monitor) and then click the Change button. When the Select Device dialog box appears, read and follow the instructions that appear onscreen to install the software for that device.

Tip   If you check the "Show settings icon on task bar" option in advanced properties, a little monitor icon will appear at the edge of your taskbar (opposite the Start button). You can click this icon to change the screen resolution, color palette, and desktop area quickly. Or, double-click it to jump to the Settings tab of the Display Properties dialog box.

Changing the color palette

The Color Palette drop-down list on the Settings tab enables you to select whatever color palettes your graphics hardware offers: 16-color, 256-color, High Color (16-bit), and possibly True Color (32-bit). Only options available for your graphics hardware will appear in the list.

These settings differ in that the more colors you choose, the closer you get to true photographic-quality color. The downside, however, is that more colors lead to slower repainting of the screen when things change. So it's up to you to decide on the best trade-off. I recommend you don't go below 256 colors because most modern multimedia and graphics programs assume you're using a 256 (or better) setting.

Getting the latest and greatest

If you have a disk for the hardware you're installing and your device is in the list when the Select Device dialog box appears, choose the driver from the list and click the Have Disk option. This way, you can be sure you get the latest Windows Me driver for your device.

Or, if you have a connection to the Internet, you can use the Windows Update to be sure you have the latest drivers for your computer equipment. To start the Windows Update, connect to the Internet (see Chapter 6) and then click Start on the taskbar and choose Windows Update. Follow the instructions onscreen.

Note If you connect two display cards and monitors to your PC, you can change their color depths and resolutions independently. See Chapter 28 for information on using multiple monitors.

Changing the screen area (resolution)

The Screen Area option on the Settings tab is equivalent to what the hardware manufacturers usually refer to as resolution. This boils down to how many dots are on the screen (or, in plain English, how much stuff appears onscreen at once). At higher resolutions, more stuff can appear onscreen. The downside of higher resolution is everything is smaller.

To change the Screen Area option, drag the slider to the setting you want. You can choose only settings your graphics hardware supports. To get the best picture onscreen, it's especially important to adjust the brightness, contrast, and sizing controls on the monitor after changing the Screen Area option.

Tip You also can change the appearance and size of the mouse pointer on the screen. See Chapter 16 for information.

Figure 15-4 shows three windows on the desktop — one for Calculator, one for Paint, and one for a CD Player — at the low resolution of 640×480 pixels. I need to overlap the windows on this screen because of the small desktop area I'm using. (Most screens in this book are shown at 640×480 resolution.)

Figure 15-4: Three windows with the desktop area at 640×480 resolution

Figure 15-5 shows the same three windows onscreen with the desktop area set to
1,024×768 pixels. I now have room to spread things out more because each item on
the screen is smaller.

Graphics card manufacturers often recommend choosing a desktop area based
on the physical size of your screen, as summarized in Table 15-1. It's up to you,
however, to decide what's comfortable for your eyes. Also, because changing the
desktop area on the fly is so easy, you can choose whatever desktop area is most
convenient for the work you're currently doing.

Figure 15-5: The same three windows at 1,024×768 resolution

| Table 15-1 | |
| **Physical Screen Size and Suggested Desktop Area** | |
Screen Type/Size	*Suggested Desktop Area*
Laptop	640×480
15-inch diagonal	800×600
More than 15-inch diagonal	1,024×768

Tip

You usually can magnify or shrink the document within a Windows program without fussing with the Desktop Area setting. Choose View ➪ Zoom in the current program or search the program's help system for the word *zoom*.

Changing the font size

The Font Size option on the General tab of the Properties dialog box that appears when you click Advanced (refer to Figure 15-3) determines the size of text on the desktop (choose a Desktop Area greater than 640×480 pixels to see this option). The name that appears below an icon, for example, is affected by the Font Size setting. The options in the Font Size drop-down list depend on your graphics hardware. Typically, you can choose Small Fonts or Large Fonts. If you have trouble reading small text on your screen, try switching to Large Fonts.

Note

If you're not familiar with fonts, see Chapter 19 for the pertinent concepts and terminology. But remember, I'm discussing only the fonts on the Windows desktop in this chapter. Settings you make here have no effect on printed documents.

Some graphics hardware even enables you to define your own custom font size, as indicated by the Other option in the Font Size drop-down list. If this option is available and none of the other settings works for you, try using it to set a custom font size.

Remember, you usually can change the size of the text on your screen by using View ➪ Zoom in any program. This method, which simply magnifies the text within the current window, is often easier than changing the resolution for the entire screen.

Choosing a desktop appearance

You can choose a built-in desktop appearance for your Windows Me desktop or make up your own scheme. In the Display Properties dialog box, click the Appearance tab. To select one of the predefined schemes, open the Scheme drop-down list (by clicking the little down arrow next to Scheme) and then click your preference.

To create your own scheme, first choose any of the predefined schemes as a starting point. Then choose an option in the Item drop-down list to customize individual portions of the screen. For example, you can choose Desktop as the area to customize and then choose a color from the Color 1 pop-up palette. Some options enable you to choose a Size. For example, if you choose Icon Spacing (Horizontal), you can change the Size rather than the Color 1 option. Enter a size (in pixels).

Tip

As an alternative to choosing an item from the Item drop-down list, you can click the place you want to change in the sample area near the center of the dialog box. For example, click the title bar labeled "Active Window" to select "Active Title Bar" in the Item list automatically.

If the item you're changing contains text, you also can choose a Font, Size, and Color for that text. In Figure 15-6, I chose white 12-point Comic Sans MS as the font for active title bars. You also can choose a weight: Bold (B) or Italic (/).

Figure 15-6: Text in active windows is set to the white 12-point Comic Sans MS font.

Saving a custom appearance

As soon as you start changing one of the predefined schemes, the name for that scheme disappears from the Scheme box. If you want to save the scheme you created, click Save As, enter a name, and choose OK.

Choosing a background

The Background tab of the Display Properties dialog box enables you to add a pattern (or texture) to the desktop and put a picture (wallpaper) on the desktop. If your monitor is slow, you can use this option to remove patterns and wallpaper and speed up things. Either way, follow these steps:

1. Open the Display Properties dialog box, as discussed earlier, and click the Background tab (refer to Figure 15-1).

2. Do one of the following:

   • To add a pattern (rather than a picture) to the background, click the Pattern button and choose a pattern from the Pattern list that appears. To remove the current pattern, choose (None) from the top of the Pattern list. To change a pattern, select it in the Pattern list and click Edit Pattern. Change the pattern to your liking and then click Done. Choose OK to return to the Display Properties dialog box.

- To add wallpaper to the desktop, choose a predefined option from the Wallpaper list. Or, click the Browse button and locate and double-click the picture or HTML file you want to use.

3. If you chose a picture format wallpaper, you can choose an option from the Display drop-down list. The *Center* option centers the image in the middle of the desktop; *Tile* makes a repeated pattern from the image (useful for small wallpaper patterns). *Stretch* stretches the image to cover your desktop.

4. Click OK to save your selection.

Note   There's no point in choosing a pattern along with tiled or full-screen wallpaper because the wallpaper will cover the pattern completely. In this case, you may as well set the pattern to None.

Creating your own wallpaper

You can use any graphic image stored on your disk in bitmap (.BMP) format or Hypertext Markup Language (HTML) format as your wallpaper. You can scan a photo, company logo, or other image into a file in the Windows folder and then choose that file by using the Browse button in Step 2. Or you can use a photo from your digital camera.

If you want the image to fill the screen as wallpaper, be sure to size and scale the image to your screen before you save it. In Figure 15-7, I used my digital camera to take a photo of my view from my office. Using options within the camera, I scaled the image to 640 pixels wide by 480 pixels high — an exact fit for my current desktop area of 640×480.

Figure 15-8 shows how my Windows Me desktop looks with this wallpaper onscreen.

Scanner tips

When you scan an image to use as wallpaper, you should set the unit of measurement to pixels. Then, as you scan, crop, and scale the picture, set its size to that of the desktop area. The larger of the two numbers is always the width. If you use 640×480 resolution, for example, scan to about 640 pixels wide by 480 pixels high.

To keep the file size of the scanned image small, don't go for extremely high print quality. A setting of 75 dpi (dots per inch) probably will do fine.

If you don't have a scanner (or digital camera), check the phone book for desktop-publishing service bureaus in your area. Call around to see who can do the job and how much they charge. When you get there, show them this sidebar to help explain what you want. Be sure they save the image to a bitmap (.BMP) file. Warning: If the material you're scanning even looks like it's copyrighted, they may not be willing to scan it!

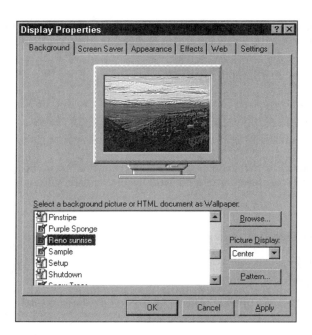

Figure 15-7: A photo selected for use as wallpaper

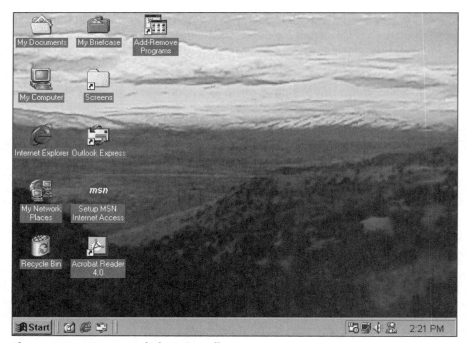

Figure 15-8: My scanned photo is wallpaper now.

Painting a wallpaper

You also can use the Windows Me Paint program to create wallpaper. To start Paint, click the Start button and then choose Programs ➪ Accessories ➪ Paint. You can use the Paint program's tools to create a picture from scratch. Or, you can choose File ➪ Open within Paint to open an existing bitmap image and then use the program's tools to modify that image.

If you don't see Paint in your Accessories menu, maybe it isn't installed yet. See Chapter 25 for information on installing it.

To learn to use Paint, click Help in Paint's menu bar and then click Help Topics. Click the Contents tab and then open (double-click) any book to learn about that topic.

When you're happy with the image you created in Paint, save it using the standard File ➪ Save command. After you save the image, you can set it as wallpaper by clicking the File menu and then choosing one of the following options:

✦ **Set As Wallpaper (Tiled):** Fills the entire screen with your picture

✦ **Set As Wallpaper (Centered):** Puts your picture in the center of the screen

Figure 15-9 shows an example in which I opened a digital image in Paint. Then I saved that image and chose File ➪ Save As Wallpaper (Tiled). The image appears on the desktop behind Paint's window. To avoid repeating the image all over the desktop, choose File ➪ Save As Wallpaper (Centered) instead.

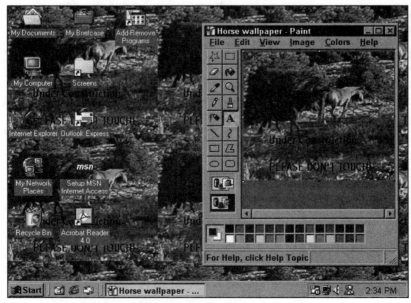

Figure 15-9: A Paint image set as tiled wallpaper

To remove that wallpaper image, to stretch it to fit the desktop, or to select another image for your desktop, follow the steps described at the beginning of this section. That is, right-click the desktop, choose Properties, click the Background tab, and then make your selections in the Wallpaper and Display areas.

Choosing a screen saver

A screen saver is a moving pattern that appears on your screen after some amount of idle time. By idle time, I mean a period in which no mouse or keyboard activity has occurred. The purpose of a screen saver is to prevent burn-in, a condition caused by keeping an unchanging image onscreen too long. Burn-in causes the screen on some older monitors to become blurry and lose some clarity. Though many people use screen savers on more modern monitors, just for the fun of it.

Windows Me offers you many built-in screen savers. To select one of them, follow these steps:

1. If you aren't in the Display Properties dialog box, right-click the desktop and choose Properties.

2. Click the Screen Saver tab (see Figure 15-10).

3. Choose a screen saver from the Screen Saver drop-down list.

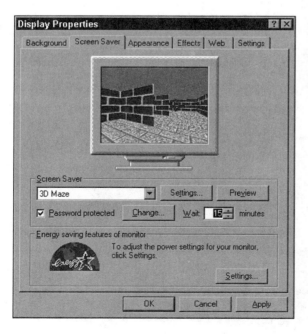

Figure 15-10: The Screen Saver tab has the 3D Maze selected, password protection turned on, and a wait time of 15 minutes.

4. Do any of the following:

- To customize the screen saver you selected, click the Settings button and then choose among the options that appear. Choose OK when you finish.

- To preview the currently selected screen saver and settings, click the Preview button. (To turn off the preview, move the mouse pointer a little.)

- Most screen savers support password protection. To use this feature, select Password Protected, click the Change button, enter a new password and confirmation as instructed onscreen, and choose OK.

- To specify how long the PC must be inactive before the screen saver kicks in, specify the number of minutes in the Wait box.

If you password-protect your screen saver, be sure to write your password on paper and store it in a safe place. If you forget the password, you won't be able to turn off the screen saver easily. (More on this in a moment.)

Turning off the screen saver

When the screen saver kicks in, your Windows Me desktop disappears, and a moving pattern or blank screen appears. To return to your Windows Me desktop, move the mouse pointer a little or press any key. If you password-protected your screen saver, you will be prompted for your password. Type the correct password and press Enter to return to the regular Windows Me desktop.

Hacking the screen-saver password

I told a little white lie earlier when I said you're practically doomed if you forget the password for a screen saver after you enter it. Truth is, it's easy to hack (get around) a password-protected screen saver. I'm not telling you this to encourage computer break-ins. I only want you to know what to do in case you forget your screen-saver password (or how to get around the prank password left behind by some computer-store vandal).

Where to find screen savers

Windows Me comes with many screen savers, desktop wallpapers, and multimedia sound schemes. If you can't find them on your computer, you can add them using the Windows Setup tab of the Add/Remove Programs Properties dialog box in the Control Panel. (See Chapter 25 for information on installing Windows components.)

You can also find screen savers on the Internet's World Wide Web and in your local and mail-order computer stores. To locate screen savers on the Web, search for "screen saver" in your favorite search engine (see Chapter 7).

First, if you're stuck in the screen saver and can't get past the password request, you need to restart the PC. (I know this is a bummer, but you're stuck.) Either press the Reset button on the PC or turn off the PC, wait a moment, and then turn it on again. Wait until you return to the Windows Me desktop.

When Windows Me has fully restarted, right-click the desktop and choose Properties. Click the Screen Saver tab, and then click the Change button. Type a new password, twice (preferably one you'll remember). Or, leave both password boxes blank. Choose OK. (If you want to get rid of Screen Saver password protection altogether, clear the Password Protected check box on the Screen Saver tab.) Click the OK button to return to the desktop. The original password is ancient history and it won't bother you again.

Using Energy Star Features

Did you know your computer monitor uses more electricity than any other component in your computer (except perhaps your laser printer)? Even when the monitor is showing only a screen saver or a blank screen, it's running up your electric bill. When you multiply your single monitor by the millions of computer screens out there, you have a lot of screens sucking up a lot of energy, many of them doing nothing. To top it off, the monitors are putting out heat, just by sitting there. Some scientists even believe all these monitors contribute to global warming!

To curb this high-tech polluting waste of power, the Environmental Protection Agency (EPA) devised a feature called Energy Star. Energy Star automatically reduces power consumption—and even turns off the monitor automatically after the computer has been idle for some time. If your monitor complies with Energy Star standards, you'll probably see an Energy Star logo somewhere on the front or back of the monitor. You can use Windows Me to activate this feature. Follow these steps:

1. If you're not in the Display Properties dialog box, right-click the desktop and choose Properties.
2. Click the Settings tab and then click the Advanced button.
3. Click the Monitor tab. Be sure the correct monitor type is selected and the Monitor Is Energy Star Compliant option is checked.
4. Click OK (if you made a change) or Cancel (if you did not make a change) to return to the Display Properties dialog box.
5. Click the Screen Saver tab. Then click the Settings button to open the Power Schemes tab of the Power Options Properties dialog box, shown in Figure 15-11.

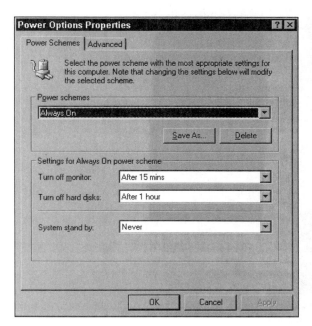

Figure 15-11: The Power Schemes tab of the Power Options Properties dialog box enables you to choose a scheme for conserving energy.

Tip

Clicking the Settings button on the Screen Saver tab has the same effect as choosing Start ➪ Settings ➪ Control Panel and then opening the Power Options icon.

Even if you don't turn off your computer at night, you should still turn off the monitor.

6. To use a predefined power scheme, choose one from the Power Schemes drop-down list. Initially, your choices are Portable/Laptop, Home/Office Desk, and Always On.

7. To choose how much idle time elapses before the monitor is turned off, select an option from the Turn Off Monitor drop-down list. You also select settings for turning off your hard drives and for placing your system into standby mode.

8. To select advanced behaviors for the power scheme, click the Advanced tab. You'll see the dialog box shown in Figure 15-12. Change settings in the Options area as needed. Remember, you can click the question mark (?) button in the upper-right corner of the dialog box and then click the option you're curious about if you need help.

9. If you want to save your current settings to a scheme in the Power Schemes list, click the Save As button on the Power Schemes tab, type a name for the power scheme, and click OK.

10. Click the OK button until you return to the desktop.

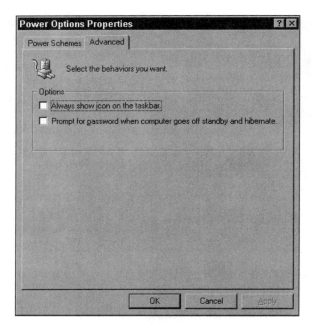

Figure 15-12: The Advanced tab of the Power Management Properties dialog box enables you to refine a selected power scheme.

Changing the Date and Time

The time indicator opposite the Start button in the taskbar shows the current time. When you point to this indicator, the date pops up as a ToolTip.

Note   If the time isn't visible in the taskbar, right-click an empty place on the taskbar, choose Properties, select Show Clock in the Taskbar and Start Menu Properties dialog box, and choose OK.

If the date or time is wrong, you can follow these steps to correct it:

1. Double-click the time indicator on the taskbar. Or, choose Start ➪ Settings ➪ Control Panel and then open the Date/Time icon. You'll see the Date/Time Properties dialog box, shown in Figure 15-13.

2. Choose the current month and year from the Date drop-down lists and then click the current day in the calendar.

3. In the Time box, click the hour, minute, second, or AM/PM option. Then type your correction or use the spin box to make the fix.

4. Click the Time Zone list box down arrow and then choose your time zone.

5. If you have daylight savings time in your time zone, select the "Automatically adjust clock for daylight saving changes" option.

6. Click the OK button to save your settings.

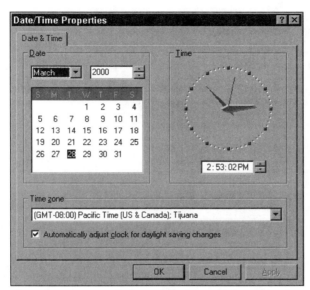

Figure 15-13: Use the Date/Time Properties dialog box to set your computer's calendar and clock.

Date, Time, Currency, and Number Formats

The world has many standards for displaying dates, times, numbers, and currency values. In the United States, we use a period as a decimal point, but Great Britain uses a comma. The Regional Settings dialog box in Windows Me enables you to specify the formats you want to use on your PC. Most Windows programs use whatever date, time, currency, and number format you specify in the Regional Settings Properties dialog box. You needn't pick the same settings for every program on your system.

To choose regional formats, follow these steps:

1. Choose Start ⇨ Settings ⇨ Control Panel.

2. Open the Regional Settings icon. You see the Regional Settings Properties dialog box, shown in Figure 15-14.

Figure 15-14: Use the Regional Settings Properties dialog box to customize numeric, currency, time, and date formats for your region.

3. On the Regional Settings tab, select a region from the drop-down list.

4. To set the Number, Currency, Time, or Date format individually, click the appropriate tab and then choose among the options provided.

5. Click OK to save your changes.

Managing the Menu Bar and Toolbars

In previous chapters, you learned how to browse through your computer's files and folders using My Computer and Windows Explorer. As you know, these windows offer toolbars full of shortcut buttons that make navigating and managing your files much easier. To display or hide the toolbars in My Computer and Windows Explorer, choose View ➪ Toolbar and then choose a toolbar name (such as Standard Buttons) from the submenu.

Figure 15-15 shows an easy-to-use arrangement of bars in the My Computer window, in which the menu bar appears at the top and the other three toolbars are stacked in separate rows below it. The toolbars and even the menu bar in My Computer and Windows Explorer windows can be moved, resized, and customized in several ways. In the following sections, I explain how to set up the toolbars to your liking. As you'll see, fiddling with toolbars is fun and easy.

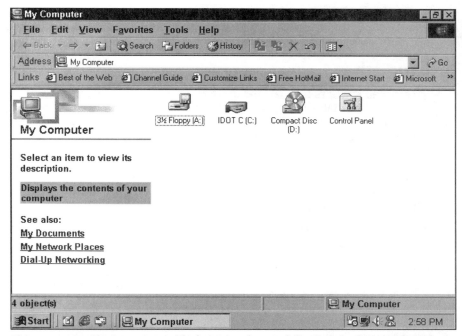

Figure 15-15: My Computer with the menu bar and the Standard Buttons, Address Bar, and Links toolbars visible and stacked one atop the other.

Moving a bar

The menu bar and toolbars always appear at the top of the window. You can, however, move them up, down, left, and right with respect to one another. Here are the steps to follow:

1. Move your mouse pointer to the raised vertical line at the left edge of the bar you want to move. The mouse pointer changes to a two-headed horizontal arrow.

2. Drag the bar up, down, left, or right in the area at the top of the window. As you drag, the mouse pointer changes to a two-headed horizontal arrow with double-vertical crosshairs.

3. When the bar is positioned where you want it, release the mouse button.

That's all there is to it. The bar now appears at its new position.

Tip

You also can place the mouse pointer just to the right of the vertical line and then drag. In this case, the mouse pointer changes to a four-headed arrow as you drag.

Resizing a bar

If you've stacked the bars next to one another, as shown in Figure 15-16, some buttons and options probably will be hidden from view. Of course, you can move the bars so they occupy their own rows at the top of the window. Or, you can resize the bars using either of these techniques:

✦ To expand the bar quickly to its full width or to collapse it as small as possible, move the mouse pointer to the vertical line (or just to the right of that line). Then, double-click your mouse. If the bar was previously expanded, it will collapse; if it was collapsed, it will expand.

✦ To resize the bar by a specific amount, move the mouse pointer to the vertical line. Then, drag the line right or left.

Tip

Some bars, such as the menu bar and the Standard Buttons toolbar shown in Figure 15-16, display tiny scroll arrows at the left or right edge of the bar. Click the arrow to see additional options or buttons.

Figure 15-16: The bars after lining them up on the same row at the top of the window

Showing or hiding toolbar button names

If you point your mouse to any button on the Standard Buttons toolbar, a ToolTip describing the button soon appears near the mouse pointer. You can, if you prefer, display text labels instead of ToolTips below the buttons, as shown in Figure 15-17. To do this, choose View ➪ Toolbars ➪ Customize and choose the text option you prefer. To hide the labels again, repeat this sequence.

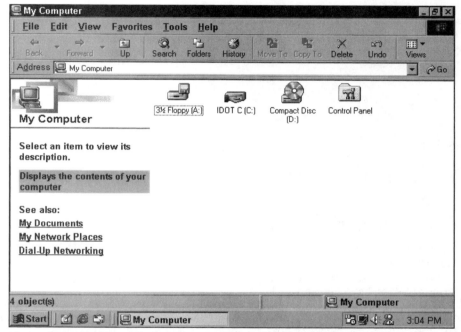

Figure 15-17: The Standard Buttons toolbar with text labels visible

Changing Desktop Icons and Visual Effects

The Effects tab of the Display Properties dialog box, shown in Figure 15-18, enables you to customize the permanent desktop icons (My Computer, My Documents, and such). It also enables you to choose from among several optional visual effects. To get to this dialog box:

✦ Right-click any neutral part of the desktop, choose Properties, and then click the Effects tab.

✦ Or, click the Start button, choose Settings ➪ Control Panel, and then open the Display icon.

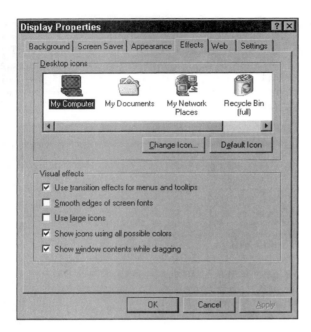

Figure 15-18: The Effects tab of Display Properties enables you to choose new desktop icons and visual settings.

Changing desktop icons

If you want to change the icon for My Computer, My Documents, My Network Places, Recycle Bin (full), or Recycle Bin (empty), click the icon you want to change. Then click the Change Icon button. A dialog box containing alternative icons appears, as in Figure 15-19.

To choose one of the icons shown, click whichever icon you want and then click the OK button to return to the Display Properties dialog box. From there, you can choose another icon to alter or click OK to return to the Windows Me desktop. If you made any changes, they should be visible on the desktop after you click the Apply button or OK button in Display Properties. If the new icon doesn't appear, try refreshing the desktop (right-click some neutral area of the desktop and choose Refresh).

Note   Be aware, you are not limited to the icons that first appear when you choose to change an icon. You can browse around through other files containing icons to see if they contain any good icons for your purpose. Chapter 34, "File Icons, Associations, and Properties," discusses the more advanced techniques required to dig around for icons on your PC.

To restore a desktop icon to its original default appearance, get back to the Effects tab of the Display Properties dialog box. Click the icon you want to restore and then click the Default Icon button.

Figure 15-19: Alternative icons

Using the visual settings

The Visual effects pane of the Effects tab enables you to activate features that can improve the quality of your visual display. The only downside to these effects is they do consume some computer resources and can, therefore, slow down the performance of your PC. In most modern Pentium computers, however, the slowdown will probably be so minor it will be unnoticeable. To see what does or doesn't work for you, experiment with the various settings. You can clear or choose any check box and then click the Apply button to see the effects of that selection immediately. (A few options require you to restart your computer.) The following provides a brief description of what each option offers:

✦ **Use transition effects for menus and tooltips:** Windows Me uses animations in the menus and ToolTips. Selecting this option allows those animations to play.

✦ **Smooth edges of screen fonts:** When selected, gets rid of the *jaggies* — those jagged edges that make text on the screen look blocky rather than smooth.

✦ **Use large icons:** Enlarges all the icons on your desktop. Useful if you use a high screen resolution that makes the icons too small to see comfortably at their normal size.

✦ **Show icons using all possible colors:** Ensures all desktop icons are displayed at the color depth you selected on the Settings tab of the Display Properties dialog box.

✦ **Show window contents while dragging:** Normally, when you drag a window across your screen, only a ghost image of the window follows the mouse pointer onscreen. Choosing this option makes the entire window visible during dragging.

Fun with Desktop Themes

A *desktop theme* is a collection of wallpaper, screen savers, mouse pointers, sound effects, colors, and fonts organized around some theme. Figure 15-20 shows an example of one of the themes that come with Windows Me. Those of you familiar with Microsoft Plus! 98 may already be familiar with desktop themes. In Windows Me, the themes are part of the Windows Me product. You needn't purchase a separate Plus! package to enjoy desktop themes.

Before you try to activate a desktop theme, see if any themes have been installed on your computer yet. If not, you can install some themes on the fly, as discussed in the next section.

Figure 15-20: The Inside your Computer desktop theme

Installing desktop themes

To use desktop themes, you'll first need to ensure the feature is installed. Follow these steps to check and, if necessary, to install the desktop themes component:

1. Click the Start button and choose Settings ⇨ Control Panel.

2. Open the Add/Remove Programs icon.

3. Click the Windows Setup tab and wait a moment while Windows checks your currently installed components.

4. Click the Desktop Themes option to highlight it, as in Figure 15-21.

5. If the check box next to Desktop Themes is not checked, go ahead and click that check box so it gets a check mark.

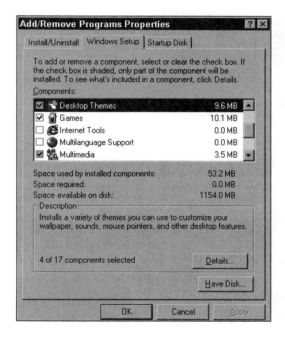

Figure 15-21: Choose the Desktop Themes component to install desktop themes on your PC.

6. Click the Details button to reveal a list of ready-made themes, as in Figure 15-22.

Figure 15-22: Here's a selection of ready-made desktop themes from which you can choose.

7. Choose any themes that look interesting to you by clicking their check boxes. See the section titled "Finding more desktop themes" later in this chapter for themes that come with Windows Me.

8. After choosing your theme(s), click the OK button to leave the Desktop Themes dialog box and then click the next OK button to leave the Display Properties dialog box.

9. Follow any and all instructions that appear on the screen to install your themes.

Activating a desktop theme

After you install one or more desktop themes, you can easily activate or deactivate the theme by following these steps:

1. Click the Windows Me Start button and choose Settings ➪ Control Panel.

2. Open the Desktop Themes icon to reveal the Desktop Themes dialog box shown in Figure 15-23.

3. Choose a desktop theme from the Theme drop-down list. The Preview pane presents an example of how the screen will look with that theme applied. Note, you can use the buttons and check boxes at the right side of the dialog box to apply/remove any individual component of the theme such as the screen saver, mouse pointers, fonts, and so forth. Feel free to experiment — you can't do any harm.

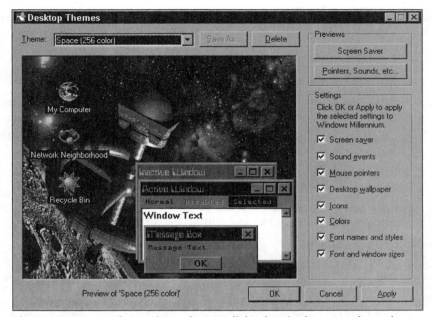

Figure 15-23: Use the Desktop Themes dialog box in the Control Panel to choose a desktop theme.

4. When you're happy with your selection, click the OK button. The theme will be applied to your desktop immediately.

Deactivating a desktop theme

If you get tired of a theme or you decide the theme is making your PC run slowly, you can easily deactivate the theme by following these simple steps:

1. Click the Windows Me Start button and choose Settings ⇨ Control Panel.

2. Open the Desktop Themes icon to reveal the Desktop Themes dialog box.

3. From the Theme drop-down list, choose Windows Default.

4. Click the OK button.

You'll be back to your original Windows Me desktop settings.

Uninstalling desktop themes

Every installed desktop theme takes up some disk space — anywhere from about 1.5 to 3.5MB — because the wallpaper, screen saver, and sound files can be quite large. To recover some lost disk space, you can remove any theme you're not using. Here's how:

1. Click the Start button and choose Settings ⇨ Control Panel.

2. Open the Add/Remove Programs icon.

3. Click the Windows Setup tab and wait a moment while Windows checks your currently installed components.

4. Click the Desktop Themes option to highlight it and then click the Details button.

5. Each installed theme will have a check mark next to it. Simply clear the check box next to any theme you wish to remove.

6. Click the OK button to close the Desktop Themes dialog box. Then click the next OK button to close the Add/Remove Programs dialog box.

Finding more desktop themes

Windows Me comes with quite a few built-in desktop themes. If you have access to the Internet, you can probably find even more themes you can download and use free. Your best bet to begin is to point your Web browser to a search engine such as http://www.altavista.com. Then search for the appropriate buzzwords, such as Windows+desktop+themes or "Windows desktop themes" (in quotation marks). Chances are, you'll find dozens of themes to explore and download.

Using the Accessibility Wizard

Up until now, the settings I've shown you in this chapter have been pretty much focused on simply making your PC a bit more fun to use. There's certainly nothing wrong with having a little fun, but if you have physical impairments that make using a computer difficult, you probably have more important things in mind — such as being able to use your system productively.

Windows Me comes with a tool — the *Accessibility Wizard* — that can help make using a PC a whole lot easier for someone with vision, hearing, or mobility problems. There's no reason why almost anyone can't have the benefit of using a modern Windows Me-based PC.

Caution   The Accessibility Wizard makes a number of configuration changes to your system. If you are simply trying out the Accessibility Wizard so that you can later assist someone else with their system, you will probably want to save your current settings using the Save As button on the Appearance tab of the Display Properties dialog box before you begin. Otherwise you may find it somewhat difficult to reverse all of the changes made by the Accessibility Wizard.

To use the Accessibility Wizard, follow these steps:

1. Click the Start button and choose Programs ⇨ Accessories ⇨ Accessibility ⇨ Accessibility Wizard. This will display the Accessibility Wizard welcome screen shown in Figure 15-24.

Figure 15-24: Use the Accessibility Wizard to help configure a PC so it is easier to use.

2. Click Next to continue.

3. On the Text Size screen shown in Figure 15-25, choose the text size that works best for you.

4. Click Next once you have selected the text size.

5. On the Display Settings screen shown in Figure 15-26, choose the display options that are appropriate for your needs:

   • **Change the font size:** Increases the size of the type in menus, titles bars, and other screen elements controlled by Windows Me.

   • **Switch to a lower screen resolution:** Reduces the screen resolution so that everything on the screen appears somewhat larger. This option is not available if your screen is already set to 640×480 resolution.

   • **Use Microsoft Magnifier:** Dedicates a portion of the screen to a window that greatly magnifies the area around the mouse pointer.

   • **Disable personalized menus:** Prevents Windows Me from hiding menu items that haven't been used in some time. This makes the menus less confusing since items remain in the same location on the menus.

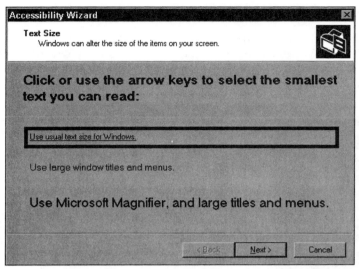

Figure 15-25: Choose the text size that is easiest to read.

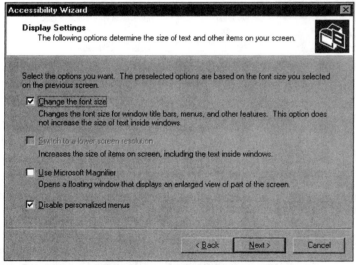

Figure 15-26: Choose the Display Settings options you need.

6. Click Next to continue.

7. On the Set Wizard Options screen shown in Figure 15-27, choose the statements that describe your situation:

- **I am blind or have difficulty seeing things on screen:** Instructs the Accessibility Wizard to choose settings that help people with vision problems.

- **I am deaf or have difficulty hearing sounds from the computer:** Instructs the Accessibility Wizard to choose settings — such as flashing a title bar — when Windows Me would normally use an audible prompt to get the user's attention.

- **I have difficulty using the keyboard or mouse:** Instructs the Accessibility Wizard to set options such as *StickyKeys* that make it easier to use a computer with a pointing stick or one hand.

- **I want to set administrative options:** Opens the Accessibility Properties dialog box so you can set any of the accessibility options.

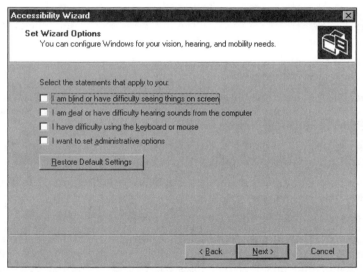

Figure 15-27: Choose the statements that apply to your needs.

8. Once you have made your selections, click Next to continue. At this point, the Accessibility Wizard may continue to ask further questions depending on your selections so far. Follow the onscreen prompts to continue setting up the accessibility options you need.

Tip   If you know someone who may need to use the accessibility options, they may have a difficult time configuring these options without a bit of assistance since the Accessibility Wizard starts out using normal Windows Me settings. It may be a good idea to offer to help with the Accessibility Wizard.

Summary

In this chapter, you've seen umpteen different options for controlling the exact appearance of your Windows Me desktop. Let's review the most important options discussed in this chapter:

✦ To personalize your screen settings, right-click the desktop and choose Properties. The Display Properties dialog box appears.

✦ To change the background pattern or wallpaper, click the Background tab in the Display Properties dialog box.

✦ To change the screen saver, click the Screen Saver tab in the Display Properties dialog box.

✦ To change the screen appearance (colors, sizes, and fonts), click the Appearance tab in the Display Properties dialog box.

✦ To change the color palette, resolution (desktop area), font size, and display type, click the Settings tab.

✦ To change the date, time, and format of numbers and currencies, go to the Control Panel (choose Start ➪ Settings ➪ Control Panel). Then open the Date/Time or Regional Settings icons.

✦ To display or hide toolbars in My Computer, Windows Explorer, and Internet Explorer, choose View ➪ Toolbars and select the toolbar you want.

✦ To move a bar, point to its double-vertical line and then drag the bar to a new position near the top of the window.

✦ To resize a bar, drag or double-click its double-vertical line.

✦ The Effects tab of the Display Properties dialog box enables you to change the appearance of your My Computer, My Documents, My Network Places, and Recycle Bin icons. It also enables you to choose from among numerous visual settings that improve the quality of your display but can slow down performance on slower PCs.

✦ To activate, change, or deactivate a desktop theme, click the Start button, choose Settings ➪ Control Panel, and then open the Desktop Themes icon.

✦ To configure your system for use by someone with vision, hearing, or mobility problems, click the Start button, choose Programs ➪ Accessories ➪ Accessibility ➪ Accessibility Wizard.

✦   ✦   ✦

Mouse, Keyboard, and Game Controllers

In this chapter, I explain techniques for tailoring your computer's input devices — mouse, keyboard, and game controllers — to your own personal work style and habits. This chapter also discusses Windows Me's accessibility options, which can make using a PC much easier for people with physical disabilities or sensory impairments.

Personalizing the Mouse

Windows Me initially assumes you use a standard mouse and a standard desktop monitor, you're right-handed, and so on. If the mouse pointer causes you eyestrain or if you feel a little klutzy with the mouse, you may want to change some of those assumptions. To get started:

1. Open the Control Panel (click the Start button and choose Settings ➪ Control Panel, or open My Computer and then open the Control Panel).

2. Open the Mouse icon to get to the Mouse Properties dialog box, shown in Figure 16-1.

3. Choose options, as described in the following sections, to tailor your mouse to your liking and then click the OK button.

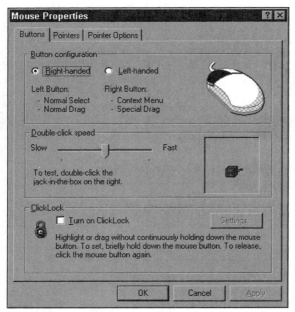

Figure 16-1: Use the Mouse Properties dialog box to fine-tune the behavior of your mouse.

Note If you have serious problems with your mouse, or you want to ensure that you're using the latest mouse driver software, use Device Manager discussed in Chapter 26 to troubleshoot or upgrade.

Mice for lefties

If you're left-handed and you want the main mouse button to be below your left index finger, choose Left-Handed under Button Configuration near the top of the Buttons tab in the Mouse Properties dialog box. Once you make this change, you'll have to "think in reverse" when you're told to use the left or right mouse button. Table 16-1 shows how the standard terminology becomes backward for lefties.

Taking control of double-clicking

If you find double-clicking is a problem, you can speed or slow the double-click speed. If you can't seem to double-click fast enough, for example, slow down the double-click speed. Or, if you often double-click when you mean to make two separate clicks, speed up the double-click rate.

Table 16-1 Lefties Need to Use Different Buttons for Common Mouse Activities	
Standard Terminology	**Lefties Use This Mouse Button**
Click	Right mouse button
Double-click	Right mouse button
Drag	Right mouse button
Right-click	Left mouse button
Right-drag	Left mouse button

Tip Some mice come with their own programs that enable you to tweak the mouse even more than the Mouse Properties dialog box. This is especially true if your mouse has any unique features such as a third button, a wheel, or a touchpad. If you have some kind of written documentation for your mouse, you may want to look at it and see what else is possible.

The Double-Click Speed option on the Buttons tab enables you to determine how fast two clicks must be for interpretation as a double-click. To find the double-click speed that works best for you, try the following steps:

1. Drag the slider below Double-Click Speed to the Fast end of the scale.

2. Double-click the jack-in-the-box, using your normal double-click speed.

3. If the jack-in-the-box doesn't open, drag the slider bar slightly toward Slow.

4. Repeat Steps 2 and 3 until you find a comfortable double-click speed.

Using ClickLock

If you find that selecting or dragging items with your mouse is difficult, you may want to give the ClickLock feature a try. When this option is activated, you can highlight or drag objects without continuously holding down the mouse button.

To select this option, add a check to the Turn on ClickLock check box. Then click the Settings button and use the slider to adjust the length of time you need to hold down the mouse button to turn on ClickLock. You can experiment with the delay slider to see when you have a comfortable setting.

When ClickLock has been activated, you click a second time to release the lock. It may take some time to get used to using this option.

Controlling the mouse motion

If you find zeroing in on things with the mouse pointer difficult, slow down the mouse-motion speed. Or, if you must move the mouse too far to get from point A to point B onscreen, speed up the mouse-pointer speed. On laptop LCD screens (and some others), the mouse pointer may fade, or even disappear, when you move the mouse. To solve this irritating problem, turn on the pointer trails.

Tip   When you use a projector to give a demonstration onscreen, turn on the pointer trails to make following the mouse across the screen easier for your audience.

To control the mouse speed and trails, click the Pointer Options tab in the Mouse Properties dialog box (see Figure 16-2). To adjust the speed of the pointer, drag the slider in the Pointer Speed slider bar toward the Slow or Fast end of the bar. To test your current setting, click the Apply button and then try moving the mouse around. To see your full range of options, apply the slowest speed and test the mouse. Then apply the faster speed and try the mouse again.

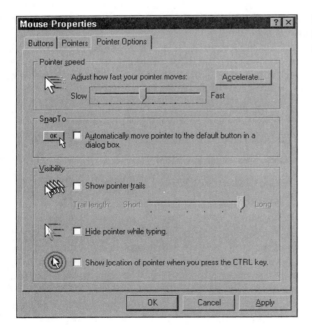

Figure 16-2: Options for controlling mouse speed and pointer trails

To make your mouse pointer *accelerate* — move faster the further — you move the mouse, click the Accelerate button and choose the acceleration options you prefer. Turning on pointer acceleration can make your mouse seem more responsive, while turning off acceleration completely may make it seem sluggish.

To turn on pointer trails, select the "Show pointer trails" check box. The trails turn on immediately and will be visible as soon as you move the mouse. To control the length of the trails, drag the slider to the Short or Long end of the slider bar.

If you find that the mouse pointer is distracting while you are typing, select the Hide pointer while typing box. This will hide the mouse pointer when you are typing, but it will reappear when you stop typing or move the mouse.

Finally, if you often find that you simply lose track of the mouse pointer location, select the "Show location of pointer when you press the CTRL key" box. When this option is selected, Windows Me displays a set of circles that draw your attention to the mouse pointer whenever you press the Ctrl key.

Choosing mouse pointers

If you're having trouble seeing the mouse pointer, try a larger pointer. Are you bored with the same old pointer? Try some fancy 3D animated pointers, quite a few of which come with your Windows Me program. The choices available to you are on the Pointers tab in the Mouse Properties dialog box (see Figure 16-3). In this example, I've already chosen a scheme called Animated Hourglasses, which shows moving sand in the hourglasses, instead of the standard pointers.

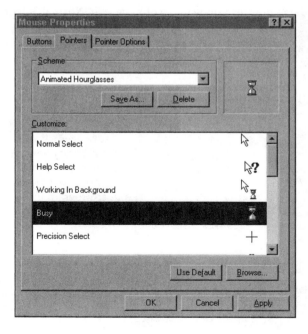

Figure 16-3: The Pointers tab in the Mouse Properties dialog box

To begin, open the Scheme drop-down list and then experiment with the different options offered. When you find a scheme you want, you can customize it further, if you like. Click any mouse pointer in the list and then click the Browse button to try another pointer. If you select a different pointer and then change your mind, click the Use Default button to return to the default pointer.

After mixing your own mouse pointer scheme, you can click the Save As button and give your new scheme a name. You can delete the scheme currently shown in the drop-down list by clicking the Delete button.

Finding more mouse pointers

Many of the desktop themes described back in Chapter 15 include some custom mouse pointers. If you've installed any themes, you'll find their mouse pointers in the c:\Program Files\Plus!\Themes folder. If you just want to use some of the mouse pointers from an installed theme, without using all the features of the theme, you can see what's available by following these steps:

1. Click the Start button and choose Settings ➪ Control Panel.

2. Open the Mouse icon.

3. Click on the Pointers tab.

4. Click on the style of mouse pointer you want to change (e.g. Normal Select, Help Select, etc.)

5. Click the Browse button and navigate to c:\program files\plus!\themes. The Browse dialog box will list cursors available from that folder (if any) as in Figure 16-4.

6. Click on any filename then click the Open button.

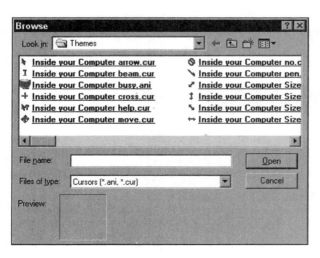

Figure 16-4: If you've installed any desktop themes, you'll find their mouse pointers in c:\program files\ plus!\themes

You can choose unique cursors for as many, or as few, pointers as you wish. When you're finished, just click the OK button.

Tip　Files that contain cursors have the .cur extension. Animated cursors use the .ani extension. Use Start ➪ Search ➪ For File or Folders to search your entire hard disk for *.cur or *.ani files to explore all the cursors available on your hard disk.

If you have Internet access, you can download some cool collections of animated cursors. To find some possible resources, use your Web browser to go to any of the large search engines, such as `http://www.altavista.digital.com` and search for Windows+mouse+pointers or Windows+Me+mouse+pointers. If you visit some of the sites listed, you're likely to find quite a few sets you can download for free.

Note　For those of you who have absolutely no idea what I'm talking about in the previous paragraph, Part II in this book discusses the Internet in detail.

Personalizing the Keyboard

The keyboard is another important input device. And, as you might expect, Windows Me offers some options for tweaking the behavior of your keyboard. To get to those options:

1. Open the Control Panel (click Start ➪ Settings ➪ Control Panel, or open the Control Panel icon inside My Computer).

2. Open the Keyboard icon to get to the Keyboard Properties dialog box shown in Figure 16-5.

3. Make your selections, as discussed in the following sections, and then click the OK button to close the dialog box and save your settings.

Controlling the keyboard's responsiveness

Most keyboards are *typematic*, which means that if you hold down a key long enough, it starts repeating automatically. If you're a slow typist, you may accidentally type the same letter two or more times. To correct the problem, adjust the Repeat Delay slider to a longer delay, so you must hold down the key longer before auto-repeat typing starts.

You also can use the Repeat Rate slider bar to determine how fast the key repeats as you hold it down. You can test either selection simply by typing in the text box below the sliders after making a change to either slider.

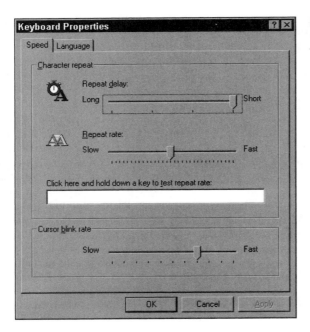

Figure 16-5: The Keyboard Properties dialog box enables you to personalize your keyboard.

Note   If you have serious problems with your keyboard or you want to ensure that you're using the latest keyboard driver software, use Device Manager discussed in Chapter 26 to troubleshoot or upgrade.

Controlling the cursor blink speed

The "Cursor blink rate" section of the Keyboard Properties dialog box enables you to determine how fast the blinking cursor (also called the insertion point) blinks. Drag the slider to the Slow or Fast end of the Cursor blink rate bar and watch the sample blinking cursor. The idea is to find a speed that's in sync with your own cosmic biorhythms or, perhaps, the pace of life in your locale. In San Diego, for example, people like slow-blinking cursors; in New York City, they like their cursors blinking at full-on, high-anxiety speed (hurry! hurry!).

Multiple-language keyboarding

For people who work in multiple languages, Windows Me offers some handy options for adjusting your keyboard to work in a specific language, including:

✦ Easy switching from the keyboard layout used in one language to the keyboard layout for another language

✦ Automatic font substitution when switching among different languages (fonts are discussed in Chapter 19)

✦ Correct sorting and comparison rules for different locales and cultures

Note

You can set the format of dates, times, numbers, and currency values by using the Regional Settings icon in the Control Panel. See the end of Chapter 15 for more information.

The options for controlling language-related keyboard options are on the Language tab of the Keyboard Properties dialog box, shown in Figure 16-6. The following sections examine techniques for installing multiple-language support and using multiple-language keyboard layouts.

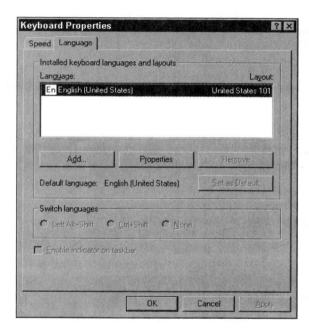

Figure 16-6: The Language tab of the Keyboard Properties dialog box

Setting keyboard languages and layouts

The first step is to choose specific languages and keyboard layouts appropriate to your work. Follow these steps:

1. Windows Me may need to install specific languages during this procedure, so close all open programs and save your work; then gather your original Windows Me CD-ROM.

2. On the Language tab of the Keyboard Properties dialog box, click the Add button, choose a language from the drop-down list (Figure 16-7), and then click the OK button.

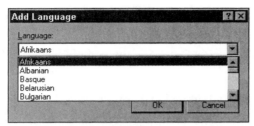

Figure 16-7: Many languages are offered in the Add Language dialog box.

3. Click the Properties button, choose a keyboard layout for the currently selected language, and choose OK.

4. Repeat Steps 2 and 3 to add as many languages as you want.

5. To select a default language, click the language you want and then click the Set As Default button.

6. If you want to use a shortcut key for switching languages, choose Left Alt+Shift or Ctrl+Shift under Switch Languages. Or, choose None for no keyboard shortcut. (Left Alt+Shift means to press the Alt key on the left side of your keyboard while pressing either Shift key.)

7. If you want to switch languages by clicking an icon on the taskbar, select "Enable indicator on taskbar."

8. Choose OK when you finish making your selections.

As usual, if any additional instructions appear onscreen, be certain to read and follow them.

Switching among languages and layouts

After you select one or more foreign languages and layouts, switching among them is easy. If you selected "Enable indicator on taskbar" while you chose layouts, you see a two-letter abbreviation at the right end of the taskbar indicating which language is currently in use — for example, *En* if you're working in English.

To switch to another language and keyboard layout, do either of the following:

✦ Click the language indicator in the taskbar and then click the language you want to use (see Figure 16-8).

✦ Press the shortcut keys you indicated (for example, Left Alt+Shift). Each time you press the shortcut key, you will cycle to the next available language. (You won't get any feedback about which language you chose unless you enabled the indicator on the taskbar.)

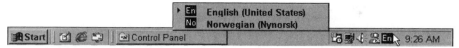

Figure 16-8: Clicking the En indicator to switch to another language

Now you can fire up your word processing program and type with the currently selected language and keyboard layout. In fact, you can switch to another language and layout on the spot. Anything new you type will use the language, layout, and (if applicable) font for that language. In a true multilingually aware program, you can even select existing text and change it to whatever language and font you're currently using.

Removing languages

If ever you decide to eliminate a foreign language keyboard layout, return to the Control Panel, open the Keyboard icon, and go to the Language tab. Click any language option you want to eliminate and then click the Remove button. Then click the OK button to save your changes and close the dialog box.

Adding and Calibrating a Game Controller

Some computer games play better using a joystick, steering wheel, or video game-style control pad or another game controller. Game controllers are, of course, entirely optional. So if you don't feel you need one, don't bother to read this section. Also, be aware that game controllers work only with certain kinds of games, not with the Windows Me desktop. For example, many drive games support steering wheels and foot pedals. Games that involve flying might support joysticks. Some shoot-em-up games support video game-style gamepads. The only way to know for sure which input devices a particular game supports is by reading about the game in which you're interested.

Many different kinds of game controllers exist, as a quick visit to your local Comput-O-Rama superstore will prove. I should point out, however, that Windows Me has built-in support for the following types of controllers:

✦ 2-axis, 2-button joystick

✦ 2-axis, 4-button joystick

✦ 2-button flight yolk

✦ 2-button flight yolk with throttle

✦ 2-button gamepad

✦ 3-axis, 2-button joystick

✦ 3-axis, 4-button joystick

✦ 4-button flight yolk

✦ 4-button flight yolk with throttle

✦ 4-button gamepad

✦ CH Flightstick

✦ CH Flightstick Pro

✦ CH Virtual Pilot

✦ Gravis Analog Joystick

✦ Gravis Analog Pro Joystick

✦ Gravis Gamepad

✦ Logitech ThunderPad

✦ Logitech Wingman

✦ Logitech Wingman Extreme

✦ Logitech Wingman Light

✦ Microsoft Sidewinder 3D Pro

✦ Microsoft Sidewinder Freestyle Pro

✦ Microsoft Sidewinder gamepad

✦ Microsoft Sidewinder Precision Pro

✦ Thrustmaster Flight Control System

✦ Thrustmaster Formula T1/T2 with adapter

✦ Thrustmaster Formula T1/T2 without adapter

Adding a game controller

Because so many different kinds of game controllers exist, I can't guarantee the simple installation instructions will work for every product on the market. But they're worth a try. (If these instructions don't work, you'll probably need to follow the installation instructions that came with your game controller.) Anyway, here are the steps you must follow to install a game controller:

1. Close all open programs and documents, and save any work in progress (to play it safe). Shut down the computer.

2. Plug the game controller into the appropriate plug on the back of your PC.

3. Restart the computer. If Windows detects the game controller at startup follow the instructions that appear on the screen.

4. Open the Control Panel and then open the Game Controllers icon.

5. Select your game controller from the list and click the OK button. Or, if your game controller isn't listed, click the Add Other button and follow the instructions onscreen.

6. If Windows successfully locates your controller, the Status column will read OK, as in Figure 16-9, where I successfully added a 3-axis, 2-button joystick.

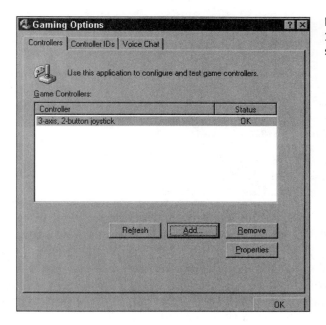

Figure 16-9: 3-axis, 2-button joystick is successfully attached.

Calibrating and testing the controller

Once the controller is installed and you're given the OK status, you'll want to calibrate the controller. Doing this tells Windows about the buttons on your device, the range of motion it has, and so forth. Calibration is pretty easy; follow these steps:

1. Click the name of the controller you want to calibrate and then click the Properties button. The Game Controller Properties dialog box appears.

2. Click the Settings tab and then click the Calibrate button (see Figure 16-10).

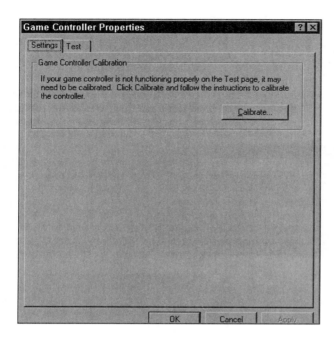

Figure 16-10: Use the Calibrate button to tune your game controller to your PC.

3. Follow the instructions onscreen to calibrate your controller.

4. When you finish the calibration, click the Test tab in the Game Controller Properties dialog box and try out your controller. The test page will provide options relevant to your controller, as in the example shown in Figure 16-11.

5. If necessary, repeat the calibration and test until the game controller appears to work properly. Then click OK to close the Game Controller Properties dialog box and click OK again to close the Game Controllers dialog box.

The game controller won't work on the desktop. When you fire up a game that supports this kind of controller, however, the controller should work fine. If not, check the documentation or Help screens that came with the game to see if you need to select any special options to activate the game controller.

If you have severe problems with your game controller, you may have a hardware conflict or some other problem. Check the Device Manager as discussed in Chapter 26.

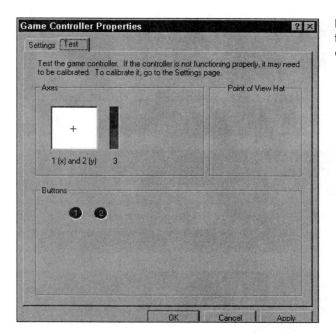

Figure 16-11: The test page for a 3-axis, 2-button game controller

Using Accessibility Options

More than half the corporations in the United States employ people whose disabilities can make using a computer difficult. In its never-ending battle to make computers easier for everyone to use, Microsoft has included the Accessibility Options feature in Windows Me. Before I show you how to activate those options, let's see what's available.

Visual enhancements

If you have any difficulty seeing the screen or your eyes fatigue quickly, first adjust the knobs on the monitor and personalize the screen display, as discussed in Chapter 15. Then, if you're still having trouble seeing the screen, consider choosing one of the predefined high-contrast color schemes according to the procedure in Chapter 15.

The accessibility options provide additional enhancements including large text and large icons. Also in Windows Me is the Microsoft Magnifier. When activated, this feature splits the screen into two halves. The lower half displays text and graphics at normal size. The upper half of the screen magnifies whatever is near the mouse pointer, as in Figure 16-12.

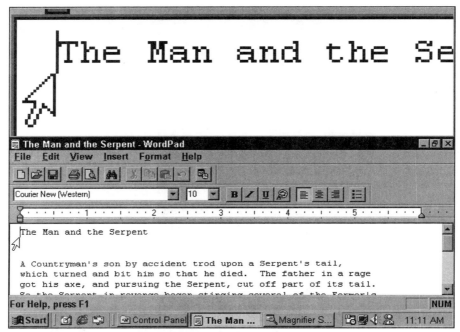

Figure 16-12: Microsoft Magnifier is turned on.

To control how much of the screen is regular and how much is magnified, you
can drag — up and down — the horizontal bar that separates the two parts of
the screen. You can also control the degree of magnification, mouse behavior, and
screen colors using the Microsoft Magnifier dialog box shown in Figure 16-13. To
get to that dialog box, click the Start button and choose Programs ➪ Accessories ➪
Accessibility ➪ Microsoft Magnifier.

> **Note** If the accessibility options aren't available on your PC, see the following section,
> "Installing Accessibility options," for instructions on installing those options.

Once open, you can show and hide the Magnifier Settings dialog box by clicking
on the Magnifier Settings button that appears in the taskbar. To close the Magnifier,
right-click its button in the taskbar and choose Close from the menu that appears.

Mouse/keyboard accessibility

Many physical impairments can make operating the keyboard and mouse difficult.
Some of the options for personalizing the mouse and keyboard, described earlier in
this chapter, may help. In addition, you can choose among the options described
in the following sections.

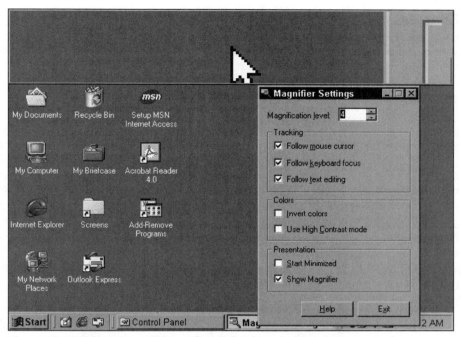

Figure 16-13: The Microsoft Magnifier dialog box enables you to control magnification, mouse behavior, and screen colors.

StickyKeys

If you have difficulty typing combination keystrokes, such as Ctrl+Esc, Shift+F1, or Alt+Z, try using the StickyKeys feature. With StickyKeys enabled, you can make the *modifier keys* (Ctrl, Alt, and Shift keys) stick after you press them, so you needn't hold down any of those keys to press a combination keystroke. Instead, you press and release the Ctrl, Shift, or Alt key (or any combination thereof) and then press and release the *nonmodifier key*, which will be any key on the keyboard except Ctrl, Alt, or Shift. Pressing and releasing the nonmodifier key automatically releases the modifier key(s).

You can also tap the modifier key twice to keep that key locked down. To unlock the modifier key, press the modifier key a third time. As you lock and release StickyKeys, a small indicator near the lower-right corner of the Windows desktop provides some visual feedback as to which keys are currently locked down. If all of this gets to be confusing, and you need a quick reminder of how to use StickyKeys, you can open Help (click the Start button and choose Help). In the search box, type in **StickyKeys** and click the Go button.

FilterKeys

If you are double-pressing keys by holding them down too long or typing extra characters because your finger brushes nearby keys, use the FilterKeys option to change the sensitivity of the keyboard.

ToggleKeys

The Caps Lock, Num Lock, and Scroll Lock keys on the keyboard all act as toggles, meaning you can press the key to turn the feature on and off. Most keyboards have small indicator lights that light up when one of those keys is in the "on" position. If you're visually impaired, it may not be so easy to see those indicators. The ToggleKeys option provides an auditory cue that informs you of the status of the key. When one of those keys is turned on, a high-pitch sound is played. Turning off one of those keys plays a low-pitched tone.

MouseKeys

MouseKeys enables you to use the keyboard to move the mouse, click things, and so forth. When MouseKeys is activated, you can control the mouse as follows (be sure to use only the keys on the numeric keypad):

✦ **Move the pointer:** Press (or hold down) the numeric keys surrounding the number 5. The 7, 9, 1, and 3 keys move the pointer diagonally. The 8, 4, 6, and 2 keys move the pointer in the direction of the arrow shown in the key.

✦ **Click:** Press the 5 key in the middle of the keypad.

✦ **Double-click:** Press the plus (+) sign key or press the 5 key twice, fast.

✦ **Drag (left mouse button):** Point to the object, press the insert (0) key to begin dragging, use the numeric keys surrounding the 5 to move the mouse pointer, and then press Delete (.) to complete the operation.

✦ **Right-click:** Position the mouse pointer and press the minus (–) sign key. Then press the 5 key to click or the plus (+) sign key to double-click.

✦ **Right-drag (right mouse button):** Point to the object you want to drag, press the minus (–) sign key, and then press the insert (0) key to lock down that button. Use the numeric keys surrounding the number 5 to drag. Then press the Delete (.) key to complete the drag.

✦ **Return to standard clicking:** Press the slash (/) key. This is useful if the 5 key is right-clicking when you want it to click. (If a shortcut menu is open, press Alt or Esc before pressing the slash key.)

✦ **Click both mouse buttons:** Press and release the asterisk (*) key.

✦ **Jump the mouse pointer in large increments across the screen:** Hold down the Ctrl key as you move the mouse pointer with the numeric keys surrounding the number 5.

✦ **Slow the movement of the mouse pointer (as when you need to position it precisely):** Hold down the Shift key as you move the mouse pointer with the numeric keys surrounding the number 5.

Even if you're not physically impaired, you may find MouseKeys a handy option, especially if you need to position the mouse precisely in your work. Precise positioning is easier to do with the numeric keypad than with the mouse. It's also handy if you're suffering from mouse shoulder (a pain in your shoulder) or repetitive stress syndrome pains.

 Tip   When the MouseKeys feature is active, you can mix mouse actions with numeric keypad actions in any way that's convenient.

Sound enhancements

If your hearing is impaired, you may want to try SoundSentry or ShowSounds. Windows uses small beeps and other sounds to provide extra feedback. You can also have SoundSentry put up visual cues along with the sounds, so you can see when the sound is being played. ShowSounds allows programs that use speech or other audible cues to provide text on the screen, much like close-captioned TV.

SerialKeys alternative input devices

Windows Me also provides built-in support for alternative input devices, including eye-gaze systems and head pointers. Typically, you can plug any such SerialKey device into an available serial port. You needn't disconnect the mouse first. To give an alternate input device its own serial port, install the device according to the manufacturer's instructions. Then, in the General tab of the Accessibility Properties dialog box (discussed in a moment), select the Support SerialKeys Devices option, and click the Settings button to specify the serial port and baud rate for the alternative input device.

Installing Accessibility options

If you've never used the Windows Me Accessibility options, you may need to install them. If you need to install those options (or you think you may need to install them), follow these steps:

1. Save any work in progress and close all open programs.

2. Gather up your original Windows Me floppy disks or CD-ROM. (If Windows Me came preinstalled on your computer, you may be able to skip this step.)

3. Click the Start button and choose Settings ➪ Control Panel.

4. Open the Add/Remove Programs icon.

5. Click the Windows Setup tab.

6. If the Accessibility component's check box already has a check mark, as in Figure 16-14, then those options are already installed. You can click the Cancel button, skip the remaining steps, and go straight to the following section.

7. If the Accessibility check box isn't checked, click it now to select it.

8. Click the OK button near the bottom of the dialog box and follow the instructions that appear onscreen.

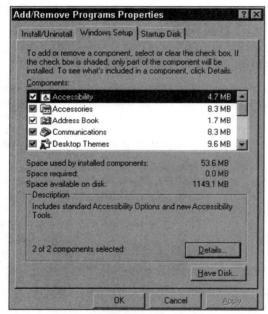

Figure 16-14: The Windows Setup tab in the Add/Remove Programs Properties dialog box

Once the installation is complete, you can then use the Accessibility Settings Wizard, described next, to choose and activate whatever accessibility options are useful to you.

Note   If you have access to the World Wide Web and you want to see what's new in accessibility, point your Web browser to http://www.microsoft.com/enabled.

Using the Accessibility Wizard

The easiest way to select and tune your accessibility options is though the Windows Me Accessibility Wizard. To start the wizard:

1. To play it safe, save any work in progress and close any open programs.

2. Click the Start button and choose Programs ➪ Accessories ➪ Accessibility ➪ Accessibility Wizard. Click Next in response to the Welcome screen that appears.

3. In the Text Size wizard screen that appears (see Figure 16-15), choose (using the mouse or arrow keys on the keyboard) the smallest size of text you can read. Then click the Next button.

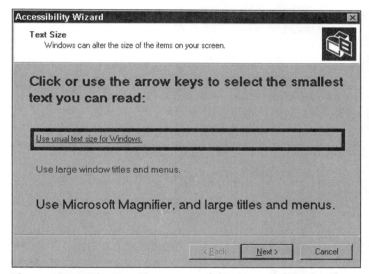

Figure 16-15: The Text Size screen of the Accessibility Wizard

From here on, the rest of the wizard screens are self-explanatory. Just read each wizard screen, select any options appropriate for you, and then click the Next button. Do so until you get to the last screen and then click its Finish button.

Activating options without the Accessibility Wizard

Although not quite as hand-holding as the Accessibility Wizard, the Accessibility Properties dialog box also offers a means of defining accessibility options. To get to this dialog box, open the Control Panel (click Start ➪ Settings ➪ Control Panel, or open My Computer and then open the Control Panel). Open the Accessibility Options icon. You'll come to the dialog box shown in Figure 16-16.

Make your choices using the tabs near the top of the dialog box and the options within each tab. As you explore, you'll notice many options offer a hot key for turning the option on and off. For example, if you choose Use StickyKeys and then click the Settings button, you'll come to the Settings for StickyKeys dialog box shown in Figure 16-17.

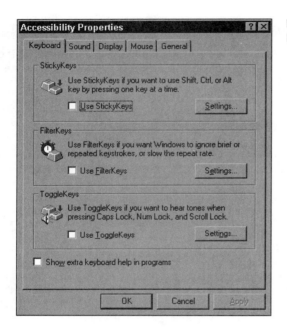

Figure 16-16: Accessibility Properties dialog box

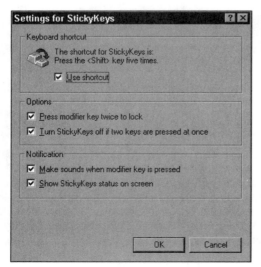

Figure 16-17: Here I enabled the Keyboard Shortcut (hot key) for the StickyKeys accessibility option.

The hot keys provide an easy means of turning an accessibility option on and off. So when you're presented with an option to activate a keyboard shortcut, you'd be wise to select this option.

If you need help or more information while working in the Accessibility Properties dialog box, click the question mark (?) button near the upper-right corner of the dialog box and then click the option with which you need help. When you finish, click the OK button.

Note   You can also get a lot of good information from the online help. Click the Start button, choose Help, and click the Accessibility for Special Needs topic.

Accessibility time-out and status indicator

If disabled and nondisabled users share a PC, you may want to activate the automatic reset and notification features:

✦ The Automatic Reset feature turns off the accessibility features (except the SerialKey device) and returns to the regular settings after the PC has been idle for a specified period.

✦ The Notification feature warns all users when the accessibility features are active and can provide audio feedback when a feature is turned on or off. The indicator also tells MouseKeys and StickyKeys users when a key or mouse button is locked down.

To activate either of these options, click the General tab of the Accessibility Properties dialog box. Then select the Automatic Reset and Notification options you want to use and set the idle time (if any) for turning off the accessibility options.

Using shortcuts to activate/deactivate accessibility options

If you activate the shortcut key for each accessibility option you enable, you can use the keys listed in Table 16-2 to turn those options on and off.

Tip   The accessibility options are available even when you're running a DOS program.

Table 16-2 Emergency Hot Keys for Turning Accessibility Options On and Off	
Accessibility Option	*Hot Key*
FilterKeys	Hold down right Shift key for 8 seconds
High-Contrast Mode	Left Alt+Left Shift+Print Screen
MouseKeys	Left Alt+Left Shift+Num Lock
StickyKeys	Press Shift 5 times
ToggleKeys	Hold down Num Lock for 5 seconds

Using the On-Screen Keyboard

The on-screen keyboard is designed to enable you to enter text using a mouse or other pointing device. Figure 16-18 shows the On-Screen Keyboard. To start the program click the Start button and choose Programs ⇨ Accessories ⇨ Accessibility ⇨ On-Screen Keyboard.

Figure 16-18: The On-Screen Keyboard enables you to enter text without typing.

You can choose various layout options for the On-Screen Keyboard using the Keyboard menu. You might, for example, find that the block layout is somewhat easier to use since this layout assigns similar widths to most of the keys and this allows the keys to line up in straight columns.

> **Tip** The on-screen keyboard automatically acts as though the StickyKeys option is installed. This means that you can click the Shift key, for example, and the next key you click will act as though the Shift key is being held down. The Shift key returns to normal, un-shifted status after another key is pressed.

Typing on the on-screen keyboard is only effective if you have an application open that can accept keystrokes. Your PC reacts exactly the same way to the on-screen keyboard as it would to a standard keyboard.

More on sharing a computer

If your vision is impaired and you share a computer with another user, you may find it difficult to read the screen when that user leaves his or her settings behind. In this case, you can set up some hot keys to take you straight to high-contrast mode as soon as you press them.

To activate the quick switch to high-contrast mode, open the Accessibility Properties dialog box (choose Start ➪ Settings ➪ Control Panel and open the Accessibility Options icon). Click the Display tab and select Use High Contrast. Then, click the Settings button to select a scheme: White On Black, Black On White, or Custom (to choose any color scheme available in the Display options of the Control Panel). Be sure to select the "Use shortcut" check box for the emergency hot key.

Another way to deal with the issue of several people sharing a single computer is to set up *users*, as discussed in Chapter 29.

When this feature is activated, you can hold down the left Alt key, hold down the left Shift key, and press the Print Screen key to turn high-contrast mode on and off.

Uninstalling accessibility options

If, for whatever reason, you ever want to remove the accessibility options from your PC, simply repeat Steps 1 through 4 under "Installing Accessibility options" earlier in this chapter. Then clear the check box next to Accessibility options, click the OK button, and follow the instructions onscreen.

Summary

All the techniques for personalizing your mouse, keyboard, joystick, and accessibility options are in the Control Panel. Here's a quick summary of the steps required to personalize each device:

✦ To personalize your mouse, choose Start ➪ Settings ➪ Control Panel and then open the Mouse icon.

✦ To personalize your keyboard, choose Start ➪ Settings ➪ Control Panel and then open the Keyboard icon.

✦ To install and/or calibrate a game controller, choose Start ➪ Settings ➪ Control Panel and then open the Game Controllers icon.

✦ To set up accessibility options using a wizard, click the Start button and choose Programs ➪ Accessories ➪ Accessibility ➪ Accessibility Settings Wizard.

✦ As an alternative to using the wizard, you can activate accessibility options via the Control Panel (choose Start ➪ Settings ➪ Control Panel and then open the Accessibility Options icon).

✦ To turn on Microsoft Magnifier, click the Start button and choose Programs ⇨ Accessories ⇨ Accessibility ⇨ Microsoft Magnifier. To turn off the magnifier, right-click its button in the taskbar and choose Close.

✦ To turn on the on-screen keyboard, click the Start button and choose Programs ⇨ Accessories ⇨ Accessibility ⇨ On-Screen Keyboard.

✦   ✦   ✦

Organizing Your Virtual Office

In This Chapter

How and when to
create your own
folders

Reorganizing your
Start menu

Clearing the
Documents menu

Using the
Favorites menu

Personalizing the
taskbar

Understanding
Windows Me's
special folders

In some ways, every computer is like a small, virtual office. The computer's hard disk is like an electronic file cabinet in which you keep everything in the computer. The computer's screen is like your real desktop, where you put the stuff you're working on currently. As in a real office, the better you organize things in the virtual office, the more easily you can find them. Getting organized is what this chapter covers.

Why Folders?

Imagine a real file cabinet filled with documents (on paper), but no folders — just sheet after sheet of paper. What a pain it would be to try to find a particular document. To stay organized, we typically add folders to our file cabinets, perhaps grouped by client name or by project, to hold related sheets of paper.

Folders on a disk serve the same purpose as folders in a file cabinet: to organize stuff so you can find it easily later. If you had no folders on your hard disk, you'd continually be digging through hundreds, or thousands, of documents trying to locate the document you needed.

Your hard disk probably is organized into folders already because the procedure for installing a new program usually creates one or more folders to hold that program's files. If you've installed the WordPad component of Windows Me, for instance, this program, named wordpad.exe, is already stored in a subfolder named C:\Program Files\Accessories (that is, in a subfolder named Accessories inside the folder named Program Files on hard disk drive C).

In general, you should not move or rename any folders created by a program's installation procedure. Doing so usually is more trouble than it's worth. Why? First, because the Windows Me Registry keeps track of various folders and files and when you move registered things around, you risk fouling up the Registry. Second, because any shortcuts you create will continue to point to the original folder. The shortcut won't work anymore because the folder it expects to find no longer exists.

To illustrate why messing with the names or locations of a program's folders isn't good, let me relate two examples from my own experience. Of course, I'll tell you how I fixed the problems I caused.

Folder problem #1

One day, I was browsing around my hard disk and I came across a folder named Waol15. I couldn't remember what was in this oddly named folder. I explored a little and discovered it contained the programs I use to interact with America Online (an online information service). Thinking myself clever, I renamed the folder America Online, so I wouldn't forget its contents in the future.

Whoops — bad move. The next time I tried to use America Online, I had nothing but problems from the get-go — not because anything was wrong with America Online's program, but because I had renamed its folder. My America Online program still expected to find things in a folder named Waol15 (the C:\WAOL15 directory, in DOS terminology). But because I renamed that folder, I had no folder named Waol15 anymore.

Fixing the problem was simple, once I realized what was wrong. I renamed the America Online folder back to Waol15 and all was well again.

Folder problem #2

Another time, I moved a folder from its current location to a new location in a different folder. I made a slightly different mistake, but one with the same unpleasant results. Here's what happened:

I installed Microsoft Access and its installation procedure put all the programs for Access in a folder named Access (C:\ACCESS). Later, I installed a few applications in Microsoft Office. The installation procedure for Office created a folder named MSOffice; it also created two subfolders inside the MSOffice folder. One of these subfolders was named WinWord (C:\MSOFFICE\WINWORD, in DOS terminology); Office used this folder to store Microsoft Word. The second subfolder, named Excel (C:\MSOFFICE\EXCEL), was where Office stored Microsoft Excel.

Then it dawned on me: Because Access is part of the Microsoft Office suite, I could move Access's folder into the MSOffice folder. So without much forethought, I dragged the Access folder into the MSOffice folder. Not smart. The next time I launched Microsoft Access, I began having problems immediately. As in the preceding example, when the Access program needed something from the disk, it looked for a folder named C:\ACCESS.

You may think, "Yeah, but you didn't change the name of that folder." Well, by moving the folder, I actually did change its name. In this case, I changed the name of the Access folder from C:\ACCESS to C:\MSOFFICE\ACCESS. Those names are not the same. So whenever Access needed something from C:\ACCESS, it would bomb.

Once again, the cure was simply to drag Access's folder back to its original location.

The moral of these stories is: When a program is on your hard disk, it's best not to move or rename any of the folders it needs. Living with whatever organization and names the installation programs created is better.

Why Create Folders?

After boring you to tears with stories of stupid things I've done, why would I tell you how to create (and manage) folders? Answer: Even though you don't want to mess with the folders your installation programs create, plenty of good reasons exist for creating folders to manage your document files, just as plenty of good reasons exist for managing your paper documents in folders in a file cabinet.

With a few more real-world examples, you'll quickly see why folders are a good way to organize your documents.

As an author, I usually have a few projects going: a main project, some back burner projects in the idea stage, and, perhaps, some books still in production that need last-minute checks and changes.

To organize these projects, I always keep a folder named Projects. Within that folder, I have a subfolder for each project on which I'm working. For example, right now my Projects folder contains a subfolder named "Windows Me Bible." This folder holds every file I created for this book. Another subfolder within Projects is called "Susan's Stuff." That subfolder contains some programs I'm creating for my wife.

Figure 17-1 shows my Projects folder open on the desktop, with subfolders for all my ongoing projects (in their various stages of disarray).

Figure 17-1: My Projects folder contains a folder for each ongoing project.

The beauty of this organization is that when I need to open a document for any project, I first open the Projects folder and then open the appropriate project name to see all the associated documents for that project. When I find the document I'm looking for, I open it. No muss, no fuss, no trying to remember where things are or what program I used to create them.

When I start a new project, I always go right to the Projects folder and create a new subfolder for that project. Then it's only a matter of remembering to put each new document for the project in the appropriate folder so I can find it later.

When I finish a project and no longer need immediate access to its documents, I move its subfolder to some obscure place on the disk. In most cases, I eventually move it all off to a Zip disk or a CD-ROM and then delete the entire project from my local hard drive C to reclaim the disk space the project's files were using.

Here's another example. I have a folder named "ClipArt" that contains thousands of pieces of royalty-free art. Within the ClipArt folder, I've categorized the files by theme. The Animals subfolder (see Figure 17-2), for example, contains pictures of animals. The Business and Travel subfolder contains art related to business and travel, and so on for the other subfolders.

Note   *Clip art* refers to small pieces of filler art you can put in newsletters, brochures, and other publications. Chapter 22 discusses clip art.

Whenever I need a piece of clip art, I always start my search by opening the folder named ClipArt — a plain, simple, efficient process.

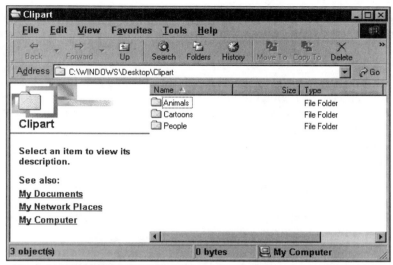

Figure 17-2: My ClipArt folder contains subfolders of art clips organized by theme.

How to Create a Folder

After this preamble, you may think creating a folder is a big hassle. Not true — in fact, creating a folder is easy. The preamble was meant to give you food for thought about how you might organize your own folders and tips about when not to mess with folders. You can create a folder with whichever browsing tool you prefer: My Computer or Windows Explorer.

Creating a new folder with My Computer

To create a folder with My Computer, follow these steps:

1. Open the My Computer icon.

2. Open the icon for the drive on which you plan to put the folder (usually hard disk drive C).

3. If you want to put this new folder inside an existing folder, open the folder that should contain the new one. Repeat this step as necessary to drill down and open the folder that will contain the new folder.

4. If you wish, switch to Large Icons view to make seeing what you're doing easier. Either click the Large Icons button on the toolbar or choose View ➪ Large Icons from the menus. Or right-click anywhere within that folder and select View ➪ Large Icons.

5. Choose File ➪ New ➪ Folder from the menu bar, or right-click some empty space between existing icons and choose New ➪ Folder. A folder titled New Folder appears, as shown in Figure 17-3. The folder name is highlighted and ready for you to type a new name.

6. While the icon label is highlighted, type a name for this new folder. Your new name will replace the highlighted name. If the label is no longer highlighted for some reason, press F2 or right-click the folder and choose Rename before you start typing.

7. To save the new folder, click an empty place inside the folder window or press Enter.

If you want to move the folder to its proper alphabetical position within the current window, choose View ➪ Arrange Icons ➪ By Name. Or, switch to Details view (choose View ➪ Details) and then click the Name button at the top of the first column. The folder icons will appear in alphabetical order.

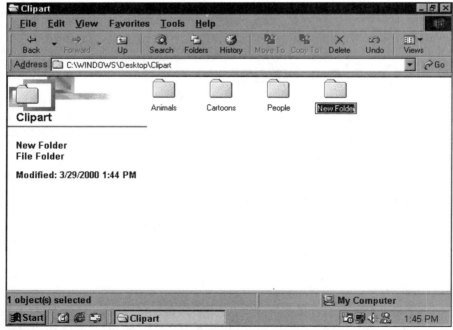

Figure 17-3: A new folder is created on my hard drive (C).

Creating a new folder with Windows Explorer

You also can create a folder from the Windows Explorer window, if you prefer. The basic procedure is as follows:

1. Click the Start button, point to Programs, Accessories, and then click Windows Explorer.

2. In the left column, select the drive or folder one level above where you want to create the new folder. If you want the new folder to be at the first level of drive C, for example, select the icon for drive C. If you want to create a folder within a folder, select the folder that will contain the new folder.

3. Choose File ➪ New ➪ Folder. A new folder titled New Folder appears at the bottom of the list in the right-hand pane, as in the example shown in Figure 17-4. The folder name is highlighted and ready for you to type in a new name.

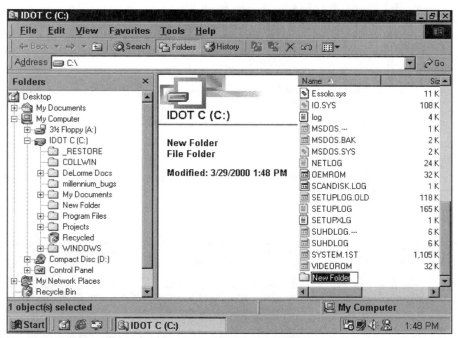

Figure 17-4: A new folder is created with Windows Explorer.

4. While the name is highlighted, type a name for the new folder. If the name is no longer highlighted, press F2 or right-click the folder icon and choose Rename, so you can type a new name.

5. To save the folder with its new name, press Enter or click an empty area in the right panel of the Explorer window.

6. If you want to shuffle the new folder into proper alphabetical position in the list, choose View ➪ Arrange Icons ➪ By Name.

Tip   Here's another way to create a folder. Right-click some empty area within the list of folder and filenames (the pane on the right) and choose New Folder. You can also create a folder by right-clicking an empty area within the list of files and folder and choosing New ➪ Folder.

Your new folder is just like any other; it's accessible from both the left and right panes of the Explorer window (when you have navigated to where you can see the folder). And, of course, it's also accessible from My Computer.

Managing Folders — A Quick Review

Earlier chapters (especially Chapter 2) discussed the many techniques for managing folders and files. Because we're on the subject of folders now, let's review the main techniques:

✦ To open a folder, double-click it (if you're using Classic style clicking) or click it (if you're using Web-style clicking). If a folder is open, but covered by other windows on the desktop, click the hidden folder's taskbar button to bring it to the forefront.

✦ To close a folder, click the Close (X) button.

✦ To rename a folder, right-click it and choose Rename. Or, select it and press F2. Then use standard text-editing techniques to create a new name and press Enter.

Understanding parents and children

Parents and children have different meanings in the computer world than in the animal world. A subfolder that's inside another folder sometimes is called the *child folder*. The folder containing the child is called the *parent folder*.

To move from viewing a child folder to viewing its parent in Windows Explorer, click the Up button in the Standard Buttons toolbar or select the parent folder in the left panel of the Exploring window. You can also press the Backspace key to move up a level, My Computer or Windows Explorer (though Backspace only works in the left pane of Windows Explorer.) To reveal hidden child folders below a parent folder in the left pane of the window, click the plus (+) sign next to the parent folder. You can click the minus (–) sign next to a parent folder if you want to hide the child folders again.

✦ To move or copy items into a folder, right-drag the selected objects to the folder's icon or the folder's open window, release the mouse button, and then choose Move Here or Copy Here.

✦ To move or copy items out of a folder, open the folder, select the items you want to move or copy, right-drag them to the destination drive and/or folder, release the mouse button, and then choose Move Here or Copy Here.

✦ To move or copy an entire folder, navigate to the drive and/or folder that will contain the folder. Then right-drag the folder's icon to that destination, release the mouse button, and choose Move Here or Copy Here.

✦ To view the DOS path name for a folder, open the folder, choose Tools ➪ Folder Options, click the View tab, and select the "Display the full path in title bar" option or the "Display the full path in the address bar" option. Then click OK.

✦ To bring hidden files into view, choose Tools ➪ Folder Options, click the View tab, choose "Show hidden files and folders," and choose OK.

✦ To delete a folder, select the folder's icon, and then press Delete. Or, right-click the folder's icon and then choose Delete. Choose Yes when asked for confirmation.

Don't forget, when you delete a folder, you delete all the files and folders inside that folder, including any hidden files. Also remember, only deletions from your local hard disk are sent to the Recycle Bin. You cannot undelete folders deleted from removable media or network drives.

✦ To create a shortcut to a folder, right-drag the folder's icon to the Start button, to a desktop toolbar (such as the Quick Launch toolbar), or to the desktop. If prompted, choose Create Shortcut(s) Here.

Web view or no Web view?

You can view folders as Web pages where the folder's window contains an image, perhaps some fancy text, and other information, as shown in the left-hand side of Figure 17-5. In classic Windows style, no extra goodies are shown, as in the right-hand side of Figure 17-5.

To turn the Web view on or off, choose Tools ➪ Folders Options and select the Web View option you prefer.

In My Computer, you can also choose whether all folders appear in Web view by default. To do so, follow these steps:

1. Open your My Computer icon.

2. Choose Tools ➪ Folder Options. You're taken to the Folder Options dialog box shown in Figure 17-6.

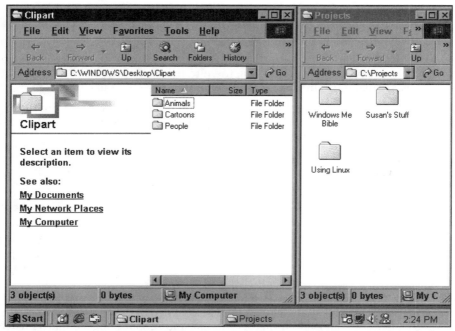

Figure 17-5: Folders viewed as a Web page (left) and in Classic Windows style (right)

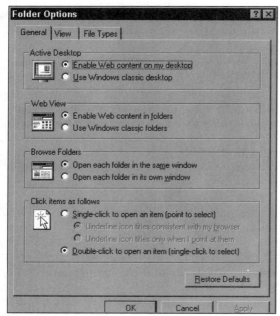

Figure 17-6: Folder Options dialog box

3. If you want folders to open in Web view by default, choose "Enable Web content in folders." If you want to open folders in Classic style, choose "Use Windows classic folders."

4. You can also choose any of the other options in the dialog box.

5. Click the OK button to save your changes and close the dialog box. Then click OK to close the Folder Options dialog box.

Folder background images

You can jazz up any folder so it displays a special background when opened. Your background can be an HTML document or a picture in bitmap, JPEG, or GIF format. If you change your mind about using the background, you can remove it easily.

Note   HTML stands for Hypertext Markup Language and it's the format used to display the pages you visit on the World Wide Web (see Chapter 6).

Customizing any folder is a snap, thanks to a wizard that steps you through the procedure:

1. Using My Computer, Windows Explorer, or Find, open the folder you want to customize.

2. Choose View ➪ Customize This Folder from the menus.

3. Click Next to continue. You'll see the Customize This Folder Wizard, shown in Figure 17-7.

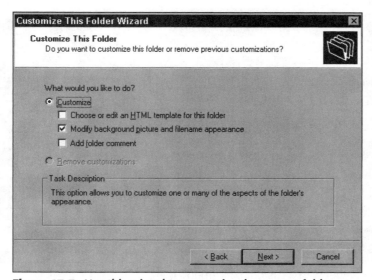

Figure 17-7: Use this wizard to customize the current folder or to remove customization.

4. Do one of the following:

- To choose or edit an HTML document, click the "Choose or edit an HTML template for this folder" option.

Note

Learning to create HTML can take weeks, even months. So don't feel intimidated if that option leaves you baffled. If you don't know anything about HTML, you can still add a custom picture to your folder by choosing the second option instead.

- To use an existing picture in bitmap, JPEG, or GIF format, click the "Modify background picture and filename appearance" option.
- To add a comment to the folder, select the "Add folder comment" option.
- To remove the custom backgrounds, click "Remove customizations."

5. Click Next as needed and follow any remaining instructions onscreen.

6. When you reach the last step in the wizard, click Finish to save your changes.

Your folder will have the custom background appearance anytime you open it. Figure 17-8 shows an example in which I selected a graphic image named Carved Stone as my background image, set the text color to white, and set the background color to blue (although in the figure, the blue behind the icon text looks gray).

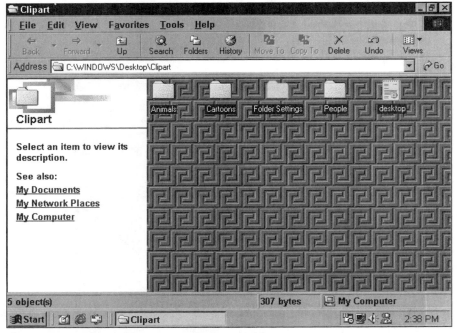

Figure 17-8: Folder with a custom background image

Finding a lost folder

If you lose track of a folder, you can always locate it with Search. Click the Start button, point to Search, and then click For Files Or Folders. If you want to search the entire hard disk, select the C: drive in the Look In list and select (check) the "Include subfolders" option. Type all or part of the folder name and then choose Search Now.

 Note

You can broaden the search beyond the local hard disk by choosing My Computer in the Look In list. Part VI of this book explains how you can even search other PCs in your local area network (LAN) if you're part of one.

Reorganizing Your Start Menu

The Start button offers the easiest way to get documents from your virtual file cabinet (the hard disk) onto your virtual desktop (the screen). The better you organize your Start menu, the easier it is to get things to the desktop when you need them. The following sections examine ways to organize your Start menu and its submenus.

So many techniques, so little time

As you'll quickly discover, Windows Me offers many ways to accomplish the same tasks — from organizing your Start menu to opening icons — and you may wonder why. Well, I guess the short answer is "different strokes for different folks." Some people like to do things one way, while others prefer to use a different method. The long answer is that the more ways you know to accomplish a task, the easier it is to pick the best tool for the job at hand.

Consider how handy it is to know several routes between work and home. If you know only one route, you might be stymied if a storm, a water main break, or a traffic jam blocks your normal route. If you know several routes, however, you can find alternate ways to home or work when your usual route is blocked.

The same holds true for Windows Me. If you know one way to do something and it works — fine, use it! But sometimes knowing another method can save you time and keystrokes or mouse clicks, depending on what you're currently doing. So, for example, if you already have Windows Explorer open and you have a burning desire to rearrange your Start menu, have at it with Windows Explorer. But if Windows Explorer isn't open, you may prefer right-clicking the Start button or the taskbar to begin your Start-menu housekeeping chores because these methods tend to be easier than Windows Explorer.

Of course, you don't have to learn every method under the sun. Simply use the method you like best. When you're ready to learn a new technique or a shortcut, you can always return to this book for tips.

Putting shortcuts in the Start menu

As you may recall from Chapter 4, you can easily create desktop shortcuts to favorite programs, folders, and documents by right-dragging their icons out to the desktop and choosing Create Shortcut(s) Here. You can use a similar method to add new shortcuts to the top of the Start menu. But you needn't use the right mouse button. You can drag any icon — using the left mouse button — to the Start button and drop the icon right onto the button.

New shortcuts appear near the top of the Start menu. For example, to create the Start menu shown in Figure 17-9, I poked around my computer using My Computer. While looking around at various icons, I did the following:

✦ I dragged the icon for a Word document named The Man and the Serpent to the Start button.

✦ I dragged the printer icon for my HP LaserJet from the Printers folder to the Start button.

✦ I dragged the icon for my Projects folder to the Start button.

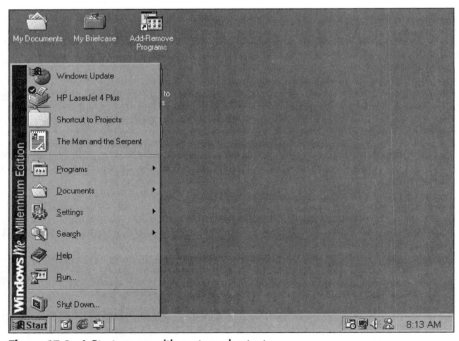

Figure 17-9: A Start menu with custom shortcuts

After dropping an icon onto the Start button, clicking the Start button reveals the new shortcut near the top of the Start menu.

The one drawback to this approach is the Start menu may become huge. Putting every icon right on the Start menu proper isn't absolutely necessary, though. Instead, you can add shortcuts to only the Programs menu within the Start menu. You can even create your own custom submenus.

Using large or small Start-menu icons

If your Start menu is getting crowded, you can use smaller icons to make more space. Follow these steps:

1. Right-click an empty part of the taskbar and then choose Properties. Or, click the Start button and choose Settings ➪ Taskbar and Start Menu.

2. Click the General tab.

3. To use smaller icons, select the "Show small icons in Start menu" check box. To use larger icons, clear that check box.

4. Click the OK button.

Rearranging the Start menu

If you like, you can rearrange items in the top of the Start menu, as well as inside the Programs and Favorites submenus.

Here's how:

1. Click the Start button and then point to (do not click) the item you want to move.

2. Hold down the left mouse button while dragging the item to its new destination. The destination can be the top of the Start menu or any spot within the Programs or Favorites folders and subfolders.

3. When the black horizontal bar is positioned where you want the menu item to appear, release the mouse button.

Figure 17-10 shows an example where I've rearranged the items at the top of my Start menu.

Tip

To quickly rearrange any of the Start menu items into alphabetical order, open the menu you wish to rearrange, right-click the menu, and choose Sort by Name from the pop-up menu.

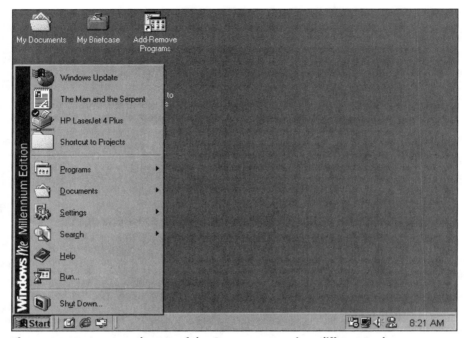

Figure 17-10: Items at the top of the Start menu are in a different order.

Deleting menu Items

To remove an item from the Start menu, click the Start button and then point to (don't click) the option you want to delete. Right-click the item you want to delete, choose Delete, and then choose Yes when asked about sending the item to the Recycle Bin.

Adding new menus

You can also add new menus — groups of items — to the Start menu. Here's how to do this:

1. Right-click the Start button and choose Open. A folder named C:\Windows\ Start Menu opens. Every shortcut in this folder is actually an icon on the Start menu.

2. To create a new menu group, right-click some neutral area within the folder and choose New ⇨ Folder. A folder named New Folder appears.

3. Give the new folder a name you'll recognize later. In Figure 17-11, I created a new folder and named it "My Absolute Faves."

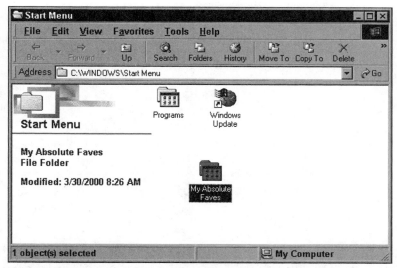

Figure 17-11: A new folder named My Absolute Faves is added to the C:\Windows\Start Menu folder.

4. Close the C:\Windows\Start Menu folder.

After closing the C:\Windows\Start Menu folder and clicking the Start button, I see I now have an option named My Absolute Faves near the top of my Start menu (see Figure 17-12). Pointing to this option reveals the option is currently empty. But this is only because I haven't yet added any shortcuts to the new C:\Windows\Start Menu\My Absolute Faves folder.

Note

> The C:\Windows\Start Menu folder is a regular folder like any other on your PC. The only thing unique about it is that its contents automatically show up in the Start menu. In fact, the Start menu is just a unique way to view the contents of the folder named C:\Windows\Start Menu on your hard drive.

Putting shortcuts in submenus

To put shortcuts into a submenu of the Start menu, follow these steps:

1. Right-click the Start button and choose Open to get to the C:\Windows\Start Menu folder.

2. Open the icon for whatever folder to which you want to add shortcuts.

3. Create shortcuts to whatever folders, documents, or programs you wish to access from inside this new folder.

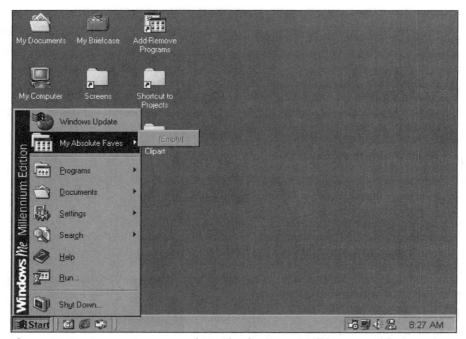

Figure 17-12: A new menu named My Absolute Faves will be accessible from the Start menu.

For Step 3, you can use any technique you like to add a new shortcut. The simplest would probably be to right-drag an icon into the folder, release the mouse button, and choose Create Shortcut(s) Here. You can also choose File ➪ New ➪ Shortcut from the folder window's menu bar and use the wizard that appears to browse to the icon for whatever folder, file, or program you wish to add to that menu.

Now you can close any open windows. Click the Start button and then click Programs. You should see your shortcut in its proper alphabetical position below the icons leading to folders.

Yet another way to customize the Start menu

I don't mean to confuse things. But I should point out that, on top of all the techniques I've discussed so far, you can take yet another approach to add and delete Start menu items — the Advanced tab of the Taskbar and Start Menu Properties dialog box. To use this approach:

   1. Click the Start button and choose Settings ➪ Taskbar and Start Menu.

2. Click the Advanced tab. Then click any of the following buttons:

- **Add:** Provides an alternative browsing approach for adding an icon to the Start menu.

- **Remove:** Removes an item from the Start menu.

- **Advanced:** Displays the Start menu in a Windows Explorer-style window so you can add, delete, move, and copy Start menu items using the same general techniques you use to manage folders and files in Windows Explorer.

- **Re-sort:** Rearranges the menus into alphabetical order.

3. After making your choices, click the OK button.

Whether you use the dialog box or the drag-and-drop methods described earlier in this chapter is simply a matter of personal preference. The end result is the same either way—a more personalized Start menu.

Clearing the Documents Menu

The Documents submenu on the Start menu keeps track of recently saved document files. So if you need to reopen that document in the near future, you can click the Start button, point to Documents, and then click the name of the document you want to open.

The Documents menu doesn't keep track of every document you open and close. Instead, it only keeps track of the last 15 documents created or edited with programs that enable such tracking. Most 32-bit programs (programs designed for Windows 95, Windows Me, or Windows NT) do support the Documents menu.

If your Documents menu is cluttered with files you don't open anymore, follow these simple steps to clear the Documents menu and start with a clean slate:

1. Right-click the taskbar and then choose Properties. Or, click the Start button and choose Settings ➪ Taskbar and Start Menu.

2. Click the Advanced tab.

3. Click the Clear button.

4. Click OK.

That's all there is to that! If ever you want to delete a single file from the Documents menu, open the menu, right-click the item you want to delete, and choose Delete.

Using and Organizing the Favorites Menu

Most people use the Favorites menu to store links to favorite Web sites on the World Wide Web. But you can also use the Favorites menu to store links to favorite things on your own, local PC. For example, suppose I want to put a quick link to my Windows Me Bible folder into the Favorites menu. All I have to do is get to this folder via My Computer, Windows Explorer, or Search. After opening the folder, choose Favorites ➪ Add to Favorites, as in Figure 17-13.

Tip   If the Favorites menu does not appear on your Start menu, select the Display Favorites option on the Advanced tab of the Taskbar and Start Menu Properties dialog box.

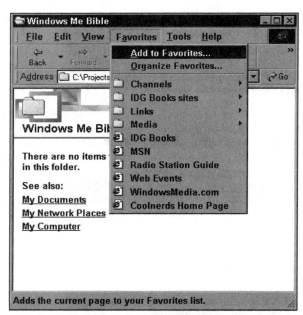

Figure 17-13: About to add the Windows Me Bible folder to my Favorites menu

You'll come to the dialog box shown in Figure 17-14. You can click the OK button to finish the job.

From this point on, you can click the Start button and point to Favorites to get to that shortcut icon. For example, you can see the Windows Me Bible folder icon in the Favorites menu, shown in Figure 17-15.

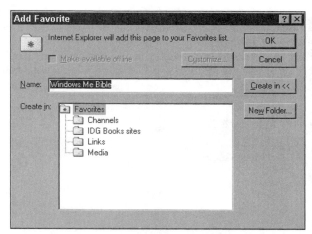

Figure 17-14: The Add Favorite dialog box enables you to add items to your Favorites menu.

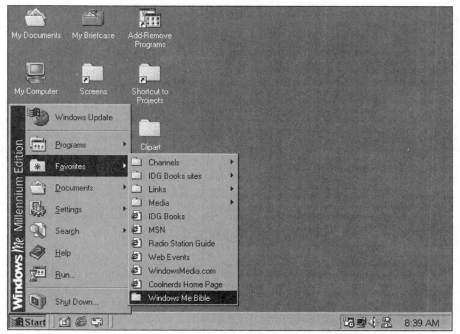

Figure 17-15: Shortcut to Windows Me Bible folder added to my Favorites menu

The Favorites menu offers the handy Organize Favorites dialog box, shown in Figure 17-16, which makes it especially easy to organize the contents of this menu. To get to the Organize Favorites dialog box, choose Favorites ➪ Organize Favorites from any menu bar that offers those options. (If you're at the desktop, you can open the Start menu, right-click Favorites, choose Open, and choose Favorites ➪ Organize Favorites from its menu.)

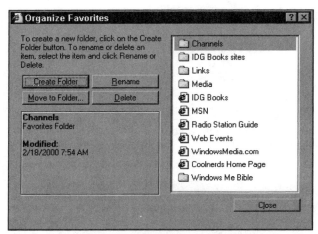

Figure 17-16: Use the Organize Favorites dialog box to manage your collection of favorites.

Once you're in the dialog box, the rest is simple. Just click whatever icon you want to move, rename, or delete, and then click the appropriate button beneath the icons. Follow the instructions onscreen and you're done. Click the Close button when you finish organizing. To see the results of your efforts, click the Start button, point to Favorites, and look at the contents of the Favorites menu.

Windows Me Special Folders

You may have noticed some of the things that appear on (or are accessible from) the Windows desktop seem to have some regular folder hidden behind them. For example, the Start menu is really a specialized view of a standard folder named C:\Windows\Start Menu. You may be interested to know that quite a few desktop items are only special views of regular folders on your hard disk. Table 17-1 lists the desktop items that display special folders and the path to each folder.

Table 17-1
Desktop Items That Display Special Folders and Their Paths

Item	Folder
Auto-Start Programs	C:\Windows\Start Menu\Programs\StartUp
Desktop	C:\Windows\Desktop
Favorites	C:\Windows\Favorites
Programs menu	C:\Windows\Start Menu\Programs
Send To menu	C:\Windows\SendTo
Start menu	C:\Windows\Start Menu

Personalizing the Taskbar

The taskbar is another important tool on your desktop. The following list provides a quick review of the taskbar's purpose:

✦ Every open window has a button on the taskbar. To bring any window to the forefront onscreen, click its taskbar button.

✦ To close or resize any open window (even one buried in a stack), right-click its taskbar button and choose the appropriate option from the menu that appears.

✦ To tidy up (arrange) all the open windows, right-click an empty part of the taskbar (not a button in the taskbar) and then choose Cascade Windows or one of the Tile Windows options. You also can minimize all the windows from that menu.

✦ A little clock usually appears in the taskbar, showing you the current time. Point to the clock to see the current date; double-click the clock to change the current date and time. (At the end of this chapter, I explain how to display or hide the clock.)

✦ Some hardware devices (such as sound cards and printers) display an icon in the taskbar while they are running. Typically, you can click, right-click, or double-click that icon to get more information about — or even to control — the device.

Handy little gadget, that taskbar. The following sections explain some ways you can personalize it.

Sizing and positioning the taskbar

You can put the taskbar along any edge of the screen. Whichever edge you prefer is simply a matter of personal taste. To move the taskbar, point to an empty area of the taskbar and then drag the taskbar to some other edge of the screen.

To size the taskbar, rest the mouse pointer right on the top of the taskbar, so the mouse pointer turns into a two-headed arrow. Then drag the edge of the taskbar toward the center of the screen to enlarge it or toward the closest edge of the screen to narrow it. In Figure 17-17, for example, I dragged the taskbar to the right edge of the screen and then widened it by dragging its innermost edge toward the center of the screen.

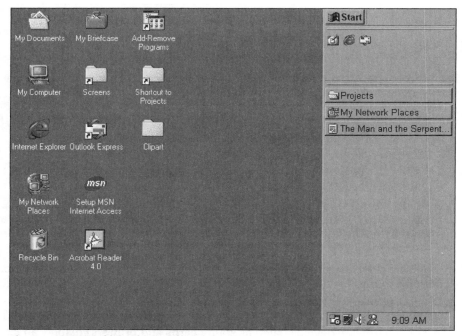

Figure 17-17: Taskbar along right edge of screen – and widened

Note   If you make the taskbar too skinny, the Start button disappears and the taskbar changes to a thin gray line. Don't panic. Simply move your mouse pointer to the thin gray line. When the pointer becomes a two-headed arrow, drag the edge of the taskbar toward the middle of the screen. The taskbar widens and the Start button reappears.

Hiding the taskbar

If you don't want the taskbar eating up valuable space on your screen, you can have it go into hiding, automatically, whenever you're not using it. Follow these steps:

1. Right-click an empty part of the taskbar and then choose Properties.

2. Click the General tab.

3. To control whether the taskbar appears on top of other windows, select or clear "Always on top." If you select this option, open windows never cover the taskbar. If you clear this option, open windows may cover the taskbar.

4. To control whether the taskbar hides automatically, select or clear Auto Hide. If you select Auto Hide, the taskbar shrinks to a thin line along the edge of the screen when it isn't in use. If you clear this option, the taskbar never shrinks to a thin line.

5. Choose OK.

I suggest you leave the "Always on top" option selected. No good reason exists to allow other windows to cover the taskbar. If the taskbar gets in your way, however, select the Auto Hide option, so it's tucked away, but within easy reach. To redisplay the shrunken taskbar, point to the thin line.

Using desktop toolbars

In Chapter 4, you learned about the Quick Launch toolbar, yet another good repository for shortcuts to your favorite programs. Windows Me also has four other special toolbars:

✦ **Address:** Displays an Address box in which you can type Internet addresses or the names of disk drives, folders, and files on your computer. After you press Enter, Internet Explorer takes you to the place you chose. See Chapters 7 and 8 for more information.

✦ **Links:** Displays shortcut buttons for visiting handy places on the Internet. Click a button to visit that place. Again, see Chapters 7 and 8 for more information on the Internet.

✦ **Desktop:** Displays a button for each item on your desktop, just as the taskbar does. This toolbar can float (be placed anywhere onscreen).

✦ **Quick Launch:** Provides easy access to favorite programs. (Chapter 4 discusses how to add programs to the Quick Launch toolbar.)

To turn any of these toolbars on or off, follow these steps:

1. Right-click some neutral area of the taskbar and point to Toolbars (Figure 17-18).

2. To display — or hide — a toolbar, click its name (checked toolbars are already on display).

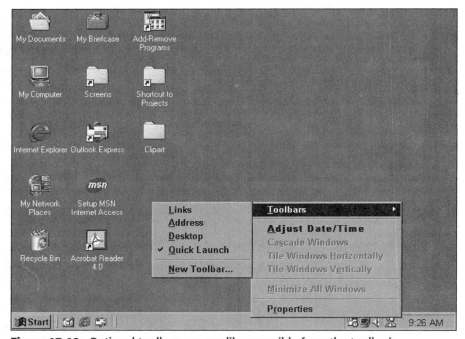

Figure 17-18: Optional toolbars are readily accessible from the toolbar's right-click menu.

Positioning and sizing toolbars

You can position and size desktop toolbars in several ways, all of them easy. When the desktop toolbars appear on the taskbar (their normal location), use these methods to position and size them:

✦ To resize a desktop toolbar, point to the vertical bar near the left or right edge of the toolbar and then drag left or right, or double-click to expand or contract.

✦ To move a toolbar out of the taskbar and onto the desktop, point to the vertical bar at the left edge of the toolbar you want to move. Then drag this toolbar out to the desktop and release the mouse button.

Figure 17-19 shows an example in which I opened all four toolbars—Address, Desktop, Links, and Quick Launch—and then dragged them all out to the Windows desktop.

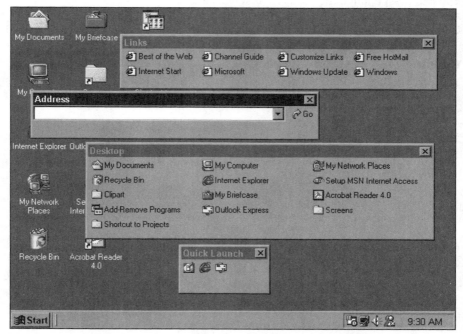

Figure 17-19: The four desktop toolbars are displayed as floating windows.

When the toolbars appear as floating windows, you can resize and position them in these ways:

✦ To move a floating toolbar, drag the toolbar's title bar to some new spot. You can drag the toolbar back onto the taskbar, so it again becomes part of the taskbar, or to any edge of the screen to anchor it there.

✦ To resize a floating toolbar, drag any corner or edge of the toolbar's window.

Other ways to customize desktop toolbars

You can choose from a host of handy options for customizing a desktop toolbar or any button on it. Simply right-click any empty spot on a desktop toolbar or any desktop toolbar button and choose the option you want.

For example, when you right-click an empty spot on a toolbar, you can choose whether to display buttons as large or small icons, to show or hide text descriptions below the buttons, to show or hide the toolbar's title, and to close the toolbar. Right-clicking a button offers options that are relevant to that particular button. You can even change the icons themselves: Right-click any icon, select Properties, and click the Change Icon button — all but the Desktop icon will enable you to do this. Experiment! You'll like what you find.

Creating new desktop toolbars

You can create a toolbar that automatically includes buttons for items within any folder on your computer or for an address on the Internet. Your custom toolbar will stick around until you close it.

To create a custom toolbar:

1. Right-click an empty part of the taskbar and choose Toolbars ⇨ New Toolbar.

2. When the New Toolbar dialog box appears (see Figure 17-20), click a folder in the list or type a full Internet address (see Chapter 6).

3. Click the OK button.

Figure 17-20: The New Toolbar dialog box enables you to create toolbar access to any folder.

Your toolbar will appear on the taskbar. To get a better view, you can drag it by its little vertical bar up onto the desktop, as in the example shown in Figure 17-21. But remember one important point: When you close the toolbar, it's gone for good — so you don't want to go to a lot of trouble making it pretty. If you need more permanent toolbar access to favorite items, I suggest you use the Quick Launch toolbar rather than a new toolbar.

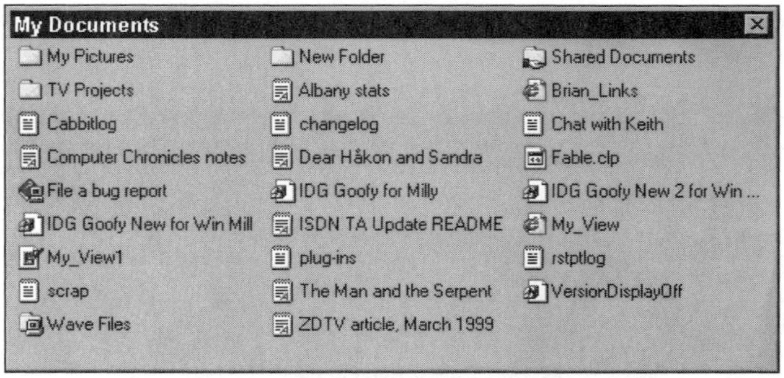

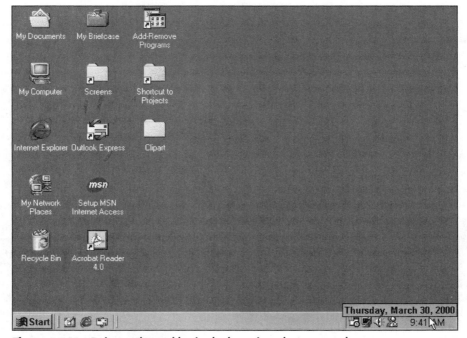

Figure 17-21: A new toolbar created from my My Documents folder

The taskbar's clock

In case you ever wonder what the date is, you can rest the mouse pointer on the time. The current date (according to your computer's clock) appears in a ToolTip, as in Figure 17-22.

Figure 17-22: Point to the taskbar's clock to view the current date.

If your taskbar clock is showing the wrong date and/or time, here's how you can set it straight:

1. Double-click the clock indicator. Or choose Start ⟹ Settings ⟹ Control Panel and open the Date/Time icon to reveal the dialog box shown in Figure 17-23.

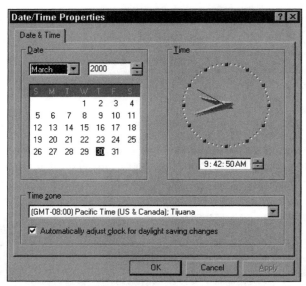

Figure 17-23: The Date/Time dialog box enables you to set the current date and time.

2. Choose the correct date and set the correct time.

3. To set your time zone, click the Time Zone drop-down list arrow and then choose your time zone from the list.

4. Click the OK button to save your settings and close the dialog box.

Note The Date/Time dialog box sets the date and time for your entire computer system, not just for the taskbar clock. If your files keep getting stamped with wrong dates or your personal calendars keep opening up with the wrong dates, changing the date in the Date/Time dialog box will take care of those problems, too!

The little clock that appears at the right edge of the taskbar is entirely optional. To turn it on or off, click the Start button and choose Settings ⟹ Taskbar and Start Menu. On the General tab, clear the check box next to Show Clock if you want to hide the time. Otherwise, select this check box (so it contains a check mark) to make the time visible in the taskbar. Then click the OK button.

Summary

Windows Me has lots of great stuff for organizing and personalizing your folders and desktop. Here are the main points to remember:

✦ To create a folder, open the drive or folder in which you want to place the folder. Then right-click some neutral area between existing icons and choose New ➪ Folder.

✦ To activate/deactivate the Web view of a folder, choose Tools ➪ Folder Options from that folder's menu bar and choose the Web View option you prefer.

✦ To customize the appearance of a single folder, choose View ➪ Customize This Folder from that folder's menu bar.

✦ To add a new icon to the top of the Start menu, drag a copy of the icon to the Start button.

✦ To rearrange items in the Start menu, drag items to new locations.

✦ You can also change the contents of the Start menu by right-clicking the Start button and choosing Open; or, by clicking the Start button and choosing Settings ➪ Taskbar and Start Menu.

✦ To change the size of icons on the Start menu, right-click the taskbar, choose Properties, and then select or clear the "Show small icons in Start menu" check box.

✦ To clear the Documents menu, right-click the taskbar, choose Properties, click the Advanced tab, and click the Clear button.

✦ To hide/display desktop toolbars, right-click the taskbar and point to Toolbars.

✦ To size the taskbar, drag its inner edge (the edge nearest the center of the screen).

✦ To move the taskbar, drag the entire taskbar to any edge of the screen.

✦ To change your computer's date/time, double-click the clock indicator at the right side of the taskbar. Or, click the Start button and choose Settings ➪ Control Panel, and then open the Date/Time icon.

✦ ✦ ✦

Work and Play

Numbers, Text, Pictures, and Scraps

In this chapter, I cover some of the handy programs that come with Windows Me. These programs are often called *applets* because they're similar to large, commercial application programs but without quite so many capabilities and features. Nonetheless, they do come in handy occasionally. And, for our purposes, applets can also be used as tools to help you learn general techniques for working with numbers, text, and graphic images on your PC. I also discuss techniques for moving and copying elements from one document to another.

Using Windows Me Applets

Most of the applets described will be readily accessible from your Accessories menu. Just click the Start button and choose Programs ➪ Accessories, as in Figure 18-1.

If you discover you are missing one or more applets, you can install them using Windows Setup in Add/Remove Programs. For specific instructions, see Chapter 25.

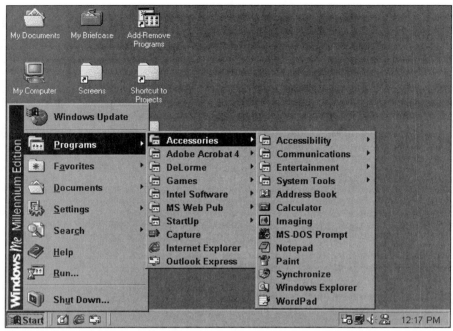

Figure 18-1: Applets are available on the Accessories menu.

The Calculator

To help you work with numbers, Windows Me offers the Calculator applet. The calculator works much like your standard pocket calculator. To start it, click the Start button and choose Programs ➪ Accessories ➪ Calculator. The calculator pops up onscreen, as in Figure 18-2.

Figure 18-2: The Calculator applet

Once the calculator is visible on your screen, you can click its buttons with your mouse, exactly as you'd press the buttons on a regular calculator. For example, to calculate 24 times 19, you would click the following buttons in the order shown:

    24x19=

Note

Computers generally use an asterisk (*) to represent multiplication — not an x or a dot. So when you type a formula into Calculator, such as 2 times 3, you would actually type 2*3. Division is handled by the / character. For example 10/5 (ten divided by five) equals two. Addition uses the plus (+) character; subtraction uses a hyphen (-).

To calculate 15% of $34.00 you would type (using the keyboard):

    0.15*34=

Or, you would click (using the mouse and Calculator) the following buttons:

    0.15x34=

The result would be 5.1 (or $5.10).

If your math needs go beyond basic arithmetic, you can switch to the scientific calculator shown in Figure 18-3. To get there, choose View ➪ Scientific from Calculator's menu bar.

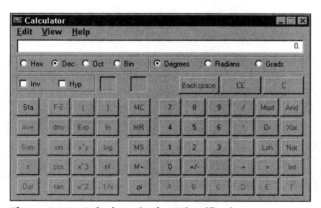

Figure 18-3: Calculator in the Scientific view

I won't go into the details of the more advanced math capabilities of Calculator here because I doubt many of you will need this sort of math in your work. As always, though, you can get plenty of help right on your screen. While Calculator is visible on your screen, choose Help ➪ Help Topics from Calculator's menu bar. When you finish with the calculator, you can close it in the usual manner — click its little Close (X) button.

Special note for HTML authors

If you're a Web author who's into HTML and scripting languages, you may be happy to find that the scientific calculator can convert from hexadecimal to decimal and vice versa. This is handy when you need to convert an RGB triplet, such as FFFFFF, to a decimal number for use with a Java applet, ActiveX control, or script. For example, to convert #FFFFFF to decimal, click the Hex option button, type FFFFFF, and then choose the Dec number system. The result is 16777215, which is, indeed, the correct decimal equivalent of the hex number.

To convert from decimal to hex, click the Dec radio button, type in the decimal number, and click the Hex option button. When typing hex numbers into HTML tags, remember to use the leading pound sign. For example, to use FFFFFF as a page's background color, the correct tag would be `<BODY BGCOLOR="#FFFFFF">`.

Notepad

Windows Me offers a few handy applets for working with text. Notepad, the simpler of the two, is especially designed for working with plain ASCII text. This means you can't do anything fancy with fonts, boldface, graphic images, or anything like that. All you can do is type text. But this is good because certain kinds of files must be plain text.

For example, if you ever need to manually change the CONFIG.SYS or AUTOEXEC.BAT files (left over from DOS) on the root directory of your C: drive (C:\), use Notepad. Web authors can also use Notepad to open and edit HTML files and to work directly with the document source.

Caution   Never, ever change system files like CONFIG.SYS or AUTOEXEC.BAT unless you know exactly what you're doing. Chances are, you'll never have to modify those files. But, just in case you come across instructions that tell you specifically to modify one of those files, you'll know you can use Notepad to do it.

To start Notepad, click the Start button and choose Programs ➪ Accessories ➪ Notepad. When Notepad first opens, it will show a blank page, as in Figure 18-4. If you want to use Notepad to edit a specific file, you can use the "Send To" shortcut. That is, right-click the icon for the text file you want to edit and then choose Send To ➪ Notepad. Notepad opens with the text file already displayed and ready for editing.

Note   You can customize the Send To menu to include whatever programs you wish. See "Customizing Your Send To Menu" in Chapter 4 for instructions.

Once you're in Notepad, you can type text in much the same way you type on paper. When you finish typing a line of text, press Enter to move on to the next line. That's how I typed the little shopping list shown in Figure 18-5.

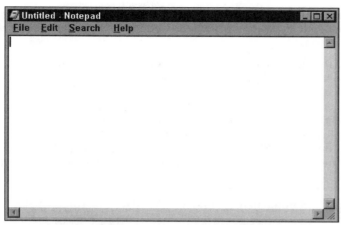

Figure 18-4: Notepad with a "blank page" on which to type

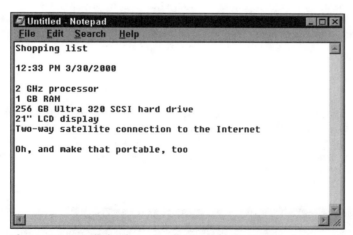

Figure 18-5: A little shopping list typed into Notepad

To edit (change) text, use the standard techniques discussed under "Changing Text" in Chapter 2. In addition, you can do the following:

✦ Press Enter as necessary to insert blank lines.

✦ To delete a blank line, move the blinking cursor to the blank line you want to delete and then press the Delete (or Del) key.

✦ To type the current date and time into the document, choose Edit ➪ Time/Date.

✦ To locate a particular word or phrase in the document, choose Search ➪ Find from Notepad's menu bar, type whatever it is you're looking for, and then click the Find Next button.

✦ To print the current document, choose File ➪ Print from Notepad's menu bar. Or, you can choose File ➪ Page Setup to choose a specific printer, paper size, and other print options.

To save your work, choose File ➪ Save from Notepad's menu bar and then enter a filename. Notepad will automatically add a *.txt* extension to whatever name you provide. If you name the document Shopping List, it will actually be named Shopping List.txt. Most likely, the file will be stored in your My Documents folder, where all documents are stored by default.

As always, you can get additional help by choosing Help ➪ Help Topics from Notepad's menu bar. And, as always, you can close Notepad when you're done by clicking its Close (X) button, or by choosing File ➪ Exit from its menu bar.

Tip   You can create desktop or QuickLaunch toolbar shortcuts to any applets you use frequently. Just right-drag the applet's icon out of the Accessories menu and drop it onto the desktop or Quick Launch toolbar. Choose Copy Here after releasing the mouse button.

WordPad

WordPad is another handy applet for working with text. But, unlike Notepad, which creates plain, simple text files, WordPad can help you create true word processing documents with fonts, boldface, and other print features. To start WordPad, click the Start button and choose Programs ➪ Accessories ➪ WordPad. You'll be taken to a fresh new page for typing and editing, as in Figure 18-6.

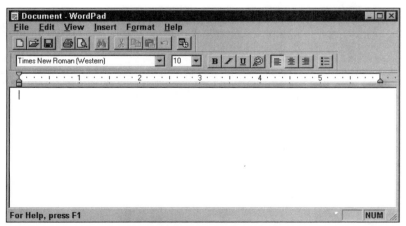

Figure 18-6: WordPad, as it looks when opened with a new, blank document

Note   WordPad is actually a trimmed-down and simplified version of Microsoft Word, a program you can purchase separately.

Typing in WordPad is much the same as typing on paper. One important difference exists, though: When typing a paragraph, you do not want to press Enter at the end of each line. Instead, keep typing right past the right margin. The text will automatically word wrap (break between two words). Press Enter only at the end of the paragraph. You can press Enter twice if you want to insert a blank line. For example, to type each paragraph shown in Figure 18-7, I typed the entire paragraph without pressing Enter. Then I pressed Enter twice before starting on the next paragraph.

All the standard text-editing techniques described under "Changing Text" in Chapter 2 work in WordPad. You can also format (change the appearance of) text by selecting the text you want to alter and then selecting an option from the Format menu. For example, to create the large centered title in the sample document, I selected that text and then chose Format ⇨ Font from WordPad's menu bar. In the Font dialog box (Figure 18-8), I chose an Arial Black font at 20 points.

Note   If you're unfamiliar with fonts, don't worry about it. Chapter 19 discusses fonts in more detail.

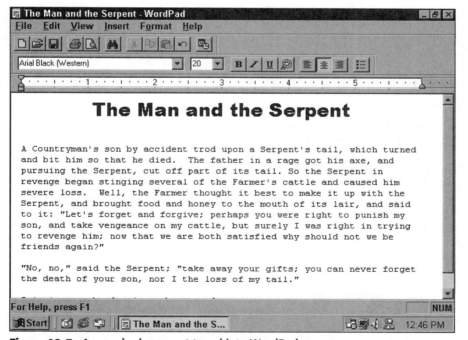

Figure 18-7: A sample document typed into WordPad

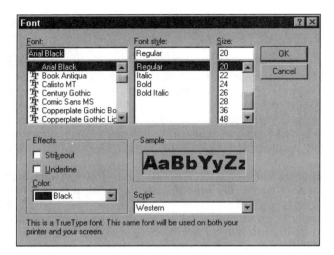

Figure 18-8: The Font dialog box enables you to choose a print style and size.

To center this title, I put the blinking cursor into the title line (just by clicking the line). Then I chose Format ➪ Paragraph ➪ Alignment ➪ Center ➪ OK from WordPad's menu bar.

Printing, saving, and closing is done in the usual manner, by selecting options from WordPad's menu bar. For instance:

✦ To print the current document, choose File ➪ Print.

✦ To define margin size, paper size, or a specific printer, choose File ➪ Page Setup.

✦ To save the current document, choose File ➪ Save.

✦ To close WordPad, choose File ➪ Exit or click the Close (X) button in WordPad's upper-right corner.

When you save a document created in WordPad, the program will suggest using .*doc* (for document) as the filename extension and My Documents as the folder. But be aware that Microsoft Word also uses .doc as the default extension for documents you create in Word. Thus, if you click (or double-click in Classic style) on the name of a .doc file, the file will open in Microsoft Word rather than in WordPad. If you prefer to open the document in WordPad, you can right-click it and choose Send To ➪ WordPad.

Note   If WordPad isn't on your Send To menu, you can add it using the techniques described under "Customizing Your Send To Menu" in Chapter 4.

I'll show you more examples of working with WordPad in the following sections. Meanwhile, if you ever need help while you're working in WordPad, look into its online help. Press F1 or choose Help ➪ Help Topics from WordPad's menu bar.

Character Map

Windows Me Character Map is a handy applet for typing special characters not found on the keyboard — such as © for copyright and ® for registered trademark and _ for summation. It works with any application that supports special characters, including WordPad. To use Character Map:

Note If Character Map isn't available on your PC, it simply hasn't been installed yet. You can install it at any time using Windows Setup in Add/Remove Programs, as discussed under "Installing Missing Windows Components" in Chapter 25.

1. Click the Start button and choose Programs ➪ Accessories ➪ System Tools ➪ Character Map. The applet opens looking something like Figure 18-9.

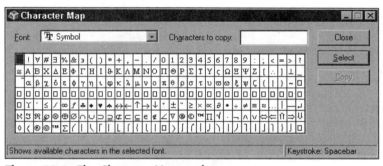

Figure 18-9: The Character Map applet

2. From the Font drop-down list, choose a font. (Each font will offer its own unique set of special characters.)

3. To get a close-up look at a character, point to the character you want to inspect and then hold down the primary mouse button.

4. To select a character, click it and then click the Select button. The Characters To Copy text box will show the character to be copied. You can repeat this step to select as many characters as you wish.

5. To paste the special character into a document, click the Copy button. Then right-click wherever you want to place the special character in your document, and choose Paste.

In Figure 18-10, you can see both WordPad and Character Map onscreen simultaneously. In Character Map, I already selected a font named Wingdings and copied a little happy face character into the Characters to Copy text box. To put this character in my WordPad document, I have to click the Copy button in Character Map, right-click where I want to put this character in the WordPad document, and then choose Paste.

The character is placed in the document. If the correct font isn't selected in the document, though, it may not look right. The trick here is to make sure the same font used to display the character in Character Map is also used in the document. As you can see in Figure 18-10, the character I selected is from the Wingdings font collection.

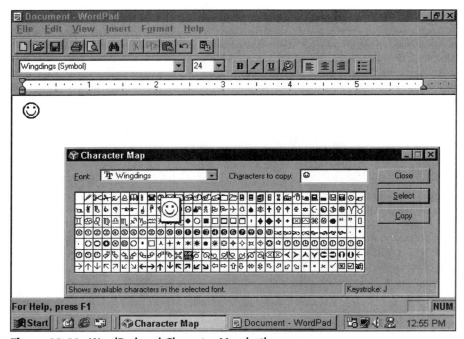

Figure 18-10: WordPad and Character Map both onscreen

To make the happy face look right in WordPad and, optionally, to change its size, select the character(s) by dragging the mouse pointer through it or by double-clicking it. Then, choose Format ➪ Font from WordPad's menu bar. In the Font dialog box, choose the correct font (Wingdings, in this example). Then choose a size and any other options you want from the Font dialog box and click the OK button.

When you've finished using Character Map for the time being, click the Close (X) button in the upper-right corner of its window.

Paint

For working with graphic images, Windows Me offers Paint. To start Paint, click the Start button and choose Programs ➪ Accessories ➪ Paint. Initially, you'll be taken to a blank canvas for drawing, as in Figure 18-11.

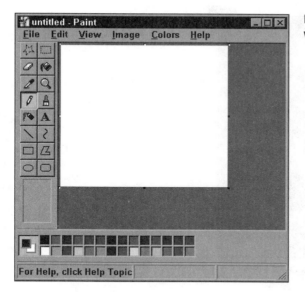

Figure 18-11: Paint applet with a blank canvas in it

To draw in Paint, you can first choose a line color by clicking the color you want down in the little color palette near the bottom of the window. You can also choose a fill color, which comes into play when drawing filled shapes, by right-clicking any of the colors in the palette. Then pick a drawing tool from the left-hand side of the window. For example, to create the goofy-looking face in Figure 18-12, I did the following:

✦ In the tool section, I clicked the oval shape (the button titled Ellipse when the mouse pointer is resting on it).

✦ From the three triangles just below the button, I chose the middle option, which draws the shape's outer line in one color and then fills the shape with a second color.

✦ In the color palette, I clicked the black square to make the line color black and then clicked the orange square to make the fill color orange (I realize you can't see the orange color here; but you get the idea.).

✦ Then on the canvas, I dragged out the large circle that forms the head.

✦ Next, I right-clicked blue and used the oval drawing tool to drag out circles for the eyes.

✦ To make the mouth, I first selected the curved-line tool. Then I clicked the thickest line under the tools. Next, I dragged a line straight across under the nose and released the mouse button. Finally, I dragged the middle of this line downward.

✦ I added some other bits and pieces using various other fun tools.

✦ To save this masterpiece, I chose File ⇨ Save, as usual, from Paint's menu bar.

Figure 18-12: Goofy-looking face in Paint

You can also use Paint to open and edit existing graphic images stored in bitmap format, which includes images with the filename extensions .bmp, .jpg, and .jpeg. Choose File ➪ Open from Paint's menu bar. At the bottom of the dialog box, choose which type(s) of files you want to view. Then browse around for the picture you want using the Look In drop-down list, the Up One Level icon in the toolbar, and/or the folder icons inside the Open dialog box. When you find the image you want, click its name and then click the Open button. Figure 18-13 shows an example in which I opened a JPEG image named Reno sunrise.jpg.

Tip　If you need to create GIF and JPEG files for a Web site, you're better off using Paint Shop Pro because it provides more tools and options. You can download an evaluation copy from `http://www.jasc.com`.

Probably the best way to learn to draw in Paint is simply to experiment with different colors and tools and see what happens. You certainly can't hurt anything by doing so! Here's a quick overview of Paint's most used features:

✦ To undo a mistake in a picture, choose Edit ➪ Undo.

✦ To start a new picture, choose File ➪ New.

✦ To print the current picture, choose File ➪ Print.

✦ To select optional tools and views, select options from the View menu.

✦ To flip, rotate, stretch, or skew the picture, choose an option from the Images menu.

✦ To save the current picture, choose File ➪ Save.

✦ To close Paint, click its Close (X) button or choose File ➪ Exit from its menu bar.

Figure 18-13: An image opened for viewing, editing, or printing in Paint

For more information on using Paint, check out its online help. Press the Help (F1) key or choose Help ➪ Help Topics from Paint's menu bar.

Games

Windows Me even comes with a few games you can enjoy. To play a game, click the Start button and choose Programs ➪ Games. You'll see a list of installed Windows Me games, as in Figure 18-14. You can install any missing games using Windows Setup, as discussed under "Installing Missing Windows Components" in Chapter 25.

I won't go into any detail on how you play the games. You can find out easily enough by opening the game you want to play and looking at its online help (press F1 or choose Help ➪ Help Topics from the game's menu bar).

For the rest of this chapter, I'll focus on a few techniques you're bound to find useful in your work with documents: Cut and paste is one of those techniques and scraps is the other.

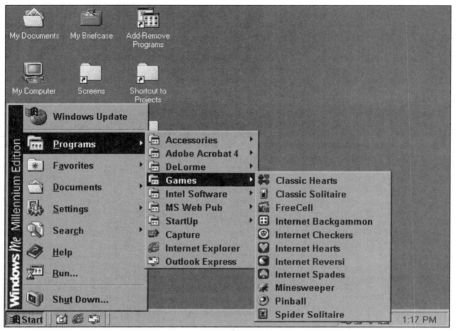

Figure 18-14: Windows Me comes with eleven games, accessible from the Games menu.

Cut and Paste

You may have noticed most of the sample applets support a particular type of document or information. For instance, Calculator is used for doing math with numbers. WordPad and Notepad both focus on written text. And Paint is dedicated to working with pictures. Which brings up the question, "What if I want to create a written document with a picture in it?" Good question!

The way you move elements (text, graphics, and so on) from one document or program into another is called cut and paste or copy and paste. To do this:

1. Select whatever you want to move or copy, using the following as your guideline:

   - To select text, drag the mouse pointer through the text you want to select.

   - To select a single picture, click it once.

   - To select the number currently showing in Calculator, choose Edit ➪ Copy from Calculator's menu bar.

   - To select an entire document or picture, choose Edit ➪ Select All from the program's menu bar.

2. Once the item is selected, choose Edit ⇨ Copy from the program's menu bar, or press Ctrl+C. A copy of the selection goes into the (usually invisible) Windows Clipboard.

3. Click wherever you want to insert the copy, right-click, and choose Paste. Or, choose Edit ⇨ Paste from the program's menu bar or press Ctrl+V.

When pasting into a text document, the object goes wherever the blinking cursor is, *not* necessarily where the mouse pointer is. So, typically, you must click the exact spot where you want the picture to appear to get the blinking cursor to this point. Then you can right-click and choose Paste, or press Ctrl+V, or choose Edit ⇨ Paste from the program's menu bar.

Let me show you an example. Figure 18-15 shows two separate documents in two separate programs — a graphic image in Paint and some text typed up in WordPad. Suppose I want to put a copy of the picture inside the written document in WordPad. Here's how I would do this:

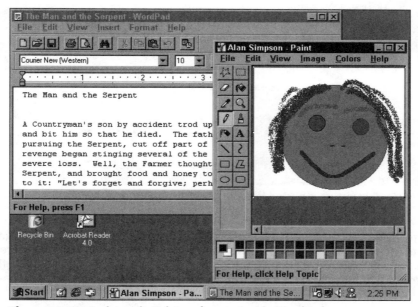

Figure 18-15: A picture in Paint and some text in WordPad

1. Choose Edit ⇨ Select All from Paint's menu bar to select the entire picture.

2. Choose Edit ⇨ Copy from Paint's menu bar.

3. Right-click at the top of the text document in WordPad and choose Paste.

The end result is shown in Figure 18-16.

Do remember, this is only an example. Cut and paste works with virtually all Windows programs — even the extra programs you purchase and install separately. Shortcut keys for using the Clipboard are also universal among Windows programs. You can press Ctrl+C to copy a selection to the Clipboard, Ctrl+X to move a selection to the Clipboard, and Ctrl+V to paste the contents of the Clipboard at the current cursor position.

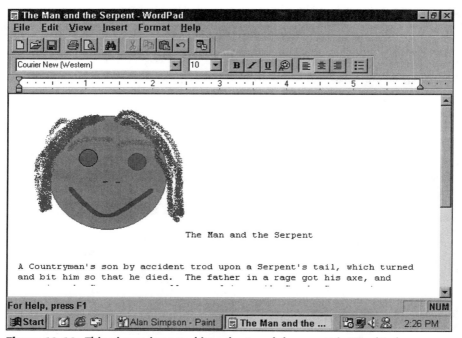

Figure 18-16: This picture is pasted into the typed document in WordPad.

Finally, remember this example represents general cut and paste techniques. Slight variations may exist among various programs out there in the real world. If you're using some program and you don't know how to select and copy stuff in that particular program, open its help screen and look for the words "select," "copy," and "paste."

Using the Clipboard Viewer

Now, let's discuss what goes on behind the scenes when you do a cut and paste. When you select something and choose Edit ⇨ Copy (or press Ctrl+C), a copy of the selection is placed in the Windows Clipboard. When you select something and choose Edit ⇨ Cut, you move the selection from its original place into the Windows Clipboard.

When you choose Edit ➪ Paste or press Ctrl+V, you take a copy of whatever is currently in the Clipboard and plop it down at the mouse pointer. Another copy of the item also remains in the Clipboard. So you could paste a whole bunch of copies of something after copying (or cutting) it once.

Now here's an important point: The Windows Clipboard can hold only one thing at a time. So, as soon as you copy or cut some item, you replace whatever used to be in the Clipboard with whatever you put in there.

Tip   You can use *scraps,* discussed a little later in this chapter, to simplify the task of cutting and pasting multiple objects.

Even though the Clipboard is usually invisible, you can look at its current contents if you like. Click the Start button and choose Programs ➪ Accessories ➪ System Tools ➪ Clipboard Viewer.

Here's a quick example. Figure 18-17 shows the Paint applet open on the desktop, displaying a picture. Using the rectangular select tool in Paint, I dragged a frame around part of the character's face and then chose Edit ➪ Copy from Paint's menu bar. Then I opened the Clipboard Viewer and, lo and behold, I can see the Clipboard does indeed contain a copy of the selected and copied portion of the picture (to the right of Paint's window in the figure).

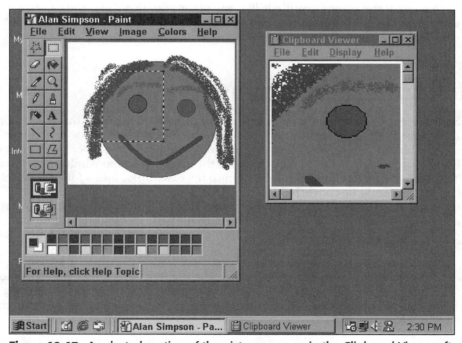

Figure 18-17: A selected portion of the picture appears in the Clipboard Viewer after choosing Edit ➪ Copy from Paint's menu bar.

Note   If you open the Clipboard and your picture looks distorted, try choosing Display ➪ Bitmap from the Clipboard Viewer's menu bar.

Printing the screen

In the olden days of DOS, you would print whatever was on your screen by pressing the Print Screen (Prnt Scrn) key on your keyboard. In Windows, this works a little differently. First, you capture the screen to the Windows Clipboard. Then you can paste it into Paint, or any other graphics program, and print it from there.

You can capture the screen in two ways:

   ✦ Press the Print Screen key if you want to capture the entire screen.

   ✦ Hold down the Alt key and press Print Screen if you want to capture only the current window (whichever window on the screen has the colored title bar).

Nothing appears to happen, but the Windows Clipboard receives a copy of the screen or window. You can verify this by opening the Clipboard Viewer, if you like. To print or save this image, you need to open Paint, or some other graphics program, and then choose Edit ➪ Paste from that program's menu bar. A copy of the image will be loaded into the graphics program.

At this point, the screen capture is like any other graphic image. You can edit it using the graphics program. You can save it by choosing File ➪ Save or print it by choosing File ➪ Print from the graphics program's menu bar.

You'll Love These Scraps

Scraps are a slight variation on using cut and paste to move/copy things from one document to another. With scraps, you drag the selection out to the desktop or to some folder. Or, if dragging doesn't work, you can select some object and choose Edit ➪ Copy or Edit ➪ Cut to copy or move the selection to the Windows Clipboard. Then you can paste the selection right onto the desktop or into a folder. The selection will instantly be converted to a small file named *scrap*. Additional scraps dropped onto the desktop, or into the same folder will be named scrap(2), scrap(3), and so forth. So this solves the problem caused by the fact that the Clipboard can only hold one thing at a time; the desktop (or a folder) can hold any number of scraps.

Note   Unfortunately, even though Windows Me supports scraps, not all application programs do. To find out if a particular application supports scraps, try creating a scrap using the following procedure. Or, search that program's online help for the word *scraps*.

Dragging and dropping scraps

Now let's take it one step at a time. I'll assume you're using the desktop as the place to store your scraps. Here's how you would proceed, using the drag-and-drop method:

1. Open the document containing the material you want to copy. For instance, in Figure 18-18, I opened a WordPad document. Size the document's program window so you can see some of the desktop behind it.

2. Select whatever you want to copy, using any of the standard selection techniques (drag the mouse pointer through whatever you want to select or choose Edit ➪ Select All from the program's menu bar). In Figure 18-18, I selected a paragraph to copy.

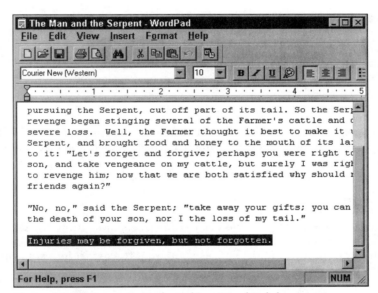

Figure 18-18: Some text selected in a WordPad document

3. Put the mouse pointer somewhere in the selection, hold down the mouse button, and then drag the selection out to the desktop. As the mouse pointer passes over the desktop, it changes to a copy symbol (a hollow arrow with a plus sign) if you're using a program that supports drag-and-drop scraps.

4. Release the mouse button.

An icon that looks like a torn piece of paper appears on the desktop. Its name is Scrap or some other longer name with the word scrap in it. For instance, after dragging the selection from Figure 18-18 out to the desktop and dropping it there, I end up with a scrap named The Man and the Serpent, as shown in Figure 18-19.

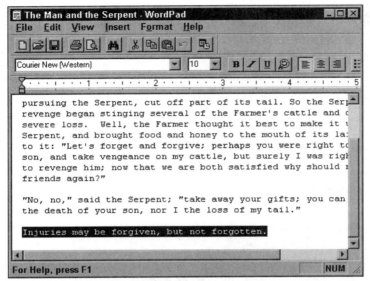

Figure 18-19: Scrap of text created on the desktop by dragging the selection out to the desktop

If I were to open the scrap's desktop icon now — by clicking or double-clicking it — I would see the scrap does, indeed, contain an exact copy of the text I selected in WordPad.

Cutting and pasting scraps

If a particular program won't enable you to drag a selection out to the desktop, you can use the more traditional cut-and-paste method. But you can paste the selection onto the desktop (or into a folder) in case you want to paste it into some document later. Follow these steps:

1. Open the document containing the material you want to copy and size its window so you can see some portion of the desktop behind it. For instance, in Figure 18-20, I opened a graphic image in Paint.

2. Select whatever you want to copy using any of the standard selection techniques for this program. For example, I selected the entire picture in Figure 18-20 by choosing Edit ➪ Select All from Paint's menu bar.

3. Choose Edit ➪ Copy from the program's menu bar (Paint's menu bar, in this example) to copy the selection to the Windows Clipboard.

4. Right-click the desktop and choose Paste.

An icon for the scrap appears near where you right-clicked, as in Figure 18-21. This time, Windows gave the new scrap the simple name "Scrap."

Figure 18-20: A picture open and selected in Paint

Figure 18-21: New scrap created by right-clicking the desktop and choosing Paste

Remember, if you don't want to clutter your desktop with too many scraps, you can paste the scrap into some folder instead. For example, if you want to put all your scraps into your My Documents folder, drag the selection to this folder's icon on the desktop and drop it there. Or, after choosing Edit ➪ Copy to copy the scrap to the Windows Clipboard, right-click the My Documents folder, and choose Paste. The scrap ends up inside the specified folder and will be invisible until you open this folder.

You could even create a new folder, perhaps named Scraps, just by right-clicking the desktop and selecting New ➪ Folder. Doing this creates a folder named New Folder. To rename this folder, right-click it and choose Rename. Then, type in a new name, such as Scraps. From now on, you can drop your scraps into this folder to keep them all in one place without cluttering your desktop.

Using the scraps

Once you create one or more scraps, you can easily drop them into any documents you please. A few ways exist to accomplish this. One is to cut and paste the scrap off the desktop into the document:

1. Right-click the scrap you want to move or copy and choose Copy (if you want to copy the scrap) or Cut (if you want to move the scrap).

2. Open the document into which you want to paste the scrap.

3. Click where you want to place the scrap. Then right-click that same spot and choose Paste.

If you are using a program that supports drag-and-drop scraps, you can drag the scrap's icon from the desktop into whatever document you want to place the scrap and then release the mouse button to drop the scrap inside the document.

Remember, each scrap you create is a small document file in its own right, so you can do all the normal operations you'd perform on document files. For example:

✦ To see what is inside a scrap, open the scrap (click once if you're using Web-style navigation, double-click if you're using Classic-style navigation).

✦ To rename a scrap to make it easier to identify later, right-click the scrap, choose Rename, and type the new name.

✦ To delete a scrap (assuming you don't need it anymore), right-click the scrap's icon and choose Delete.

If you have any trouble copying or moving stuff within a particular program, remember your best bet is to check that program's online help for more information. Open that program's help (choose Help ➪ Help topics from its menu bar) and then click the Index tab in the help screen. Type a relevant word, such as "select" or "copy" or "move" or "scrap," to see what information is available under that topic.

Summary

In this chapter, you learned about some of the applets that come with Windows Me, as well as some general techniques for moving and copying stuff from one document to another. To recap:

✦ To start a Windows Me applet, click the Start button and choose Programs ➪ Accessories (or in some cases, Programs ➪ Accessories ➪ System Tools). Then click the applet you want.

✦ If you're missing any Windows Me accessories, you can reinstall them using the Windows Setup tab in Add/Remove Programs.

✦ The Calculator applet works like a standard pocket calculator.

✦ The Notepad applet is good for working with plain, unformatted text.

✦ The WordPad applet is a miniature word processing program capable of displaying fancy text, fonts, pictures, and special characters.

✦ The Character Map applet enables you to insert special characters — characters not normally found on the keyboard — into a document.

✦ The Paint applet enables you to create and edit graphic bitmap images, including those stored in the .bmp, .gif, and .jpg formats.

✦ The Clipboard Viewer enables you to see what is currently inside the Windows Clipboard.

✦ To put something into the Windows Clipboard, select the thing to move/copy and then choose Edit ➪ Copy or Edit ➪ Cut from this program's menu bar.

✦ To copy something from the Clipboard into another document, click at about where you want to place the object. Then choose Edit ➪ Paste from that program's menu bar, or right-click and choose Paste.

✦ Keyboard alternatives for cut and paste are as follows: Ctrl+C copies the selection to the Clipboard, Ctrl+X moves the selection to the Clipboard, and Ctrl+V pastes the Clipboard contents at the current cursor position.

✦ Use the Print Screen and Alt +Print Screen keys to puts screenshots in the Windows Clipboard. Then paste the snapshot into any graphics program by choosing Edit ➪ Paste.

✦ To create a scrap, paste the contents of the Windows Clipboard right onto the desktop or in a folder.

✦ Some applications enable you to create scraps by dragging the selection out to the desktop.

✦   ✦   ✦

Printers and Fonts

T his chapter, as you may have guessed, is all about print-ing. You'll learn to use a printer, manage print jobs, and even install a new printer. We'll also cover fonts, which enable you to print fancy text. Toward the end of the chapter, I'll dis-cuss even more products to enhance your printed materials, such as clip art and specialty papers.

Installing a Printer

Installing a printer is easy. First you need to follow the manufac-turer's instructions for connecting the PC to the printer. This is usually a simple matter of connecting the parallel printer port on the back of the PC to some plug on the back of the printer. Then you need to plug the printer into a regular wall socket to get power and then turn on the printer. If your printer came with any floppy disks or a CD-ROM, keep them handy as you proceed through the following steps to make Windows Me aware of your new printer:

Note These steps assume you are installing a printer physically connected to the PC on which you are working. If you want to install a printer on some other computer in a LAN, see Chapter 32.

1. Gather up your original Windows Me floppy disks or CD-ROM (unless your PC came with Windows Me pre-installed, in which case you may be able to skip this step).

2. Shut down Windows and then shut down your PC.

3. Make sure the printer is connected to the computer and is turned on.

4. Restart your PC.

5. If Windows does *not* automatically detect your printer at startup, go to Step 6. If Windows does detect your printer at startup, follow the instructions that appear onscreen and then skip the following steps.

Tip   If you're given the choice to install a Windows Me driver or the manufacturer's driver, always try the Windows Me driver first. Click the Have Disk button *only* if you're installing a printer that has no Windows Me driver.

6. Click the Start button and choose Settings ➪ Printers.

7. Open the Add Printer icon. You'll see the first page of the Add Printer Wizard. Click the Next button.

8. In the next wizard screen (see Figure 19-1), choose Local Printer and then click the Next button.

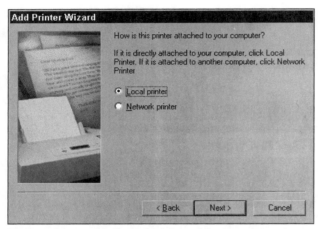

Figure 19-1: Second page of the Add Printer Wizard

9. In the next wizard page (Figure 19-2), choose the manufacturer and model of your printer and click Next. If you cannot find your printer's manufacturer and model and you have disks that came with the printer, click the Have Disk button.

From this point, it's all a matter of following the instructions that appear onscreen and clicking the Next button. When you complete all the steps, the printer will be ready to use.

Every printer installed on (or accessible from) your PC is represented by an icon in the Printers folder. To open the Printers folder, simply click the Start button and choose Settings ➪ Printers. Figure 19-3 shows an example from one of my PCs. The printer marked with a check mark is the default printer for this computer, which means it is the printer that will be used when you print something without first choosing a specific printer. If you have multiple printers installed you can use any one of them as the default printer by right-clicking its icon and choosing Set As Default.

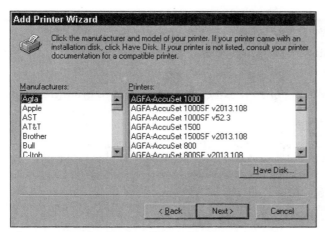

Figure 19-2: Third page of the Add Printer Wizard

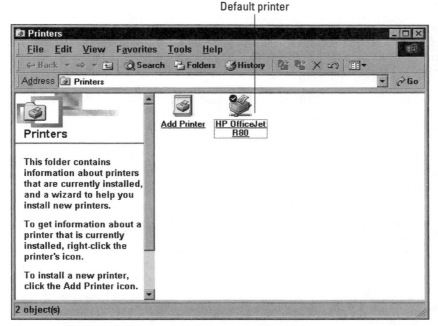

Figure 19-3: Sample Printers folder open on the desktop

Printing Documents

After your printer is installed, you can use any of these techniques to print most documents:

✦ To print from a program, open the document you want to print (if it isn't already open). From the menu bar of the program displaying the document, choose File ➪ Print and respond to any prompts or dialog boxes that appear.

✦ To print from the desktop, browse to the document you want to print. Then right-click the document's icon and choose Print from the shortcut menu that appears.

✦ To print several documents, open the Printers folder and then browse to and select the documents you want to print. Then drag the selected documents to the printer's icon in the Printers folder.

Tip
Unfortunately, not all programs support the latter two methods of printing. If you have any problems printing a document, try the first method.

The last technique is particularly good for printing a bunch of documents while you're away from the computer. Probably the simplest thing to do is to open the Printers folder and then right-drag a printer icon out to the desktop. When you release the mouse button, choose Create Shortcut(s) Here to create a desktop shortcut to the printer.

Now, whenever you want to print one or more documents, you can select those documents from My Computer, Windows Explorer, or Find, and then drag the documents to the printer's shortcut icon and drop them there. For example, in Figure 19-4, I already created a shortcut icon to my OfficeJet printer. I also opened a folder and selected a few Microsoft Word documents to print. To print all those selected documents I'd just have to drag that selection onto the shortcut icon for the printer and drop it right there.

Managing printers and print jobs

When you want to check the status of the printer or manage ongoing print jobs, open the Printers folder (Start ➪ Settings ➪ Printers) and then open the icon for the specific printer with which you want to work. (If you're printing to a network printer, you must go to the PC to which the printer is physically connected and open the Printers folder on that machine.) You'll come to a dialog box like the one shown in Figure 19-5.

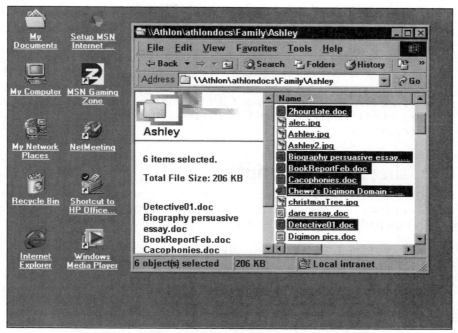

Figure 19-4: You can print multiple documents by dragging their icons to a printer's shortcut icon.

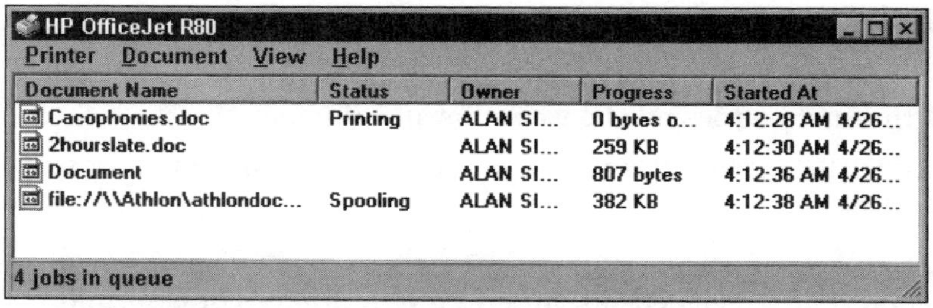

Figure 19-5: Dialog box for managing a printer's print jobs

You can choose options from the Printer menu to control the print queue (the list of documents being printed). From the menu bar, you can do the following:

✦ To pause all print jobs, choose Printer ➪ Pause Printing.

✦ To cancel all print jobs, choose Printer ➪ Purge Print Documents.

✦ To pause printing one document, right-click that document and choose Pause Printing.

✦ To cancel printing one document, right-click that document and choose Cancel Printing.

Tip   Most printers contain a *buffer* that holds text to be printed. When you pause or cancel a print job, the printer won't actually stop until that buffer has been emptied. So don't expect the printer to stop at the exact moment you choose to pause or cancel a job.

Choosing a default printer

If you have access to several printers from your PC, you can specify the one you use most often as the default printer. This way, when you start a print job without specifying a particular printer, the job is sent to the default printer.

To define a default printer, follow these steps:

1. Click the Start button, and choose Settings ⇨ Printers.

2. Right-click the icon for the printer you want to make the default, and choose Set As Default from the shortcut menu.

Changing printer properties

Every printer has its own unique set of properties, which you can change. Regardless of what settings your printer offers, you can follow these simple steps to get to those properties:

1. Click the Start button and choose Settings ⇨ Printers.

2. Right-click the icon for the printer you want to work with and choose Properties.

Figure 19-6 shows a sample properties sheet for a printer. Be aware, the properties that appear on your screen depend entirely on your printer. For more information about the available properties, refer to the manual that came with your printer.

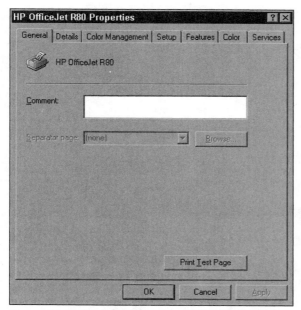

Figure 19-6: Sample printer Properties dialog box

Using Fonts

A font, simply stated, is a style of print. This text is in one font; the heading above this paragraph is in a different font. Any font can be printed in a variety of weights. What you're reading right now is the regular (or Roman) weight. **This is the bold-face (or bold) version of this font.** *And here is the italic weight for this font.*

The size of a font is measured in points: 1 point equals roughly $\frac{1}{72}$ inch. Normal-size text (such as this) usually ranges from 8 to 12 points. Letters printed at 36-point size are around a half-inch tall and letters printed at 72 points are around one inch tall.

The three main classes of fonts are serif, sans serif, and decorative. Serif fonts have little curlicues at the end of each letter to minimize eyestrain when reading small print. This font and the Times New Roman font, shown in Figure 19-7, are serif fonts.

Sans serif fonts don't have the little curlicues and generally are used for large text. The Arial font shown in Figure 19-7 is a sans serif font, as are the fonts that appear on most street signs.

Decorative fonts are used to call attention to something or to set a mood. Bees Knees and Comic Sans MS are decorative fonts. Such fonts can be used for headlines, advertisements, and signs, usually to call attention to a single word or a short phrase. Some decorative fonts, such as Wingdings in the Figure 19-7, contain little clip art images and symbols.

Figure 19-7: Examples of serif, sans serif, and decorative fonts

After a font is installed, the way you apply it to text depends on the program you use. In most programs, you select the text to which you want to apply the font and then choose Format ⇨ Font. In some cases, you can choose a font from the toolbar. Figure 19-8 shows a Microsoft Word document. I'm using the Font drop-down list in the formatting toolbar to apply a font to selected text.

Expanding your font collection

You are not limited to the fonts currently installed on your computer. You can buy all kinds of fonts — thousands of them — and install them on your computer. Quite a few freebie fonts are floating around on the Internet, which you can download free. You can also choose from several different formats of fonts. TrueType fonts are the ones best supported by Windows Me because you don't need any special programs to use them. Other font types, such as PostScript, do require special programs to manage those fonts. I'll talk about non-TrueType fonts a little later in this chapter. For now, let's focus on TrueType fonts.

Tip   If you have Internet access, you can probably find lots of fonts simply by going to some search engine, such as http://www.altavista.com, and searching for TrueType Fonts. Microsoft Corporation also offers a few freebies at http://www.microsoft.com/truetype.

Figure 19-8: Choosing a font for selected text in Microsoft Word

Managing TrueType fonts

You can review, add, and remove TrueType fonts via the Fonts folder. To get there, follow these steps:

1. Click the Start button and choose Settings ⇨ Control Panel.

2. Open the Fonts icon.

The Fonts folder opens and displays an icon for every font currently installed on your computer. TrueType fonts are indicated by a TT icon. The folder also lists older raster fonts, identified with an A icon, and are included with Windows Me mainly to maintain compatibility with earlier printers and versions of Windows.

Here are some things you can do in the Fonts folder to manage your fonts:

✦ To see what a font looks like, double-click the font's icon. When the font's window appears (refer to Figure 19-9), you can click Print to print the font sample or click Done to close the window.

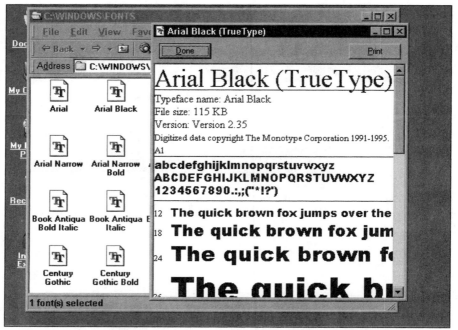

Figure 19-9: Double-clicking a font's icon shows a dialog box like this one.

✦ To see copyright and other information about a font, double-click its icon.

✦ To delete a font, click its icon and choose File ➪ Delete.

✦ To view similar fonts, choose View ➪ Fonts by Similarity. Then choose a font from the List Fonts By Similarity To drop-down list.

✦ To close the Fonts folder, click its Close (X) button.

You don't use the Fonts folder to apply a font to text. Instead, you apply fonts to text within whatever program you are currently working with, as described earlier in this chapter.

Installing TrueType fonts

New TrueType fonts you purchase typically are delivered on floppy disk or CD-ROM. Before you can use a TrueType font, you must install it. Most fonts will come with their own instructions for installing on Windows Me. If so, you probably should follow the manufacturer's instructions. If you don't have such instructions, you can probably follow this generic procedure for installing TrueType fonts:

1. Insert the floppy disk or CD-ROM containing the font(s) into a drive.

2. Click the Start button and choose Settings ⇨ Control Panel.

3. Open the Fonts icon to display the Fonts folder.

4. Choose File ⇨ Install New Font.

5. Use the Drives and Folders options to navigate to the disk containing the fonts you want to install. For example, in Figure 19-10, I've navigated to a folder named TRUETYPE on the floppy disk in drive A. The names of fonts in this folder are listed near the top of the dialog box. In my example, the fonts are all named Remedy . . . (something-or-other).

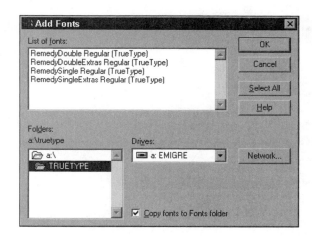

Figure 19-10: Installable fonts from a floppy disk in drive A

6. In the List of Fonts box, select the font(s) you want to install. You can Shift+click and Ctrl+click to select multiple fonts. You also can click the Select All button to select all the listed fonts.

7. Make sure the "Copy fonts to fonts folder" check box is selected (checked).

8. Click the OK button.

Copying the fonts to your hard disk takes a few moments. When this process is done, you'll be returned to the Fonts folder. If you look around, you'll see the new fonts are included in this folder, now under the names listed in the dialog box. For example, my newly installed fonts would be named RemedyDouble, RemedySingle, and so forth.

You can remove the floppy disk from the floppy drive or the CD from the CD-ROM drive when the installation is complete. You won't need the disk(s) anymore because the fonts are now on your computer's hard disk. Store the floppy disks or CD-ROM someplace safe as a backup.

If you want to test your new font, open up any program that supports fonts, such as WordPad (Start ➪ Programs ➪ Accessories ➪ WordPad). Type some text, select it, and then change its font. For example, in Figure 19-11, I've already chosen Format ➪ Font from WordPad's menu bar. As you can see, the newly installed "Remedy" fonts are now included in the list of available fonts.

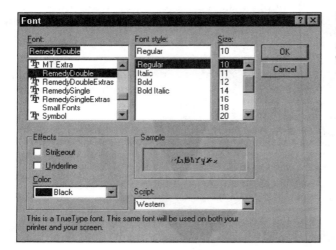

Figure 19-11: My new Remedy fonts are available for use in WordPad.

Adding a Little Art to Your Life

Clip art is a great way to spruce up newsletters, reports, brochures, and other printed material. You can buy clip-art collections at most computer stores, and also from mail-order houses that advertise in computer and desktop publishing magazines. Windows Me supports all popular PC clip-art formats including .cgm, .tif, .pcx, .bmp, .wmf, .jpg, and .gif.

The real compatibility issue, however, is between the program in which you plan to use the clip art and the format of the clip art. You should check the help file or documentation for your word processing, desktop publishing, or graphics program to see which formats are supported.

A good clip-art browser is a tool worth having. One of these browsers, called the Microsoft Clip Gallery, is built into Microsoft Office 97 and 2000. The Gallery enables you to organize clip art by theme and displays thumbnails of each piece of art within a theme, as in the example shown in Figure 19-12. If you don't have Microsoft Office, you might want to try Jasc's Media Center, which is a similar product. You can find this product at many computer stores or on Jasc's Web site at www.jasc.com.

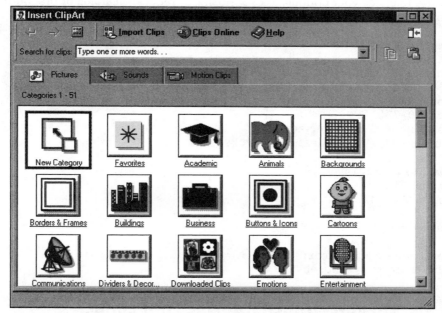

Figure 19-12: Microsoft Clip Gallery comes with Microsoft Office 2000.

Tip   When copying graphic images to your hard disk, consider placing them in the C:\My Documents\My Pictures folder, which will use thumbnails rather than icons to display picture contents in My Computer and Windows Explorer.

If you have Internet access, you may want to look around for clip art you can download to your PC free. I would recommend you go to some search engine, such as http://www.altavista.com and search for the phrase *free clipart*.

Awesome Papers

Your printer can do much more than print text and graphics on 8.5×11-inch paper. The following sections examine ways you can expand your horizons by printing labels, cards, checks, and more.

Printing checks and business forms

You can use your printer to print on preprinted checks and business forms. Remember, if you want to print on carbon-paper forms, you should use a forms printer (basically, a heavy-duty dot-matrix printer). Carbonless (single-sheet thickness) forms and checks can be printed on either a laser printer or a dot-matrix printer. To check your options, ask your bank, or request a catalog or brochure from the following companies:

Designer Checks
P.O. Box 9100
Anniston, AL 36202-9100

Phone: (800) 239-4087
Fax: (800) 774-1118
E-mail: info@checks.hotnew.com
Web site: http://www.designerchecks.com

Nebs Business Forms
500 Main Street
Groton, MA 01471

Phone: (800) 225-6380
Fax: (800) 234-4324
E-mail: ordering@nebs.com
Web site: http://www.nebs.ca

Cards, stickers, transparencies, and slides

Most printers can print on mailing labels, floppy disk labels, file folder labels, and a wide variety of stickers. Many word processing programs, such as Microsoft Word, have built-in templates that help make it easier to print on those formats. You can find stock for printing those items, as well as for printing business cards, greeting cards, invitations, file cards, and gatefold mailers. Most laser printers even enable you to print on the transparencies used with overhead projectors. But don't trust just any paper or transparency to your laser printer. Instead, find stock specifically designed to handle the high heat laser printers produce.

The Avery label company offers a large selection of laser-printer labels, stickers, and transparencies. You can find these products at most large office supply and computer stores. Or, contact Avery at the following address:

Avery Dennison Consumer Service Center
20955 Pathfinder Road
Diamond Bar, CA 91765

Phone: (800) 252-8379
Fax: (909) 594-4876
E-mail: productinfo@averydennison.com
Web site: http://www.avery.com

For cards and predesigned labels, see the catalogs mentioned in "Color from black-and-white printers" later in this chapter.

Label printers

If you get tired of switching between regular stock and labels in your printer, consider purchasing a dedicated label printer. Typically, you can plug the label printer into a serial port, so it doesn't conflict with your main printer.

Seiko Instruments makes nice label printers, which you can find at most computer stores. I use a CoStar label printer, and I'm pleased with it. CoStar also makes a label printer that can print bar codes and POSTNET bar codes. For more information on CoStar label printers, contact the company at the following address:

CoStar Corporation
599 W Putnam Avenue
Greenwich, CT 06830

Phone: (800) 426-7827 or (203) 661-9700
E-mail: sales@costar.com
Web site: http://www.costar.com

35mm slides

Printing on 35mm slides for a slide show requires special equipment. The most cost-effective means of creating and printing 35mm slides is presentation software such as Microsoft PowerPoint, which comes with the Microsoft Office suite. Within this program, you'll find instructions for sending your work to a service center that will create the slides for you.

Color from black-and-white printers

Even if you don't have a color printer, you still can use color to spruce up your letterhead, brochures, mailing labels, postcards, business cards, newsletters, and other items. Just purchase predesigned colored stock for laser printers. The selection of designs, paper sizes, and label formats is fantastic and you can buy coordinated sets to give your documents a consistent, professional image. Just visit any computer store or office supply store to see the wide range of papers you have to choose from. Or contact the following companies, and ask them to send you a catalog:

Premier Papers
P.O. Box 64785
St. Paul, MN 55164

Phone: (800) 843-0414
Fax: (800) 526-3029

Queblo
1000 Florida Avenue
P.O. Box 1393
Hagerstown, MD 21741

Phone: (800) 523-9080
Fax: (800) 554-8779

Troubleshooting Printers and Fonts

Most printing problems are caused by simple, although common, mistakes. If your printer won't print, check the printer as follows:

✦ Make sure the printer is plugged in.

✦ Make sure the printer is turned on.

✦ If the printer has an online/offline button, make sure the printer is online.

✦ Make sure paper is in the printer, and the paper is properly loaded.

✦ Make sure the ink cartridge has ink.

✦ If you're printing to a network printer, make sure the computer to which the printer is physically connected is up and running.

If you still have trouble with printing or fonts, the Windows Me Troubleshooter can almost certainly help you. Follow these steps:

1. Click the Start button and choose Help, and then click the Contents tab.

2. Open the Troubleshooting book.

3. Open the Windows Me Troubleshooters book.

4. Open the Print page.

The rest is easy. Just answer questions and make selections from options presented onscreen, and let the troubleshooter help you pinpoint and resolve the problem.

Changing the Screen Fonts

Even though I've focused mainly on printing and fonts in this chapter, I don't want to give you the impression that fonts are used only for printing. You can also select a font to use on your screen for icon labels, window titles, and so forth. To get started, follow these simple steps:

1. Right-click any neutral area of the Windows Me desktop and choose Properties. Or click the Start button and choose Settings ⇨ Control Panel; then open the Display icon.

2. Click the Appearance tab to get to the options shown in Figure 19-13.

3. If you want to experiment without messing up any existing appearance scheme, click the Save As button, type in a new name, and then click the OK button. Any changes you make will affect only the scheme that appears in the Scheme text box.

4. Under Item, choose any item that displays text, such as:

   - Active Title Bar
   - Icon
   - Inactive Title Bar
   - Menu
   - Message Box
   - Palette Title
   - Selected Items
   - ToolTip

5. Choose a font, size, color, and, optionally, boldface (B) or italics (/) from the bottom row of options. For example, in Figure 19-14, I opted to set the font of the Active Title Bar to Comic Sans MS (Western) at 15 points, white in color, no boldface or italics. The font is automatically applied to the sample windows inside the Display Properties dialog box.

6. Repeat Steps 4 and 5 to stylize as many items as you wish.

7. Click the OK button when you finish.

You'll be returned to the Windows Me desktop. Any font selections you made will be applied automatically from this point.

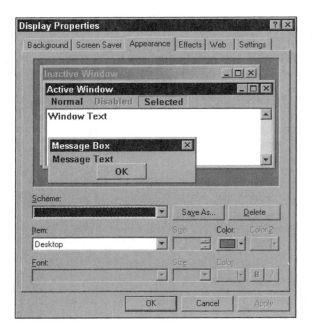

Figure 19-13: Use the Appearance tab of Display Properties to choose desktop fonts.

Figure 19-14: Using a 15-point Comic Sans font for Active Title Bars onscreen

PostScript Type 1 and OpenType Fonts

As I mentioned, Windows Me has built-in support for TrueType fonts and that's why I've focused on those fonts in this chapter. Other types of fonts are out there; the best known are PostScript fonts (also called Type 1 fonts). You can use those fonts with Windows Me, but you'll need to purchase and install Adobe Type Manager (ATM) to do so. You can pick up a copy of ATM at most computer stores. Or, purchase it directly from Adobe at:

Adobe Systems, Inc. Customer Service
P.O. Box 1034
Buffalo NY 14240-1034

Phone: (800) 833-6687
Fax: (716) 447-7303
Web site: http://www.adobe.com

Once you purchase ATM, you can follow the instructions included with the product to install it and to install and use PostScript fonts in your documents. As of this writing, a new font technology known as OpenType is being developed jointly by Adobe and Microsoft. The OpenType font format is an extension of the TrueType font format, adding support for PostScript font data. The goals of the OpenType format are as follows:

✦ Support a broader range of platforms including Windows, Mac, and UNIX

✦ Support for larger international character sets

✦ Smaller file sizes to make Internet distribution more efficient

✦ Increased flexibility for more advanced typographic control

Unfortunately, I can't tell you anything more specific than this because the OpenType specification is still in the works. If you have Internet access and you want to keep up on what's happening with OpenType fonts, visit the following Web sites:

✦ Adobe's OpenType page at http://partners.adobe.com/supportservice/ devrelations/japan/opentype/otover.htm

✦ Adobe WebType at http://www.microsoft.com/typography/Web/fonts/ Webtype/default.htm

✦ Microsoft Typography page at http://www.microsoft.com/typography

✦ Microsoft Typography links page at http://www.microsoft.com/ typography/links

Also, you can go to any search engine, such as http://www.altavista.com, and search for the keyword "OpenType" for a listing of other sites that deal with this new, emerging font technology.

Summary

Printing is pretty easy in Windows Me, once you get a printer installed. Here's a quick recap of the important points about printing and fonts:

✦ To install a printer, connect it to your PC per the manufacturer's instructions. Then to install the Windows Me drivers, click Start, choose Settings ➪ Printers, open the Add Printer icon, and follow the instructions onscreen.

✦ To print the document currently open and visible onscreen, choose File ➪ Print from the program's menu bar.

✦ To print a document that isn't open, right-click the document's icon and choose Print. Or, drag the document's icon to a printer icon.

✦ To manage print jobs in progress, click the Start button and choose Settings ➪ Printers. Open the icon for the printer and use Printer and Document commands in the menu bar that appears to manage print jobs.

✦ To install and manage TrueType fonts, click the Start button and choose Settings ➪ Control Panel. Then open the Fonts icon.

✦ To apply a font to selected text, use commands in whatever program you're currently working with. Typically, you only need to select text and then choose Format ➪ Font from the program's menu bar.

✦ Clip art is a great way to spruce up printed documents. Learn to use a clip-art browser, such as the Clip Gallery, which comes with Microsoft Office, to get the most from your clip-art collection.

✦ Remember, you're not limited to plain white 8½ × 11-inch paper. You can choose from hundreds of sizes and colors of papers.

✦ ✦ ✦

Sounds and Music

Most PCs sold today come with some built-in multimedia capability to play sound effects, MIDI music, audio CDs, and various types of sounds stored in files. And the Internet now offers tons of music that you listen to online or even download to your computer. This chapter shows what you can do with sound using tools that come with Windows Me. You'll also learn the basics of using the Windows Media Player (which I often refer to as simply Media Player), which is a great tool for working with all types of multimedia files, including music and video.

Get Your Sound Working

Nearly every PC built these days comes with sound capability built right in. A computer that doesn't have sound capability just needs a *sound card* added to it. There are dozens of sound cards to choose from, as a visit to your local computer store (or online computer store) will verify. You'll need speakers to go with that sound card, of course. If you want to listen to audio CDs, you'll need a CD-ROM drive as well. Assuming that you do have at least a sound card and speakers in your PC, let's look at how you can control the sound.

Choosing your Preferred Audio Devices

First, you might have multiple devices capable of playing and recording sound. For example, the computer I'm sitting at right now has a sound card and speakers. But it also has an audio headset with a speaker and a microphone. Most of the time, I prefer to use my large external speakers for playing sound. But for recording voice (or talking on the Internet), I prefer the microphone on the headset. Choosing your preferred devices in Windows Me is pretty easy:

1. Click the Start button and choose Settings ⇨ Control Panel.

2. Click the Sounds and Multimedia icon.

3. Click the Audio tab.

4. Select your preferred devices for wave file playback, sound recording, and MIDI music playback as in Figure 20-1.

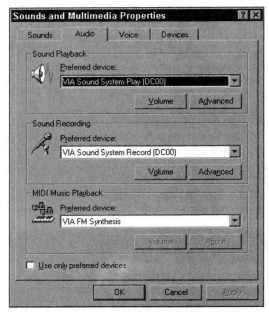

Figure 20-1: The Audio tab of the Sounds and Multimedia Properties dialog box

5. If you have a microphone, click the Voice tab to get to the options shown in Figure 20-2. Then choose your Preferred Devices for playback and recording. Use the Voice Test button to test the sensitivity of your microphone and volume of your playback device.

6. Click OK after making your selections to save them and close the dialog box.

You can, of course, change your preferred devices at any time. For example, if you have a headset for voice as well as a microphone, and you prefer to use the microphone, you can just go into the Sounds and Multimedia Properties dialog box and choose the microphone as your preferred device for voice capture. If you're not sure which device to use for each of the different types of sound, just use the default settings that were in the dialog box when you first opened it.

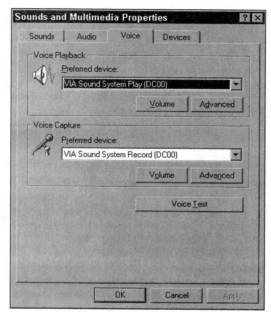

Figure 20-2: The Voice tab of the Sounds and Multimedia Properties dialog box

Adjusting the volume

Being able to control the volume of the sound coming from your speakers is pretty critical. After all, you don't want the sound to be too low to hear, or too loud to bear. Controlling the volume of your speakers can be a little trickier than you might think, as there are actually three different controls that determine how loud the sound is at any moment:

✦ The volume control on your speakers

✦ The volume control on the Windows Me desktop

✦ The volume controls in your mixer

If any one of those is turned off, or turned down too low, you may not hear any sound coming from your speakers!

Caution If you're using headphones while adjusting volumes, hold the headphones away from your ears until you're sure the volume isn't so loud as to blast your eardrums. A sudden loud sound from your headphone speakers can cause a permanent loss of hearing!

Most speakers for PCs are powered. Meaning you either have to put batteries into them or plug them into a wall socket using a special adapter. Once the speakers are powered and turned on, you can generally adjust their volume using knobs located right on the speakers. You'll want to make sure that they're not turned down too far. Otherwise, they might be working properly, but be too quiet to hear. In which case, you may think there's a problem with your sound system when there's not. Your best bet is to crank the speakers up quite high, so that you can use the volume controls on your screen to make fine adjustments while listening to music.

The taskbar Volume Control

If you turn the volume controls on your speakers up high, you'll no doubt need to use the Volume Control in the taskbar to adjust the volume of your sound to a comfortable level. The taskbar Volume Control is initially just a small speaker icon in the indicators section at the right-hand side of the taskbar. When you click on the speaker icon the volume control slider appears as in Figure 20-3. You need to make sure that the Mute option is *not* selected, otherwise no sound will reach the speakers at all. Then you can adjust the volume of the sound by sliding the little box up and down the slider bar. To close the Volume Control slider, just click anywhere outside of it.

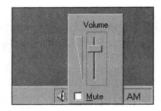

Figure 20-3: Clicking the Speaker icon in the Indicators area opens the Volume Control slider.

If you don't see a little speaker icon on your taskbar, but do have a sound card, the icon is probably just hidden. To find out, click the Start button and Settings ⇨ Control Panel. Open the Sounds and Multimedia icon and make sure you're viewing the Sounds tab as in Figure 20-4. The last item in the dialog box, Show volume control on the taskbar, must be checked (if enabled) for the speaker icon to appear. You can also adjust the sound volume while you're in that dialog box, by dragging the slider to the left or right.

As always, you'll want to click the OK button after making any changes in the Sounds and Multimedia Properties dialog box to put those changes into effect and to close the dialog box.

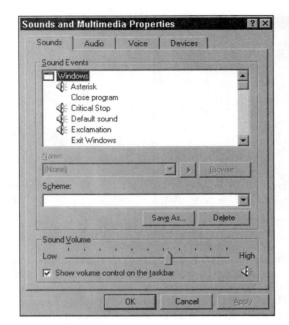

Figure 20-4: The Sounds tab of the Sounds and Multimedia Properties dialog box

Using the Mixer

Yet another program, called the *mixer,* lets you adjust the *relative* volume and sensitivity of different types of sounds your sound hardware can play and record. There are a couple of ways to open the mixer:

✦ Double-click the little speaker icon in the indicators section of the taskbar.

✦ Or, click the Start button and choose Programs ➪ Accessories ➪ Entertainment ➪ Volume Control.

✦ Or, click the Start button and choose Settings ➪ Control Panel. Open the Sounds and Multimedia icon, and then click the Volume button on any playback device on the Audio tab.

The mixer will open displaying a separate volume control slider for each type of playable sound, as in the example shown in Figure 20-5. To adjust the sensitivity of recording devices, choose Options ➪ Properties from the mixer's menu bar and click the Recording button.

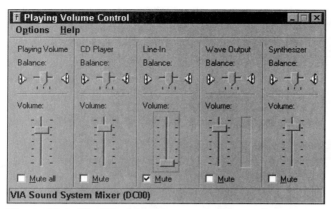

Figure 20-5: The Windows Me sound system mixer

The first thing you want to do is make sure you're adjusting the playback volumes, not the recording volumes. To do so, choose Options ➪ Properties from the mixer's menu bar. In the dialog box that appears, select Playback. Also, you can use the check boxes near the bottom of the dialog box to choose which types of sound you want to control the volume of — the speakers in general, CD player (for audio CD playback), Wave/DirectSound (sound effects), synthesizer (MIDI music), and so forth. If you select Mute, that device won't play at all, no matter how high you turn up its volume.

Tip   If you're not getting sound from a particular device, make sure its Mute check box isn't selected in the mixer.

The Play Control slider at the left edge of the mixer is the general volume of all sounds. If that's muted or turned down to low, no devices will play. So make sure the Mute All button isn't selected and its slider isn't pulled down too low.

On some devices you can also control the balance, bass, and treble. The Balance slider appears just below the device name in the mixer. To adjust bass and treble look for a button labeled Advanced under the main Play Control button or any other device in the mixer. If you don't see an Advanced button, it may be hidden. Choose Options ➪ Advanced Controls from the mixer's menu bar to display the Advanced button. If the Advanced option on the menu is disabled (dimmed), then your sound card doesn't have the capability to change bass and treble. However, if you can get to the Advanced options, you can adjust the sliders for Bass and Treble.

After you've made your selections, close the mixer by clicking its Close (X) button. As long as you didn't mute anything, and you're certain that the volume controls in the mixer and on your speakers (if any) aren't turned down too low, you should be able to hear all the different types of sounds described throughout the remainder of this chapter.

Using Windows Media Player

Windows Media Player is a general-purpose program for playing all kinds of multi-media files, including audio and video files. When you open a file that Media Player is capable of playing, the program will start from automatically. But you can also start it yourself at any time by clicking the Start button and choosing Programs ⇨ Accessories ⇨ Entertainment ⇨ Windows Media Player.

Windows Media Player is a big improvement over earlier programs used for playing with multimedia files. With Media Player you can:

✦ Play audio CDs and copy tracks (songs) to your hard disk

✦ Find and play streaming media from the Web

✦ Create and organize libraries of favorite music and video files

✦ Create and listen to custom playlists of your favorite songs

✦ Download MP3 music to a portable listening device

Media player is capable of taking on several different looks, called "skins." But the first time you open it, you'll probably see something similar to Figure 20-6. The most important controls for playing multimedia files are those along the bottom of Media Player. As always, you can point to any control to see its name in a ToolTip. If you've ever worked a VCR, tape player, or CD Player, these main controls should be familiar to you. The *playlists* referred to in the list are lists of songs (or videos) to be played in sequence. You'll learn how to create playlists a little later in this chapter. Media Player's controls include:

✦ **Play/Pause:** Plays or pauses the current multimedia file

✦ **Stop:** Stops playback

✦ **Seek:** Shows progress as a file is being played, and also lets you skip ahead by dragging the box or clicking somewhere along the slider

✦ **Mute:** Shuts off the volume without stopping playback

✦ **Volume:** Adjust the sound volume of the playback

✦ **Previous track:** Jumps to previous track in the current playlist

✦ **Rewind:** Jumps to beginning of file currently being played

✦ **Fast forward:** Moves forward at higher speed through current file

✦ **Next track:** Jumps to beginning of next track in the playlist

✦ **Switch to compact mode:** Displays smaller media player window

Figure 20-6: Windows Media Player

The Windows Media Player is capable of playing the many different types of multimedia files, as listed in Table 20-1. (The .avi, .ivf, and .mp* formats are actually video files, which are discussed in Chapter 22.) And because Media Player comes with Windows Me, you should be able to hear and view files in those formats without purchasing or downloading any special player.

Table 20-1
Multimedia File Formats Windows Media Player Can Play

Format	Common Filename Extensions
CD Audio	.cda
Indeo Video Format	.ivf
Macintosh AIFF	.aif, .aifc, .aiff
Microsoft	.asf, .asx, .avi, .wav, .wax, .wma, .wmv, .wvx
MIDI (Musical Instrument Digital Interface)	.mid, .midi, .rmi
MPEG (Motion Picture Experts Group)	.mpeg, .mpg, .m1v, .mp2, .mp3, .mpa, .mpe, .mpv2, .mp2v, .m3u, .pls
Unix/Linux	.au, .snd

If you discover that some other program (or no program) is autoloading when you open one of the file types listed in Table 20-1, you can probably fix the problem by specifying the file type in Media Player's Options. Choose Tools ⇨ Options from Media Player's menu bar. Then click on the Formats tab. Select all the file types that you want to associate with Windows Media Player, and then click the OK button.

With the basic controls having been covered, let's take a look at how you could use Media Player to listen to your favorite audio CDs from your computer.

Playing Audio CDs

If your computer has a CD-ROM drive, you can use it to play standard audio CDs — the same CDs you play in your home or car stereo. The process is simple:

1. Put the audio CD into the CD-ROM drive, label side up just as in a stereo.

2. Wait for Media Player to open. (If it doesn't open within a minute, open My Computer on your desktop, and then click or double-click the icon for your CD-ROM drive.)

3. Listen to the CD.

Use the volume control slider near the bottom of Media Player to adjust the volume of the CD. If that doesn't take the sound high or low enough, try adjusting the volume control attached to the little speaker indicator in the taskbar. If you want to adjust the audio CD independently of other sound devices, double-click the little speaker icon in the taskbar top open the mixer. Slide the CD Audio control up and down to adjust the volume. If that doesn't work, your sound card is probably using DirectSound to play the CD. In that case, you can adjust the volume of the CD by sliding the Wave/DirectSound slider control.

If you have a connection to the Internet, and that connection is open when you load the audio CD into your CD-ROM drive, Windows Media Player will look up a list of the songs that are on the audio CD and then display that information on the CD Audio section of the player. It gets this information from the All Music Guide (AMG) database on the Internet, and generally does so with no intervention on your part. If you're not connected to the Internet when you start the CD, and song titles are not downloaded automatically, you can still try to get the song titles by connecting to the Internet and clicking the Get Names button above the title list. If all the conditions are right, you should be able to see the song title for each track on the CD as in Figure 20-7.

Tip   The listing of CD audio tracks on the Internet are called CDDBs (Compact Disk Database). The AMG that Windows Me uses can be accessed directly from your Web browser at www.allmusic.com.

Figure 20-7: CD Audio tab of the Windows Media Player after downloading a song list

If you don't have Internet access, or if the CD you're listening to isn't listed in AMG's database, then there's no way for Media Player to determine the song titles of the tracks by itself. They'll just be listed as Track 1, Track 2, Track 3, and so forth, with "Unknown" listed in the Artist and Genre columns. You can, however, add your own information by right-clicking a track and choosing Edit from the pop-up menu.

By default, all of the songs on the CD are played in the order in which they appear. If nothing is playing, clicking the Play button starts the playback. If you want to listen to a specific song, just double-click its line. If you'd like Media Player to play every song on the CD, but in random order, click the Shuffle button up near the top of the Media Player's window.

Keeping Media Player up-to-date

Windows Media Player is so tied into the Internet that it's likely to evolve more quickly than other components of Windows Me. So, you'll want to check for updates often. To have Media Player check for updates automatically, choose Tools ➪ Options from its menu bar. Under Auto Upgrade, select how often you'd like Media Player to check for updates.

Once you're listening to music, clicking the Now Playing tab on the left side of Media Player will offer some tools to play with. Choose View ➪ Now Playing Tools from Media Player's menu bar after clicking on the Now Playing tab to see your options. As you experiment with different tools, you'll see that some offer buttons of their own, such as the little arrow buttons next to Bars and Waves: Ocean Mist and the Graphic Equalizer in Figure 20-8. Feel free to experiment — you certainly can't do any harm.

Tip   To see whether new visualizations are available on the Internet, choose Tools ➪ Download Visualizations from Media Player's menu bar. Then follow the instructions on the screen.

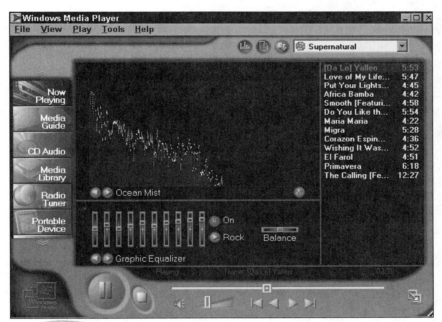

Figure 20-8: The Now Playing tab of Media Player with the Graphic Equalizer on

Copying Audio CD Tracks

The check boxes to the left of the song titles in the CD Audio tab of Media Player let you select songs to copy to your hard disk. This is a great way for building up a collection of favorite songs on your computer, and then playing them in any order you wish. Just be aware that each song can eat up five or six megabytes of disk space if copied at the highest quality possible. That's not really much by today's standards, where hard disks are sold by the gigabyte (1 gigabyte equals 1,000 megabytes). But if you're using an older, smaller hard disk, those songs can take up a significant amount of disk space.

I have 20,000 mb

Before you start copying songs from audio CDs to your hard disk, you might also want to make sure that you know where the songs will be stored so that you can find them later. For example, you might create a folder named C:\My Documents\ My Music (if such a folder doesn't already exist) using My Computer or Windows Explorer. Then tell Media Player to use that folder to store tracks copied from audio CDs. To do that, choose Tools ➪ Options from Media Player's menu bar. Use the Change button near the bottom of the CD Audio tab to specify the folder to which you want to copy CD audio tracks, as in Figure 20-9. You can also adjust the quality of the copied songs and select from among the other options shown in the figure. As always, click OK to save your changes and close the dialog box.

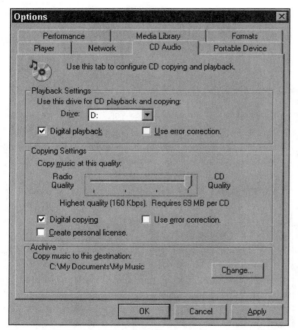

Figure 20-9: The CD Audio tab of the Options dialog box in Media Player

To copy files from an audio CD, just insert the CD as you normally would and click on the CD Audio tab at the left side of Media Player. To copy songs, place a check mark next to any song that you want to copy. Leave the check boxes blank next to songs that you don't want to copy. Then click on the Copy Music button near the top of the CD Audio tab. It may take a while to copy all the files. The Copy Status column in the list of tracks keeps you apprised of the copy's progress. If you need to stop copying prematurely, click the Stop Copy button (which will be where the Copy Music button was.)

When all the selected tracks have been copied the Copy Status column for each copied song will show Copied to Library and the Stop Copy button will become the Copy Music button again. The check boxes for all copied files will be cleared. The songs will be stored on your local hard disk so that you can play them whenever you want, even without the audio CD handy. You'll learn how to organize and play songs that you've copied to your hard disk a little later in this chapter when we discuss the Media Library component of Media Player.

Tip   As in most programs, you can widen and narrow columns in the CD Audio tab by dragging the thin lines that separate the column headings.

Using Media Player to copy songs from audio CDs to your hard disk has a couple of unusual side effects. First, the songs are automatically converted from their native .cda (CD Audio) format to the Windows Media Player Audio (.wma) format on your hard disk. This won't hurt the playback quality of the songs. However, in case you go looking for a song later, be aware that each song is stored in a .wma file.

Also, Media Player won't ask where you want to store the song. Instead, it decides that for itself, based on where you told it to store the songs in Options (see Figure 20-9.) Within that folder it sort of "buries" each song in a set of folders that help Windows Media Player keep track of the songs. The general format is:

```
Yourdirectory\artist\album\
```

For example, song's copied from Carlos Santana's *Supernatural* on my computer, where I specified c:\My Documents\My Music as the default directory for storing audio CD files, will actually all be stored under c:\My Documents\My Music\Santana\Supernatural.

Tip   To see a list of all the .wma files on your hard disk, regardless of which folder they're stored in, click the Start button and choose Search ➪ For Files and Folders. Enter *.wma as the files to search for, and choose your local hard drive(s) under Look In. Then click the Search Now button to start the search.

Of course, if Media Player isn't able to get the album and track information off the Internet, it can't very well organize the songs in that manner. In that case, it will store the songs under the not-so-obvious folder names shown below:

```
Yourdirectory\Unknown_Artist\Unknown_Album(date time)\
```

Where *date* and *time* are the date and time at which the songs were copied. Your best bet, though, is *not* to go in and rename the song file or folders using My Computer or Windows Explorer. Instead, you can rename and reorganize the folders and song titles using the Media Library discussed a little later in this chapter. Media Library will help you keep your media collection more organized. Before we discuss Media Library though, let's look at another important source of music for your PC—the Internet.

Music on the Internet

Audio CDs are certainly a good source of music. But these days the Internet is also home to tons of recorded music. However, unlike radios and CDs, which deliver music smoothly and evenly to your ears, the Internet has no capability to send data at a smooth, even rate. In fact, delivery of data over the Internet is usually pretty choppy and unpredictable. You usually don't notice this when you're viewing Web pages or downloading files. However, if you try to listen to a song or view a video as it's being downloaded from the Internet, the choppiness will be quite apparent. Especially if you're using a modem and dial-up account as opposed to a broadband connection such as cable or DSL.

Music and video, which are intended to be listened to and viewed smoothly, are called *streaming media*. Windows Media Player uses *buffering* to minimize the choppiness that's likely to occur with streaming media. With buffering, you don't have to wait for the entire file to be downloaded before you can start listening to it. Instead, a good chunk of the file is first downloaded and stored in a *buffer*—a place in the computer's memory for temporarily storing data. Once the buffer is filled (or partially filled) playback begins even though the file hasn't been fully downloaded. As long as your Internet connection can fill the buffer faster than your computer plays the streaming media, you'll get smooth continuous playback without the interruptions normally caused by the manner in which the Internet transfers data from one computer to another.

Intelligent streaming is a form of streaming that goes to even greater lengths to ensure that you get the best quality playback possible. Intelligent streaming depends on media being encoded at multiple *bit rates*. The program receiving the data being sent analyzes the network to get a sense of how much bandwidth (speed) is currently available. Then the program chooses whichever *bit rate* is best suited to current network conditions. The higher the bit rate, the better the sound quality. The range for downloaded media goes from about 28Kbps (28,000 bits per second) to 100Kbps (100,000 bits per second), with the largest number being the highest quality. Sometimes the highest quality transmission is shown as T1, which is a high-speed connection to the Internet. If you have a broadband connection such as DSL or cable, you may be able to listen to streaming media at that highest quality level.

Do remember that none of this really has anything to do with downloading music—it only applies to listening to music as it's being sent to your computer. When you download music to a file on your hard disk, there's no need for the transmission to be a smooth one, because you won't be listening to the music until after the file has been downloaded to your computer. More on downloading in a moment.

Licensed Media Files

For years, the music industry has made its money by recording music on some kind of medium—such as the LP album, the CD, or the cassette—and then selling the music to fans. The Internet takes away the need to store the music on some kind of medium to get it from seller to buyer. A fan can download a song and listen to it without driving to a music store and without buying an entire album or CD. While great for the consumers, it does pose a bit of a problem for the artists and publishers. That is, how do the artists and record companies make money if they're going to give the stuff away?

The common solution here is to distribute Internet music in *licensed files*. A licensed file is one that requires some kind of license to play and is designed to prevent the file from being randomly distributed without payment to the copyright holder. In some cases, you'll need to pay for the license. In others, you may just have to register with the music provider to get on its mailing list. Fortunately, Windows Media Player does a great job of keeping your licenses organized and out of your way, so that you really don't need to think about them. However, you do need to be aware that there are restrictions on using licensed files, including:

✦ Licenses can expire. If you download a "free preview" file, the license will expire after a specified time. Media Player will tell you when the license is about to expire and will not play the file after the license expires.

✦ Although licenses are often shipped with licensed files, there may be situations where you need to go to a separate site to purchase a license. Exactly how the licensing is handled, and what the costs are, is entirely up to the company that holds the copyright to the licensed file. There are no "generic" instructions for managing all types of licensed files — you have to follow whatever instructions are presented on the screen.

✦ Copying a licensed file to another computer, or e-mailing it to a friend, will generally *not* copy the license. The license usually allows you to play a specific file on a specific computer only. However you *can* copy many licensed files to a separate portable player without purchasing an additional license. Portable players are discussed a little later in this chapter.

Internet Music File Formats

One other important feature of music that's stored on the Internet is that not all songs are available in the same format. Unlike audio CDs, which always store songs in .cda format, songs on the Internet are available in several flavors. Windows Media Player is capable of playing songs that are stored in the popular MP3 (.mp3) format, as well as all the other formats listed earlier in Table 20-1. However, it can't play songs stored in RealAudio (.ram) or Liquid Audio (.lqt) format. For those formats you need to download the appropriate players from www.realaudio.com and www.liquidaudio.com, respectively.

In many cases you'll also be given a choice of quality file to download. If you're planning on just listening to the song as it's being streamed to your computer, you'll need to pick a quality that matches the speed of your Internet connection (although Media Player can also select the appropriate speed automatically.) However, if you're copying the file to your hard disk, you're better off downloading the highest-quality copy you can get.

As a rule, it's easy to tell which file is the highest quality. The higher the bps (or Kbps), the higher the quality of the recording. Higher quality also means a larger file and longer download time. But again, if you're copying it to your hard disk you really don't care how "smooth" the delivery is. So it's worth it to go for the highest quality. You may also come across some sites that list T1 as a quality rating. Consider that to be the highest quality available.

Downloading to the Media Library

Finally, if you want Windows Media Player to add downloaded music that you've purchased to its own Media Library, you'll need to choose Tools ⇨ Options from Media Player's menu bar. Then click on the Media Library tab and select the "Automatically add purchased music to my library" option. When you do so, Media Player will attempt to organize downloaded music in the same manner that it organizes music copied from audio CDs. If you don't choose this option, or if you end up in a site that forces you to choose the folder where you want to store the file, don't worry about it. You can always add the song to your Media Library later, as discussed in the Media Library section later in this chapter.

Now that you have a basic understanding of all these issues, you're ready to go online and start looking for music that you like.

Finding music online

Your search for music online can begin from Windows Media Player itself. Just click the Media Guide tab on the left side of window, and the larger window will show you the home page for WindowsMedia.com on the Web. The Home and Music tabs on that home page are good starting places for finding music on the Web. But be forewarned — finding actual songs that you can download can be a time-consuming experience. Most sites that offer downloadable music have a remarkable tendency to hide the downloads behind tons of ads and hype, which can get on your nerves if you're in a hurry. If you get impatient with Media Player, you might have better luck firing up Internet Explorer (or any other Web browser) and checking out some of the sites listed below:

- ✦ Atomic Pop: www.atomicpop.com
- ✦ Capitol Records: www.hollywoodandvine.com
- ✦ Emusic: www.emusic.com
- ✦ Epitonic: www.epitomic.com
- ✦ Hear and Now: www.cvp.net
- ✦ House of Blues: www.hob.com
- ✦ K-Tel: www.ktel.com

- ✦ Launch: www.launch.com
- ✦ Listen: www.listen.com
- ✦ MP3.com: www.mp3.com
- ✦ MTV: www.mtv.com
- ✦ Music Choice: www.musicchoice.com
- ✦ Music Maker: www.musicmaker.com
- ✦ MusicDownloads.com: www.musicdownloads.com
- ✦ Rave World: www.raveworld.net
- ✦ RealPlayer: www.realplayer.com
- ✦ Remote Music: www.remotemusic.com

As you cruise around these sites, you'll find samples to listen to, as well as files to download. Just listening is almost always free. However, you may not be able to listen to the entire track — only a portion of it; downloading may require a license and possibly a payment. Specific download instructions will have to come from the Web site you're downloading from, but the procedure is similar to that used in most downloads. You may be asked for the location on your hard disk to store the file — in which case you'll want to be consistent in choosing one (such as c:\my documents\my music). Then just wait for the download to complete.

Tip

If you're looking for music from a specific artist or group, consider going to a general search engine like www.yahoo.com and looking up the artist's or group's name. You may find their home page, which may, in turn, point you to some places for downloading their music.

Playing downloaded music

After you've downloaded a song from the Internet, you can play it using Media Player, or whatever player is suitable for the type of file you downloaded. Use My Computer or Windows Explorer to browse to the folder that contains the downloaded song. Then just click (or double-click) the downloaded file's icon or name to open it in the appropriate player. Optionally, you can open the player first (for example, Start ⇨ Programs ⇨ Accessories ⇨ Entertainment ⇨ Windows Media Player). Then choose File ⇨ Open from that program's menu bar and navigate to the folder that contains songs that are suitable for that player.

Whether or not the downloaded songs will be available in Media Player's Media Library depends on many factors. However, don't fret if the songs are not available. As you learn next, it's pretty easy to add songs to Media Player's library and to organize them there as well.

Can't play a sound file?

If you're given a choice of file format when downloading music, you should choose Windows Media Player, the .wma or .mp3 file type, or any other compatible file type listed earlier in Table 20-1. However, not all music distributors offer Media Player-compatible files. Some may offer files that are compatible only with other players, such as Real Audio (.ra files) and Liquid Audio (.lqt files). If you don't have a player for the type of file you've downloaded, you'll be taken to the Open With dialog box where you're supposed to choose a program to play the downloaded file, although that won't do you any good until you have the appropriate player. You can download players for the Real Audio and Liquid Audio file formats from www.realaudio.com and www.liquidaudio.com, respectively.

Media Library and Playlists

As you copy songs from audio CDs, and download songs form the Internet, remember that they're all stored on your hard disk. The Media Library component of Windows Media Player provides a means of organizing songs (and videos) into categories and groups. Some songs are automatically organized by group, album, and genre, provided that Media Player can get enough information from the Internet to categorize the clip. Others won't be in the library or organized at all; but that's easily rectified.

To view your media library, open Windows Media Player if it isn't open already. Then click the Media Library tab at the left edge of the player. The main window will divide into two columns. The left column is a typical "tree" of categories and subcategories, where a plus sign (+) indicates a category that can be expanded to show more information, and a minus sign (−) indicates an open category that can be collapsed to make room for other information. You can widen or narrow the left column by dragging the bar that separates the two columns to the left or right. Figure 20-10 is an example of a media library with several different types of media.

Bringing Media Library up to date

If at any time you feel that the Media Library isn't showing all of your music files, you can update the library manually by following these steps:

1. Choose Tools ➪ Search Computer for Media from Media Player's menu bar.

2. In the dialog box that appears, choose your hard disk (typically drive C:).

3. If you want to limit the search to a specific folder and its subfolders, use the Browse button to indicate the starting folder.

Figure 20-10: The Media Library tab of Media Player

4. If you want Media Player to include small sound effects files (.wav), choose the "Include Wav files found in System folders" option.

5. Click the Start Search button.

6. When the search is complete you can click the Close buttons on the small search dialog boxes that remain.

The left column of Media Library will now include any new files that were found along the way. Files that can be categorized automatically by Album, Artist, and Genre will be. Unknown songs copied from audio CDs will by placed in folders called Unknown Album, Unknown Artist, and so forth. Every file that was found that Media Player is capable of playing — even small sound effects files that were found if you selected "Include Wav files found in System folders" in Step 4 above will be listed in the All Audio category, as shown in Figure 20-11.

Tip   To change the width of the columns in the main window of Media Player, drag to the left or right the line separating the column headings Name, Artist, Album, and so forth.

Figure 20-11: The All Audio category in Media Library lists all audio files that Media Player can play.

Organizing your Media Library

The automatic categorizing that takes place with some CD and Internet audio is certainly handy, even though you're bound to end up with some "unknowns," as well as uncategorized files under All Audio. For example, suppose you find a line like the following under All Audio:

```
Track 3   Unknown Artist   Unknown Album... Unknown (Genre)
```

To find out what that track is, double-click it in the right column so you can hear it. Once you've determined which song the track represents, you can change the "unknowns" to more useful information. For example, suppose Track 3 above is a song titled *Go Now* by the Moody Blues, from an album titled *The Best of the Moody Blues*. To change Track 3 to Go Now, right-click on Track 3 and press the Delete (Del) key to delete that name. Type the new name and press Tab or click outside the edit area. You can do the same for the Artist, Album, and Genre columns. Thus, in my example, I'd change the Track 3 line to something like this:

```
Go Now         Moody Blues      Best of Moody Blues Rock
```

As you move things around, the categories in the left column of Media Player are updated automatically. If you're re-categorizing a lot of files, and start feeling overwhelmed, take a moment to close Media Player (by clicking its X button.). Catch your breath, re-open Media Player, and click on the Media Library tab in the left column again to see where you're at. You can also alphabetize all the entries in the All Audio category by any column (that is, by Name, Artist, Album, Genre) simply by clicking the column head. Be aware, however, that uncategorized items (such as Windows system sounds) will appear at the top of the list in some categories. So, you may need to scroll down to see the first item in the alphabetized list.

Caution   Pressing the Backspace key while editing an entry in Media Library will take you to a different page altogether. Click the Back button at the top of that page to return to where you were.

Deleting from the Media Library

You can delete an item from the Media Library at any time, but first you must decide whether you want to delete the song from the library only, or whether you want to actually delete it from your hard disk. If you want songs that you delete from the library to be deleted from the hard disk as well, choose Tools ➪ Options from Media Player's menu bar. Then, on the Media Library tab of the Options dialog box, choose "Remove file permanently when deleting from library" and then click OK.

To delete an item from the library just right-click its line in the larger pane of Media Player and choose Delete From Library from the menu that appears. Initially the item will be moved to the All Deleted Media folder near the bottom of the left column. Opening that category displays all files currently in that holding bin. To "undelete" a deleted item, click its line to choose it. Then right-click on the All Deleted Media folder in the left column and choose Restore Selected.

Creating playlists

A *playlist* is a selection of songs from your Media Library that you can play in a series or in random order. For example, you might create a playlist titled Dinner Music containing soft songs that you can listen to while dining. You could create another playlist titled Dance Music for wild, late-night parties. You can create as few or as many playlists as you like. And any song can belong to any number of playlists, giving you total flexibility.

To create a playlist in Media Player, click the New Playlist button that appears above the last column when you're viewing the Media Library in Media Player. Type in a meaningful name of your own choosing, and then click OK. A new icon with that title appears under My Playlists in the left column of Media Player.

To add songs to your playlist, stay in the Media Library tab and explore your songs by Album, Artists, Genre, or All Audio, however you prefer. To add a song to a playlist, click the song name in the right column to select the song. The Add to Playlist button above the columns will then be enabled. Click on the Add to Playlist button and choose Add to *Playlist name* from the menu that appears, where *Playlist name* is the name of the playlist to which you want to add the song. Optionally, you can right-click the song, choose Add to Playlist, and then choose the playlist to which you want to add the song.

Whenever you want to listen to just the songs in your playlist, open the My Playlists icon in the left column of Media Library. Then double-click on the name of the playlist you want to listen to. Figure 20-12 is an example in which I created a playlist named Dance Party and put a bunch of funky old disco tunes in it.

Figure 20-12: A playlist named Dance Party added to Media Player

To arrange songs in a playlist, first open the playlist by clicking its name in the left column of Media Library. Then, in the larger right column, click any song that you want to move. Then use the "Moves media up" and "Moves media down" button above the list to move the song to a new position in the list. To delete a song from a playlist, right-click its name and choose Delete From Playlist. To delete an entire playlist, right-click its name in the left column of Media Player and choose Delete.

Internet Radio

Many radio stations now broadcast over the Internet, which means that you can listen to the station no matter where you are in relation to its broadcast origin. Just open up Windows Media Player in the normal manner, and click on Radio Tuner in the left column. Media Player will split into two columns as in Figure 20-13. The left column contains "presets"—radio stations that have been preset for instant access with a single mouse click—the same idea as a car radio, where you can adjust buttons to jump to favorite stations. The column on the right lists all available radio stations.

Figure 20-13: The Radio Tuner tab in Media Player

To listen to a radio station, just click its line in either the left or right column of Media Player. Then click on the blue Play button that appears to the left of the line. Optionally, you can just double-click on the name of the radio station you want to listen to. In the right column under STATION FINDER, you can choose a format to search for, such as Country, Rock, or even Police Scanners!

To create your own list of preset radio stations, choose My Presets from the drop-down list under PRESETS. Or choose Create Preset List from that option to create a new collection of radio stations. As you explore radio stations, you can add them to the current preset list just by clicking the Add button that separates the left and right columns of Media Player. To delete a station from a presets list, just click its name in the left column, and then click the Delete button. It's all fun and easy, and you'll no doubt figure out all the ins and outs just by experimenting with your options. You just have to be a little bit patient because, unlike a real radio, selecting a radio station in Media Player doesn't necessarily make that station audible right away. Sometimes you have to wait a short time after selecting the station before you can hear anything.

Copying Music to Portable Devices

Since the rise of audio on the Internet, numerous companies have created small, portable stereo devices capable of playing music in MP3 and other formats. Typically, they're called MP3 Players. If you haven't seen one yet, and would like to see what's currently available on the market, take a look at MP3's hardware page at www.hardware.mp3.com. More often than not, when you buy such a device, you'll get software and instructions for copying songs from your computer or the Internet right into the player. Most likely, you'll need to use the software and instructions that came with the device in order to copy music to the device.

As I write this chapter, Windows Media Player has the capability to copy music to Cassio's Cassiopeia E-100 and E-105 portable handheld computers with the Windows CE operating system on them. Whether or not future versions of Windows Media Player will be capable of copying to other devices remains to be seen, but assuming you do have a compatible portable player, you can use Media Player to copy audio files to your portable device in any of these formats:

✦ MP3 (.mp3)

✦ Windows Media (.wma and .asf)

✦ Windows Wave (.wav)

Copying licensed files is usually no problem. When you downloaded the licensed file from the Internet, the license probably came with it, and Media Player automatically keeps track of those licenses. So, when you copy a licensed file to your portable device, Media Player will copy the appropriate license as well. The one catch is that some players require you to enter a hardware device serial number. If so, you can get the necessary information from your particular device only.

Many portable devices use some kind of memory card, as opposed to a disk or tape, to store recorded music. In those cases, you might be pretty limited on how much music you can get into the device. The trade-off becomes one of quantity versus quality. If you want to get lots of music on your portable device, you'll need to use a lower-quality bit rate, such as 28 Kbps. If you want quality, you can use a higher bit rate, like 128Kbps, although you can't squeeze as much music onto the player at that high rate. When you copy files to your portable device, Windows Media Player automatically uses the Windows Media Audio (WMA) compression technology to squeeze as much music into as little space as possible. You can choose your own sound quality by following these steps:

1. Choose Tools ➭ Options form Media Player's menu bar.

2. Click the Portable Device tab.

3. If you want Media Player to automatically decide how best to compress the files, leave the first option selected. Otherwise, choose the second option and then move the slider to the quality that you want. Your options are:

   • **Radio Quality (32 Kbps):** The lowest quality setting, this one uses the least space. It's not great for all forms of music. But it's certainly acceptable for spoken voice audio and .mp3 files stored at a bandwidth of 64Kbps.

   • **Medium Quality (64 Kbps):** Takes up less space than CD quality, but comes close to CD quality. Works well with as 128-Kbps .mp3 and Windows Media files that have already been compressed.

   • **CD Quality (128 Kbps):** Produces CD-quality sound, though each song will require a lot of storage space in your portable player.

4. After making your selection click OK.

When you're ready to copy files to your portable device, plug the device into the computer as per the manufacturer's instructions. Start up Windows Media Player normally, and click on the Portable Device tab in the left column. Choose the device name from the Music on Device tab's drop-down list. If you've already copied music to the device, that tab will list the songs that are currently stored in the device. If you want to delete any songs to make room for new ones, click whatever song you want to delete and then click the Delete (X) button next to the drop-down list.

On the Music to Copy tab, select All Audio or any other category from the drop-down list. Then place a check mark next to songs you want to copy to the portable device. Keep any eye on the odometer below the Music on Device tab to make sure you don't use more than 100 percent of the available storage space. After you've selected the songs to copy, just click the Copy Music button above the Music to Copy tab, and follow the instructions on the screen.

Burning audio CDs

The ultimate in portability would be to copy music from your hard drive onto a standard audio CD. That way, you can listen to the music in any CD player, be it the one in your home, your car, or something you wear. Unfortunately, Windows Me does not have any built-in capabilities for "burning" music onto audio CDs. That sort of operation requires special hardware and software. On the hardware side, you need a CD-R or CD-RW drive in your system. On the software side, you need some program that's compatible with your hardware.

Typically, when you buy a CD-R or CD-RW drive, you'll get software that works with that hardware. Of course, I have no idea what that software might be, so I can't help you with that. There are some important things to remember though. For one, the files must be stored in CD audio (.cda) format on the audio CD. You don't want to copy .mp3, .wma, or any other formats directly to the audio CD. If you do, you automatically make the CD into a data CD that only computers can work with.

This presents a bit of a catch-22 because virtually all music that you store on your hard disk is likely to be stored there in .mp3, .wma, .wav, or some other format that requires a player on your computer. So, the question becomes, is it possible to convert .mp3, .wma, and other formats to .cda before or during the process of "burning" tracks to the audio CD? The answer to that question is a resounding yes and no. At least, for the moment.

As I write this chapter, I know of no software that will automatically convert .wma files to .cda while burning them to an audio CD. (Of course, that could change by the time you read this.) However, Adaptec's EZ CD Creator 4 and Adaptec's SoundStream (www.adaptec.com) are both capable of converting .mp3 and .wav files to .cda while you're burning the audio CD. Both are commercial products that you need to purchase at a computer store. There may be other products available; I haven't researched the market. I mention the Adaptec products because that's what I'm familiar with, have been using for years, and I know that they work well with a wide variety of CD-R and CD-RW drives.

But the fact that the Adaptec products can create audio CDs from .mp3 and .wav formats still leaves the .wma format out of the picture. There is, however, a program that can convert .wma (and many other formats) to .mp3 or .wav, which, in turn, can be burned to an audio CD using either of the Adaptec software products. The conversion program is called Media Wizard by CDH Productions. It's available for download at http://www.cdnow.com.

Thus, if you use a program such as Media Wizard to copy all your songs to .mp3 or .wav format and then use one of the Adaptec products to actually burn the CD, you'll be able to create your own custom audio CDs from any music on your hard disk. Just do remember that the music is almost certainly copyrighted. So, if you sell those CDs you're leaving yourself wide open to a copyright infringement case that you're certain to lose, though I doubt that anyone will make a federal case out of creating custom CDs for your own listening pleasure. But I'm not a lawyer, and that's just a personal opinion.

Recording Sound

You may well want to record sound that doesn't come prepackaged from an audio CD or from the Internet. For example, you might want to record your own voice, or music that's stored on cassette tape, LP, or some other format. For those items, you can use the simple Sound Recorder that comes with Windows Me, although there are probably more sophisticated sound editing programs on the market that you could use.

Adaptec's EZ CD Creator 4 mentioned in the preceding section comes with CD Spin Doctor, which can help you record music from LPs, tape cassettes, and other sources. Spin Doctor also provides tools for cleaning up the hisses, pops, and scratches that often accompany older recordings.

To record your own voice with Sound Recorder, you first need to have a microphone or headset plugged into your sound card or computer. Then you'll want to make sure it's capturing sound, and the mixer is set up to record from that device. Here's how:

1. Click the Start button and choosing Settings ⇨ Control Panel ⇨ Sounds and Multimedia.

2. Click on the Voice tab.

3. Make sure that the device you'll be speaking into is selected under Preferred Device under Voice Capture. For example, in Figure 20-14 I selected my Telex USB microphone.

4. Click the Volume button beneath your selection and make sure the Mute option isn't selected and the Volume isn't turned down too low.

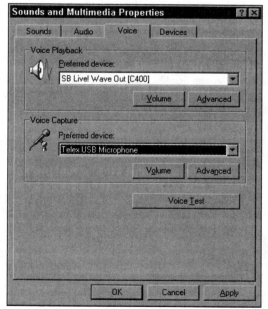

Figure 20-14: Sounds and Multimedia Properties set up to record from Telex USB Microphone

5. Close the little Volume slider and then click OK to close the Sounds and Multimedia Properties dialog box.

For the cleanest recording, it's a good idea to disable all other recording devices. You'll do this through the mixer, which you can open by double-clicking the speaker icon in the taskbar, or by clicking the Start button and choosing Programs ➪ Accessories ➪ Entertainment ➪ Volume Control. Choose Options ➪ Properties from the mixer's menu bar, choose Recording, and then click OK. Make sure that the Microphone's Select box is selected (checked) and then close the Mixer. All other input devices can be left unselected, because you probably don't want to record from them simultaneously. You might also have them mute the wav output so there's no feedback.

Tip   You can leave the mixer open while recording to adjust the sensitivity of the microphone or other recording device.

To start Sound Recorder:

1. Click the Start button and choose Programs ➪ Accessories ➪ Entertainment ➪ Sound Recorder.

2. Choose File ➪ New from Sound Recorder's menu bar is you want to record a new file.

3. Select a recording quality by choosing File ➪ Properties from Sound Recorder's menu bar. Then click Convert Now in the Properties for Sound dialog box that appears.

4. Choose a recording quality from the drop-down list. Your options from lowest to highest quality are Telephone (11Kbps), Radio (22Kbps), and CD (172Kbps).

Tip   As usual, the trade-off is size versus quality. CD-quality recording creates much larger files than Radio or Telephone Quality recordings. But radio and telephone qualities may be sufficient for voice.

5. Click the OK buttons on the open dialog boxes to save your settings and return to Sound Recorder.

6. Click the Record button (it has a red circle on it).

7. Start talking. The green line should provide feedback if Sound Recorder is picking up the sound, as in Figure 20-15.

Figure 20-15: Sound Recorder is recording my voice through a microphone.

8. When you've finished recording, click the Stop button in Sound Recorder.

9. To test your recording, click the Seek to Start button in the lower left corner of Sound Recorder. Then click the Play button.

10. To save the recording choose File ⇨ Save, choose a folder, and enter a filename. Sound Recorder will automatically save your voice as a Wave file, adding the filename extension .wav.

In the future, you can play the file by clicking (or double-clicking) its icon in My Computer, Windows Explorer, or Search. Or you can start Sound Recorder, or any other program that's capable of playing Wave files, and use that program's File ⇨ Open menu options to open the file and play it.

Recording other sound sources

If you want to record from a cassette tape player or audio CD player, you connect that player's Line Out plug to the sound card's Line In plug, using whatever cable is appropriate for your hardware. Be sure to check the manual that came with your sound card before recording from devices through the Line In jack on your card. If you plug in the wrong type of sound source, you could permanently ruin your sound card! This is so important, that it bears repeating:

Caution
You can permanently damage sound hardware by plugging in an unacceptable device or by plugging a device into the wrong plug. Refer to your sound card manual for specific instructions before you plug in any device.

Next, you may need to use your mixer to specify the device from which you want to record. The way you perform this step varies from one sound card to the next. Refer to your sound card documentation if you run into any problems. As a general rule, you can follow these steps to isolate a single device from which to record and control the sensitivity of the recording:

1. Open your mixer (Start ⇨ Programs ⇨ Accessories ⇨ Entertainment ⇨ Volume Control).

2. Choose Options ⇨ Properties from the mixer's menu bar.

3. Choose Recording and then choose those input types whose volume you want to control from the list near the bottom of the dialog box. For example, if you've plugged the device into the Line In plug of your sound card, make sure Line In is selected and its volume is at least half way up.

4. Open Sound Recorder (click the Start button and choose Programs ⇨ Accessories ⇨ Entertainment ⇨ Sound Recorder).

5. To adjust the quality of the recording, choose File ⇨ Properties ⇨ Convert Now from Sound Recorder's menu bar. Choose Radio, Telephone, or CD quality as described in the previous section and then click OK to close the open dialog boxes.

6. Click the Record button to start recording.

7. Click the Play button on the device from which you're recording.

8. When you reach the end of the material that you want to record, click the Stop button on Sound Recorder. (You can stop whatever device you're recording from as well.)

You're done. To listen to the recording click the Seek to Start and Play buttons in Sound Recorder. To save the recording in a file, choose File ➪ Save from Sound Recorder's menu bar. The sound will be saved as a Wave (.wav) file.

Special effects and editing

Sound Recorder provides some rudimentary sound-editing capabilities. For example, you can add echo, change the speed of the playback, change its volume, cut out sections of the file, even insert one file into another. Everything you need to know is right in Sound Recorder's help. Just choose Help ➪ Help Topics from Sound Recorder's menu bar, and you're on your way. Just remember that any changes you make will not be permanent until you save the file using File ➪ Save or File ➪ Save As.

For more professional editing, there are plenty of sound editors on the market for Windows. There are also lots of shareware audio editors available at TUCOWS. See `http://tucows.fast.net/audioedit95.html` for audio editors. To see the full range of Windows Me-compatible audio programs, go to `http://woffice.tucows.com/window95.html`.

Assigning Sound Effects to Events

You can assign sounds, stored in .wav files, to various events that occur in Windows. You can play one sound when Windows starts, another when an error message appears onscreen, and so on. To assign system sounds, follow these steps:

1. Choose Start ➪ Settings ➪ Control Panel.

2. Open the Sounds and Multimedia icon. It should open with the Sounds tab visible as in Figure 20-16.

3. Select the name of any event to which you want to assign a sound. Events with speaker icons already have sounds assigned to them, but you can change the sounds if you want.

4. Assign a sound to the selected event by choosing a sound from the Name drop-down list, or by clicking the Browse button and then navigating to the Wave file of your choice.

Tip

To choose the sound that plays when Windows first starts, assign a wave file to the Start Windows option in the list of sound events.

5. To preview a sound, click the Play button next to the Preview box. For details on a particular sound, click the Details button.

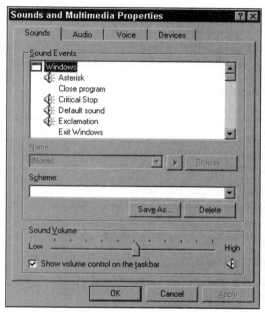

Figure 20-16: The Sounds tab lets you assign sound effects to events.

6. Repeat Steps 3 to 5 to assign sounds to as many events as you want.

7. To save your current mix of sounds, choose Save As, and then enter a name.

8. When you finish, choose OK to return to the Control Panel. Close the Control Panel, if you want.

The next time one of the events to which you assigned a sound occurs, you'll hear that sound. If ever you want to turn off all sound events, or if you want to return to the default sound scheme that came with Windows, repeat steps 1 and 2 above and choose No Sounds to turn off all sounds or Windows Default to return to the default sound scheme from the Scheme drop-down list.

You can install some fun sound schemes from your original Windows 98 disks or CD-ROM disc. Click the Start button and choose Settings ⇨ Control Panel ⇨ Add/Remove Programs and click the Windows Setup tab. Choose the Multimedia component, and then click the Details button. Scroll down to and select (check) the Multimedia Sound Schemes and Sample Sounds components, click the OK buttons, and then follow the instructions onscreen. The new sound schemes will be available from the drop-down list described in the previous Step 4.

Of course, the Internet is home to many thousands of small sound effect-sized Wave files. Just go to any search engine, such as www.yahoo.com, and search for "free wav files" or something similar.

Summary

Computers are transforming the ways in which we purchase, listen to, and record music. Windows Me provides support for virtually all types of sound files, particularly through the Windows Media Player component. To wrap up the amount of information covered in this chapter:

✦ Your PC needs to have a sound card installed, as well as speakers or headphones, to get sound.

✦ Windows Media Player can play a wide variety of sound file formats including the popular .wav, .mp3, and .wma, as well as others.

✦ To listen to an audio CD in your PC, just put the CD into the CD-ROM drive and wait for Media Player to open up and start playing songs.

✦ As an alternative to buying music on CD, you can now buy albums, as well as individual songs, online at numerous music sites on the Web.

✦ Windows Media Player provides access to many radio stations.

✦ To record downloaded or copied music to a portable device, follow the instructions that came with the device.

✦ Windows Me alone can't create audio CDs from songs stored on a hard disk, but there are many products, such as Adaptec's EZ CD Creator 4, that can.

✦ To assign sounds to events that occur as you use your computer, open the Control Panel and then open the Sounds and Multimedia icon.

✦   ✦   ✦

Enhanced TV, DVD, and Video

You can use your computer to watch TV and movies on DVD. While it may seem impractical at first, there are good applications. For example, suppose you trade stocks from your PC. You could have a small window on your monitor (or one of several monitors) showing the realtime broadcast from some investment channel, while you're doing other things with your computer. Furthermore, you don't have to sit bolt upright at a desk and watch TV or movies on your computer screen. If your graphics card has a TV Out option, you can plug your computer into any TV, and use that as your screen. Then your can use the TV screen to watch TV and movies, and to browse the Internet or whatever at the same time. Add in a wireless mouse and keyboard, and you can easily sit in your favorite recliner while enjoying all that your TV and computer combined have to offer!

Watching TV

Web TV for Windows, which comes with Windows Me, enables you to watch TV on your desktop. Windows Me can receive and display TV signals from broadcast TV (antenna), cable TV, and from DIRECTV direct broadcast satellite (DBS) service. Windows Me can't do any of this, however, until you install appropriate hardware. You need a National Television System Committee (NTSC) card or a Phase Alternation Line (PAL) card. Those cards are readily available at most computer stores. In fact, if you tell the salesperson you want to watch TV on your Windows Me PC, I'm sure he or she can find you the correct card. To hear TV broadcasts, you also need a sound card. If you already have a sound card in your system, you can use that one. If you're not the type to monkey around inside computers, you may want to get your dealer to install the card(s) for you.

Starting and configuring Web TV for Windows

Once you have all your TV hardware installed, either by a professional or by installing it yourself, you can do either of the following to start Windows Me Web TV for Windows:

✦ Click the Launch Web TV for Windows button in the Quick Launch toolbar.

✦ Or, click the Start button and choose Programs ⇨ Accessories ⇨ Entertainment ⇨ Web TV for Windows.

If Web TV for Windows isn't available on your PC, you can install it using the Windows Setup tab of Add/Remove Programs. If you need a reminder on how to do this, see Chapter 25.

If you've never used Web TV for Windows before, you'll come to a screen that lets you scan for channels. This only happens the first time you start the program. Just click the Start Scan button and follow the instructions on the screen. When the scan is completed, enter your Zip code and download the TV listing for your area. You might also be taken through a brief tour of using the Program Guide, which you'll also learn about in this chapter. Again, just keep following the onscreen instructions until you get to the "You're Done" screen; then click the Finish button.

After you've completed the first-time configuration, Web TV for Windows will start up without all the configuration rigmarole. It's not easy to say how it will look when you first start it — it all depends on how you left it. But you should either see the screen filled with a TV show, or the Program Guide shown in Figure 21-1. If you get the full-screen view and want to get to the Program Guide, follow these simple steps:

1. Click the TV picture, and then move the mouse pointer to the very top of the screen (or press the F10 key) to view the TV Banner (described below.)

2. Click on the Guide button on the TV Banner.

Using the TV banner and toolbar

The main controls for watching TV are on the TV Viewer's banner and toolbar. Whenever the TV Viewer is open, you can press and release the Alt key or the F10 key to display the banner and toolbar, both shown in Figure 21-2. The TV banner is the bar across the top. The TV toolbar is below the banner and contains buttons. Both the banner and the toolbar appear/disappear when you press the F10 or Alt key.

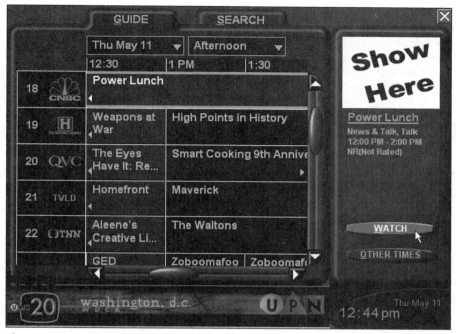

Figure 21-1: Web TV for Windows

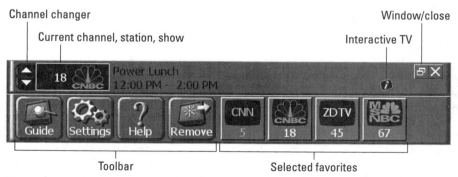

Figure 21-2: The TV Banner and toolbar made visible by pressing the F10 or Alt key

When the TV Viewer is displayed in full-screen mode, you can also display the banner and toolbar by moving the mouse pointer to the top of the screen and holding it there for a second or two. If you have a remote control for your TV Viewer, click its Menu button to view the banner.

The controls on the banner and toolbar are simple to work. Some of the major features such as the Program Guide, Enhancements, and favorites are discussed in more detail a little later in this chapter, but here's a brief summary of the controls:

✦ **Channel changer:** Click the small up and down arrows to go from channel to channel. You can also select the current channel number and then replace it by typing a new number. Press Enter after typing the number of the channel to which you want to go.

✦ **Current channel, station, show:** As you change channels, this area shows the channel number, station logo, specific show that's on, and that show's start and end times.

✦ **Interactive TV button:** When you're viewing a show that offers interactivity, the *i* button turns gold and interaction is turned on automatically. If you want to turn off interactivity, you can click that button. The button has no effect on normal non-interactive programs.

✦ **Window/Close buttons:** Click the Restore button to switch from full-screen to windowed view. Click the Close (X) button to close the TV Viewer.

✦ **Guide button:** Click the Guide button to go straight to the Program Guide, discussed a little later in this chapter.

✦ **Settings button:** Lets you decide which channels are, and are not, visible in the Program Guide.

✦ **Help button:** Takes you to the online help for the TV Viewer.

✦ **Add/Remove button:** This button is sometimes labeled Add, and sometimes labeled Remove, depending on what you're doing at the moment. It lets you add channels to, and remove buttons from, the collection of favorite channels that are just to the right of the button.

✦ **Selected favorites:** Channels you've deemed as favorites appear in this area.

TV volume control

Volume control on the TV can be a little tricky. To get any sound at all, you will need to run a small cable from your graphics or TV card to the Line In port of your sound card. Typically your graphics or TC card will come with the appropriate cable and instructions for making the connection. Once you've made that connection, the Line In Slider in the Volume Control (mixer) is what determines the relative volume of the TV. As you may recall, you can open the Volume Control at any time by double-clicking the small speaker icon in the indicators section of the taskbar, or by clicking the Start button and choosing Programs ➪ Accessories ➪ Entertainment ➪ Volume Control. If there is no slider for the Line In volume, choose Options ➪ Properties from the mixer's menu bar, and make sure Line-In is selected in the list of volume controls to display.

The master volume control will also control the volume of the TV, although it's not easy to get to when the TV is in full-screen mode. To increase or decrease the volume in full-screen mode, use the Alt or F10 key to display the banner, and then click the Restore button up near the Close button. Then click the speaker indicator in the taskbar to get to the main volume control slider as discussed in Chapter 20.

Using the Program Guide

The Program Guide is the interactive equivalent of the traditional printed *TV Guide*. To keep your Program Guide up-to-date, you may need to download listings from time to time. To do that, press Alt or F10 to display the banner and then click the Guide button in the toolbar. Then look for a station named TV C — with a show named TV Configuration. It could be a very low channel, such as Channel 1, or it could be a high channel such as 96. When you find the show titled TV Configuration, click it and then click the Watch button. You'll come to a TV Configuration Wizard. Click the Go To button and choose Get TV Listing to get to the screen shown in Figure 21-3.

Figure 21-3: Web TV Configuration page for updating your TV listings

If you haven't already done so, enter your Zip code where indicated. If you have Internet access, click Microsoft TV Listings and follow the instructions on the screen. Otherwise, click the Next button and follow the instructions that appear next.

To learn more about using the Program Guide, click the Go To button in TV Configuration and choose Program Guide tour.

When you've finished using the TV Configuration Wizard, click the Go To button and choose Configuration Complete. There you can click the Finish button to go back to the Program Guide or TV. If you need additional help, open the TV Banner by pressing Alt or F10. Then click the Help button in the toolbar.

Searching for shows

While you're in the Program Guide, you'll notice there are a couple of tabs at the top of the screen labeled Guide and Search. Clicking the Search tab (or Other Times button) will take you to a screen like the one in Figure 21-4.

Figure 21-4: The Search tab of the Program Guide

The Search tab offers several tools for finding programs that suit your interests. For example:

> ✦ Click the All days drop-down list to specify how many days of programming you want to include in the search.

✦ Click the Sort by time button to sort the programming listing by the time the show starts.

✦ Click a category in the left column to limit the display to shows in that category.

✦ Or, type some word or phrase into the Search box and then click the Search button.

The Search For option is really cool. For instance, say I type "football" as the word to search for and then I click the Search button. All the shows listed will be ones with the word *football* in their titles or descriptions. If you find a show you'd like to watch, but it isn't on yet, you can click the Remind button to set up a reminder to watch the show. You can also click the Other Times button to see what other times the show comes on.

Viewing closed captions

If a show offers closed captions and you want to see them, get to the toolbar in the usual manner (press Alt or F10). Click the Settings button and then choose (check) the Show Closed Captioning option near the bottom of the Settings dialog box.

Viewing interactive (enhanced) TV

Interactive TV is slowly working its way into our day-to-day lives. Interactivity can take many forms — participating in a game show, viewing sports statistics, joining in a chat room, touring schedules of popular bands, and more. If a particular show offers interactivity, the little *i* button in the toolbar will by fringed with gold. Clicking that button will give you the opportunity to turn interactivity on or off.

Some game shows offer interactivity through their Web sites as well. If a TV show tells you to visit www.whatever.com, use Internet Explorer (Chapter 7) or any other Web browser of your choosing to visit that site and learn more about playing along.

Turning off the TV

Turning off the TV is as easy as can be. Just click the Close (X) button in the upper-right corner of the screen. If you don't see the X button, just press Alt or F10, or click on the TV show and move the cursor to the top of the screen. The TV Banner will appear with the Close (X) button in its upper-right corner.

To keep up with changes in Web TV, or learn more about underlying technologies, visit the Microsoft TV Platform site at www.microsoft.com/tv.

Watching DVD Movies

I imagine just about everyone these days knows about DVD. A DVD disk is the same shape and size as a CD disk. However, the DVD disk can hold far more information than a CD. In fact, a DVD can store an entire full-length motion picture. And as I'm sure you know, you can rent and buy DVDs at many of the same stores where you get video tapes.

You can't read DVD disks in a standard CD-ROM drive. You'll need a DVD drive instead. Most DVD drives can read CD-ROMs (as well as audio CDs), so it's not necessary to have both types of drives in your system. On the other hand, there's no reason why you can't have both types of drives.

If your PC doesn't already have a DVD drive, it's fairly easy to add one. You'll want to look for a new ("third generation" or so) drive, as some of the early DVD drives for computers didn't work very well. Most DVD drives will also come with a *decoder card,* which needs to be installed in a PCI slot. If you're not familiar with installing hardware and don't know if you have a spare PCI slot in your system, any computer repair or upgrade service can find out for you and install the drive. Your system will also need a sound card. Any sound card will do — it's not necessary to get a separate card just for the DVD.

Theoretically, when you install a DVD drive in your system, Windows Me automatically installs a DVD player. But for reasons unknown, I've never seen it. My experience has been that when you install a DVD player, you also get player software for that hardware that allows you to watch the DVDs. For example, after installing a Philips DVD drive with REALMagic software, I can use the DVD player shown in Figure 21-5 to watch movies. (The movie itself appears in a separate window.) The DVD player on the screen offers the same controls as most physical DVD players. The buttons show standard icons for Play, Stop, Eject, Rewind, and so forth, as shown in the figure.

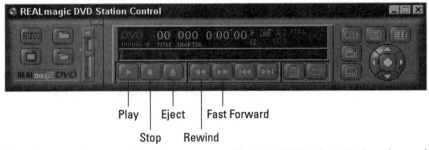

Figure 21-5: The DVD player that comes with the REALMagic DVD decoder card

DVD on the PC is evolving at a rapid pace. As I write this chapter, most people use DVD drives to watch DVD movies. However, because a single DVD disk can hold as much as 23 times the amount of information that a CD-ROM disk holds, there will no doubt be highly advanced games and other software packages shipping on DVD in the near future. In fact, Microsoft already offers a DVD version of its Microsoft Encarta Suite on DVD. The single disk contains the Encyclopedia, Virtual Globe, and Bookshelf products. If shipped on CD-ROM rather than DVD, the suite would occupy about five disks as opposed to one. If you're interested in learning more about DVD, or keeping up with changes in this rapidly evolving technology, check out some of these Web sites:

✦ DVD Empire: `www.dvdempire.com`

✦ DVD Superstore: `www.dvdsuperstore.com`

✦ Net Flix: `www.netflix.com`

✦ Reel.com: `www.reel.com`

Summary

This chapter has covered a couple of technologies that, on the one hand, are mature and well supported by Windows Me. And yet, on the other hand, they're rapidly evolving and merging into Internet technology to forms of entertainment as yet unimagined. The skills you've learned in this chapter will certainly put you well on your way to being part of this evolution. In this chapter, you learned the following:

✦ If you want to watch TV on your computer, you need to install a graphics card that has TV capabilities built in, or a TV add-on card to supplement your existing graphics card.

✦ Once you've installed TV hardware on your computer, you can use the TV viewer to watch TV (Start ➪ Programs ➪ Accessories ➪ Entertainment ➪ WebTV for Windows).

✦ When in the TV Viewer program, press Alt or F10 to make the TV banner and toolbar visible. In full-screen mode, you can move the cursor to the top of the screen to open the banner and toolbar.

✦ Use the TV C (TV Configuration) channel to set up or change your Web TV settings.

✦ The Program Guide enables you to download current TV listings from the Internet.

✦ If your computer has a DVD drive, you can use it to watch DVD movies on your PC.

✦ If your graphics card has a TV Out port, or you purchase and install a TV Out card, you can use your television as though it were a computer monitor.

✦   ✦   ✦

Working with Digital Images

T his chapter covers all the basic skills necessary to work
with *digital images*. As the name implies, a digital image
is some sort of picture stored on a computer disk that you can
view on the computer screen. Two of the more common methods of creating digital images are digital cameras and scanners. You can also draw images directly on the screen, if you
have some sort of illustration program and some artistic tal-
ent. You can also purchase pre-drawn images, know as *clip art*,
in case your artistic abilities fall into the "non-existent" category, like my own. *Screenshots*, like most of the pictures in this
book, are yet another type of digital image.

Digital Image File Types

Perhaps the most perplexing thing about digital images is the
wide range of file formats used to store these images. Table
22-1 lists types of image files and the filename extensions typically used to name images stored in each format. As daunting
as the list may seem, most images are stored in the popular
JPEG, GIF, BMP (bitmap) formats, and perhaps a few other formats. Furthermore, if you get a good, flexible graphics program such as Paint Shop Pro (www.jasc.com), you can easily
open an image in any of those formats, change the image to
your liking, and then save it in whichever format you wish. It's
not necessary to know the complexities of how the image is
stored in each different type of format.

Table 22-1
Some of the File Formats Used for Storing Digital Images

Format	Filename extension
Amiga	.iff
Autodesk Drawing Interchange	.dxf
CompuServe Graphics Interchange	.gif
Computer Graphics Metafile	.cgm
Corel Clipart	.cmx
CorelDraw Drawing	.cdr
Deluxe Paint	.lbm
Dr. Halo	.cut
Encapsulated PostScript	.eps, .ai, .ps
FlashPix	.fpx
GEM Paint	.img
HP Graphics Language	.hgl
Joint Photographic Experts Group	.jpg, .jif, .jpeg
Kodak Digital Camera	.kdc
Kodak Photo CD	.pcd
Lotus PIC	.pic
Macintosh PICT	.pct
MacPaint	.mac
Micrografx Draw	.drw
Microsoft Paint	.msp
Paint Shop Pro	.psp
PC Paint	.pic
Photoshop	.psd
Portable Bitmap	.pbm
Portable Greymap	.pgm
Portable Network Graphics	.png
Portable Pixelmap	.ppm

Format	Filename extension
Raw File Format	.raw
SciTex Continuous Tone	.sct, .ct
Sun RasterImage	.ras
Tagged Image File Format	.tif, .tiff
Truevision Targa	.tga
Ventura/GEM Drawing	.gem
Windows Clipboard	.clp
Windows Enhanced Metafile	.emf
Windows Meta File	.wmf
Windows or CompuServe RLE	.rle
Windows or OS/2 Bitmap	.pmp
Windows or OS/2 Device Independent Bitmap	.dib
WordPerfect Bitmap or Vector	.wpg
Zsoft Multipage Paintbrush	.dcx
Zsoft Paintbrush	.pcx

Bitmap versus vector images

Despite the many different file formats and extensions, digital image formats can be broken down into two main categories — *bitmap* images and *vector* images.

Bitmap images are made up of tiny colored dots, which you can see if you look at an image with a magnifying glass. In fact, with newspapers you hardly even need a magnifying glass to see the individual dots that make up a picture. The bitmap file essentially just stores information about the color of each dot. The vast majority of image files, including those from cameras and scanners, are bitmap images.

Vector images store information about the size, curvature, and length of lines in the drawing, as well as color information. Vector images are relatively rare, and created only with illustration programs used by professional artists. In other words some — but not all — line drawings and other hand-drawn art images are stored in vector file format. While there are a handful programs that can read and write only one type of image or the other, there are also plenty of programs that can read and write both types. For example, the aforementioned Paint Shop Pro program can open vector images as easily as it can open bitmap images. You can also convert an image from one type to the other using Paint Shop Pro.

Image Quality and File Size

When computer people talk about image quality, they're not talking about whether a image is "good" (the subject is smiling) or "bad" (the subject has one eye closed and is drooling). They're talking about the *resolution* (how many dots per inch) and *color depth* (the number of unique colors) contained within the image. Simply stated, the higher the resolution and color depth, the higher the "quality" of the image. The reason it matters is that the higher the quality of the image, the larger the file required to store the image. And the larger the file the more disk space it eats up and the longer it takes to transmit across a wire (which matters when publishing photos on the Internet).

Let's look more closely at those two buzzwords, *resolution* and *color depth*. An image's resolution is measured in dots per inch (dpi). The term "dot" here is synonymous with *pixel*—one tiny little dot on a computer screen or printed page. If you look at a computer monitor or printed page with a strong enough magnifying glass, you can see that all images are actually made up of tiny dots. The effect is even more apparent in a newspaper comic strip where the dots are especially large and visible with even a weak magnifying glass. The advantage of using a high resolution (lots of dots per inch) is that you get a sharper, crisper image. But because you're packing more dots into each inch of the picture, the amount if disk space the file eats up grows.

Color depth refers to the number of unique colors in the image. As an example of an image with a low color depth, think again of a comic strip in a newspaper. Since there is no shading in such images, the cartoonist can get away with using only a few unique colors. In some cases only 16 unique colors will be sufficient. In others, 256 colors might be required.

Since each dot's color needs to be stored as part of the graphic image's file, the more possible colors there are in the image, the more *bits* of information it takes to define each color. A *bit* is the smallest unit of information a computer can work with. The bit can have only two possible values, either "on" (or 1) or "off" (or 0). Thus if you use one bit to store information about colors, you get only two choices of colors, 0 or 1. Those two values translate to black and white. So if the entire image requires a million dots to render, but there are only two possible colors per dot, the image could be expressed with exactly 1 million bits—one bit per dot.

But suppose the image needs at least 16 unique colors. In that case, you need four bits of data to define each dot's color. Why four? Because if you look at all the combination of four bits where each bit can be either 1 or 0—0000, 0001, 0011, 0010, 1111—you end up with sixteen possible combinations of ones and zeros. Thus, if the picture contains a million bits and requires four bits to express the color of each dot, the picture requires four million bits (or 500,000 bytes–4 million bits / 8-bits byte) of disk space to store—which makes the file four times as large as the image in pure black and white.

If the picture requires 256 unique colors, you need eight bits of information to store each unique color value. Hence a picture with a million dots would then require

8 million bits of information — eight times the amount of disk space required by the black and white picture containing a million bits. The real world contains many millions of colors. Hence, a photograph of the real world will also contain many millions of colors. To be able to express the color of each dot in a photograph containing millions of colors, you might need 24 bits, or 32 bits of information to express each color. So a graphic image file that contains a million dots will require 24 million, or 32 million bits of disk space (3 million or 4 million bytes, respectively).

Basically it boils down to getting the most bang for your storage and transmission time buck. You don't want to give an image more resolution or color depth than it needs because doing so wastes disk space and time if the file is to be transmitted across the Internet or some other network. On the other hand, if you skimp too much on resolution or color depth, you might degrade the quality of the picture.

For example, Figure 22-1 shows a photograph at 1-bit (black and white), 4-bit (16 colors) and 24-bit (about 16.7 million possible colors) color depths. Even though the image is in grayscale rather than in color here in the book, you can see that the photo looks most realistic at the highest color depth. At the 1-bit depth, it's purely black and white. At the 4-bit depth (16 colors), it looks weird simply because there aren't enough colors in the photo to make it look right.

Note The 1-bit black-and-white resolution really is just black and white, with no shades of gray in between. The black and white you see in black-and-white photos or TVs is actually called *grayscale*. Printing color images on non-color printers usually results in a grayscale image.

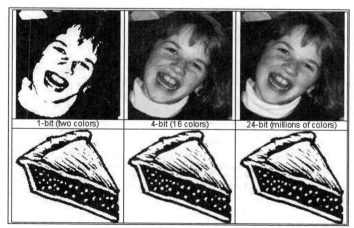

| 1-bit (two colors) | 4-bit (16 colors) | 24-bit (millions of colors) |

Figure 22-1: The 1-bit and 4-bit color depths aren't sufficient for the photograph, but are OK for the line drawing.

Figure 22-1 also shows a simple line drawing of a slice of pie at 1-bit, 4-bit, and 24-bit color depths. Because the original drawing is pure black and white to begin with, using the 4-bit or 24-bit depth to display the image doesn't improve the image quality at all. The file would be larger at those color depths, since more bits would be used to represent each pixel. But it's a waste of pixels since the 1-bit resolution is sufficient to show the line drawing.

Tip   If all the photographs on you screen look like the bad photos in Figure 22-1, your monitor's color palette is probably set too low. Crank it up using the Settings tab in the Display settings dialog box, as discussed under "Customizing the Screen In a Nutshell" in Chapter 15.

Choosing the right image quality

Choosing the best resolution and color depth for a particular graphic image is largely a matter of knowing how low a quality you can get away with (assuming you're looking to conserve disk space and transmission times.) There's also the issue of how people will be viewing the image. Virtually all monitors display graphic images at about 72 dots per inch (dpi). So if a graphic image is to be viewed on monitors only, and never printed, then there's not much reason to store an image at anything higher than 72 dpi.

Printers, on the other hand, can print to 2,400 dots per inch and even higher. So if a photograph or scanned image is destined for the printer, you need to make some decision about how high a resolution you want to go to, realizing that the higher you go, the larger the file will be. Then again, if your printer can go no higher than 600 dpi, there would be no sense in storing the image at any higher resolution.

Tip   While there are no hard and fast rules, most scanning aficionados agree that 150 dpi is a sufficient resolution for scanning pictures that will be displayed on the screen and printed with "typical" inkjet and laser printers.

With color depth, you can pretty much bank on a minimum of 16 million colors (24-bit). For other illustrations, it's just a matter if figuring out roughly how many unique colors there are in the image. In some graphics programs, you can decrease the color depth of an image to see how it will look at a lower resolution before committing to a higher resolution. The reverse isn't true, however. If the original image is shot or scanned at a low color depth — say 16 colors — increasing the color depth won't do any good because the program can't "guess" what the missing colors might be. Exactly how and when you define the resolution and color depth of a graphic image depends on how you create the image, as discussed in the sections that follow.

Sources of Digital Images

There are many ways to get digital images onto your PC. You can take pictures with a camera, or scan printed material with a scanner. You can purchase existing photos and clip art. You can even download many free images off the Internet. If you have a fax card in your PC, and use it to receive faxes, the faxes you received will be stored as digital images (even if the fax itself contains only text!). As discussed in the sidebar later in this chapter, you can use Optical Character Recognition (OCR) software to convert text stored in digital images back to text that can be edited with a word processing program or other text editor.

Digital photography

As you probably know, a digital camera is like any other camera—except there is no film. Instead, the photos you take are stored electronically inside the camera. To view the photos, you need to *download* them to your PC, where each photo is stored as a file. Exactly how you download the images to your computer depends on the camera you're using. When you purchase a digital camera you'll also get the software necessary to download pictures to your PC. You'll need to install that software and learn how to use it, as per the instructions that came with the camera, to get photos out of your camera into files on your computer.

> **Note**   Windows Me itself has no "universal" program that's capable of reading images from every make and model of digital camera on the market.

There are some third-party programs that will allow you to pull images right from a camera into the program itself. For example, version 6 of the Paint Shop Pro program mentioned earlier has the capability to read from many makes and models of digital cameras. See www.jasc.com/dcs2.asp for a complete list of supported cameras.

In short, exactly *how* you get images from your camera onto your hard disk, and what format they're stored in once they get to your hard disk, is a function of the camera and software you use. And there's really not more I can tell you there since I don't know the make and model of your camera. But once the image is stored on your hard disk, you can probably view it, change it, and print it using the Kodak Image program discussed later in this chapter. If not, you may need to purchase a third-party program such as Paint Shop Pro.

> **Tip**   As far as choosing a resolution and color depth for a photograph goes, exactly when and how you do that depends on several factors. Basically, you need to decide on these things *before* you shoot the photograph. Although if you must err, you should err in favor of going too high because once the picture is taken and on your hard disk, you can always *reduce* its resolution and color depth. But you can't *increase* those settings beyond what they are in the original photo.

Whether or not you can adjust color depth prior to shooting a photograph depends on the camera. Most cameras shoot at a 24-bit color depth, which yields about 16 million unique colors. Some cameras can shoot at 32-bits (called True Color), and some may give you a choice. Only the instructions that came with your camera can fill you in on the details. But if 24-bit color is all you get, don't worry about it. That's plenty for the day-to-day photography that most of us do.

With most cameras, you can select the resolution using some switch that's right on the camera. You'll have to review the manual that came with your camera to see what your options are (if any), and how to choose your options. In some cases, the camera doesn't really give you a choice of specific resolutions. Instead, it may just give you the choice of Low, Medium, or High resolution. The higher you go, the fewer pictures you can take per session because each photo takes up more storage space within the camera. But again, it's better to err in favor of "too good" rather than not good enough because you can always degrade the picture quality, and hence the file size, later using a graphics program.

Scanners

As you may know, a scanner is a hardware device that looks something like a small photocopy machine—except that is attaches to your computer and the images you "copy" are actually stored as image files on your hard disk, rather than being printed directly to paper. While you use a camera to take photographs, you use a scanner to copy images that are already printed on paper (or some other medium) to files on your PC. The resulting file is a digital image file, very similar to a photograph taken with a digital camera.

Editing faxes and scanned documents

Regardless of the type of information you scan, the resulting file is stored as a digital image. Even if you scan a sheet of paper that has nothing but written text on it, you end up with a graphic image file. The same is true of files that are faxed directly to your computer. The resulting file is a graphic image that can only be edited with a graphics program, and not a word processing program.

To convert a graphic image of a text file to a document that you can edit with a word processing program or text editor, you'll need to purchase an Optical Character Recognition (OCR) program. There are many on the market to choose from, as a visit to your local brick-and-mortar or online software store will reveal. The main trick is knowing what format the scanned text documents or faxes are stored in. You can get that information from the documentation that came with the scanner or fax card although you can also just look at the file-name extension of any files that were created by the scanner or fax card. Then it's just a matter of finding an OCR program that can read that type of file and convert it to a text document.

By the way, the digital images produced by faxes are always pretty low quality. That's because faxing was never intended to be a high-resolution, high-color depth medium for transmitting pictures. The whole idea behind faxing was simply to be able to transmit a reasonable facsimile of a printed document across phone lines. In fact, the term *fax* is short for *facsimile*.

As with cameras, learning to use your scanner will require that you read the documentation that came with the scanner. Windows Me doesn't have a built-in one-size-fits-all program for using every make and model of scanner ever created. However, the Kodak Imaging program that comes with Windows Me is capable of scanning images from TWAIN-compliant scanners. A TWAIN-compliant scanner is one that adheres to a *protocol* (set of rules) that any TWAIN-compliant graphics program can understand. If you purchase a TWAIN-compatible scanner, you can still use the software that came with the scanner to scan images. But you can also use any TWAIN-compatible software program to scan images.

Tip

In case you're wondering, TWAIN stands for Technology Without An Interesting Name. I guess the people who thought up the technology just couldn't come up with a more interesting name or acronym!

If you want to use Kodak Imaging to scan an image from your TWAIN-compatible scanner, click the Start button and choose Programs ⇨ Accessories ⇨ Imaging to start the program. From the Imaging program's menu bar, choose File ⇨ Select Scanner, and then make sure to select the appropriate scanner from the options presented. Then click OK. Lastly, to scan the image in the scanner, choose File ⇨ Scan New from the menu bar, and follow the instructions on the screen. To save the scanned image as a file on your hard disk, choose File ⇨ Save from Imaging's menu bar, choose a Folder (such as My Documents/My Pictures), enter a filename, choose a type from the Save As Type drop-down list, and click the Save button.

Tip

My personal favorite, Paint Shop Pro, can also acquire images directly from TWAIN-compliant scanners, as well as from many digital cameras.

With a scanner, you can generally choose your resolution just prior to performing the scan. For example, I have an HP OfficeJet R80 printer that also doubles as a scanner, fax machine, and copier. When scanning with Paint Shop Pro or the HP PrecisionScan software that came with the R80, I can set the resolution just prior to scanning the item using the simple "Set Custom Resolution" setting in the dialog box, as shown in Figure 22-2.

Scanners might also let you set a color depth just prior to scanning. For example, the HP PrecisionScan program mentioned earlier gives me a choice of scanning at 32-bit True Color (the right choice for photographs), or at the lower 256-color depth, which is sufficient for many illustrations and other drawings (see Figure 22-3).

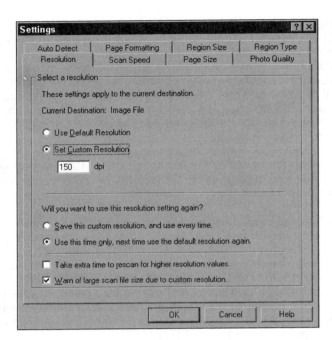

Figure 22-2: HP's PrecisionScan software lets you choose a resolution prior to scanning.

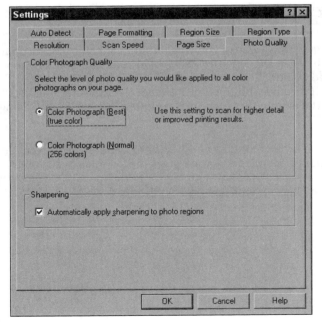

Figure 22-3: HP's PrecisionScan software provides two color-depth options.

Screenshots

Screenshots are like photographs of whatever appears on your screen at the moment. The resolution of a screenshot will always match the resolution of your screen, which is generally about 72 dpi. The color depth of the shot will initially match the color depth of your monitor. That depth is something you set through the Settings tab of the Display Properties dialog box, as discussed in Chapter 15. The term "color palette" is often used to describe the number of colors your monitor can display. The color palette of the monitor translates directly to the color depth of the resulting screenshot.

Assuming you're comfortable with your monitor's color depth, and you have something on the screen that you want to shoot a picture of, there are two ways to take the screenshot in Windows Me:

✦ To capture the entire screen, press the Print Screen (Print Scrn) key.

✦ To capture just the active window or dialog box, press Alt+Print Screen.

At first, nothing seems to happen and you'll be tempted to write me an e-mail telling me I'm nuts. But, in fact, the screenshot is stored in the Windows Clipboard, and will remain there until you put something else in its place. To get the screenshot to a file, you need to paste it into a graphics program. Virtually any graphics program that offers an Edit ➪ Paste option from its menu bar will do. The Paint program that comes with Windows Me will work just fine as well. Here are the instructions for using Paint:

> **Note**
>
> If Paint isn't available on your Accessories menu, it hasn't been installed. You can install it using the Windows Setup tab in Add/Remove Programs, as discussed in Chapter 25. You'll find it under "Accessories" there.

1. If you haven't already done so, take the screenshot by pressing Print Screen or Alt+Print Screen.

2. Click the Start button and choose Programs ➪ Accessories ➪ Paint.

3. Choose Edit ➪ Paste from Paint's menu bar. The image appears in the document area of the Paint program, as in Figure 22-4 where I've captured a sample dialog box (surrounded by a dashed line in the figure).

4. To save the image to a file, choose File ➪ Save from Paint's menu bar.

5. Choose a folder from the Save In dialog box.

> **Tip**
>
> If you save all your graphic images in the My Documents/My Pictures folder, you'll automatically see a thumbnail of the image whenever you open that folder with My Computer or Windows Explorer.

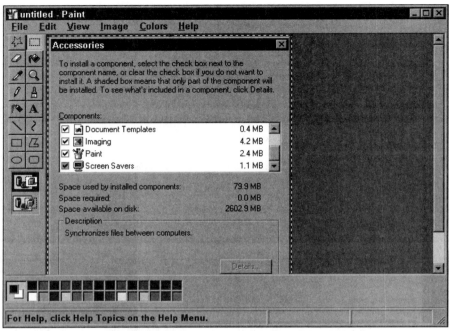

Figure 22-4: A screenshot of the Accessories dialog box in the Paint program

6. Choose a color depth and/or file type from the Save As Type drop-down list.

> **Tip** As discussed in a sidebar a little later in this chapter, choose GIF or JPEG if you're planning on publishing the screenshot on the Internet. If you don't care about the Internet, you can choose one of the bitmap/device independent bitmap (.bmp/.dib) formats.

7. Type in a filename where indicated, but don't add an extension (Paint will add the appropriate filename extension automatically).

8. Click the Save button.

The one disadvantage to using the Print Screen key to capture screenshots is that it never captures the mouse pointer. If showing the mouse pointer is important in your images, you'll probably want to purchase a more sophisticated screen capture program. Inner Media, Inc at www.innermedia.com offers Collage for more sophisticated screenshots. You can also find some shareware and freeware versions of screen capture programs online. For example, if you go to www.tucows.com and search for the phrase "screen capture" for Windows 95/98/Me, you'll probably find a bunch of programs you can download right on the spot.

Web cam shots

If you have a "Web cam" of the type described in Chapter 11, you can easily capture whatever it's displaying. One method is to simply take a screenshot of either the entire screen, or the window or dialog box that's displaying what the Web cam is showing on you screen. Paste that into a graphics program, and then crop as you see fit. The Paint program that comes with Windows Me offers another means of capturing whatever is coming through your Web cam at the moment. Assuming your Web cam is hooked up and turned on at the moment, click the Start button and choose Programs ⇨ Accessories ⇨ Paint. From Paint's menu bar choose File ⇨ From Scanner or Camera. Click the Capture button in the left side of the dialog box that appears to capture whatever is visible in the camera. You can change poses or move the camera, and click the Capture button to capture as many images as you wish.

Then, click any image in the right side of the dialog box to copy that image into the Paint program. Finally, choose File ⇨ Save to save the image to a file. When the Save As dialog box appears, be sure to choose a folder name from the Save In drop-down list, choose a color depth and/or file type from the Save As Type drop-down list, and then enter a filename before clicking the Save button.

Clip art

Commercial clip art is any photograph or pre-drawn graphic image that you purchase the right to use in your own work. There are many clip art packages on the market, as a trip to any computer store will verify. There are packages that contain up to a million unique pieces of art spread across many CDs and on the Internet as well. There's even a lot of free clip art that you can download off the Web. Just go to your favorite search engine and search for "free clip art" or "free clipart" and you'll be pointed to thousands of sites.

Of course, anything that appears on your screen can easily be saved to your own hard disk as a graphic image. You just have to take a screenshot, as discussed above, paste it into a graphics program, crop out whatever you don't want, and save the remainder of the image to a file. If the image you want is in a Web page, you don't even have to bother with pasting the image into a graphics program or cropping. Instead, just right-click the graphic image in the Web page, choose Save Picture As from the menu that appears, choose a folder to save the image in, and give it a filename in the Save Picture dialog box that appears.

But just because it's technically possible to swipe any graphic image that appears on your screen doesn't mean it's legal to do so. Plenty of graphic images are copyrighted. And you should never swipe and use any copyrighted image without written permission from the copyright holder. If you do, you're infringing on the owner's copyright and breaking the law. Plain and simple.

Working with Graphic Images

Regardless of how a graphic image gets *onto* your computer's hard disk — be it via camera, scanner, floppy disk, download, or even a fax card — you can change, edit, and print the program using just about any *graphics manipulation program*. Or, I suppose I should say any *bitmap* or *paint* type graphics program. *Vector* or *illustration* type programs only work with vector images. And vector images, in turn, are only created by those types of programs. Images created through the types of sources focused on in this chapter are bitmaps.

Windows Me comes with two programs suitable for manipulating bitmap graphic images — Microsoft Paint and Kodak Imaging — although both are extremely limited when compared to a true graphics manipulation program like Paint Shop Pro. But in a pinch, they can help you with basic editing and printing. Both programs are accessible from the Accessories menu (click the Start button and choose Programs ➪ Accessories). If either one or both of the programs isn't available on you Accessories menu, it probably just hasn't been installed. You can use the Windows Setup tab in Add/Remove Programs to install the programs, as discussed in the section "Installing Missing Windows Components" in Chapter 25.

Using Microsoft Paint

Microsoft Paint is largely geared toward drawing simple pictures, although it can also be used to edit existing digital images to some degree. As mentioned, you can open Paint by clicking the Start button and choosing Accessories ➪ Paint. When the program opens, you'll see that it has a typical menu bar, as well as an additional toolbox and color box, as pointed out in Figure 22-5.

Paint is capable of opening digital images, and saving them, in the following formats:

- ✦ 1-bit monochrome bitmap (.bmp, .dib)

- ✦ 4-bit, 16-color bitmap (.bmp, .dib)

- ✦ 8-bit, 256-color bitmap (.bmp, .dib)

- ✦ 24-bit, 16.7 million colors bitmap (.bmp, .dib)

- ✦ JPEG, millions of colors (.jpg, .jpeg)

- ✦ GIF, 256 colors (.gif)

While the File ➪ Open commands in Paint limit you to opening files in those formats, you can cut and paste virtually any image and screenshot into Paint using the Edit ➪ Paste options on its menu bar.

Toolbox

Menu bar

Color box

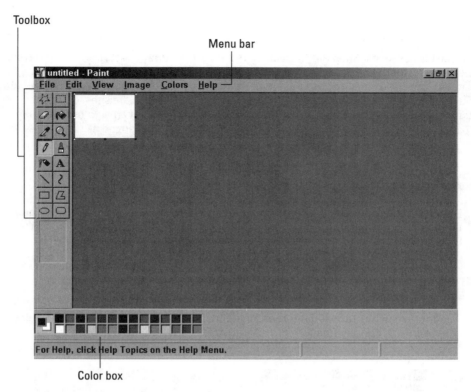

Figure 22-5: The menu bar, toolbox, and color box in Paint

GIFs, JPEGs, and the Internet

If you're planning on publishing graphic images in a Web site on the Internet, you can greatly simplify your life by using the JPEG format for photographs and the GIF format for illustrations that require fewer colors. Virtually all Web browsers support those two image formats, and you want your images to be readable by as many different types of Web browsers as possible.

If you're at all serious about publishing images on the Internet, I strongly suggest that you purchase a graphics program that's well-suited to the job. As you may have guessed, I'm going to suggest Paint Shop Pro—for several reasons. For one, you can open graphic images stored in virtually any format using Paint Shop Pro and then easily save those images in GIF or JPEG format using the simple File ⇨ Save As commands from the program's menu bar.

Continued

Continued

You can also use Paint Shop Pro to create transparent-background GIFs, in which you choose one color to be "transparent." It will also let you create *animated GIFs* — small animations that you may have seen on Web pages you've visited. Plus, Paint Shop Pro has all the tools you need to touch up photos and get rid of "red eye," wrinkles, blemishes, or anything else you don't want. To top it all off, you don't need to be a professional artist to use the program. It's easy to learn and easy to use even if you're as artistically challenged as I am.

Rotating images in Paint

Depending on how you hold your digital camera, or place paper in your scanner, an image can end up being sideways, as in the example shown in Figure 22-6. You can fix that using the Rotate capability in Paint by doing the following:

1. Choose Image ➪ Flip/Rotate from Paint's menu bar.
2. Choose Rotate by Angle ➪ 270°.

The picture will rotate 270 degrees as in Figure 22-7. If the figure ends up being upside down, choose Image ➪ Flip/Rotate ➪ Flip Vertical.

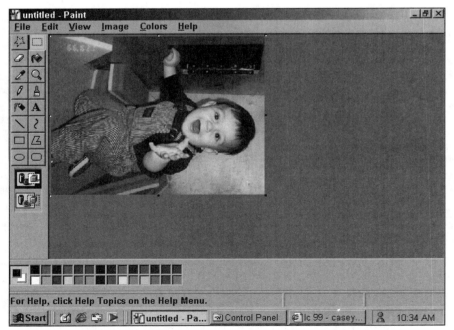

Figure 22-6: A digital photograph that ended up sideways in the Paint program

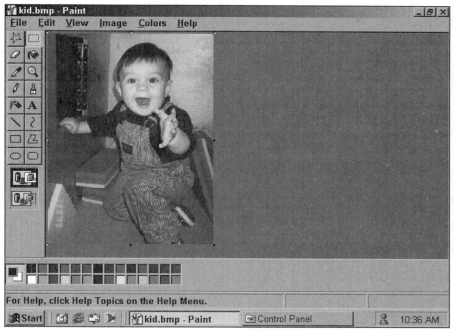

Figure 22-7: Results of rotating the previous image 270 degrees

Cropping in Paint

To crop a digital image in Paint, first open (or paste in) the image you want to crop. If you paste the image in and want to keep a copy of the uncropped image on your hard disk, go ahead and save that image using the File ➪ Save commands from Paint's menu bar.

To crop, click the Select tool near the upper-right corner of the toolbox. Then drag a border around the area of the image that you want to keep. For example, in Figure 22-8 I've drawn the selection around the main subject area of the photo.

Next, choose Edit ➪ Copy (or press Ctrl+C) to copy the selected area to the Windows Clipboard. Nothing will seem to happen at first. But you can be certain that a copy of the selected area (only) is in the Clipboard.

Next, choose File ➪ New to get rid of the larger picture. Then choose Edit ➪ Paste from Paint's menu bar, or press Ctrl+V. The cropped area is now the entire new image, as in Figure 22-9. If the white background behind the image is larger than the image itself, just drag the sizing handles of the white area into the image until the white area is the same size as the image. Then choose File ➪ Save to save the cropped image with a file-name of your choosing.

Figure 22-8: Using the Select tool in Paint to select an area within a photo

Figure 22-9: Results of pasting selection area into Paint as a new image

Other Paint capabilities

As the toolbox and color box suggest, Paint offers more capabilities than just rotating and cropping photos. But since all those capabilities are well documented in its Help (choose Help ➪ Help Topics from Paint's menu bar), there's really no need to go into the step-by-step instructions for each capability here. So here's a quick summary of what you can do, just so you know what to look for in Paint's help:

   ✦ Draw lines and shapes

   ✦ Add text to pictures (annotate)

   ✦ Add and change colors

   ✦ Erase portions of the picture

   ✦ Print the picture

   ✦ Use a picture as your desktop wallpaper

Using Kodak Imaging

The Kodak Imaging program that comes with Windows Me also offers some limited capabilities for working with graphic images. It's slightly oriented toward working with large image documents, such as faxes. But it can handle some of the simpler tasks of working with photos and clip art as well. To start Imaging, click the Start button and choose Programs ➪ Accessories ➪ Imaging.

Imaging's File ➪ Open and File ➪ Save commands are limited to opening and saving files in the format listed below:

- ✦ TIFF document (.tiff, .tif)
- ✦ FAX document (.awd)
- ✦ Bitmap image (.bmp)
- ✦ JPEG file (.jpg, .jpe, .jpeg)
- ✦ PCX/DCX document (.pcx, .dcx)
- ✦ XIF document (.xif)
- ✦ GIF file (.gif)
- ✦ WIFF document (.wif)

Once the image is in the Imaging program, you can view it in a variety of ways. For example, you can zoom in and out, rotate the image to the left or right, and even add annotations. The full range of capabilities is clearly documented in its Help (choose Help ➪ Imaging Help, or Help ➪ Imaging Preview Help from the menu bar).

Summary

Windows Me is capable of handling a wide range of graphic images and virtually all graphic image file formats. While there are no sophisticated graphics programs built into Windows Me, you can view, print, and manipulate images (to some degree) using the Microsoft Paint and Kodak Imaging programs. The main topics covered in this chapter include the following:

- ✦ Digital images come in a wide variety of file formats, with .jpeg, .gif, and .bmp being among the most common.
- ✦ The quality of a digital image, in computer terms, is the image's resolution and color depth.
- ✦ An image's resolution is defined as the number of dots per inch (dpi) used to display the image.
- ✦ On the screen, the dots that make up a picture are also called *pixels*.

✦ The color depth of an image defines how many unique colors are used within the picture.

✦ The higher the quality (that is, resolution and color depth) of a picture, the larger the size of the file required to store the image on disk.

✦ Sources of digital images include digital photographs, scans, screenshots, purchased clip art, and faxes received directly through a fax card.

✦ The image formats most widely used on the Internet are GIF and JPEG. Use GIF for simple illustrations (up to 256 colors) and JPEG for photographs.

✦ The Paint and Imaging programs that come with Windows Me provide the capability to view and print images, along with some basic editing capability.

✦ To really gain control over digital images, I'd recommend a full-blown third-party graphics program such as Paint Shop Pro (www.jasc.com).

✦　　✦　　✦

Windows Movie Maker

Whereas sound, music, pictures, and such are all part of what we call *multimedia* in the computer biz, the ultimate in multimedia has got to be full-motion movies (or video) with sound. Windows Me is the first version of Windows to offer a full-fledged program for creating your own custom movies from digital video, recorded video from TV or a VCR, still images, and sound. The program that allows you to create these movies is called Windows Movie Maker. The movies you create with Movie Maker can be viewed by anyone who has a copy of Windows Media Player (version 7 or later). While that version of Media Player comes with Windows Me, anyone with earlier versions of Windows can download the player, for free, from www.microsoft.com/windows/mediaplayer, which means you can e-mail the movies you make to anyone who has an e-mail account. If you have your own Web site, you can publish your movies there as well.

Getting to Know Windows Movie Maker

As with so much of multimedia, taking full advantage of Movie Maker requires that you have the hardware to create and display digital video. In terms of sheer computer hardware, you'll need at least the following to create movies:

- ✦ 300 megahertz (MHz) Pentium II or equivalent
- ✦ 64 megabytes (MB) of RAM
- ✦ 2 gigabytes (GB) of free hard disk space
- ✦ An audio capture device
- ✦ An analog or digital video capture device

Software-wise, you just need Windows Me to run Movie Maker.

Compatible hardware

Not all makes and models of hardware are compatible with Movie Maker. If you haven't yet purchased the hardware necessary to create your own videos and record them to your hard disk, you might want to focus your attention on the devices summarized in the following sections. Bear in mind that these are devices that are compatible as I write this chapter. There will no doubt be more devices available as time rolls by. So you'll want to check the Windows Me Web site from time to time to see if any new devices have been added to the list.

Graphics cards (analog devices)

Your graphics card needs the capability to display video. If you'll be copying video from a video camera, TV, or VCR, the graphics card will also need an A/V In or S-Video port into which you can plug the video device. Specific models of graphics cards that are currently supported by Windows Movie Maker include the following:

✦ Asus AGP-V6600 GeForce 256 Deluxe

✦ ATI Series cards (All In Wonder, Pro, 128, Standard)

✦ Hauppauge WinTV

✦ Matrox Marvel G200/G400

✦ Osprey 100

Web cams

Movie Maker can also record live input from a Web cam, provided the camera is one of the following makes and models:

✦ 3Com HomeConnect

✦ Creative Labs VideoBlaster 3

✦ Intel Web Cam CS430

✦ Kodak DVC325

✦ LogiTech QuickCam Pro

✦ Philips Web Cam

Digital video FireWire cards

If you use a digital video camera that connects to the computer through an IEEE 1394 (aka FireWire, iLink and iLink 1394) compliant add-in card, you can use any of the cards listed below to capture digital video directly into Movie Maker:

✦ ADS Technology's Pyro DV

✦ Orange Micro 1394 PCI

✦ Orange Micro Cardbus

You can learn more about these devices and order them online, from www.1394firestation.com and www.orangemicro.com.

Starting Windows Movie Maker

Starting Windows Movie Maker is easy:

1. Click the Start button.

2. Choose Programs ➪ Accessories ➪ Windows Movie Maker.

When first opened, Windows Movie Maker will look like Figure 23-1, shown with the screen area in Display Properties at 800×600. Labels in the figure point out specific portions of the program described throughout this chapter.

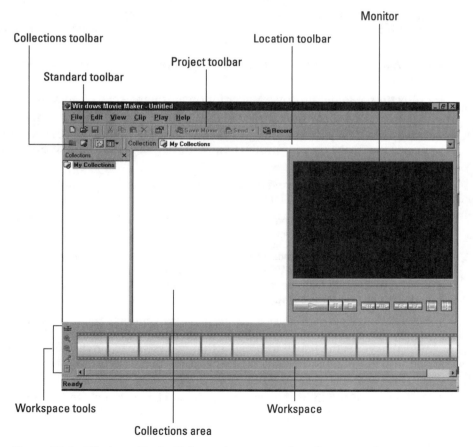

Figure 23-1: Windows Movie Maker as it appears when first opened

Tip

For an explanation of how to change your screen area using the Settings tab of the Display Properties dialog box, see Chapter 15.

Buzzwords

As with most things in life, creating movies has its own set of jargon and buzz-words. It's hard to describe things without using those words. So before we get any deeper into Movie Maker, let's take a moment to define our terms so you'll know what I'm talking about as you progress through this chapter:

✦ **Capture:** Means the same thing as *to record*. More specifically, it means to convert incoming video and/or audio to digital data that can be stored in a file on a computer disk.

✦ **Capture card:** A graphics card that has capture abilities built right in (like the ATI All In Wonder card), or an add-on card specifically designed for recording (capturing) output from a playback device. For example, a FireWire card can capture digital video and therefore act as a capture card (also called a *capture device*).

✦ **Clip:** A small segment of audio or video content, much like a single scene in a regular movie. Most movies are made from a series of short clips.

✦ **Collection:** A folder in Movie Maker for organizing the clips from which your movie will be produced.

✦ **Content:** In the media biz, this general term refers to audio, video, text, and images that make up your production or movie. Also called *source content* or *source material*.

✦ **Frame:** A video is composed of many still images played in rapid succession. Each one of those still images is a *frame*.

✦ **Movie File:** The .asf file that results from combining clips into a movie and saving that movie as a file.

✦ **Playback device:** Any device that's capable of playing audio or video such as a VCR, a video camera in VCR mode, a CD player, or a Web cam. The "Out" port(s) of the playback device need to be connected to the "In" ports of the capture card on your computer.

✦ **Player:** Unlike *playback device,* the term *player* generally refers to some kind of software that can display content on a computer. For example, Microsoft Media Player is the *player* for movies that you create in Movie Maker. So anyone who has Microsoft Media Player can view (but not necessarily change) the movies you create.

✦ **Project:** A collection of clips that have already been assembled into a movie, although not necessarily a completed movie. A movie "work in progress."

Connecting hardware

There are no hard and fast rules for connecting your video hardware to your computer. You'll have to get that information from the manuals that came with your hardware. So the first step will be to learn everything about your graphics card, video capture card, or FireWire card to learn how and where various types of devices can be connected. You'll also need to learn everything you can about your playback device (your video camera, VCR, or whatever) to discover what types of output jacks it has. Then you need to find the right cable for connecting the "Out" port of the playback device to the "In" port of your graphics card or capture card.

For example, if you're using a video camera or VCR that has an S-Video output jack, and your graphics or capture card has an S-Video "In" jack, you can connect the two using an S-Video cable. Likewise, for a camera that has an IEEE 1394 FireWire Out port, you'll need the appropriate cable for connecting that to your FireWire card. A VCR or camera that only has the older-style RCA video and audio Out ports will need to connect to similar ports on the capture card. There are all kinds of cables for connecting non-similar ports. For instance, your VCR might have a single Out port, and your capture device three separate In ports. With the appropriate cable you can still connect the devices. Again, all the necessary information should be in the documentation that came with your hardware.

Setting defaults

Once you've connected your hardware to the capture card on your computer, the next step is to tell Windows Movie Maker where to look for the incoming video and audio stream. Movie Maker is pretty good at detecting the appropriate device, although it's not perfect. And if you have multiple input devices, you'll need to tell Movie Maker which one you want to record from. To do that, click the Record button on the toolbar, or choose File ➪ Record from Movie Maker's menu bar. You'll come to the Record dialog box shown in Figure 23-2.

Movie sound

If you have any trouble hearing or recording sound in your movies, make sure the volume control for the line that sound is being played through isn't muted or turned down to low. Use the Volume Control (mixer) application discussed in Chapter 20 to adjust the volume. Remember to choose Options ➪ Properties ➪ Playback there to make sure you can see the volume control for your playback device, which might be Wave/DirectSound/MP3 in many movies.

Likewise, when recording, the sound from your video will enter the computer through some port, such as the Line In port. In that same Volume Control application, choose Options ➪ Properties ➪ Recording to list possible recording volume controls. Then select the appropriate control for your recording device and make sure it isn't muted or turned down too low.

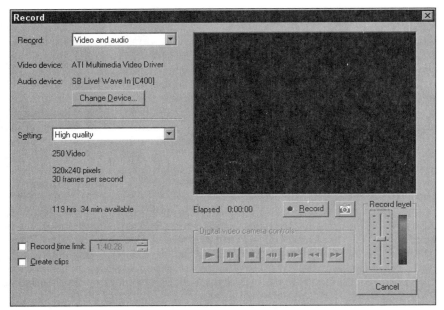

Figure 23-2: The Record dialog box lets you choose your devices and start recording.

If you have a FireWire card properly installed, you should see the DV device already selected in the Record drop-down list. If not, select digital video (DV) from that drop-down list. If you then start playing a video in your digital camera you should see a message indicating that a digital device has been detected. The Digital video camera controls in the Record dialog box should then be enabled, and you should be able to control the camera's playback using the Play, Pause, Stop, and other buttons in the Record dialog box. If those buttons aren't available, you'll need to use the Play, Stop, Pause and other buttons on the camera to control playback.

If you connected an analog device, such as a non-digital video camera, VCR, CD player, or whatever to your computer, the Video device and Audio device options will show where Movie Maker intends to record from, although you'll need to test, and possibly adjust, the devices to match your hardware. Hit the Play button on your device to have it start playing a video or sound and watch the large monitor in the Record dialog box for a clear image of the movie you're playing.

If you get lucky and Movie Maker has already detected your hardware correctly, you won't have to fiddle with any settings. But if the playback screen shows nothing, or the image isn't clear, click the Change Device button to get the Change Device dialog box shown in Figure 23-3.

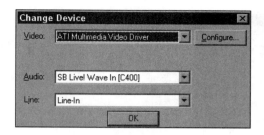

Figure 23-3: The Change Device dialog box lets you specify where you'll be recording from.

Choose the Video capture device from the Video drop-down list. Then click the OK button to close that dialog box. If you've made the right selection, whatever video your playback device is showing should appear clearly in the monitor window. If not, you'll need to click the Change Device button again and try a different setting. If the onscreen monitor shows your video, but the picture isn't clear and running smoothly, some fine-tuning might be in order. In that case, you'll need to click the Change Device button again and then click the Configure button in the Change Device dialog box. You'll come to a dialog box that's unique to your hardware. You'll need to make selections according to that hardware. Once again, your best source of information will be the documentation that came with your hardware.

Once the monitor on the Record dialog box is able to show, clearly, what's being played in your playback device, you know you have the right settings in place. You can close the Record dialog box for now. There are a few more settings you may want to adjust before you actually begin recording.

General options

To set a few last defaults, choose View ➪ Options from Movie Maker's menu bar. You'll come to the Options dialog box, shown in Figure 23-4. You can change these settings on-the-fly while making your movies. But if you don't think they'll change much from one project to the next, you can save yourself some time by putting in default values now. Your options are as follows:

✦ **Default director:** This is the name of the person who will be given the title "Director" in the movies you create. You can put your own name here.

✦ **Still image duration:** Your movie can contain still images that appear for a specified time. Set this option to the number of seconds that you want still images to remain unchanged in your movies.

✦ **Automatically create clips:** When recording video, Movie Maker can automatically divide a lengthy segment into smaller, more manageable clips. It creates a new clip whenever the scene in one video frame is completely different from the scene in the previous video frame. Select this option if you want Movie Maker to create clips automatically in this manner.

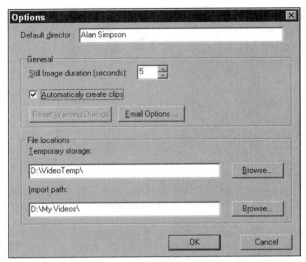

Figure 23-4: The Options dialog box in Movie Maker
for setting general defaults

✦ **Email options:** You can send clips as e-mail attachments directly from Movie
Maker by choosing File ➪ Send Movie To. Use the Email Options button to specify which e-mail program you'd like Movie Maker to use when mailing clips.

✦ **Temporary storage:** Select a drive and directory where you want Movie Maker
to store temporary files as you record video.

✦ **Import path:** If you already have video you'll be importing into Movie Maker,
set this option to the drive and directory where most of those clips are
stored. Later, when you choose File ➪ Import, Movie Maker will initially look
for clips in the folder you specify.

Click OK after making your selections.

Creating and managing collections

You can organize your content into *collections* as you see fit. A collection is really
nothing more than a folder, just like a regular folder on a disk. You can name a collection however you see fit and put whatever clips you feel are appropriate into
each collection. A collection can contain "subcollections," just as a folder can
contain subfolders. Initially, Move Maker contains just one collection, named
My Collections, that's visible in the Collections pane when it's open. Choose
View ➪ Collections to show or hide that pane.

To create a new collection, right-click on the collection that will act as the parent to the collection you're creating and choose New Collection. The new collection will be named New Collection, but you can type in a more meaningful name. For example in Figure 23-5 I've created a collection named Home Videos 2000, which I'll use to store clips shot in the year 2000 with my home video camera.

Figure 23-5: A new collection named Home Videos 2000 added to Movie Maker

You can move, copy, and rename collections using the same techniques you use with folders in Windows Explorer or My Computer. For example, to rename a collection just right-click its name, choose Rename, and type in the new name. To move a collection, drag it to a new parent directory and drop it there. To delete a collection (and all the clips within it), right-click the collection name and choose Delete.

When you capture clips, new collections will be created automatically. The clip(s) from the capture will be placed in the new collection for you. You can rename, move, edit, delete, and copy clips as well, as you'll learn later in this chapter.

A collection is different from a folder in one important way. Unlike a folder, which contains files, a collection only contains *pointers* (shortcuts) to files. So once you've added a clip to a collection, you should avoid going back to its original folder and deleting, moving, or renaming the original file. If you do, the pointer in the collection will no longer be able to find the clip's underlying file. The problem is fairly easy to fix, however. Just delete the faulty clip by right-clicking its name and choosing Delete. Then use File ⇨ Import to re-import the clip into the collection of your choosing. You'll learn more about creating clips a little later in this chapter.

Gathering Content

The movie you create will consist of *content*—audio, video, and still images. There are two main ways to gather content. You can import existing clips that are already stored on a computer disk. Or you can capture content from a video camera, VCR, or other playback device. We'll look at how you go about importing content first.

Importing existing clips

It's not necessary to create all the content for your movie from scratch. If you have a video camera and software for recording video to your PC, you can probably use those clips in your movies without re-creating them from scratch. Likewise, if you have sound tracks or still video images already, you can use them as well. You just have to *import* the existing material into Windows Movie Maker. The types of files you can import into Movie Maker include the following:

✦ **Video files:** .asf, .wm, .wmv, .avi, .mpg, .m1v, .mp2, .mp2v, .mpa, .mpe, .mpeg, .mpv2

✦ **Audio files:** .wav, .wma, .aif, .aiff, .aifc, .snd, .mp3, .au

✦ **Still images:** .bmp, .jpg, .jfif, .jpe, .jpeg, .dib, .gif

To import clips:

1. Click on the name of the collection into which you want to import the file.

2. Choose File ➪ Import from Movie Maker's menu bar.

3. In the Select the File to Import dialog box that appears, use the Look In drop-down list to navigate to the drive and directory that contains the file(s) you want to import.

4. Optionally, if you want to limit the display to a particular type of file, choose an option from the Files of Type drop-down list.

5. If you want to import a single file, click its name and skip the remaining steps. Otherwise, click some neutral area (not on a filename) within the list of filenames.

6. To import multiple files, point to the first file you want to import until its name is selected. Then, hold down the Ctrl key while pointing to select additional files, or use the Shift key to extend the selection through multiple adjacent file names.

7. Click the Open button to import the selected files.

There will be a brief delay as Movie Maker converts the data to the appropriate format for Movie Maker. And, if you've opted to automatically divide content into clips, Movie Maker will also divide the file into clips if you've opted to have it do so. When the job is done, the imported file will be displayed as one or more clips within the collection. Initially, the clips will be named Clip 1, Clip 2, Clip 3, and so forth. But you can rename any clip just by right-clicking its icon and choosing Rename. For example, in Figure 23-6 I've imported four clips into the collection named 01 RiverHouse and then renamed each of those collections to my liking.

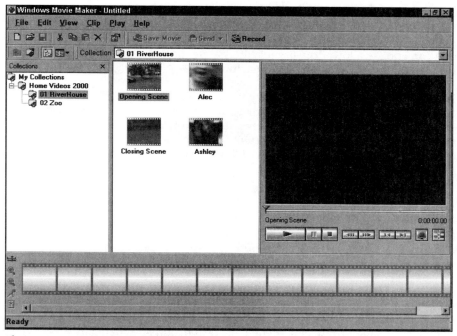

Figure 23-6: Four clips imported into a collection named 01 RiverHouse

Capturing content

To capture content (that is, record content that's being played by some playback device such as a video camera in VCR mode), make sure the device is connected properly, as discussed earlier in this chapter. Then, click the Record button on the toolbar or choose File ⇨ Record from Movie Maker's menu bar. You'll come to the Record dialog box shown back in Figure 23-2. From the Record drop-down list choose what you want to record, Video and Audio, Audio Only, Video Only, or DV (if you have a digital video capture device.). Then, click the Play button on your playback device to make sure you can see the content to be recorded in the monitor that appears within the Record dialog box. If you can't see the content, use the Change Device button to select the appropriate device. Before you actually begin recording, you'll also want to adjust some other settings in the Record dialog box, as discussed next.

Choosing audio/video quality

Before you begin recording, choose the recording quality from the Setting drop-down list. You have several choices. And as with sound and images, the higher the quality, the larger the resulting file. At this stage, when you're importing raw content, you don't need to worry about how quickly the movie will transfer across the Internet. If you have ample disk space and a reasonably fast computer, you might as well go for high quality. Later, when you create your movie from the clips, you can choose a lower quality for Internet versions for the movie, and perhaps higher quality for other forms of distribution.

But as with a piece of cloth, which you can always make shorter but not longer, you can only *decrease* the quality of the movie — not increase it. So you're better off erring in favor of higher quality rather than lower. Later in this chapter, when you get to the stage in which you're actually producing movies from your clips, where quality settings are more important, I'll discuss the full range of options in more detail.

Time limits and clips

If you want to put a time limit on how many minutes of audio and video you record, choose the Record Time Limit option and specify your recording time. That's entirely optional. If you leave that option unselected, you can determine the length of your recording on-the-fly as the video is playing.

The Create Clips option, if selected, attempts to break your video into separate scenes or clips. To do so, it watches for a radical change in content from one video frame to the next. Whenever the content of a frame changes totally, Movie Maker assumes that an entirely new scene has started, and automatically places the next set of similar video frames in a separate clip. Again, this is entirely optional. If you don't select this option, the video will be recorded as one long clip. And then you can divide it into separate scenes later yourself, manually, when putting together your final movie.

Start and stop recording

When you've finished making all the other selections in the Record dialog box, rewind your video to the beginning, or do whatever it takes to get the playback to where you want to start recording. Then click the Record button and start playing your video. A message indicating that the playback device has been detected might appear if you're recording from a digital device. Just click Yes if you see such a message. You can click the Play button under Digital video camera controls, if available, rather than the Play button on the camera, to start playback in that case.

Note   While capturing video content, you won't hear the audio portion through your computer speakers. Don't worry about that.

The content being recorded appears in the monitor of the Record dialog box (Figure 23-7), the Record button changes to a Stop button, and the Elapsed time indicator keeps track of how long you've been recording. Most of the other options in the Record dialog box will be disabled because you can't change those options as content is being captured.

Monitor

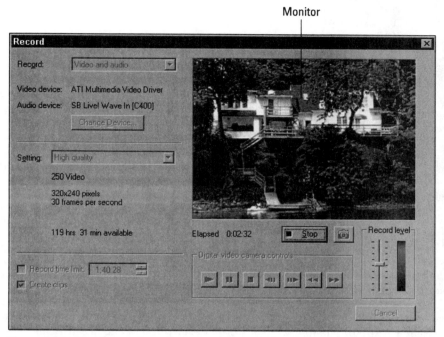

Figure 23-7: During capture, the Record button changes to Stop and most other options are disabled.

If you set the Record time limit, recording will stop when the time limit is reached. Otherwise, you can stop recording content at your leisure by clicking the Stop button. (You can also stop the playback device using its Stop button, or the Stop button under Digital video camera controls, if they're enabled.) A Save Windows Media File dialog box will pop up, as in Figure 23-8. Choose a folder from the Save in drop-down list and change the suggested filename, Untitled.ASF, to something more meaningful. Then click the Save button. The Creating Clips dialog box appears as Movie Maker stores the captured video on disk and separates it into clips. Initially, the clips will be named Clip 1, Clip 2, Clip 3, and so forth. But as you'll learn a little later in this chapter, you can rename the clips to your liking.

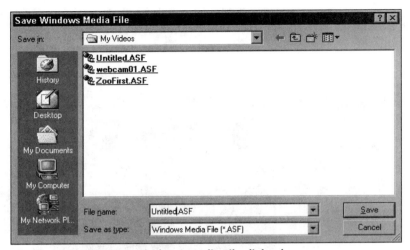

Figure 23-8: The Save Windows Media File dialog box

Playing a clip

To verify that a clip was imported or captured correctly, just click the name of the clip that you want to view. Then click the Play button beneath the monitor in the Record dialog box. The clip should play normally, and now you should also be able to hear any recorded sound. You'll also notice a slider (called the seek bar) and other buttons beneath the monitor. Pointing to those controls will display their names in a ToolTip. The following is a brief description of each control and its corresponding action:

✦ **Seek bar:** Drag the pointer on the seek bar to the left and right to move frame-by-frame through the video

✦ **Play:** Plays the video, or resumes play if the video is paused

✦ **Pause:** Pauses playback at the current frame

✦ **Stop:** Stops playback and removes the clip from the monitor

✦ **Step Back:** Moves back one frame if the video is paused

✦ **Step Forward:** Moves forward one frame if the video is paused or not playing yet

✦ **Back:** Jumps back to the first frame in the video

✦ **Forward:** Jumps ahead to the last frame in the video

✦ **Full Screen:** Hides Movie Maker and displays the video full-screen. Click anywhere on the screen to return to Movie Maker.

✦ **Split:** Tells Movie Maker to split the clip into two clips at the current frame.

Of these, the Split button is probably the least obvious. But you'll learn its function next when we discuss editing your clips.

Working with Clips

As mentioned, Movie Maker can divide lengthy content into smaller, more manageable clips automatically as you capture content. But the automatic clips won't always be exactly what you had in mind. You may end up with some scenes that are too long and would be better split into two or more clips. Or you may end up with two clips that really should be combined into a single clip. Either way, it's pretty easy to create new clips from your existing clips.

Backing up a clip

If you're concerned about possibly ruining a clip while splitting or editing it, you can always make a backup copy of the clip before you begin. Just right-click the name of the clip you plan to work with and choose Copy. Then, right-click some neutral area outside of the clip and choose Paste. The copy will have the same name as the original, followed by a number in parentheses. I suggest you right-click that copy, choose Rename, and give the clip a more meaningful name, such as the original name followed by the word *backup*. When you no longer need the backup, you can just right-click it and choose Delete.

Splitting one clip into two

If a scene is too long, and you want to separate it into two or more clips, just split the clip into two. Or, if you want to insert a scene in the middle of an existing clip, you can split the clip into two and then insert the new scene later when composing your movie. To split a clip:

1. If you haven't already done so, open the collection that contains the clip you want to split. Then click the clip that you want to split. The first frame of the clip appears in the monitor.

2. Click the Play button to get to where you want to split the clip and then click Pause. Optionally, use the seek bar, or the Step Forward or Step Backward buttons to get to the specific frame where you want to make the split.

3. Click the Split button beneath the monitor, or choose Clip ➪ Split.

The content up to the split point remains in the clip with the original name. The content beyond the split frame is saved to a separate clip that has the same name followed by a number in parentheses. For example, splitting a clip named *BigBoy* into two scenes creates a shorter scene named *BigBoy* which includes the material up to, and including the frame at the spilt point. It also creates a separate clip named *BigBoy (1)*, which contains all the content beyond the split-point frame. Rename either or both the clips to your liking.

Note   Remember that Movie Maker contains only *pointers* to the original content that's stored on your disk. When you split a clip, you don't change the original underlying file at all. Instead, each clip is just a pointer to a set of frames within the original file.

You can, of course, divide any of the resulting scenes into two smaller clips simply by repeating the steps above.

Combining clips

Movie Maker's automatic clip creation doesn't always do a perfect job of dividing a video into perfect clips. If a frame within a single scene changes radically from the frame that preceded it, Movie Maker will divide the scene into two separate clips even if it's not particularly appropriate to do so. You might even end up with some really short clips that are just end pieces to the clips that precede them. When that happens, the clips will be *contiguous* within their collection, named Clip 1 and Clip 2 or Clip 7 and Clip 8. If you like, you can recombine those two contiguous clips into a single clip before you start putting your movie together. Here's how:

Note   It's not necessary to combine contiguous clips to create a movie. You'll create your movie by playing clips in a sequential order. Combine contiguous clips only when you want to piece together two clips that would be better treated as a single scene.

1. Open the collection that contains the clips you want to combine.

2. Click the first clip (the lower-numbered one) to select it.

3. Hold down the Ctrl key and click on the second clip (the one with a number that's just one higher than the clip that precedes it.)

4. Choose Clip ➪ Combine from Movie Maker's menu bar.

Both clips appear unchanged at first glance. But if you play the first clip, you'll see that it now contains its original content plus the content from the second clip. You can delete the second clip now since its content is now included at the end of the first clip.

Managing clips

As you know, the clips you import or capture are stored in collections. You can move, copy, rename, and delete clips using the same basic techniques you use to manage files. For example, to rename a click, right-click its icon, choose Rename, and enter the new name. To delete a clip, right-click it and choose Delete. To move or copy a clip to another collection, right-drag the clip to the collection to which you want to move or add it. Then release the mouse button and choose Move if you want to move copy the clip to the collection, or choose Copy if you want to copy the clip to the collection.

 Tip
You can view clips as thumbnails, a list of icons, or a detailed list of icons by choosing View and either List, Details, or Thumbnails from Movie Maker's menu bar.

Changing a clip's properties

Every clip you create has a name, which is visible under the clip's icon. To keep better records about each of your clips, you can also add a directory name, date, description, and so forth. To do so, right-click the clip's icon and choose Properties. In the Properties dialog box that appears, enter a title, directory name, date, rating, and description of your choosing. Then click the Close (X) button in the Properties dialog box.

Producing a Movie

A movie is a collection of clips played in a specific order. This is as true in Movie Maker as it is in real movies. In a real movie or TV show, scenes aren't shot in the order you see them at the theater. Instead, they shoot all the scenes based on location, set, costumes, who's in the scene, and so forth. Then, all those scenes are assembled into a story that (one hopes) makes sense. (Often, the actors in a movie have no idea of the story behind the movie, and therefore have no idea why they're supposed to act a certain way. Hence the somewhat famous acting term "What's my motivation?" or "Why am I doing this?")

In Movie Maker, you assemble your movie in the workspace down near the bottom of the Movie Maker window. There are two ways to view the contents of the workspace, as illustrated in Figure 23-9:

✦ **Storyboard:** Shows the contents of the workspace as a series of clips without regard to the duration of each clip.

✦ **Timeline:** Shows the contents of the workspace as a flow of content along a timeline where the size of each clip is proportional to the amount of time it takes up in the movie.

You can switch views at any time; you don't have to work exclusively in one view or another. To switch views, just click the Storyboard or Timeline button at the top of the workspace tools. Or, right-click the workspace and choose Storyboard or Timeline from the menu that appears. Or choose View ➪ Storyboard or View ➪ Timeline from Movie Makers menu bar.

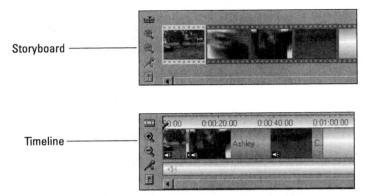

Storyboard

Timeline

Figure 23-9: The workspace at the bottom of Movie Maker can be viewed as a storyboard or timeline.

Adding clips to the workspace

Once you've collected all your clips, assembling a movie is simply a matter of copying clips into the workspace in the order in which you want them presented in the final movie. To add a clip to the workspace, open the collection that contains the clip that you want to display next in the movie. Then do whichever of the following is most convenient for you:

✦ Right-click the clip that you want to add to the movie and choose Add to Storyboard or Add to Timeline.

✦ Click the clip you want to add to the movie and choose Clip ⇨ Add to Storyboard/Timeline.

✦ Drag the clip to where you want it to appear in the Storyboard/Timeline and drop it there.

✦ Or select several clips using Ctrl+click, Shift+click, or Edit ⇨ Select All (Ctrl+A). Then drag any selected clip to the workspace.

That's all there is to it. If you make a mistake, you can delete a clip from the storyboard or timeline just by right-clicking it and choosing Delete. Doing so *only* removes the clip from the workspace and doesn't remove the clip from its collection or the file from your drive. If you decide to change the order of some clips, just drag any clip to a new location in the workspace and drop it there. (You may find it easiest to do this in the Storyboard view, in which all the clips are the same size.)

If you want to insert a clip between two adjacent scenes in the storyboard, just drag the clip into the storyboard and drop it between the two existing scenes. If the scene is already in the storyboard, just drag it into place between the existing scenes.

Previewing the movie

You can preview how your finished movie is going to look at any time. Just keep in mind that there's a difference between playing a movie and playing a clip. To view the entire movie, you first need to make sure that no specific clip is selected in the workspace. You can do this easily by clicking any blank area in the timeline — on any blank frame in the storyboard view, or to the right of segments in the timeline view. Then choose Play ➪ Play Entire Storyboard/Timeline from Movie Maker's menu bar.

The entire movie starts to play. In the Timeline view, a vertical bar movies along the workspace to show you where you are in the movie at the moment. In the Storyboard view, a yellow border surrounds the scene that's currently appearing in the monitor.

You can pause the movie playback by choosing Play ➪ Play/Pause again. (Or just tap the spacebar). You can step through the movie frame by frame using the Previous Frame and Next Frame options on the Play menu. Or press Alt+→ to move one frame to the right, or Alt+← to move one frame to the left. Choose Play ➪ Play/Pause or press the spacebar again to resume normal playback after pausing. The Back and Forward options on the Play menu move you to the previous and next clips, respectively, in the movie. Choosing Play ➪ Stop stops playback.

Adding transition effects

You can add *cross-fade transitions* between clips in your movie, where one scene fades out while the other fades in. This eliminates the abrupt changes between scenes within your movie. To add a transition:

1. Go to the Timeline view in the workspace (View ➪ Timeline).
2. If necessary, click the Zoom In and Zoom Out buttons to the left of the toolbar to expand or contract the size of the scenes in the timeline.
3. Decide which two clips you want to place a transition effect between and then click the clip on the right side of the two. It becomes surrounded by a blue frame and its portion of the timeline is highlighted.
4. Drag the selected scene to the left so that it partially overlaps the scene to the left. The larger the overlap, the longer the transition between the frames.

To watch the effect, choose Play ➪ Play Pause. You can drag the vertical bar toward the transition effect if you don't want to wait for the normal play speed to reach that point. If you want to increase the decrease the duration of the transition, drag the scene on the right side of the transition to the left or right to increase or decrease the amount of overlap. If you change your mind and decide to delete the transition effect altogether, drag the scene on the right as far to the right as you can and then release the mouse button.

Trimming scenes

If you decide that a scene is running to long, you can trim frames off the front and/or back to shorten the scene. To do so, you set starting and ending *trim points* within the scene. Only content between the two scenes will be played when you view the movie. Here's how to set the trim points:

1. Set the workspace to the Storyboard view (choose View ➪ Storyboard from the menu bar or click the Storyboard button).

2. In the storyboard, click the frame that represents the scene you want to trim.

3. In the workspace, click the clip that you want to trim and then click the Play button to start playing the clip.

4. Click the Play button below the monitor to play the current scene.

5. When the scene gets close to where you want to set the starting trim point, click the Pause button under the monitor. You can use the Step Ahead and Step Back buttons to get to the specific frame, if need be.

6. Choose Clip ➪ Set Start Trim Point from the menu bar to set the starting trim point.

7. Click the Play button or click the Step Ahead button under the monitor to continue playing the scene. When you get near the point where you want to set the ending trim point, click the Pause button beneath the monitor.

8. Once again, you can use the Step Ahead and Step Back buttons beneath the monitor to move to a specific frame within the scene.

9. Choose Clip ➪ Set End Trim Point.

To see the trimmed scene, click its frame in the storyboard and then choose Play ➪ Play/Pause to play just that scene. If you change your mind and want to remove the trim points, click the scene in the storyboard again to select it and choose Play ➪ Play/Pause from the menu bar. While the scene is playing, choose Clip ➪ Clear Trim Points from the menu bar.

Trimming the scene in the movie has no effect on the original clip. If you want to see the clip again without the trim points, play the original clip rather than the movie.

Adding still photos to your movie

You can add still photos to your movies. This can be useful in a video in which you want to display an unchanging chart or other illustrations. If you have an existing photo or other still image that you'd like to insert into your movie, you can import the image as you would a video clip. The image needs to be in .bmp, .dib, .jpg, .jpeg,

.jpe, .jfif, or .gif format. If necessary, you convert its file type as discussed in Chapter 22. Then, to import the image:

1. Click on the collection to which you'd like to add the photo.

2. Choose File ⇨ Import from Movie Maker's menu bar.

3. In the dialog box that appears, navigate to the folder that contains the image that you want to import. To reduce the number of filenames shown, you can choose Still Images from the Files of Type drop-down list near the bottom of the dialog box.

4. Click the icon or filename of the image you want to import. (If you're using Classic navigation, double-click the icon, or click it once and then click Open.)

The photo is added to the collection. Its icon looks the same as any other clip's. When you click the icon, the image appears in the monitor. (Clicking the Play button has no effect, of course, since it's not a video.)

As an alternative to importing an existing digital image, you can convert a single video frame to a photo. You'll need to go through all the steps described in the section "Capturing content" to capture material from a video camera, VCR, digital device, or Web cam. But don't click the Record button to capture all the content. Instead, as the content is playing in the monitor of the Record dialog box, click the Take Photo button rather than the record button. If you're using a digital video camera, you can use the Pause button to stop playback at the frame you want to convert to a photo before you click the Take Photo button.

Tip You can create slide shows without video clips by adding a series of still photos to a storyboard. You can then spice that up by adding an audio track and/or narration as described a little later in this chapter.

As soon as you click the Take Photo button, a Save Photo dialog box appears. Choose a folder in which you want to store the photo from the Save In drop-down list. Then give the photo a filename with the .jpg extension. Click the Save button and Movie Maker will save the photo to disk and also add a clip of the photo to the current collection. You can click the Cancel button in the Record dialog box to close it. The photo's icon on the collection will look the same as any video clip's icon.

Once you've added a photo to a collection, you can follow these steps to insert the photo into your movie, just drag the photo's icon from the collections area to any place in the storyboard or timeline.

Note If the *aspect ratio* (ratio of height to width) of the photo doesn't match the aspect ratio of the video screen, black space will appear around the edges of the photo.

When you play the entire movie, any photos you've added to the movie will appear for five seconds each. If you want to change the duration of photos in the movie, choose View ➪ Option from the menu bar. Change the number of seconds displayed for Still Image Duration to however long you want photos to appear within the movie.

Tip   All photos in a movie will be displayed for the same duration. But you can make any photo appear for a longer duration by adding multiple copies of the photo, in sequence, to the storyboard or timeline. You can fade into and out of stills using the same techniques used to cross fade between video sequences.

Adding audio to your movie

You can insert audio clips into your movie in much the same way you insert video clips and still photos. First, you'll need to import or capture the audio into a collection. You can import existing audio clips that are stored in the .wav, .wma, .aif, .aiff, .aifc, .snd, .mp3, or .au formats. To import such a clip:

1. Click on the collection to which you want to add the audio clip.

2. Choose File ➪ Import from Movie Maker's menu bar.

3. Navigate to the folder that contains the existing audio clip.

4. Optionally, choose Audio Files from the Files of Type drop-down list to limit the display to compatible audio file formats.

5. Click (or double-click) the name of the audio file you want to import.

Tip   As discussed in Chapter 20, Windows Media Player can convert .cda music imported from an audio CD to the .wma format, which can be imported into Windows Movie Maker. The Media Wizard program from CDH Productions (www.cdhnow.com) can convert audio files to and from a variety of formats.

The clip appears as an icon in the current collection. To listen to the clip, double-click it (or click it once, and then click the Play button under the monitor).

If you want to important audio from an external source, such as a cassette tape player, CD player, or whatever, you can do so using File ➪ Record and the general procedure discussed in the section "Capturing content" earlier in this chapter. You'll need to connect the device to the computer, choose Audio Only from the Record drop-down list in the Record dialog box, and choose the appropriate audio device using the Change Device button. However, if you want to copy audio from an audio CD, you'd probably find it easier to just use Media Player as discussed in Chapter 20 to copy the audio track to a .wma file on your hard disk.

Once you have an audio file in your collection, you can add it to your movie by following these simple steps:

1. In the workspace, switch to the Timeline view (choose View ⇨ Timeline).

2. Drag the audio clip's icon to the timeline and drop it at about where you want it to start playing.

3. Release the mouse button.

The audio track appears below the storyboard/timeline as a light blue bar next to the microphone button in the workspace area. As necessary, you can drag the blue bar to the left or right to control exactly when the audio clip will start to play.

If the audio clip is longer than the movie, the clip will actually play after the video has stopped. So you'll probably want to limit the length of any audio track to the length of the movie. You can get an accurate measure of the movie's length by going to the Timeline view and dragging the vertical bar that crosses the timeline to the end of the movie. The timer beneath the monitor will show the duration of the movie up to where the vertical line is resting. For example 0:3:25:03 would indicate that the movie is about three minutes and 25 seconds long.

To create a shortened copy of your sound clip, click its name in the collections area and then click the Play button under the monitor. As the sound is playing, the duration will appear beneath the monitor. You can drag the seek bar to quickly move toward the desired time duration and then click the Pause button when you reach that spot. Choosing Clip ⇨ Split from the menu at that point will split the audio clip into two clips. The first (original) clip will then be the length of the movie. The second new clip that appears will be the remainder of the audio clip. If you drag the first original clip to the workspace and align the beginning with the start of the movie, its duration should match the movie's duration quite well.

Narrating a movie

You can also narrate a movie as it's playing. You'll need a microphone or headset plugged into your sound card to do this. But assuming you've already taken care of all that (as discussed back in Chapter 20), narrating the movie will be pretty easy:

1. Click on the collection to which you'd like to add the recorded narration.

2. Switch the workspace to the Timeline view (choose View ⇨ Timeline from Movie Maker's menu bar).

3. Choose File ⇨ Record Narration from the menu bar. The Record Narration Track dialog box, shown in Figure 23-10, appears.

4. If the selected Device and Line aren't correct, click the Change button and then choose the appropriate audio device and line.

Figure 23-10: The Record Narration Track dialog box

5. To prevent any audio from the movie's existing soundtrack from being played while you're narrating, choose the Mute Video Soundtrack option.

6. Speak into the microphone and watch for a reaction on the Record Level indicator. If necessary, drag the slider up or down to increase or decrease the microphone sensitivity. You want the loudest noises (only) to just reach the top of the bar.

7. When you're ready to start narrating, click the Record button.

8. As the movie is playing in the monitor speak into the microphone and narrate the movie as it plays.

9. When you get to the end of the movie, or whenever you want to stop narration, click the Stop button in the Record Narration Track dialog box.

10. When prompted, choose a folder to save the narration in and enter a filename with the .wav extension. Then click the Save button.

The narration appears as a clip in the current collection and is also added to the movie automatically. In the workspace it appears as a bluish line along the bottom of the storyline or timeline, next to the microphone icon in the workspace toolbox

To hear the narration while watching the movie, just play the movie as you normally would (choose Play ➪ Play/Pause from the menu bar). If you're not happy with the narration and want to try again, you can delete the current narration by right-clicking that bluish line and choosing Delete from the menu that appears.

As with video clips and photos, audio clips can also be overlapped. To make two audio tracks overlap one another, first drag them both to the workspace. Initially, the audio clips will not overlap. But you can drag the clip on the right to the left, so that it covers the first audio track, either entirely or partially. Wherever the two tracks overlap, the audio will be played simultaneously.

Keep in mind that if any video clips already contain audio, that audio will also be played. Things can get pretty complicated this way. So if you're thinking about adding a soundtrack to your movie, and the video clips already have audio of their own, you may want to limit yourself to just adding background music or narration to the movie, but not both.

You can adjust the relative volume of the audio from the video clips and the audio clips you add to the movie by following these steps:

1. Choose Edit ⇨ Audio Levels from Movie Maker's menu bar. The Audio Levels dialog box shown in Figure 23-11 appears.

Figure 23-11: The Audio Levels dialog box

2. To increase the volume of the audio clip you added yourself, drag the slider bar to the right.

3. Or, to increase the volume of the audio coming from the video clips, drag the slider to the left.

4. Click the Close (X) button in the upper-right corner of the dialog box.

Saving your work

The sum total of clips stored in a storyboard/timeline at any given moment is called a *project.* You might think of it as a work in progress as well. As you develop your movie you'll want to save that work from time to time, just to make sure you don't accidentally lose it when you exit Movie Maker (intentionally or by power outage.) To save your work:

1. Choose File ⇨ Save Project from Movie Maker's menu bar.

2. Choose a folder and enter a filename, as usual. Movie Maker will add the extension .MSWMM (for Microsoft Windows Movie Maker) to whatever name you provide.

Everything in the workspace is saved to the file. From this point on you can save your work at any time just by choosing File ⇨ Save Project or by clicking the Save Project button in the standard toolbar. You won't need to re-enter the filename each time. To prevent mishaps, you may want to get into the habit of saving the project each time you've successfully made some change to the movie.

Opening a project

To re-open a project in the future, start Movie Maker again. Initially, your collection of clips will appear, but there will be no movie in the workspace. To open a previously saved movie, choose File ➪ Open Project from Movie Maker's menu bar. Then navigate to and open the project you want to work on. The movie will appear in the workspace.

Creating the Final Product

The true final product from a movie is a standalone .asf file that can be played by anyone who has Windows Media Player on his or her computer. Movie Maker automatically does all the conversion and compression necessary to make this .asf file as small as possible. However, you also have control over the size of that file. As with most things multimedia, the higher the quality of the sound and video, the larger the resulting .asf file will be. And the larger that file is, the longer it will take to transfer over the Internet. You might want to consider making several .asf files from your movie, all at different qualities, so you can get a sense of how much quality you're sacrificing to conserve file size. To save your movie to a .asf file:

1. Choose File ➪ Save Movie, or click the Save Movie button in the toolbar. The Save Movie dialog box shown in Figure 23-12 appears

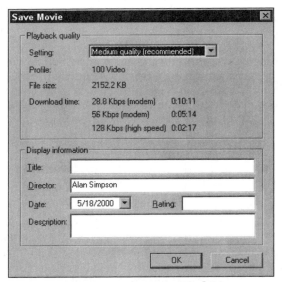

Figure 23-12: The Save Movie dialog box

2. Choose a quality from the Setting drop-down list. When you do, the information below the drop-down list changes to show you the profile, file size, and download times at various speeds for the file at that quality setting. There are actually seven quality profiles to choose from, the details of which are summarized in Table 23-1.

3. Optionally, add a Title, Director Name, Date, Rating, and Description to the dialog box.

4. Click the OK button. A Save As dialog box appears.

5. Choose a folder from the Save In drop-down list and then enter a filename for the movie. Keep the recommended .asf filename extension.

6. Click the Save button.

Table 23-1
Choices for Determining the Playback Quality of a Movie You Create

Quality	Name	Size (in Pixels)	Video Bit Rate (Bytes)	Audio Quality	Audio Bit Rate (Bytes)
Low	56.6 dial-up modem	176×144	21,006	FM radio (11.025 kHz)	9,992
Medium	100 video	320×240	80,680	FM radio (16 kHz)	16,000
High	250 video	320×240	216,200	FM radio (22.05 kHz)	32,040
Other	28.8 dial-up modem	160×120 (8 kHz)	14,000	AM radio	8,000
Other	512 video	320×240	452,488	Near CD (44.1 kHz)	64,040
Other	1Mb video	320×240	976,776	Near CD (44.1 kHz)	64,040
Other	3Mb video	320×240	3,041,928	CD quality (44.1 kHz)	96,040

To try out your movie at different qualities, repeat the steps. Choose a different quality for each save in Step 2 and enter a unique filename for each in Step 5 (for example, My FirstMovie28K.ASF, MyFirstMovie56K.ASF, MyFirstMovieMedium.ASF, and so forth).

To really see how your movies play, close Movie Maker. If you haven't saved the project lately, you'll be prompted to do so first. Go ahead and choose Yes to save the latest version of your movie.

Next, use My Computer or Windows Explorer to navigate to whatever folder you stored the .asf files in. Then click (or double-click) any .asf file to have it open in Windows Media Player. Remember, in Media Player you can only watch the movie. If you want to make changes to it, you'll need to open Movie Maker again and then use File ⇨ Open Project to open the original movie. If you make any changes to that original movie, you'll need to use Save Movie once again to create new .asf file(s) from the current movie project.

Tips, Tricks, and Troubleshooting

This chapter covers the nuts-and-bolts of what's involved in creating a movie. But streaming media and video multimedia technologies are evolving quickly these days, and things will change as the months go by. If you have access to the Internet, I recommend you check out www.windowsmedia.com from time to time to see what's new, and to check for new versions of Movie Maker and Media Player.

For tips on sending movies as e-mail attachments, or adding them to a Web site, see Movie Maker's Help screens. That is, choose Help ⇨ Help Topics and click the Contents tab. Expand the Windows Movie Maker, Using Windows Movie Maker, and Sending Movies books to get some tips on sending movies via the Internet. For troubleshooting help, open the Troubleshooting book there in the online help. For general tips on recording quality video and audio, see the Creating the Best Audio and Video Source Material book under Getting Started.

Summary

This chapter has covered all the basic skills and techniques you'll need to create your own movies using the new Windows Movie Maker. It all boils down to gathering a collection of video clips, still images, and/or audio clips, and then organizing them along a timeline into a cohesive movie. The main points to remember from this chapter include:

✦ Microsoft Movie Player can import clips in a variety of multimedia formats and organize them into a single movie that's stored as a .asf file.

✦ A *collection* is similar to a folder and acts as a container for organizing video, still image, and audio clip files.

✦ Multimedia files in a variety of popular formats can be imported into Movie Maker clip collections.

✦ You can also create clips by *capturing* content from analog and digital video cameras, VCRs, microphones, Web cams, and other devices.

✦ To create a movie, you drag clips to the workspace at the bottom of the screen; you can display the clips in either Storyboard or Timeline view.

✦ The order of clips along the storyboard/timeline indicates the order in which they'll be displayed in the movie.

✦ The Play pull-down menu in Movie Maker offers commands for watching the movie as a whole.

✦ A movie "work in progress" is referred to as a *project,* and can be saved via File ➪ Save Project from Movie Maker's menu bar.

✦ The end result of a project is a single movie stored as a .asf file, which can be viewed by anyone who has Microsoft Media Player.

✦　　✦　　✦

Road Warrior Tools and Techniques

Hardware for mobile computing has evolved tremen-
dously over the years. Laptop computers now rival
desktops in storage and processing capability. PC Cards
(PCMCIA) are credit card-sized boards that you can install and
remove on the fly. Docking stations make it easy to use a laptop as both a desktop and a mobile PC. And improved dial-up
networking capabilities make computing on the road easier
than ever. As you'll see in this chapter, Windows Me offers
many goodies to help you get the most from your portable
computer.

Mobile Computing Features

Many of Windows Me's features make mobile computing easier. Some of the features are specifically designed for newer
laptops with the special plug-and-play BIOS and power-
management capabilities. But if you're one of the many millions who bought a laptop before these hardware options
became available, don't fret — plenty of features help you
compute on the road, regardless of what type of laptop PC
you own.

The following is a summary of these features:

✦ Hot docking and flexible configurations

✦ Power management

✦ Deferred printing

✦ Dial-from settings that you can change on the fly

✦ The Briefcase

✦ Improved PC Card (PCMCIA) support

✦ Dial-Up Networking

✦ Direct Cable Connection to a LAN or PC

Many of these features are installed automatically when you install Windows Me. If you don't find a particular component, either your hardware doesn't support it, and/or the software for that component isn't installed. If it's just that the software isn't installed, you can install the component via Windows Setup, as discussed in Chapter 25. For more information on you own computer hardware, check the documentation that came with your laptop computer.

Hot Docking and Flexible Configurations

A docking station (also called a port replicator) is an optional device that connects a laptop to a desktop PC or to a desktop-size monitor, keyboard, mouse, and other peripherals. The idea is to provide the storage, display, and extensibility options of a desktop PC without sacrificing portability.

To become mobile, you just need to disconnect the PC from the docking station. Unfortunately, in the old days, disconnecting wasn't as easy as it sounded. The job required manually changing configuration files, such as CONFIG.SYS and AUTOEXEC.BAT, before disconnecting or reconnecting — a time-consuming and technically challenging endeavor for many laptop users. Windows Me offers two features that simplify the process: hot docking and flexible configurations.

Hot docking

Many laptops that ship with Windows Me support hot docking, which enables you to dock and undock the laptop without even turning it off. This is both a hardware and software capability, so you probably should check the manual that came with your laptop computer for specific instructions.

In general, though, you should be able to undock your laptop by clicking the Start button and choosing Eject PC. Windows Me automatically detects the impending hardware changes, takes care of any potential problems with open files on an external drive, and loads or unloads any appropriate drivers.

To redock, simply put the laptop back into the docking station. Windows Me again loads the appropriate drivers automatically. If you used deferred printing while your laptop was undocked, Print Manager starts automatically and prompts you to print any documents you printed while the laptop was undocked.

Not-so-hot docking

If you have an older laptop, you can't count on hot docking. You may have to power down your PC before connecting to, or disconnecting from, the docking station (check your laptop's documentation to learn whether you must do this). You can simplify matters, though, by creating two separate hardware configurations: one for docked status and the other for undocked status. Here is the quick and easy way to create these configurations:

1. Click the Start button.
2. Choose Settings ⇨ Control Panel.
3. Open the System icon.
4. Click the Hardware Profiles tab.
5. Click the Original Configuration option and then click the Copy button.
6. Name the new configuration Docked Configuration.
7. Click the Original Configuration option again and then click the Copy button again.
8. Name this new configuration Undocked Configuration.
9. Choose OK to leave the System Properties dialog box.

Now you have three identical hardware configurations, named Original Configuration, Docked Configuration, and Undocked Configuration. I'll show you how to make each configuration unique soon. First, though, you must know the proper way to dock and undock your laptop.

Cold docking and undocking

Unlike hot docking, cold docking (and undocking for that matter) involves completely shutting down your laptop before you do anything. You could think of this as the safe way of doing things, but if you don't like waiting for Windows to shut down and then restart, it can be tiresome. Whenever you want to dock or undock your laptop, follow these steps:

1. Click the Start button.
2. Choose Shut Down.
3. Choose Shut down and then click Yes.
4. When the screen says it's safe to do so, turn off the laptop.
5. Dock or undock the laptop.

When you restart the PC later, keep an eye on the screen. You'll see something similar to the following before the Windows Me desktop appears:

```
Windows cannot determine what configuration your computer is
in. Select one of the following:

1. Original Configuration
2. Docked Configuration
3. Undocked configuration
4. None of the above

Enter your choice:
```

Type the appropriate item number (2 if you're docked, 3 if you're undocked, and so on), and then press Enter.

The first time you use Undocked Configuration, Windows Me may complain about some new or missing hardware, but you should be able to work your way through any error messages until you get to the Windows Me desktop. Once you get to the desktop, you can customize your configuration, as discussed in the following section.

Customizing hardware configurations

Much of the work needed to customize your docked and undocked configurations may have been done automatically when you restarted your PC and chose Undocked Configuration.

But you can refine your hardware settings for a particular configuration by following these simple steps:

1. Click the Start button.

2. Choose Settings ➪ Control Panel.

3. Open the System icon.

4. Click the Device Manager tab.

5. Click the plus (+) sign next to any device type to see devices within this category.

6. Double-click on any device name to see its properties.

7. At the bottom of the dialog box that appears (see Figure 24-1), choose the "Disable in this hardware profile" option if you want to disable that device in the current configuration. Otherwise, leave that option blank. Choose the "Exists in all hardware profiles" option only if the device will, indeed, exist in all the hardware profiles you create.

8. Repeat Steps 5 to 7 for as many devices as you want.

9. Choose OK and Close to work your way back to the desktop.

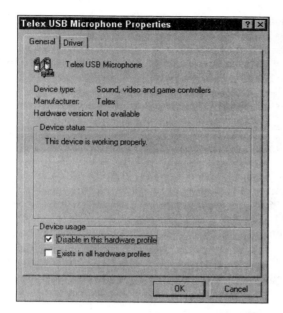

Figure 24-1: You can enable and disable a hardware device for the current hardware profile.

Comfort settings

The hardware configurations discussed so far work for hardware devices. You also may want to carry more-refined comfort settings from one configuration to another. For example, you may want to use one set of screen colors and mouse properties when your laptop is docked and another set when the machine is undocked.

The hardware configurations don't keep track of personal preferences. But you can create multiple user profiles for yourself, perhaps named Docked and Undocked. Thereafter, when you log in, you can choose whichever user profile is currently appropriate. For more information, see Chapter 29.

Power Management

Battery life is a major concern for many mobile-computer users. Windows Me supports the Power Management Standards that most computers — especially laptops — offer. Specifically, Windows Me provides:

✦ An optional battery indicator in the taskbar

✦ The capability to put your laptop in Suspend mode by clicking the Start button and choosing the Shut Down ⇨ Suspend

✦ The capability to have the computer shut off automatically when you exit Windows

✦ The capability to create custom "power schemes" that suit your needs at the moment

Creating Power Schemes is pretty easy. First, follow these steps to get to the Power Options Properties dialog box:

1. Click the Start button.

2. Choose Settings ➪ Control Panel.

3. Open the Power Options icon (if available).

On the Power Schemes tab of the dialog box that opens (Figure 24-2), choose how long you want to allow the computer to sit idle before Windows shuts down the monitor and hard drives, and/or puts the computer into Standby mode. You can choose an existing scheme from the Power Schemes drop-down list. Or you can create your own scheme, click the Save As button, and give this new scheme a name. For example, in Figure 24-2 I've created a Power Scheme named Battery that shuts down the monitor and hard disks, and puts the computer into standby mode after the computer has been sitting idle for just three minutes.

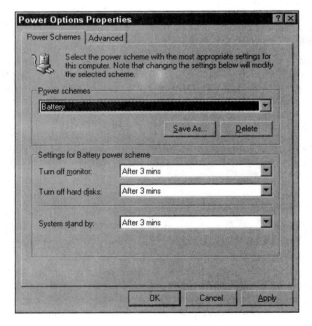

Figure 24-2: The Power Schemes tab of the Power Options Properties dialog box

On the Advanced tab of the Power Options Properties dialog box (Figure 24-3), you can choose whether you want the power icon to always be visible in the taskbar. It's a good idea to select this option if you'll be using batteries to run your computer, as it can help warn you when the batteries are running low.

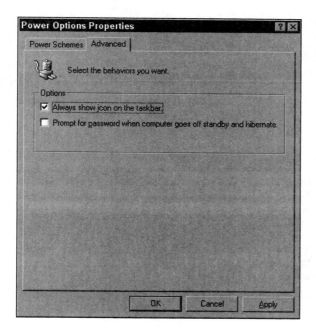

Figure 24-3: The Advanced tab of the Power Options Properties dialog box

If you select the second option, Prompt for password, then whenever the computer goes into standby or hibernate mode, you'll need to enter a password to get back to the desktop. If you choose this option, make sure you think up a good password and write it down somewhere so you won't forget. Otherwise, you'll lock yourself out of your own computer!

Click OK at the bottom of the Power Options dialog box after making your selections to save those choices and close the dialog box.

Deferred Printing

Deferred printing lets you print a document even when your laptop is not connected to a printer. Sort of. More specifically, this feature does everything necessary to prepare a file for printing. Suppose you aren't currently connected to a printer, but you want to be certain to print a document when you get to a printer. No problem — go ahead and print the document normally. A message appears, telling you that the printer isn't available, but that you can work in offline mode. When you choose OK, the document is prepared for printing and sent to the selected printer's queue.

Tip   If you're in a hotel room with your laptop and fax modem, but you don't have a printer, send a copy of the document to yourself via the hotel's fax machine — instant hard copy. You also can use the hotel's fax machine to scan documents into your PC. Fax the hard copy to your hotel room and have the portable PC answer the phone.

Now you can forget about that document. You can do all your other work normally, exit Windows, turn off the computer, whatever. When you reconnect to the printer later, you'll see a message telling you that there are documents waiting to be printed. Just click the Yes button beneath the message and printing will start right up.

Managing Multiple Dial-From Locations

Another traditional headache associated with mobile computing is dialing out from the PC. When you're dialing from outside your own area code, you must dial 1 plus the area code for numbers that used to be local. When you're in a hotel room, you may need to dial 8 to get an outside line or 9 before dialing long distance.

The Windows Me Dialing Properties dialog box greatly simplifies matters by enabling you to change dial-out settings on the fly. You need to install your modem first, as discussed in Chapter 5. Then, whenever you want to change the location from which you're dialing, follow these steps:

1. Click the Start button.

2. Choose Settings ➪ Control Panel.

3. Open the Telephony icon to display the dialog box shown in Figure 24-4.

4. To set new dialing properties, click the New button and then type a name for the settings you're about to create into the "I am dialing from" drop-down list.

5. Click the Apply button.

6. Fill in the Dialing Properties dialog box with information that describes where you're dialing from and how to dial.

   If you're outside your normal area code, for example, type the current area code. If you need to dial a special number to get an outside line, set the appropriate options for local and long-distance dialing.

7. When you finish, click OK.

After you create the dialing settings, you needn't recreate them. The settings you choose stay in effect until you go back into the Control Panel and choose different dialing properties from the Telephony icon.

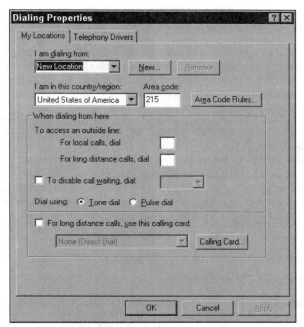

Figure 24-4: The Dialing Properties dialog box

The Virtual Briefcase

Many people use their portable PC as a kind of virtual briefcase. Perhaps you generally do your work on a desktop PC. To take your work on the road, you copy the appropriate files from the desktop PC to your laptop for editing on the road. When you get back to the office, you copy the updated files from the portable PC back to the desktop PC.

The one problem is things can get confusing. Fortunately, the Windows Me Briefcase helps reduce the confusion and simplifies the entire process. The general idea behind using Briefcase is simple, as the following list explains:

✦ When you want to take work on the road, simply drag that work into Briefcase.

✦ To use a Briefcase document on the road, open Briefcase and open the document name. Then perform your work and save the document normally.

✦ When you get back to the office, unpack Briefcase by opening My Briefcase and choosing Briefcase ➪ Update All.

High-speed Internet wherever you go

Road warriors, check this out! IPORT is an easy-to-use system that enables you to connect your laptop computer at high speed to the Internet and to your company's intranet from anywhere in the world that offers IPORT access — all for less than the cost of a long-distance phone call.

Developed jointly by ATCOM/INFO and Microsoft, IPORT is ideal for travelers who want to use the Internet and e-mail on their own computers while they're on the road. Basically, IPORT is a special RJ-45 wall jack to which you can connect your portable computer and IPORT software enables you to gain access to the Internet, e-mail, or whatever else you do online. So far, availability of these ports is limited to some hotels in large metropolitan areas, but plans call for them to become more widely available in places like airports, convention centers, and other public venues. In concept, IPORT should prove a valuable tool, especially for business travelers who need frequent Internet access. To use IPORT, you'll need:

✦ Microsoft Windows Me

✦ 10BaseT Ethernet network card and cable (which you connect to an RJ-45 wall jack)

✦ TCP/IP protocol configured to obtain IP addresses automatically

✦ Web browser, e-mail program, or similar software to use the Internet or your corporate intranet (Outlook Express and Internet Explorer will do the job fine)

✦ And, of course, the IPORT software, which is free

For more information about IPORT and related communications products for the business traveler, visit the ATCOM/INFO Web site at http://www.atcominfo.com.

Before you use Briefcase, you must have the My Briefcase icon on one of the computers. If neither computer shows the My Briefcase icon on the desktop, use the techniques described in Chapter 25 to install Briefcase on one of your PCs.

Briefcase relies entirely on your computer's internal calendar and clock to determine which version of a document is the most current version, so make sure your clocks are in sync. See the section on changing the date and time in Chapter 15.

If the two computers are not connected via a cable or LAN, you must use floppy disks with Briefcase. The following sections discuss how to use Briefcase with or without floppies.

Using Briefcase without floppy disks

If the desktop and portable PCs are connected via a LAN or some other cable connection, you can use Briefcase without fumbling with floppy disks. When you're about to hit the road, all you must do is pack your Briefcase. To pack Briefcase, drag the files you want to take on the road into the My Briefcase icon on your portable PC. Just follow these steps:

1. On the portable computer, use Network Neighborhood, My Computer, Windows Explorer, or Find to locate any document you want to put into Briefcase.

2. If you want to put several documents into Briefcase, select them by Ctrl+clicking and/or Shift+clicking.

3. Drag the documents to the My Briefcase icon.

Or, right-click the selected documents, choose Send To, and then choose My Briefcase.

When Windows Me finishes copying files, the hard disk in the portable PC will have its own copies of the files you want to take on the road. Then you can shut down the portable and disconnect it from its docking station or network card.

While you're on the road

When on the road, remember this: whenever you want to work on a Briefcase document, get it from Briefcase. You can retrieve the document in either of these following ways:

✦ Open the My Briefcase icon on the desktop and then open the document with which you want to work.

✦ If you're already in a program, choose File ⇨ Open to display the Open dialog box. In the Look In drop-down list, select My Briefcase and then open the name of the file that you want to open.

Now you can go about your business normally. When you finish, close and save the document and exit the program normally. The edited copy of your document is stored in Briefcase automatically.

When you return from the trip

When you get back from your road trip, you want to unpack Briefcase — that is, get the documents you left behind in sync with the newer copies on your portable PC's hard disk. Just follow these steps:

1. Redock (or reconnect) the portable PC to the docking station, LAN, or cable that hooks it to the desktop PC.

Tip

If your laptop supports hot docking, My Briefcase may launch automatically as soon as you reconnect to the docking station.

2. Start Windows Me and open the My Briefcase icon.

3. Click Update All on the toolbar. If you only want to update specific files, highlight them in the list and click Update Selection. A dialog box with an arrow pointing from the new version of the file to the old version displays.

4. To update, click the Update button.

Remember that after you update your files using My Briefcase, the old files that were originally put into the briefcase before your trip will be replaced. If you want to retain a copy of the old version of the file (always a good idea), save a copy of it in another folder or disk before you update.

Using Briefcase with floppies

You can use Briefcase even if the portable and desktop computers are not connected by any sort of cable. The downside to this approach is you must use a floppy disk as your virtual briefcase, which means your storage is limited to 1.4MB (or 2.5MB). If you work mainly with word processing and spreadsheet documents, though, that limit may be plenty roomy.

Tip   As mentioned in Chapter 27, you can use DriveSpace to increase the capacity of a 1.4MB floppy to about 2.5MB.

If the icon named My Briefcase is already on your desktop PC, grab a floppy disk and label it My Briefcase. Then skip to "Packing the floppy Briefcase" later in this chapter. If My Briefcase is on your portable PC, read the next two sections to learn how to create your virtual briefcase and move it from the portable to the desktop PC.

What if both copies change?

Suppose you load a document into Briefcase and edit that document on the road. While you're away, somebody (let's say Harry) opens the document you left behind and changes it. When you return, Harry may not be too thrilled at the prospect of your replacing his copy of the document with the one in your Briefcase. You and Harry may have to decide who did what while you were away and then reconcile the differences. If you're lucky, the program both of you used to edit the document can reconcile the differences automatically. Windows Me supplies programmers with a set of tools called Reconciliation APIs. Using these tools, a program can hook into Briefcase and automatically reconcile the differences between two copies of a document that changed while one document was away in Briefcase. When you start upgrading to Windows Me versions of your favorite programs, check the manuals or online help systems for information on reconciling documents. Your days of negotiating with Harry may be over.

Creating a My Briefcase floppy disk

Step 1 in using My Briefcase with floppies is to create a floppy disk that acts as your virtual briefcase. To create such a disk, follow these steps:

1. Grab a blank floppy disk and label it My Briefcase.
2. Go to the portable PC, which has the My Briefcase icon on its screen, and put the floppy disk in drive A.
3. Open My Computer so you can see the icon for drive A. Move and size the My Computer window, if necessary, so that you also can see the desktop icon for My Briefcase.
4. Drag the My Briefcase icon to the icon for drive A.

The briefcase moves to the floppy disk and its icon disappears from the Windows desktop. Don't worry. You're only going to move the icon to the desktop PC.

Putting Briefcase on the desktop PC

Now you need to put Briefcase on the desktop PC (the one containing the files that you plan to take on your trip). To do so, follow these steps:

1. Take the floppy disk labeled My Briefcase to the desktop PC (which, presumably, contains the latest versions of the documents that you want to take with you).
2. Put the floppy disk in drive A.
3. Open My Computer.
4. Open the icon for drive A.

   You should see the My Briefcase icon in the window that opens.
5. Drag the My Briefcase icon from drive A to the Windows Me desktop.

At this point, Briefcase is on the desktop PC only. The floppy disk is empty because you moved Briefcase — you didn't copy it.

Packing the floppy Briefcase

Suppose you're about to go on a trip and you want to take a few documents from the desktop PC with you. Follow these steps:

1. At the desktop PC, use My Computer, Windows Explorer, or Find to get to any document you want to put into Briefcase.
2. Select the documents that you want to take.
3. Drag the documents to the My Briefcase icon.

Now the My Briefcase icon on your desktop PC contains copies of the files that you want to take on your trip. You need to take those copies with you, so now you need to move the filled Briefcase from the desktop PC to a floppy disk. Follow these steps:

1. Insert the floppy disk you labeled My Briefcase into drive A of the desktop computer.

2. Open My Computer and move and size its window so that you can see both the icon for drive A and the icon for My Briefcase.

3. Drag the My Briefcase icon from the Windows Me desktop to the icon for drive A.

Windows Me moves Briefcase to the floppy disk, so you won't see the My Briefcase icon on the desktop computer's screen anymore. Don't worry. Just pack that floppy disk with your portable PC. You'll use that floppy as your virtual briefcase while you're on the road.

On the road with a floppy Briefcase

When you're on the road with your portable PC and floppy Briefcase, follow these steps to work on your documents:

1. Insert the My Briefcase floppy into drive A of your portable PC.

Tip

If you don't want to work from floppies on the road, you can drag the files from My Briefcase on the floppy disk to your portable PC's hard disk. Then you can edit directly from the hard disk. When you finish editing, put the My Briefcase floppy disk in drive A, open My Briefcase on that floppy, and choose Briefcase ➪ Update All.

2. Open the My Computer icon.

3. Open the icon for drive A.

4. Open the My Briefcase icon.

5. Open the name of the document with which you want to work.

Now you can work on the document normally. When you finish working with the document, exit the program and save your work normally. Windows automatically saves the modified version in its original location: My Briefcase on drive A.

Unpacking the floppy Briefcase

When you return to the home office, your best bet is to move the My Briefcase icon back to the Windows Me desktop of your desktop PC and then update files from there. Follow these steps:

1. Insert the My Briefcase floppy into drive A of the desktop PC.

2. Open My Computer.

3. Open the icon for drive A.

4. Drag the My Briefcase icon to the Windows Me desktop.

At this point, the floppy disk is empty again and Briefcase is back on the desktop PC. You can see the My Briefcase icon on the Windows Me desktop. To get the documents on the desktop PC in sync with the copies in Briefcase, follow these steps:

1. Open the My Briefcase icon on the desktop.

2. Click Update All on the toolbar and follow the instructions onscreen.

When you finish, you can go back to editing the files outside Briefcase. You need to use the files inside Briefcase only when you're on the road. If you don't think you'll edit the same files on the road again, you can regain some space by deleting them from Briefcase. Open the My Briefcase icon, select the files you want to delete, and then choose File ⇨ Delete.

Tip   Another quick way to update your files is to right-click the My Briefcase icon on the desktop and choose Update All from the shortcut menu.

Summary

The combined power of today's mobile computers and Windows Me makes your work on the road more headache-free than ever. Of course, you still have to make it all happen by remembering some important points:

✦ Try to use a laptop that supports hot docking. You can create multiple hardware profiles for your docked and undocked configurations using the Hardware Profiles tab of the System icon in the Control Panel.

✦ To switch to another hardware configuration, shut down the computer and choose a new profile when Windows restarts.

✦ You can send jobs to the print queue even when your laptop is not connected to a printer. With deferred printing, the tasks will automatically be sent to the printer when you re-dock.

✦ Use Briefcase to simplify the task of copying files between computers. Copy the files you need on the road to Briefcase and then move Briefcase to your laptop.

✦ When you return home, move Briefcase back to your desktop system. Then open Briefcase and click Update All.

✦   ✦   ✦

V

Growth, Maintenance, and General Tweaking

✦ ✦ ✦ ✦

Installing and Removing Programs

Every Windows program, whether it is delivered to you on floppy disks or on CD-ROM, comes with its own installation program. Installing the programs usually is a breeze, as you'll see in this chapter. Remember, the techniques described here will work with nearly any DOS, Windows 3, Windows NT, Windows 95, Windows 98, Windows 2000, or Windows Me program you purchase. But if you have problems with a particular program or you need more information during an installation procedure, you should refer to the installation instructions that came with the program. I can cover only the general procedures here.

Installing New Programs

For those of you who are new to PC biz, a program must only be installed to your hard disk one time. You needn't install a program each time you want to use that program. Once a program is installed, you can start it by clicking the Start button, pointing to Programs, and then clicking the program's startup icon in the menu.

And here's a small caution. In this chapter, I talk specifically about installing programs on your computer. So consider the following guidelines before you begin:

✦ If you are trying to install fonts, use the techniques described in Chapter 19, rather than the techniques described in this chapter.

✦ If you are trying to install a driver for a new piece of hardware, use the Add New Hardware Wizard discussed in Chapter 26.

✦ If you are trying to copy files, such as other people's documents or clip art, use the general copying techniques discussed in Chapter 14.

✦ If the program you want to use is on a CD-ROM, it may have an auto-start capability. To find out, put the CD into your CD-ROM drive and wait a few seconds to see if anything appears onscreen. If an option to install (or play) the program appears, you can click that option.

✦ If you are trying to install a program you downloaded from an online service or the Internet, follow the instructions that came with the program. Downloaded files usually require you to decompress them before you install them and no general procedure applies to all downloaded programs. See Chapter 7 for more information.

So now, assuming you are, indeed, trying to install a program, you can use either the Add/Remove Programs Wizard or the Run command. I suggest you try the wizard first.

Using the Add/Remove Program Wizard

The Add/Remove Programs Wizard makes installing new programs a cinch. To use this wizard, follow these steps:

1. Save any work in progress and close all open programs.

2. If you're installing from floppy disks, put the program's Setup disk (usually disk #1) in a floppy disk drive. If you're installing from a CD-ROM, put the CD in the CD-ROM drive.

Note   To prevent confusion, remove disks from the floppy or CD-ROM drives you're not going to use during installation. Otherwise, Windows may think you're trying to install from one of those other drives.

3. If you are installing from a CD-ROM, wait about 30 seconds to see if the CD auto-starts. If it does, and you see an option to Install, select that option, follow the instructions onscreen, and skip all the following steps.

4. Assuming you're not installing from an auto-start CD, click the Start button, point to Settings, and then click Control Panel.

5. Open the Add/Remove Programs icon. The Add/Remove Programs Properties dialog box appears, as in Figure 25-1. Click the Install button to continue.

6. The first wizard screen asks you to insert a floppy disk or CD-ROM. But if you already did this in Step 2, you needn't bother. Just click the Next button.

7. The wizard searches the floppy and CD-ROM drives for SETUP.EXE or a similarly named file. If it finds such a file, the wizard displays its name and some instructions, as shown in Figure 25-2.

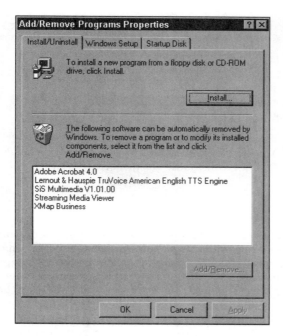

Figure 25-1: Here's the Add/ Remove Programs Properties dialog box, ready for action.

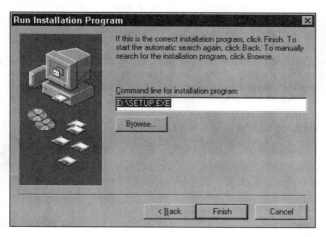

Figure 25-2: The wizard found a SETUP.EXE program on my CD-ROM drive (D).

8. Click the Finish button to launch the setup program.

Note

If the wizard can't find a setup program, refer to the section "Programs that have no setup" later in this chapter.

Check the README.TXT file

Many programs come with a file named README.TXT on the first floppy disk or the CD-ROM. Often, this file contains information relevant to installing the program. If you want to read this file before installing, first use My Computer, Windows Explorer, or Find to locate that README.TXT file on the installation floppy disk or CD. Then, open that icon. (If Windows asks which program to use, choose Notepad).

If you want to print the README.TXT file, choose File ➪ Print from Notepad's menu bar. When you finish with README.TXT, close Notepad by clicking its Close (X) button. If you're asked about saving changes to README.TXT, choose No (because you haven't made any intentional changes to that file).

Now you need to follow whatever instructions appear onscreen. I can't help you much with this part because Windows Me is out of the picture now and the setup program is in control. Do pay attention to where the installation program plans to put the installed program, however, so you can find it later. Be sure to complete all the installation instructions onscreen until you see a message indicating the installation was completed successfully.

When the installation is complete, you may be asked to restart your computer. Remove the last floppy disk, or the CD-ROM disk, from the drive and put the disks in a safe place for use as backups. If the screen tells you to restart the computer before trying to run the program, click the Restart button onscreen, if any. Or, if no Restart button appears, go to the desktop, click the Start button, choose Shut Down, choose Restart, and then click OK to shut down and restart your PC. After the computer starts up, you should be able to find the new program's startup icon in the Start menus — most likely by clicking the Start button and pointing to Programs.

Using Run to install a program

The installation instructions for a Windows 3.x or DOS program probably will tell you to start by choosing File ➪ Run from Program Manager. Windows Me has no Program Manager, of course, but you still can follow the program's installation instructions by making a detour to the Run dialog box, as follows:

1. Click the Start button, and then choose Run from the Start menu. You'll see the dialog box shown in Figure 25-3.

2. Follow the instructions given with your program, starting with the part that tells you what to type (for example, a:\setup.exe or a:\install.exe). If you don't know what the program's setup file is called, click the Browse button and look for a program with the word "install" or "setup" in its name.

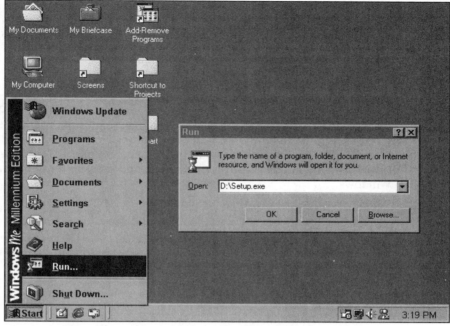

Figure 25-3: Click Run in the Start menu to open this dialog box.

3. Click OK or press Enter to launch the setup or install program.

4. Follow all the instructions onscreen. If you have any problems, see the section that follows for suggestions.

Programs that have no setup

If the wizard or Run doesn't find a setup or install program — or it finds the wrong one — don't panic. Choose Cancel from the error message (if you're using the Add/Remove Programs Wizard, choose Cancel again from the wizard window). Then try the following procedures:

✦ Remove disks from or open all the drives except the one from which you are installing the program. Make certain the installation disk is fully inserted into the appropriate drive. Then try again, using the Add/Remove Programs Wizard.

✦ Check the program's documentation for the name of the program you must run to start the installation. It may not be named "setup" or "install." When you find the name of the installation program, click Start and choose Run to run that specific program.

✦ If you are trying to run a setup or install program in a particular folder on the CD-ROM or floppy disk, you still can use the wizard or Run. Either way, you'll get to a dialog box that offers a Browse button. For example, after you click the Start button and choose Run, you can use the Browse button to navigate to the appropriate folder before you proceed.

✦ If the setup program is named something other than setup or install, try installing it from an MS-DOS window. To open the MS-DOS window, click the Start button, point to Programs, Accessories, and then click MS-DOS Prompt. Then switch to the drive that contains the setup program (for example, type **a:** and press Enter if the program is on floppy disk drive A). Now type the name of the installation program and press Enter. When you finish installing the DOS program, type **exit** and press Enter to return to Windows.

✦ Some programs install from a file named Setup.inf. To use this icon, you need to right-click it and then choose Install.

✦ Review the list under "Installing New Programs" at the start of this chapter and think about the type of files you want to install to your hard disk. Then proceed to the appropriate chapter.

Running the installed program

When a program is installed, you can use the following standard techniques to run it:

1. Click the Start button and then point to Programs.

2. Point to the Programs folder (group) icon until you find the startup icon for the program.

3. Click the program's startup icon.

If you can't find the program's startup icon on the Start menu, you can use My Computer, Windows Explorer, or Search to locate the program's startup icon. When you do, open that icon to launch the program. You also can create a shortcut to the program.

Remember, some (but not all) programs that come to you on CD-ROM must have the CD in the drive to work—even if you installed from that CD—because the installation procedure copies some programs from the CD-ROM, but large graphic images, sound files, and such are kept on the CD-ROM to conserve your hard disk space.

Consumer software alert

Consumer software for the home—including games, edutainment programs, and multi-media titles—is notoriously difficult to install and/or run, especially if it was designed for Windows 3.x or DOS. Some programs assume you're using a 256-color monitor and a 16-bit sound card. DOS-based programs assume you have plenty of conventional memory to spare. These are big assumptions, of course, and some home PCs don't measure up to the required specifications.

Sometimes, the problem is easy to fix. If the program complains you don't have a 256-color monitor, for example, you may need to activate this capability of your monitor (refer to Chapter 15). Or, you may be able to free some conventional memory. For help with this procedure, click the Start button, click Help, and then click the Troubleshooting link, and then explore the hardware and system device problems troubleshooter topic. You also can examine your available hardware by using Device Manager (see Chapter 26).

If all else fails, you may need to contact the manufacturer of the program.

Installing Missing Windows Components

When you installed Windows Me on your PC, the installation procedure made some decisions about which components to install and which not to install. You're not stuck with those decisions, though. If you can't find a program that supposedly comes with Windows Me, you can follow these instructions to install that program:

1. Gather your original Windows Me CD-ROM.

If you purchased a computer that came with Windows Me preinstalled, you may be able to install missing Windows components right from your internal hard disk.

2. Choose Start ➪ Settings ➪ Control Panel.

3. Open the Add/Remove Programs icon.

4. Click the Windows Setup tab to see the options shown in Figure 25-4.

Any component in the Windows Setup tab with a check mark is installed already. A check box that is both checked and grayed indicates some (but not all) components in that category are installed. (Click the Details button to see which are and which aren't installed.) Do not clear any check marks unless you're positive you want to remove those components.

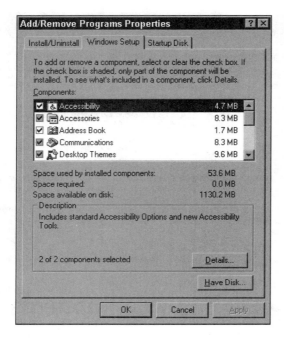

Figure 25-4: This Windows Setup tab enables you to add and remove Windows Me components.

5. Scroll through the list of available components. If you see the component you want to install, skip to Step 9.

6. If you don't see the component you want to install, check the component's details. That is, click any component (such as Accessories) and then click the Details button. As a shortcut, you can double-click the name of the component (not its check box) to see the details.

7. If you still don't see the component you want to install, click Cancel and then try a different component (for example, Communications).

8. Repeat Steps 6 and 7 until you find the component you want to install.

9. Click the check box next to the component you want to install, so it is checked. Repeat the steps of locating and checking boxes until you've checked all the components you want to install.

10. When you finish choosing components, click OK to leave the Details box (if you're in it). Then click OK to close the Add/Remove Programs Properties dialog box. Follow any instructions onscreen to install the component(s).

Things should go smoothly now. If the installation procedure looks for the components in the wrong place (for example, if it looks for a floppy disk in drive A rather than for the CD-ROM in drive D), you can click the Browse button and navigate to the appropriate drive to begin the installation.

Removing Installed Programs

You may want to remove an installed program for many reasons. Maybe you decided you don't like the program and you want to free the disk space it's using. Or, perhaps you bought a competing program from a different vendor and now you need to make some room on the disk to install this program.

As a general rule, when you upgrade to a new version of an existing program, you should not uninstall the earlier version first. The upgrade program will expect, perhaps even require, the earlier version to be installed. If you're in doubt, check the program's upgrade instructions.

Regardless of your motivation for removing a program, you must exercise some caution. Deleting a program and its folder can have peculiar side effects on files expecting that folder and/or program to be there, especially if you use the Delete key to delete the program's folder (as discussed later). A better practice is to uninstall (remove) the program formally, if possible, to prevent side effects. The following sections explain how.

Save your work first

Before you remove a program, stop to think about any documents you created and saved within that program's folder. If you're deleting Microsoft Word for Windows (which is part of the Microsoft Office suite), for example, did you create and save documents in the C:\MSOffice\winword folder or in a subfolder, such as C:\MSOffice\winword\documents? If so, are you sure you want to delete those documents?

If the answers to those questions are yes and no, respectively, create a new folder outside the program's folder (refer to Chapter 17); then move the documents you want to save to the new folder (refer to Chapter 14). Otherwise, when you delete the program's folder, you also might delete documents in that program's folder and subfolders.

Uninstalling with the Add/Remove Programs Wizard

Most Windows 95-, 98-, and Me-aware programs register themselves as programs that can be removed automatically (Windows 3.x and DOS programs do not). You should always try the following method of removing a program before resorting to any other method:

1. Choose Start ➪ Settings ➪ Control Panel.

2. Open the Add/Remove Programs icon.

3. Click the Install/Uninstall tab if it isn't selected already.

4. If the program you want to remove appears in the list, click that program's name. Then, click the Remove button and follow any instructions that appear onscreen.

Protecting your documents from hungry uninstall programs

The uninstall programs for each application vary in how they clean up. Some are careful not to delete files you created, but others may blow them away. For best results, be cautious and assume the uninstall program doesn't care a whit about what happens to documents you created within the program's own folders.

In general, avoid creating documents in the folders set up for you by a program's install procedure. For example, do not save documents in C:\MSOffice or its subfolders. Instead, create separate folders outside the application's standard folders for your own documents. As a convenience to you, the Windows Me installation program automatically creates a folder named My Documents. If you store your documents there (or in any subfolder of My Documents), your work will be safe from overzealous uninstall programs.

If you'd rather not use the My Documents folder, you can set up another folder for your work, such as the Projects folder discussed in Chapter 17.

If, in Step 4, you don't see the program you want to remove, check to see whether it's listed as a Windows component. To do this, click the Windows Setup tab, locate the component you want to remove (using the Details button if necessary), and clear the check box for this component. Then choose OK as needed and follow the instructions onscreen.

Uninstalling with SETUP.EXE

If you can't find the program you want to remove in the Add/Remove Programs Properties dialog box, try the following method:

1. Click the Cancel button, if necessary, to return to the Control Panel.

2. Close the Control Panel to return to the desktop.

3. If the program you want to remove is open, close it.

4. Click the Start button, click Programs, and then find the folder for the program you want to remove.

5. Look for a Setup or Remove icon for the program you want to remove.

6. Click this Setup or Remove icon, and look for options that enable you to remove (or uninstall) programs.

7. From here on, the remove or setup program is in control. Follow instructions and choose options as appropriate to that program.

If you can't find a setup program or uninstall option for the program you want to remove, terminate the current installation program and then use the last-resort method described in the following section.

If all else fails

If you can't find an uninstall option for the program you want to remove, you must remove the program by deleting its folder. Follow these steps:

1. Move anything you want to keep to a new folder that is outside the program's folder and subfolders. Make sure you closed the program you want to delete.

2. Use My Computer, Explorer, or Find to locate the program's entire folder.

3. Select the program's folder and press Delete. Or, right-click the folder and choose Delete.

4. Choose Yes to confirm the deletion and send the folder and its files to the Recycle Bin.

Note Remember, when Windows Me moves files to the Recycle Bin during a Delete operation, those files continue to take up disk space. The space doesn't become free until you empty the Recycle Bin, as explained in Chapter 14.

At this point, the deletion is finished, but you have not deleted references to the program. To tidy up and deal with any problems that arise, consider using the following methods:

✦ If you left behind any shortcuts to the program you deleted, browse to, and then delete, those shortcuts.

✦ If you left behind any Program menu options that lead to the deleted program, delete those options using the techniques described in Chapter 17.

✦ If you have startup problems in the future, your C:\CONFIG.SYS and C:\AUTOEXEC.BAT files still may contain references to the old program. You need to modify those files.

If you feel uneasy about taking any of the preceding actions, don't do them — there's little margin for error. I strongly recommend against the "wing it and hope for the best" approach here.

Using an Emergency Startup Disk

Keeping an emergency startup disk (also called an Emergency Boot Disk or EBD) around is a good idea; you can use this disk in case some problem with your hard disk prevents you from starting your PC in the normal manner.

Creating the emergency startup disk

Chances are you created this startup disk when you installed Windows Me. But if you didn't (or you've forgotten where you put it), you can follow these steps to create a new one at any time:

1. Choose Start ➪ Settings ➪ Control Panel.

2. Open the Add/Remove Programs icon.

3. Click the Startup Disk tab to get to the dialog box shown in Figure 25-5.

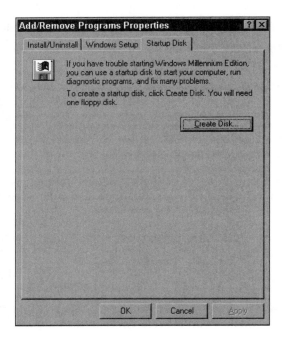

Figure 25-5: This is the Startup Disk tab in the Add/Remove Programs Properties dialog box.

4. Insert a blank floppy disk (or one containing files you're willing to trash for all eternity) into the floppy drive.

5. Click the Create Disk button.

6. Follow the instructions onscreen.

Label the disk Windows Me Startup Disk (or something to that effect). Then put it in a safe place where you can find it. It's unlikely you'll ever need the startup disk, but if you do need it, you'll really need it.

Starting your computer using the emergency startup disk

When you can't boot up from the hard disk, first turn off your computer. Then, put the Startup disk in floppy drive A and turn on the computer. When the computer starts up, you'll have four options: Help, Start computer with CD-ROM support, Start computer without CD-ROM support, and Minimal Boot. Choose the Start computer with CD-ROM support option. To get to your hard disk (assuming the whole thing hasn't crashed), type c: and then press Enter. If you then type dir and press Enter, you should see all the files in the root directory of that drive. You can now manage the drive using DOS commands (although I realize this doesn't do you much good unless you're already fluent in DOS!). If your Windows directory and programs are still intact, you should be able to get to Windows by typing win and pressing Enter.

If you need to reinstall Windows Me, you can probably also do this from the C:\>DOS command prompt. Follow these steps:

1. Go ahead and boot up from your floppy disk, as described earlier, to get to the A> prompt.

2. Then, switch to drive C by typing c: and pressing Enter.

3. Insert your original Windows Me CD into your CD-ROM drive or your Windows Me Setup floppy disk into drive A.

4. At the C:\> prompt type d:\setup.exe where d represents the drive that contains the Windows Me disk. For example, if you are installing from a CD-ROM, and your CD-ROM drive is drive D, you would type d:\setup.exe as the name of the program to run. If your Windows Me setup disk is in drive A, you'd type a:\setup.exe as the name of the program to run.

Caution The Windows Me startup disk usually changes the drive letter for your CD-ROM drive to one letter higher than you may be used to. For example, if your CD-ROM drive is normally drive D, it will likely appear as drive E when you start your system using the Windows Me startup disk.

5. After you type the appropriate command, press Enter. Windows setup will start and you can follow the instructions that appear onscreen.

Summary

Here's a quick recap of the various ways you can install and uninstall programs on your Windows Me PC:

✦ To install a program, choose Start ➪ Settings ➪ Control Panel. Open the Add/Remove Programs icon, click the Install button, and follow the directions onscreen.

✦ As an alternative, you can click the Start button, click Run, and then use the Browse button to locate the setup or install program you need to run.

✦ To install missing Windows components (programs that come with Windows Me, but are not on your hard disk), choose Start ➪ Settings ➪ Control Panel. Open the Add/Remove Programs icon. Then click the Windows Setup tab and check the components you want to install.

✦ To remove a program from your hard disk, choose Start ➪ Settings ➪ Control Panel, and open the Add/Remove Programs icon. If you see the program you want to remove, click its name and then click the Remove button.

✦   ✦   ✦

Installing and Removing Hardware

Before we dive into this chapter, let me define my terms. Hardware refers to any physical device that you plug into your computer — devices that plug in from the outside, as well as boards that must be installed inside the computer. Anything recorded on a disk is software. In this chapter, I talk specifically about installing hardware.

A Crash Course in Hardware

If you've never tinkered with computer hardware, all the acronyms like PCI and ISA and other terminology in this chapter may leave you feeling pretty bewildered. So, before I start in on all that, let me give you a crash course on PC hardware. This isn't meant to make you into a hardware guru. Instead, I want you to have a sense of what the information discussed in this chapter refers to in the real world.

External devices

When I talk about adding hardware, I'm talking about actual physical objects, such as modems, mice, keyboards, monitors, scanners, cameras, and so forth. The device must be physically connected to the computer via some kind of cable or slot. An external device is one that plugs into the back of your computer (into one of the available jacks). Figure 26-1 shows a photo of the back of one of my computers. This particular computer has a whole bunch of plugs in the back (your computer may have more, or fewer, jacks, also called *ports*).

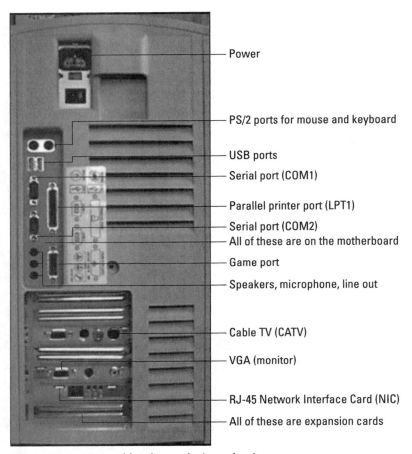

Figure 26-1: External hardware devices plug into ports (also called *jacks*) on the back of the PC.

Before you purchase an external device to add to your computer, you want to be sure that you have a plug available for the device. For example, if you buy a modem that hooks into a serial port, you must have a serial port available into which to plug this device. If you want to buy speakers or a camera that hooks into the USB port, your computer must have an available USB port. Let's discuss some of the different types of plugs you might encounter and what kinds of devices might plug into them:

✦ **Power:** The power port is used for one thing only—to plug the PC into the wall socket for power. No devices are ever hooked into the power port.

✦ **Parallel printer port:** Also known as the LPT1 port, the parallel printer port is generally used to connect a parallel printer. You can also plug some portable devices, like Zip drives, into the parallel port. On the back of the computer, the parallel port generally contains 25 little sockets and the parallel cable has 25 pins on its plug. The plug itself is often referred to as a DB25.

✦ **Serial port:** The serial port is used primarily for communications devices, such as modems. Some mice and other devices can also plug into that port. The plug on a serial port is usually a DB9 (it has nine pins on the male plug and nine sockets on the female plug). Occasionally, a PC will have a 25-pin serial port that looks like a parallel port. The serial port on the back of the PC usually is male (has pins), however, and the plug itself is female.

✦ **USB ports:** Available only in computers made after 1997, the Universal Serial Bus (USB) port offers the ultimate in plug-and-play convenience. Typically, you can plug the device into the port and start using it. Common hardware devices that use the USB port include cameras, scanners, and speakers.

✦ **SCSI (not shown):** SCSI (pronounced scuzzy) stands for Small Components Serial Interface. Unlike other components, SCSI devices can be daisy chained, meaning you can plug several devices into a single plug. The first device connects to the plug, the second device connects to the first device, the third device plugs into the second device, and so forth. Conventional SCSI supports up to seven devices on a single plug. Ultra Wide SCSI supports up to 15 devices.

✦ **Speakers, microphone, line out:** If your computer has sound capability, you probably have a plug for a microphone, a plug for speakers, and perhaps Line In and Line Out plugs for connecting stereos and other audio equipment.

✦ **Game port:** The game port plug is used to connect joysticks and other input devices. On most PCs, this plug is near the plugs for the speakers and the microphone. The port resembles the serial and parallel ports, but contains 15 sockets, making it larger than the serial port, but smaller than the parallel port.

✦ **VGA or SVGA:** Similar in size to a serial port, but with three rows of pins or sockets, rather than two — for a total of 15, rather than nine pins or sockets. The port on the computer is generally female; the plug itself is male. A monitor is the only device that plugs into a VGA or SVGA port.

✦ **RJ-45:** This resembles a slightly oversized telephone jack. It's used mainly for networking cables (as discussed in Part VI). The RJ-45 may also be used to connect an ISDN modem to an ISDN telephone jack on the wall.

✦ **PS/2:** PS/2 ports are used for mice and keyboards. Older computers may not have these ports. Instead, the keyboard plugs into a special keyboard port at on the back of the PC and the mouse may plug into one of the serial ports.

✦ **CATV:** If your computer has TV capabilities, you'll probably find a standard cable TV plug (CATV) somewhere on its back. You hook your cable TV cable into that port.

Remember that the computer shown in Figure 26-1 is only an example. The back of your computer may look completely different and it may have some other combination of ports. The technical manual that came with your computer probably has a diagram showing you which port is which on the back of your PC.

Internal cards

Some hardware devices are internal, or partially internal. For example, a new display card, sound card, or internal modem will be housed entirely within the system unit. These cards plug into expansion slots inside the system unit. Then some external device, like a monitor, speakers, or your telephone line plugs into the part of the card that's exposed from the back of the PC.

Some external devices require special cards. For example, if you purchase a SCSI scanner or an external SCSI drive, that device has to plug into a SCSI plug. You may need to add an internal SCSI card to the PC to get that SCSI plug on the outside.

Caution   You must always, always power down your PC and, ideally, remove the power plug from the back before opening the computer's case. Ground yourself by touching some large metal object, like a file cabinet. Never, ever monkey around inside the computer while the computer has power.

An internal adapter card (or expansion card) must be plugged into a slot on the computer's motherboard (see Figure 26-2). To get to those slots, you must shut down the PC and remove the case. The motherboard will probably be green with a bunch of chips and solder dots on it (my daughter says it looks like a little city). On the motherboard, are slots into which the boards plug. Depending on the age and model of your PC's motherboard, you will probably find some combination of the following slots:

✦ **AGP slot:** The Advanced Graphics Port (AGP) is available only on the newest motherboards. The slot can hold only display cards specifically designed for AGP. The AGP port is about three inches long—about the same as a PCI port, which can help confuse things. An AGP port, however, is set back further from the edge of the board, about two-and-a-half inches. On my PC, the AGP port is a brownish-gray color, while the PCI ports are light tan.

✦ **PCI slots:** The Peripheral Components Interface (PCI) slot is a general-purpose slot found in most Pentium computers. Devices that plug into a PCI slot are usually easy to install. You can find a PCI version for nearly any internal device. Do remember, though, that you can only have as many PCI cards as you have slots. For instance, if your computer has four PCI slots, you can put in a maximum of four PCI cards. Each PCI slot is about three inches long, set back about an inch and half from the back of the motherboard, and is usually a light tan in color.

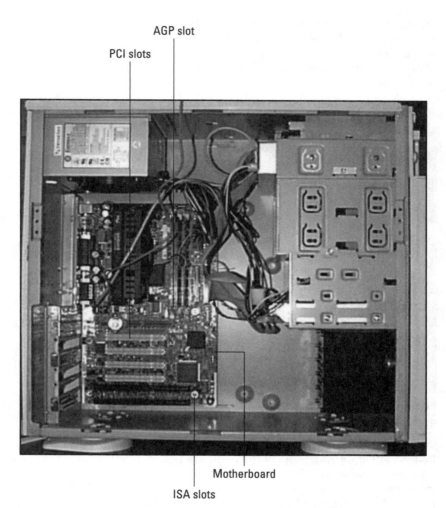

Figure 26-2: This motherboard has AGP, PCI, and ISA slots.

✦ **ISA and EISA slots:** Industry Standard Architecture (ISA) slots have been around since the earliest PCs, so virtually every PC has two or more ISA slots. Most ISA slots are over five inches long and are black, or dark gray, in color. Many different kinds of cards fit into ISA slots. Some motherboards may also sport an EISA (Extended Industry Standard Architecture) slot or two. Because EISA is an older technology that never really caught on, EISA slots are rare.

The things that plug into these slots are basically circuit boards with a row of metal contacts on the bottom that fit into the AGP, PCI, ISA, or EISA slot. Figure 26-3 shows examples of adapter cards. The back of the card often contains a plug that ends up sticking out of the back of the PC. For example, in Figure 26-1, the CATV, VGA, and RJ-45 plugs are all on adapter cards plugged into that PC's motherboard.

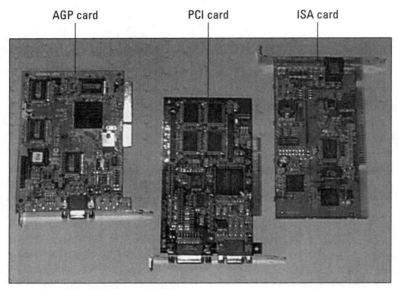

Figure 26-3: Here are examples of three adapter cards that can plug into a computer's motherboard.

Re-look at Figure 26-1; most of the plugs are not on adapter cards. The power, PS/2, USB, serial, game, speaker, microphone, line out, and parallel ports are separate from the others. These other ports are on the motherboard because they are built right in. For instance, if I were to remove every expansion card from the PC shown in Figure 26-1, I would still have all the ports shown as "on the motherboard" in the figure.

Now, you must remember that Figure 26-1 is only an example. Dozens of different kinds of motherboards and cases are available. Your computer may have more or fewer plugs on the motherboard. As a general rule, though, anything not on the motherboard can be added with an expansion slot. For example, the PC in Figure 26-1 has multimedia capabilities (microphone, speaker, line out, and game port) right on the motherboard. This is rare. Most motherboards do not have those capabilities built in. So, to get sound on a PC whose motherboard doesn't have the capabilities built-in, you'd need to add a sound card. The back of the sound card will most likely have the same plugs — microphone, speaker, line out, and game port.

Before purchasing new internal hardware for your computer, you need to open the computer and see what slots are available. As I said earlier, the new AGP and PCI slots are easiest to get along with. If those slots already have cards plugged into them (or don't exist at all in your PC), then you need to use an ISA slot (assuming one is available).

Replacing or removing a card

If you want to replace an existing board with a new board, you should first remove the existing board's drivers and then remove the board itself. To do this, leave the computer case on and start up the PC in the usual manner. When you get to the Windows Me desktop:

1. Click the Start button and choose Settings ⇨ Control Panel.

2. Open the System icon.

3. Click the Device Manager tab.

4. Click the plus (+) sign next to the hardware category that best describes the board that you want to remove. This will show all hardware devices in that category.

5. Click the name of the device that you want to remove and then click the Remove button. For example, in Figure 26-4, I chose my SiS 530 display adapter card as the device to remove.

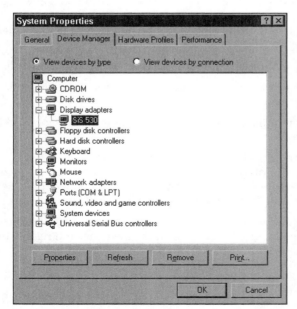

Figure 26-4: Before physically removing a card from your system, remove it in Device Manager.

6. After clicking the Remove button, follow any instructions onscreen until (and excluding) the option to restart your computer.

To remove the card physically from the PC, after removing it via Device Manager, you need to shut down the computer completely. You must do this before you restart your computer. Thus, if the screen asks Do you want to restart your computer now?, choose No, and then get back to the Windows Me desktop. Close any and all open programs and dialog boxes. Then click the Start button, choose Shut Down, and shut down the computer completely. To play it safe, you should unplug the PC from the wall socket now.

Remove the card from the PC before you restart the computer. Otherwise, Windows will probably detect the card and reinstall it automatically when you fire up the computer. If you already have a replacement for the card you removed, go ahead and plug that board in now, while the computer is still powered down. When you restart the computer, Windows will probably detect the new card and automatically install the drivers for it. However, you should read the sections that follow before you install a new hardware device.

When to skip this chapter

While this chapter can provide general guidelines for installing new hardware, every hardware device is unique. You should always refer to the instructions that came with a piece of hardware for step-by-step installation instructions. Some types of hardware are described in more detail elsewhere in this book. Some suggestions:

✦ If you're installing a PC Card in a PCMCIA slot, ignore this chapter and go straight to Chapter 24.

✦ If you're installing a modem, ignore this chapter and go to Chapter 5.

✦ If you're installing a game controller, such as a joystick or game pad, ignore this chapter and go to Chapter 16.

✦ If you're installing multimedia hardware, see Chapter 20 for some additional relevant information.

✦ If you're installing a printer, plug in the printer, connect it to the PC, and then turn it on. Gather your original Windows Me CD-ROM as well as any disks that came with the printer. Then click the Start button and choose Settings ➪ Printers. Open the Add Printer icon and follow the instructions onscreen.

✦ If you're replacing an existing keyboard, mouse, or monitor, shut down your equipment, remove the old device, plug in the new one, and restart the PC. Chances are the new device will work fine.

Note   If you're not into messing with electronic gizmos, an easy way exists to avoid all the stuff described in this chapter. Take your PC (just the system unit—you needn't take the monitor, mouse, keyboard, or any other extras)—to your local computer store and have *them* install the new device for you!

About plug and play

Historically, adding a new device to a PC was a haphazard ritual, often leading to hours or days of hair-pulling frustration. If, like most people, you don't know about—or care to learn about—such arcane subjects as IRQs, SCSI hosts, and DMA channels, those hours or days of frustration could be for naught. You'd give up and take the new device back to the store or put the device on the shelf, hoping time would make it easier to install later.

One of the most important features of Windows Me (and both Windows 95 and Windows 98) is support for plug-and-play devices. The idea behind plug and play is simple: adding a new device to your PC should be as easy as plugging a game into a video-game player or hooking a pair of speakers to a stereo system. You just plug in the device and start playing.

A new breed of PCs and optional gadgets followed Windows 95, Windows 98, and Windows Me to market, supporting the new plug-it-in-and-go concept. Millions of PCs and other devices, though, aren't plug-and-play-compliant. In this chapter, I discuss how to install both plug-and-play and legacy (non-plug-and-play) devices in your PC.

How to Install a Plug-and-Play Device

First, a word of caution: the term plug-and-play has been used for years and not all products claiming to be plug-and-play truly are, at least not in the sense that I use the term here. The installation procedure discussed in this section works for devices whose cartons declare them to be Windows plug-and-play compatible. To install such a device, follow these steps:

1. Save any work in progress and close down any open programs.

2. Gather your original Windows Me CD-ROM, the device you want to install, and any disks that came with the device.

3. Check the instructions for the new device. If the instructions tell you to turn off the power to your PC, close Windows Me and turn off the power.

4. Install the new device per the manufacturer's instructions.

5. If you turned off the PC in Step 3, turn it back on now.

6. The screen will notify you when Windows Me detects the new device and will probably ask you to insert a Windows Me disk or the disk that came with the device. Follow the instructions onscreen until a message indicating that you are finished appears.

Note   Windows may look to the wrong drive or folder when searching for the device's setup files on its own. If so, click the Browse button to navigate to where the disk or files may be found.

You're done! Windows Me automatically notifies all other devices of the new device and you should be able to start using that device.

If you need to install programs to use the device, do so now, using the Add/Remove Programs Wizard discussed in Chapter 25. Then skip the rest of this chapter.

How to Install Legacy Hardware

For our purposes, the term legacy hardware refers to any device that isn't plug-and-play. This includes hardware devices designed for DOS and Windows 3.x. The procedure for installing legacy hardware goes something like this:

1. If necessary, use Device Manager to locate available resources for the device.

2. Follow the manufacturer's instructions for installing the device.

3. When you get to the part about installing DOS/Windows 3.x drivers, ignore them. Use the Windows Me Add New Hardware Wizard instead.

4. Install any programs other than drivers that came with the device.

If you can complete these four steps on your own, great — you can ignore the following sections. If you need more support, read the following sections, which discuss each step in greater detail. Please remember that I cannot provide detailed instructions for installing every conceivable device on the market. Sometimes you must do a little device-specific tweaking and only the instruction manual that came with the hardware device can help you.

Step 1: Before you install the device

Before you put a hardware device in the PC, you must determine whether the device requires you to choose an Interrupt ReQuest line (IRQ). To find out, browse through the device's instructions. If the device doesn't require you to specify an IRQ, skip to the section "Step 2: Put the device in the machine."

Virtual devices versus real-mode drivers

Windows Me offers a virtual method of device support unavailable in Windows 3.x and earlier. To understand the advantages, you first must understand that Windows 3.x used real-mode drivers. These drivers were loaded into conventional memory (the first 640K of available memory), or upper memory (the next 384K) at boot time via CONFIG.SYS and AUTOEXEC.BAT. The drivers were static, meaning that after they were in memory, you had no way to get them out short of changing the configuration files and rebooting. Also, only one program at a time could use the device driver.

Windows Me virtual device drivers offer significant advantages. First, these drivers are loaded into extended memory, above the first 640K of conventional and 384K of upper memory. The device drivers don't consume the lower memory that DOS programs need (desperately!) to run there. Second, the virtual drivers are dynamic: they can be loaded and unloaded from memory on an as-needed basis. Third, the virtual driver allows more than one program at a time to access the device.

Virtual device drivers (also known as protected mode drivers) can be identified by the .VXD file extension. These drivers are never loaded from CONFIG.SYS or AUTOEXEC.BAT. Instead, the drivers are loaded after those two files have been processed. Any device driver included in CONFIG.SYS or AUTOEXEC.BAT is, by definition, a real-mode driver. When given a choice, always use the virtual driver rather than the real-mode driver.

Finding an available IRQ

A big headache in using legacy hardware is caused by IRQ conflicts. An IRQ is sort of a voice for the device, telling the computer, "I'm doing something now; pay attention to me." Most PCs have 16 IRQs, numbered 00 to 15. Each device must have its own IRQ. If two devices attempt to share an IRQ, you have an IRQ conflict and neither device will work properly.

Note   An IRQ conflict can have strange effects. Your floppy drive may no longer be able to read perfectly formatted floppy disks, for example, or your speakers may crackle madly as you move the mouse pointer across the screen.

The big problem was that some hardware products expected you to specify an available IRQ. But earlier versions of DOS and Windows made it nearly impossible to determine which IRQs were available and which were already being used by some installed device. In some cases, you had to guess. If your selections didn't work, you had to backtrack, pick another IRQ, and then try that one — on and on until you found one that worked. This situation was not good. (Whenever I hear news stories about some guy going berserk in public, I wonder whether he had been trying to find an IRQ just before the mania set in.)

Anyway, if the device's instructions tell you to pick an IRQ, then you needn't rely on trial and error. Follow these steps instead:

1. Click the Start button, point to Settings, and click Control Panel. The Control Panel window opens.

2. Open the System icon.

3. Click the Device Manager tab.

4. Double-click the Computer icon at the top of the list in Device Manager.

5. If it isn't selected already, click the Interrupt Request (IRQ) option at the top of the Computer Properties dialog box, as shown in Figure 26-5.

6. Used (unavailable) IRQs are listed in the Setting column. Be sure to scroll through the entire list to determine all the used and available IRQs. On a piece of paper, jot down the IRQs that are not in the list (those IRQs are available). On my machine, for example, only 11 is missing from the sequence, so 11 is the available IRQ I would write down.

Tip   Click the Print button near the bottom of the System Properties dialog box to get a printed version of your System Properties.

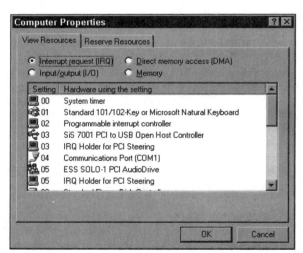

Figure 26-5: This is a list of used IRQs. Any IRQ that isn't listed is available.

7. Although you may not need this information, it can't hurt to write down which DMA channels are in use. Click the Direct Memory Access (DMA) option and write down the information you see in this list.

8. You can ignore the other resources — Input/Output (I/O) and Memory — unless you are familiar with those concepts and you're certain you want that information.

9. After writing down or printing the necessary information, click Cancel to leave the Computer Properties dialog box. Then click Cancel again to leave the System Properties dialog box. Close the Control Panel and then proceed to the following section.

Setting jumpers and switches

Next, you must determine whether the board requires you to set jumpers or dip switches manually. To find out, check the device's instruction manual. Three possibilities exist, as discussed in the three following sections.

If you have a jumperless device

Many modern boards are jumperless, which means you don't have to mess with any jumpers or switches on the board. If you have this type of board, skip to the section titled "Step 2: Put the device in the machine."

If your documentation includes written instructions for setting jumpers

If the device has jumpers or dip switches and the instruction manual includes instructions for setting them, follow those instructions now. Be sure you set the switches or jumpers to an available IRQ and write down the IRQ that you decide to use. Then skip to the section "Step 2: Put the device in the machine."

If you need to run a program to set jumpers

Some manufacturers do not provide written instructions on how to set jumpers or dip switches to pick an IRQ. Instead, these manufacturers require you to run a program that determines the best setting for your card. The program shows you, onscreen, exactly how to set the jumpers or switches. Typically, you can run the necessary program from the floppy disk that came with the hardware device. The device's instruction manual will tell you which program to run.

If you can run the program from Windows, insert the disk into a floppy drive, click the Start button, choose Run, type the appropriate startup command (for example, a:\comcheck.exe), and then press Enter.

If you need to run the program from DOS, you will have to use your Windows Me startup disk to boot your system to a DOS prompt. See Chapter 25 for details on creating a Windows Me startup disk. When you get to the MS-DOS prompt, type the command required to run the manufacturer's program (for example, a:\comcheck.exe) and then press Enter.

After you set the jumpers or dip switches according to the onscreen instructions, proceed to the following section.

Step 2: Put the device in the machine

Now you are ready to install the new device in (or on) the computer. Shutting down everything before you begin is important, so be sure you carry out this procedure carefully. Follow these steps:

1. Gather the device that you're installing, any disks that came with this device, and your original Windows Me CD-ROM.

2. Close any open programs and then shut down Windows. Click the Start button, click Shut Down, click Shut Down again, and click OK.

3. When the screen tells you it's safe, turn off the PC and any peripheral devices (for example, monitor, printer, modem, and CD-ROM drive).

4. Connect the device to the PC or install the card inside the PC, per the manufacturer's instructions. Install the device only. Don't worry about installing any software right now.

5. When you finish connecting the device or installing the card, turn on all the peripherals, including the new device (if it has an on/off switch).

6. Be sure drive A is empty or else the computer will try to boot from the floppy disk.

7. Turn on the PC.

If Windows Me detects the new device as it starts, it will take you to the Add New Hardware Wizard, described in the following section. You can skip to the third step of the following instructions.

Step 3: Install the Windows Me drivers

You should ignore any instructions for installing DOS/Windows 3.x drivers because the Add New Hardware Wizard can install the Windows Me drivers for you. As mentioned in the preceding section, this wizard may fire up automatically the first time you start the PC after installing the new hardware. If not, you can launch the wizard from the desktop. Follow these steps:

1. Choose Start ➪ Settings ➪ Control Panel.

2. Open the Add New Hardware icon.

3. Read the first wizard screen and then click Next. (Be sure you close any open programs as instructed.)

4. Read the next screen (shown in Figure 26-6) and then click Next.

5. You'll need to wait while Windows looks for plug-and-play devices. If it finds any, you'll be taken to the dialog box listing any devices that were found. Because you are presumably installing a legacy (non-plug-and-play) device here, you should select No and click the Next button.

6. In the next wizard screen (see Figure 26-7), choose Yes (Recommended) and follow the instructions onscreen.

Note

The Add New Hardware Wizard concerns itself only with new devices that have been installed, but have no drivers yet. If the wizard doesn't detect a new device, this may be good news. This could mean that your new device is already installed and working fine.

Figure 26-6: The Add New Hardware Wizard will first search for plug-and-play devices that aren't relevant to your legacy hardware device.

Figure 26-7: The Wizard can search for non-plug-and-play devices.

How the wizard proceeds from here depends on the device you're installing. For example, if the wizard finds a device, it may install the appropriate drivers from the Windows Me CD-ROM. If the wizard doesn't find a new device, you'll be given the option to install a specific device. Choose the type of device you're installing and then proceed through the wizard screens.

If Windows Me has its own driver for the device, the wizard copies that driver from the Windows Me CD-ROM or displays a message telling you which floppy disk to insert. If Windows Me does have its own driver, it will not ask you to insert the manufacturer's disk. This is normal and not a matter for concern. Follow every instruction that appears.

After the drivers are copied to the hard disk, the wizard may ask you to shut down the computer. Again, do exactly what the wizard tells you to do. When the installation is complete and the drivers are installed, you should be able to go right to the Windows Me desktop without a hitch.

Many hardware devices come with their own programs. A fax/modem, for example, comes with a faxing program. A scanner may come with scanning and touch-up programs. If such programs came with your device, install those programs now, using the techniques described in Chapter 25. Again, be sure that you install only the extra programs — not the DOS or Windows 3.x drivers. (If you accidentally install DOS or Windows real-mode drivers, or if you need to eliminate old ones, see "Removing a Device" later in this chapter.)

If you have any problems with your newly installed hardware, if a device that worked previously doesn't work anymore, or if you can't get Windows Me started, try the troubleshooting techniques described in the following sections.

Tip   If you're going to do a lot of tweaking, you'll do well to create a desktop shortcut to the Control Panel. Right-drag the Control Panel's icon out of My Computer, drop it onto the desktop, and choose Create Shortcut(s) Here. You can also do this with the Add New Hardware and Add/Remove Programs icons that are found in the Control Panel.

I have no Windows Me driver

In the worst-case scenario for installing legacy hardware, the device requires a driver, but no Windows Me driver is available on your Windows Me CD or disks or on the manufacturer's disk. You may be tempted to try to force the DOS driver or Windows 3.x driver into the system. You can do this, but you won't like the result. Most likely, the device won't work and your whole system will behave strangely.

If you have Internet access, you can use the Windows Update to search for the most recent driver. To ensure you have the latest updates available for your computer, click the Start button, and then click Windows Update. When the Windows Update page appears, click the Update option. Wait patiently while Windows Update scans your computer to determine what updates you need and then follow the instructions on screen.

Your only other alternative is to contact the manufacturer of the device and ask where to get the Windows Me driver for this device. (Windows 95 or Windows 98 drivers also should work.) If you already have access to the Internet and can browse the World Wide Web with Internet Explorer, try the manufacturer's Web site. Here are three more good sites to check for information on current drivers: Frank's Windows95 Driver Request Page at http://www.conitech.com/windows/drivers.html and Microsoft's own Web site at http://www.microsoft.com/msdownload, as well as the Microsoft Knowledge Base at http://www.microsoft.com/kb.

Upgrading Device Drivers

Windows Me makes it easy to discover whether you're using the best and most recent driver for a device. And, better yet, if you don't have the latest driver, Windows Me can find and install it for you. Here are the steps to follow to ensure that you're using the latest driver for a device:

1. Save any work in progress and close all open programs.

2. Gather your original Windows Me CD-ROM. (You may not need to do this if Windows Me came preinstalled on your PC.)

3. Open the Control Panel (Start ➪ Settings ➪ Control Panel).

4. Open the System icon and click the Device Manager tab.

5. Click the device for which you want to check for better drivers.

6. Click the Properties button.

7. Click the Driver tab (if it's available) to get to the screen shown in Figure 26-8.

8. Click the Upgrade Driver button. The Upgrade Device Driver Wizard kicks in. Read the first page and then click the Next button.

9. On the second wizard screen (see Figure 26-9), try the Search option first (click its radio button and then click the Next button).

10. If the manufacturer has provided a disk, choose the second option to display the wizard page shown in Figure 26-10, so that you can choose all the places that you want to search.

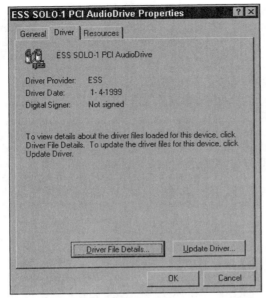

Figure 26-8: Ready to check for an upgraded driver for this device

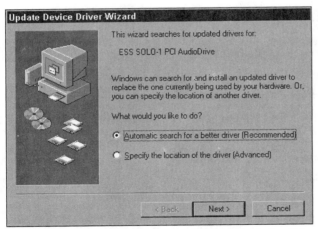

Figure 26-9: A page from the Upgrade Device Driver Wizard

11. Click the Next button and follow the instructions onscreen.

There's no guarantee a newer and better driver exists for your hardware device. If one does, though, the wizard will definitely be your best bet to find and install this driver.

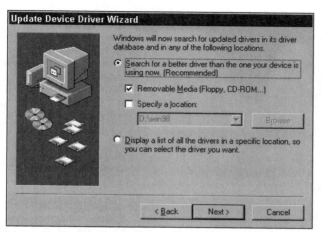

Figure 26-10: More help from the Upgrade Device Driver Wizard

Troubleshooting Hardware Conflicts

Hardware conflicts occur when two or more devices try to use the same IRQ, or the same memory range, to get the computer's attention. A hardware conflict may cause a device to behave strangely or erratically. Or, in many cases, one of the conflicting devices doesn't work at all. Fortunately, Windows Me offers several tools for tracking and resolving hardware conflicts.

Using the hardware troubleshooter

If a new hardware device won't work or if something that worked before has stopped working properly, then there is a device conflict. The quickest and easiest way to resolve a device conflict is to use the Troubleshooter. Follow these steps:

1. Click the Start button and choose Help.
2. Click the Troubleshooting link.
3. Click the Hardware & system devices link.
4. Continue drilling down through the links until you find the appropriate troubleshooter to help resolve the problem.

Many of the Troubleshooter suggestions take you to Device Manager in the Control Panel. (You also can open Device Manager without going through the troubleshooters, as explained later in this chapter.) As you proceed through the Troubleshooter Wizard, pay particular attention to any devices whose icons are covered by an exclamation point (!) inside a yellow circle. These devices conflict with some other device and you must reconfigure them to fix the problem.

Tip If Windows detects a hardware conflict, it often will start the appropriate troubleshooter automatically!

If the Troubleshooter doesn't find any problems, something else is wrong. Check the manual that came with your new device for specific troubleshooting tips or try some of the troubleshooting methods described in the following sections.

Getting around startup problems

If starting Windows Me leads to a slew of error messages and/or Windows Me freezes up before you can get to the desktop, you can do many things to get around, diagnose, and fix the problem. Follow these steps:

1. Restart the computer (click Start ➪ Shutdown ➪ Restart ➪ OK).

2. When you see the Starting Windows Me message on a black background screen with white text, press F8. (You must be fast with the F8 key or the computer will restart in the normal way. Sometimes it helps to press F8 more than once.)

3. Choose one of these options:

   • ___Normal: **Starts Windows Me in normal mode, as though you hadn't pressed F8.**

   • ___Logged (\BOOTLOG.TXT): **Starts Windows Me normally, but creates a C:\Windows\Bootlog.txt file containing a log of all the events that occurred during startup. Use BOOTLOG.TXT to locate failed startup events.**

   • ___Safe Mode: **Starts Windows Me, but bypasses many startup files. Loads only the basic system drivers. This mode is used for trouble-shooting only. You can't do real work while in Safe Mode.**

Note If Windows Me starts with a blank or funky screen, choose Safe Mode to load only the standard VGA driver.

   • **Step-By-Step Confirmation:** Enables you to step through each command in the startup files (starting with CONFIG.SYS and AUTOEXEC.BAT if you have them), so that you can identify the commands causing problems.

Note If Windows Me displays error messages at startup or freezes up before it starts, choose Step-By-Step Confirmation to identify the specific commands causing the problem.

If you can't start Windows Me because of a problem with the hard disk, you can boot from the Windows Me startup disk in drive A or from any DOS startup disk that has system tracks (again in drive A).

My mouse died

Sometimes, the mouse gets involved in a hardware conflict and stops working. To get to the Troubleshooter without a mouse, press Ctrl+Esc and then type h to choose Help. Once you're in the Help window, you can use the Tab and Enter keys to open links and navigate. When the highlighter is on the topic you want, press Enter to open that topic.

Finding all references to a faulty driver

If you discover that the problem is with Windows Me loading a specific driver, you can delete references to this driver from all initialization files. Starting from the Windows Me desktop, follow these steps:

1. Click the Start button, point to Search, and click For Files or Folders.

2. Click the Name & Location tab, if it isn't selected already.

3. In the Look In box, choose drive C and then be sure to check the Include Subfolders option (under Advanced Options).

4. Enter the driver name (or some part of it) in the Containing Text box. If, for example, a driver named TSBA311.DRV is causing the problem, type tsba311 as the search text.

5. Click Search Now and wait for Search to locate every file containing the text you typed.

6. To edit a file Search located, right-click its icon or name at the right of the Search Results dialog box and then choose Open. You especially want to edit any file identified as a Configuration Settings file type.

7. If you are prompted for a program with which to open the file, choose Notepad.

8. Within Notepad, choose Search _ ➪ Find, type the name of the driver you want to find, click Find Next, and then click Cancel. The first matching text is selected (highlighted) in the file.

9. Delete the reference to the faulty driver and then press Find Next (F3) to locate the next reference. Repeat this step until you delete all references to the bad driver. When you finish, click OK and then choose File ➪ Exit.

10. Repeat Steps 6 to 9 for each configuration file you want to edit.

11. Shut down and restart Windows Me to test your changes.

Danger! Edit only what you understand

In some of these troubleshooting procedures, I assume you understand the structure and purpose of initialization (.INI) and similar files (such as C:\CONFIG.SYS and C:\AUTOEXEC.BAT). I also assume that you understand that you can use Notepad or DOS's EDIT command to change those files without making a mess of things.

If you are unfamiliar with those concepts and techniques, I strongly recommend you do not make changes in those files. Get help from a more experienced user. Little margin for error exists when you are tampering at this depth. Even the slightest mistake can make matters worse.

Using Device Manager to resolve conflicts

If your system starts smoothly, but you have problems with specific devices, a hardware conflict is the most likely cause. The Troubleshooter, described earlier in this chapter, takes you step-by-step through the procedure of finding and fixing the problem. You also can go into Device Manager yourself and change the settings. Follow these steps:

1. Choose Start ➪ Settings ➪ Control Panel.

2. Open the System icon.

3. Click the Device Manager tab to get to the dialog box shown in Figure 26-11.

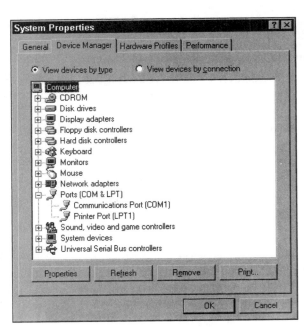

Figure 26-11: The Device Manager tab of the System Properties dialog box

Within Device Manager, you have enormous flexibility to explore — and change — specific settings for every device operating in your system. The following are some general guidelines for using Device Manager:

✦ The first items displayed are classes (or types) of devices. To see the specific devices within a class, click the plus (+) sign next to the class or double-click the class.

✦ If a specific device is conflicting with some other device, its icon is marked by an exclamation point within a yellow circle. If a specific device isn't working, its icon is marked by the international prohibited symbol.

✦ To view or change a device's properties, double-click the device's icon or name, use whatever tabs and options are provided in the dialog box to resolve problems, and then click OK.

✦ To update the entire list of installed hardware, click the Refresh button.

✦ To remove a device, click its icon or name and then click the Remove button.

✦ To print a summary of the hardware list, click the Print button.

✦ To organize the devices by the way they're connected, click the View Devices By Connection option button.

✦ To view devices by the resources they're using, double-click the Computer icon at the top of the list to open the Computer Properties dialog box and then choose whichever option describes the way you want the list organized.

✦ For help with anything in Device Manager, click the question mark (?) button at the upper-right corner of the dialog box and then click whatever you need help with.

The Hardware Profiles tab of Device Manager is discussed in Chapter 29. The Performance tab is discussed in Chapter 27.

When you finish with Device Manager, choose OK to close this window. You may need to shut down the PC and restart Windows Me for your changes to take effect.

Removing a Device

Before you read this section, please be aware that I'm discussing only devices that you want to remove from your system permanently. You can ignore all this information if you're disconnecting a portable CD-ROM drive, modem, network card, or any other device that you plan to plug back in and use later. On the other hand, if you're removing an internal PC card permanently — perhaps with the intention of replacing it with a new card — it's a good idea to remove all the drivers for this card first. Follow these steps:

1. If you have any open program windows on the desktop, close them.

2. Choose Start ➪ Settings ➪ Control Panel.

3. Open the System icon.

4. Click the Device Manager tab.

5. Double-click the class (or type) of device you plan to remove.

6. Click the specific device you plan to remove.

Note When removing a non-plug-and-play device, jot down any settings for the device you're going to remove before you remove this device. That way, if you need to reinstall it later, you'll know what settings to choose. (To view the settings, double-click the device icon, explore all the tabs in the dialog box that appears, and choose Cancel.)

7. Click the Remove button, read the warning dialog box to make certain you're removing the right device, and then click OK.

8. If you are asked about restarting your computer, click No for the moment.

9. Repeat Steps 5 to 7 as necessary to remove all the drivers that support the device you plan to remove.

10. Click the Close (X) button.

If you are instructed to restart your computer, do not do so. Instead, choose No to get back to the Windows Me desktop. From there, close all open programs and dialog boxes. Then click the Start button and choose Shut Down ➪ Shut Down ➪ OK to exit Windows Me. Before you open the PC be sure to shut down all power. To play it safe, unplugging the power cord altogether never hurts. After all this is done, you can open the PC and remove the device. If you have any problems when you restart your PC, you may not have removed all the drivers for the device. Repeat the preceding steps or use Find to find and remove all references to the device, as discussed in "Finding all references to a faulty driver" earlier in the chapter.

Removing a real-mode device driver

Some older hardware devices (those designed for DOS and Windows 3.*x*) will get their drivers during bootup from listings in a few files named CONFIG.SYS and AUTOEXEC.BAT. Both of those files exist on the root directory of drive C (C:\). If you need to eliminate a device driver being loaded through one of those files, you must open CONFIG.SYS or AUTOEXEC.BAT using Notepad or some other simple text editor such as the DOS Edit.com program. After the file is open, you can type the letters **rem** followed by a blank space in front of any commands that you don't want executed. (Rem stands for remark and is a special command that tells the operating system to treat this line as a remark or comment to be ignored, rather than as a command to execute.)

For example, in Figure 26-12, I commented out (put the `rem` in front of) the line `device=oakcdrom.sys /D:mscd001`. After I save this modified CONFIG.SYS file and then restart my computer, the line that reads `device-oakcdrom.sys /D: mscd001` will no longer be executed. Thus, the OAKCDROM.SYS driver will not be loaded. But this is OK in this instance, because that was the real-mode driver for my CD-ROM drive. Now Windows Me can handle that CD-ROM drive with its own virtual drivers.

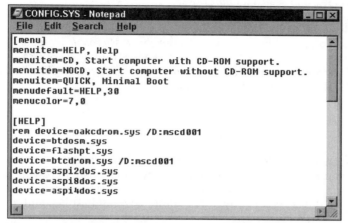

Figure 26-12: One line in this CONFIG.SYS file is commented out with a rem statement.

As an alternative to typing rem in front of a line in CONFIG.SYS or AUTOEXEC.BAT, you can delete the line altogether. You'd do well to use the rem method first, though, to make sure that everything still works properly after you restart the computer. This way, if the computer doesn't run properly after restarting, you can remove the word rem from the front of the line in CONFIG.SYS or AUTOEXEC.BAT to reinstate the driver and get your machine working normally again.

If you need more details on what the various commands in CONFIG.SYS and AUTOEXEC.BAT are all about, your best bet is to check a DOS manual or book, as well as the documentation for the device using the real-mode driver. Both those files are like vestigial organs left over from the early days of DOS and are more relevant to DOS than to Windows.

CONFIG.SYS and AUTOEXEC.BAT are both optional in Windows Me. If they exist in C:\ (the root directory of drive C), then Windows Me will process their commands at startup. If CONFIG.SYS, AUTOEXEC.BAT, or both are missing from the root directory of drive C, Windows Me will boot up without looking for those files.

More Technical Stuff and Troubleshooting

As I stated earlier, my goal in this book is to help you to take advantage of what Windows Me has to offer, not to talk about design philosophy or architectural issues. The topics discussed in this chapter should enable you to install or remove any hardware device successfully. If you encounter problems you can't solve, you can search the online manual for more information.

Note To find hardware-related topics and help in the online manual, click the Start button, click Help, click Index, and search for *hardware*.

If you want more advanced technical information or if you need to go deeper into hardware troubleshooting, you may want to purchase *Microsoft Windows Millennium Edition Secrets,* by Brian Livingston and Davis Straub (IDG Books Worldwide, 1998). This book covers more esoteric matters concerning hardware installation and older DOS drivers and programs.

Summary

In this chapter I looked at the wild world of adding more hardware gizmos to your PC. Although not recommended for the technologically squeamish, hardware installation and upgrades are easier than ever, thanks to recent advances in Windows Me and hardware. Here's a quick recap of the main points covered in this chapter:

✦ All hardware devices connect to your computer either externally (using plugs on the outside of the PC) or internally (using slots inside the PC).

✦ Plug-and-play hardware devices are by far the easiest to install and use.

✦ No matter what kind of hardware device you're installing, you should always follow the manufacturer's installation instructions to install everything except 16-bit DOS/Windows 3.*x* device drivers.

✦ Installing legacy (pre-Windows 95) devices is still a bit rough, but not as bad as it was in Windows 3.*x*.

✦ If a legacy device is going to ask for an available IRQ, you can easily see which IRQs are available. Choose Start ➪ Settings ➪ Control Panel. Open the System icon and click the Device Manager tab. Double-click Computer at the top of the list to get to the Computer Properties dialog box. From there, you can examine used (taken) IRQs, I/O addresses, DMA channels, and Memory ranges.

✦ The typical scenario for installing a legacy device is to shut down everything and then install the device (but not the drivers), as per the manufacturer's instructions. Then restart the PC. If Windows doesn't detect the new device at startup automatically, choose Start ➪ Settings ➪ Control Panel and then open the Add New Hardware icon to start the Add New Hardware Wizard.

✦ If possible, always use the Windows 95, Windows 98, or Windows Me driver for a legacy device, rather than the original DOS/Windows 3.x drivers. The Add New Hardware Wizard will install the correct drivers for you, if they exist.

✦ If you end up with hardware conflicts, use the Troubleshooter to track them down and solve them. Click the Start button, choose Help, and open the Troubleshooting link.

✦   ✦   ✦

Updates, Upgrades, and Optimization

This chapter is about routine maintenance tasks you can perform to keep your computer running smoothly and at top speed. In particular, this chapter covers the Windows Maintenance Wizard, which can keep your hard disk performing at its best. You'll also learn about Windows Update, which can automatically bring your system up-to-date by downloading files from the Internet. I'll also discuss disk compression, task scheduling, and other features that can help you get the most from all of your computer hardware.

Using the Windows Maintenance Wizard

Your computer spends a lot of time reading stuff from and writing stuff onto your hard disk (typically drive C). A hard disk that isn't running at maximum efficiency can slow down your entire PC. Two things can slow down a hard disk: If you're keeping a bunch of old, unnecessary files around, Windows must manage more files than necessary so it slows down, and flaws on the hard disk, such as *bad sectors* (tiny flaws that prevent that section of the disk from being written to) can slow down your hard disk as well.

Over time, files on your hard disk become fragmented, a situation that slows disk activity and, in turn, the entire system. Suppose your hard disk is nearly full and you need to delete some stuff to make room for a new program. You drag some old files into the Recycle Bin and then empty the bin. Now you have space. You don't really know, however, how that extra space is split up on the disk. Some of the files you deleted may have been near the outer edge of the disk, others may have been near the inner edge, and still others may have been near the center of the disk. So you can say the empty space left by those deleted files is fragmented in different areas of the disk.

Now suppose you install the new program. Windows has to use whatever space is available, so part of your new program might be near the outside of the disk, part near the middle, and part near the center. Now your program is fragmented in different areas of the disk. Technically this situation isn't a problem. Windows can find all the pieces automatically when it needs them. You won't ever know how fragmented the file has become.

But fragmentation has a downside. As time passes, more files become fragmented and the drive head has to move more to access the disk. From your perspective, opening files and saving your work seem to take longer. If you're near the PC, you may even hear the heavy clickety-clack of the drive head moving frantically about the disk to access all these fragments.

The Windows Maintenance Wizard automatically runs three programs to help fix all these problems.

✦ **Disk Cleanup:** Removes old, unnecessary junk from your hard disk.

✦ **Scan Disk:** Checks for, and repairs, flaws on the hard disk.

✦ **Defrag:** Rearranges files on the disk to speed access to programs and files.

Only one drawback exists to running these three programs. They can take several hours to get the job done! Fortunately, you needn't sit there the whole time because once the maintenance session gets going, it runs unattended until the job is done. You could start a maintenance session just before leaving your computer for a while and let it happen while you're away. Also, you needn't perform the maintenance too often. Once or twice a month is probably plenty.

Another alternative is to schedule the maintenance at odd hours, such as in the middle of the night, while you're away from the computer. This way, Windows can be hard at work fine-tuning your hard disk while you're off sawing logs in dreamland. So, probably the best way to start off with the Windows Maintenance Wizard is to decide when you want it to run. This sets up Task Scheduler to run the maintenance during those hours. Here's how to get started:

Caution   The Maintenance Wizard will run at the correct time only if your system clock is set correctly. To set your system date and time, double-click the clock indicator at the right edge of the taskbar. Or, click the Start button, choose Settings ➪ Control Panel, and then open the Date/Time icon.

1. Click the Start button and choose Programs ➪ Accessories ➪ System Tools ➪ Maintenance Wizard.

2. If you have run the Maintenance Wizard before, choose Change My
   Maintenance Settings or Schedule (Figure 27-1) and then click OK.

Figure 27-1: The Windows
Maintenance Wizard

3. Chances are, the Express approach will be fine. So on the next wizard screen,
   choose Express and then click the Next button.

4. In the next wizard screen, shown in Figure 27-2, choose a time when you'll be
   away from the computer, such as Nights. Then click the Next button.

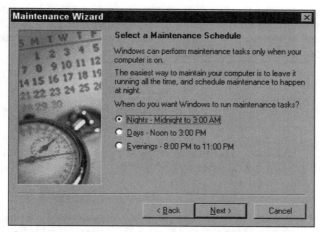

Figure 27-2: Choose a time of day to run Windows
Maintenance.

5. On the next wizard screen, choose which maintenance tasks you want to perform. The three suggested tasks, shown in Figure 27-3, will do everything you
   need, so you can click the Finish button.

If your System Tools menu is missing any of the programs described in this chapter, you can use the Windows Setup tab in Add/Remove Programs to install the
component from your original Windows Me disks. See Chapter 25 for more
information.

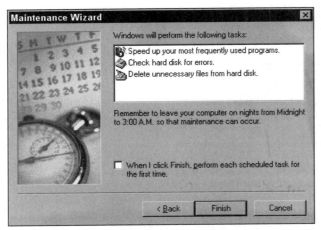

Figure 27-3: Decide which maintenance tasks you want to perform.

If you didn't request to have the scheduled task performed for the first time, nothing will happen after you click the Finish button. Rest assured that the tune-up will be performed at the hours you requested. You must remember, however, to leave the computer running at the time or the tune-up won't happen. You can turn off the monitor, if you like; only the PC itself needs to be running.

Tip   You may want to check and empty your Recycle Bin before running Windows maintenance. Doing this frees more disk space, which, in turn, helps the disk defragmenter do its job better. Chapter 14 discusses the Recycle Bin in detail.

I'll talk about the Task Scheduler, ScanDisk, and Disk Defragmenter programs in more depth later in this chapter. The simple steps you just performed will probably take care of all your tune-up needs, however so you can consider those later sections as optional.

Running ScanDisk, Defrag, and Disk Cleanup on the fly

Cleanup, ScanDisk, and Defrag (the disk defragmenter) are stand-alone programs you can run at any time. The Task Scheduler makes it easy to run these time-consuming programs while you're away from the computer.

To run these programs independently, click the Start button and choose Programs ➪ Accessories ➪ System Tools. Then choose either Disk Defragmenter, ScanDisk, or Disk Cleanup, depending on which program you want to run.

Using Windows Update

If you have access to the Internet, you can use Windows Update to check for, and to download automatically, any Windows Me files that have been changed or improved since your original purchase of Windows Me. To run Windows Update, click the Start button and then choose Windows Update from the Start menu. Your Web browser will start and take you to the current Windows Update page.

Windows Me also includes an automatic method of downloading updates and advising you when new updates are available. You access this feature using the Automatic Updates icon in the Control Panel.

Cross-Reference Part II of this book discusses how to connect to the Internet and how to use Microsoft Internet Explorer 5.5. You will also find information in Part II on using Windows Update and Automatic Updates.

Exactly what appears on that page depends on what's currently available from Microsoft. You should be able to follow instructions right on your screen to perform the update with minimal effort.

Are We Optimized Yet?

You can do still more to ensure your PC is optimized (running at its best possible speed). The quickest and easiest way to check — and possibly improve — the performance of your PC is to look at the Performance tab of the System dialog box. Follow these steps:

1. Click the Start button and choose Settings ➪ Control Panel.

2. Open the System icon.

3. Click the Performance tab.

The dialog box that appears enables you to see if your PC is already optimized to do its best. For example, Figure 27-4 shows the Performance tab of the System Properties dialog box for one of my computers. The message "Your system is configured for optimal performance" in this dialog box tells it all. In the example shown in the figure, the PC is already optimized, so I can't really do any more — via this dialog box anyway — to make it run any faster.

If anything in your PC can be improved to up its performance, the Performance tab will tell you about it. For example, if your disk drive is using an old real-mode (DOS) driver, you'll be told. You could then try upgrading to a newer driver using the Upgrade Driver button in Device Manager (see Chapter 26 for instructions).

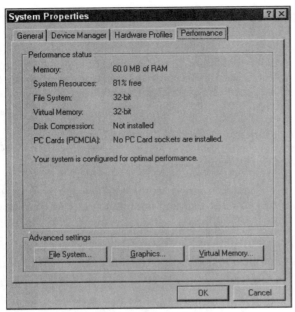

Figure 27-4: The Performance tab for a computer already configured for optimal performance

Things that determine PC speed

Three main components gadgets control the speed of a computer: the microprocessor, random access memory (RAM), and the hard disk. The speed of your microprocessor is measured in megahertz (MHz). The higher the number, the faster the processor. For example, a 300 MHz Pentium processor is three times faster than a 100 MHz Pentium processor.

RAM is where programs and documents you're currently working on is stored. More is faster because RAM is much faster than the hard disk. So more work stored in RAM means fewer performance-draining visits out to the hard disk. RAM is usually measured in megabytes (MB). If everything else were the same, a PC with 32MB of RAM would generally run faster than one with 16MB of RAM. But exactly how much RAM influences performance depends on many factors, including how large your document files are.

RAM chips have a clock speed that's measured in nanoseconds (ns). The measurement is one that indicates how long it takes to process an instruction, so the smaller the number, the faster the RAM chip. For instance, a 60ns memory chip runs faster than a 70ns chip.

Hard disks come in a variety of flavors. The inexpensive IDE disk drives built into many off-the-shelf computers are among the slowest, transferring about 16 MBps (megabytes per second) between the disk and RAM. At the other end of the spectrum, an Ultra 160 SCSI (pronounced *scuzzy*) drive running at 10,000RPM can transfer about 160 MBps.

How do you use your hard disk?

As you've probably figured out by now, hard disk performance is important to the overall speed of a PC. In addition to everything the Windows Maintenance Wizard can do to keep your hard disk going great-guns, you can change a simple setting in the Control Panel. Follow these steps to see:

1. Click the Start button and choose Settings ⇨ Control Panel.

2. Double-click the System icon.

3. Click the Performance tab.

4. Click the File System button.

5. In the File System Properties dialog box that appears next (see Figure 27-5), click the Hard Disk tab and then select one of the following options from the drop-down list:

   • **Desktop computer:** For a normal stand-alone PC or a PC that's a client in a LAN

   • **Mobile or docking system:** For a portable or laptop computer

   • **Network server:** For a PC that plays the role of file server and/or print server in a peer-to-peer LAN

6. Click OK.

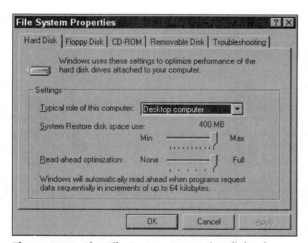

Figure 27-5: The File System Properties dialog box enables you to fine-tune your hard disk performance based on how you use that disk.

Windows Me automatically self-tunes, according to your selection in Step 5, to allocate resources. You may see a message indicating you need to reboot your computer to activate the new setting. If so, go ahead and close any open programs and then shut down and restart your computer using Start ⇨ Shut Down.

Speedier graphics

From a computer's perspective, a picture (graphic image) is a pretty complex thing that takes time to render onscreen. To ensure Windows is using your graphics hardware to its fullest potential, click the Graphics button on the Performance tab to get to the Advanced Graphics Settings dialog box shown in Figure 27-6. Then drag the slider to Full and click OK.

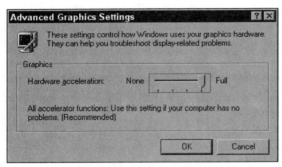

Figure 27-6: The Advanced Graphics Settings dialog box enables you to crank up the speed of your display.

If you experience problems with your monitor after cranking up hardware acceleration, you may need to tone things back down. Return to the Advanced Graphics Settings dialog box, move the slider to the left, and try again. Your goal is to get the slider as close to the Full side of the scale as possible, without experiencing any weird problems with your screen.

Taking inventory

If you don't really know about all the hardware attached to your system, you can use a few programs to snoop around. One is the System Information Utility, which you can get to by clicking the Start button and choosing Programs ⇨ Accessories ⇨ System Tools ⇨ System Information. The other is Device Manager, which you can find in the Control Panel. Click the Start button, choose Settings ⇨ Control Panel, open the System icon, and then click the Device Manager tab.

Virtual memory

When you try to load more programs than can fit into RAM, Windows Me creates virtual memory on the hard disk, which acts like RAM (only slower), so you don't get a "Not Enough Memory" message that brings your computer to a halt. The thing holding the stuff that spills over from RAM is called a swap file because it constantly swaps things in and out of RAM.

In Windows 3.x, you could improve system performance by creating a permanent swap file. But it doesn't work that way in Windows Me. To the contrary: Creating a permanent swap file may deteriorate Windows Me's performance. The swap file in Windows Me is dynamic, automatically using what resources are available and freeing them when they're not needed.

To ensure you're using the dynamic swap file, click the Virtual Memory button on the Performance tab of the System Properties dialog box. You'll be taken to the Virtual Memory dialog box. Make sure the first option is selected, as in Figure 27-7, and then click OK.

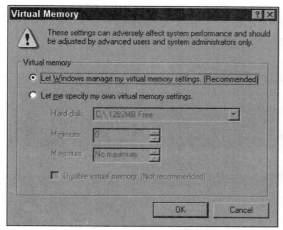

Figure 27-7: The Virtual Memory dialog box with the recommended setting selected

Disk caching

A disk cache (pronounced *cash*) serves as a sort of holding area between RAM and the disk. The purpose of a disk cache is to minimize disk accesses and, thereby, speed operations. Windows Me uses a self-tuning cache named VCACHE (the V stands for virtual). Unlike the caches in earlier versions of Windows, VCACHE does not require you to set its size, because it's dynamic. When demand is high, VCACHE uses whatever resources it can find. When demand is low, VCACHE frees resources for other activities so they can run faster.

Caching is another reason why more RAM equates to faster performance: VCACHE automatically takes advantage of whatever RAM you have. The more RAM you have, the larger the cache. The larger the cache, the fewer disk accesses. The fewer disk accesses, the faster things go.

Caches are not additive. In fact, a cache within a cache slows operations. You should check your CONFIG.SYS and AUTOEXEC.BAT files to see whether either is loading a real-mode cache, such as SmartDrive (SMARTDRV). If so, remove the appropriate commands or at least comment them out with a `rem` command. While you're at it, you can remove any commands that load the old SHARE program, which is not needed in Windows Me. After making and saving your changes, don't forget to reboot the machine.

Windows Me will also maintain a cache for your CD-ROM drive, speeding access to files on the CD. To check and set your CD-ROM drive's cache, click the File System button on the Performance tab and then click the CD-ROM tab. You'll come to the dialog box shown in Figure 27-8.

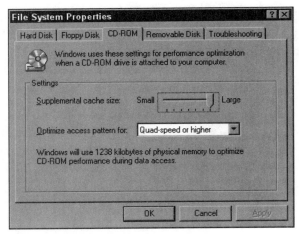

Figure 27-8: CD-ROM Cache settings

To optimize the speed of your CD-ROM drive, move the Supplemental cache size slider all the way to the Large end of the scale. Doing so creates a cache that is 1,238K. To optimize performance, you should also choose an option from the Optimize Access Pattern For drop-down list, based on the speed of your drive, as listed in Table 27-1.

Table 27-1
CD-ROM Drive Speeds and Access Patterns

CD	ROM Drive Speed	Setting
1X	Single	speed drives
2X	Double	speed drives
3X	Triple	speed drives
4X or better	Quad	speed or higher drives

Optimizing printer performance

Printing can be another bottleneck in overall PC performance. Even though you can do other things with your PC after the printer gets going, the print job takes up all system resources for a period right after you issue the Print command. All you can do is wait.

This waiting period, called return-to-application time, occurs when the PC is creating an image for the printer on the disk. Windows Me supports the EMF (Enhanced Metafile Format) for this disk image, which it can create quickly. The EMF can't make your printer go any faster than it was designed to go, but the time required to create the EMF is reduced, so return-to-application time is shorter.

EMF works only with some non-PostScript printers and printer drivers. If you aren't using a PostScript printer, follow these steps to ensure you're using the EMF format:

1. Click the Start button and choose Settings ⇨ Printers.
2. Right-click the icon for any non-PostScript printer driver and choose Properties.
3. Click the Details tab.
4. Click the Spool Settings button and then choose EMF (if available) from the Spool Data Format drop-down list (see Figure 27-9).
5. Click OK to return to the printer's Properties dialog box.
6. Click OK to return to the Printers dialog box.

You can repeat Steps 2–6 for each non-PostScript printer driver in the Printers dialog box.

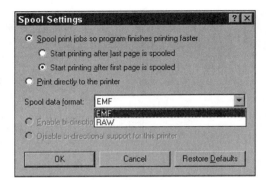

Figure 27-9: The Spool data format is set to EMF.

Disk spin-down

Battery-operated laptops offer disk spin-down (also called hard disk timeout) to prevent the hard disk from running all the time and draining battery power. Unfortunately, spin-down also means slowdown — big-time slowdown. If you're not relying on batteries while you use your laptop, by all means disable spin-down (you may have to disable all the power-saving features to do so).

 Caution

Don't forget to re-enable your laptop's power-management capabilities when you go back to battery power. Otherwise, you'll drain those batteries before the flight attendants serve the first round of drinks.

You'll need to check the manual that came with your laptop for specific instructions on controlling spin-down. The exact method varies from one machine to the next. Typically, though, you can control spin-down by using the CMOS setup. On my laptop, I have to shut down Windows and reboot the machine. After the memory test flashes onscreen, I press Del to run setup. Within that setup (called WinBIOS on my laptop), I can enable or disable all the power-management features. Turning off all those features disables disk spin-down and makes the machine run noticeably faster.

Windows Me can also shut down the hard disks on many newer computers even if they are not battery powered. To try out this option on your system, open the Power Options icon in Control Panel (see Figure 27-10). Then choose the setting you prefer from the "Turn off hard disks" drop-down list.

 Caution

Use the Windows Me Power Options settings or the BIOS settings to control the power-saving settings for your system — not both. If you set the BIOS options and the Windows Me Power Options settings, the results may be unpredictable.

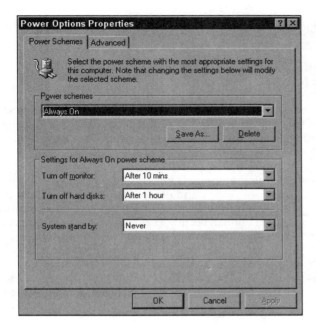

Figure 27-10: You can use the Power Options Properties dialog box to control how quickly your hard disks spin down.

Formatting Floppy Disks

Floppy disks can be used to back up important documents and to transfer files from one PC's hard disk to another's. Programs you buy often come on floppies. Documents other people send to you also may come on floppies. In both cases, the floppy disk is already formatted and you don't want to format it again—when you format a floppy disk, you also erase everything on it.

When you buy a box of floppy disks from your local Comput-O-Rama, the disks may be preformatted already for PC use. Those floppies don't need formatting either. In fact, you only want to format a floppy when the disk never has been formatted or when you want to erase everything on a floppy to make it a blank, formatted disk.

Formatting a floppy is easy. Follow these steps:

1. Put the floppy disk in drive A (or drive B) of your computer.

2. Open My Computer.

3. Open the icon for the drive that contains the floppy (usually drive A).

Caution   Be *very* careful in Step 3. If you accidentally format your hard disk, you'll lose everything on your hard disk! And there will be no way to get those files back!

4. If a message tells you the floppy disk has not been formatted, follow the instructions onscreen to format the floppy disk.

Caution   If the Format Results message box that appears at the completion of the format tells you that some disk space was used by *bad sectors*, consider this a warning that the floppy disk is failing and probably shouldn't be trusted. Once a floppy disk begins to fail it is usually best to simply discard the disk.

If you do not see a message indicating the floppy is not formatted, you needn't format it. If you really want to reformat the floppy and erase everything on it, however, close the window that displays the floppy's contents. In the My Computer window, right-click the floppy drive's icon and choose Format (see Figure 27-11) or select the floppy drive's icon and choose File ➪ Format from the menu bar. Then click the Start button to proceed and follow the instructions that appear onscreen.

Cross-Reference   If you want to copy files to or from a floppy disk, see Chapter 14. If you want to install a program from a floppy disk or create a bootable (startup) disk, see Chapter 25.

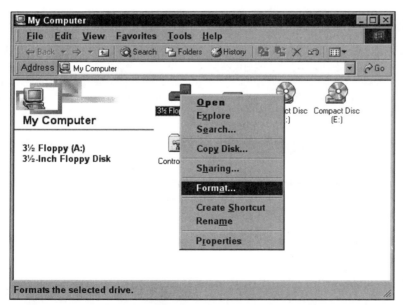

Figure 27-11: Right-click a floppy drive icon and choose Format to format the floppy disk in that drive.

Tweaking Task Scheduler

As you learned at the beginning of this chapter, Task Scheduler enables you to schedule programs to run automatically while you're away from your PC. This is especially good for performing your system maintenance tasks, such as Disk Cleanup, ScanDisk, and Defrag. You can, of course, add more tasks to Task Scheduler, tweak existing tasks, and so forth, as discussed in the following sections. First you need to open Task Scheduler using whichever of these methods seems most convenient:

✦ Open the Control Panel and then open Scheduled Tasks.

✦ Click the Start button and choose Programs ➪ Accessories ➪ System Tools ➪ Scheduled Tasks.

The Task Scheduler opens, as in Figure 27-12. Here, in brief, is how you manage those scheduled tasks:

✦ To delete a task, right-click it and choose Delete.

✦ To change something about a task, right-click the task and choose Properties.

✦ To add a new task, click the Add Scheduled Task option.

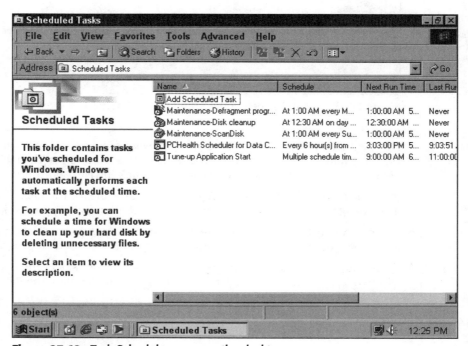

Figure 27-12: Task Scheduler open on the desktop

Scheduling Disk Cleanup

Suppose you want to add a new program to Task Scheduler. Let's say you want to have Disk Cleanup run every night to remove unneeded files while you sleep. You would proceed by following these steps:

1. In Task Scheduler, click the Add Scheduled Task option. The Scheduled Task Wizard starts.

2. Click the Next button. You'll come to the screen shown in Figure 27-13, in which you can choose the program you want to run. In the picture, I've chosen Disk Cleanup. Click Next after making your selection.

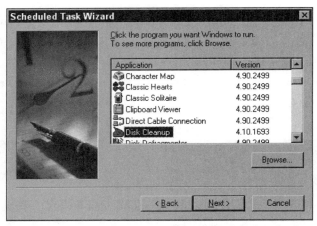

Figure 27-13: Second screen of the Scheduled Task Wizard

3. Next, a dialog box appears asking how you want to name this task (you can type any name you like), as well as how often you want to run the task, as in Figure 27-14. Make your selections and then click the Next button.

4. In the next wizard screen, you can choose a start time for the task. You can also change how often the task runs. Click Next after making your selection.

5. The next wizard screen (see Figure 27-15) summarizes your selections and also gives you the option of adjusting settings in the scheduled program.

6. If you want to look at the scheduled program's settings, select the check box. Otherwise, leave it blank. Click the Finish button to complete the job.

Figure 27-14: Third screen of the Scheduled Task Wizard

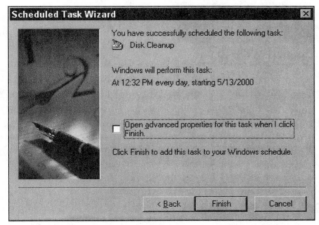

Figure 27-15: Fifth screen of the Scheduled Task Wizard

If you opted to view the advanced properties for the scheduled program, you'll come to a dialog box like the one in Figure 27-16. There, you can use the various options and tabs available to you to tweak the schedule or to see how the program behaves when run.

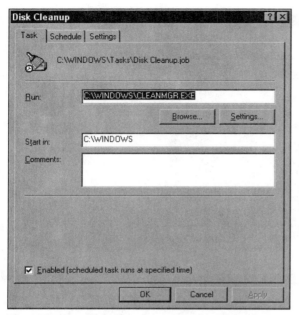

Figure 27-16: Disk Cleanup properties dialog box

The program you just scheduled will be listed with other scheduled programs. You can close the Scheduled Tasks window, if you wish, by clicking its Close (X) button. The program will run at the appointed time, provided your computer is running when the time arrives. You needn't open Task Scheduler to make scheduled events occur. This should happen automatically each time you start your computer (provided at least one task is scheduled).

Disabling a scheduled program

You can temporarily disable a scheduled program so it does not run at its appointed time. The program remains in the Scheduled Tasks window and you can re-enable it in the future. To disable a scheduled program, open Task Scheduler, right-click the program you want to disable, choose Properties, clear the Enabled check box, and choose OK. The column named Scheduled now displays "Disabled" as a reminder that the program will not run next time. To enable a program, repeat the same procedure but select (check) the Enabled option.

Disabling or enabling Task Scheduler

Sometimes you may not want Task Scheduler to run any of its programs. For example, if you plan to use your PC to give a public presentation, you certainly don't want Disk Cleanup, ScanDisk, or Defrag to pop up in the middle of your talk. No problem—here's what you do:

1. Open Task Scheduler.

2. Choose Advanced from the Scheduled Tasks window's menu bar.

3. Choose one of the following:

   • **Stop Using Task Scheduler:** Prevents all scheduled programs from running.

   • **Pause Task Scheduler:** Temporarily prevents all scheduled programs from running.

You can click Task Scheduler's Close (X) button to close the window.

If you need to re-start Task Scheduler, choose Start ➪ Programs ➪ Accessories ➪ System Tools and click Scheduled Tasks. Or, open the Control Panel and then open the Scheduled Tasks icon. Then, click the Advanced option on the menu bar and choose Start Using Task Scheduler.

Using Compressed Folders

Many of the files you may download from the Internet are *compressed* so they can be transferred in less time. In most cases those compressed files all use the same file format—known as *Zip* format because of the file extension.

In previous versions of Windows, it was necessary to obtain a third-party utility to handle Zip files, but this is no longer necessary in Windows Me due to a new feature known as *compressed folders*. Windows Me can handle the files inside of a Zip file just the same way it handles files in any other folder. You can even create compressed folders on your hard disk or on floppy disks to store your files in the industry-standard Zip file format.

To create a compressed folder, follow these steps:

1. Click Start and choose Programs ➪ Accessories ➪ Windows Explorer to open Windows Explorer.

2. Navigate to the location where you would like to add the compressed folder.

3. Select File ➪ New ➪ Compressed Folder from the Windows Explorer menu bar.

4. Enter a name for the compressed folder.

Compressed folders use an icon similar to normal folder icons except that they include a zipper on the face of the folder. You can use compressed folders the same way you use any other folder. When you store a file in a compressed folder, that file will use less actual disk space since the files in compressed folders are all compressed automatically.

Using System Restore

Whenever you make a change to your system, you run the risk of creating problems where none existed before. You might, for example, decide to install some hot new program and later discover that one of your existing programs or even one of your peripherals has stopped working.

When you encounter these types of problems, it would be very handy to be able to quickly restore your computer to the condition it was in before you made the change. The new Windows Me System Restore tool does just that — it allows you to undo any changes that were made to your PC.

To use System Restore, follow these steps:

1. Click Start and choose Programs ➪ Accessories ➪ System Tools ➪ System Restore.

2. To create a point that you can return to if problems occur, click the "Create a restore point" radio button (see Figure 27-17).

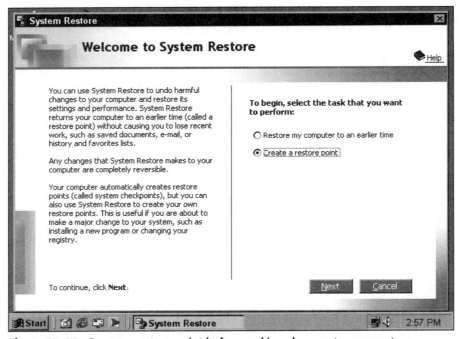

Figure 27-17: Create a restore point before making changes to your system.

3. Click Next to continue.

4. Enter a descriptive name for the restore point so you will be able to easily select the correct restore point later (see Figure 27-18).

Figure 27-18: Use a name that you will easily remember.

5. Click Next to continue.

6. Click OK to create the restore point.

If you have a problem with your system, open System Restore and choose the correct restore point to return your system to a state when it was working properly. You can choose a different restore point if you discover that the problem has not been corrected. Follow the directions on your screen to complete the restoration.

Note   System Restore does not affect your data files so you will not lose any work you have done since the last restore point. This is true even if the restore removes an application you installed after the restore point was created.

Summary

This chapter included tools and techniques to keep your PC tuned up, to squeeze more onto your disks, to schedule routine maintenance tasks, and to make backups of your hard disk. To recap:

✦ Use the Windows Maintenance Wizard (Start ➪ Programs ➪ Accessories ➪ System Tools ➪ Maintenance Wizard) to tune up your hard disk or to schedule the maintenance for a later time.

✦ If you have access to the Internet, you can use Windows Update (Start ➪ Windows Update) to bring your system up-to-date with the latest changes (if any) from Microsoft.

✦ Use the Performance tab in Device Manager (Start ➪ Settings ➪ Control Panel ➪ System) to check on your computer's current performance and, optionally, tweak some performance settings.

✦ Another good way to increase your storage space is to use the new Compressed Folders option to create Zip-compatible folders.

✦ Use System Restore before you make changes to your system such as adding new hardware or software. That way, you'll be able to return to the previous state if the upgrade causes serious problems.

✦   ✦   ✦

Using Multiple Monitors

Multiple monitors is one of those features of Windows
Me (as well as Windows 98) that's truly great, but not
very well known or understood. When people come into my
office and see me sitting in front of three 19-inch monitors,
with one mouse and keyboard, they always get a puzzled look
on their face. The inevitable question is "Why three computers?" My reply of course is, "It's just one computer, with three
monitors attached to it." They still don't get it. Until I drag a
window right off of one monitor across the other two monitors. Then their eyes light up, and they understand. The three
monitors are acting like one extra-wide monitor.

Of course, in a book I can't show you how it looks to drag windows across three monitors. However, let me try to illustrate
the concept using two monitors, each set to a resolution of
640×480. If the two monitors are side by side, you actually end
up with a desktop that's 1280×480 (you double the width of
the desktop) as in Figure 28-1. There, you can see that I can
easily fit three windows across the desktop without overlap.

Of course, no monitor has the rectangular shape shown in
Figure 28-1. So the desktop actually gets stretched across two
monitors as in Figure 28.2. But in real life, you stop noticing
that the desktop is stretched across multiple monitors. It feels
more like you're working with one wide monitor. In my office,
where I have three side-by-side monitors, each set to a resolution of 1024×768, I end up with a desktop that's a walloping
3,072 pixels across and 768 pixels tall. That's enough to keep
MSNBC on the screen (in a window) to watch the financial
news while trading with my Web browser and managing numbers in a spreadsheet. There's plenty of room still for other
programs — such as the word processing program I'm using
to write this chapter.

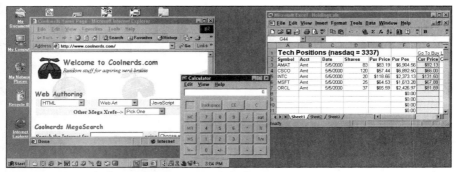

Figure 28-1: A desktop at 1280×480 resolution

Figure 28-2: How the desktop in Figure 28-1 looks split across two monitors

Once the multiple monitors are connected, they're simple to use. For example, to move a window to some other monitor, you just drag it normally by its title bar right off the edge of one screen onto the other screen. Like I said, before long you don't even think about the monitors being separate — it all just seems like one huge Windows desktop to work with. For that reason, I'll also show future screenshots of multiple monitors in this chapter as one wide desktop.

What You Need

Using multiple monitors isn't exactly cheap because the monitors themselves can be fairly expensive. Furthermore, each monitor needs it's own graphics display card. In a nutshell, here's how what you need to add multiple monitors to your existing PC:

✦ Two or more computer monitors with standard cables

✦ For the primary display, either a motherboard with on-board video capability or a PCI or AGP graphics display card

✦ For each additional monitor, you need a PCI or AGP graphics display card. Unlike Windows 98, you do not need to worry about the graphics chip set used on the card. Microsoft now says simply a PCI or AGP video adapter.

✦ An available PCI slot into which to plug each display card (unless, of course, one of them is integrated into the motherboard)

Those needs may seem pretty complex if you aren't the type who likes to mess with hardware. If this is the case, you can probably grab your computer's system unit, take it to the nearest computer store, and tell them you want to use two monitors at a time on your PC. They can help you choose a monitor and a display card. Because those two items aren't cheap, you may be able to get them to install the card free. Or, at least, inexpensively. If you go this route, you'll probably save a lot of time. And you can skip all the way to the section "Using the monitors" later in this chapter.

For you do-it-yourselfers out there, the next section explains all the details involved in setting up multiple monitors. I assume you understand some basic hardware concepts such as the motherboard, PCI slots, display cards, and so forth.

Installing Multiple Monitors

Setting up multiple monitors is no walk in the park. It can be a frustrating experience, so I'll try to walk you through it slowly. The exact approach you take to get both monitors to work will depend on whether your PC has a video display chipset right on the motherboard.

If your PC has an on-board video display, you need to know some important things before you start:

✦ Setting up Windows Me for the first time with only your on-board video adapter in the computer is very important. If another adapter is present before you start Windows Me for the first time, Setup cannot initialize your on-board video properly.

✦ After you can start your computer and Windows Me with that one display, then you can shut everything down, install the second display adapter card, and restart the computer.

✦ The new card you add will control the primary monitor, and the on-board chipset will control the secondary monitor. This is a function of the BIOS and there's nothing you can do about it.

✦ If you follow the instructions and your on-board video does not function correctly as the secondary display, it is likely the on-board chipset won't work as a secondary display. Your only other choice is to install two display cards and leave the on-board video unused.

The only difference when installing on a PC with no on-board video chipset is that it's unnecessary to install one monitor at a time. If you build a computer, you can put in both video cards right away — before you install Windows Me. Of course, if your PC already has one monitor working, you can add a second display card and monitor at any time.

As with any hardware device, be sure to follow the manufacturer's instructions when you put the card(s) into the PC. Most likely, you won't need to install the drivers for those cards. After you install two or more cards and plug a monitor into each one, you can restart your computer. Windows Me will find and install the appropriate drivers for the board(s). If Windows Me doesn't have appropriate drivers, then you may need to go back and install the drivers that came with the video board.

Caution   Some pre-Windows Me display drivers may not work correctly with Windows Me. Windows Me has introduced a revised driver architecture with which some older drivers cannot work. If you run into this problem, you have three options. First, visit the manufacturer's Web site and obtain the latest drivers. This usually solves the problem. Second, if you cannot get drivers that will work, you can try the Standard PCI Display Driver or Standard AGP Display driver provided by Microsoft. Third, you can take the occasion to purchase new video adapters. This is the most expensive, but guaranteed to work, option.

Working with Multiple Monitors

After you install two or more display cards, connect one monitor to each card, and turn on all the monitors, you can restart your computer. Your primary display will look normal. If someone has already used this PC with multiple monitors, the second monitor may be the same background color as the primary monitor; otherwise, it may be blank. If this is the case, both of your monitors are already activated. You can skip to the section "Getting your bearings" later in this chapter.

If one of the monitors doesn't appear to be lit at all, make sure the monitor is turned on. Then check Device Manager to see if the card being used for the secondary monitor is capable of doing the job. See "Troubleshooting Multiple Display Support" later in this chapter for more info.

Activating the secondary monitor(s)

If you just installed a secondary display card, when you turn on your PCs, one of the monitors will probably show a message reading something like this:

```
If you can read this message, Windows has successfully
installed this display adapter.
To use this adapter as part of your Windows desktop, open the
Display option in the Control Panel and adjust the settings on
the settings tab.
```

If this is the case, you need to activate the second monitor. That's easy. The steps are as follows:

1. Right-click your Windows Me desktop and choose Properties.

2. Click the Settings tab. Two (or more) monitor icons appear, as in Figure 28-3.

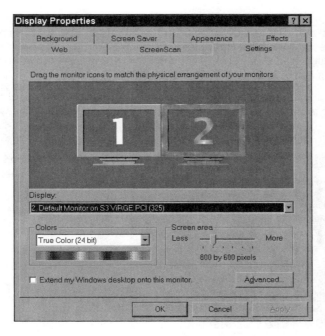

Figure 28-3: The Settings tab in Display Properties with two monitors installed

3. Click the icon for the secondary monitor. (Don't use the drop-down list under Display. It does not activate the secondary monitor.) You will see the message indicating the monitor is not enabled, as shown in Figure 28-4. Choose Yes to enable the monitor.

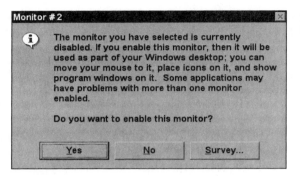

Figure 28-4: Click Yes to activate your second monitor.

4. If the "Extend my windows desktop onto this monitor" check box is not selected, select it now as in Figure 28-5. Clicking Yes in the previous step should have selected this check box by default, but it never hurts to verify that Windows is doing what it was supposed to do.

5. Again, if you see a message indicating the monitor is not enabled, choose Yes to enable the monitor.

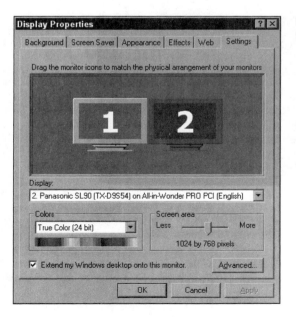

Figure 28-5: Secondary monitor is now enabled

You may receive warnings along the way telling you some programs will not work with the Multiple Display Support enabled. You can ignore such messages for now, choosing Yes to proceed with enabling the multiple monitors. If you have problems with some program later, see "Disabling Multiple Display Support" later in this chapter.

Tip   If you need to use programs that won't work with multiple displays enabled, check out the information on using hardware profiles in the next chapter. You can have a multiple monitor hardware profile and a single monitor hardware profile.

Getting your bearings

With both monitors in action now, you can get your bearings. First, make sure you know which monitor is which. Rest the mouse pointer on either of the monitor images in the Display Properties dialog box and then hold down the mouse button. The corresponding monitor will display its number, 1 or 2. For example, in Figure 28-6, I rested the mouse pointer on the picture of Monitor 1. Holding down the mouse pointer there displays the giant 1 you see in the figure. Pointing to Monitor 2 and holding down the mouse button would display a large 2 on my other monitor.

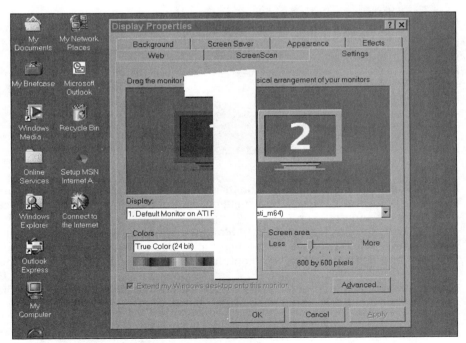

Figure 28-6: This must be Monitor number 1!

Next, you want to drag the little monitor pictures so they resemble the actual arrangement of the two monitors. This step is important because it tells Windows the arrangement to use in extending your desktop. Also, you can only drag the mouse pointer across where the two monitor images touch each other. For example, if the two monitors are stacked one atop the other on some kind of shelving — with Monitor 2 as the one on top — then you would arrange the little pictures as shown in Figure 28-7. Later, when using the monitors, you could drag items up and down from one monitor to the next.

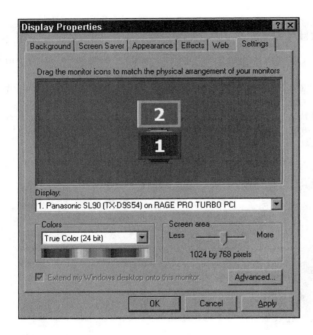

Figure 28-7: Use this arrangement if Monitor 2 is on top of Monitor 1.

If Monitor 2 is to next to Monitor 1, on its right, then the arrangement shown back in Figure 28-5, will work fine. After arranging the monitors in that manner, you can drag items left and right across the two monitors where the two pictures touch each other. If Monitor 2 is to the left of Monitor 1 on your desk, then you want to arrange the little icon pictures accordingly, as in Figure 28-8. Again, you could drag items left and right across the two monitors where the pictures touch each other.

After you've done all this, you can choose OK to close the Display Properties dialog box. Your two monitors should be ready for action.

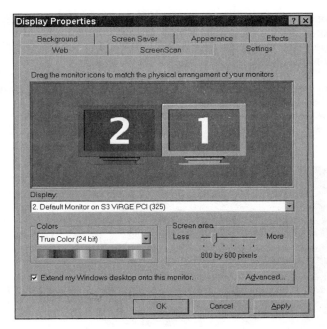

Figure 28-8: Use this picture arrangement if Monitor 2 is to the left of Monitor 1 on your desk.

If you want some advice, I suggest you put Monitor 1 right in front of your keyboard. Put Monitor 2 to the right of Monitor 1. Leave the little monitor icons in their original position, with Monitor 1 on the left, as shown back in Figure 28-3. If you discover Monitor 2 is on the left, a few simple solutions to the problem exist. Just switch places between the two monitors. Or, leave the monitors where they are, shut down Windows, turn off the computer, switch the two VGA cables on the back of the computer, and then turn on the computer again. If you use the latter approach, you may need to reboot the machine a few times as Windows switches the drivers for the two monitors.

When you do get back to the Windows Me desktop, if you notice anything strange, make sure the appropriate monitor is associated with the appropriate display card. See "Tuning the Monitors" later in this chapter.

Using the monitors

When you first get two monitors going, it may look like nothing much is happening. But if you move the mouse pointer off the edge of the screen nearest the other monitor, the mouse pointer disappears from the current monitor and appears on that monitor. In a sense, the two monitors are now one big Windows Me desktop.

Here's another way to look at it. Let's say the resolution of each monitor is set to 800×600 pixels. The actual size of your screen is now 1,600×600 pixels — twice as wide as it used to be. The screen is split onto two separate monitors. But nonetheless, this screen is 1,600 pixels wide.

You can drag things from one monitor to the other, just by dragging them off the edge of the screen. Here's an example. Suppose my monitors are arranged so Monitor 1 is to the left of Monitor 2, as in Figure 28-5. Initially, my screen looks like Figure 28-9.

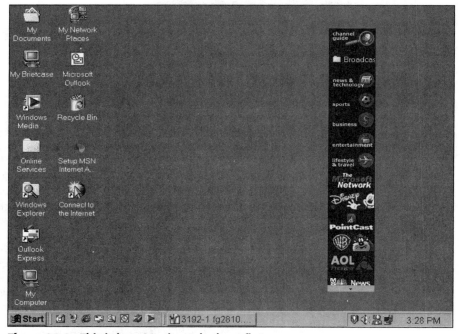

Figure 28-9: This is how Monitor 1 looks at first.

> **Note** You can't drag an application already displayed full-screen from one monitor to the other. If you want to drag this program to the other monitor, you must click its Restore button first (up near the Close button) to shrink the window a little. Then you can drag the window over to the other monitor.

If I want to get that Channel Bar off the main display, without closing it or clicking it, I could drag it right off the edge of Monitor 1 onto Monitor 2. Now Monitor 2 would show the Channel Bar and Monitor 1 would no longer show that, as in Figure 28-10.

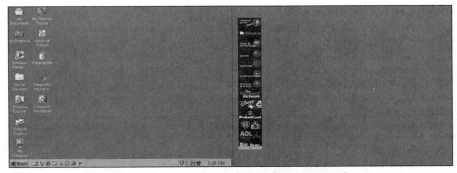

Figure 28-10: The Channel Bar has been dragged over to Monitor 2.

Here's another scenario. Suppose you have Internet access and you find a message in a Usenet group from someone telling you to check out some cool Web site. Rather than cover up your e-mail program with your Web browser, drag the e-mail program over to Monitor 2. Then click the link to the Web site, or use your favorite search engine to look for it. Internet Explorer and the Web page appear in the primary Monitor 1. So now you can see both your Web browser and your e-mail program, as in Figure 28-11.

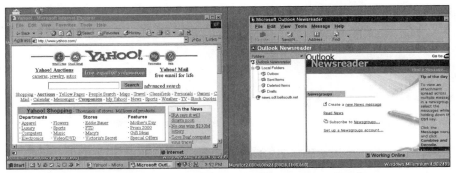

Figure 28-11: E-mail reader on Monitor 2 — Web browser on Monitor 1.

Here's another scenario you'll appreciate if you're into creating your own Web pages. Suppose you want to edit some Web page using a basic text editor such as Notepad. You open the page in Microsoft Internet Explorer first and leave it on Monitor 1. Then, you open the same page in Notepad and drag that over to Monitor 2. Now, to see the results of any changes you made to the document source, you needn't close and reopen anything. Just choose File ➪ Save from Notepad's menu bar to make sure the disk contains the latest version of the file. Then click the Refresh button in Microsoft Internet Explorer to reload the page from the disk. And, bingo, you can still see the page's document source on one monitor and you can see exactly how the page will look on the Internet over in Monitor 1, as in Figure 28-12.

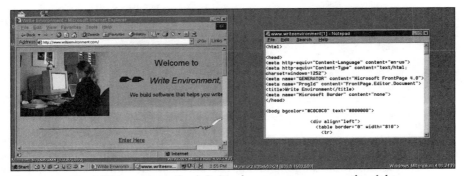

Figure 28-12: A Web page on the left, it's document source on the right

My two little scenarios hardly do justice to how much easier life at the PC can be after you double the width of your screen. Of course, you're not limited to two monitors either. You can add as many monitors as you have PCI slots for the display cards. For example, you could put four monitors on there, maybe two across the top and two across the bottom. If each of those monitors were set to 800×600, your actual screen size would be 1,600×1,200. Or at 1024×768 resolution, your desktop would be 2,048×1,536 pixels in size. Huge!

Multiple Display Gotchas and Tips

Here are a few pointers to remember when working with multiple monitors:

✦ You cannot drag a maximized application window to the other monitor. You must first click the Restore button to shrink the window, and then drag the smaller window over to the new monitor.

✦ You can stretch many application window across two or more monitors — handy for viewing extra wide spreadsheets and such! To do so, make sure the program window isn't maximized. Then drag the edge of the window closest to the second monitor right off the edge of the screen. It will reappear at the left edge of the next monitor where you can continue stretching across that monitor.

✦ If the mouse pointer seems to disappear, remember it's probably over on the other monitor. You can use pointer trails and such, as discussed in Chapter 16, to make the mouse pointer more visible onscreen.

✦ If the monitors use different resolutions, the monitors won't be the same size. You can only drag the mouse pointer across two monitors where their icons touch. So, for example, in Figure 28-13 where monitor 1 is set to 1024×768, and monitor 2 is set to 800×600, you couldn't drag a title bar near the bottom of Monitor 1 over to Monitor 2 because there's a gap there when the two monitors don't touch. The problem is easily rectified though by simply dragging up a little first, and then to the right.

✦ Programs that are specifically designed for Windows Me will be able to use Multiple Display Support in unique ways. Check the documentation or online help for each program to see what's possible.

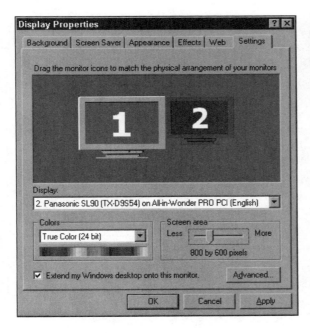

Figure 28-13: The place where the two monitors touch here represents where you can drag the mouse pointer across the two monitors.

Tuning the Monitors

Now that you have two monitors, you get to think about how you might want to set each one. The monitors don't have to use the same color depth or resolution. Each monitor can be set independently. Here's how:

1. Right-click any neutral part of the desktop (not on an icon) and choose Properties.

2. In the Display Properties dialog box that appears, click the Settings tab.

3. Click one of the monitor pictures or use the drop-down list, as shown in Figure 28-14, to pick a monitor with which to work.

4. Choose settings for this monitor including Colors, Screen Area, and options on the Advanced button.

Note Settings on the Background, Screen Saver, Appearance, Effects, and Web tabs affect both monitors equally. For example, if you pick a tiled wallpaper from the Background tab, all monitors will have this background. After all, it *is* one big screen that just happens to be split across two or more monitors.

5. Repeat Steps 3 and 4 for the other monitor.

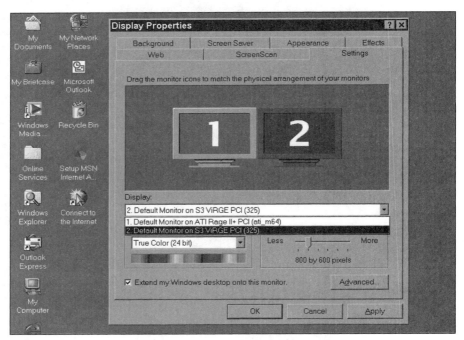

Figure 28-14: Choose a monitor with which to work.

If you have any problems with your monitors, or if you see a monitor referred to as Unknown Monitor, then you need to choose whichever display card (not monitor) is causing you grief. Then click the Advanced button and click the Monitor tab to get to the options shown in Figure 28-15.

If you're not absolutely sure the monitor name shown is the exact make and model of the monitor attached, click the Change button. Then complete the following steps:

1. In the first wizard screen to appear, click the Next button.

2. On the second wizard screen, choose the second option, "Display a list of all the drivers in a specific location, so you can select the driver you want." Then click the Next button.

3. In the next wizard screen, choose the Show All Hardware radio button.

4. Then choose your monitor's manufacturer and model number from the two lists shown.

5. Click the Next button and follow any instructions that appear onscreen to install the correct driver for the monitor attached to the current display card.

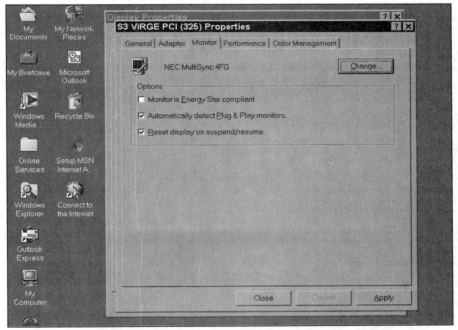

Figure 28-15: S3 ViRGE (325) PCI display card has a NEC MultiSync 4FG monitor attached, according to its dialog box.

Disabling Multiple Display Support

Certain programs will not run at all when Multiple Display Support is enabled. The only workaround to this problem is to deactivate the secondary monitor(s) so you can run the uncooperative program. To disable Multiple Display Support:

1. Right-click some neutral area of the desktop and choose Properties.

2. Click the Settings tab.

3. Clear the "Extend my windows desktop onto this monitor" check box for each secondary monitor. You cannot, nor do you want to, clear that check box on the primary display's settings.

4. Click the OK button to save, and to activate, your changes.

You should be able to start the uncooperative program now. When you finish using this program — having saved your work and closed the program — you can then reactivate the secondary monitor(s). Repeat the previous Steps 1 through 4, except this time, you want to select — not clear — the secondary monitor's "Extend my Windows desktop onto this monitor" check box.

Troubleshooting Multiple Display Support

Like I said, using Multiple Display Support is great — and easy — once you get the hang of it. The hard part is getting it to work. If you have no luck getting a second monitor working, check to see if it's even supported. Here's how:

1. Click the Start button and choose Settings ➪ Control Panel.

2. Open the System icon.

3. Click the Device Manager tab. If the Display Adapters category isn't open, click the little plus (+) sign next to it so you can see all installed adapters, as shown in Figure 28-16.

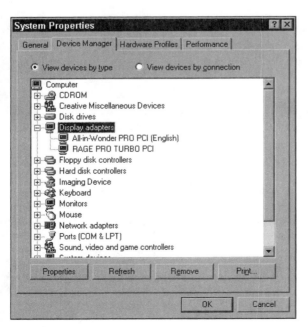

Figure 28-16: Device Manager sees two display cards.

4. If one of the display cards has an exclamation point (!) near it, click it, and then click the Properties button.

5. Click the General tab (if it isn't already open) and check for any messages. If you see "Your computer's display driver will not work with Multiple Display Support" that is your problem. The message you want to see ("This device is working properly") is shown in Figure 28-17.

6. Click the Cancel button to close the System Properties dialog box.

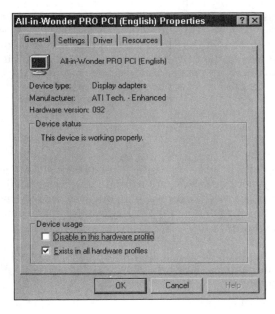

Figure 28-17: This display card is working fine.

So, if you saw the message indicating your display card isn't going to work as a secondary monitor, then you need to find out if an updated driver exists to make that card work. The people to contact are the ones who manufactured the display card. Or, if you have access to the Internet, visit Windows Update to see if a newer driver is waiting. To go to Windows Update, click the Start button and then click Windows Update. (Or, click the Start button and choose Settings ⇨ Windows Update.)

If one of your monitors is connected to an on-board video display plug and you can only see one monitor listed on the Settings tab of Display Properties, the problem could be any of the following:

✦ The PCI motherboard video is hidden from the enumerator and may be identified incorrectly.

✦ Some systems hide the motherboard video from PCI when another video card is detected in the system. If Plug and Play cannot find the device, Setup cannot start it. If you have this particular problem, you can do nothing to resolve it. To verify this is the problem, open the Device Manager tab in the System Properties dialog box (Start ➪ Settings ➪ Control Panel ➪ System). If only your add-in card is shown as present and working, then you cannot use your on-board video as one of the connections for multiple monitors. You must install a PCI or AGP display card for each monitor you want to use.

Another potential problem, especially with older hardware and drivers, is if the driver used for the display is a Windows 3.*x* driver or a standard VGA driver; then no secondary displays will work. Also, if you intentionally set the screen resolution to 640×480 with 16 colors, Windows will use the standard VGA driver by default. You may want to increase the color depth and/or resolution. If you can't increase the color depth or resolution, then try using Windows Update and/or the Change Driver option in Device Manager to install a more recent driver.

Summary

Using multiple monitors is cool. The only downside is the potential headaches you may encounter while trying to install the appropriate hardware, particularly if you're not big on installing your own hardware. A simple way around this problem is to pay a professional to select and install the hardware. Let's review the main points covered in this chapter:

✦ To set up a secondary monitor, you need another monitor, a spare PCI or AGP slot, and a display card that uses one of the chip sets supported by Windows Me as a secondary monitor.

✦ After you install the hardware for multiple monitors, you need to go to the Settings tab of the Display Properties dialog box and activate all secondary monitors by choosing the "Extend my Windows desktop to this monitor" option on the Settings tab.

✦ Also important is that you arrange the monitor icons on the Settings tab to match the actual physical arrangement of your monitors.

✦ Once multiple monitors are working, you can treat them as a single desktop by dragging stuff right off the edge of one monitor and onto the other monitor.

✦ If you ever need to disable Multiple Display Support due to some uncooperative program, you can go back to the Settings tab of Display Properties and clear the "Extend my Windows desktop to this monitor" check box for all but the primary monitor.

✦   ✦   ✦

Managing Multiple Users and Hardware

Sometimes, one PC must serve the needs of several people. Each of those people may have certain preferences for screen colors, accessibility options, and so forth. Windows Me enables you to create multiple user profiles that enable different users to personalize Windows to their liking, without changing anyone else's preferences.

Some PCs also need to operate a lot of extra hardware devices — perhaps even too many to manage at once. To get around this problem, Windows Me offers hardware profiles. You can define multiple profiles, each of which fires up its own particular devices at startup. In this chapter, you learn how to create both user profiles for managing multiple users and hardware profiles for managing multiple hardware configurations.

Sharing a PC

Every user has personal preferences in screen colors, desktop icons, and the like. This is why you can personalize Windows Me in so many ways, as discussed in Chapters 15 through 17. But, when two or more people share the same PC, not everyone may want to use the same settings. In this case, each person can have his or her own settings and can turn them on with a few mouse clicks. This feature is perfect for families in which the parents want to restrict which programs the kids can use (or vice versa!). It's also handy in offices where coworkers have different personal tastes and working styles.

To use this feature, every person who uses the PC must have a unique user name and password. (All users should write down this information and put it in a safe place in case they need it to recover their personal settings in the future.) Then, one of the users must activate the user profiles feature, as discussed in the following section.

Enabling multiple user profiles

The first step in setting up user profiles is to tell Windows Me you plan to use this feature. Follow these steps:

1. If you have any work in progress, save all that work, and then close all open program windows.

2. Click the Start button, point to Settings, and open the Control Panel.

3. Open the Passwords icon and click the User Profiles tab.

4. To activate user profiles, click the second option button, as shown in Figure 29-1.

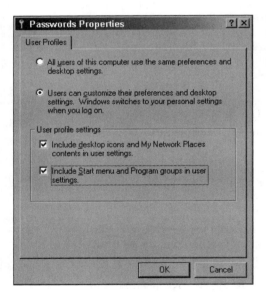

Figure 29-1: The User Profiles tab in the Password Properties dialog box enables you to assign multiple users to a single PC.

5. To enable each user to set his or her own desktop icons, Start menus, and so on, select options under User Profile Settings as follows:

   • If you want each user to have a personal set of desktop icons and Network Neighborhood contents, select the first option.

   • If you want each user to have a personal Start menu and Start ⇨ Program folders, select the second option.

Note   Initially, all users will have the current settings. However, they can change their settings independently.

6. Click OK when you finish.

7. When you see the dialog box asking if you want to restart your computer, click Yes.

When Windows restarts, you need to fill in your user name and password and, perhaps, answer additional questions onscreen. You may come to the message shown in Figure 29-2, as well. You can choose Yes to proceed to the desktop.

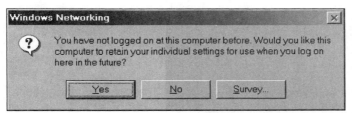

Figure 29-2: This message appears at startup after enabling multiple users.

 New Feature   Unlike its predecessors, Windows Me does not ask all new users if they would like to save their settings for use when they log on in the future. Once multiple users are enabled, Windows Me saves the settings that have been enabled for existing users without asking. Features that cannot be personalized are saved to the All Users profile. Features that can be customized are saved to a profile named after the user. (If you would like to see the profiles, look in \Windows\Profiles. You will see a folder named All Users, and one folder named after each user.) If someone whose user name has not already been created logs in, Windows Me shows the dialog box presented previously in Figure 29-2.

Adding a new user

A few ways exist to add a new user. Simply logging onto the PC with a new name and password will do the trick. In most cases, however, someone will probably take the responsibility of creating a profile for each user. Here's how to do this:

1. Click the Start button and choose Settings ➪ Control Panel.

2. Open the Users icon to get to the User Settings dialog box, as shown in Figure 29-3.

3. To create a new user, click the New User button.

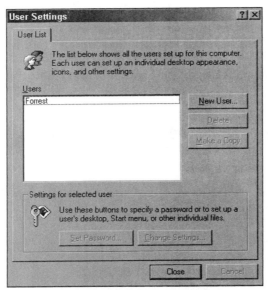

Figure 29-3: The User Settings dialog box enables you to add new users to the PC.

4. Read the first wizard screen that appears and then click the Next button.

5. In the next wizard page to appear (see Figure 29-4), type in the name of a new user and then click the Next button.

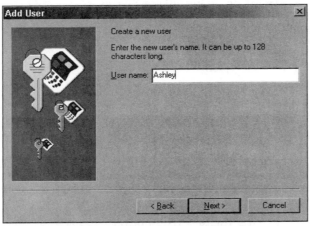

Figure 29-4: First page of the Add User Wizard

6. In the next window (see Figure 29-5), type the password this user must type in to gain access to the PC. The password will appear as asterisks. Type it twice, as indicated, to ensure you typed it correctly, and then click the Next button. Be careful: the password is case-sensitive, meaning you must use type the password using exactly the same uppercase and lowercase letters each time you type it. To simplify things, make it your rule to use only lowercase letters in your passwords.

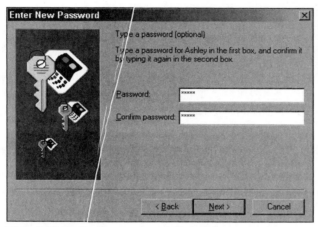

Figure 29-5: Type a password (twice) for the new user you're creating.

7. The next wizard page (see Figure 29-6) enables you to choose which items this user can personalize. For example, if you want the new user to have the same desktop shortcuts and Documents menu as everyone else, leave the first option cleared. If you want the user to have his or her own desktop shortcuts and Documents menu, select (check) the first item. The bottom two options enable you to start the user from scratch, or from the current user's settings, as follows:

- **Create copies of the current items:** If you choose this option, the new user's desktop and other settings will initially be identical to your own. Even if you're not sharing those items, the new user receives copies of your existing settings.

- **Create new items:** If you choose this second option, the new user will initially have access to only pure Windows Me stuff, similar to when you first install Windows Me. You (or this user) can then design new desktop shortcuts and other settings.

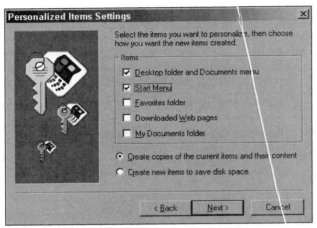

Figure 29-6: Choose which items can be personalized.

Tip

If in doubt, select the second item to minimize disk space. If you later change your mind, it's no big deal to go back and change the options you set here.

8. Click Next after making your selections to get to the final wizard screen (see Figure 29-7). Then click the Finish button.

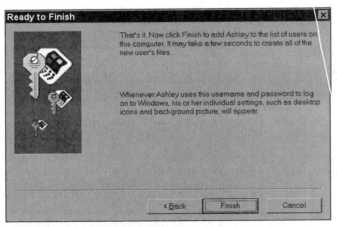

Figure 29-7: I'm finished creating a new user.

From here on, it's only a matter of following the instructions onscreen. If you shut down and restart the computer, you'll come to a dialog box like the one in Figure 29-8.

(The dialog box will look a little different if your PC is not connected to a network.) To use his or her own personalized settings, the person sitting at the keyboard only needs to enter his/her own user name and password and then click the OK button to get to the Windows desktop.

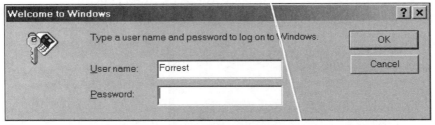

Figure 29-8: Type in the user name and password.

From this point, any changes to the appearance of the desktop will apply only to the person who is logged on currently. For example, if Ashley is logged on, and she changes the screen colors to a shocking pink color scheme, only Ashley will be faced with those colors. Anyone logging in under a name other than Ashley won't have to look at those shocking pink colors.

Tip   If you really like Ashley's color scheme, however, and want to make sure that Marsha shares it, you can use the Make a Copy button in the User Settings dialog box to build a new user that is a copy of Ashley. When you make a copy, you don't have to keep all settings identical. But making a copy is a handy way to make sure that new users share the same desktop color scheme, for example.

Protecting your own settings

When sharing a PC among multiple users, each user must log off the machine before leaving it. Otherwise, some other user may sit down and unwittingly change your preferences. To log off, click the Start button and choose Log Off. When asked if you're sure, choose Yes. If you left any unsaved work behind, you're given a last chance to save this work. If you do need to save any work in progress, be sure to choose Yes because this is your last chance.

When all your work is saved, your desktop icons disappear and only the login window, shown back in Figure 29-8, appears onscreen. Anyone who wants to use the computer while you're away will need to type in a valid user name and password, and then click OK.

Changing/deleting users

You can change and delete user profiles as easily as you can create them. Follow these steps:

1. Click the Start button and choose Settings ➭ Control Panel.

2. Open the Users icon to get to the dialog box shown in Figure 29-9.

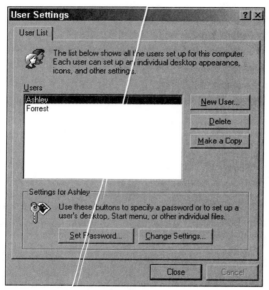

Figure 29-9: The User Settings dialog box lists names of existing users and enables you to make changes.

3. Click the name of the user whose profile you want to change or delete. You can then do the following:

- To delete this user, click the Delete button.

- To change this user's password, click the Set Password button.

- To change other settings for this user, click the Change Settings button.

- If you want to add a user and give this new user the same settings as the currently selected user, click the Make a Copy button.

Caution Be careful! Deleting the user profile also will delete the desktop, favorites, and other individual settings chosen by that user. This action will delete the documents in the user's My Documents folder! Make sure you want to do this before you proceed.

4. Respond to any prompts, and follow any instructions that appear onscreen.

5. Click the Close button.

As usual, if any more prompts or instructions appear onscreen after you click the Close button, go ahead and respond to those prompts and/or follow the instructions that appear.

Displaying a list of users at logon

When you are sharing your PC, sometimes you have to share it with people who don't want to remember a username and password for each PC they use. Some users will have to log on to several different PCs during a day, and it is a real convenience for them just to pick their user name from a list. Windows Me allows you to present a list of users at logon time rather than receiving the standard logon dialog box.

To present this list, you must install the Windows Family Logon. To install this client, follow these steps:

1. Click the Start button and choose Settings ⇨ Control Panel.

2. Open the Network icon, and click the Add button.

3. Select Client and click the Add button, as shown in Figure 29-10.

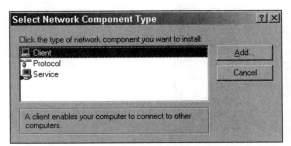

Figure 29-10: Choose to add a new network client to your computer.

4. Select Microsoft Family Logon and click OK (see Figure 29-11).

5. Make sure Microsoft Family Logon shows as your Primary Network Logon, as shown in Figure 29-12. Then click OK. Place the Millennium CD in the drive when Windows Me asks for it. When prompted, restart your computer.

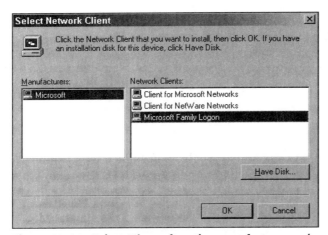

Figure 29-11: Select Microsoft as the manufacturer and Windows Family Logon as the client.

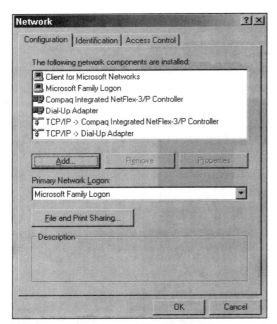

Figure 29-12: To see the list of users, you must have Windows Family Logon as your primary network client.

You must choose to restart your computer before the Windows Family Logon will take effect. Once you do, you see a logon list, like the one shown in Figure 29-13.

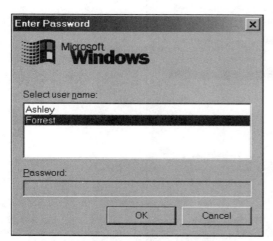

Figure 29-13: The Windows Family Logon presents a list of users to select from.

Using Multiple Hardware Profiles

Windows Me enables you to create multiple hardware profiles. A hardware profile is a list of attached devices activated at bootup. Multiple hardware profiles are useful in several situations:

✦ If multiple users share a PC, each user can select his or her own hardware to activate.

✦ If you have more devices than IRQs, preventing you from using all those devices at once, you can create profiles for different combinations of hardware devices.

✦ If you have a portable computer, you can set up one hardware profile for when you're on the road and another for when you're connected to a LAN or docking station.

Setting up and using multiple hardware profiles is fairly easy. The first step is to tell Windows you plan to use multiple profiles. To do so, follow these steps:

1. Click the Start button and choose Settings ➪ Control Panel.

2. Open the System icon and then click the Hardware Profiles tab to get to the options shown in Figure 29-14.

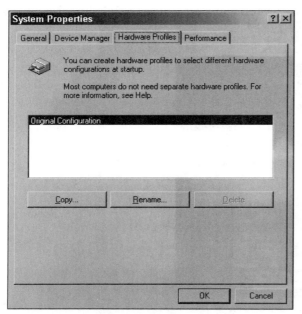

Figure 29-14: Options for managing multiple hardware profiles

3. Click whichever profile you want to use as the starting point for a new profile. If only the Original Profile option is available, click this one.

4. Click the Copy button.

5. In the next dialog box that appears, type in a name of the new profile you're about to create and then click the OK button. In the example shown in Figure 29-15, I'm about to create a new profile named Off the LAN.

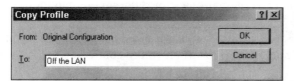

Figure 29-15: I'm about to create a new hardware profile named Off The LAN.

6. Click the OK button to save your changes and close the dialog box.

Nothing happens right away. But you can easily customize this new profile, as I discuss in the next section.

Picking the active profile

The only time you can choose a hardware profile is when you first start the PC or after you reboot. To reboot:

1. Save any work in progress and close all open programs.

2. Click the Start button and choose Shut Down.

3. Choose Restart and then click the OK button.

4. As Windows is loading, it will stop and present a little menu, looking something like this:

```
Select one of the following:

1. Original Configuration

2. Off the LAN

3. None of the above

Enter your choice:
```

5. Type the number of the hardware profile you want to use and then press Enter.

Nothing spectacular will happen, particularly if the current profile is identical to the other profile. You can, however, alter the hardware profile you're using right now by following this basic procedure:

1. Click the Start button and choose Settings ⇨ Control Panel.

2. Open the System icon.

3. Click the Device Manager tab.

4. Click the category of hardware you want to remove from the current profile and then click the specific hardware device. For example, in Figure 29-16, I chose my network adapter card.

5. Click the Properties button.

6. To remove the device from the current profile (only), select (check) the "Disable in this hardware profile" option and clear the "Exists in all hardware profiles" check box, as in Figure 29-17.

7. Click OK (twice) to return the Control Panel. You can then close the Control Panel, if you wish.

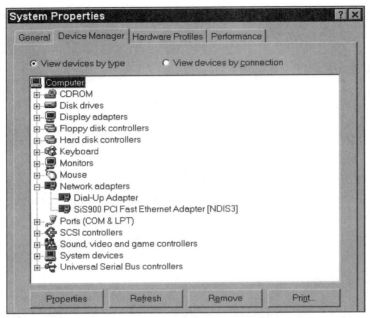

Figure 29-16: I'm about to work with my network adapter card.

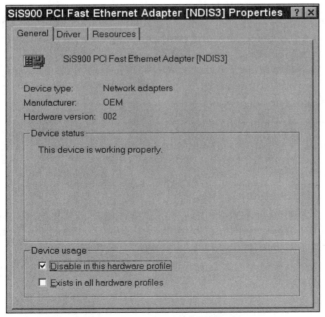

Figure 29-17: Now I'm about to disable this hardware device in the current hardware profile.

To activate the modified hardware profile, you need to reboot. You can also verify the hardware device has been disabled after you reboot. Follow these steps:

1. Save any work in progress and close all open programs.
2. Click the Start button and choose Shut Down ➪ Restart ➪ OK.
3. When prompted to choose a hardware profile, select the one you just changed.

When the computer restarts, you'll be in your selected hardware profile. To verify the device has, indeed, been disabled, take another peek at Device Manager. To do this, click the Start button and choose Settings ➪ Control Panel. Open the System icon and then click the Device Manager tab. The disabled device will appear with a red X through its icon to indicate that the device is no longer active.

Basically, that's how it all works. Note, however, that when you get to the Properties dialog box for a specific piece of hardware, you may have any combination of the following settings from which to choose:

✦ **Disable in this hardware profile:** When selected, prevents the Windows driver for this device from being loaded at startup. If this is a plug-and-play device, the resources consumed by the device will be freed for other devices to use.

✦ **Exists in all hardware profiles:** Specifies a device that needs to exist in all hardware profiles, such as a mouse, a keyboard, or a monitor.

Be aware that when you disable a non-plug-and-play device, the resources used by this device may not be freed automatically. To disable a real-mode (non-plug-and-play) device, you need to remove the device first by clicking its name in Device Manager and clicking the Remove button. Then, you need to shut down the computer and physically disconnect or remove the device from the PC.

Tweaking hardware profiles

The main trick to working with hardware profiles is to remember you can only work with one profile at a time—whichever profile you selected while Windows was booting up. As you go through the various devices in Device Manager, remember you are enabling or disabling hardware devices for the current hardware profile only.

If you want to delete or rename a hardware profile, return to the Hardware Profiles tab of the System Properties dialog box (click the Start button, choose Settings ➪ Control Panel ➪ System, and click the Hardware Profiles tab).

If you need assistance, check the online help. Click the Start button, choose Help, click the Index tab, type **hardware, p** (including the comma and the space) to jump to the Profiles subtopic under Hardware, and then click the Display button. You'll see a list of relevant topics. Also, while you're in any of the dialog boxes you access from the Control Panel, you can click the question mark (?) button and then click the item with which you need help.

Summary

In this chapter, you learned how to let people who share a single PC pick and choose their own preferences. You also learned about setting up multiple hardware profiles. Here's a recap of the most important points to remember:

✦ To enable multiple users, open the Control Panel, open the Password icon, click the User Profiles tab, and select the "Users can customize their preferences and desktop settings" option.

✦ To set up a new user, open the Control Panel, click the Users icon, and click the New User button. Or, click the Make a Copy button and rename the copy to whatever name you want to give the new user.

✦ To modify or delete a user profile, open the Control Panel and click the user profile you want to change or delete. Then use options in this same dialog box to make your changes.

✦ To present a list of users at logon, open the Control Panel and open the Network icon. Click the Add button and add Windows Family Logon as a network client, and make sure it is the primary network logon.

✦ To manage hardware profiles, open the Control Panel, open the System icon, and click the Hardware Profiles tab.

✦ To create a new hardware profile, first click an existing profile and then click the Copy button.

✦ ✦ ✦

Building Your Own Network

Why Bother with a Local Area Network?

If you have two or more PCs in your office or home, the best thing you can do for yourself is to hook them together as a local area network (LAN). You may think, "Yeah, right. Like I'm really going to create a LAN just to hook my portable PC to my desktop." You assume creating a LAN is a big, expensive, complicated undertaking. You think you need to shell out big bucks to have someone set it up and then you'll be at that person's mercy every time the LAN goes down. Or worse, you'll have to hire someone full-time to baby-sit the LAN!

Put all such thoughts out of your head. LANs were a big complicated mess when DOS was in the picture. But things have become much, much easier now that Windows Me (and Windows 2000) have built-in networking capabilities. You no longer have an operating system (DOS) fighting a LAN every step of the way. Instead, you have an operating system that supports and embraces a LAN, which even has all the software you need built right into it.

Advantages of a LAN

Even though setting up a LAN is easier than ever, some investment of time and money still is involved, so you need some justification. Perhaps one of the following advantages of a LAN will solve a problem for you:

✦ If only one PC in the LAN has a printer, CD-ROM drive, or fax/modem, every PC in the LAN can use that hardware.

✦ If several people work on the same document, they can use the documents on one PC without copying and transporting files via floppy disk. Several people often can work on the same document at the same time.

✦ If several people work with the same data — such as a customer list, inventory list, or orders — all this information can reside on one PC. Each user in the LAN will have access to this always current data.

✦ Any portable PCs connected to the LAN can regain access to the resources of the LAN even while they're away, thanks to dial-up networking.

In short, if you're using floppy disks to transport files from one PC to another — whether to print, fax, modem, whatever — you need a LAN. You'll quickly earn back the time and money you invest in creating the LAN by not having to fumble with floppies anymore.

Why LANs Seem So Complicated

When you read about LANs, you are inundated by so many acronyms, technical terms, and product names that you have difficulty understanding what's really involved in setting up a LAN. Maybe I can clear up some of the confusion.

Any PC with Windows 95, Windows 98, Windows Me, Windows NT, Windows 2000, or Windows for Workgroups on it can hook into the LAN without any third-party software. You don't need Novell NetWare, Banyan-Vines, Microsoft LAN Manager, Lantastic, or other network programs.

If you have relatively few computers (15 or fewer), a simple peer-to-peer LAN probably will work perfectly for you. You needn't worry about client/server terminology.

The written documentation for LANs can be one of the most confusing elements of networking. Often, when you look up the solution to a problem, the documentation tells you to ask your network administrator — not much help if you *are* the network administrator. Another problem with the written documentation is that Step 1 in the instruction manual says something like this: "Make sure the LAN is up, running, and working perfectly, and you have full administrative rights before you do anything else. If you have any problems, ask your network administrator."

Isn't this situation a catch-22? You're expecting to set up a LAN and the instructions tell you to set it all up and grab your local full-time network guru before you do anything else.

In this book, I make no such assumptions. For all intents and purposes, you are the network administrator, even if you currently don't know diddly-squat about LANs. And I'm not assuming the LAN is set up and ready to go. I'm only assuming you have two or more PCs you want to connect in a LAN.

What You Really Need to Know

I don't mean to imply a computer novice should set up a LAN. The job calls for some prerequisite skills and knowledge, summarized in the following list:

✦ You must know how to use My Computer or Windows Explorer to browse around a PC.

✦ You must know how to open a computer case and install a board. If the PC you're connecting to the LAN has an available PCMCIA slot, you must know how to insert and remove PC cards.

✦ You should get a little practice with Device Manager (refer to Chapter 26) so you can find available resources and tweak some settings if necessary.

If you don't meet those criteria, you may be better off hiring a pro to do the job. Just make sure this person understands you want to set up a peer-to-peer LAN, using the network capabilities built into Windows Me or Windows 2000. Explain that you're not looking for a dedicated server and you don't need third-party software, such as NetWare. The installer may grumble because this approach seems too easy. But easy is good. Trust me—the simpler, the better.

Planning the LAN

Phase One in setting up a LAN is planning your equipment purchase. You have to choose among several types of cables and network cards. In the interest of keeping things simple, I'll narrow your choices to the items that have emerged as industry standards and which offer the simplest and most flexible solutions to the problem.

Choosing a cable type

The first decision is the kind of cable to use. You have several choices, but you'd do well to stick with TPE cable. This type of cable has many names, including 10BaseT, 10BT, Twisted Pair, Twisted Pair Ethernet, TPE, and RJ-45. But you can recognize the cable because the plugs at the ends look like slightly oversized telephone plugs. The cable resembles the cable that connects your telephone to the wall.

You may want to go wireless

The best type of network cable may be no cable at all. A number of manufacturers now make *wireless* home networking equipment. These types of networks use small radio transmitters to connect all of the PCs on the network so you don't have to mess around with running cables all over the place. You can find out more about one of the popular wireless LANs at `http://www.proxim.com`.

In addition to radio frequency LANs, you can also get home networking equipment that relies on existing wiring in your home. There are several types of these *no new wiring* LANs available, and they typically use either your existing phone lines or electrical outlets to send the signals between the PCs on the network.

If you decide that one of the wireless (or no new wire) options suits your needs, be aware that different brands of this type of equipment are generally incompatible with each other. Also, the tradeoff for ease of installation is much slower network speed. You may not need the higher speed provided by a traditional LAN, but you should be aware of these differences.

TPE cabling requires an Ethernet hub (also called an *Ethernet concentrator*) to which each PC in the LAN will connect, as shown in Figure 30-1.

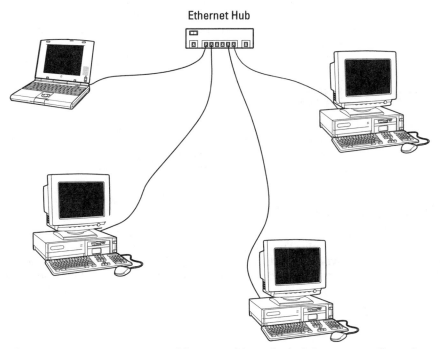

Figure 30-1: PCs are connected by TPE cable and a hub in a star configuration.

Tip If you want all the members of the LAN to have access to the Internet through a single ISDN phone line, you can buy an Ethernet hub that doubles as a modem. Ramp Networks, Intel, and 3Com all make several products to help with this. For more information, ask your computer dealer, or stop by `http://www.rampnet.com` on the Web. Regardless of the brand you choose, make certain you get equipment that is easy to set up and maintain.

This type of arrangement, in which each PC plugs into a hub, sometimes is called a *star configuration*. I guess this name arose because if you put the hub smack in the middle and spread the PCs around evenly, the configuration would look like a giant asterisk (*), and an asterisk sometimes is called a *star*. (Now we're really getting technical, eh?)

After you decide to use the TPE cable, you must decide where you want to put the hub. Some hubs actually require their own power and, therefore, must be plugged into a wall outlet. You probably should plan to put the hub near a standard power outlet (the same kind you use for a lamp).

Next, you need to measure the distance from each PC to the hub. You must run the cable in such a way that people aren't likely to trip over it. Always round up when you make your calculations. If one PC is only a few feet from the hub, you need a 2-foot or 4-foot cable for this connection. If another PC is about 10 feet from the hub, you need approximately a 12-foot cable for that connection. You need one cable for each PC you plan to connect to the LAN.

Tip A cable that's too long is still usable; a cable that's too short is unusable.

Choosing a network card

In addition to cable, you need one network interface card for each PC in the LAN. This card is a piece of hardware that enables you to connect one PC to a LAN. Like cables, network cards go by several names, including network adapter card, Ethernet card, and NIC. Choosing a network card is fairly easy if you follow these guidelines:

✦ Make sure the card is an Ethernet card.

✦ Make sure the card will fit in the slot you have available — either a PCI slot or ISA slot on the PC, or the PCMCIA slot on a portable computer.

✦ ISA cards are limited to 10 MBps (megabytes per second).

✦ Choose a card that supports the type of cable you're using (TPE). The hole into which the TPE cable plugs sometimes is called an *RJ-45 connector*.

✦ A plug-and-play card will be easier to install than one that isn't plug and play.

✦ A 32-bit card is faster (and more expensive) than a 16-bit card, but it's not worth fretting over if the LAN is fairly small.

✦ A card that supports 100 MBps is ten times faster than a 10 MBps card.

✦ If any of the network cards are 10 MBps only, your entire network will be limited to 10 MBps.

You can mix and match brands and models of network cards however you want, as long as all of them are Ethernet cards. But for simplicity's sake, you may want to buy the same make and model of network card for each PC in the LAN. (You can buy network cards in packs of five and ten.) Any laptop PCs you want to hook to the LAN require PC cards (PCMCIA) rather than traditional internal cards.

Making the buy

Before you go to the local Comput-O-Rama to buy the stuff for your LAN, you should have your shopping list ready. You need to know the following:

✦ How many PCI or ISA Ethernet cards you need and how many PCMCIA Ethernet cards you need.

✦ What type of plug you need on each Ethernet card (most likely, the RJ-45 plug for TPE cable).

✦ How many Ethernet cables you need and how long each cable should be. Make sure the cables have the proper plugs on each end (the plugs that fit into the RJ-45 socket).

✦ How many slots you need in your Ethernet hub. Allowing for growth never hurts. If you plan to link, say, four computers in your LAN, consider getting a hub with six connection slots.

Figure 30-2 shows an example of a shopping list for connecting four PCs in a LAN. I need four Ethernet cards. But because one of the PCs in my LAN is a laptop, one card must be a PCMCIA-style card. I need four cables (one for each card) and a hub with at least four connection slots.

Things to Pick up at Comput-O-Rama

3	Ethernet cards for desktop PCs [ISA slots]
1	Ethernet card for laptop PC [PCMCIA slot]
2	6-foot TPE cables
2	12-foot TPE cables
1	Ethernet hub with at least 4 slots [6 to allow growth]

Figure 30-2: Shopping list for equipment needed to set up a four-PC LAN

After you buy all this stuff and get it back to where your PCs are, you're ready to move to the next chapter in which you actually set up that LAN.

Summary

If you have two or more PCs in one location, consider hooking them together in a local area network (LAN):

✦ Computers in a LAN can share resources — printers, disk drives, CD-ROM drives, folders, and modems.

✦ LANs, which once required highly specialized knowledge, are relatively easy to set up and maintain in Windows Me.

✦ All the networking software you need is built right into Windows Me.

✦ You do need additional hardware to set up a LAN. In particular, you need a network card and Ethernet cable for each PC in the LAN and an Ethernet hub to which to connect all the cables.

✦ ✦ ✦

Creating Your Own LAN

After you purchase all the hardware you need to turn those independent PCs into a working team, as discussed in Chapter 30, you're ready to start installing. Be forewarned: This process can take a few hours. Try to do it when people are not working on the PCs you want to link. Get ready to concentrate. Take the phone off the hook. If other people are around, put a big sign on your back that reads: "Do not talk to me." Your brain will be tied up for a while.

Installing the LAN Hardware

At this point, you have hardware (cards and cables) and perhaps software (disks that came with the network cards) in hand. This part is a little tricky. You may have Ethernet cards that were designed for DOS/Windows or you may have plug-and-play Ethernet cards designed for Windows Me (or Windows 9x). If you're adding a portable PC to the LAN, you may have a PCMCIA Ethernet card. In the following sections, I'll try to cover all these possibilities. But you also must rely on the card manufacturer's instructions, in addition to my instructions.

Note   If the card manufacturer's documentation includes instructions for installing software in DOS or Windows 3.x, you want to ignore that section of the documentation. You don't want to use the old real-mode 16-bit drivers if you can avoid them. Instead, you want to use the 32-bit drivers, which are built into Windows Me.

Step 1: Check available resources

Whenever you install new hardware, you'll probably be asked to choose an Interrupt Request (IRQ) for that device. You also may have to provide an Input/Output (I/O) address. Network cards are no exception.

What is an IRQ?

An *Interrupt Request* (IRQ) is a channel that's allowed to interrupt whatever the processor is currently doing and request immediate attention. The keyboard is a perfect example. Suppose you start some long process and then you decide to finish it later. When you press the Esc key, you don't want the processor to ignore you and keep doing what it's doing. You want the processor to stop what it's doing and pay attention to whatever key you are pressing.

Some standards exist for assigning IRQs to devices. IRQ 1, for example, is used for the keyboard on virtually every PC. IRQ 2 is used for the system timer, and IRQs 3 and 4 are for the serial ports (COM1 and COM2). The IRQs generally left available are 7, 9, 10, and a few others.

Every time you install some new non plug-and-play internal device, such as a sound card or modem, you may need to give this device its own IRQ, and thus the available IRQs start getting used up. Remembering which IRQs are used and which are available at any given time is tough, so use Device Manager to check for available IRQs before you install any new hardware device.

Before you shut down a PC to install the network card, jot down (or print) the resources available on the PC. Follow these steps:

1. Choose Start ➪ Settings ➪ Control Panel.

2. Open the System icon. Or, you can right-click My Computer and select Properties.

3. Click the Device Manager tab.

   If this computer is connected to a printer, click the Print button, select System summary, and then choose OK. You get a printed summary of the used IRQ and I/O ports, as well as other information.

4. Double-click Computer at the top of the list and then click the IRQ option button. The screen shows installed devices, listed by the IRQs the devices are using (see Figure 31-1).

5. Write down any IRQs not already taken (IRQs that do not appear in the list). By looking at Figure 31-1, for example, I could write "Available IRQs on this PC: 9."

6. Choose Cancel twice to return to the Control Panel.

7. Close the Control Panel by clicking its Close button.

Remember that the available IRQ settings you wrote down (or printed) apply only to this PC, so don't let your notes drift too far from this PC. Also make sure you don't confuse these settings with those of any of the other PCs you plan to add to the LAN. While working with each PC, you must refer to the settings several times.

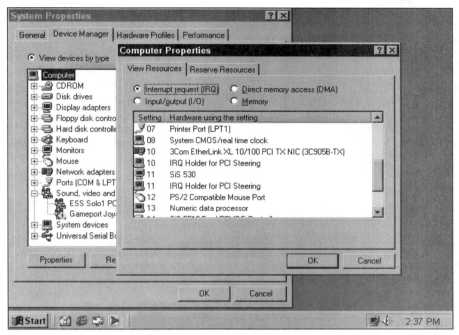

Figure 31-1: Installed devices listed by IRQs

Why it's so confusing

If you read this chapter, you may think this is all terribly complicated and confusing. Networking hardware and software have been evolving from the takes-a-genius technology of the '80s to Windows Me plug-and-play simplicity.

How complicated things are depends on the age of your hardware. If you buy plug-and-play cards designed for Windows Me or PCMCIA cards, you needn't mess with IRQs. Also, if you have a Pentium computer with an available PCI slot, you can buy a PCI Ethernet card for that computer, which is easier to install than the legacy ISA cards. A PCI card is easier to install because it can detect an available IRQ and set itself to use that IRQ.

Older cards require you to do all those things. Your goal is to find an IRQ not being used by any other device. Set the Ethernet card to this IRQ (assuming you can set the IRQ right on the board). The trick is always to specify this IRQ whenever any prompt asks you which IRQ to use for the network card or which IRQ the network is using. (Ugh!)

Step 2: Set the board's IRQ

Some old ISA cards (not newer plug-and-play PCMCIA or PCI cards) require you to set dip switches on the board to tell the board which IRQ to use. Now you're getting into a tricky area. You must look at the instructions for the Ethernet card you're installing to determine whether you must set an IRQ yourself — and, if so, how you should go about setting this IRQ. The following are possibilities:

✦ If the card's instructions say you don't have to set anything, skip to "Step 3: Shut everything down" later in this chapter. If you bought the card recently, this is the most likely scenario.

✦ If the card has dip switches you can adjust manually and if the directions tell you how to set those switches, follow those instructions to set the dip switches to an available IRQ (in my example, 09). Then skip to "Step 3: Shut everything down."

✦ If the card requires you to run a program to set the IRQ, do so, following the Ethernet card's instructions. Make sure you follow only the instructions for setting the dip switches. Do not install the DOS or Windows 3.x drivers. Then read on.

Running the little program that sets dip switches may be somewhat tricky. Most likely, the program will be a DOS program and you may be unable to run it from a DOS window. Furthermore, you may be required to run the program twice: before you install the board in the PC and after you physically install the board. If you need to run the program before you install the card, follow these steps:

1. Insert the floppy disk that came with the Ethernet card into drive A or drive B, according to the manufacturer's instructions.

2. If you must run the program from a DOS prompt, first try choosing Start ⇨ Programs ⇨ MS-DOS Prompt.

3. Type the command the instructions tell you to type (for example, a:\softset2), and then press Enter.

Note If the program complains it cannot be run from a DOS window, you won't be able to use it with Windows Me. You may want to return the network card to your dealer and ask for a modern replacement that does not depend on an obsolete DOS program.

At this point, you must rely on the Ethernet card manufacturer's instructions to set the IRQ. The screen may tell you how to set the dip switches or jumpers to select a specific IRQ. If the program tells you the best choice is an IRQ that's already taken, don't believe the program — choose an IRQ you know for certain is not taken (in my example, 9).

If you set the board to a specific IRQ now, write this setting on a piece of paper. You may be asked for the setting later and you may forget if you don't jot it down. You can write something like "I set the Ethernet card's IRQ to 9" (replacing the 9 with the actual setting you used).

When you complete the manufacturer's instructions on what to do before you install the board, exit the program, if necessary. Type exit and press Enter at the C:> prompt to return to the Windows Me desktop.

Step 3: Shut everything down

Before you install the card, you should shut down everything on this PC (and I do mean everything). Follow these steps:

1. Choose Start ⇨ Shut Down.

2. Click Shut Down and click Yes.

3. When the screen says it's safe to do so, shut down the PC and all peripherals attached directly to the PC (monitor, printer, external modem, external CD-ROM drive, and so on).

Step 4: Install the Ethernet card

With everything shut down, you are ready to install the Ethernet hardware. Once again, you should follow the manufacturer's instructions, but the general procedure will be something like the following:

1. If you're installing an internal card (not a PCMCIA card), remove the case from the system unit.

2. Put the card in an available slot.

   If your network card has dip switches, be careful not to change the dip-switch settings accidentally.

3. Replace the cover.

4. Connect one end of an Ethernet cable to the slot on the Ethernet card and the other end to your Ethernet hub. You can skip this step if your network is a wireless network as discussed in Chapter 30.

Step 5: Set the IRQ for the card (if the card isn't plug and play)

You can ignore this step if you're installing a plug-and-play card or if you already set the IRQ on the board by setting dip switches. If this is indeed the case, skip right now to "Step 6: Repeat Steps 1 through 5 on each PC."

If the board has no dip switches, but the hardware manufacturer requires you to run a program to set those switches, the instructions will tell you to run the program from DOS. Windows Me, of course, has no DOS. But if the card requires you to run a setup program from the DOS prompt to set IRQ switches, you must carefully follow these instructions:

1. Start your computer and wait for the Windows Me desktop to appear.

2. Click the Start button.

3. Select Programs ➪ Accessories ➪ MS-DOS Prompt.

4. When you get to the C:> prompt, follow the manufacturer's instructions to set the board's IRQ.

You may need to put a floppy disk in drive A. Type a:\softset2 and press Enter, for example. Remember, if the program you're running suggests using an IRQ you know is already in use, do not use that suggested setting. Instead, pick an IRQ you know is available (in my example, 9).

After you set the IRQ, jot down the settings you chose. You may write something like "I set my board to IRQ 9." Again, don't let your notes wander from this PC. Keep your notes handy because they have no bearing on any other PC in the LAN. I know I'm harping on this point, but it's not purely a neurotic compulsion. Getting this IRQ stuff squared away as early in the process as possible is important. Most networks fail simply because the IRQ setting on the board doesn't match the IRQ setting Windows expects or because the IRQ setting you chose for the network card conflicts with the IRQ setting for some other device installed in the PC. Going back and fixing the mistake can be a lengthy process.

Follow the instructions to complete and exit the manufacturer's program. When you get to the C:> prompt, you can type EXIT to return to the Windows Me desktop. Trying to test the card or the LAN makes no sense until at least two of the PCs have their cards installed and are connected to the Ethernet hub.

Step 6: Repeat Steps 1 through 5 on each PC

The best thing to do now is to repeat the process for each PC in the LAN, starting with "Step 1: Check available resources." The process takes a while. But if you properly install all the network hardware and connect every PC to the Ethernet adapter now, getting everything to work right will be much easier later. I've spent many frustrating, hair-pulling hours trying to set up LANs in a hurry. The technique I'm giving you here is slow and cautious but, in the long run, it produces satisfactory results faster.

Telling Windows Me You're on the LAN

After you install all the Ethernet cards and hook every PC to the Ethernet hub, you need to fire up Windows Me and tell it, "Hey, look—we're on a LAN now." As long as all the hardware is in place and at least two PCs are connected to the Ethernet hub, Windows Me will say, "Hey, yeah, cool. Let me install my networking software for you."

This part usually is easy. You need to complete the following procedure on each PC in the LAN (one PC at a time, of course):

1. Gather up your original Windows Me CD-ROM (unless your computer came with Windows Me pre-installed and you don't need those original disks).

2. Turn on all the peripherals (monitor, printer, external modem, external CD-ROM drive, and so on) for any PC in the LAN.

3. Remove any floppy disks from the floppy drives.

4. Turn on the computer, sit back, and watch the screen.

What you do next depends on what happens onscreen. The most likely scenario is Windows Me will detect the new piece of hardware in your PC and it will install the drivers for it without any intervention from you. If further instructions appear onscreen, though, follow them closely. If you come to a dialog box asking you to identify the current computer, skip to the section "Identifying this PC on the LAN" now.

If you got all the way to the Windows Me desktop and Windows didn't detect the new Ethernet card, follow these steps:

1. Choose Start ⇨ Settings ⇨ Control Panel.

2. Open the Add New Hardware icon.

3. Read the instructions, click Next, choose Yes when you're asked about auto-detection, and then click Next again.

4. Follow the instructions onscreen.

If the Add New Hardware Wizard says it didn't find any new devices, you need to install the device. Click the Next button, click Network adapters, click Next again, and select the Manufacturer and Model of your network card. If you can't find your make and model, put the manufacturer's drivers disk in drive A, click Have Disk, choose OK, and follow the instructions onscreen.

Windows Me probably will install many files from the floppy disks or CD-ROM and then ask you to restart the computer. Follow whatever instructions appear onscreen. Then proceed to the following section.

Using the Home Networking Wizard

Once your network hardware is installed, you are ready to run the Home Networking Wizard. This wizard installs and configures all of the software components that are necessary for your network. It also enables you to share a single Internet connection across your entire network.

To run the Home Networking Wizard, click the Start button and choose Programs ➪ Accessories ➪ Communications ➪ Home Networking Wizard (or choose Home Networking Wizard from My Network Places). This displays a welcome screen where you click Next to continue.

You next choose the type of Internet connection, as shown in Figure 31-2:

   ✦ If you are setting up the computer that will provide Internet access to the other computers on the network, choose the "A direct connection to my ISP using the following device" option. Then make certain you select the correct device from the drop-down list. Your options might include a modem if you use a dial-up connection, an ISDN adapter if you have an ISDN connection, or a network adapter if you have a DSL or cable connection. Don't choose the adapter that connects the PC to your network.

   ✦ If another PC on the network is already providing shared Internet access, choose "A connection to another computer on my home network that provides direct access to my Internet service provider (ISP)." This is the option to use if another computer already has Internet Connection Sharing (ICS) installed since only one computer on the network can have ICS installed.

   ✦ Choose "No, this computer does not use the Internet" if you don't want to allow Internet access to this PC.

Once you have selected the correct Internet connection option, click Next to continue. You next choose a unique name for the computer and the proper workgroup name, as shown in Figure 31-3.

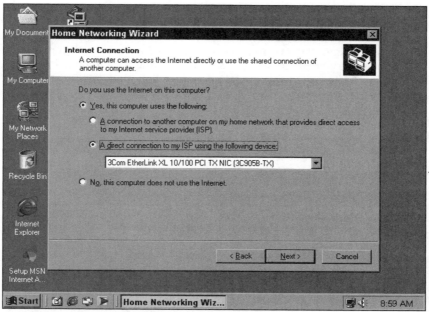

Figure 31-2: Select the correct Internet connection option for this PC.

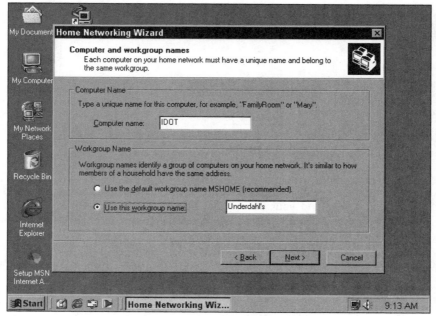

Figure 31-3: Choose the computer and workgroup name.

Caution   If you are adding a new PC to an existing network, make certain you choose the correct workgroup name. The default workgroup name suggested by the Home Networking Wizard — MSHOME — is only useful if all of the PCs on the network use this same workgroup name. You will only be able to interact with computers that are in the same workgroup, so if you select the wrong workgroup name you'll end up frustrated later when you cannot connect to your network. Don't say I didn't warn you!

Continue by clicking Next. Now you choose if you wish to share your folders and printers on the network, as shown in Figure 31-4.

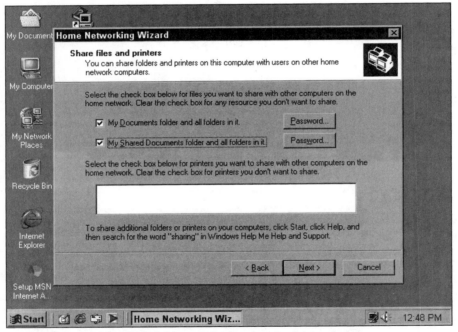

Figure 31-4: Decide which folders and printers you wish to share.

Cross-Reference   The Home Networking Wizard enables you to share two folders — your My Documents folder and your Shared Documents folder. To learn about sharing additional folders on your network, see "Sharing a Folder" in Chapter 32.

If you share folders, you can click the appropriate Password button and set a password that others on the network will have to enter in order to access the shared folders. If you do not set a password, the Home Networking Wizard will remind you that you have not set one when you click the Next button.

Once you have decided which of your folders and printers to share, you have the opportunity to create a setup disk that you can use to configure any PCs on the network that are running Windows 95 or Windows 98. Figure 31-5 shows the Home Networking Wizard window where you make your choice. If all of your PCs are running Windows Me you can skip creating the setup disk.

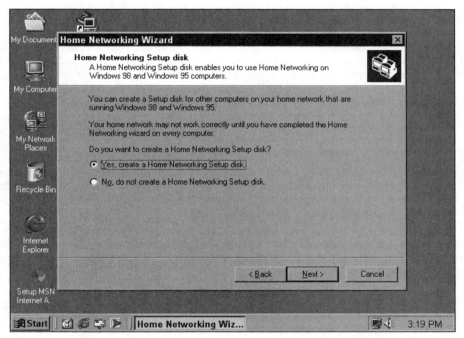

Figure 31-5: If some computers on your network are running Windows 95 or 98, create a setup disk to properly configure them.

Click Next and then click Finish to complete the Home Networking Wizard.

Identify this PC on the LAN

No matter which route you take to install your network, you eventually return to the Windows Me desktop. You may be prompted to enter a user name and password along the way. Type a user name—typically, a person's first name, followed by the first letter of the last name, with no spaces, such as AlanS. Also type a password of up to 15 characters, with no spaces.

Caution   Remember, passwords often are case-sensitive. The password Snorkel, for example, is not the same as snorkel or SNORKEL. Pay attention to the Caps Lock key when you type your password.

Write both the user name and the password on a piece of paper, and keep this paper near the PC. You'll need to refer to it in the near future. You can change the user name and password later if you want, but you need to know the password you typed originally.

Note   Any time you're uncertain how to respond to a prompt, you can click the question mark (?) button in that window and then click the item about which you're confused. Additional information pops up onscreen.

When you get to the desktop, you should see an icon called My Network Places. Typically, this icon is below the My Computer icon. If you don't see the icon, close all open windows, right-click the desktop, and choose Arrange Icons ➪ By Name.

Tip   If you still don't see the My Network Places icon after arranging the desktop windows, something didn't install correctly. Make sure the hardware (card and cable) are hooked up. Then choose Start ➪ Settings ➪ Control Panel, and open the Network icon. Click Add, click Adapter, click Add again, and follow the instructions onscreen to install your network adapter card.

Even after you use the Home Networking Wizard to set up your network, you may find that you must adjust a few settings. Right-click the My Network Places icon and choose Properties. The Network dialog box appears (see Figure 31-6).

Notice the three tabs near the top of the Network dialog box, named Configuration, Identification, and Access Control. Read the following sections carefully for instructions on adjusting these settings.

The Configuration tab

The list of installed components on the Configuration tab should contain at least the following three items:

✦ Client for Microsoft Networks

✦ A line indicating the type of network adapter card you've installed

✦ TCP/IP network protocol

If an option is missing, click Add and select Client, Adapter, or Protocol (depending on which type of component is missing); select the missing component; and then follow the instructions onscreen to install this component.

In the Primary Network Logon drop-down list, select Client for Microsoft Networks.

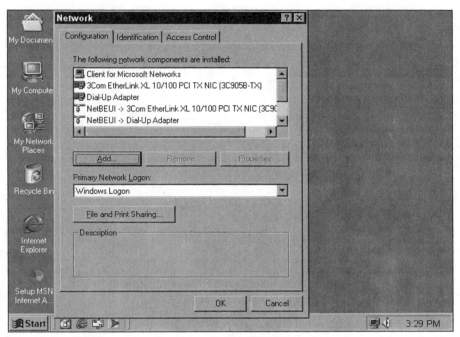

Figure 31-6: The Configuration tab of the Network dialog box enables you to add and remove networking services.

Finally — and this step is important — click the File and Print Sharing button. I suggest you choose both options in the File and Print Sharing dialog box: "I want to be able to give others access to my files" and "I want to be able to allow others to print to my printer(s)," as shown in Figure 31-7. (All you're doing here is giving yourself the option to share things from this PC later. You're not giving anything away.) Then choose OK to close the dialog box.

The Identification tab

When you finish with the Configuration tab, click the Identification tab. You see a dialog box that looks something like Figure 31-8. The following list explains how to fill in the blanks:

✦ **Computer Name:** Give the computer a unique name of up to 15 characters, with no spaces. You can use any name that identifies the computer or use the name of the person who uses this computer most often.

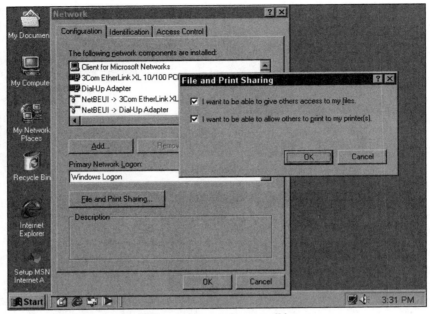

Figure 31-7: Give yourself the option to share stuff later.

✦ **Workgroup:** Giving each PC in the LAN the same workgroup name is extremely important, because only PCs with the same workgroup name can share resources. The name can be up to 15 characters long, with no spaces. In my example, every PC belongs to a workgroup named Underdahl's. You, of course, can make up your own workgroup name. Just make sure you type the name exactly the same way on each PC.

✦ **Computer Description:** You can type any description for this computer. No particular rules apply. Type a brief description you think will further identify this PC to someone on the LAN.

The Access Control tab

The Access Control tab (see Figure 31-9) defines security on this PC. I suggest you select "Share-level access control," which is by far the easiest type of control to manage. If, after using the LAN for a few weeks, you feel you must tighten security, you can change this setting. But unless you're allowing total strangers to dial in to your network, I doubt you'll ever need user-level access control. User-level control is a hassle because you must list the name of every LAN member who's allowed to use every shared device.

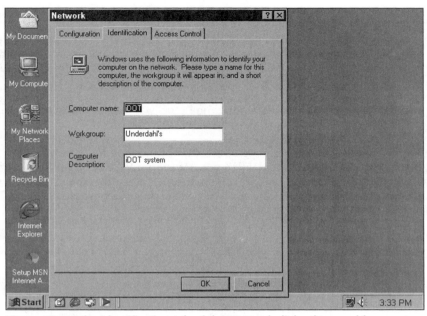

Figure 31-8: The Identification tab of the Network dialog box enables you to identify the PC you're currently configuring.

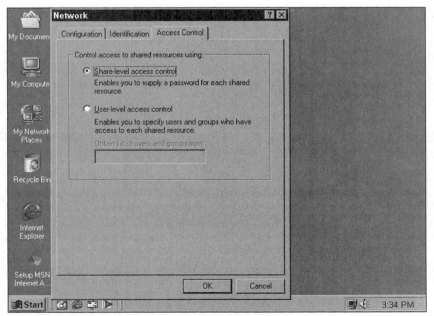

Figure 31-9: The Access Control tab of the network Properties dialog box enables you to choose a security method.

Save the network settings

After you complete all three tabs of the Network dialog box, you're ready to save your choices. Simply click OK at the bottom of the Network dialog box. Depending on your selections, you may need to insert the Windows Me CD-ROM. Just follow the instructions onscreen.

You probably will be prompted to restart the PC, as well. Remove any floppy disks from the floppy drives and follow the instructions to restart the PC.

Know what you get to do next? You get to gather up the Windows Me CD-ROM, and carry it to the next PC in the LAN. When you get to that PC, start over again, starting with the instructions from the previous section "Telling Windows Me You're on the LAN" and continuing to this paragraph. Then repeat the process for every PC connected to the LAN.

Read my instructions carefully at each PC. If you forget certain little steps, they'll come back and bite you later, and figuring out what you forgot to do is hard.

When you get to the Identification-tab step, remember to give each PC a different computer name, but the same workgroup name.

After you set up every PC in the LAN, you're ready to test the network.

Testing the LAN

By the time you get to this section, you should have set up the network hardware on every PC in the LAN and identified each PC in the LAN. Every PC is running, showing the Windows Me desktop, and each desktop shows a My Network Places icon. (It's late at night, your eyes are tired, your brain is fried, and you wish I'd hurry up and get this over with, right?)

Networking With Other OS's

Of course, it is not really necessary to be running Windows Me on every PC on your LAN. Windows Me is perfectly happy sharing resources with other OS's, but you may need to search to find the exact configuration options you need on those other PCs since they likely will be slightly more complicated to set up for networking than Windows Me.

To test your new LAN, follow these steps:

1. Go to any PC in the LAN.
2. Open the My Network Places icon.
3. Repeat Steps 1 and 2 for every PC in the LAN.

If everything went well, you see a little icon for every shared folder in the LAN. In Figure 31-10, for example, you see the nine shared folders in my little LAN. Your screen, of course, should list the computer names you assigned to the PCs in your LAN.

If you don't see the names of the PCs in your LAN, first try opening the Entire Network option. That action may be enough of a wake-up call to get things going. When you can close the My Network Places folder, reopen the folder, and immediately see all the shared folders on your LAN, you're finished. You're ready to move on to Chapter 32 and start sharing additional resources on the LAN.

If you can't get the network going or if some PCs refuse to appear inside My Network Places, try the troubleshooting techniques in the following section.

Figure 31-10: Each shared folder in the workgroup appears in My Network Places.

Troubleshooting the LAN

As you've seen, setting up a LAN is a complicated ritual, involving many settings and options. Any little wrong setting can cripple the network. The following sections examine possible solutions to various problems that may arise.

You have no My Network Places icon

If one of your PCs doesn't have a My Network Places icon on its desktop, first make sure the icon isn't simply hidden. Close all open windows, right-click the desktop, and choose Arrange Icons ⇨ By Name. Typically, this action puts the My Network Places icon right below the My Computer icon.

If this procedure doesn't work, something isn't installed — the LAN hardware, the LAN software, or both. Make sure you installed the LAN hardware and that the cable from the PC is connected to the Ethernet hub. Then repeat the installation instructions, beginning with the section "Telling Windows Me You're on the LAN" earlier in this chapter.

My Network Places is empty

If nothing appears when you open My Network Places, try the following semisuper-stitious ritual on each PC:

1. Close all open windows.
2. Choose Start ⇨ Shut Down.
3. Select Shut Down and then click Yes.
4. When the screen says it's safe to do so, shut down the PC and all attached peripherals — monitor, printer, external CD-ROM drive, everything.

Next, check the cable that attaches the PC to the Ethernet hub. Make sure the cable is properly plugged into the PC's network card and is properly plugged into the hub. If the hub has its own power, make sure the hub is plugged into the wall and is turned on. (See the manual that came with the hub for any additional instructions.)

When you're sure everything is plugged in correctly, follow these steps:

1. Go to any PC in the LAN and turn on all its external peripherals (monitor, external CD-ROM drive, and so on).
2. Turn on the PC.
3. Watch the screen for any error message that may give you a clue as to what's wrong.

4. When you're prompted, log in, using the appropriate user name and password for that PC.

5. Repeat Steps 1–4 on each PC in the LAN.

After all the PCs are turned back on, open the My Network Places icon on each PC again. You should see an icon for every shared folder in the LAN. If so, you're finished and you're ready to start sharing additional resources on the LAN. Proceed to Chapter 32.

Note If you did not choose to share any folders as you used the Home Networking Wizard, the My Network Places folder won't show any shared folders. Go to Chapter 32 to learn how to share some folders so there will be something to show in the My Network Places folder.

A PC is missing

If My Network Places shows some, but not all, of the PCs in the LAN, you need to troubleshoot the missing PCs. Go to any PC not (but should be) listed, and follow these steps:

1. Shut down Windows.

2. Shut down the entire PC system, including all external peripherals.

3. Make sure the cable is properly plugged into the LAN card on the PC and is properly connected to the Ethernet hub.

4. Restart all the external peripherals, restart the PC, and go to the Windows desktop.

5. Open My Network Places on the current PC and on some other PC in the LAN.

If you see the shared folders of both PCs in My Network Places, you're finished. You're ready to move to Chapter 32 and start sharing resources.

If you're still having a problem with one PC, follow these steps on that PC:

1. Right-click My Network Places and choose Properties.

   Make sure the workgroup name on the Identification tab for this PC is spelled exactly like the workgroup name for other PCs in the LAN.

2. Check everything on all three tabs — as discussed in the sections "The Configuration tab," "The Identification tab," and "The Access Control tab" earlier in this chapter — for instructions on setting up this dialog box.

3. After you review all three tabs, choose OK.

4. Follow any instructions that appear onscreen.

If you changed any settings, you probably need to restart this PC and possibly feed it some disks. When you get back to the Windows Me desktop, open My Network Places again on this PC and on some other PC in the LAN. If you still can't see this PC in the LAN, you may have a hardware conflict with your Ethernet card. This problem can be the nastiest of all to solve, which is why I am so obsessed with getting the IRQs right from the beginning. To diagnose and solve this problem, follow these steps:

1. Right-click My Network Places and choose Properties.

2. Click the icon for the network adapter card. This icon looks like a tiny board with the letter *P* on it and should show the make and model of your network card. If you see an icon named Dial-Up Adapter, ignore it — it's for dial-up networking only.

3. Click the Properties button.

4. If your network card has a configurable IRQ and/or I/O address range, you see a tab labeled Resources. Click this tab. If you don't see a Resources tab, skip to Step 7.

5. Look at the current Interrupt (IRQ) and/or I/O address range settings.

6. What you do now depends on what you see:

   • If a pound sign (#) appears before the IRQ and I/O settings, those settings are not the problem. Go to Step 7.

   • If the IRQ setting does not match the setting you wrote down for this computer way back in "Installing the LAN Hardware" earlier in this chapter, use the spin boxes to select the appropriate IRQ. (If the IRQ option is dimmed and unavailable, first set the Configuration type to Basic Configuration 0.) When you choose the right IRQ, you may see a # sign before this setting, but only if the card has dip switches or some kind of program for setting the IRQ.

   • If an asterisk (*) appears for either the IRQ or I/O setting, you have a conflict between this piece of hardware and some other piece. Proceed to Step 7 and then read the section "If you have a hardware conflict."

7. Choose OK until you get back to the desktop.

If you have a hardware conflict

If you discover a hardware conflict, you'll have to change the IRQ setting on either the network card or on the device conflicting with the network card. You may have to start from scratch. Follow these steps:

1. Choose Start ➪ Settings ➪ Control Panel.

2. Open the System icon.

3. Click the Device Manager tab.

4. Click the plus (+) sign next to the Network Adapters option (if any).

5. Click the name of the adapter card that's giving you grief.

6. Click the Remove button to remove all drivers for that card.

7. Follow the instructions onscreen.

8. Go back to the Windows Me desktop, shut down everything, remove the network card from the computer, and start all over with "Installing the LAN Hardware" near the start of this chapter.

This time, pay *very* close attention to the IRQs you choose and make certain to write down everything as you go. If possible, repeat the entire process with a different IRQ this time. If IRQ 5 let you down on the first go-around, for example, use IRQ 7, 9, or 10 (if any one of those settings is available) on the second try.

Cross-Reference Chapter 26 discusses general techniques for installing hardware and troubleshooting hardware conflicts.

If all else fails, you may need to call the manufacturer (major bummer, I know). Or, study closely both the instructions that came with the board and the instructions that came with the Ethernet hub. Good luck and hang in there — I'm sure you'll get everything working.

Summary

This chapter has been all about installing network hardware and getting your LAN up and running. The main points to remember are as follows:

✦ Before you install any hardware, use Device Manager to check and, perhaps, print information on used and available IRQs and I/O addresses.

✦ If you're installing a network card that requires you to set an IRQ and other settings right on the board, be sure you do so before installing the card. Refer to the manufacturer's instructions.

✦ You should install the actual card as per the manufacturer's instructions. But ignore any instructions about installing DOS/Windows 3.*x* drivers for the card.

✦ As you specify IRQ and other settings, be sure to jot down notes. You may be asked for this information several times as you proceed through the installation.

✦ After you've installed all the LAN hardware in all the PCs, you can start setting up the LAN software. Turn on all peripherals and PCs. Then start up each PC. If Windows Me doesn't detect the new hardware automatically, you can run the Add New Hardware Wizard to install the appropriate software.

✦ When identifying PCs on the LAN, be sure to give each computer a unique computer name, but give each computer the same workgroup name.

✦ When configuring the LAN software, be sure to click the File and Print Sharing button and enable file and print sharing if you plan to share either anywhere down the road.

✦ After installing all hardware, setting up the software, and restarting each PC in the LAN, you should be able to open the My Network Places icon on any PC and see the names of all shared folders in the LAN.

✦   ✦   ✦

Sharing Resources on a LAN

The whole reason for setting up a LAN is to make it possible for people on that LAN to share resources, such as printers, disk drives, and folders. By the time you get to this chapter, you should already have set up your LAN, as described in Chapters 30 and 31. This chapter is about using the LAN after it's all set up and ready to roll.

Sharing a Printer

When you share a printer on a LAN, any other PC on the LAN can use that printer. The printer, of course, must be physically connected to, and installed for use on, one PC on the LAN. In other words, the printer must be installed as the local printer on one PC, as discussed in Chapter 19. Which PC the printer is connected to doesn't matter.

For our purposes, I refer to the PC the printer is physically connected to as the *print server*. Mind you, the print server can be *any* PC in the LAN — it need *not* be some special PC whose sole purpose is to manage print jobs. Before other people in the LAN can access the printer, that printer must be shared. Here's how to share a printer:

1. Go to the PC the printer is plugged into, click that PC's Start button, and choose Start ➪ Settings ➪ Printers to get to the Printers folder.

2. Right-click the icon for the printer you want to share and choose Sharing from the menu. The Properties dialog box for this printer opens.

3. Click the Sharing tab (if it isn't already selected).

Caution The "I want to be able to allow others to print to my printer" option in My Network Places' Properties dialog box must be selected, or the Sharing options won't appear.

4. Choose the Shared As radio button.

5. Or type in a name to identify this printer. You can also add a plain-English comment, as I did in the example shown in Figure 32-1.

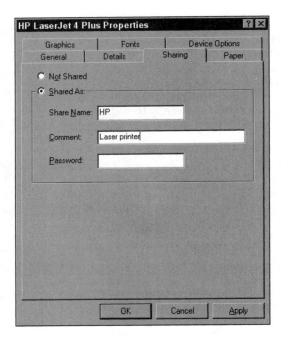

Figure 32-1: This printer will be shared as HP.

6. If you want to limit access to this printer to people who know some password, type that password into the Password text box.

7. Click the OK button.

Note If you don't see Sharing as an option when you right-click a printer icon, chances are you forgot to allow printer sharing on this PC. See "Troubleshooting File and Printer Sharing" later in this chapter.

After the dialog box closes, the printer's icon will have a little hand under it, as in the example shown in Figure 32-2. The hand indicates that the printer is now shared. But before others can use this printer, they must install it as a network printer (not a local printer) on their own machines, as described next.

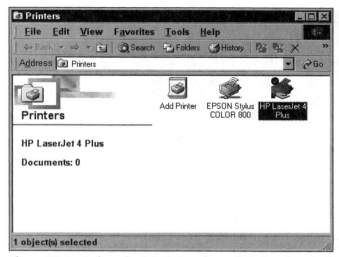

Figure 32-2: A shared printer's icon has a little hand under it.

Connecting to the shared printer

Any other PC that's in the LAN now can act as a printer client. By *printer client,* I mean any other PC in the LAN not physically attached to this printer. But the printer must be installed on each client who wants access to the printer. To accomplish this, go to any printer client and install the printer as a network printer. Bring to this PC your original Windows Me CD-ROM. Also, if you originally needed to use any disks from the printer manufacturer to install the printer, you should also bring those disks to each PC.

Once you get to some PC in the LAN that needs access to this shared printer, follow these steps to give this PC access to the printer:

1. Click the Start button and choose Settings ➪ Printer.

2. In the Printers dialog box, open the Add Printer icon.

3. Click Next after reading the first wizard screen.

4. On the second wizard screen, choose Network printer, as in Figure 32-3.

5. Click the Next button.

6. In the next wizard screen, click the Browse button and then click the plus (+) sign next to the PC to which the printer is physically attached. Then click the name of the shared printer, as in Figure 32-4, where I browsed to the printer named HPLaserJ on the computer named Underdahl1.

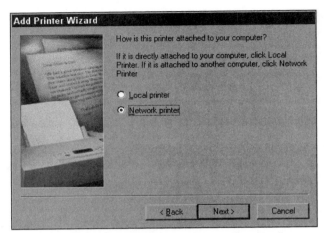

Figure 32-3: About to install a printer not physically attached to this PC

Figure 32-4: About to attach to the printer named HPLaserJ on the computer named Underdahl1

7. Click the OK button.

8. If you think you need to use the printer to print documents from old DOS programs, click the Yes button. Otherwise, choose No.

9. Click the Next button.

10. On the next page (see Figure 32-5), you can change the name of the printer, if you like. Also, decide whether you want this printer as the default printer for this computer and then click the Next button.

Note The default printer is the printer that is used when the person at the computer requests to print a document, but doesn't say which printer to use.

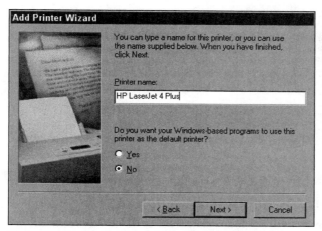

Figure 32-5: Another page from the Add Printer Wizard

11. On the last wizard screen, I suggest you choose Yes to print a test page. Then click the Finish button.

Windows will install the drivers for the printer. (It may ask you for some disks to do this. If it does, follow the instructions that appear onscreen.) After the drivers are installed, the test page will be printed (if you asked to print a test page). A prompt will appear, asking if the test page printed correctly. If the test page did, indeed, print correctly, click the Yes button. Otherwise, click the No button and work through the Print troubleshooter that appears onscreen.

An icon for the printer will appear in the Printers folder. The icon will have a cable and connector under it, as in Figure 32-6, which indicates this is a network printer not physically attached to this PC.

That the printer isn't physically attached to this PC is kind of a moot point now. From this PC, you can use the printer as though it were physically attached to this PC. Remember, though, that you have connected only this PC to the network printer. If you want to connect other PCs to this printer, you must go to each PC and repeat the previous Steps 1 to 11.

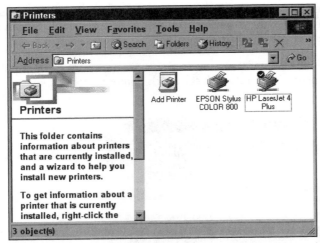

Figure 32-6: Network printer icons have a little cable under them, like this.

Using the shared printer

After you install the network printer, using it is done no differently than using a printer physically attached to your computer. For example, to print from the program you're currently using, choose File ➪ Print in this program. The default printer will appear in the Print dialog box that opens. (The default printer may be the network printer.) But all the printers to which this PC has access will be available from the Name drop-down list, as in the example shown in Figure 32-7.

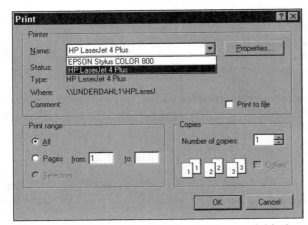

Figure 32-7: The network printer will be available from all Print dialog boxes.

If the network printer is busy printing someone else's document, your print job waits in the queue until the printer is available. You can go about your business normally, right after you start the print job.

If you have a problem with a print job, check the print queue on your local printer. Open the Printers folder and then open the icon for the printer causing the problem. Most likely, the print job still is in your local print queue. You can use commands in the Printer and Document menus to pause or cancel the print job, as discussed in Chapter 19. If you wait too long, though, you may get a message indicating you do not have permission to mess with the print job. At this point, you must go to the PC to which the printer is physically attached and manage the print job from there, again using the standard techniques discussed in Chapter 19.

Sharing a Disk Drive

You can share an entire disk drive — be it a floppy disk drive, hard disk, CD-ROM drive, or removable drive (like a Zip drive) from any PC in the LAN. When you do, every other PC in the LAN has access to everything on that disk.

There are lots of applications for using a shared drive. If you share a floppy drive or CD-ROM drive, other computers can access those drives as though they were local drives. For example, if you have a portable computer with no CD-ROM drive or no floppy drive, you could still install programs onto that portable computer from a floppy disk or CD-ROM drive and connect to, and install from, the shared drive. You could use a single, removable drive — like a Zip or Jaz drive — to make backups from all the computers in the LAN. Just share that removable drive.

Two steps are involved in sharing a drive. You must first go to the *server* (the PC to which the drive is physically connected) and share the drive. Then you can go to any client (any other PC in the LAN) and get to this drive via My Network Places. You also can map a drive letter to the shared drive, making access to that shared drive even easier, as discussed later in this chapter.

The first step in giving multiple computers access to a disk drive is to perform the sharing. As the *owner* of the drive (the one who is allowing it to be shared), you have several choices in how much freedom you want to give other PCs in accessing this drive. Your choices are:

✦ **Read-Only:** Other people in the LAN (clients) can read stuff from the drive, but they cannot change the contents of the drive in any manner.

✦ **Full:** Clients can read from the drive, as well as change its contents. That is, they can save files to this drive, change files on this drive, and delete files from this drive.

✦ **Depends On Password:** Clients who know one secret password can gain Read-Only access to the drive. Clients who know some other secret password can gain Full access to the drive. As owner of the drive, you determine what those passwords will be.

Once you decide which kind of access you want to give to others, sharing the drive is easy. Follow these steps:

1. Go to the PC containing the disk drive that you want to share.

2. Open the My Computer icon on this PC.

3. Right-click the icon for the drive that you want to share and choose Sharing. You'll come to the Sharing tab of the Properties dialog box for the drive, as in the example shown in Figure 32-8.

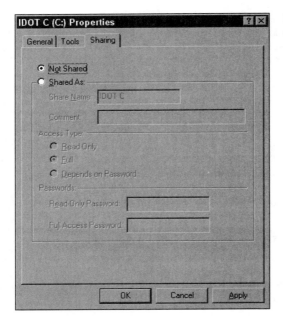

Figure 32-8: Sharing tab of a drive's Properties dialog box

 Note   If you don't see Sharing as an option when you right-click a drive's icon, chances are you forgot to allow file sharing on this PC. See "Troubleshooting File and Printer Sharing" later in this chapter.

4. Choose Shared As and give the drive a name up to 12 characters in length. You can also type in a lengthier comment, if you wish. For example, in Figure 32-9, I shared the CD-ROM drive from a computer named Ace. I named this shared resource Ace CD-ROM and provided a lengthier description as well.

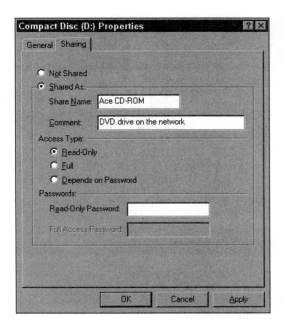

Figure 32-9: Other users can access this computer's CD-ROM drive without needing to know a password.

5. Choose an Access Type: Read-Only, Full, or Depends On Password, as described earlier. Then you can password-protect the drive, if you wish, by filling in a password. (If you leave the password blank, anyone in the LAN can access the device, without a password.) If you choose Depends On Password, type in one password for people who will have Read-Only access and another password for people who will have Full access.

When sharing a CD-ROM drive, Read-Only is the only access type that makes any sense because a CD-ROM drive is a Read-Only device (the ROM in CD-ROM stands for Read-Only Memory).

6. Click the OK button.

A little hand now appears below the icon for the shared drive, indicating the drive is shared. For example, the CD-ROM drive on my computer named Ace now has the little sharing hand under it, as shown in Figure 32-10. From this point on, any other PC in the LAN can connect to this drive, as discussed under "Accessing a Shared Drive/Folder" later in this chapter.

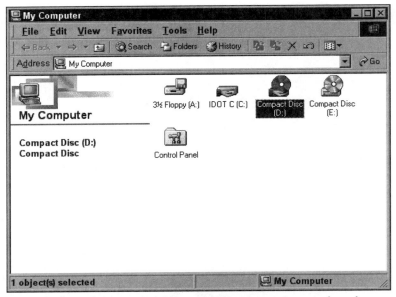

Figure 32-10: The CD-ROM drive on this computer is now shared, as indicated by the little hand in its icon.

Sharing a Folder

You don't have to share an entire drive. If you want to give others access to *some* of the files on your hard disk, you can share one or more folders. When you share a folder, you give others access to all the files in this folder, as well as any subfolders within this folder. But other people cannot access files or folders outside this shared folder. Sharing a folder is virtually identical to sharing a drive—you must navigate to (or create) the folder you want to share before you do the sharing. Here are the exact steps:

1. On the computer containing the folder that you want to share, open My Computer and navigate to the icon for this folder.

2. Right-click the icon of the folder you want to share and choose Sharing.

3. Choose Shared As, provide a name and optional comment, choose an access type, and, optionally, provide any passwords. For example, in Figure 32-11, I named a shared folder Shared Docs, provided a slightly lengthier comment, and offered to give all other users in the LAN Full access to the folder without a password.

4. Click the OK button. The folder's icon now has the little sharing symbol under it, as in the example shown in Figure 32-12.

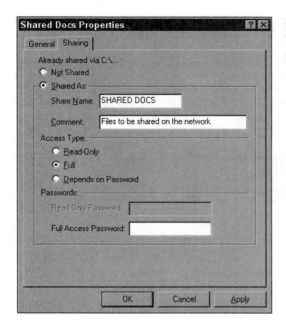

Figure 32-11: Giving full access to a shared folder named Shared Docs

Figure 32-12: The folder named Shared Docs is now shared on the LAN.

Next, I'll look at ways in which other members of the LAN can access the shared resource (be it a drive or a folder).

Accessing a Shared Drive/Folder

To access a shared drive or folder, anyone in the LAN simply needs to open My Network Places and then open whichever shared drive or folder they need. For example, in Figure 32-13, I opened My Network Places. From here, I opened the drive named c on main on Underdahl1 and, within this drive, you can see icons for the shared folders on that computer.

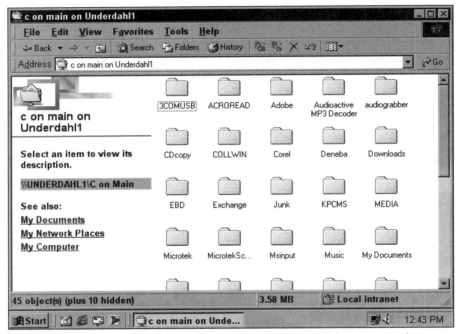

Figure 32-13: Shared resources from another computer visible via Network Neighborhood

This person can now open any icon to gain access. For example, opening the icon for the CD-ROM drive would give this person access to whatever CD is currently in that drive. It's as though the CD-ROM were physically attached to this computer. Opening the icon for the Shared Docs folder would give this person access to the contents of that folder.

Mapping a drive letter

Going through My Network Places to get to a shared resource can become tedious. So, common practice is to map a drive letter to a shared resource. This way, you can get to the resource right from My Computer. You could even create a desktop icon to the shared resource. Here's how you map a drive letter to a shared drive or folder:

1. If you haven't already done so, open My Network Places and open the icon for the shared resource.

2. Choose Tools ➪ Map Network Drive. The Map Network Drive dialog box appears.

3. Pick any available drive letter from the drop-down list.

4. If you want to be reconnected automatically to this shared resource each time you start this computer, choose the Reconnect at Logon check box. For example, in Figure 32-14, I've mapped the drive letter F: to the C drive on the laptop computer and opted to be reconnected automatically in the future, as well.

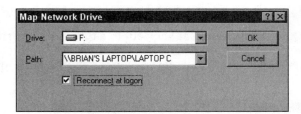

Figure 32-14: Mapped drive letter F: to C drive on another computer

5. If the shared resource is password-protected, you'll be prompted to enter a password. Go ahead and type in the appropriate password. If you don't want to have to type in the password every time you want access to this resource in the future, choose (check) the Save This Password In Your Password List option. Then click the OK button.

6. Click the OK button.

The shared resource opens up in a My Computer window. You can close this, if you don't need immediate access to it. In a moment, I'll show you how to access the shared resource now that you've mapped a drive letter to it.

As an example, say I also want to map a drive letter to Darlene's computer from here. I would need to open My Network Places and then choose Tools ➪ Map Network Drive. Let's say I map the drive letter S: to this shared folder, as in Figure 32-15.

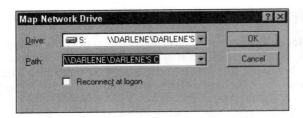

Figure 32-15: Mapped drive letter S: to shared drive C on Darlene's computer

Now let's see how I can get to those shared resources after mapping drive letters.

Accessing network drives

Once you assign a drive letter to a shared drive or folder, this resource becomes a *network drive* from the perspective of this computer. You can simply open My Computer to get to these drives. For example, Figure 32-16 shows how My Computer in the PC named Mimi *sees* the shared drives and folder from the PCs on the network. One is drive F: (Laptop c on Brian's laptop), the other is drive S: (Darlene's c on Darlene).

To create a desktop or Quick Launch toolbar shortcut to either of those drives, right-drag the icon to the desktop or toolbar, drop it there, and choose Create Shortcut(s) Here. To open either resource, open its icon (or any shortcut icon).

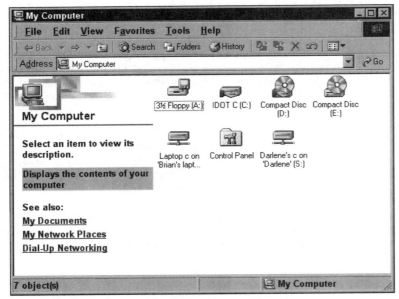

Figure 32-16: Mimi's My Computer sees the shared resources as network drives.

So, for all intents and purposes, the shared resource is a drive on this computer. If this computer has Full access, then the person sitting at this computer would have total access to the drive, as though it were a local drive. If the drive were shared with Read-Only access, then the person at this computer could read files from the drive, but could neither save files to the drive nor delete files from the drive.

Note   If, while browsing around in My Computer, you start to lose track of which window represents which drive, choose Tools ➪ Folder Options from My Computer's menu bar. On the View tab, select the Display the Full Path in Title Bar option. Each window's title bar now includes the drive letter.

Unmapping a drive letter

If, for whatever reason, you want to *unmap* a drive letter to some resource, follow these simple steps:

1. Go to the client PC — the one connected to the resource via the network, not the one physically connected to the source.

2. Open My Computer.

3. Right-click the icon for the resource you want to unmap and choose Disconnect from the menu.

Simple enough, yes?

Sharing Fonts

Fonts can be a pain on a LAN, because different PCs may have different fonts installed. Suppose Bertha creates a nice document using her cool Avalon Quest font. Then Ellen opens this document on her PC. But Ellen doesn't have the Avalon Quest font on her PC, so Windows replaces that font with something else, such as Times Roman, which doesn't have quite the look and feel Bertha intended.

One way around this problem is to create a single font repository on one PC in the LAN. Share this folder and then allow other PCs in the LAN access to this shared folder. Not only does this approach give everyone access to the same fonts, but it also saves disk space. For example, if you have a huge collection of fonts (several megabytes worth), you can store those fonts on one PC and access them from other PCs in the LAN without actually copying all those fonts to the other PCs.

Sharing a fonts folder is no different than sharing any other folder. Installing fonts without actually copying them to a PC is a tad trickier, though. So, let me take you step-by-step through the whole process.

Suppose I decide my computer named Ace will be my font server (the PC with a big collection of TrueType fonts). On that PC, I would install TrueType fonts normally, as discussed in Chapter 19. To share fonts in Ace's Fonts folder, I would . . .

1. Open My Computer and browse to C:\Windows (open the icon for drive C and open the icon for the folder named Windows).

2. Right-click the icon for the folder named Fonts and choose Sharing.

3. Choose Shared As and provide a name and, optionally, a comment and then choose an access type. (Read-Only access would be fine here unless you want to install fonts from other PCs in the LAN.) In the example shown in Figure 32-17, I named the shared resource Shared Fonts and I granted Read-Only access to it.

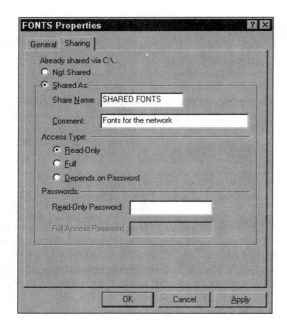

Figure 32-17: Sharing the C:\Windows\Fonts folder

4. Click the OK button.

The dialog box closes and now the Fonts folder's icon shows the little sharing hand.

Now, to gain access to the shared fonts from some other PC in the LAN, I need to go to that PC, map a drive letter to the shared Fonts folder, and install (without copying) fonts from that shared folder. For example, to gain access to shared fonts on Underdahl1 from my computer named Mimi, I would go to Mimi and perform the following ritual:

1. Open My Network Places.

2. Choose Tools ➪ Map Network Drive.

3. Pick a drive letter (I'll use T: for my example), choose (check) the Reconnect option, as in Figure 32-18, and then click OK.

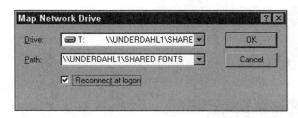

Figure 32-18: Mapped drive letter T: to fonts folder on Underdahl1 computer

4. The Fonts folder will open. But you can close it, as well as any other open windows on the desktop, now.

Even though you mapped a drive letter to the shared Fonts folder, you still don't have access to its fonts right now. You must install fonts from that drive before you can access them on this PC. Here's how:

1. On the client PC (the one you just created drive T: on), click the Start button and choose Settings ➪ Control Panel.

2. Open the Fonts icon.

3. Choose File ➪ Install New Font from the Fonts folder's menu bar.

4. In the Add Fonts dialog box that appears (see Figure 32-19), choose the drive letter you assigned to the shared Fonts folder (T:) in my example. Also, clear (uncheck) the "Copy fonts to fonts folder" option, as shown in the same figure.

5. Select the font that you want to install by clicking it. If you want to install multiple fonts, you can select them in the usual manner.

6. Click the OK button. You'll see the message shown in Figure 32-20. The purpose of this message is to remind you that if the *font server* goes down, the fonts won't be available. Click Yes to continue.

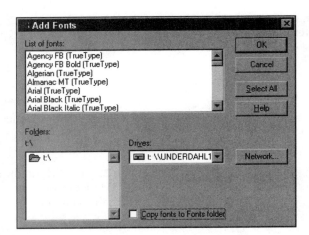

Figure 32-19: Ready to install (but not copy) fonts from drive T:

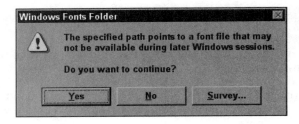

Figure 32-20: Reminder that shared fonts may not always be available

The fonts will install quickly because the font files aren't actually being copied to the client PC. You can close the Fonts folder and the Control Panel when the installation is complete.

Note   Don't worry about accidentally re-installing a font that has already been installed. If you try to do so, Windows will tell you that the font is already installed and that you cannot install it again unless you delete the current installation of this font.

The new fonts should be available from any program. For example, suppose I open WordPad on the client PC, type some text, and want to assign a font to that text. The Jokerman fonts from Underdahl1 will be available in the list of available fonts, as in Figure 32-21.

The only downside to this approach is if Underdahl1 (the font server in my example) gets shut down or if someone on Underdahl1 stops sharing this folder; then, no other PCs in the LAN can access its shared fonts.

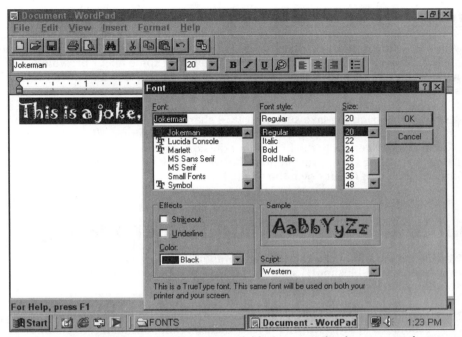

Figure 32-21: Jokerman fonts are now available from WordPad on some other computer

Stop Sharing a Resource

If, for whatever reason, you want to stop sharing a resource on a LAN, you must go through the same steps you went through to share the resource. But when you get to the Sharing dialog box, choose the Not Shared option, rather than the Shared As option.

If any computers are currently connected to this resource, you'll be given a warning and the option to change your mind. If you do not proceed, the other people will still have access to this shared resource. If you proceed, all others will lose access to this shared resource.

A client cannot regain access to the shared resource until the owner of the resource turns that PC back on and/or shares the resource. This raises a topic that I should address directly.

Shutting Down LAN PCs

When you shut down a PC that shares its resources, you take this shared resource away from everyone else in the LAN. You could lose some major brownie points with coworkers this way, especially if you cause them to lose any work they had stored in a shared folder in your PC.

A simple approach to make sure your PC's shared resources are always available to others in the LAN is to never shut down the PC. You can turn off the monitor if you like (and that's generally the biggest energy consumer anyway). You can log off using Start ➪ Log Off to prevent unauthorized personnel from using your computer directly. Just don't shut down the whole PC.

Troubleshooting File and Printer Sharing

Newbie networkers make some fairly common mistakes when using a LAN. If you ever need to troubleshoot, I suggest that you check the common problems and solutions listed in the following:

✦ Remember that only PCs with the same workgroup name can share resources in My Network Places. To check (and, optionally, to change) a PC's workgroup name, right-click My Network Places on this PC and then use the Identification tab.

✦ Only PCs with File and Printer sharing turned on can share resources. To activate File and/or Printer sharing on a PC, right-click its My Network Places icon, choose Properties, click the File and Printer Sharing button, and then choose the types of resources that you want to share, as in Figure 32-22.

✦ My Network Places displays only *shared* resources. You can't see a resource in My Network Places until this resource has been shared from its *server* PC.

If none of these points helps you solve the problem, try going through the Windows Me Troubleshooter. Here are the steps to do so:

1. Click Start ➪ Help.

2. Click the Troubleshooting link.

3. Click the Home Networking & network problems link.

4. Click the Home Networking Troubleshooter problems link.

5. Then start answering questions the troubleshooter (see Figure 32-23) presents.

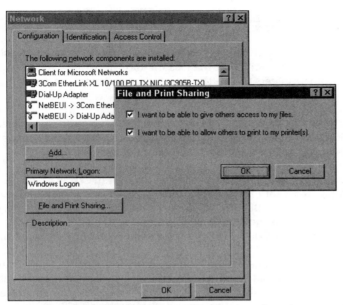

Figure 32-22: This computer is willing to share its printer as well as its files (drives and folders).

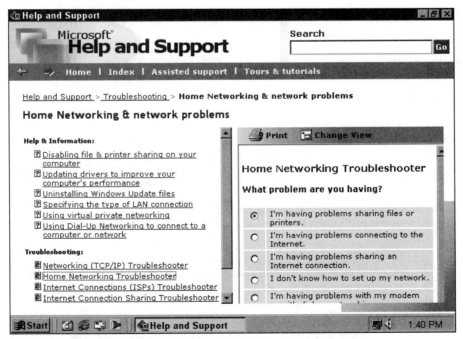

Figure 32-23: The Windows Me Home Networking troubleshooter

Sharing Your Internet Connection

One of the neatest things about setting up your home network is that you can share a single Internet connection between all of the PCs on your network. That way, you won't have to argue about who gets to use the Internet connection—everyone can use it.

Note   Only one PC on your LAN can have Internet Connection Sharing (ICS) installed. The remaining PCs don't need to have ICS installed because they simply connect to the Internet through the LAN using the ICS PC as a *gateway*.

When you use the Home Networking Wizard to install your network as discussed in Chapter 31, you can choose to set up one PC as the Internet Connection Sharing server. When you do, the wizard will have you insert a floppy disk in order to create an ICS *client disk*. You simply run the setup program on this disk in each of the client systems and your Internet Connection Sharing will be automatically set up.

Caution   Some ISPs specify that only one PC can use an Internet account at one time. Technically this could mean that using ICS violates your service agreement with your ISP. In reality, though, only the ICS server on your network is truly connected to the Internet, so it's unlikely you will encounter problems using ICS.

You can control whether the client systems can use ICS by right-clicking the ICS icon in the Windows Me system tray. Then choose Enable Internet Connection Sharing or Disable Internet Connection Sharing as appropriate.

Summary

This chapter has been about sharing, and using, the type of LAN described in the preceding two chapters. In a nutshell:

✦ You can share a printer, drive, or folder on any PC in the LAN.

✦ The computer the shared resource is on, or connected to, is called the *server*. For example, the PC that has a printer hooked to its parallel port is the *print server*.

✦ Before other LAN members can access a shared resource, you must go to the server of the resource and share the resource. You can do this in My Computer.

✦ Any other PC in a LAN that can use a shared resource is called a *client to the resource*. For example, every PC in the LAN, except the one to which a printer is connected, is a *print client*.

✦ To access a shared printer, click the Start button, choose Settings ➪ Printers, open the Add Printer icon, and allow the wizard to guide you through installing a network printer.

✦ To access a shared drive or folder, browse to that shared drive or folder from My Network Places. To map a network drive to the resource, choose Tools ➪ Map Network Drive.

✦ Don't forget, a PC that serves some resource to other PCs in the LAN does so only when this PC is up and running! Most people leave all the PCs in a LAN running constantly to prevent confusion.

✦ You can share a single Internet connection between all of the PCs on your network. Only one PC should have ICS installed.

✦   ✦   ✦

Cool LAN Tricks

This chapter explains some features and tricks you can try on your own LAN. Everything discussed in this chapter is optional — you needn't do any of these things to set up or use a LAN — so feel free to read this chapter at your leisure.

Fun with Pop-Up Messages

WinPopup is a handy built-in utility that enables people on a network to send instant messages to one another. The best way to use WinPopup is to install it on every PC in the LAN. Also place a shortcut to it in the StartUp folder, so it's loaded and ready to go as soon as you start up the PC.

Installing WinPopup

If you're unsure whether WinPopup is on your PC yet, follow these steps to find out and to install it, if necessary:

1. Choose Start ⇨ Settings ⇨ Control Panel.

2. Open the Add/Remove Programs icon.

3. Click the Windows Setup tab.

4. Click System Tools, click the Details button, and then scroll down to the WinPopup component.

5. If WinPopup is already installed (has a check mark next to its name), click the Cancel button and skip to the following section, "Adding WinPopup to your StartUp folder." If WinPopup isn't already installed, select it, so its check box is checked, and then proceed with Step 6.

6. Gather up your original Windows Me CD-ROM and click OK. As always, this step may be unnecessary if Windows Me came pre-installed on your computer.

7. Click the OK button and follow the instructions onscreen to install WinPopup.

After WinPopup is installed on your PC, proceed to the following section.

Adding WinPopup to your StartUp folder

The best way to use WinPopup on a LAN is to make sure all LAN members have the utility up and running at all times. The simplest way to do this is to go to each PC and add WinPopup's icon to the StartUp folder. Follow these steps:

1. Choose Start ➪ Search ➪ For Files or Folders.

2. Type **winpopup.exe** as the file to find.

3. Choose C: as the Look In: folder and select (check) the Include Subfolders check box (this hides under the Advanced Options item).

4. Click the Search Now button. When the file is found, it should have a little jack-in-the-box icon.

5. Right-click the Start button and choose Open.

6. Open the Programs icon and then open the StartUp icon. The StartUp folder that opens displays an icon for every program started automatically when you first start your PC.

7. Move and size windows so you can see both the StartUp folder and the WinPopup.exe icon in Find.

8. Right-drag the WinPopup.exe icon into the StartUp folder, release the mouse button, and choose Create Shortcut(s) Here.

9. If you want to create a desktop shortcut to WinPopup, right-drag the icon for WinPopup.exe out to the desktop, release the mouse button, and choose Create Shortcut(s) Here.

10. If you like, you can rename the desktop shortcut icon by right-clicking it, choosing Rename, and typing a new name. For example, in Figure 33-1, I renamed the desktop shortcut icon to WinPopup.

11. Close all open windows and folders.

To ensure WinPopup starts, you may want to restart your PC. Choose Start ➪ Shut Down ➪ Restart ➪ OK. You can just click the WinPopup icon, to start the program, but restarting your PC will allow you to check that you've added WinPopup to the StartUp folder correctly. Remember, you must go to each PC in the LAN and repeat this procedure, so all PCs start with WinPopup open and ready to go.

After restarting a computer, WinPopup appears already open onscreen, as shown in Figure 33-2. Don't close it — WinPopup works best if it's open on each computer in the LAN. If you want to get it out of the way, click its Minimize button to reduce it to a button in the taskbar.

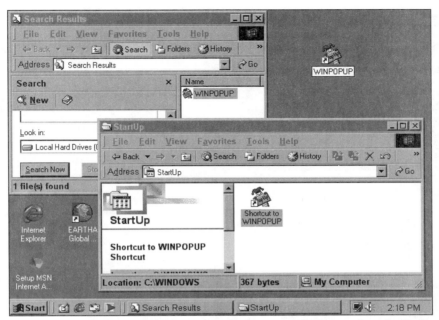

Figure 33-1: Shortcuts to WinPopup.exe in the StartUp folder and on the desktop

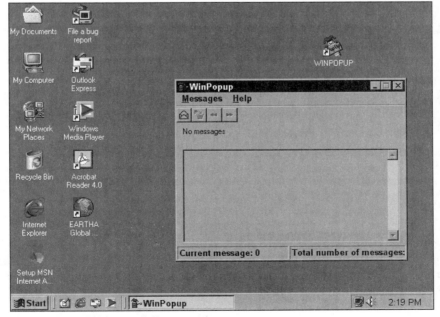

Figure 33-2: WinPopup fully opened at startup

Sending a pop-up message

To send a pop-up message to someone in your workgroup, follow these steps:

1. Open the WinPopup window, if it isn't open already. (If you minimized it, click its taskbar button.)

2. Choose Messages ➪ Send or click the envelope button in WinPopup's toolbar. The dialog box shown in Figure 33-3 opens.

Figure 33-3: Send Message dialog box from WinPopup

3. To send the message to a specific person or computer, choose "User or computer" and type the recipient's log-in name (for example, IDOT). To send the message to everyone in the workgroup, choose the Workgroup option and type in the name of the workgroup (for example, Underdahl's).

4. Type your message in the large Message text box, as in the example shown in the figure.

5. Choose OK to send the message.

6. Choose OK to respond to the prompt that your message has been sent.

You could minimize the WinPopup window now, but don't close it yet. You want to leave it open so you can receive messages.

Reading pop-up messages

When someone sends you a pop-up message, the WinPopup button in your taskbar informs you that you have a message. Click this taskbar button to view your message. The WinPopup window appears with the message displayed, as in the example shown in Figure 33-4.

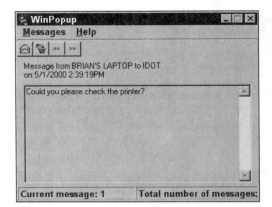

Figure 33-4: IDOT just received a WinPopup message from Brian's Laptop computer.

After reading the message, you can use the various toolbar buttons and the commands in the Messages menu to respond, as follows:

✦ To send a reply, click the Send button (the one with the envelope icon).

✦ To delete the message, click the Delete button.

✦ If you have several messages in your bin, click the Previous and Next buttons to scroll through the messages.

When you finish reading your messages, minimize the WinPopup window. But don't close the window if you want to continue getting pop-up messages from other workgroup members. If WinPopup is closed on your PC, you can't receive messages from other LAN members.

Personalizing WinPopup

If you want to change the way WinPopup behaves when it receives a message, choose Messages ➪ Options from within WinPopup. You see the simple dialog box shown in Figure 33-5. Your options are:

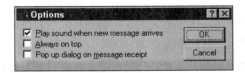

Figure 33-5: Options for personalizing WinPopup

✦ **Play sound when new message arrives:** You'll here a sound when a new message arrives on your PC.

✦ **Always on top:** Makes sure the WinPopup window appears on top so other windows don't obscure your view of it.

✦ **Pop up dialog on message receipt:** Opens the WinPopup window automatically when a new message arrives to ensure you see it immediately.

Select (check) the options you want, clear (uncheck) the options you don't want, and then click the OK button. Your settings will be active next time you receive a WinPopup message.

Cutting and Pasting Between PCs

Cut-and-paste and scraps are both handy techniques for moving and copying material from one document to another — on one PC. But what if you want to copy something from a document on one PC in the LAN to a document on some other PC in the LAN? Well, nothing is built into Windows Me to enable such a thing directly. But you can easily make it possible by putting scraps into a shared folder to which other people in the LAN have access. As an example, let me show you how I would set up a shared scraps folder on one of the PCs in my own LAN. And then I'll show you how another PC in the same LAN can use those scraps.

Creating a shared scraps folder

To make scraps accessible to other members of the LAN, first create a folder for your scraps and share this folder. Here's how:

1. On the PC that will offer scraps to other LAN members, right-click the desktop and choose New ➪ Folder.

2. Give this folder an easily identifiable name. In my example, I'll name the folder My Scraps.

3. After naming the folder, right-click it and choose Sharing.

4. Choose Shared As, give the folder a name, and choose your Access Type. For example, in Figure 33-6, I decided to give other users Full access to my shared scraps folder.

5. Choose OK to close the Sharing dialog box. The scraps folder on your desktop should now display the sharing hand, as in Figure 33-7.

 Note If Sharing isn't available in the pop-up menu after you right-click, you probably didn't allow for file sharing when you set up this PC. You need to right-click My Network Places, choose Properties, and use the Configuration tab to allow file sharing.

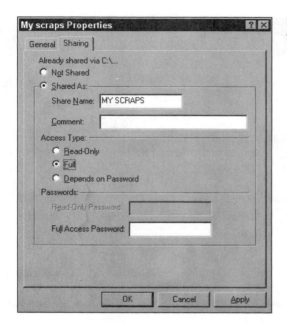

Figure 33-6: Sharing the My Scraps folder

Figure 33-7: Shared scraps folder on the desktop

Gaining access to shared scraps

Now that you have a shared scraps folder, you may want to go to other PCs in the LAN and provide each of them with easy access to that folder. Here's how:

1. On any other PC in the LAN that needs access to the shared scraps, open the My Network Places icon.

2. Open the PC on which you created the shared scraps folder.

3. Choose Tools ➪ Map Network Drive and choose a drive letter. For example, in Figure 33-8, I mapped the drive letter P: to the shared scraps folder.

4. Click the OK button. A window for the scraps folder opens, but you can close this window for now, if you wish.

5. To create a convenient desktop icon for the scraps folder, right-drag the shared scraps icon out of its folder onto the desktop, release the mouse button, and choose Create Shortcut(s) Here.

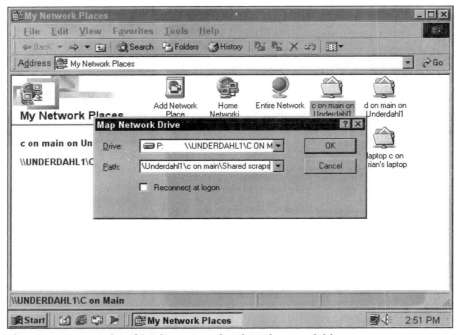

Figure 33-8: Mapping drive letter P to the shared scraps folder

6. Now you can close all open windows.

7. If you want to rename the shortcut icon you just created, right-click it, choose Rename, and then type a new name.

Figure 33-9 shows an example in which I renamed the shortcut icon "Shared scraps on Underdahl1."

Figure 33-9: Shortcut to shared scraps folder on the desktop

Cutting and copying to the scraps folder

Now it will be easy to copy and paste material from one PC to another. For example, suppose Ace is working on a document. He selects a chunk of text, as in the example shown in Figure 33-10, and chooses Edit ➪ Copy to copy this text to the Clipboard.

To make the Clipboard contents accessible to Mimi, Ace now needs to right-click his shared scraps folder and choose Paste. The scrap will be given some default filename. To rename the scrap, Ace needs to open his scraps folder, right-click the icon to be renamed, choose Rename, and type in a new name.

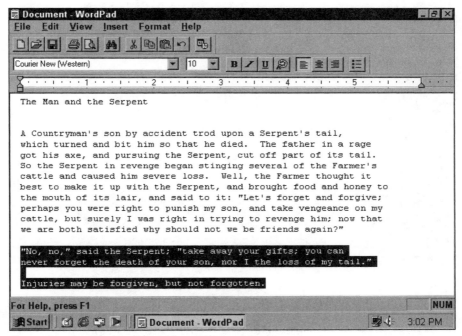

Figure 33-10: Text is selected in a Wordpad document

Pasting from the scraps folder

Now that Ace has put a scrap into his shared scraps folder, how can Mimi use it? Well, Mimi would need to do the following:

1. Open the shortcut icon to the shared scraps folder, as in Figure 33-11.

2. Right-click the scrap Mimi wants and choose Copy.

3. Open (or create) the document into which Mimi wants to paste the scrap.

4. Click the spot where Mimi wants to place the scrap in the document (to get the blinking cursor to the correct place).

5. Right-click near the blinking cursor and choose Paste.

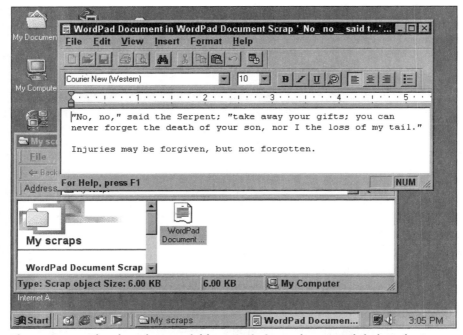

Figure 33-11: The shared scraps folder on Mimi reveals a scrap left there by Ace.

Let's review what we just did. On the Ace computer we created a shared folder other people in the LAN can access. We could put anything in this folder, of course. We decided to make this particular folder a repository for scraps that need to be shared among multiple PCs in the LAN.

To simplify access to this shared scraps folder from Mimi, we went to Mimi and mapped a network drive letter to that shared scraps folder. To make things easier still, we then created a desktop shortcut to this shared scraps folder.

In short, we didn't really use a specific feature of Windows Me to solve the problem of cutting-and-pasting between PCs. Instead, we used a combination of features — scraps, sharing, and desktop shortcuts — to make cut-and-paste between machines possible. Even easier!

Finding Things on the LAN

As you may recall, you can use Search to look for files with a certain filename, contents, creation date, and so forth. Normally, Search enables you to search only your local hard disk (or disks) or shared folders from other PCs in the LAN — but not both at the same time.

You can, however, extend Search's reach to shared resources to which you already mapped a network drive. As you may recall, when you open My Computer, you see an icon for each shared resource to which you mapped a drive letter, as in Figure 33-12.

To include shared resources in a search, you simply need to perform the search on My Computer, rather than on a single drive. For example, let's say you want to scour your own computer, and all the shared resources on other computers, for a file named "Company Profile." To start, you would click the Start button and choose Search ➪ For Files or Folders.

In the "Search for files or folders named" text box, you would type Company Profile (or whatever filename you wanted to find). Down in the Look In drop-down list, you would select My Computer. Doing this tells Search to search every resource listed in your My Computer folder.

Next, you would click Search Now to conduct the search. All files with the word "Company" and/or "Profile" in their filenames will be listed — including a document from drive H: (which is actually a shared folder on another computer), as shown in Figure 33-13.

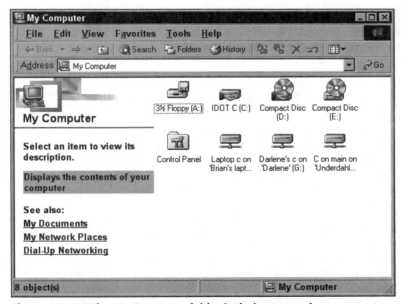

Figure 33-12: The My Computer folder includes network resources to which you've mapped a drive letter.

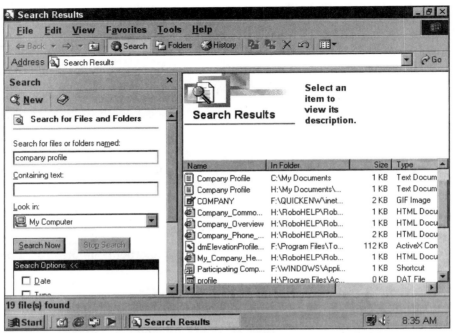

Figure 33-13: Find located files on the network drives.

Managing Other PCs from Your Own PC

Remote administration enables you to manage other PCs in the LAN from your own PC. Specifically, you can share or unshare folders on some PC other than your own without leaving your chair. On a larger scale, if you set up all the PCs in the LAN for remote administration, you can share and unshare any folder on any PC in the LAN from whichever PC you are using.

In a sense, you become the Grand Wazoo of all the resources on the PC with remote administration enabled—even when you aren't sitting at this PC. If you allow remote administration of every PC in the LAN, you become the Grand Wazoo of every PC in the LAN and you have access to every file on every one of those PCs—shared or not! (If the title *Grand Wazoo* bothers coworkers, you can use the more traditional title of *network administrator.*)

Before you can manage a PC remotely, you need to set it up for remote administration and think up a password. Only people who know the password will have Grand Wazoo privileges. So, if you keep it to yourself, you'll be the only Grand Wazoo. Anyway, let's discuss how you go about setting up a PC to be managed remotely.

Maybe you *don't* want to map network drives

To search for something on a specific computer on your LAN, you open the Look in list in the Search window and click Browse at the bottom of the list. You then open the My Network Places item and choose any of the shared resources on the network—unless you have mapped network resources to drive letters. If you *have* mapped network resources, you will only be able to choose those mapped resources—not the entire range of shared resources. The end result is that you must make a choice between mapping drives for easy access *or* being able to search the entire network easily.

Allowing a PC to be managed remotely

Before you can administer a PC remotely, you must make sure this PC has its file and print sharing capabilities activated, as discussed in Chapter 31. If you want to check and, optionally, activate this setting, right-click My Network Places and choose Properties. On the Configuration tab, click the File and Print Sharing button. Make sure the "I want to be able to give others access to my files" option is selected. If the PC also has a printer attached, you can activate printer sharing, too, as in Figure 33-14. Then click the OK buttons to save your current settings. (If you changed any settings, you may get some instructions onscreen to follow. Follow those instructions before you move on to the next paragraph.)

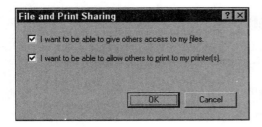

Figure 33-14: This PC has file and printer sharing enabled.

Next, you need to enable remote administration of the PC. Here's how:

1. On the PC you want to manage remotely, choose Start ➪ Settings ➪ Control Panel.

2. Open the Passwords icon.

3. Click the Remote Administration tab.

4. Select the "Enable remote administration of this server" option.

5. Type (twice) a password up to eight characters in length that will enable this PC to be managed from another PC. As usual, the password appears in asterisks, as shown in Figure 33-15.

6. Choose OK.

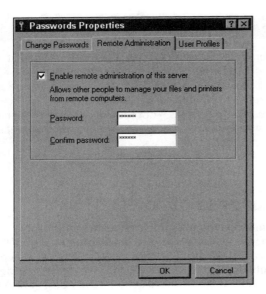

Figure 33-15: This PC can now be managed from any other PC in the LAN.

This procedure takes care of the PC at which you're sitting right now. If you want to manage other PCs in the LAN remotely, you need to repeat this process on each of those machines.

Managing a PC remotely

Whenever you're ready to put on your Grand Wazoo robe and gain access to the entire hard drive of some other PC in the LAN, follow these steps:

1. On your PC (or whatever PC you are using), open the My Network Places icon.

2. Open the Entire Network icon.

3. Open the icon for your workgroup.

4. Right-click the name of the PC you want to manage and choose Properties from the shortcut menu.

5. Click the Tools tab in the dialog box that appears.

6. Click the Administer button.

7. When you are prompted, type your password for managing that PC and then choose OK.

You see all the shared resources on that PC, with a new item called C$ included in the list, as shown in Figure 33-16.

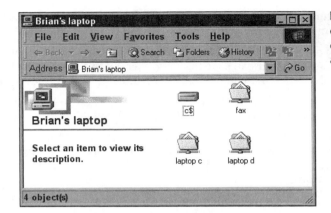

Figure 33-16: The C$ drive is the entire hard drive of the PC being administered remotely.

That little C$ is your ticket to the remote PC's hard drive. Open C$ and you get a view of the entire hard disk on that PC. You can open any folder or document. You can also share/unshare any folder in the usual manner — by right-clicking its icon and choosing Sharing.

Be careful about unsharing a resource that's already shared. If you disconnect someone from a shared folder she is using, you can destroy her work. This is not likely to make you a popular Wazoo. If you accidentally disconnect another user from his work and he can no longer save his changes, have him choose File ➪ Save As to save the document to some local folder on his PC. This way, no work will be lost. After resharing the drive, the user can open the *good* copy of his document and use File ➪ Save As to save this copy back to the shared folder.

Summary

This chapter wraps it up for networking. I know if you're in a large corporation, your LAN is probably more complicated than those discussed in this part of the book. You may have dozens of PCs and workgroups on the LAN, as well as several full-time network administrators. But most of the techniques discussed in this part of the book work on any LAN, large or small. The following is a review of the main techniques discussed in this chapter:

✦ To send a pop-up message to another LAN member, open WinPopup, click the envelope button, address the message, type the message, and choose OK.

✦ When you receive a pop-up message, open WinPopup to read the message. To reply, click the envelope button. To delete the message, click the trash-can button.

✦ Remember that after you close WinPopup, you won't get messages anymore. A better idea is to minimize WinPopup when you want it out of the way.

✦ The trick to cutting and pasting between PCs is creating a shared folder both PCs can access. A LAN member can save folders or scraps to the shared folder and then any other LAN member can open and copy objects in that folder.

✦ You can tell Search to conduct a search of My Computer when you want to search all local and mapped network drives for a folder or file.

✦ If you want to share folders from a PC without actually going to that PC, you must activate Remote Administration on that PC. Choose Start ➪ Settings ➪ Control Panel, open the Passwords icon and use the Remote Administration tab to set up a password.

✦ To manage a PC's folders remotely, open My Network Places, open the Entire Network and then your workgroup, right-click the name of the PC you want to manage, and choose Properties from the shortcut menu. Click the Tools tab, click the Administer button, and then open the C$ drive to gain access to that PC's entire hard disk.

✦   ✦   ✦

Advanced Stuff

File Icons, Associations, and Properties

This chapter shows you some ways to refine how you work with documents and programs. In particular, I focus on how you can decide exactly which program opens when you click, or double-click, a document folder's icon. I also discuss some techniques for controlling the appearance of icons on your screen. And, finally, I discuss some of the advanced settings for files and folders.

Registering Documents with Programs

As I mentioned in earlier chapters, opening a document directly from Windows usually opens the program associated with (or registered to) that type of file. The file's type is determined by its filename extension. For example, opening a file with the .htm extension automatically opens that document in Microsoft Internet Explorer or whatever Web browser is currently your default browser.

As mentioned in Chapter 4, you can give yourself more flexibility by adding favorite programs to your Send To menu. This way, rather than only opening a document by clicking (or double-clicking) its icon, you can right-click the icon, choose Send To, and then select the program with which you open the program. For example, if you create your own Web pages (HTML documents with the .htm extension), you may want to add Microsoft Internet Explorer, Notepad, WordPad, FrontPage Express, and any other Web-authoring aids to your Send To menu. This way, you can right-click any .htm file and send it to whatever program best suits your needs.

There will be times, however, when you'll want to ensure that clicking (or double-clicking) a document file sends the document to a specific program. For example, the graphic images you see throughout this book are TIF files. (TIF is one of many graphic image file types.) When I click (or double-click) a program with the .tif extension, the graphic image opens up in the Kodak Imaging program on my PC. But I'd prefer the image open in Paint Shop Pro, which is my preferred graphics imaging program. Making this change is pretty easy. First, you may want to search your hard disk to make sure you have files with the appropriate filename extension to work with by following these steps:

1. Click the Start button, choose Search ➪ For Files or Folders.

2. In the Search For Files Or Folders Named text box, type the filename extension you want to change without any periods. For example, I would type ***.tif**.

3. Click the Search Now button and wait for a list of files to appear.

4. Make sure you are in Details view (choose View ➪ Details from the menu bar). Also, widen the window so that you can see the Type column, as shown in Figure 34-1.

Figure 34-1: Search has located all filenames containing the letters tif.

Though I have the filename extensions turned odd, I happen to know that the file-names starting with FG are TIF images (the FG stands for "figure," and is the format we used in creating this book.) When you're satisfied that there are indeed some files to work with, you can go ahead and set up a new association by following these steps:

1. Open My Computer and choose Tools ➪ Folder Options.

2. Click the File Types tab.

3. Scroll to and click the file type you want to change. For example, in Figure 34-2, I clicked TIF Image.

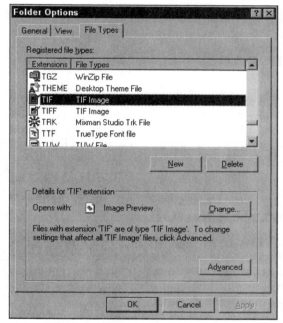

Figure 34-2: I'm about to change current associations for TIF Images.

4. Click the Change button. The Open With dialog box (see Figure 34-3) opens.

5. Click on the name of the program that you want to have open that file type.

6. Make sure the "Always use this program to open this file" check box is checked, as in Figure 34-3.

7. Click OK to save your settings and close the dialog box.

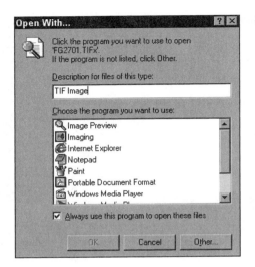

Figure 34-3: The Open With dialog box

This should do the trick. You can close the Folder Options dialog box by clicking its OK button. To verify that the association was successful, find a filename with the extension you re-associated (.tif, in my example). Click or double-click this file's icon; it should open in the program you specified (Paint Shop Pro, in my example). From now on, all files with this extension will open in the specified program.

Creating a New Association

If a filename extension has never before been associated with a program, it's easy to create an association. Just click (or double-click) the type of file that has no association. For example, say I click a file named myLetter.let in My Computer, and the .let extension has never been associated with any program before. The Open With dialog box appears, enabling you to choose which program you want to use to open this file.

Now suppose that you want to use WordPad to open files with the .let extension. In the Open With dialog box, you can type in a plain-English description of the .let extension, choose an opening program from the list of available programs, and make sure that the Always... check box is selected. In Figure 34-4, for example, I defined the .let extension as My Letters, chose WordPad as the associated program, and selected the check box so that all .let files open in WordPad when clicked (or double-clicked).

Figure 34-4: Files with the .let filename extension will now open in WordPad.

After making my selections, I will click the OK button and the job is done. From now on, opening any file with the .let extension from My Computer, Windows Explorer, or Search will send that file to WordPad.

Changing Icons

Windows Me automatically puts an icon on every file on your system. But you're not stuck with those icons. In most cases, you can change to some other icon. The first step is to get to the Change Icon button for the file type you want to re-iconize (for lack of a better term). How you do this depends on the type of file you want to change. Try whichever of the following methods seems most appropriate to the situation at hand. (If one approach doesn't work, you can always try another.)

✦ To change icons for permanent desktop items such as My Computer and the Recycle Bin, right-click some neutral area of the desktop, choose Properties, and click the Effects tab to get to the options shown in Figure 34-5.

✦ To change the icon for a shortcut, right-click the shortcut icon, choose Properties, and then click the Shortcut tab to get to the dialog box shown in Figure 34-6.

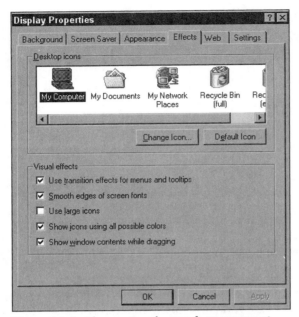

Figure 34-5: Change Icon button for permanent desktop icons

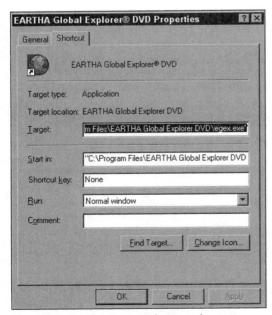

Figure 34-6: Change Icon button also appears in Properties sheet of shortcuts

✦ To change the icon of a document type, click the Start button and choose Settings ➪ Control Panel and open the Folder Options icon. Click the File Types tab, scroll to and click the type of file for which you want to choose a new icon, and then click the Advanced button. The Change Icon button appears at the top of the Edit File Type dialog box, as in Figure 34-7.

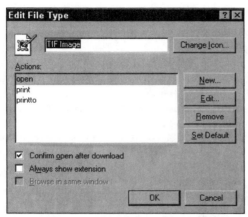

Figure 34-7: Change Icon button is also available in the Edit File Type dialog box.

Regardless of how you get to a Change Icon button, when you click it, you'll come to a dialog box that looks something like the example shown in Figure 34-8. To select one of the icons shown, click it and then click the OK button. No biggie there.

Figure 34-8: The Change Icon dialog box

What may not be too apparent from this dialog box is that you aren't limited to the icons appearing in the Change Icon dialog box. You can apply any icon file (a file with the .ico extension). The tricky part is finding additional icons. Some icons are stored right on the hard disk with an .ico extension. Others are stored inside files with the .exe or .dll extension. I don't know for certain what icon files are available on your computer, though you should have the two that come with Windows Me. Those are:

✦ C:\WINDOWS\SYSTEM\shell32.dll

✦ C:\WINDOWS\Moricons.dll

To view the icons in one of those files, browse to the appropriate folder and open the file. Or, type the path into the File Name text box. For example, in Figure 34-9, I'm viewing the collection of icons in the shell32.dll file. As you can see in the figure, this file offers a lot of icons. You can use the scroll bar at the bottom of the icons to scroll to the right and view even more icons. To choose one of those icons, click it, and then click the OK button.

Figure 34-9: Icons from the shell32.dll file visible in the Change Icon dialog box

If you download or purchase additional icons, you can install from those files as well. The exact procedure depends on the product you purchased. You need to refer to this product's documentation for details. As an example, though, say you installed the RISS Icon Pack from the www.tucows.com Web site or some other location.

To access those icons, use the Browse button to get to the folder where those icons are stored (C:\Rissicon, in this example). You'll see a bunch of files with the .dll extension. Click one of those files and then click the open button. Icons in this file are then visible. To choose one, click it and then click the OK button. After making your selection, close whatever dialog boxes remain open using their OK or Close (X) buttons.

If you have Internet access and you want to surf for icons, point your Web browser to a search engine such as `http://www.altavista.digital.com`. Then search for icons using a relevant search term, such as Windows+icons.

You can also create your own icons if you have a program capable of saving images in the .ico format. Some popular products in this category include IconEdit Pro available at `http://softseek.com/Desktop_Enhancements/Icons/Utilities_ and_Tools/Review_16475_index.html` and IconForge icon editor available from `http://www.cursorarts.com/ca_if.html`. You can also go to your favorite search engine, such as `http://www.altavista.digital.com`, and search for something similar to icon+edit to see what you find.

Other File Properties

As I previously mentioned, the best way to find out what you can do with some object on your screen is to right-click that object and look at the menu that appears. If a Properties option is in this menu, selecting it will give you some options for changing characteristics of the object.

For example, suppose I'm browsing around my computer, and I right-click a file-name and choose Properties. Most (though not all) files will display something similar to the example shown in Figure 34-10. (If the dialog box contains multiple tabs, the General tab will show information similar to that in the example.)

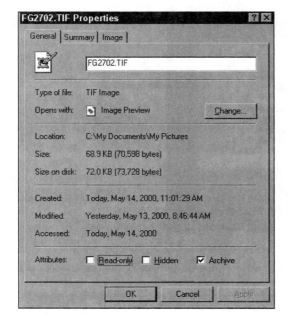

Figure 34-10: General options for a TIF image file

Much of the information on the General tab tells you about the file, its type, location, size, and the filename. You can also see the date and time the file was created, last modified, and last opened (accessed).

The Attributes at the bottom of the list enable you to tweak the behavior of the file a little more. Those options are:

✦ **Read-Only:** If selected, you can open the file and view it, but you cannot change the contents of the file. (If you share a computer with others, selecting this option can keep other people from changing the file's contents.)

✦ **Archive:** If selected, it means the file has changed since the last backup. Hence, this copy of the file will be backed up the next time you do a backup of the disk.

✦ Hidden: If selected, the file will have no filename or icon visible onscreen, unless you go into Folder Options and opt to "Show hidden files and folders" on the View tab, as in Figure 34-11. (You'll need to do this yourself to find the file in the future!)

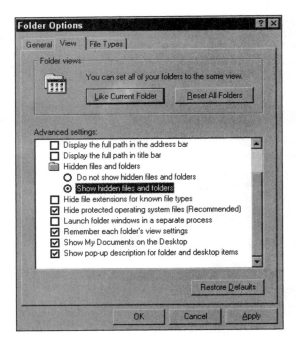

Figure 34-11: The Hidden Files And Folders options in the View tab of Folder Options

When you are finished making your selections, click the OK button to save your changes and close the dialog box.

Advanced Settings in Folder Options

The View tab of the Folder Options dialog box offers some advanced settings to give you more control over the appearance and behavior of folders and icons.

Here's how:

1. Click the Start button and choose Settings ⇨ Control Panel and open the Folder Options icon.
2. Click the View tab to get to the options shown in Figure 34-12.

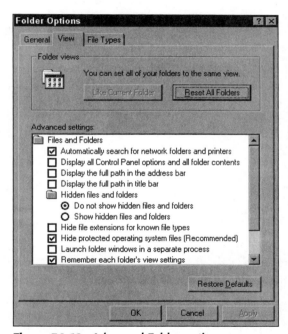

Figure 34-12: Advanced Folder options

In the following sections, I summarize what the various options offer. For future reference, though, be aware that for more information on any option, you can click the question mark (?) button near the upper-right corner of the dialog box and then click the option with which you need help.

The Reset All Folders button

The Reset All Folders button, when clicked, returns all folders to the view defined when you first installed Windows Me. This view generally shows an icon, the folder name, and other information in the left column of every folder. Figure 34-13 shows an example, using the My Computer folder. In this example, the icon for drive C is currently selected (highlighted). The left side of the window shows drive C has a capacity of 2.01 gigabytes. Of that, 789 megabytes are in use and 1.24 gigabytes are still available for storage.

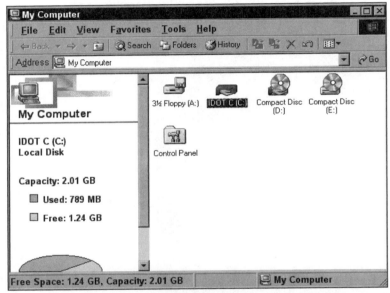

Figure 34-13: How My Computer looks after resetting all folders

Files and folders options

The options listed under Advanced Settings are all toggles, in the sense they can either be turned on (checked), or turned off (not checked). Clicking a check box checks or unchecks that box. Here's what each of those options does:

✦ **Remember Each Folder's View Settings:** When selected, ensures any changes you made to a folder while it was open are saved with that folder. The next time you open the folder, it will look as it did last time you closed it. Clearing this option prevents folder options from being saved.

✦ **Display the Full Path in Title Bar:** When selected, the title bar of each folder in My Computer shows the complete path to the folder you're viewing in DOS format (for example, C:\Windows\System). When clear, only the name of the current folder appears in the title bar (for example, System).

✦ **Hide File Extensions for Known File Types:** When selected, the filename extension of any registered document type is hidden when viewed in My Computer. When cleared, filename extensions appear for all files.

✦ **Show Pop-Up Description for Folder and Desktop Items:** When selected, this enables the large ToolTips that some folders and icons offer to appear when you rest the mouse pointer over the item, as in the example in Figure 34-14. Clearing this option prevents those ToolTips from showing.

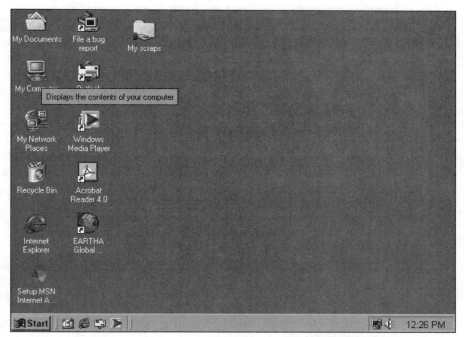

Figure 34-14: The My Computer icon's ToolTip is visible because the mouse pointer is over it.

✦ **Hidden Files and Folders:** The two options under Hidden Files And Folders enable you to choose which types of files are visible and which are invisible. Hidden files are ones that have been declared hidden in the file's properties, as discussed under "Other File Properties" earlier in this chapter.

✦ **Hide Protected Operating System Files (Recommended):** System files are files that are critical to Windows Me, so hiding those files prevents you from accidentally deleting them.

✦ **Automatically Search for Network Folders and Printers:** If selected, this makes it easier for you to use shared network resources because Windows Me will look for them whenever you start your system.

✦ **Display All Control Panel Options and Folder Contents:** If selected, this insures that you will be able to quickly find all of the items in the Control Panel, rather than just the simpler ones.

✦ **Display the Full Path in the Address Bar:** When selected, the address bar of each folder in My Computer shows the complete path to the folder you're viewing. This option is similar to the Display the Full Path in Title Bar option, and you only need to choose one or the other of these two options.

✦ **Launch Folder Windows in a Separate Process:** Opens a new window when you open a different folder rather than using an existing open window. Use this option to make it easier to drag-and-drop items between folders.

✦ **Show My Documents on the Desktop:** Places an icon for the My Documents folder on your desktop so that you can easily find your document files.

Restore Defaults button

The Restore Defaults button under the Advanced Settings will return all the check boxes under Advanced Settings to the settings that were in place when you first installed Windows Me on your PC. In other words, clicking this button undoes any custom settings that you have made since Windows Me was first installed.

The Like Current Folder button

The Like Current Folder button is available for selection only when you access the Folder Options through My Computer or some other folder. (Open My Computer and choose View ➪ Folder Options from its menu bar and then click the View tab.)

 Tip   If you click this button, all folders will receive whatever settings you just applied to the current folder.

If you got to the advanced options through the Start button, then all folders automatically inherit whatever settings you choose. Because the button would serve no purpose in this case, it is dimmed and unavailable.

Some additional visual settings

Windows Me has a few additional options that are accessible through the Display Properties dialog box. To get there, right-click the desktop, choose Properties, and click the Effects tab.

✦ **Smooth Edges of Screen Fonts:** When selected, gets rid of the jagged look some icons produce on screen. The only downside to this option is that it slows screen performance a little, but probably not enough to be noticeable on most PCs.

✦ **Show Window Contents While Dragging:** If selected, any time you drag a window across the desktop, the contents of this window will remain visible as you drag. If not selected, dragging a window across the screen shows only a ghost outline of the window being dragged. This option can slow performance, but not to a noticeable degree on most PCs.

Summary

In this chapter, I discussed some of the more advanced personalization features of Windows Me. To recap the important points:

✦ Most of the advanced settings for tweaking files and folders are in the File Types and View tabs of the Folder Options dialog box.

✦ To get to the Folder Options dialog box and make selections that will affect all folders and files, click the Start button, choose Settings ➪ Control Panel, and open the Folder Options icon.

✦ One way to change which program opens when you click (or double-click) a document icon is to delete the icon's current association in the File Types tab. Then reopen the document to get to the Open With dialog box and choose the associated program from the list that appears.

✦ You can also change associations between document types and programs by working in the File Types tab directly.

✦ To change the icons used for My Computer and other permanent desktop icons, right-click the desktop, choose Properties, click the Effects tab, choose an icon to change, and then click the Change Icon button.

✦ To change the icon for a shortcut, right-click the shortcut, choose Properties, click the Shortcut tab, and then click the Change Icon button.

✦ To change the icon for a file type (for example, all TIF files), click the Start button, choose Settings ➪ Control Panel, and open the Folder Options icon. On the File Types tab, click the file type that you want to change, click the Edit button, and then click the Change Icon button.

✦ When the Change Icon dialog box appears, you can use the Browse button to locate and select icons that aren't initially visible within this dialog box.

✦ You can change several more advanced properties for a file by right-clicking the file and choosing Properties. The exact options that appear depend on the type of file with which you're working.

✦ To adjust more advanced settings of all folders and files, click the Start button, choose Settings ➪ Control Panel, open the Folder Options icon, and make your selections from options on the View tab.

✦   ✦   ✦

Dealing with the Windows Me Registry

In this chapter, you will learn about the Windows Me Registry—what it is and how to use it. You will also learn how to use the Windows Me Registry Editor. The Registry Editor gives you the power to make changes to the Registry. You can fix problems or, if you're not careful, cause them. You can even remove all the information Windows Me needs to boot and run. This is why you will also learn how to save extra backup copies of the Registry and how to recover from Registry disasters. After learning how to manipulate the Registry, you will learn useful tricks for customizing your Windows Me environment—tricks you can perform only by manually editing the Registry.

What Is the Registry?

The Registry is a repository of information for Windows Me and its applications. What kind of information? Almost anything. For example, when you installed Windows Me, the setup program asked you for your name and it stored this information in the Registry.

Windows Me also stores information about your hardware configuration in the Registry, such as settings for your modem, printers, video adapters, and so on.

Another example is Explorer, which uses the Registry for several purposes. In Explorer, every file has an icon. Windows Me uses the Registry to remember which icon goes with which file. When you open a file, Explorer looks up information about this file so it can decide which application to launch. Where do you think Windows stores this information? That's right — in the Registry.

Most applications store additional information in the Registry, such as user preferences, configuration data, the files you edited most recently, and so on. Each application can store anything it wants.

Out with the old

You may be familiar with .INI files. In Windows 3.1, an application typically stored its configuration data in a text file, such as WINWORD.INI. You could find many of these files cluttering your Windows folder. Windows itself kept information in files, such as WIN.INI and SYSTEM.INI. Windows 95 and 98 replaced these files with the Registry. When you upgraded to one of these versions, all the information in the .INI files hanging around in your Windows folder was placed in the Registry (The old .INI files were kept around just for those applications that were designed for Windows 3.1 and didn't know how to look up settings in the Registry).

Figure 35-1 shows an excerpt from CONTROL.INI, which stores information for the Control Panel. When you upgraded your computer to Windows Me, the setup program read CONTROL.INI and similar files, and then copied this information into the Registry. Windows Me retrieves this same information from the Registry, not from CONTROL.INI. (If you look around on your drive, however, you will still find a CONTROL.INI file lurking. It's there for older programs that need to use it).

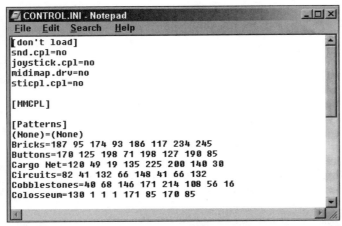

Figure 35-1: Windows 3.1 used CONTROL.INI to store Control Panel data.

Back when you installed a new application in Windows 3.1, the setup program often created new .INI files and modified existing ones. In some unfortunate situations, it asked you to manually edit one or more .INI files, such as SYSTEM.INI.

Some power users enjoyed working with .INI files. The files are plain text files, so you could use any text editor, such as Notepad, to examine or modify a .INI file. Sometimes the only way to get out of a jam was to edit an .INI file.

In with the new

In Windows 95, the plethora of .INI files was replaced with a single database — the Registry. Windows 98 capitalized on the Registry, and this change is also present in Windows Me. Because the Registry is a single, centrally located database, it is easy to find the configuration data for a particular application. The Registry does away with the separate .INI files and enables long names for its Registry entries, so you can find information much more easily than you could with .INI files. Instead of trying to decipher eight-letter filenames, you can search the Registry for a company name and then look for a full product name. This makes it easier to find information for a particular application.

The original reason Microsoft created the Registry was to handle multiple users on a single system. The .INI files could not easily identify different settings for different users. Since that original decision, however, Microsoft engineers have found many more uses for the Registry. Microsoft's COM object technology depends heavily on the Registry. When you embed an Excel spreadsheet inside a Word document, for example, Windows Me uses the Registry to determine how to store the Excel spreadsheet, what files to use when you edit the spreadsheet, and how to integrate Excel menus into Word .

What's in the Registry?

Because the Registry stores information for every application, it needs a way to organize this information. To keep one application's data from interfering with the data from another application, the Registry uses a tree-like arrangement, similar to the way files and folders reside on a disk drive.

Where a disk drive uses folders, the Registry has keys. Just as a folder can contain other folders, a key can have its own subkeys. Instead of files, the Registry has values. For example, the Control Panel stores its information under the key, Control Panel. This key has subkeys for Appearance, Cursors, and so on. The Appearance subkey has its own subkey — Schemes — to record all the named color schemes you can define in the Appearance tab of the Control Panel's Display applet. Each named color scheme is a separate value, as in Figure 35-2.

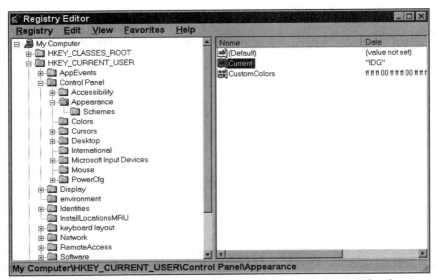

Figure 35-2: The Control Panel stores its Registry data in a tree under the Control Panel key.

In the Registry, a key has no relation to the keys on your keyboard, car keys, house keys, or any other key you are likely to encounter in real life. A key is one more bit of technojargon you need to learn. In computerese, a program uses a key to look up information. For example, when you look up a word in a dictionary, you are using the word as a key to search through the dictionary. A key in the Registry is similar — programs look up configuration data using keys and subkeys. The Registry stores the actual data (like the definitions in the dictionary) in a key's values.

Keys in the Registry are like relatives in a family tree. One key can be the parent of several child keys. All the child keys that share a parent are siblings.

The information for a key is its values. Every value has a name, a type, and data. For example, the Appearance key has a value — Current — the name of the current color scheme. A value's type says whether the data are ordinary text, a number, or something else. To be specific, the Registry uses special names for these types. Table 35-1 lists the types you will see in the Registry.

DWORD is short for double word, which is another way of saying number. A word is a unit of computer storage. A double word is two adjacent words. But don't let this confuse you. Just remember, when the Registry says DWORD, it means number.

Table 35-1 Registry Value Types	
Type	**Registry Jargon**
Ordinary text	String
Numbers	DWORD
Everything else	Binary

To refer to a specific Registry key, use a path, which is analogous to a file path. A Registry path is a series of key names, separated by backslashes. Every Registry path starts with a root key, one of six special keys Windows Me defines. The root key is similar to a drive letter in file paths. For example, HKEY_CURRENT_ USER\ Control Panel\Appearance\Schemes is a Registry path that starts with the root key HKEY_CURRENT_USER and follows the keys Control Panel, Appearance, and Schemes.

That's enough theory. Now it's time to start getting your hands dirty. You can begin by learning how to use the Registry Editor to view and modify Registry entries.

Backing Up Your Registry

Before you make any changes to the Registry, you should make a backup copy. Some of the entries in the Registry are vital for Windows Me and, if you accidentally delete the wrong key, you may be unable to start your computer.

Windows Me makes a backup copy of your Registry each time you restart your computer. Every time your computer starts, Windows Me's Registry Checker application (named SCANREG.EXE) automatically scans your Registry. If it finds a problem, it automatically replaces the Registry with the backup copy of the Registry it made from the last restart.

You can manually start the Registry Checker: Click Start, click Run, type **scanregw** in the Open field, and then click OK. If your registry contains an entry referencing a file that no longer exists (such as a .vxd file), it will not be fixed by the Registry Checker.

Windows Me does not change the current Registry backup to reflect any changes to the Registry that occur while Windows Me is running. This helps ensure that a valid backup of the Registry exists in case an application stores invalid information in the Registry and prevents Windows Me from running. You have a guarantee the Registry was valid when Windows Me created the backup files, so they are probably safe to use.

Sometimes, though, you want to make additional backups of the Registry. For example, say you are about to make some manual changes to the Registry — perhaps you want to implement one of the ideas from the section "Useful Registry Tricks," which appears later in this chapter. You want to save the Registry in its current state, not the state it was in when you started Windows Me this morning (or yesterday, or last week, or whenever you booted your PC).

To make a manual backup of the Registry, simply copy the USER.DAT and SYSTEM. DAT files to a safe place. Remember to select View ➪ Folder Options ➪ View ➪ Hidden Files ➪ Show All Files in Explorer, so you can see the USER.DAT and SYSTEM.DAT files in the Windows directory. If you are using a DOS window or a BAT file, you can make these files visible by changing their file attributes. At the MS-DOS command prompt, enter the following series of commands shown in boldface, pressing Enter after each command:

```
C:\>cd \windows
C:\WINDOWS>md backup
C:\WINDOWS>attrib -h -r -s system.dat
C:\WINDOWS>copy system.dat backup
        1 file(s) copied

C:\WINDOWS>attrib -h -r -s user.dat
C:\WINDOWS>copy user.dat backup
        1 file(s) copied

C:\WINDOWS>attrib +h +r +s system.dat
C:\WINDOWS>attrib +h +r +s user.dat
```

It's wise to make a manual backup of your Registry. When disaster strikes the Registry, it is often caused by electrical faults that corrupt files. If you can get your machine up using an Emergency Startup Disk, you can always manually copy the Registry files back into place.

New Registry Backup Feature

Windows Me, however, has a new Registry and system backup feature. Windows Me keeps multiple copies of your Registry in a folder located at \Windows\Sysbackup. The Windows Me System Restore utility manages these backups. The System Restore program allows you to set system checkpoints whenever you want to make sure that you can return your system to a given state.

What is a checkpoint? Suppose you just visited the Windows Update site and installed all the latest upgrades for security. Once you are done installing, System Restore creates a checkpoint. Now if you go out and accidentally delete a file with a .DLL extension from \Windows\System, you can recover that file by rolling back your computer to its state at the time the checkpoint was created. Data files and e-mails are not rolled back, but the Registry and installed programs are rolled back.

You can use System Restore to create manual checkpoints, in effect, to choose a reference point for backing up your system. This feature is handy for creating Registry backups before editing the Registry. It is also a good thing to use just before and just after you install new software. If the software screws up your system, you can always roll it back to the pre-installation state, fixing the problem.

To create a checkpoint, follow these steps:

1. Click the Start button and choose Programs ⇨ Accessories ⇨ System Tools ⇨ System Restore.

2. Select Create a restore point using the option buttons. Click Next. (See Figure 35-3.)

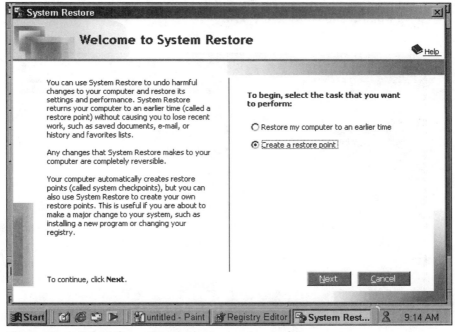

Figure 35-3: Select the option to create a restore point.

3. Enter a description for the restore point in the text box. Click Next.

4. Review the description and click OK to create the restore point.

Tip

Another useful technique for backing up your Registry is to select Registry ➪ Export from the Registry Editor's menu. When the dialog box appears, make sure the All option button is selected, and enter a file name. Clicking Save produces a text file with a .REG extension that contains all your Registry settings. If you need to restore your Registry, you can double-click on this file. The default action for a .REG file when double-clicked is to merge with the Registry. Even if you have to do a complete re-install of Windows Me, you can get back most of your settings with a simple double-click. This technique saves re-installing all your applications.

Using the Registry Editor

You can look at what's in the Registry by running the Registry Editor. From the Start menu, choose Run, type **regedit**, and press Enter (or click the OK button). You will see a window similar to Figure 35-4.

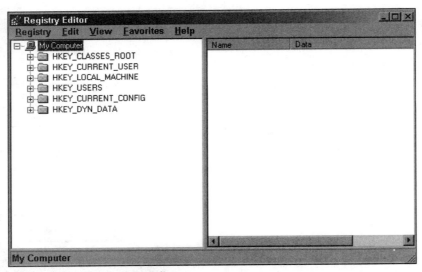

Figure 35-4: The Registry Editor

As you read this chapter, you may find dragging the regedit icon onto your desktop more convenient. You can find Regedit.exe in the Windows folder.

The left pane shows several keys (HKEY_CLASSES_ROOT, and so on). You can expand each key to reveal subkeys, in much the same manner as Explorer. Click the little plus (+) sign to expand a key and view its subkeys. You can also press the plus sign on the numeric keypad to expand a key. Click the minus (–) sign to collapse the subkeys or press the minus sign on the numeric keypad.

When you select a Registry key, the Registry Editor displays the full path to this key in the status bar, at the bottom of the window. If you cannot see the status bar, select View ➪ _Status Bar from the menu bar.

The Registry always contains six standard, top-level keys. Every Registry path must start with one of these root keys, just as a complete filename starts with a drive letter. Table 35-2 lists the root keys in Windows Me.

Table 35-2	
Standard Root Keys	
Key Name	**Description**
HKEY_CLASSES_ROOT	File associations (short for HKEY_LOCAL_MACHINE\ Software\Classes). Explorer uses this information to choose icons, respond to double-clicks, and display context menus.
HKEY_CURRENT_USER	Information for the current user (short for HKEY_USERS\ current user name). Applications store their preferences here.
HKEY_LOCAL_MACHINE	Information that applies system-wide. Windows Me stores information about hardware configurations here. Applications can also store information that pertains to the computer, not to users.
HKEY_USERS	Information for all users. If you configured Windows Me for multiple users, each user has a subkey under this key. When the user logs in, that user's subkey becomes HKEY_CURRENT_USER.
HKEY_CURRENT_CONFIG	Current configuration of the local machine (short for HKEY_ LOCAL_MACHINE\Config\current configuration). When you boot Windows Me, it determines your hardware configuration and sets this key to the appropriate subkey of HKEY_LOCAL_ MACHINE\Config. This is important only if you use multiple configurations, such as a laptop computer that may or may not use a docking station.
HKEY_DYN_DATA	System data that vary at run time, such as information about plug-and-play devices.

You can use the Registry Editor to view, create, or modify Registry entries (keys and values). The following sections tell you how to use the Registry Editor.

Before you make any changes to the Registry, carefully read the section, "Backing Up Your Registry," earlier in this chapter. The Registry Editor has no Undo function. Always back up the Registry before modifying it.

Creating a new key

To create a new key, select the parent key and choose New ➪ _Key from the short-cut menu or choose Edit ➪ New ➪ Key from the menu bar. The Registry Editor creates the key and gives it a name like New Key #1. Change the name to the desired name and press Enter.

Notice the key automatically has a value, named (Default Value), but this value has no data. This is why the Registry Editor displays the data as (value not set).

Deleting a key

Select the key you want to delete and press Delete, choose Delete from the shortcut menu, or choose Edit ➪ Delete from the menu bar. The Registry Editor confirms whether you want to delete the key.

When you delete a key, you also delete all its subkeys and values. The Registry Editor does not have an Undo feature. When you delete a key, that key is gone for good. Always make a backup copy of the Registry before you delete any keys.

Renaming a key

To change a key name, select that key, press F2, and type the new key name, followed by Enter. You can also choose Edit ➪ Rename from the menu bar or choose Rename from the shortcut menu. All the subkeys that share a common parent key must have different names. The Registry Editor will not enable you to assign a key name that is the same as a sibling key's name.

Values

When you select a key, the Registry Editor displays a list of values in the right pane. Notice the columns, labeled Name and Data. A key can have any number of values, although most keys have none. The Registry Editor always displays one key, named (Default). For its data, you usually see (value not set), which is the Registry Editor's way of saying this key does not really have a default value.

If you are a programmer, you should know the real name of the default value is an empty string. The Registry Editor displays the name as (Default) because this is easier to read. Think of it as the equivalent of, "This value name intentionally left blank." You should never create a value with the name (Default) because this would be confusing.

To see an example of a key with several values, expand HKEY_CURRENT_USER, expand the Control Panel, and select the Colors key. In the right pane of the Registry Editor, you can see a list of names and strings, where the strings contain mysterious-looking numbers. This is where Windows Me stores the color choices you make in the Display Control Panel applet.

Try this experiment: In the Control Panel, open the Display icon and then select the Appearance panel. Look at the value for Window in the Registry Editor. You may see something like "255 255 255" for the data. This means your current window background color is white. In the Display applet, change the color to bright green (or any other color you like), as shown in Figure 35-5. Click the Apply button to see all your windows change color. In the Registry Editor, press F5 to refresh the window. Notice how the Window value changes to "0 255 0"—the color value for green. Restore the original value in the Display applet before you go blind.

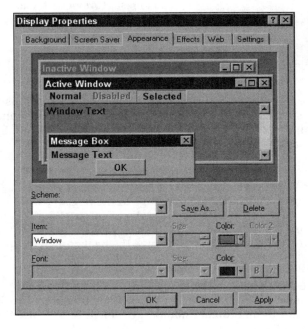

Figure 35-5: Change the Window color to bright green and watch how the value changes in the Registry .

Any changes you make in Windows Me update the Registry immediately, even if the Registry is open with regedit. As you'll see in a moment, though, the opposite isn't always true. That is, changing the contents of the Registry with regedit doesn't necessarily update all of Windows Me immediately.

Modifying a value

You can change any value in the Registry. Just double-click the name or select the value name and press Enter. The Registry Editor pops up a dialog box where you can type a new value.

The Registry stores information for Windows Me, but changing the information does not always cause an immediate change to Windows. For example, view the Control Panel\Desktop key and try changing a value by hand. For example, double-click the Wallpaper path and enter **C:\windows\clouds.bmp** (or another .bmp file if your wallpaper is already clouds.bmp) as the string data. Figure 35-6 shows you what this dialog box looks like. Press Enter or click OK. Notice the Registry Editor has the new values, but your desktop looks the same. It hasn't adopted the new background.

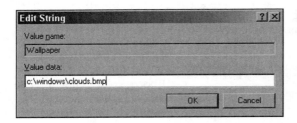

Figure 35-6: Double-click the Wallpaper path and type **C:\windows\clouds.bmp**. You need to restart Windows Me to see the effect of this change.

Exit and restart Windows Me. Now you can see the new background image. This is because when Windows Me starts, it reads the Registry to learn what background to make the desktop. After that, it doesn't check the Registry again until an application tells it the information has changed.

The moral of this story is: You can change values in the Registry Editor, but Windows Me may not act on the new values until you exit and restart Windows. Restarting Windows every time you make a minor change to the Registry would be tedious, so an application, such as a Control Panel applet, can inform Windows of a change to the Registry. In this case, Windows reads the new value from the Registry and redraws the background. This is how you can change the background image without restarting Windows.

For an example of editing a DWORD value, select the HKEY_CURRENT_USER\ Control Panel\Desktop key and double-click the ScreenSaveUsePassword value. You can enter the new DWORD value as an ordinary number (decimal) or as a hexadecimal (base 16) value. Click Cancel or press the Esc key to exit the dialog box without making any changes. Figure 35-7 shows you the Edit DWORD Value dialog box.

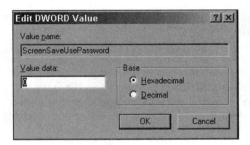

Figure 35-7: Enter a number in the Edit DWORD Value dialog box.

To see an example of the Edit Binary dialog box, select the Control Panel\Appearance key and double-click the CustomColors value. Notice the data for CustomColors is a series of pairs of letters and numbers. Each pair represents one byte of data. When you edit the binary data, type to insert new bytes. Use the arrow keys to move around in the dialog box. The Delete key deletes the next byte and the Backspace key removes the previous byte. You can also select many bytes at once and delete them or type to replace them with new data. Figure 35-8 shows you the Edit Binary Value dialog box.

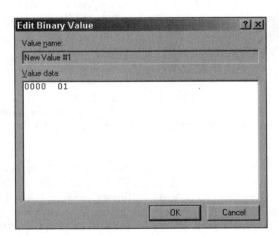

Figure 35-8: Edit binary data by inserting and deleting bytes in the Edit Binary Value dialog box.

Instead of double-clicking a value to modify it, you can also select the value name and press Enter. Or you can choose Edit ➪ Modify from the menu bar or choose Modify from the shortcut menu. When you modify a value, make sure the new value is what you want. The Registry Editor does not have an Undo feature.

Adding a new value

Most of the changes you will make to the Registry will be modifications of existing values. Sometimes, though, you'll need to add a new value to a key. Choose Edit ➪ _New or choose New from the context menu. The cascading menu gives you the choice of creating a new String value, Binary value, or DWORD value. Choose the type of value you want to create and the Registry Editor creates the value with default data and a name like New Value #1. Type a new name for the value and press Enter.

The Registry Editor creates a String value with an empty string as the data. A DWORD value gets zero as the data and a new Binary value gets a zero-length value for its data. You can modify the default data, as described in the preceding section, "Modifying a value."

Deleting a value

To delete a value, select the value you want to delete (or select multiple values). Then press the Delete key. You can also choose Delete from the shortcut menu or from the Edit menu in the menu bar. The Registry Editor confirms whether you really want to delete the values.

The Registry Editor does not have an Undo feature. When you delete a value, that value is gone. If you make a mistake, you might damage your Registry in a way that prevents Windows Me from starting. Always make a backup copy of the Registry before you try editing it by hand.

User profiles

If you configure Windows Me for multiple user profiles, then each user has a separate Registry tree under the HKEY_USERS root key. If you click Cancel in the logon directory, Windows Me uses the default user profile, which corresponds to the "Default" Registry key.

Each user has a separate USER.DAT file in the user's logon folder, which is typically under Profiles, that is, C:\Windows\Profiles\Jane\USER.DAT. Windows Me divides the Registry into two files to separate the system-wide settings (SYSTEM.DAT) from the entries that vary for each user (USER.DAT). When you log on, Windows Me copies the appropriate USER.DAT file from your profile folder into the Registry to provide the settings for HKEY_CURRENT_USER.

Because SYSTEM.DAT contains the global, system-wide Registry entries, a single SYSTEM.DAT file exists. Thus, to make a backup copy of the Registry when you have multiple user profiles, you need to copy SYSTEM.DAT in the Windows folder and you must copy the current user's USER.DAT file in that user's logon folder.

 Tip To make .REG files for each user, when the user is logged on, export HKEY_ CURRENT_USER to a .REG file named after the user. Select Registry ➪ _Export and choose the Selected Branch option button in the dialog box. Then enter HKEY_ CURRENT_USER in the text box next to the option button, enter a filename, and click Save.

Exporting and importing Registry entries

Instead of copying the entire Registry, you will often find saving a copy of only one key and its subkeys and values easier. For example, if you want to experiment with the settings under Control Panel\Appearance, you can save only those keys and values without copying the entire Registry. This can make undoing your changes easier. You can import the saved key to restore the original settings without copying the entire Registry.

To export a key, its subkeys, and all their values, select the parent key and choose Registry ⇨ Export Registry File. The dialog box shows the Export range as the key you selected. Enter a filename and click OK. The exported file is not a Registry file, but a text file you can view or edit in any text editor.

If you are familiar with .INI files, you will recognize the format of a Registry export file (.REG). The most striking difference is the section names in a .REG file are complete key paths, for example, [HKEY_CURRENT_USER\Software\Microsoft]. Also, .REG files can contain binary and DWORD values, such as *dword:0000016d*.

To import the entries from an export file, choose Registry ⇨ Import Registry File. Importing a Registry file merges the exported file with the entries already in the Registry. Figure 35-9 illustrates how values in the export file take precedence over values in the Registry, but any values or keys not present in the export file are unaffected by importing that file. (You can also open a .REG file on the desktop, or anywhere else, and its contents will merge with the Registry.)

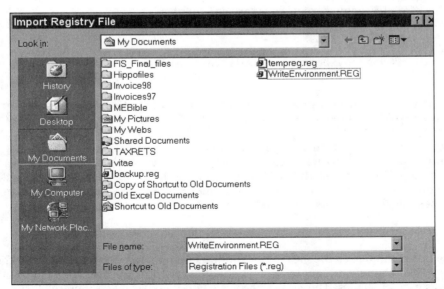

Figure 35-9: Import Registry tries to merge those entries with existing keys and values in the Registry.

You can also save a copy of the entire Registry by exporting all its keys. Click the All button for the Export range to export the entire Registry. If you must save the entire Registry, though, it's easiest to copy the file without bothering with exporting and importing keys. Exporting is most useful when you need to save only a few keys.

Restoring a Damaged Registry

Disaster strikes — you try to start your computer, but all you get is an error message:

```
Registry File was not found. Registry services may be
inoperative for this session.
```

Or worse, while Windows Me is booting, it stops dead in its tracks, with no error messages, no explanations, but with one bewildered user. The first thing to try is to boot in Safe Mode. When you see "Starting Windows Me . . . " press the F8 key. Use the arrow keys to change the menu selection to Safe Mode and press Enter. Windows automatically restores the Registry from the last backup and the most you've lost is one session's worth of changes.

If you're the hands-on type, you can restore the Registry yourself. Boot to Command mode and change directories to the Windows directory. If you made a backup following the directions earlier in this chapter, then type the commands shown in boldface below at the MS-DOS command prompt, following each command by pressing the Enter key:

```
C:\WINDOWS>attrib -h -r -s system.dat
C:\WINDOWS>copy backup\system.dat system.dat
        1 file(s) copied

C:\WINDOWS>attrib -h -r -s user.dat
C:\WINDOWS>copy backup\user.dat user.dat
        1 file(s) copied
```

If you have multiple user profiles, remember to restore USER.DAT to the appropriate users' folders under Windows\Profiles.

If you did not make a manual copy of the Registry and still want to do a manual restore, you can restore your registry from a backup copy kept in \Windows\ Sysbackup. You must use the EXTRACT command, however, because these backups are stored in .CAB files in a compressed format. The EXTRACT command uncompresses the files. Use this command to extract the files:

```
C:\WINDOWS>extract /Y /E /L c:\windows c:\windows\sysbackup\rb000.cab
```

This command places the files in the Windows folder (where you started, right?). The /Y switch indicates not to prompt about overwriting files, and the /E switch means extract all files. The /L switch says where to put the files, and the last part of the command is the .CAB file from which to extract files. This command restores all of your system files. If you have multiple user profiles, remember to copy USER.DAT to the appropriate profile.

If one of the Registry files becomes damaged while you are running Windows Me, you may see an error message from Windows. In most cases, you can let Windows automatically restore the backup copy of the Registry. You can also start System Restore and select the "Restore my computer to an earlier time" option button. Select one of your checkpoints on the next wizard screen to return your system to that previous configuration. You can do this restore from safe mode if you have to. If all else fails, you can restore the Registry files from the last system or manual backup you performed.

Registry failures are the most devastating problems that Windows Me users can face. Despite the built-in protections, you need to make a manual backup of your Registry, one that you can restore by hand from a command prompt if you have to. The reason is that you may have to boot from a startup disk and perform the manual copy if a system hits serious disaster. Once you have a good Registry in place, you can boot and use all the graphical tools to get yourself back to where you want to be. But you have to think in terms of what happens if you can't boot your machine except from a startup floppy.

How Applications Use the Registry

Applications typically use the Registry in one of two ways. The most common way is to store application-specific information, such as user preferences. The details depend on the application. Sometimes, you can learn about an application's Registry settings by reading the application's help files or other documentation. Usually, though, this information is not documented, and you should not try manually editing the application's Registry entries.

If you are curious, you can use the Registry Editor to browse the Registry entries for an application. Look under the key, HKEY_CURRENT_USER\Software. You will see a list of software companies, including Microsoft. The exact list depends on which software products you have installed on your computer. The subkeys under a company's key represent the company's products. For example, HKEY_CURRENT_USER\Software\Netscape may have a subkey for Netscape Navigator. Some products have subkeys for different versions of the product. For example, the key for Microsoft Money ME is HKEY_CURRENT_USER\Software\ Microsoft\Money\4.0.

Try running the Registry Editor now. Look at the entries under Software, to see which products have Registry entries. See if you can find a match between the Registry entries and your preferences and options in an application.

Another kind of application presents a user interface to the Registry entries that other programs create and use. Several of the Control Panel applets work like this. These applications relieve you of the burden of editing the Registry manually by providing a nice, easy-to-use interface. In addition to modifying Registry entries, these applications might also tell Windows Me about the new Registry entries, so you needn't restart Windows for the new settings to take effect.

The standard Control Panel applets do not cover all the useful Registry entries, though. The next section describes another applet you can download from the Internet. This applet helps by giving you a useful interface to several Registry entries. The remaining sections in this chapter describe Registry entries for which no Control Panel applet exists. For these situations, you must edit the Registry manually, which you learned about earlier in this chapter.

Power Toys

The Tweak UI is a Control Panel applet that enables you to control several aspects of your Windows Me environment. It began its life under Windows 95 as one of several power toys, which are simple tools Microsoft offers free, but without support. You could download the power toys from Microsoft's Web site. You can currently find several sets of Power Toys at the Microsoft Web site by going to www.microsoft.com and searching for the keywords *power toy*.

Tweak UI is a useful tool for working with several Registry entries and other preferences for your Windows Me environment. Without the Tweak UI power toy, you would need to edit the Registry manually. Now that you've read this far, you know how to do this, but why should you? The Tweak UI power toy is easier to use and you don't have to remember the Registry names and values.

For example, if you have turned off the Tip of the Day feature and you want to re-enable it, you can do so in the Registry. Find HKEY_CURRENT_USER\Software\ Microsoft\Windows\CurrentVersion\Explorer\Tips, and edit the Show value to change it to 01 00 00 00 instead of 00 00 00 00. The next time you start Windows Me, it will no longer use Show value to show tips. Remembering the Registry key isn't easy, though. In addition, if you have profiles enabled, the value will be under HKEY_USERS\UserName\Software\Microsoft\Windows\CurrentVersion\Explorer\ Tips. The Tweak UI Control Panel applet makes it easier. Select the Explorer page and check or uncheck the Tip Of The Day box. Figure 35-10 shows this example of using the Tweak UI power toy.

Tweak UI also has a Repair feature. You can use it to rebuild icons and repair the font folder, system files, regedit, and associations. It also has an Add/Remove Programs feature that will enable you to easily and automatically do one of the Registry tricks we explained. Tweak UI is a great idea for those people who want to play with the Registry, but would rather do it the easy way.

The Tweak UI power toy also has settings for the mouse (see Figure 35-11), changing the arrow icon for shortcuts, choosing icons and drives to appear on the desktop, and more.

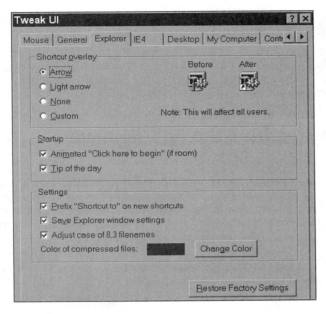

Figure 35-10: The Tweak UI power toy enables you to easily modify your Windows Me environment.

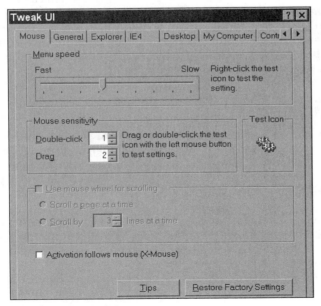

Figure 35-11: You can change your mouse settings using TweakUI.

Useful Registry Tricks

This section describes several ways you can use the Registry to customize your Windows Me environment. The are few situations when you need to edit the Registry manually, but sometimes you have no other choice. In the following situations, the Registry Editor is often your only choice.

Removing a program from the Add/Remove Programs list

Remember the program you deleted in your quest for more hard drive space? Know how it keeps showing up in the Control Panel's Add/Remove Programs folder, even though it's gone? The information Add/Remove Programs accesses is stored in the Registry, which means we can edit the Registry and remove an entry manually from the list.

Tip   You may want to back up your Registry before proceeding.

Open regedit and find the key, HKEY_LOCAL_MACHINE\SOFTWARE\Microsoft\ Windows\CurrentVersion\Uninstall (see Figure 35-12). This key contains a key for every application that can be uninstalled. Find the key with the name of the program you deleted and delete it. This operation can be performed for any number of programs. If you are unsure the key is the right one for the program, look at the "DisplayName" or "QuietDisplayName" string. The full name and version of the program it belongs to is usually contained in this string.

Moving an application

Sometimes you need to move an application from one folder to another, often from one drive to another. One way to do this is to uninstall the application and reinstall it to a new location. This means you lose all the preferences you have laboriously customized. Instead, you can move all the files by hand and then update the application's Registry entries by hand.

Let's say you plan on moving an application from C:\AppDir to D:\AppDir after buying a new disk drive. The first step is to move all the files. The next step is to update the application's Registry entries.

In the Registry Editor, choose Edit ⇨ Find. Type C:\AppDir and press Enter. The Registry Editor searches for a Registry entry that contains "C:\AppDir" and selects the first one it finds. Press Enter to edit the value's data. Then type the new folder name (e.g. **D:\AppDir**) and press Enter.

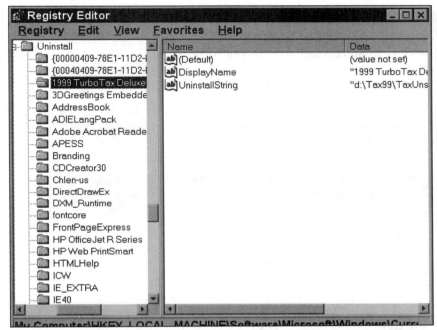

Figure 35-12: The keys for uninstalling programs that Add/Remove programs uses to generate its list

Now press F3 to repeat the search. You can make this go faster by copying the new folder name to the Clipboard, so you can quickly paste it (by pressing Ctrl+V) when you change values.

Keep repeating this — F3, Enter, Ctrl+V, Enter — until the Registry Editor can no longer find any occurrences of the old application path. Congratulations! You have now moved the application without sacrificing your preferences. Some applications keep additional information in .INI and other files. Consult your application's documentation for details. You may need to edit those files to change C:\AppDir to D:\AppDir the same way you changed the Registry.

If you find the repetition tedious, you can export the Registry to a temporary .REG file and use a text editor to replace the file paths. Then import the edited .REG file. Many text editors, like WordPad, have powerful search and replace functions, which can make this task easier.

Before making any changes to the Registry, remember to make a backup copy. Exporting and importing the entire Registry opens the possibility of a major catastrophe and you should be prepared.

File associations

You can easily create new file associations from Explorer by choosing View ➪ _Folder Options and clicking the File Types tab, as discussed in Chapter 34. When you create a file association, Windows Me creates two or more entries in the Registry—one entry for the file type and one for each extension.

The (Default) value for the extension is the name of the key for the file type. This is how you can have several different extensions for the same file type. Figure 35-13 illustrates how file associations work.

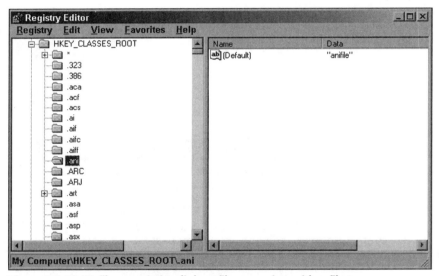

Figure 35-13: A file association links a file extension with a file type.

When you open a file, Explorer looks up the file extension under the HKEY_CLASSES_ ROOT. It uses the (Default) key to learn the file type, which it also looks up under HKEY_CLASSES_ROOT. From there, Explorer learns which command it must run to open this file. The file type can also specify an icon, a context menu, property sheet information, and so on.

When you use View ➪ _Folder Options, Explorer automatically creates both kinds of Registry keys for you. But what happens if you change your mind and want to use different extensions for a file type? Explorer does not have a simple way to change the filename extensions it associates with a file type. For this, you must edit the Registry manually.

Let's say you want to add a new extension (say, .TEXT) to the existing extensions for plain text files. First, you need to learn which Registry key Windows Me uses for text files. Open the Registry Editor and expand HKEY_CLASSES_ROOT. Look for an extension Windows Me currently uses for text files, such as .TXT. The data for the (Default) value is the name of the file type key. As you can see in Figure 35-14, this key name is "txtfile."

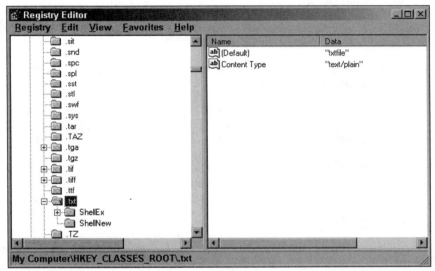

Figure 35-14: Add a new extension for a file type by creating a Registry entry under HKEY_CLASSES_ROOT.

Now you can create a new key for .TEXT files. Select HKEY_CLASSES_ROOT and choose Edit ⇨ _New ⇨ _Key. Enter .**TEXT** and click OK to create the new key. In the value pane, double-click the (Default) name. In this case, the (Default) value is used to store a description of the file, so you can edit it safely. The Registry Editor prompts you for a new value. Enter **txtfile** and click OK. You have now created a new Registry key and value.

Go to the Explorer window and choose View ⇨ _Folder Options. Look for Text Document, and notice TEXT is now one of the extensions it lists. When you open a .TEXT file, Explorer treats this file as a plain text file and opens it using Notepad or another text editor you may have installed.

Bookmarks on floppy

Have you ever wanted to use your bookmark file on a different computer? Do you have it on a floppy? You're in luck!

If you use Netscape Navigator, telling Netscape where you want your bookmarks is not one of the configurable options, so this is where you can use the system Registry to your advantage.

First, open REGEDIT.EXE and find out where the values for the default bookmark destination are held.

In my case, they are located at: HEKEY_CURRENT_USER\Software\Netscape\ Netscape Navigator\Bookmark List.

But depending on what version you use, you may have to look around (some versions, like some Communicator versions, don't support it at all). In the key "File Location," just modify the value of the key, quit, restart Netscape, and there you go!

Do the same thing for your favorite browser. You may have to do some looking around to find the key, so remember regedit's search feature if you get stuck.

Icon for BMP files

You already know you can specify a different icon for different kinds of files using My Computer or Windows Explorer. (Choose View ⇨ _Options, click the File Types tab, choose a registered file type, click the Edit button, and then click the Change Icon button.) For bitmap (.BMP) files, you can take things a step further and display a miniature of the bitmap as the file's icon. Find the key, HKEY_CLASSES_ROOT\ Paint.Picture\DefaultIcon. Set the (Default) value to %1. After this, Windows Me displays the actual bitmap as the file's icon, as you can see in Figure 35-15. Change the view to large icons to get a better view of the miniature bitmaps.

You should do this only if you have a fast CPU and a fast disk. Reading and reducing the bitmaps can take a long time, especially for a folder containing many bitmap files, such as the Windows folder. With a 133 MHz or better CPU, though, you probably won't notice much slowdown. If you want to change the icon back, use the Explorer's View ⇨ _Options menu item to select a new icon for all bitmap files.

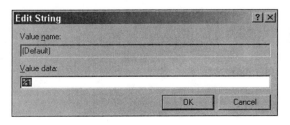

Figure 35-15: Display a miniature bitmap as a BMP file's icon

Cleaning up your desktop

Not every user likes the Windows Me desktop and its icons. You can remove all the icons from your desktop in one swift move. Find the Registry key, HKEY_CURRENT_USER\Software\Microsoft\Windows\CurrentVersion\Policies\Explorer and create a DWORD value, with the name NoDesktop. Change the data to 1. When you restart Windows, your desktop will be completely clean of icons. And you won't be able to drag files to the desktop.

If you ever want to revert to the original Windows Me desktop, change the NoDesktop value to zero (0) and restart Windows.

Special folders

You can also look up useful information in the Registry for use elsewhere in Windows Me. For example, expand the key HKEY_CLASSES_ROOT\CLSID. You will notice a long list of subkeys with strange names, such as {21EC2020-3AEA-1069-A2DD-08002B30309D}. Windows Me uses these strange key names to keep track of information when you link data in applications, for special files and folders, and so on. The specific values are cryptic because they are used by applications, not people. You needn't remember any of these special values, but you can use three of them in a special way.

When you choose the Settings ⇨ _Control Panel item from the Start menu, Windows Me opens the Control Panel, which looks and acts like a folder, albeit a special folder. You can take advantage of this similarity between the Control Panel and folders by creating a Control Panel shortcut in your Start menu. By adding the Control Panel to the Start menu, the Control Panel applets become individual menu items. This means you can start one particular applet without opening the Control Panel folder.

This trick requires knowledge of the magic name for the Control Panel folder. You can learn this name by searching the Registry. Select the HKEY_CLASSES_ROOT\CLSID key and choose Edit ⇨ _Find. Type **Control Panel**, make sure the Data box is checked, and click OK. Windows Me searches for Control Panel as the value data and finds the key with this value. The key name is the magic identifier for the Control Panel. You can create a folder in your Start menu and give the folder any name you like, but make the name's extension the same as the magic key name, for example, "Ctrl Panel.{21EC2020-3AEA-1069-A2DD-08002B30309D}."

To copy the key name without making a mistake, select the key name in the Registry Editor and start to rename it (press F2 or choose the Rename menu item). Select the entire text and press Ctrl+C to copy the name to the Clipboard. Then press Esc so you don't accidentally change the name of the key. You can then set the name of the new folder by typing **Ctrl Panel**. and then pressing Ctrl+V to paste the magic name.

Windows Me recognizes the magic name (by looking it up in the Registry) and what started life as an ordinary folder becomes a magic Control Panel folder. You can now use the Ctrl Panel menu item in your Start menu to invoke any particular Control Panel applet, as shown in Figure 35-16.

You can do the same for your Dial-Up Networking and Printers folders. Look for the value data "Dial-Up Networking" and "Printers" to find the magic key names.

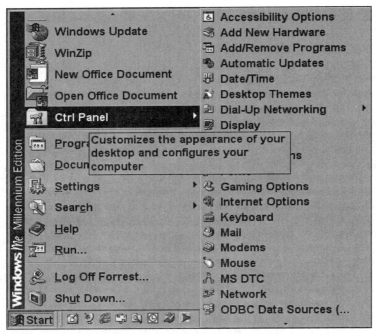

Figure 35-16: Start a Control Panel applet from your Start menu without opening the Control Panel folder.

For the truly adventurous

Quietly sitting in your \Windows\System folder is a program called MKCOMPAT.EXE. Unless you are poking about to see what all those executables do, you are not likely to notice it. However, if you have DOS or Windows 3.1 applications you are trying to run, you may want to know about it. This program allows you to tweak Windows Me's behavior on a per program basis.

MKCOMPAT does exactly what its cryptic name suggests: It makes Windows Me compatible with older programs. A quick look at Figure 35-17 suggests how. The basic options are to avoid specific Windows Me actions such as spooling enhanced metafiles to a printer, accurately representing the Windows version number, or giving a program a larger allocation of stack memory than is typical. Providing such services for a program that checks the Windows version number to see whether it is compatible, something programs did right after Windows 3.0 was supplanted by Windows 3.1, can enable them to run under Windows Me. Typically, such programs looked for the 3.1 version stamp and announced incompatibility if they did not find it. The designers may not have thought to look for a version number of 3.1 or greater. As a result, such a program might fail under Windows Me.

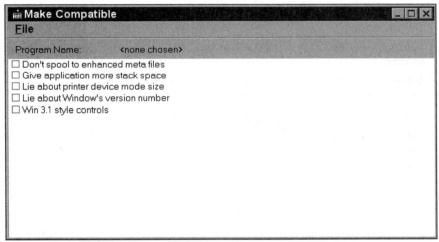

Figure 35-17: MKCOMPAT.EXE enables you to help older programs run under Windows Me.

You should try this utility under one circumstance only — when you have a program that you want to run and can't upgrade. You adjust the program's environment by selecting File ⇨ Choose Program. Check the boxes for the settings you want to employ, and then choose File ⇨ Save.

How do you know which settings to apply? Generally, you guess based on the problems you experience. If you get a version compatibility message when you try to run the program, try lying about the version number. If your program hangs when printing .WMF files, try not spooling metafiles. If you really want to tear your hair out, choose File ⇨ _Advanced Options, and look at the list. These items get down to the gritty internal mechanics of Windows Me, and you need some programming background to know what you are doing when you check the boxes (You can always uncheck them, of course, and undo the damage).

Of course, what you are doing when you change settings with MKCOMPAT.EXE is changing settings in the Registry. These are benign changes done on a per executable file basis, so you need not fear destroying your system while trying to get an older program to run. The greatest danger is dying of frustration as you try to find the right settings.

Summary

This information has become a bit technical. But, remember, most of you will probably never have to edit the Registry directly. But should the occasion arise, here are some important points to remember:

✦ The Registry is a collection of information about your Windows Me preferences and all the application programs on your PC.

✦ The Registry is automatically updated when you change preferences or install new programs, so a need to change the Registry yourself rarely occurs.

✦ The Registry replaces the initialization (.INI) files used in Windows 3.1 and earlier.

✦ Information within the Registry is organized in a tree-like hierarchy, much like the way folders and files on a disk are organized.

✦ Always back up your Registry before making any changes to it manually.

✦ To edit the Registry, use the Regedit program that comes with Windows Me. To start Regedit, click the Start button, choose Run, type **regedit** and then click OK.

✦   ✦   ✦

The Windows Scripting Host

Every operating system needs a *batch language* that allows advanced users the ability to automate routine operating system tasks. Early versions of Windows allowed you to create batch files using DOS commands. Though DOS is ill-suited to automating many of the tasks that can be performed in a graphical environment. An alternative is to try to adapt a third-party language like Perl, Python, or Wilson WindowWare's WinBatch. But even those solutions are awkward and/or costly. So most pros would just grit their teeth and performing the same boring tasks manually by hand.

With the release of Windows 98, Microsoft finally has begun to address the need for a Windows scripting language. The Windows Scripting Host (WSH) was a hook, built into Windows 98 and some other operating environments, on which script interpreters could be hung. The WSH came with interpreters for VBScript and JScript, so those languages were the ones most often used in Windows scripts. The Windows Scripting Host is embedded in Windows Me as well.

The WSH has some built-in objects that enable attached interpreters to do certain things with the operating system, such as manipulate the Registry. The WSH, taken together with a scripting language, therefore, has the power to do everything the scripting language can do, plus everything the WSH's special objects can do.

You can use the WSH to automate tasks you'd rather not do by hand. Although the best way to discover the power of the WSH is to identify a personal need and experiment with WSH scripting until you solve your problem, this chapter aims to show you the general rules of WSH scripting and give you a taste of the environment's power. By the time you finish reading this chapter and working through some of the examples here, you'll be ready to work bigger problems and really expand your knowledge of this exciting new programming tool.

Before I go any further, let me point out that the JavaScript and VBScript scripting languages are large topics in and of themselves. Covering either language here in any depth would be impossible. So this chapter is best geared toward programmers who are already familiar with one of those languages. The focus here isn't in the language; instead, the focus is on the *object model* the Windows Scripting Host presents to the language. If you're an experienced scripting programmer, you know what this means.

If you're unfamiliar with JavaScript or VBScript, plenty of books on these topics are available at nearly any large bookstore. Be aware that both JavaScript and VBScript have their roots in HTML. Both languages were originally designed to script Web pages. So you may have to learn quite a bit of HTML before the scripting languages can even begin to make sense.

Understand that the Windows Scripting Host is far from being user-friendly. In fact, the scripts themselves — when run by users — aren't particularly exciting either. For instance, Figure 36-1 shows a sample VBScript being executed by the WSH. Not exactly what one would call a friendly, exciting interface! Those of you who already have experience with scripting language will be able to add some features to your own scripts to make them a bit more friendly than the example shown.

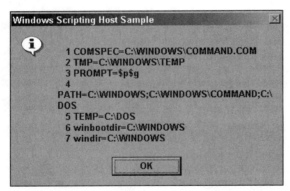

Figure 36-1: The Windows Scripting Host executing a VBScript program

Finally, remember the main purpose of this chapter is to summarize the objects, methods, and properties that make up the Windows object model. For more information, examples, and so forth, look into the Microsoft Windows Scripting Host reference, which you can view at www.microsoft.com/MANAGEMENT/ wshobj.htm. Or, point your Web browser to www.microsoft.com/search and look for the topic "Windows Scripting Host."

Understanding the Windows Scripting Host

By itself, the WSH doesn't understand a single scripting language. Technically, it's only an interface between a scripting language (such as VBScript) and the computer itself. Microsoft calls it a universal scripting host with which, via ActiveX interface technology, nearly any scripting language can be connected.

WSH operating environments

In addition to Windows Me, you'll find the WSH in current versions of Windows 98, Windows NT Workstation, Windows NT Server, Windows 2000, and Internet Information Server. Any script you write for one of those environments should run without trouble in any of the others, provided both instances of the WSH are set up with identical language interpreter modules.

Although the compatibility issues aren't as clear-cut, you should be able to run many scripts written for the WSH in Microsoft Internet Explorer and Netscape Communicator, and vice versa (yes, it's true Netscape runs JavaScript and Microsoft Internet Explorer runs JScript, but the languages are similar).

WSH languages: current and future

Microsoft has released VBScript and JScript modules with the WSH itself, but this doesn't mean those are the only languages the WSH will support. In fact, in its white paper outlining the functions of the WSH, Microsoft says it anticipates software companies creating additional language modules that will attach to the WSH core. Some possible add-on languages include:

✦ PERL

✦ TCL

✦ REXX

✦ JavaScript

✦ Python

Although Microsoft provided for such add-ons to the scripting host, third parties needed to develop the interpreters for these languages. For the most part, VBScript and JavaScript are the languages available. You may find others available for special purpose environments. Look for such additional WSH tools on the Web and in computer magazines if you find you need them. These are mostly commercial efforts, so expect to pay for them.

The two WSH flavors

Windows Me comes with two different implementations of the WSH — one runs at the command line and one runs graphically, like a Windows program.

Command-line WSH

Invoked through CSCRIPT.EXE (found in the \WINDOWS\COMMAND folder), this version of the WSH runs from the command line. Figure 36-2 shows a script executing at the command line as a result of invoking CSCRIPT.EXE.

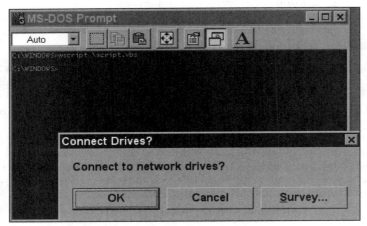

Figure 36-2: The WSH at the command line

Graphical WSH

Invoked through WSCRIPT.EXE (found in the \WINDOWS folder), this version of the WSH runs graphically, usually in response to double-clicking a script's icon. Figure 36-3 shows a script executing as a result of invoking WSCRIPT.EXE.

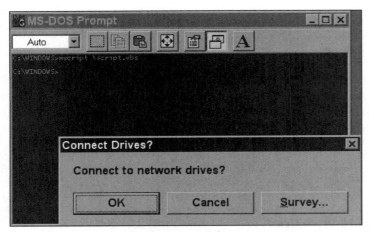

Figure 36-3: The graphical version of the WSH

Using Command-Line WSH

The real power users among us probably will gravitate to the command-line interface of the WSH. Command-line WSH is significantly more flexible than its graphical counterpart.

Usage syntax

The syntax for running a script from the Windows Me command line looks like this:

```
CScript scriptname.extension [host parameters] [script
parameters]
```

A typical command-line instruction looks like this:

```
Cscript Foo.js //nologo //T:30 /r /w
```

That line tells CSCRIPT.EXE to interpret Foo.js — a made-up file containing a JavaScript or JScript script — without showing the run-time logo. The command also gives the script 30 seconds to execute. The script parameters /r and /w are engaged. Read on to learn more about Cscript parameters.

Parameters

Parameters, sometimes called *switches,* are common in command-line environments. Recall MS-DOS commands that looked like this:

```
xcopy c:*.* a: /H /R
```

In this line, the /H parameter tells xcopy to copy hidden files, and the /R parameter tells it to overwrite hidden files as needed.

The WSH has parameters, too. Host parameters alter the behavior of the WSH itself, as opposed to *script parameters,* which affect the behavior of the script being interpreted by the WSH.

Host parameters

Host parameters have to do with how the WSH behaves as it interprets a script file. All host parameters are preceded by two slashes (//). Please note that three new parameters have shown up — //X, //D, and //Job:xxxx — for which a search of the Microsoft Web site reveals no documentation yet. I am showing them to you here on the assumption that power users will enjoy trying them out to see if they will do anything. At present, they seem to do little on the average computer.

Table 36-1 shows the host parameters the WSH supports.

Table 36-1 WSH Host Parameters	
Host Parameter	*Function*
//I	Puts the WSH in interactive mode, meaning it will communicate messages to the user.
//D	Puts the WSH in debug mode.
//X	Executes the command from within a debugging environment.
//B	Puts the WSH in batch mode, which means it hides errors and other messages.
//T:ss	Specifies the time the script has to execute, in seconds (ss). If the script isn't done executing within ss seconds, the execution is terminated. If no //T limit is specified, the script has unlimited time.
//Logo	Specifies a logo be displayed while the script executes. This switch is useless, as the logo will appear unless //nologo is used.
//NoLogo	Suppresses the run-time logo.
//Job:xxxx	Executes a WSH job.
//H:Cscript *or* Wscript	Defines the default application for running scripts.
//S	Saves current command-line options for the current user.
//?	Lists these parameters.

Script parameters

When you write scripts, you may opt to make it possible for users to adjust their function by using parameters. For example, in a script that installs a program, you may want to have a switch (call it /1) that installs the program on a local disk rather than on a network server. In this case, you'd write the script to recognize the parameter and use this command-line syntax:

```
CSCRIPT install.js //nologo /1
```

Tip

Remember, script parameters are preceded by only one slash (/), not two. In the previous example, //nologo is a host parameter and /1 is a script parameter.

The script programmer determines the purpose of script parameters.

Using Graphical WSH

The graphical version of the WSH, contained in the file WSCRIPT.EXE, operates in much the same way as the command-line version of the WSH.

Usage syntax

To run a script under WSCRIPT.EXE, double-click its icon. Or, use the same syntax as CSCRIPT.EXE (substituting WSCRIPT.EXE for CSCRIPT.EXE) in either the Run dialog box or at the command line.

Host parameters

Rather than employ host parameters, WSCRIPT.EXE has a Properties dialog box in which you can set host parameters. You call up the dialog box by double-clicking (or clicking, if you have Web style enabled) WSCRIPT.EXE. Remember that WSCRIPT.EXE appears in the WINDOWS folder.

Figure 36-4 shows the Properties dialog box.

Figure 36-4: The Windows Script Host Settings dialog box where host properties are set

Script parameters

To set script parameters under WSCRIPT.EXE, use the same syntax described for CSCRIPT.EXE at the command line or in the Run dialog box, substituting WSCRIPT.EXE for CSCRIPT.EXE.

The WSH Object Model

When writing scripts for the WSH, be aware of some new objects available to you. The properties and methods of these objects make it possible for you to write programs that manipulate the Registry and perform other tasks on the local machine—things that scripts written exclusively for Internet and intranet documents can't do.

 Tip   Note, because these objects are embedded in the WSH, they're unavailable to scripts running in your Web browser. For this reason, there's (theoretically, anyway) no danger of malicious scripts taking advantage of these objects to mess with your Registry or other key system resources.

Be aware, no WSH objects are capable of reading, writing, creating, or deleting files on a local disk. This is a severe limitation of the WSH, apparently imposed to improve security. Microsoft may make it possible to alter files under future versions of the WSH, much as it is possible to alter the Registry securely under the current version.

As I mentioned, this section won't make much sense to you if you're unfamiliar with JScript, VBScript, or JavaScript. Explaining those languages to you is beyond the scope of this book, so if you don't know one of those scripting languages, learn one and then check back here. Danny Goodman's *JavaScript Bible* (IDG Books Worldwide, Inc.) is the best tool for learning this language (and JScript, too). John Walkenbach's *VBScript For Dummies* (IDG Books Worldwide, Inc.) is a great tool to explore that language.

Now, on with the new objects!

WScript object

The WScript object enables you to refer to scripts as objects.

Properties

The properties of the WScript object are as follows:

Application

```
WScript.Application objWScript
```

This property returns an object representing the IDispatch interface on the current Wscript object.

Arguments

```
WScript.Arguments objArguments
```

This property returns a WshArguments object. To manipulate this object, see its documentation later in this chapter.

FullName

```
WScript.FullName strFullName
```

This property returns a string representing the full file path of the running instance of CSCRIPT.EXE or WSCRIPT.EXE.

Interactive

```
WScript.Interactive bInteractive
```

This property returns true if WSCRIPT.EXE is in interactive mode. Otherwise, it returns false.

Name

```
WScript.Name strName
```

This property, the default, returns a string representing WSCRIPT.EXE's friendly name.

Path

```
WScript.Path strPath
```

This property returns a string representing the name of the folder in which the running instance of CSCRIPT.EXE or WSCRIPT.EXE is stored.

ScriptFullName

```
WScript.ScriptFullName strScriptFullName
```

This property returns a string representing the full file path of the running script.

ScriptName

```
WScript.ScriptName strScriptName
```

This property returns a string representing the name of the running script.

Version

```
WScript.Version strVersion
```

This property returns a string denoting the version of the running instance of the WSH.

Methods

Here are the methods of the `WScript` object:

CreateObject

```
WScript.CreateObject(strProgID) objObject
```

This method creates a `Wscript` object named `strProgID`.

GetObject

```
WScript.GetObject(strPathname [,strProgID]) objObject
```

This method gets an Automation object from either the file specified by `strPathname` or the ProgID represented by `strProgID`.

Echo

```
WScript.Echo [anyArg...]
```

This method prints the arguments, either in a window (when the script is running under WSCRIPT.EXE) or at the command line (when the script is running under CSCRIPT.EXE).

GetScriptEngine

```
WScript.GetScriptEngine(strEngineID) objEngine
```

This method returns the `ScriptEngine` object identified by `strEngineID`. `ScriptEngine` objects represent language interpreters attached to the WSH — read all about them in the "ScriptEngine object" section later in this chapter.

Quit

```
WScript.Quit [intErrorCode]
```

This method stops execution of the script, communicating the error code specified by `intErrorCode`.

WshArguments object

Accessible only through the `WScript.Argument` property, this object enables you to access a script's parameters.

Properties

The properties of the `WshArguments` object are as follows:

Item

```
Arguments(natIndex)
Arguments.Item(natIndex) strArgument
```

This property, the default, returns the command-line argument in the position specified by natural number `natIndex`.

Count

```
Arguments.Count natNumberOfArguments
```

This property returns a natural number representing the number of command-line arguments.

Length

```
Arguments.length natNumberOfArguments
```

Provided for JScript and JavaScript compatibility, this property does the same thing as `Count`.

ScriptEngine object

The `ScriptEngine` object refers to the language interpreters that attach themselves to the WSH.

Properties

Here are `ScriptEngine`'s properties:

ProgID

```
ScriptEngine.ProgID strProgID
```

This property returns a string representing the ProgID of the current `ScriptEngine` object.

Extension

```
ScriptEngine.Extension strExtension
```

This property returns a string representing the extension (for example, VBS or .JS) of the script file being executed by the current ScriptEngine object.

 Tip   The dot—the period in .VBS—is optional. You can assign, for example, either .JS or just JS to the extension property.

ScriptID

```
ScriptEngine.ScriptID strScriptID
```

This settable property returns a string representing the script identifier of the script file associated with the current ScriptEngine object.

When setting ScriptID, you must follow these naming guidelines:

- ✦ strScriptID can contain no more than 39 characters.
- ✦ strScriptID cannot contain any punctuation other than periods.
- ✦ strScriptID cannot contain the underscore character (_).
- ✦ strScriptID cannot start with a numeral.

Description

```
ScriptEngine.Description strDescription
```

This settable property returns a description of the script file denoted by the Extension property. The strDescription must be no more than 39 characters long.

DefaultIcon

```
ScriptEngine.DefaultIcon strDefaultIcon
```

This settable property returns a string representing the location of the icon Windows Explorer uses to represent the file denoted by the Extension property. Strings take this form:

```
strPathname,intIndex
```

In this string, strPathname is the full path to the icon file and intIndex is the position (denoted by a nonnegative integer) or resource number (denoted by a negative integer) of the specified icon in the file.

Methods

The methods for `ScriptEngine` are as follows:

Register

```
ScriptEngine.Register [bWindowMode]
```

This method registers the current `ScriptEngine` object to work with the WSH, using the `ScriptEngine.Description`, `ScriptEngine.ScriptID`, and `ScriptEngine.DefaultIcon` properties in the process.

If you haven't set values for those properties, the Register method uses the default values in Table 36-2.

	Table 36-2 **Property Default Values**	
Property	*Rule*	*Example*
DefaultIcon	Specify the first icon resource in WSCRIPT.EXE	C:\WinNT\ System32\ WScript.exe,0
Description	ProgID of script engine + " "+ "Script File"	VBScript Script File
ScriptID	Extension + "File"	VBSFile

You must set the `Extension` property before using this method.

Unregister

```
ScriptEngine.Unregister
```

This method unregisters the script engine from the WSH. If you have not set the `Extension` property of the current `ScriptEngine` object, this method unregisters all extensions associated with the object.

WshShell object

The `WshShell` object includes properties and methods you need to work with the operating environment, including Registry entries and environment variables.

Methods

The methods for the WshShell object are as follows:

CreateShortcut

```
WshShell.CreateShortcut(strPathname) objShortcut
```

This method creates a WshShortcut object and returns it to the point from which this method was called.

DeleteEnvironmentVariable

```
WshShell.DeleteEnvironmentVariable(strName, [strType])
```

This method deletes the environment variable named by the string strName and, optionally, the string strType.

Valid values for strType are:

- ✦ "System"
- ✦ "User"
- ✦ "Volatile"
- ✦ "Process" (Windows Me only)

If strType doesn't appear, this method acts as if you specified "System" for strType if it's running under Windows NT and as if you specified "Process" if it's running under Windows Me.

GetEnvironmentVariable

```
WshShell.GetEnvironmentVariable(strName, [strType]) strValue
```

This method returns a string representing the value of the environment variable specified by strName and, optionally, strType. The same rules apply to strName and strType here, as in DeleteEnvironmentVariable( ).

Popup

```
WshShell.Popup(strText, [natSecondsToWait], [strTitle],
[natType]) intButton
```

This method generates a message box containing the string strText. The optional arguments are:

- ✦ natSecondsToWait. The length of time, in seconds, the box should remain visible. If this argument is not specified, the box will remain open until the user closes it.

✦ strTitle. The string that defines the title of the message box. If this argument is not specified, the title is Windows Scripting Host.

✦ natType. This natural number specifies the buttons to appear in the message box. The possible values appear in Table 36-3.

	Table 36-3 natType Button Values	
Value	**Description**	
0	OK button	
1	OK and Cancel buttons	
2	Abort, Retry, and Ignore buttons	
3	Yes, No, and Cancel buttons	
4	Yes and No buttons	
5	Retry and Cancel buttons	

This method returns a value that indicates the button the user clicked to clear the message box. The values appear in Table 36-4.

	Table 36-4 Button Values	
Value	**Description**	
1	OK button	
2	Cancel button	
3	Abort button	
4	Retry button	
5	Ignore button	
6	Yes button	
7	No button	
8	Close button	
9	Help button	

This method returns -1 if `natSecondsToWait` seconds pass without the user clicking a button.

RegDelete

```
WshShell.RegDelete strName
```

This method looks in the Registry for the key named by the string `strName` and deletes it (if `strName` ends with a backslash[\]) or its value (if `strName` does not end with a backslash).

The value of `strName` must begin with HKEY_CURRENT_USER, HKEY_LOCAL_MACHINE, HKEY_CLASSES_ROOT, HKEY_USERS, HKEY_CURRENT_CONFIG, or HKEY_DYN_DATA.

RegRead

```
WshShell.RegRead(strName) strValue
```

This method looks in the Registry for the key named by the string `strName` and returns it (if `strName` ends with a backslash[\]) or its value (if `strName` does not end with a backslash).

The value of `strName` must begin with HKEY_CURRENT_USER, HKEY_LOCAL_MACHINE, HKEY_CLASSES_ROOT, HKEY_USERS, HKEY_CURRENT_CONFIG, or HKEY_DYN_DATA.

Caution The `RegRead( )` method supports only REG_SZ, REG_EXPAND_SZ, REG_DWORD, REG_BINARY, and REG_MULTI_SZ data types. If the Registry has other data types, `RegRead( )` returns `DISP_E_TYPEMISMATCH`.

RegWrite

```
WshShell.RegWrite strName, anyValue, [strType]
```

This method looks in the Registry for the key named by the string `strName` and sets it (if `strName` ends with a backslash[\]) or its value (if `strName` does not end with a backslash) to the value of `anyValue`.

The value of `strName` must begin with HKEY_CURRENT_USER, HKEY_LOCAL_MACHINE, HKEY_CLASSES_ROOT, HKEY_USERS, HKEY_CURRENT_CONFIG, or HKEY_DYN_DATA.

Caution The optional `strType` argument can be REG_SZ, REG_EXPAND_SZ, REG_DWORD, or REG_BINARY. If you send some other data type as `strType`, `RegWrite( )` returns `E_INVALIDARG`.

Tip

RegWrite **converts** anyValue **to a string when** strType **is REG_SZ or REG_EXPAND_SZ. If** strType **is REG_DWORD,** anyValue **is converted to an integer. If** strType **is REG_BINARY,** anyValue **must be an integer.**

Run

```
WshShell.Run strCommand, [intWindowStyle], [bWaitOnReturn]
```

This method carries out the command specified in strCommand in a window of style intWindowStyle (see the table of window styles earlier in this chapter). If the Boolean argument bWaitOnReturn is not included or is false, this method will simply fire and forget the command, rather than wait for it to complete before resuming script execution.

SetEnvironmentVariable

```
WshShell.SetEnvironmentVariable strName, strValue, [strType]
```

This method sets the environment variable specified by strName (and possibly strType) to contain the value specified by strValue.

Valid values for strType are:

✦ "System"

✦ "User"

✦ "Volatile"

✦ "Process" (Windows 98 only)

If strType doesn't appear, this method acts as if you specified "System" for strType if it's running under Windows NT and as if you specified "Process" if it's running under Windows Me.

WshNetwork object

The WshNetwork object includes properties and methods you can use in your scripts to manipulate disks, printers, and other resources on a network.

Properties

The properties of WshNetwork are as follows:

ComputerName

```
WshNetwork.ComputerName strComputerName
```

This property returns a string representing the local machine's name.

UserDomain

```
WshNetwork.UserDomain strDomain
```

This property returns a string representing the local user domain name.

UserName

```
WshNetwork.UserName strName
```

This property returns a string representing the local user name.

Methods

Here are WshNetwork's methods:

AddPrinterConnection

```
WshNetwork.AddPrinterConnection strLocalName, strRemoteName,
[bUpdateProfile], [strUser], [strPassword]
```

This method assigns the network printer named by the string strRemoteName to the local resource identified by the string strLocalName. If bUpdateProfile is supplied and its value is TRUE, this method stores the assignment in the current user profile. When mapping a remote printer in the name of someone other than the current user, use the strings strUser and strPassword to communicate a user name and a password, respectively.

EnumNetworkDrives

```
WshNetwork.EnumNetworkDrive obj WshCollection
```

This method returns the current remote disk drive assignments as a WshCollection object.

EnumPrinterConnections

```
WshNetwork.EnumPrinterConnections objWshCollection
```

This method returns the current remote printer assignments as a WshCollection object.

MapNetworkDrive

```
WshNetwork.MapNetworkDrive strLocalName, strRemoteName,
[bUpdateProfile], [strUser], [strPassword]
```

This method assigns the network disk named by the string strRemoteName to the local resource identified by the string strLocalName. If bUpdateProfile is supplied and its value is TRUE, this method stores the assignment in the current user profile.

When mapping a remote printer in the name of someone other than the current user, use the strings `strUser` and `strPassword` to communicate a user name and a password, respectively.

RemoveNetworkDrive

```
WshNetwork.RemoveNetworkDrive strName, [bForce],
[bUpdateProfile]
```

This method unassigns the network disk named by the string `strName`, as long as it's not in use (you can force disconnection, regardless of whether it's in use, by including the argument `bForce` as TRUE). If `bUpdateProfile` is present and TRUE, the current user profile is altered to reflect the changes made by this method.

Tip If `strName` is a local name, only one connection is canceled. On the other hand, if `strName` is a remote resource, all connections to that remote resource are canceled.

RemovePrinterConnection

```
WshNetwork.RemovePrinterConnection strName, [bForce],
[bUpdateProfile]
```

This method unassigns the network printer named by the string `strName`, as long as it's not in use (you can force disconnection, regardless of whether it's in use, by including the argument `bForce` as TRUE). If `bUpdateProfile` is present and TRUE, the current user profile is altered to reflect the changes made by this method.

Tip If `strName` is a local name, only one connection is canceled. On the other hand, if `strName` is a remote resource, all connections to that remote resource are canceled.

WshCollection object

You can't refer to this object directly. Instead, you must use the `WshNetwork.EnumNetworkDrives` or `WshNetwork.EnumPrinterConnections` method.

Properties

The properties of the `WshCollection` object are as follows:

Item

```
WshCollection(natIndex) strEnumeratedItem
WshCollection.Item(natIndex) strEnumeratedItem
```

This property, the default, returns the string representing the item at position `natIndex` in the current `WshCollection` object.

Count

```
WshCollection.Count natNumberOfItems
```

This property returns the number of items in the current WshCollection object.

Length

```
WshCollection.length natNumberOfItems
```

Provided for JScript and JavaScript compatibility, this property returns the number of items in the current WshCollection object.

WshShortcut object

This object is not exposed directly. To get the WshShortcut object, use the WshShell.CreateShortcut method.

Properties

The properties of WshShortcut are as follows:

Arguments

```
WshShortcut.Arguments strArguments
```

This property returns a string representing the arguments associated with the current WshShortcut object.

Description

```
WshShortcut.Description strDescription
```

This property returns a string representing the description associated with the current WshShortcut object.

FullName

```
WshShortcut.FullName strFullName
```

This property returns a string representing the full name associated with the current WshShortcut object. FullName is an argument of WshShell. CreateShortcut.

Hotkey

```
WshShortcut.HotKey strHotKey
```

This property returns a string representing the hot key associated with the current WshShortcut object.

IconLocation

```
WshShortcut.IconLocation strIconLocation
```

This settable property returns a string representing the location of the icon Windows Explorer uses to represent the current WshShortcut object. The format is:

```
strPathname,intIndex
```

In this string, strPathname is the full path to the icon file and intIndex is the position (denoted by a nonnegative integer) or resource number (denoted by a negative integer) of the specified icon in the file.

TargetPath

```
WshShortcut.TargetPath strTargetPath
```

This property returns a string representing the target path of the current WshShortcut object.

WindowStyle

```
WshShortcut.WindowStyle natWindowStyle
```

This property returns a natural number representing the window style of the current WshShortcut object. Refer to the table of window styles earlier in this chapter.

WorkingDirectory

```
WshShortcut.WorkingDirectory strWorkingDirectory
```

This property returns a string representing the working directory of the current WshShortcut object.

Methods

The methods of the WshShortcut object are as follows:

Save

```
WshShortcut.Save
```

This method saves the current WshShortcut object at the location specified by the FullName property.

Resolve

```
WshShortcut.Resolve(natFlag)
```

This method verifies the validity of the current WshShortcut object by looking at the location specified by its TargetPath property.

The value of *natFlag* is zero or any combination of flags from Table 36-5.

Table 36-5 **natFlag Values**	
Value	**Meaning**
1	The method does nothing if it can't find the target.
2	The method searches subfolders if the target isn't found in the specified location.
4	The method updates the current `WshShortcut` object when the target file is found in another location.

Putting WSH to Use

So now that you have seen the inner workings of WSH, you might wonder what you might do with it. Remember when I talked about hardware profiles and showed you how to set up a no-network and a network profile? When you start up off the network, Windows Me still tries to reconnect to all your network drives. If you have a lot of drive mappings, having to tell Windows not to try to map your drives can be a real inconvenience, unless you write a script to map your drives for you.

Here is a suggested script for this task:

```
Dim WSHShell
Set WSHShell = WScript.CreateObject("WScript.Shell")
'Present a popup window that has two buttons and will not time
out
Dim answer
answer = WSHShell.popup("Connect to network drives?", 0,
"Connect Drives?", 1)
If answer = vbCancel then
   WScript.quit
End if
Dim WSHNetwork
Set WSHNetwork = Wscript.CreateObject("Wscript.Network")
'Repeat this line for each network drive mapping
WSHNetwork.MapNetworkDrive "Z:", "\\Server\Share"
```

This script is in VBScript, but you could also write in JScript if you wanted to. If you look at it closely, you see the basics of scripting demonstrated.

The first technique is in the first two lines. You dimension a variable to hold a reference to the shell object, and you create the shell object. Without a way to refer to the shell object, you can't get any scripting work done.

The next few lines create a variable to collect an answer from a dialog box and use the pop-up method of the shell to present the dialog box. It asks if you want to connect the drives, has a timeout of 0, places the title "Connect drives?" on the dialog box, and presents Yes and No buttons (the value of 1 in the last parameter causes this). If the answer collects the value that indicates the No button was pressed (the same as pressing the cancel button, or vbCancel), then the script quits by calling the scripting shell's quit method. If not, it goes on to map the drives.

To map a drive, you need a reference to the network object. You create a variable, and then create the reference. Once WSHNetwork points to the network object, you use the MapNetworkDrive method to map the drive(s).

You can create a shortcut to this script with this command line:

```
cscript scriptname.vbs
```

Then you can run the script by opening the shortcut. If you put the shortcut on your startup menu, it will run every time you start your computer. The script won't know what hardware profile you chose, but it gives you the chance to decide whether to map the drives based on the hardware profile you chose.

Tip
The method I used to connect the drives does not automatically insert the mappings in your user profile. As a result, Windows Me won't notice that the drives have been mapped before when it starts your profile. The drives represent a non-persistent network connection.

If you want to see other examples of scripts, in both JScript and VBScript, look in \Windows\Samples\WSH. Microsoft gives you some scripts to help get you started; for example, one of them shows you how to script an Excel session.

Just remember that scripting can help you accomplish a lot of tasks with less effort, although you do have to learn a scripting language. Once you have taken the time to build the script, you can reuse it every time you are working, and your computer will be more adapted to your working style. Scripts are designed to make your working life easier. So practice using the scripting language of your choice, and happy scripting!

Summary

In this chapter, you learned about the Windows Scripting Host — the piece of Windows 98 that enables you to automate certain procedures, much as you did with batch files under MS-DOS and other command-line operating systems.

You also learned about the new properties and methods you can refer to in your scripts. These new properties and methods enable you to do things such as manipulate the Windows 98 Registry from within a script. This comes in handy when it's time to automate the installation of a program across thousands of computers in your organization.

The most important things you learned here are:

✦ The WSH can help you automate key computing tasks.

✦ The WSH probably will appeal to administrators who have to accomplish the same tasks on many computers.

✦ Two flavors of the WSH exist: CSCRIPT.EXE, which runs at the command line and WSCRIPT.EXE, which takes over when you start a program graphically (with one or two mouse clicks).

✦ Parameters control the behavior of the WSH and the scripts it runs.

✦ You can incorporate a whole new object model into the scripts you write for the WSH.

✦   ✦   ✦

Installing Windows Me

Ilf you just purchased your PC, and it came with Windows Me
preinstalled, you needn't do anything in this appendix—
you can go straight to Chapter 1 and start enjoying the new
Windows. I suspect most of you currently have Windows 98
on your PC, however, and now you need to install Windows
Me. This appendix is written for you.

System Requirements for Windows Me

To use Windows Me, your PC must meet at least the
following specifications:

- ✦ **Processor:** Pentium 150 MHz or compatible
- ✦ **Memory (RAM):** 32MB (64MB+ preferred)
- ✦ **Available hard disk space:** Setup requires up to 550MB
  of free hard disk space. Some of this is temporary space
  used only during setup
- ✦ **Video display:** VGA minimum; SVGA recommended

Preinstallation Housekeeping

If you've been using your PC for a while, now may be a good
time to do a little spring cleaning and to eliminate any old junk
taking up space on your hard disk. Don't delete your existing
version of Windows, though, and don't delete any programs
you want to use after you install Windows Me. Delete only old
projects you don't need anymore and any programs you no
longer use. You should also empty the Recycle Bin, empty your
Web browser's cache, delete .TMP and .BAK files, and back
up/move off your C drive any old MS-DOS programs.

If you're using Windows 98 and you want to delete some programs, always try using Add/Remove Programs in the Control Panel as your first attempt to remove a program. This method ensures the program will be fully uninstalled. If you need to delete a program not listed in Add/Remove Programs, then you can delete the program's entire folder.

If you know how to modify CONFIG.SYS and AUTOEXEC.BAT, comment out (disable) any commands that load TSR programs, such as antivirus utilities, pop-up tools, undelete utilities, screen savers, and any other extra goodies that use memory but aren't required to make your system run. You can use a simple text editor such as Notepad to edit either file. Both files will reside on the root directory of the hard drive from which your computer boots up, typically C:\. Once in Notepad, you can type **rem** followed by a space, at the beginning of any line you want to comment out. After you modify CONFIG.SYS and AUTOEXEC.BAT, shut down your PC and then restart it to activate those changes and get a fresh start.

Some other points to remember:

✦ If your computer has any time-out features, such as the suspend features used on portable PCs, disable those features now.

✦ If you have an antivirus program handy, run it now to check for, and delete, dormant viruses that may still be lurking on your hard disk.

✦ Make sure any external devices (modems, external CD-ROM drives, and so on) are connected and turned on, so Windows Me can detect them during installation.

✦ If possible, back up the entire hard disk at this point.

✦ If your PC is connected to a local area network (LAN), check to make sure you're connected to the LAN properly so Windows Me can see your LAN during installation.

✦ If your computer offers virus-checking through the BIOS, this must also be disabled prior to installing Windows Me. The settings will be in the computer's BIOS, which you can get to by following instructions that appear onscreen during bootup (for example, "Press Del to run Setup"). For more information, see the manual that came with your computer.

You'll also need to make sure your computer meets the minimum requirements listed at the top of this appendix. If you're currently using Windows 95 or Windows 98, you can check your current hardware using Device Manager (click the Start button, choose Settings ⇨ Control Panel ⇨ System, and then click the Device Manager tab). If you're using DOS/Windows 3.x, you can use the DOS MSD program to check your current hardware. If you discover your system doesn't meet the minimum system requirements, don't try to install Windows Me until you upgrade your computer to meet the requirements. If you need help upgrading, contact your local computer dealer or repair service.

Starting the Installation

Now you're ready to begin the installation procedure. Gather your Windows Me CD-ROM and (if you haven't already done so) start your computer in the usual manner. Then follow these steps:

1. If you have any programs running, close them. If you know of any TSR programs that are running and you know how to terminate them, do so now.

2. Put the Windows Me CD-ROM in the CD-ROM drive.

3. Windows Me's AutoPlay program will automatically open and tell you that you have an older version of Windows and prompt you to upgrade. To install Windows Me, select Yes. (If the AutoPlay application doesn't automatically run after you insert the Windows Me CD-ROM, click the Start button, choose Run, type *d*:**\setup** (where *d* is the letter of your CD-ROM drive).

The Windows Me Setup Wizard

Microsoft has streamlined Windows Me to make it quicker and easier. Setup retrieves from Windows 95 or Windows 98 information on what hardware and software you already have installed. This makes setup considerably faster.

After copying some files to your hard disk and analyzing your system, Setup starts the Windows Me Setup Wizard. The wizard handles most of the installation procedure. Various wizard screens ask questions and keep you informed as the installation proceeds. The left-hand side of Windows Me also keeps you informed of Setup's progress.

Most of the wizard screens contain buttons labeled Back and Next. In general, you want to read each screen, follow any instructions, make any selections presented on each screen, and then click the Next button. Click the Back button only if you need to return to a previous screen and change some earlier selections.

The installation procedure has several phases. The following sections describe each of these phases. For actual instructions on what to do next, always do what the screen tells you to do.

The Information-Collection Phase

The first step the wizard involves gathering information about you and your PC. The wizard screens are self-explanatory, but the following sections discuss your options in various screens.

Windows Me automatically does a great deal of information collection, making system installation extremely easy.

Save system files

Windows Me enables you to save your old Windows 95 or Windows 98 information, in case you want to uninstall Windows Me in the future. This feature requires up to 150MB of hard disk space.

Specifying Windows components

When upgrading, one noticeable change to Windows Me Setup is the missing section that enables you to select Windows components. Windows Me determines which components you already have installed and automatically upgrades them. Once you install Windows Me, you can then choose to remove or install additional components.

Creating a startup disk

If you have a blank floppy disk handy, creating an emergency startup disk is a good idea. This way, if your hard disk ever crashes, you can start your PC from the floppy.

To create the startup disk, choose the Yes option and follow the instructions onscreen. When the startup disk is complete, I suggest you label it Windows Me Startup and store it in a safe place.

If you don't have a floppy disk handy right now, you can create a startup disk later. Try to remember to create the startup disk soon, however, because if you ever need it, you'll really need it. And, by then, you won't be able to create a new startup disk. See Chapter 25 for information on how to create a startup disk at any time after the installation is complete.

The file-copying phase

After the information-gathering and startup-disk phases are complete, you move to Phase 3, which involves copying files. Click the Next button and follow the onscreen instructions. This phase takes several minutes. During this copying process, information about Windows Me will be displayed onscreen. The estimated time left is also displayed on the left-hand side.

Finishing setup

After all the files have been copied, you're ready to start Phase 4 of the installation. Remove the floppy disk, if any, from the disk drive, and click OK to continue.

Windows Me may take several minutes to start and to set up all your programs, the help system, and so on. Be patient. You'll be given the opportunity to specify your time zone. Just follow any instructions that appear on the screen, then click the Next button as the screen instructs you, do this.

Toward the end of the installation, Windows Me attempts to detect and install your hardware and it may ask questions about specific items. If you can answer those questions, do so. If you are unsure about any hardware item, don't panic and don't guess — just choose the Not Installed option. You can always install a hardware device later, after you gather information about that device. For information on installing hardware, see Chapter 26 — after you finish installing Windows Me and have read the basics in Chapters 1 through 4.

When you get to the Welcome to Windows Me window, the installation process is complete. Depending on your system, you may be asked to restart your computer a few times before you get to a stable Windows Me desktop. Once you do get to a stable desktop, you're ready to roll. If you're a former Windows 95 or Windows 98 user who wants a summary of what's new and different in Windows Me, read Appendix B. If you're ready to get right into the program, start with Chapter 1.

✦   ✦   ✦

What's New in Windows Me?

This appendix is for those of you who are already familiar with Windows 95, 98, and 98 SE, and want to know what's new in Windows Millennium Edition (Me). First, let me eliminate some confusion with the other new product, Windows 2000. The Windows 2000 family of products is actually version 5 of the Windows NT product line. As such, the applications are geared toward medium to large business usage, with a strong emphasis on security, supporting multiple users, and so forth. Windows Me, on the other hand, is the next version of the Windows 95/98 product line. What it lacks in strong security and other business-oriented features, it makes up for in multimedia, gaming, and other activities geared more toward the home.

New Look and Feel

A quick run around the Windows Me user interface shows some new touches, similar to those found in Windows 2000. Perhaps the most obvious change is the attempt to reduce clutter throughout the desktop and commonly used windows. For example, the cascading Start menu (see Figure B-1) initially displays only those programs that you use most frequently. A pair of down-pointing arrows at the bottom of a menu indicates that there's more to see. Just click on those double arrows to expand the menu and see additional options.

New additions to the Start menu include a host of Internet games (Checkers and the like), Windows Movie Maker, and System Restore. Icons for Windows Explorer and MS-DOS Prompt have been moved into the Accessories group.

The capability to reduce clutter can also be found within some frequently used windows and dialog boxes. For example, opening the Control Panel (Start ⇨ Settings ⇨ Control Panel) will initially display icons for only the most commonly used configuration tools, as in Figure B-2. But don't worry, there are plenty more icons hidden behind the scenes. Just click "View all Control Panel options" at the left side of the pane to bring the remaining icons out of hiding.

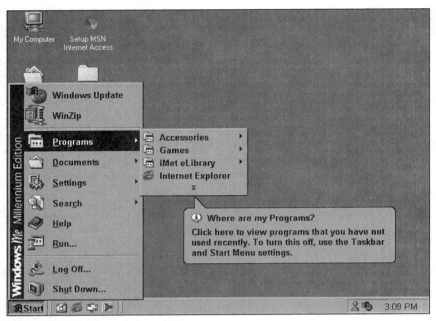

Figure B-1: The less cluttered Start menu

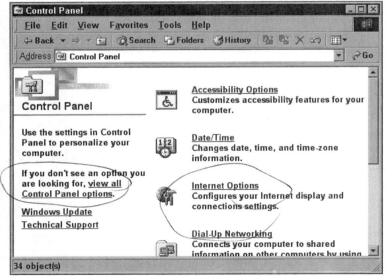

Figure B-2: The new Control Panel first opens with a reduced set of icons.

The Folder Options dialog box, which determines whether you use the Classic style double-click or new Web style single-click to open icons, as well as the general appearance and behavior of folder windows, is now within the Control Panel. Click the Start button and choose Settings ➪ Control Panel. If the reduced icon set appears, choose the "View all Control Panel options" option. Then click (or double-click) the Folder Options icon to get to the options shown in Figure B-3. You'll also find some slight design changes on the View and File Types tabs in that same dialog box, but they're self-explanatory and easy to understand.

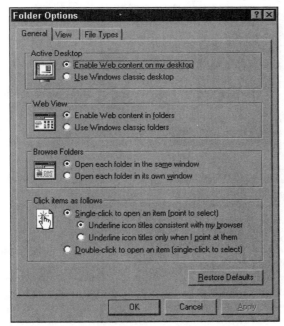

Figure B-3: The Folder Options dialog box, now opened via the Control Panel

Digital Media in Windows Me

Although most people aren't aware of it yet, the multimedia PC is quickly becoming a one-box-fits-all solution to home entertainment. Windows Me, with its capability to display photographs, home video, TV, and DVD, is a big step in that direction. In the photography arena, Windows Me now includes a special My Documents\My Pictures folder that automatically displays thumbnails of graphic images, as opposed to icons, as in the example shown in Figure B-4. In the left pane of that window is the option to view images as a slideshow. Highlighting an image displays it in the lower-left corner, where you can zoom in, zoom out, preview, print, and rotate the image using tools across the top of the image.

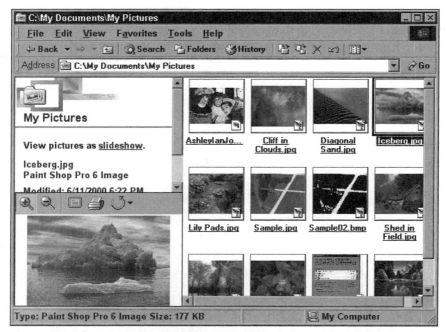

Figure B-4: The My Pictures folder automatically displays thumbnails and simple image-viewing tools.

Tip

You can make any folder display thumbnails just by choosing View ⇨ Thumbnails from the folder window's menu bar.

Your screen saver can be a slideshow of all the images in your my Documents\My Pictures folder. Click the Start button and choose Settings ⇨ Control Panel; then open the Display icon. Click the Screen Saver tab and choose My Pictures Screen Saver from the Screen Saver drop-down list to try it.

Scanners and digital cameras are easier to access through Windows Me. You can install such devices via the Scanners and Cameras icon in the Control Panel. Once installed, you can access a scanner or camera using the new Scanner and Camera Wizard (click the Start button and choose Programs ⇨ Accessories ⇨ Scanner and Camera Wizard. The Imaging program (Start ⇨ Accessories ⇨ Imaging) offers a Scan New option on its File menu that you can use to scan images.

For more information on Windows Me's new tools for working with digital images, see Chapter 22.

Windows Media Player 7

For music and video playback, Microsoft provides the new Windows Media Player 7 (WMP7) shown in Figure B-5. The new version hosts a slew of new features designed to make it more competitive with Internet-based streaming media players such as RealPlayer and Winamp. As such, WMP 7 sports an integrated Web-based Media Guide, a CD audio interface for music CDs, jukebox-like media library, an Internet radio tuner, support for some Windows CE-based PocketPC devices), and even a skin chooser (see Figure B-6). For audio enthusiasts, WMP7 also displays various "visualizations," which present undulating graphical representations of the music playing.

Figure B-5: Windows Media Player 7

To open Windows Media Player 7, click the Start button and choose Programs ➪ Windows Media Player. Optionally, if you just pop an audio CD into your computer's CD-ROM drive, the player should pop up automatically. For more information on Media Player, see Chapter 20.

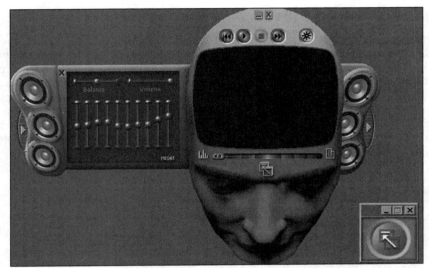

Figure B-6: Windows Media Player 7 with a different skin

Windows Movie Maker

Windows Movie Maker is an entirely new program that comes with Windows Me. As the name implies, this program lets you create movies from your home videos. You can organize clips and scenes in any way you wish, even add background music or narration to produce your movie. When you've finished, you can write the video out to an .asf (Active Streaming Format) file that can be viewed on any PC that has Windows Media Player installed on it. Thus, you can actually e-mail home videos to friends, and/or post them to your own Web site. Chapter 23 covers the new Movie Maker in detail.

The Online Experience in Windows Me

The distinction between the Internet and the operating system on your computer is becoming more blurred as the years go by. Windows Me is no exception. In fact, much of what you'll find "new" in Windows Me is actually some improvement to Microsoft's MSN site. For example, automatic updates (which are similar to those from Windows 98) can automatically repair bugs and update your software, as needed, without any intervention on your part. Internet Gaming (see Chapter 13) is radically improved.

MSN Instant Messenger

The new MSN Instant Messenger capability lets you communicate instantly with anyone who is online and has a Hotmail account. To start the Instant Messenger, click the Start button and choose Programs ➪ Accessories ➪ Communications ➪ MSN Messenger Service. To learn more about setting up and using an Instant Messenger account, see Chapter 11.

Home Networking and Internet Connection Sharing

Like Windows 98 SE, Windows Me includes an Internet Connection Sharing (ICS) feature that allows several computers to share a single Internet account. They can share a traditional dial-up account and single modem, or a faster broadband account such as ISDN, cable, or DSL, again using a single modem or terminal adapter. The one caveat is that the computers need to be connected together in a local area network (LAN). But the new Home Networking Wizard, and the capability to use existing phone and power cables for networking have greatly simplified the whole job of setting up a LAN. See Part VI in this book for more information.

Assisted Support

The lines between what's local to your computer and what's out on the Internet get very blurry when you start looking at the new Help system in Windows Me. As always, you can start Help by pressing the F1 key or by clicking the Start button and choosing Help. But the new Help system (see Figure B-7) has the look and feel of a Web site. And the Assisted Support option in the bar near the top of the Help and Support page provides easy access to online methods of technical support.

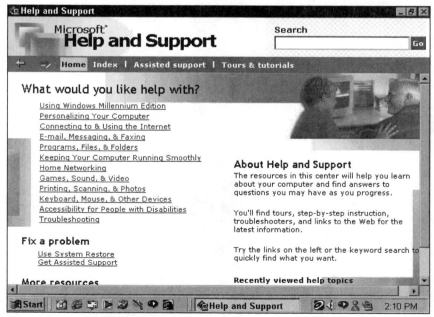

Figure B-7: The new Help and Support system in Windows Me

Windows Me and PC Health

Windows Me does away with Real Mode DOS, the 16-bit version of DOS that runs in the first 640K of RAM on a PC. This removal has several positive effects on the system: The system boots up much faster. Windows Me also shuts down much more quickly. But most importantly, Windows Me is more stable as a result. On the downside, however, you can no longer boot into DOS or shutdown to MS-DOS as you could with previous versions of Windows: The only way to boot into a command line with Windows Me is to use a boot disk. Microsoft also included a System File Protection (SFP), which protects critical files from being deleted or overwritten by errant application programs. The new System Restore automatically creates "restore points" so that if some change to the system makes a mess of things, you can return your computer to a previously known good configuration. You can also manually create a restore point before you install a suspect application, so that you can return your system to a good state if things go bad. The System Restore user interface, like Help and Support, is HTML-based and easy to use.

While Windows 98 users will find the Windows Update feature to be old hat, Microsoft has taken this concept to the next logical level with AutoUpdate, which is available from the Automatic Updates applet in the Control Panel (see Figure B-8). AutoUpdate will, optionally, allow your system to keep itself up-to-date automatically by checking the Windows Update Web site for updates (bug reports, security fixes, even driver updates) that are specific to your system.

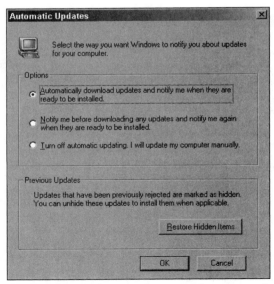

Figure B-8: Windows Update now does most of the tedious work for you.

✦   ✦   ✦

Special Folders and Shortcut Keys

This appendix provides a quick reference to special folders in Windows Me and to common shortcut keys. Everything in this appendix is optional. For example, you can rearrange items on the Start menu by dragging items to new locations within the menu. An alternative approach would be to open the special C:\Windows\Start Menu folder and rearrange icons there.

Similarly, you can do anything by clicking some item or option with the mouse. But if your hands are currently on the keyboard and you don't want to lift them, you can use the shortcut key instead.

Special Folders

Your Windows Me program is actually a set of folders and files, most of which are stored in your C:\Windows directory. Some of the folders play some special role on your screen. For example, all the shortcut icons on your Windows Me desktop are actually installed in a folder named C:\Windows\Desktop. Even though these folders play special roles, they can still be manipulated, as can any other folder on your desktop. Table C-1 lists items accessible from the desktop that store their data in special folders.

Table C-1 Windows Me Items That Store Data in Folders	
Windows Me feature	*Gets icons from*
Auto-start programs	C:\Windows\Start Menu\Programs\StartUp
Desktop	C:\Windows\Desktop
Documents menu	C:\Windows\Recent
Favorites	C:\Windows\Favorites
Fonts	C:\Windows\Fonts
History	C:\Windows\History
Internet cache	C:\Windows\Temporary Internet Files
Internet Explorer cookies	C:\Windows\Cookies
Send To menu	C:\Windows\SendTo
Start menu	C:\Windows\Start Menu

Shortcut Keys

Windows Me offers many shortcut keys you can use in lieu of the mouse. These might come in handy when your fingers are on the keyboard and you don't want to remove them to click something. General shortcut keys applicable at (or before) the appearance of the Windows Me desktop are listed in Table C-2.

Table C-2 Shortcut Keys Used at the Desktop and During Bootup	
Operation	*Key(s)*
Bypass CD-ROM AutoPlay	Hold down Shift while inserting the CD
Cancel dialog box	Esc
Cancel drag-and-drop	Esc
Capture screen to Windows Clipboard	Print Screen
Capture current window to Clipboard	Alt+Print Screen

Operation	Key(s)
Choose menu command/dialog box option	Alt+*underlined letter*
Close the current document window	Ctrl+F4
Close the current program window	Alt+F4
Command Prompt Bootup	Press F8 at startup
Copy	Ctrl+C
Cut	Ctrl+X
Delete	Delete or Del
Delete immediately (no Recycle Bin)	Shift+Delete or Shift+Del
Find Files or Folders	F3
Help	F1
Paste	Ctrl+V
Properties of current item	Alt+Enter
Refresh window contents	F5
Rename	F2
Shortcut menu for current item	Shift+F10
Safe Mode Bootup	Press F8 after beep at bootup
Shut Down	Alt+F4 (after all open windows are closed)
Start menu	Ctrl+Esc or Windows key
Step-By-Step Bootup	Press Shift+F8 after beep at bootup
Switch to another open program	Alt+Tab
System menu for current document	Alt+hyphen (-)
System menu for current program	Alt+Spacebar
Undo	Ctrl+Z

Windows Keyboards

Some keyboards, called *Windows Keyboards*, have an extra Windows key and Application key, usually placed between the Ctrl and Alt keys. The Windows key usually has a little flying Windows logo on them. The Application key has a tiny window and mouse pointer icon on it. If your keyboard has those keys, you can use the shortcuts listed in Table C-3.

Table C-3
Shortcut Keys Available on Special Windows Keyboards

Operation	Key(s)
Cycle through buttons on the taskbar	Windows+Tab
Find files and folders	Windows+F
Help	Windows+F1
Minimize or restore all windows	Windows+D
Right-click menu for current item	Application
Run	Windows+R
Start menu	Windows
System Properties dialog box	Windows+Break
Undo minimize all windows	Shift+Windows+M
Windows Explorer	Windows+E

Drag-and-drop shortcuts

You can hold down a key while dragging an item or a selection of items, to force a move, or to copy or create a shortcut, as summarized in Table C-4. As an alternative to using any of those keys, you can drag using the right mouse button. When you drop (release the mouse button), a menu appears enabling you to choose what you want to do with the item(s).

Table C-4
Shortcut Keys to Use During Drag-and-Drop Operations

Operation	Key(s) to hold
Cancel drag-and-drop	Esc
Copy file(s) being dragged	Ctrl+drag
Create shortcut to file being dragged	Ctrl+Shift+drag
Move files being dragged	Alt+drag

Accessibility shortcuts

If you installed and activated Windows Me Accessibility features, use the keys listed in Table C-5 to activate/deactivate those features.

Table C-5	
Accessibility Features Shortcut Keys	
Operation	*Key(s)*
FilterKeys on/off	Hold down right Shift key for eight seconds
High Contrast on/off	Left Alt+Left Shift+Print Screen
MouseKeys on/off	Left Alt+Left Shift+Num Lock
StickyKeys on/off	Press Shift five times
Switch ToggleKeys on/off	Hold down Num Lock for five seconds

My Computer

When browsing your system with My Computer, you can use the keys listed in Table C-6 in lieu of mouse clicking.

Table C-6	
Shortcut Keys You Can Use in My Computer	
Operation	*Key(s)*
Close current window	Alt+F4
Close current folder and all its parent folders	Hold Shift while clicking Close (X) button
Copy selected item(s)	Ctrl+C
Cut selected item(s)	Ctrl+X
Delete without copying to Recycle Bin	Shift+Delete
Find All Files	F3
Move backward to a previous view	Alt+Left Arrow
Move forward to a previous view	Alt+Right Arrow
Paste	Ctrl+V

Continued

Table C-6 *(continued)*	
Operation	**Key(s)**
Refresh window contents	F5
Rename	F2
View current item's properties	Shift+Enter or Shift+double-click
View the folder one level up	Backspace

Windows Explorer

Most of the shortcut keys listed in Table C-6 apply to Windows Explorer, as well as to My Computer and the desktop. In addition, Windows Explorer offers the shortcut keys listed in Table C-7.

Table C-7 Shortcut Keys for Windows Explorer	
Operation	**Key(s)**
Collapse the current selection if it is expanded	←
Move to parent folder if current folder is not expanded	←
Collapse selected folder if expanded, or expand folder if it is collapsed	→
Select first subfolder if it is not collapsed	→
Expand all folders below current selection	* on numeric keypad
Expand the selected folder	+ on numeric keypad
Switch between left and right panes, move to Address line	F6

Shortcut keys in most Windows programs

Many of the shortcut keys listed in preceding tables are universal in that they perform the same function within a Windows program as they perform at the desktop. Some shortcut keys are also universal to most Windows programs, even though no equivalent is at the desktop. The shortcut keys commonly used within programs are listed in Table C-8.

Table C-8
Universal Shortcut Keys Available in Most Windows Programs

Operation	Key(s)
Cancel menu, drag, or dialog box	Escape (Esc)
Close current document	Ctrl+F4
Close program	Alt+F4
Copy	Ctrl+C
Cut	Ctrl+X
Delete	Delete or Del
End of document	Ctrl+End
End of line	End
Find	Ctrl+F
Help	F1
Menu (activate)	F10
New document	Ctrl+N
Open document	Ctrl+O
Paste	Ctrl+V
Print	Ctrl+P
Pull down specific menu	Alt+*underlined letter*
Replace	Ctrl+H
Save	Ctrl+S
Select All	Ctrl+A
Select item from open menu	*Underlined letter*
Start of line	Home
Top of document	Ctrl+Home
Undo	Ctrl+Z
What's This?	Shift+F1

Dialog box shortcut keys

Table C-9 lists shortcut keys that apply to most dialog boxes and the controls displayed within those dialog boxes. Keys that apply to specific controls work only when this type of control is selected (has the dotted border around it). To select a control, click it or press Tab or Shift+Tab until the border appears around the option you want to change.

Table C-9 Shortcuts Keys Available in Dialog Boxes	
Operation	*Key(s)*
Cancel without saving	Esc
Choose option	Alt+*underlined letter*
Clear/fill current check box or radio button	Spacebar
Click button (if selected)	Spacebar
Click default (dark-rimmed) button	Enter
Cursor to end of line	End
Cursor to start of line	Home
Drop-down list (view)	Alt+↓
Move backward through options	Shift+Tab
Move backward through tabs	Ctrl+Shift+Tab
Move forward through options	Tab
Move forward through tabs	Ctrl+Tab
Open a folder one level up in Save As or Open dialog box	Backspace
Open Save In or Look In from the Save As or Open dialog box	F4
Refresh the Save As or Open dialog box	F5
Scroll bar up/down	↑, ↓, Page Up, Page Down, mouse wheel
Slider left/right	←, →
Spin box up/down	↑, ↓

✦   ✦   ✦

Glossary

+ When used in *key+key*, this means hold down the first key, tap the second key, and then release the first key. For example, *press Ctrl+A* means hold down the Ctrl key, press and release the letter *A*, and then release the Ctrl key.

:-) Your basic *smiley* looks like a smiling face when flipped on its side. Often used in e-mail messages.

10BASE-T A type of cable used to connect computers together in a local area network (LAN). Typically plugs into an RJ-45 slot on a network adapter card and Ethernet hub.

16-bit The chip architecture used for DOS and earlier Windows 3.*x* programs.

32-bit The more advanced chip architecture used in Windows 98, Me, NT, and 2000.

Active Desktop The capability to put Internet-updateable HTML pages and objects onto the Windows Me desktop.

active window The window currently capable of accepting input. The active window is said to have the focus. The active window can cover other windows on the desktop.

AGP (Advanced Graphics Port) A special slot on the motherboard that provides high-performance graphics.

anonymous FTP A type of File Transfer Protocol used on the Internet that enables anyone to log in anonymously and download files.

AOL (America Online) A popular information service offering e-mail, special-interest groups, Internet access, and other services.

app Slang for application.

applet A small application program.

application Another word for program—software you purchase and use on your PC.

ASCII (American Standard Code for Information Interchange) A standard for describing characters that allows different makes and models of computers to communicate with one another. An ASCII file or ASCII text file is one containing only ASCII characters—no pictures or formatting codes.

associate To tie a filename extension to a program. For example, the .doc filename extension is usually associated with Microsoft Word. When you double-click a document with the .doc extension, Windows automatically opens Microsoft Word and opens the file displaying the document you clicked or double-clicked.

audio CD The regular kind of CD you buy in a music store to play on a stereo CD player.

backward compatibility The capability to use documents, settings, and so forth, from earlier products.

bandwidth The amount of information that can be transferred along a wire or other medium, such as a satellite, at any given time. A higher bandwidth means more information coming through the wire at a time and, thus, faster interaction with whatever is on the other side of that connection.

baud The speed at which information is sent through a modem. A higher baud rate means faster communications.

BBS (Bulletin Board Service) A service you can contact via telephone lines using your modem and a communications program, such as HyperTerminal. Most offer special interest groups, shareware, freeware, and other services.

binding A process that establishes a communication channel between a network adapter card's driver and the driver for a network protocol. In Windows Me, bindings are available via the Network icon in the Control Panel.

BIOS The Basic Input/Output System that enables interaction between the computer and its input (mouse/keyboard) and output (screen, printer) devices. The brand name and version number of your computer's BIOS generally appear onscreen shortly after you first start your computer.

BIOS enumerator In a plug-and-play system, the BIOS enumerator identifies all hardware on the motherboard.

bit Short for *binary digit*. Represents a single switch that can be either on or off. A byte is a collection of eight bits.

bitmap A graphic file format in which each dot is actually represented by a bit. A vector image, on the other hand, stores graphics as mathematical data, which is then used to draw shapes.

bookmark A simple shortcut to some favorite resource.

bps (bits per second) A measure of a modem's speed, also expressed as *baud*.

BRB Often used in online chats as an abbreviation for Be Right Back.

broadband A generic term for high-speed Internet access such as cable and DSL.

browse To explore, look around. You can browse around your own computer using My Computer, Windows Explorer, or Find. You can use a Web browser, such as Microsoft Internet Explorer or Netscape Navigator, to browse the World Wide Web.

bus A device that controls other devices. For example, when you plug a new board into a PC, you're actually plugging it into a bus.

byte The amount of space required to store one character. For instance, the word "cat" requires three bytes of storage. The word "hello" uses five bytes.

cache Pronounced *cash*. A folder on the disk or some other resource used to store information, automatically, to speed up later operations.

capture To record to a file on a computer disk.

capture device An add-in card or other device that can record data from some external device into a file on a computer disk.

CD-R Recordable compact disc. A CD-R drive is one that enables you to record information to a compact disc. A CD-R is the recordable compact disc itself.

CD-ROM (Compact Disc Read-Only Memory) So named because the PC can read files off the compact disc. Nothing can be written to (saved on) the compact disc, however, unless you have special hardware called a CD-R (CD Recorder) and blank, recordable CDs.

CD-RW Rewriteable compact disk. A compact disk that can be written to, and also changed.

character Any single letter, numeric digit, or punctuation mark. For example, the letter *C* is a character, as is the number 4 and the semicolon (;). The word "cat" contains three characters, *c*, *a*, and *t*.

chat A service of the Internet that enables you to communicate with others by typing messages back and forth. Requires Internet access and some kind of chatting program, such as Microsoft Chat.

CIS (CompuServe Information Service) A popular information service offering e-mail, special-interest forums, Internet access, and other services.

Classic style An option that enables you to navigate Windows Me in a manner similar to Windows 95, in which you must double-click to open icons. To switch between Classic-style and Web-style navigation, click the Start button and choose Settings ⇨ Folder Options.

click To rest the mouse pointer on some item onscreen and then press and release the primary mouse button.

client A computer in a network that can use shared resources.

clip A still picture or small chunk of video or audio used in a movie.

Clipboard A place in the computer's memory where you can temporarily store text and pictures.

close To remove an object from the screen so it's no longer visible. Typically, closing an object removes it from memory (RAM) and saves it to the hard disk.

CMOS Memory maintained by a small battery within the PC. Often used to manage settings that come into play before the operating system is loaded. When you see a message, such as `Press <Del> to run Setup`, pressing the Delete (Del) key at this point takes you to the CMOS settings of that PC.

codec A system to compress/decompress digital video and sound to minimize the amount of disk space required for storage.

computer name The name assigned to a computer in a network. In a local area network, you can assign a computer name by right-clicking the Network Neighborhood icon, choosing Properties, and clicking the Identification tab.

connectoid A collection of settings that defines how to connect to some service or computer via Dial-Up Networking. The Make New Connection icon in Dial-Up Networking enables you to create a new connectoid.

content In the media biz, the text, pictures, and/or video that make up a presentation or published work. Also called *source content*.

context-sensitive help Help relevant to whatever you're currently trying to do. Context-sensitive help is generally available when you click the Help button or press the Help (F1) key.

control Any button, list, or text box within a dialog box that enables you to control how the computer will behave.

Control Panel A window in Windows Me that provides access to many settings you can control yourself. To get to the Control Panel, click the Start button and choose Settings ➪ Control Panel.

cookie A small file placed on your hard disk through a Web site. The cookie file typically contains information about you and your last visit, to make the current visit go more smoothly and easily.

Ctrl+click To hold down the Ctrl key while clicking an item.

Ctrl+point To hold down the Ctrl key while moving the mouse pointer to an item.

cut and paste A technique used to move or copy text or graphics from one document to another. After selecting the object to be moved or copied, pressing Ctrl+C copies the selection to the Windows Clipboard. Pressing Ctrl+X moves the selection to the Windows Clipboard. Pressing Ctrl+V pastes the Clipboard contents at the current cursor position. You can also choose Copy, Cut, or Paste from the Edit menu in most programs.

cyberspace A nickname for the Internet.

DDE (Dynamic Data Exchange) A technology that enables different programs to share data and documents.

default A setting made for you when you don't make the selection yourself. For example, the default margin width in most word processing programs is one inch. Any document you print will have the default one-inch margin unless you specifically set a different margin width.

desktop The main Windows Me workspace that appears when you first start your PC. To get to the desktop quickly from an application, right-click some neutral area of the taskbar and choose Minimize All Windows. To bring back your windows, right-click the taskbar and choose Undo Minimize All.

desktop icon An icon that resides on the Windows Me desktop. My Computer, Recycle Bin, My Documents, and Network Neighborhood are all examples of desktop icons.

desktop theme A combination of sounds, wallpaper, screen saver, and icons to give your entire desktop a particular appearance.

device A general term for any gizmo or gadget you put into a computer or attach to a computer with a cable.

device driver A small program that makes a hardware device work. For example, to print, you typically need a printer (hardware) and a driver (software) for that printer.

DHCP (Dynamic Host Configuration Protocol) Used on the Internet and in intranets to assign IP addresses to machines automatically.

Dial-Up Networking A program that enables you to network with the Internet or other online services via telephone lines. The icon for Dial-Up Networking can be found in the My Computer folder.

dialog box A window containing options from which you can choose. These options are generally settings—for color, size, speed, and so forth.

digital image A picture that's stored as a file on a computer disk.

directory A place on a disk where a group of files is stored. Also called a *folder*.

directory server A place on the Internet where people who want to communicate gather. Used in conjunction with a teleconferencing program such as Microsoft NetMeeting.

disk drive A physical device in the computer capable of storing information, even while the computer is turned off. Typically, the main hard disk is named C:. The floppy disk is A:. A CD-ROM drive might be D:, E:, or some higher letter.

DLL (Dynamic Link Library) A file used by one or more application programs.

DMA channel (Direct Memory Access channel) A direct channel for transferring data between a disk drive and memory, without involving the microprocessor.

DNS (Domain Name System) A database used by Internet TCP/IP hosts to resolve host names and IP addresses. Enables users of remote computers to access one another by host names rather than IP addresses.

dock To attach a notebook computer to a docking station.

docking station Usually a piece of hardware that allows a laptop computer to connect to a normal-sized mouse, keyboard, monitor, and/or network.

document A file you create using some program. For example, when you use a word processing program to type a letter, that letter is a document.

document-centric An operating system like Windows 98 that's designed to put the focus on the documents people create and use, as opposed to the programs needed to create or edit those documents.

domain In Windows NT, a group of computers sharing a common domain database and security policy controlled by a Windows NT Server domain controller.

domain controller In a local area network, the Windows NT computer that authenticates logons and controls security and then maintains the master domain database.

domain name On the Internet, the last part of an e-mail address. For example, in alan@coolnerds.com, the coolnerds.com part is the Internet domain name.

DOS (Disk Operating System) The first operating system for PCs. To enter DOS commands in Windows Me, you first must get to the DOS command prompt by clicking the Start button and choosing Programs ➪ MS-DOS Prompt.

double-click To point to an item and then click the primary mouse button twice in rapid succession.

download To copy a file from some remote computer on the Internet (or elsewhere) onto your own local PC.

drag To hold down the primary mouse button while moving the mouse.

drag-and-drop To move or copy an item by holding down the mouse button as you move the item to some new location. To drop the item, release the mouse button.

drive Short for disk drive.

driver A program used to control some device connected to your computer, such as a mouse.

drop To place an item on the desktop by releasing the mouse button after dragging.

drop-down list A text box with a down-arrow box attached, so you can choose an option from a list, rather than typing in an option. To open the drop-down list, click the drop-down list arrow or press Alt+↓.

DSL Digital Subscriber Line, a way of connecting to the Internet that allows high-speed access through traditional telephone lines.

DVD Stands for either Digital Video Disk or Digital Versatile Disk, depending on who you ask. DVD is actually a format that allows full-length motion pictures to be stored on a compact disc.

edit To change something, such as a letter you've written.

editor A program that enables you to change something, such as a letter you've written.

e-mail Electronic mail sent over the Internet or some other online service. Microsoft Outlook Express enables you to send and receive e-mail messages over the Internet.

e-mail address The address that uniquely identifies you on a network, much as your street address uniquely identifies the location of your home.

Ethernet A popular protocol for building a local area network from two or more PCs.

Ethernet cable The cable used to attach a PC's network adapter card to an Ethernet concentrator.

Ethernet concentrator A device to which all PCs in a local area network connect via Ethernet cables.

Ethernet hub Another name for an Ethernet concentrator.

event Any activity from the mouse, keyboard, or a program the computer can detect. Mouse clicks and key presses are events.

extension The short part of a filename that comes after the period. For example, in myletter.doc, the filename extension is .doc. Filename extensions are used to associate document types with programs. For example, files with the .doc extension, when opened, will open in Microsoft Word (or WordPad, if your computer doesn't have Microsoft Word installed).

FAQ (Frequently Asked Questions) A document you can browse on the Internet or download from a fax-back service answering common questions about a topic.

FAT/FAT 32 (File Allocation Table) The scheme that DOS and Windows use to keep track of files on a disk. FAT 32, available in Windows 98, Me, NT, and 2000 is an improvement over the earlier 16-bit FAT used in DOS and Windows 3.*x*.

file The basic unit of storage on a disk. For example, when you create and save a letter, that letter is stored in a file. Each file within a folder has its own unique filename.

file sharing Allowing multiple PCs on a local area network access to the same set of files on one PC. To enable file sharing on a PC, you must make sure file sharing is enabled in the network properties (right-click Network Neighborhood and choose Properties). Then to share a drive or folder, right-click the item's icon in My Computer and choose Sharing.

flame To rant and rave on the Internet or another information service by sending obnoxious e-mail messages.

folder A place on a computer disk that holds one or more files. Also called a *directory*.

font A lettering style. To add, view, and remove fonts in Windows Me, click Start, choose Settings ➪ Control Panel, and then double-click the Fonts folder. To assign a font to text in a program, select the text. Then choose Format ➪ Font from the program's menu bar.

FTP (File Transfer Protocol) An Internet service that can be used to upload and download files.

frame A single picture in a video or animation. Also a section of a Web browser screen that displays its own unique page.

G, GB, gig Abbreviation for gigabyte, roughly one billion bytes.

GIF (Graphics Interchange Format) A compact format for storing graphic images, allowing them to be transported over networks more quickly.

gigabyte Roughly one billion bytes.

graphics Pictures, as opposed to written text.

graphics accelerator A hardware device that speeds complex graphics rendering onscreen.

GUI (Graphical User Interface) Pronounced *gooey*, the icon-oriented interface offered by Windows Me and some other operating systems.

hack To get past a password or other security device.

hacker A person who breaks into secure environments on the Internet. Also refers to an amateur computer programmer.

hardware The physical components of a computer that you can see and touch.

Help key The key labeled F1 near the top of the keyboard. Pressing F1 usually brings up context-sensitive help.

home page The first page you come to when you visit a Web site on the Internet. Each home page has its own unique URL.

host Any computer you can access via the Internet or phone lines. Also, the computer that answers the phone in Dial-Up Networking. In direct-cable connection, the PC with the shared resources you want to access.

hot docking The capability to connect a portable computer to its docking station without powering down the portable PC. Requires a special plug-and-play BIOS.

hot swapping A characteristic of some PC cards that enables insertion/removal of the card without powering down the PC.

HTML (Hypertext Markup Language) A set of tags used to define the format of a page presented over the World Wide Web.

HTTP (Hypertext Transport Protocol) The protocol used in the World Wide Web to allow documents to call one another.

hub Short name for an Ethernet concentrator or Ethernet hub. A device into which all PCs on the local area network connect via cables.

hyperlink A clickable hot spot on a Web page or some other document that, when clicked, takes you to some new page or location on the Internet.

icon A little picture onscreen used to represent a disk drive, folder, or file. To open an icon into a window, click the icon if you're using Web-style navigation. Double-click the icon if you're using Classic-style navigation.

image Also called a *digital image*. A picture that's stored on a computer disk as a file.

INI file A text file that holds information necessary to initialize a program. In Windows Me, these settings are stored in the Registry, but the original INI files are maintained to support backward compatibility.

Internet A huge collection of computers and networks from around the world. Popular services offered by the Internet include e-mail, World Wide Web, conferencing, chat, and FTP.

Internet Explorer (or Microsoft Internet Explorer) A program that enables you to explore and interact with the World Wide Web.

intranet A smaller local area network (LAN) that uses the same communications protocols (TCP/IP) as the Internet, thereby making the LAN behave much like the Internet.

IPX/SPX A network transport protocol used by Novell NetWare networks. In Windows Me, the NWLINK.VXD module implements the IPX/SPX protocol.

IRQ (Interrupt Request Line) The line a hardware device uses to get the attention of the processor. To see a list of used IRQs, open Device Manager in the System icon of the Control Panel. Then double-click the word Computer.

ISDN (Integrated Services Digital Network) A high-performance telephone line available from most local phone companies. Mainly used to get faster access to the Internet.

ISP (Internet service provider) A company that provides people with access to the Internet.

JPEG (Joint Photographic Experts Group) A compact format for storing photo-quality graphic images, generally for use on the World Wide Web.

K or KB Abbreviation for kilobyte or 1,024 bytes.

kernel The part of an operating system that manages the processor.

kilobyte Roughly a thousand bytes (1,024 bytes to be exact).

LAN (local area network) A group of local computers (in the same room or building) connected together to share resources.

Legacy A euphemism for old or obsolete. Refers to any hardware device that adheres to older, outdated standards.

local area network A group of local computers (in the same room or building) connected together to share resources.

local printer A printer physically connected, via a cable, to the current PC.

localization Adapting software to the language and formats of a specific country or culture.

lurk To hang around and read messages in an Internet newsgroup without contributing to the group. This is a good thing to do for a while when you're new to a newsgroup.

M, MB, meg Abbreviation for megabyte, roughly one million bytes.

MAPI (Messaging Application Programming Interface) Allows programs to access the messaging capabilities of the operating system. For example, many programs offer a File ⇨ Send option, which interacts with the MAPI and enables you to send messages directly from that application.

megabyte Roughly one million bytes.

memory Usually refers to the Random Access Memory (RAM) component of a PC.

menu A list of options. Clicking the Start button displays the Start menu.

message The general term for any kind of correspondence, such as a note or letter, that takes place over computers.

message box Any box that appears onscreen to display a message.

MIDI (Musical Interface Digital Interface) A standard for storing and playing music on a PC.

MIME (Multipurpose Internet Mail Extensions) Defines different types of data that can be transported over the Internet.

miniport driver A 32-bit virtual driver that enables the easy addition and removal of hardware, without rebooting the entire system. Windows 95, 98, Me, 2000, and NT support miniport drivers.

MMX (MultiMedia eXtensions) Additional technology added to Pentium (and Pentium II) chips to improve multimedia performance.

modem (modulator/demodulator) A device connecting your PC to a telephone line.

monitor The big TV-like component of a computer. The screen where Windows Me and everything else is displayed.

mouse button The primary mouse button, typically the mouse button on the left.

mouse pointer The little arrow that moves around the screen as you roll the mouse on your desktop.

MP3 A format used for storing CD-quality music on computer disks.

MPEG (Motion Picture Experts Group) A format used for storing video for presentation on a computer screen.

MS-DOS (Microsoft Disk Operating System) Another name for DOS.

MSN (The Microsoft Network) An online service provided by Microsoft.

NDIS (Network Driver Interface Specification) The interface for network drivers. All transport drivers call the NDIS interface to access network adapters.

Net, or the Net Slang expression for the Internet.

NetBEUI (NetBIOS Extended User Interface) Pronounced *net buoy*. A local area network transport protocol provided in Windows Me.

netiquette Network etiquette, polite and proper conduct on the Internet.

netizen A citizen of a network or the Internet.

network Two or more computers connected to one another with cables. A local area network (LAN) is generally composed of PCs close to one another and connected without modems and telephone lines. A wide area network (WAN) is composed of computers connected with telephones and modems. A LAN can connect to a WAN.

network adapter card A hardware device that enables you to connect a PC to other PCs in a local area network. Also called a Network Interface Card or NIC.

network administrator The person in charge of managing a local area network, including accounts, passwords, e-mail, and so on.

network drive A shared disk drive or folder on a LAN to which you mapped a drive letter. To map a drive letter to a shared resource, right-click the resource's icon in Network Neighborhood and choose Map Network Drive.

network printer A shared printer physically connected to some other PC in the LAN. The opposite of a local printer.

newbie Someone just learning to use a PC or the Internet.

newsgroup An electronic bulletin board on the Internet where people post messages to one another. You can use Microsoft Outlook Express to access Internet newsgroups.

NIC (Network Interface Card) Also called a *network adapter card*. A piece of hardware required to connect a PC to a local area network.

NT Microsoft's 32-bit operating system for high-end workstations and non-Intel processors. For example, computers that use the Dec Alpha, MIPS, or PowerPC chips can run the Windows NT and 2000 operating systems. Only Intel PCs with 386, 486, or Pentium chips can run Windows Me.

object An individual chunk of data you can manipulate onscreen, which can be a chart, picture, sound, video, or chunk of text.

object-oriented An operating system that allows chunks of data to be manipulated as individual objects and easily moved/copied from one program to another.

OLE (Object Linking and Embedding) Pronounced *olay*. A feature of Windows that enables you to take an object from one program (such as a chart in a spreadsheet program) and to link or embed that object into another program's document (such as a word processing report).

OLS Abbreviation for *online service*.

online service A service for computer users. Requires a modem and generally some kind of account. America Online, CompuServe, MSN, and Prodigy are some examples of well-known online services.

open To expand an icon to full view. In Classic Windows, you double-click an icon to open it. In Web view, you can single-click an underlined icon to open it. Within a program, you typically choose File ⇨ Open from that program's menu bar to open a document.

operating system A computer program that integrates a computer and all its peripheral devices. Windows Me is an operating system. Other operating systems include UNIX, Linux, DOS, and MacOS.

option button A small, round button in a dialog box that generally enables you to select only one option of many. Also called *radio buttons* (because only one button can be pushed in at a time).

OS An abbreviation for operating system.

owner The person who controls shared resources on a server. For example, if I give other people in a LAN access to my C drive, I am the owner of that drive.

path The location of a folder described in terms of its drive, folder, and subfolder. For example, in C:\Winword\Mydocuments\Letter to Mom.doc, the C:\Winword\Mydocuments\ part is the path to the file named Letter to Mom.doc. Also, a DOS command used to identify directories to search, now handled by the Registry in Windows Me.

PC card A credit card-sized adapter card that fits into the PCMCIA slot of a portable or desktop PC.

PCI (Peripheral Component Interface) A slot for add-in cards, available on most modern Pentium PCs.

PCMCIA (Personal Computer Memory Card International Association) A standard defining how PC Cards must be designed to work in the PCMCIA slot of a portable or desktop PC.

peer-to-peer network A way to connect several PCs into a local area network where any PC can act as either client or server.

Pentium The latest microprocessor from Intel Corporation. Earlier microprocessors include the 486, 386, and 286. The Pentium II is currently the latest microprocessor from Intel. That processor has built-in MMX capabilities.

PNP An abbreviation for plug and play, a standard that makes adding a hardware device to a PC relatively easy.

playback device Any device that can play content that's been recorded and stored electronically. For example, a CD player or VCR.

plug and play A standard that makes adding a hardware device to a PC fairly easy.

point To move the mouse so the mouse pointer is touching some object onscreen. Also used as a unit of measurement in typography, where one point equals approximately $\frac{1}{72}$ of an inch. In Web browsing, to point your Web browser to some Web site means to type that Web site's URL into the Address portion of your Web browser and then press Enter.

pointing device A mouse or trackball used to move the mouse pointer around on the screen.

pop-up menu The menu that appears when you right-click an object. Also called a context menu or a shortcut menu.

port A slot on the back of your PC into which you plug a cable that connects to some external device. Mice, keyboards, monitors, external modems, external CD-ROM drives, printers, and all other external devices plug into a port on a PC.

port replicator A compact-sized docking station for a portable computer that enables easy connection to a full-sized keyboard, mouse, monitor, and other devices.

PPTP (Point-to-Point Tunneling Protocol) A more secure version of Point-to-Point Protocol (PPP), the industry-standard method of connecting PCs through telephone lines. PPTP works in conjunction with Windows Me's Virtual Private Networking.

preemptive multitasking A scheduling technique that enables the operating system to take control of the processor at any time. Enables multiple hardware devices, such as modem, printer, screen, and floppy disk to operate simultaneously.

primary mouse button The mouse button used for most activities. In most cases, this is the mouse button on the left (the button that rests under your index finger when using the mouse with your right hand).

program Software you (generally) purchase and use on your PC.

properties Characteristics such as color, size, shape, and so forth. You can get to most items' properties by right-clicking their icon and choosing Properties from the menu that appears.

protocol An agreed-upon set of rules by which two computers can exchange information over a network. Windows Me supports three protocols: NetBEUI, TCP/IP, and IPX/SPX.

RAM (Random Access Memory) The part of the computer where only the stuff you're currently working on is stored. Things you aren't currently using are stored on the disk.

read-only A file that can be viewed, but not changed. To change a file's read-only status, right-click its icon, choose Properties, and adjust the Read-Only option on the General tab.

real mode The general term for a 16-bit device driver loaded into memory from the CONFIG.SYS or AUTOEXEC.BAT file. Windows Me attempts to replace all real-mode drivers with its own 32-bit virtual drivers, which provide better performance.

registered file type A type of document file associated with a specific program, based on its filename extension. For example, all .doc files are registered to (associated with) the Microsoft Word for Windows program.

Registry A database on your hard disk that automatically keeps track of all your Windows Me settings.

resolution The general term for the number of pixels on the desktop (also called screen area). Common resolutions include 640×480, 800×600, and 1024×768. The higher the resolution, the more you can see on your screen. Can be changed by right-clicking the desktop and choosing Properties ⇨ Settings.

resource Anything offering a useful service or information.

rich text Text that contains special formatting like boldface and italics.

right-click To click an icon or other item using the secondary mouse button (typically the button on the right-hand side of the mouse).

right-drag To hold down the secondary mouse button (typically the mouse button on the right) while dragging an object to some new location onscreen.

root directory The topmost folder on a disk, usually named \. For example, C:\ represents the root directory of drive C:.

RTF (rich text format) Text containing special formatting such as boldface and italics.

scrap A picture or chunk of text copied from the Windows Clipboard onto the Windows Me desktop as a file.

SCSI (Small Computer Standard Interface) Pronounced *scuzzy*. An interface specification that enables multiple disk drives, CD-ROM drives, and other devices to be connected to one another and then connected to a single port on the PC.

search engine A special service on the World Wide Web that helps you find information on a particular topic. Alta Vista at http://www.altavista.digital.com is a search engine.

secondary mouse button The button used for viewing options, rather than opening icons. In most cases, this is the mouse button on the right side of the mouse.

select Usually refers to the act of choosing one or more items to work with by dragging the mouse pointer through them.

selection An object (or objects) already selected and, hence, framed or highlighted in some manner.

server A computer that offers resources to other computers. For example, a print server gives printer access to other computers in a network.

share To enable multiple users on a local area network to use a single device, such as a printer or modem, that's attached to only one PC in the LAN. You can also share disk drives, CD-ROM drives, and folders.

shared resource A drive, folder, printer, modem, or other device on one computer that other computers in the LAN can use.

shareware Software given to you free for a trial period, so you can try it before you buy.

Shift+click To hold down the Shift key while clicking some item.

Shift+point To hold down the Shift key while moving the mouse pointer to some item.

shortcut 1) An icon on the desktop that enables you to open a folder, document, or program without going through the Start menu; 2) An alternative to using the mouse, often called a *keyboard shortcut*.

shortcut icon A special icon that acts as a quick link to a file, as opposed to representing the actual file. Shortcut icons have a tiny arrow in the lower-left corner.

SLIP (Serial Line Internet Protocol) A method used to connect a PC to an Internet service provider. Point-to-Point Protocol (PPP) is preferred over SLIP when connecting to the Internet with Windows Me.

snail mail Standard postal service (paper) mail.

software The intangible instructions, stored on a computer disk, that tell the computer how to behave. Windows Me is a piece of software, as is every other program you run on your computer.

source content In the media biz, the text, pictures, and/or video that make up a presentation or published work. Also called just *content*.

spam To send out junk mail on the Internet or another online service.

spamming Using the Internet as a means of advertising. A spam is an e-mail or newsgroup posting with the true intention of advertising some product or service.

Start button The button that appears in the taskbar, which you can click to start a program, open a recently saved document, get help, and so forth.

Start menu The first menu to appear after you click the Start button in the taskbar.

status bar The bar along the bottom of a program's window that provides information about the status of various options within that program. Can be turned on or off using a command on the program's View menu.

streaming format Data that is sent and experienced as a continuous stream, as with TV.

string Textual, rather than numeric, data. For example, 123.45 is a number, whereas *My dog has fleas* is a string (of characters).

subfolder A folder contained within another folder. The containing folder is called the *parent folder*.

subnet Any smaller network connected to the Internet.

subnet mask A value that enables the recipient of Internet packets to distinguish the network ID portion of the IP address from the ID of the host.

SVGA (Super Virtual Graphics Array) The type of display card and monitor that gives you high resolution, rich color, and graphics. An improvement over standard VGA.

sysop The term used for the person who operates a bulletin board.

System menu A menu you can open by clicking the icon in the upper-left corner of a window or by pressing Alt+Spacebar. Enables you to move and size a window using the keyboard rather than the mouse.

T1, T3 Special lines that provide high-speed, full-time access to the Internet. Available from many Internet service providers, as well as from your local phone company.

taskbar A thin strip, usually along the bottom of the Windows Me desktop, that displays the Start button, a button for each open program, and the current time and other indicators. May also show other shortcuts and toolbars. When auto-hidden, the taskbar becomes visible when you touch the mouse pointer to the extreme bottom of the screen. To customize the taskbar, right-click it.

TCP/IP (Transmission Control Protocol/Internet Protocol) The primary communications protocol used on the Internet. Allows a Windows Me PC to participate in UNIX-based bulletin boards and other information services.

text file A file containing only ASCII text codes like letters, numbers, spaces, and punctuation—no hidden codes. Text files should be created and edited with text-only editors, such as Notepad available from the Accessories menu in Windows Me.

thread 1) A series of messages about a topic posted to an information service; 2) An executable chunk of program code that can run simultaneously with other threads in a microprocessor.

TIA Thanks In Advance, an acronym often used in e-mail or chat rooms.

title bar The colored area across the top of the window that shows the window's name and offers the Minimize, Maximize, and Close (X) buttons, and the System menu. To move a window, drag its title bar. You can also maximize or restore a window by double-clicking its title bar.

toggle A switch or option that can have only one of two possible settings: on or off.

toolbar A set of buttons and other controls that provide one-click access to frequently used menu commands. For access to Windows Me toolbars, right-click some neutral area of the taskbar and point to Toolbars in the shortcut menu that appears.

ToolTip The little label that appears when you rest the mouse pointer on the toolbar button.

UART Pronounced *wart*. A chip used on a modem or serial device that determines the top speed of serial communications. The latest UART — 16550A — offers the highest speeds.

UNC (Uniform Naming Convention) A method of identifying a resource by its computer name, followed by a resource name. The computer name is preceded by two backslashes; for example, \\Comm_Center\MyStuff.

upload To copy a file from your local PC to some remote computer on the Internet or elsewhere.

URL (Uniform Resource Locator) The address to some resource on the Internet, such as http://www.coolnerds.com.

USB (universal serial bus) A new type of connection that enables you to plug a device into your computer and use it immediately.

Usenet A service on the Internet that enables people to communicate via newsgroups. Each newsgroup is like an electronic bulletin board on which members post messages to one another.

VESA (Video Electronic Standards Association) A group that defines standards for video displays.

VGA (Virtual Graphics Array) The type of display card and monitor that gives you rich color and graphics.

virtual driver A 32-bit Windows Me device driver that can be loaded into upper memory via the Registry (as opposed to a real-mode driver, which must be loaded into conventional or upper memory via CONFIG.SYS or AUTOEXEC.BAT).

virtual memory Disk space used as RAM when RAM runs out.

Virtual Private Networking A means of connecting to the Internet through phone lines (Point-to-Point Tunneling Protocol or PTP) that provides more security than standard Point-to-Point Protocol (PPP).

virus A computer program specifically designed to do damage on whatever PC it lands. High-tech vandalism.

VxD A 32-bit Windows Me virtual device driver, often used as a filename extension on the device driver's filename. The *x* indicates the type of device being driven. For example, .VPD is a printer driver; VDD is a display driver.

WAN (wide area network) A group of computers that can share resources on a large scale. The Internet, for example, is one huge, global WAN.

WDM (Windows Driver Model) A program that allows hardware devices to work in Windows Me.

Web Short for World Wide Web, a service of the Internet.

Web browser A program, such as Microsoft Internet Explorer, used to browse the World Wide Web.

Web style An option (usually under View ⇨ Options), which enables you to navigate Windows Me in a manner similar to the World Wide Web — by clicking, rather than double-clicking, underlined links.

Whiteboard A simple drawing program that can be used by several people at the same time. Microsoft NetMeeting comes with a Whiteboard.

window A frame onscreen that displays a single program or folder. Every window has a title bar across the top; Minimize, Maximize, and Close (X) buttons near the upper right-corner; and other features. A closed window appears as an icon onscreen.

WINS (Windows Internet Name Service) A naming service that resolves Windows network computer names to Internet IP addresses.

workgroup A collection of computers in a LAN that all share the same workgroup name. When you first open Network Neighborhood, it displays other computers in your same workgroup. You determine to which workgroup a PC belongs by using the Identification tab in Network Properties (right-click Network Neighborhood and choose Properties).

workstation A PC with unusually high processing capabilities, often used for computer-aided design and similar calculation-intensive and graphics-intensive jobs. May use a non-Intel microprocessor, such as the Dec Alpha, or multiple 486 or Pentium processors.

World Wide Web A popular place on the Internet, where you can browse through documents that contain text, graphics, and even multimedia.

WWW Abbreviation for the World Wide Web, a service of the Internet.

zipped file A file that's been compressed to speed transfer over a network. Use WinZip (www.winzip.com) to zip and unzip files.

✦   ✦   ✦

Index

Continued

Continued

Continued

R

my2cents.idgbooks.com

Register This Book — And Win!

Visit **http://my2cents.idgbooks.com** to register this book and we'll automatically enter you in our fantastic monthly prize giveaway. It's also your opportunity to give us feedback: let us know what you thought of this book and how you would like to see other topics covered.

Discover IDG Books Online!

The IDG Books Online Web site is your online resource for tackling technology — at home and at the office. Frequently updated, the IDG Books Online Web site features exclusive software, insider information, online books, and live events!

10 Productive & Career-Enhancing Things You Can Do at www.idgbooks.com

- Nab source code for your own programming projects.

- Download software.

- Read Web exclusives: special articles and book excerpts by IDG Books Worldwide authors.

- Take advantage of resources to help you advance your career as a Novell or Microsoft professional.

- Buy IDG Books Worldwide titles or find a convenient bookstore that carries them.

- Register your book and win a prize.

- Chat live online with authors.

- Sign up for regular e-mail updates about our latest books.

- Suggest a book you'd like to read or write.

- Give us your 2¢ about our books and about our Web site.

You say you're not on the Web yet? It's easy to get started with IDG Books' *Discover the Internet,* available at local retailers everywhere.